James Ross Wordie was educated at the Royal Grammar School, High Wycombe, and Queens' College Cambridge, where he took a degree in History in 1963. He then spent a further year at Cambridge, taking a PGCE at Cambridge University's Department of Education, intending to teach at a school or college. However, he was persuaded to begin PhD research at the University of Reading, specialising in Agricultural History. This PhD was completed in 1967, and he next began to lecture at St. David's College in Lampeter, which was then the oldest constituent college of the federal University of Wales. In 1970 he returned to the University of Reading where he lectured on British Social and Economic History until his retirement from lecturing in 2004.

To Kim

J.R. Wordie

Philosophy in History: How Ideas Have Shaped Our World

Austin Macauley Publishers™
London • Cambridge • New York • Sharjah

The story, experiences, and words are the author's alone

A CIP catalogue record for this title is available from the British Library.

ISBN 9781398428959 (Paperback)
ISBN 9781398428966 (ePub e-book)

www.austinmacauley.com

First Published 2022
Austin Macauley Publishers Ltd®
1 Canada Square
Canary Wharf
London
E14 5AA

Acknowledgements

I would like to thank Professor Emeritus Ralph Houlbrooke, Dr. Roger Wilkes, and Dr. Chris Woods for their comments on earlier drafts of this book, which were most helpful. Of course, responsibility for this work remains my own: none of the above entirely agreed with my views (nor with each other). Thanks also go to my two sons, Mark and Jonathan, for their many helpful comments, and to my wife Kim for putting up with me during the 13 years I spent in researching and writing this book.

Table of Contents

Introduction

This book is dedicated to the proposition that it has been neither generals, nor plutocrats, nor even politicians that have shaped the destinies of nations. Rather, it has been the irresistible power of ideas whose time has come that have exercised the decisive influence. Unfortunately for humanity, however, these have been, for the most part, the wrong ideas, to the great detriment of humankind throughout our history. Let's remember a few. 'Might makes right.' 'War is glorious.' 'Government should be the preserve of a small, hereditary elite.' 'White people are superior to all coloured people.' 'Imperialism is a great idea.' 'Slavery is a fine institution.' 'Nothing is more important than religion.' 'Public floggings, burnings, hangings, and disembowelments are grand forms of popular entertainment.' 'Women are inferior to men in every way.' 'Hygiene is of no importance.' 'Those who cannot afford to pay for medical care should be left to die.' 'Not all children need to be educated.' 'The world is here for us to pillage and exploit.' etc. etc. All this prompted Edward Gibbon (1737-94), the great historian of the Roman Empire, to remark that all history was 'little more than a register of the crimes, follies, and misfortunes of mankind'. The importance of having the right ideas to live by can hardly be overstated, particularly at this point in our history, for the twenty-first century will surely prove to be 'make or break' time for our species, as we shall see below. Our present course is clearly unsustainable, and will have to be altered.

We have undoubtedly made some progress, but unfortunately some bad ideas remain with us. A case in point for our own times is neoliberalism, a very bad idea indeed, from which a host of other ills has flowed, and yet it has become, in the words of Stephen Metcalf writing in *The Guardian* for August 18, 2017, 'The Idea that Swallowed the World'. The nature of this sinister creed is fully explained in the Economics chapter below, and some suggestions as to what we can do about it are made in the Conclusion. Indeed, we are still trying to find our way, especially in the fields of economic, political, and ecological thought, where we are still far from settling on the best courses. We are still engaged upon an *Unended Quest*, to quote from the title of Karl Popper's intellectual autobiography. For good or ill, however, ideas have shaped not only our material world through the work of scientists and engineers, but also our mental world, determining which economic and political creeds come into fashion, our views on morality, and our perceptions of ourselves, our world, and our place in the universe. I will argue here that we occupy an extremely improbable position in the great scheme of things, and that we are in fact very lucky to be here at all. This great good fortune should not be taken for granted.

The political systems under which we live have of course clearly been the products of ideas. Academic philosophy as taught in our universities has some contribution to make here, but I will argue in this book that academic philosophers take too narrow a view of their subject. 'Philosophy' is after all a term from the ancient Greek, φιλοσοφία, with φιλο (philo) meaning 'to love', or 'a love of' and σοφία (sophia) generally taken to mean wisdom. But the ancient Greeks themselves did not use it only in that narrow sense. In their day it could also have meant knowledge, skill, craft, or prudence. It was an elastic term in those times, and I would argue that it should still be an elastic concept today. The very narrow sense in which 'philosophy' is defined academically in the twenty-first century has been entirely the work of a small band of professional philosophers, as I will show below. In fact, until the nineteenth century, the term 'philosophy' had a much broader application. Science, for example, was described only as 'natural philosophy', just another branch of a broader discipline, while in his day Adam Smith was never regarded as being anything other than a philosopher. The 'love of wisdom' embraced a wide range of wisdoms to be loved, and I will argue here that this broader definition of 'philosophy' should be revived.

We really ought to ask ourselves what philosophy is for. Can it ever serve any useful purpose? I believe that it can, so long as we keep our eye on the ball here. In my opinion 'good' philosophy is that which deepens our understanding of ourselves and our place in the universe, or has real, beneficial applications to daily life, including its political and social aspects. The rest is merely 'clever', or 'interesting', the plaything of academic philosophers, but of no practical use at all. It could be said that the primary task of philosophy should be a striving to answer that greatest of all questions namely, 'How should we live, both as individuals and as communities?' But the answer to so broad a question as this cannot be found within the narrow definitions of academic philosophy alone. I would suggest that, as examples, religious thought, economic thought, ecological thought, and scientific thought should also be regarded as legitimate forms of philosophy for this purpose, since all have represented a love of wisdom of one kind or another, and all can contribute towards answering the question of how we should live. In short, philosophy is too important to be left to the philosophers. Unless those disciplines mentioned above are also recognised as being genuinely 'philosophical', the full impact of ideas upon our historical development cannot be appreciated.

Taking this broader definition of 'philosophy', seeing it rather as schools of thought, it could even be argued that our entire history has been shaped by the philosophies to which people have adhered over the past twenty-five centuries or so. No agency on Earth can resist the power of an idea whose time has come. Those generals, politicians, and stock dealers who believed that they were in control deluded themselves, even although those last thought themselves to be, in the words of Tom Wolfe, 'Masters of the Universe'. Rather, they themselves have all been the products of ideas. This is not an original proposition: others have made much the same claim before me, including Edmund Burke (1720-97), Friedrich Hegel (1770-1831),

Heinrich Heine (1797-1856), Victor Hugo (1802-85) and Benedetto Croce (1866-1952). But at this point I will quote from only two of them; first, John Maynard Keynes (1883-1946), who wrote in his classic work, *The General Theory of Employment, Interest, and Money* (1936),

> The ideas of economists and political philosophers, both when they are right and when they are wrong, are more powerful than is commonly understood. Indeed, the world is ruled by little else. Practical men, who believe themselves to be quite exempt from any intellectual influences, are usually the slaves of some defunct economist. Madmen in authority, who hear voices in the air, are distilling their frenzy from some academic scribbler of a few years back. I am sure that the power of vested interests is vastly exaggerated compared with the general encroachment of ideas. Not, indeed, immediately, but after a certain interval; for in the field of economic and political philosophy there are not many who are influenced by new theories after they are twenty-five or thirty years of age, so that the ideas which civil servants and politicians and even agitators apply to current events are not likely to be the newest. But, soon or late, it is ideas, not vested interests, which are influential for good or evil. (Chpt. 24 Section V, p. 241 of pdf version, available online)

Personally, I would certainly regard Keynes as being a philosopher in the sense that he was a 'lover of wisdom', albeit mainly economic wisdom in his case. But note his disparaging references to 'defunct economists' and 'academic scribblers'. In general, philosophers hold a very poor opinion of other philosophers, each one utterly convinced that he and only he holds a monopoly on truth, and reading the delightful pieces of invective that they hurl against each other will be one of the pleasures afforded by the text below.

Keynes had a great rival in the field of economic thought in the person of Friedrich Hayek (1899-1992), the Viennese economist and philosopher. There was very little that they agreed upon, but on those two points they found common ground. Both had noted the power of ideas, and also the time delay in their implementation. Hayek wrote,

> Experience indicates that once a great body of intellectuals has accepted a philosophy, it is only a question of time until those views become the governing force of politics. (Cited in D. S. Jones, *Masters of the Universe* (2012) p. 160)

The delay involved usually amounted to a few decades, as in the case of neoliberal thought.

But readers may want to know at this point what manner of man is making these observations, and what his own philosophical standpoint might be. For my part, although I am not a professional philosopher I was, by background and training, a professional historian: an academic, Master of Arts, Doctor of

Philosophy, elected Fellow of the Royal Historical Society, with thirty-seven years of experience as a teacher of History at university level, mainly at the University of Reading. None of this, of course, offers any guarantee against my writing utter nonsense, as have so many philosophers before me, but it does put me in with at least a chance of having something interesting to say. Although a historian by training, I am a philosopher by inclination, and what I have to offer here are the fruits of a lifetime of study and thought, backed by an academic training.

My main field of expertise was in the social and economic history of modern and early-modern Britain. However, History was never my sole field of interest. Economics and Politics also fell within my purview as a lecturer, while of course religious thought has often exerted a profound influence upon historical developments, and so some grasp of theology was also called for. In addition, I have also always been interested in Philosophy and in Science. Since my retirement from lecturing in 2004 I have been able to devote more time to studies in these fields, and I have recently felt competent enough to include chapters on both topics below. I freely admit that I am not an expert in either field, but this is not a book for experts: it is simply a general survey for the general reader who has a wide range of interests in the workings of the world: all that I can do is apply something of the historian's analytical rigour to the subjects covered. The professional scientist, philosopher, or economist will not be impressed by what I have to say here, for this is not a work of original research. To them it will all seem superficial and 'old hat'. 'Surely everyone knows *that'*, they will think. But in fact everyone does *not* know 'that'. The specialists will not learn anything new about their specialities here, but the scientist might learn something about economics, the economist something about philosophy, and the philosopher something about science. Moreover, all of them will learn something about Islam and its significance from the chapter on Religion. Islam is today the world's fastest growing religion, forecast to overtake Christianity in terms of nominal adherents in the near future. But I have yet to meet a British Christian who can tell me even so much as what the Five Pillars of Islam are. Religious thought is still playing an important part in the shaping of our world today, in particular Islamic religious thought. In short, the strength of this study lies in its breadth, rather than its depth. Put all the pieces together, and what do you see? A complete answer to, 'life, the universe, and everything'? Well, perhaps not, but something rather like it: opinions on this question may differ. Indeed. Max Tegmark in his book, *Our Mathematical Universe* (2014) even playfully suggests, with the help of some well-chosen figures, that there is in fact something to be said for the answer, '42'! (pp. 246-7) Max is superbly numerate, but I rather fear that the answer is just a little more complicated than that. The whole can become greater than the sum of its parts, a development known as 'the phenomenon of emergent qualities', of which more below. Readers may make up their own minds on that point. We all have to specialise too much these days: sometimes, you have to step back and look at the bigger picture to see things in perspective. 'Only connect', as E.M. Forster would say.

Albert Einstein once famously remarked, 'Science without religion is lame, religion without science is blind'. But perhaps he could have better said, 'Science without *philosophy* is lame, *philosophy* without science is blind'. The two subjects may certainly be linked, but the relationship is asymmetrical: philosophy has much more to learn from the scientists than science has from the philosophers. It is most important to begin by establishing the nature of reality as accurately as possible, for if we choose to premise our conclusions upon false assumptions, the consequences for us all could be seriously adverse. Until we can establish what is true, we cannot make what is best right. But the search for truth must incorporate a wide range of fields of thought. Indeed, seemingly unrelated disciplines can often be found, upon closer examination, to have some features in common. For example, some similarities of methodology and purpose can be traced even between Science and History, particularly in two respects. First, when it comes to motivation, we historians do share with the scientists a rather obsessive compulsion to discover the truth, or at least to get as close to the truth as we possibly can, which is the best that either discipline can hope for. Secondly, in terms of methodology, there are also some similarities. For example, the scientific method may be said to proceed in four stages:

(a) Observation
(b) Speculation
(c) Experimentation
(d) Validation/refutation

The key stage is of course (c), experimentation. If the experimental evidence fails to support the speculation, then the speculation is *wrong*! When it comes to us historians, the equivalent of Science's reliance on experiment is our reliance upon primary sources. In the case of History, these are always written sources: that is what distinguishes our discipline from Archaeology. 'Historical' times are those which have been chronicled in documentary materials: the rest is prehistorical. Nearer to our own times these may be supplemented by paintings, photographs, film archives, and the like. For the Archaeologists, their primary sources consist of surviving artefacts, ecofacts such as dried seeds and bones, and buried or still standing remains of buildings, roads, field systems, or fortifications. It may sometimes happen that both sets of sources, historical and archaeological, are available for certain periods, but the distinction between the two disciplines remains clear enough. So how does the historian approach his task? Well, all written sources are of course written by people, so historians too adopt a four-fold approach when it comes to considering their sources. We ask,

(a) Who wrote it?
(b) What were his qualifications for writing this? Does the writer really know what he is talking about? Is he capable of historical analysis?
(c) Is this an impartial account of events, or does this particular writer have his own agenda?
(d) Is this source in fact a doctoring of an earlier account, or even an outright forgery?

Source materials should be written by those who were alive at the time of the events described, ideally by those who actually witnessed or participated in them. Thus Thucydides' *History of the Peloponnesian War* (431 BC) in which he actually fought, or *The Diary of Samuel Pepys* (1633-1703) who kept a diary from 1660, or Winston Churchill's six-volume *History of the Second World War* (1948-1953), might all be regarded as primary sources. But even primary sources may not be free from bias. Winston Churchill famously said, 'History will be kind to me – because I shall write it!' and so he did. Indeed, even 'official' documents may sometimes be suspect, and ye sceptical historian must proceed with extreme caution, consulting as wide a range of sources as possible. In general, it remains true, for example, that history is usually written by the victors, since the losing side tends to display a reluctance to chronicle its defeat. In addition, history is littered with cases of notorious forgeries, such as the putative *Donation of Constantine*, allegedly issued by the Roman Emperor Constantine the Great (c.272-337), which purported to give the popes both spiritual and secular authority over the western Roman Empire, but was actually forged in the Vatican at some time during the eighth century, or *The Protocols of the Elders of Zion*, an anti-Semitic document forged by the Tsar's secret police in 1903 claiming to reveal a Jewish plot for world domination, or the infamous 'Hitler Diaries', which were complete forgeries.

Having said all that, however, it must be admitted that none of us can ever be entirely impartial. Historians try their best to be so, but we all carry our cultural baggage with us, however hard we may try to discard it. Ideally, we would like to be able to say, 'He that loveth country, or religion, or culture, or ideology more than the quest for truth is not worthy of the name of historian', but in reality we all cling to our personal beliefs and prejudices. Since some of what follows incorporates my own views, I ought perhaps to begin by 'coming clean' about just what my basic views are. When it comes to conversation, I have always regarded talking about yourself as being the nadir of the art but here, because we historians attach such great importance to the questions (a) 'Who wrote it?' and (b) 'What were his qualifications for writing this?', I feel obliged to include some autobiographical material here.

In my own case, I have always harboured a penchant for philosophy, and began to develop a philosophy of my own at quite an early age. I had begun to think of myself as both a deist and a determinist by the time I went up to

Cambridge as a Queens' College exhibitioner in 1960. At that time I had not yet heard of the term 'pantheism', but simply thought of God as being The Great Nature of All Things, which incorporated both The Way Things Are, and The Way Things Work. It seemed to me that such a system would have to be deterministic, since it would be supremely incumbent upon such a God to obey His own laws. Not even God would have free will. I kept an open mind at the time, quite prepared to change my views in the light of better knowledge, but all my subsequent reading has in fact supported and confirmed them, rather than undermined them. Scientific support for these ideas will be provided in the Einstein section below.

I thought at first that such views made me a deist, but later learned that I was actually a pantheist, and later still a panentheist. The distinction between the latter two terms is quite a subtle one, but of some significance. The pantheist believes that God is seen in the universe and all its works, but the panentheist, while he would agree with that, goes further in seeing God as being greater than the mere material universe. This is my own position, based upon the assumption that the whole can be 'greater', from our point of view, than the mere sum of its parts. The human body is a very good example: it consists basically of water, with a few handfuls of cheap chemicals thrown in. But we all know that it amounts to much more than that. This is known as 'the phenomenon of emergent qualities', or what the philosophers might call 'holism', or *Gestalt* theory from the German for 'overall shape' or form.

Both pantheism and panentheism, however, reject the idea of an afterlife, and envisage an abstract, impersonal, and amoral God who is utterly indifferent to the doings, and indeed the survival, of humankind. At the same time, He is the creator, sustainer, and controller of the universe, following His own deterministic laws. (I will follow the convention of referring to God as 'He' and 'Him' here, even although the panentheist's God is nothing like a human being.) The phenomenon of emergent qualities suggests that there is almost a kind of intelligence behind these laws, a deep mystery at the heart of the universe. We deceive ourselves if we believe that everything has been explained. This position of awe and wonder was one adopted by both Baruch Spinoza (1632-77) and Albert Einstein (1879-1955), who might each be described as panentheists, as we shall later see in the sections devoted entirely to them below. Both were religious sceptics, but both indignantly rejected the charge of atheism: a panentheist is most certainly *not* an atheist. Both took an essentially religious view of the world.

As an uncompromising rationalist, I can at least boast that my views were formed on purely rational grounds, and were not determined by my cultural background. Indeed, those views were very unpopular with everyone else at the time. The Christians regarded panentheism as a form of atheism, while the atheists regarded it as a form of religion, which indeed it is, albeit one in which even the most rational of individuals could believe. I was therefore unpopular with both camps, but of course a quest for truth and a simultaneous quest for popularity are usually incompatible. This did not bother me, because I felt at the time that the acceptance of orthodoxy represented the surrender of thought, while contempt for authority was the beginning of wisdom. It was only a beginning to be sure, but it was an essential start. Of course, you also had to keep an open mind, for arrogance and dogmatism are the enemies of truth.

When it came to my determinism, I soon discovered that this was regarded with horror by Christians and atheists alike. At Cambridge in those years existentialism was the philosophical flavour of the month, the inevitable intellectual uniform of the 'individualist' at that time. The existentialists eagerly explained to me that we bore our fortunes in our own strong arms, that we 'made ourselves', that man was 'condemned to freedom', that he had free will and was totally responsible for the decisions that he made, and yet spent his life in flight and terror from the hideous responsibility that he bore, thus giving rise to existential angst, and a great deal more nonsense along the same lines. They seemed to find these ideas 'liberating', but they just made me laugh. I told them to stop worrying. I argued that on the contrary they had no free will at all, but were simply the instruments of God's purpose, living out an inevitable destiny that had been prepared for them from the beginning of time. They were 'responsible' for nothing, and had no control over their future destiny at all. In a sense it had already happened, just as surely as their past had happened. The existentialists simply couldn't cope with that at all. They saw this as being a doctrine of despair, when of course it is no such thing. Truly, we are all in God's hands, but your predetermined future might well turn out to be a very happy one, especially if you are fortunate enough to live here, in the developed Western World. We British tend to take our good fortune for granted, without ever pausing to consider how lucky we are to have been born in this place, at this time, and as members of this species, rather than as one of the millions of other species that inhabit our planet. Philosophy turns the mind to such thoughts as these: it inspires in me eternal gratitude for my miraculous good fortune, and contributes substantially to my personal happiness.

I suppose that I should not have been surprised by the violent reaction that my views provoked from the existentialists, but I was. They seemed to be deeply shocked. One said, 'If I really believed that, I would kill myself!' Another threatened to kill *me*! He got very angry indeed, and pulled out a knife that he flicked open and brandished in front of my face (knife carrying was not illegal in those days, it seems). He insisted that he *did* have free will, and indeed that I myself lived at that time only because he had decided to let me live, but that he was free to change his mind at any moment and kill me. This was an obvious bluff, and we both knew it: in fact he had no choice about the matter at all. But it struck me that attempting to win an intellectual opponent over to your point of view by threatening to kill him if he didn't agree with you represented the very nadir of the dialectical process. So I informed him that, on the contrary, as far as he was concerned I might as well have been at that moment clad in plate armour from head to toe. It was utterly impossible for him to kill or even wound me, because that was in neither his destiny nor mine, and that there was absolutely nothing that he could do about it.

I thought at the time that his kind of intellectual bankruptcy was unusual, but I learned in later life that, sadly, there are still many people in the world today who say, 'Agree with me or I'll kill you!': far too many, in fact. It might be said that I bet my life on my philosophy at that moment, but I did so without a qualm, because I was completely sure that my philosophy was right and his was wrong, and so indeed it proved: I live to tell the tale. However, this was not to be the last occasion on which my views were to elicit homicidal inclinations. I am always disappointed at this, because thought is free, and we should all be capable of mutual toleration and engagement in civilised debate. But it soon became clear to me that if you prioritise a quest for truth, then while humility and keeping an open mind are important, at the same time you cannot afford to be overly concerned about other people's opinions of you. The philosopher who succeeds in upsetting nobody probably has nothing of any great importance to say.

It seemed to me that panentheism and determinism walked hand in hand, and together could form the basis of an entire philosophical system and moral code. Moreover, as my reading progressed, I began to notice signs of deterministic beliefs amongst some of the great writers of the past. Listen first to the eleventh-century *Rubaiyat* of Omar Khayyam (1048-1131) in the wonderful 1859 English translation by Edward Fitzgerald:

> Oh Thou who didst with pitfall and with gin
> Beset the way that I must journey in,
> Wouldst Thou thus with predestination hedge me round,
> And then impute my fall to sin? (Verse 57)

Or William Shakespeare:

> There's a divinity that shapes our ends,
> Rough hew them how we will. (Hamlet, Act 5, Scene 2, lines 10-11)

Or T.S. Eliot in the opening lines of 'Burnt Norton', the first of his *Four Quartets*:

> Time present and time past
> Are both perhaps present in time future,
> And time future contained in time past.
> If all time is eternally present
> All time is unredeemable.
> What might have been is an abstraction

Remaining a perpetual possibility
Only in a world of speculation. (Lines 1-8)

T.S. Elliot, it seems, had quite a good grasp of the nature of the space-time continuum. Or listen to Leo Tolstoy. If you read to the very end of *War and Peace* you come to the punch line with which he concludes this great work. He ends by mocking the captains and the kings who so fondly imagined that they swayed the destinies of nations. Nonsense, says Tolstoy. Those men were but pawns in the hands of fate. They exercised no free will at all in the decisions that they made. Free will is as much of an illusion as the impression that we receive of the sun going round the earth. To quote from his last lines,

It is true that we are not conscious of our dependence, but by admitting our free will we arrive at absurdity, while by admitting our dependence on the external world, on time and on cause, we arrive at laws. In the first case it was necessary to renounce the consciousness of an unreal immobility in space and to recognise a motion that we did not feel: in the present case it is similarly necessary to renounce a freedom that does not exist, and to recognise a dependence of which we are not conscious.

Incidentally, it is interesting to notice that Pierre Bezukhov, the central character of *War and Peace* who is often taken to reflect the views of Tolstoy himself, was attracted to the philosophy of panentheism.

Of course, beliefs in determinism are considerably older than any of those cited above. The ancient Greek philosopher Parmenides of Elea (present-day Ascea) who lived from about 515 to 460 BC, was the first to have specifically taught the idea, and it was later taken up by the Stoics, who were also early pantheists of a sort. Determinism has a long history. In ancient Norse mythology even the Nordic gods were in thrall to Fate (Wyrd), which controlled the destinies of all things. The ancient Greeks and Romans also believed in 'The Fates' (Moirai), who were deaf to the pleas of mortals, while the polytheistic Hindus believed in Karma, or fate, an emanation of Atman, the universal soul, which represented your inescapable true self. Therefore, no temples were raised to Atman or The Fates, for there was no point in beseeching them: their minds had been made up. Only the lesser gods were partial to entreaties. Therefore, an ancient Greek might still pray to Athena for guidance. Quite possibly, The Fates had decreed both that he should do so, and that Athena would answer his prayer. Indeed, it might be said that a belief in determinism, in the form of 'The Fates', was more or less universal in the Indo-European pre-Christian world.

But then, human hubris began to rear its head. Certain clever people began to think that it demeaned humanity to see man as just the plaything of the gods. Surely man, 'the measure of all things' according to Protagoras, had to be greater than that! The first Europeans to argue this way were the pre-Socratic Greek Sophists, men like Protagoras of Abdera, (c490-c420 BC), Gorgias of

Leontini (c485-c380 BC) and Hippias of Elis (c450-c399 BC). They argued that by acquiring certain skills, especially in arms or rhetoric, a man could 'rise above his destiny', and to a degree 'create himself'. This theme was later taken up by Plato and Aristotle, who developed it into the doctrine of free will. The choices that a man made in his life were crucial to his future: character was destiny. I would agree with this, but I would add that both his character and his choices were predetermined. We do what we want to do and so experience the illusion of free will: but it is precisely *what we want to do* that is predetermined. As Schopenhauer put it, 'A man may do what he wills, but he cannot will what he wills'. It seems that determinism is an aspect of reality that humankind finds it particularly hard to accept, but I must ask readers to restrain their indignation at this point, and wait until the Einstein section, where it will be explained more fully in scientific terms. Basically, it rests upon the nature of the space-time continuum. Time does not 'flow', it simply *is*, and we move through it. The future is as real as the past, and just as unalterable.

Of course panentheism too was an unpopular concept, not only in Cambridge at the time, but also historically, at least in the Christian West, where panentheism was seen as a form of heresy and atheism. I later discovered that only one prominent modern philosopher had ever had the courage to make panentheism and determinism central to his thought, and that man was Baruch Spinoza (1632-1677) whose parents were Portuguese Jews, although he himself spent his life in the Netherlands. I read about him with increasing incredulity as I came to realise how closely his views paralleled my own. I found this to be quite an emotional experience. No one else had ever agreed with me before, but now here was a man dubbed by Gilles Deleuze (1925-1995) as 'the prince of philosophers' who actually *did* agree with me. I felt reassured. I will soon be forgotten, but Spinoza will never be forgotten. It was easy enough for me as a twentieth-century man living in a liberal and tolerant age with all the scientific knowledge we had at our disposal to reach the conclusions that I did, but for Spinoza to have done the same in the ill-informed and highly intolerant seventeenth century was truly remarkable.

As I later learned, pantheism and panentheism also had long histories. The term 'pantheism' was not coined in English until the early eighteenth century, but early Taoism, Hinduism, and the Bahá'i faith had included elements of pantheist thought. The pre-Socratics Anaximander of Miletus (611-546 BC) and Heraclitus of Ephesus (535-475 BC) had put forward the idea, and it was espoused by the Stoics, including the emperor Marcus Aurelius (121-180 AD). Its later proponents included Giordano Bruno (1548-1600), John Toland (1670-1722), the 'Nature Poets' William Wordsworth (1770-1850) and Samuel Taylor Coleridge (1772-1834), and the Americans Ralph Waldo Emerson (1803-1882) and Henry David Thoreau (1817-1862). Panentheism was in addition the self-proclaimed 'faith' of Albert Einstein (1879-1955), a great admirer of Spinoza. Einstein is on record as saying, 'God does not play dice', one of his best known quotations.

Another realisation that occurred to me early on was the fact that change is the first law of the universe. Nothing ever actually *is*, but rather all things are in a permanent state of becoming something else. Therefore nothing in the universe is forever including, so the cosmologists tell us, even the universe itself! God is simply *not* a forever sort of guy, at least as far as this universe is concerned, as Brian Greene explains for us in his recent book, *Until the End of Time* (2020). It must be so, for change is life, while stasis is death. Of course, change is also death, rather like Janus, the two-faced god, or the Hindu Shiva, who was lord of both creation and destruction. But at least change gives you a crack at life along the way! It is here that philosophy intersects with science, specifically the laws of causality and of thermodynamics, but more on this below. Needless to say, this was not a new idea either. I later learned that in this case I had been scooped by about 2,500 years by Heraclitus of Ephesus (535-475 BC), who had observed that, 'all is flux' and that, 'you can never step into the same river twice'. But you have to learn to forgive those people who steal your best ideas and publish them thousands of years before you were born: with philosophy, this happens all the time!

Another early idea of mine that I once fondly imagined was original related to the question of selfishness and morality. It seemed to me it could be argued that there is no such thing as an unselfish action, in that nobody ever does anything unless doing that thing makes them happier than not doing it. The comparative degree of the adjective 'happier' is significant here. The action need not make the perpetrator 'happy', just 'happier' than not doing it.

To take an extreme example, imagine a small band of soldiers fleeing from a much larger force. One of those in the fleeing group is wounded, and is slowing the progress of his companions. That man volunteers to stay behind alone, to fight a desperate rear-guard action against overwhelming odds, in order to give his colleagues more time to escape. Surely this is the supreme example of altruism, the sort of episode depicted at the end of Ernest Hemingway's *For Whom the Bell Tolls* (1940), where a small band of partisans is being pursued by Franco's Fascist troops. But even here, it could be argued that the man who stayed behind did so not because it made him happy, but only because it made him *happier* than staying with his companions, and thereby imperilling the lives of them all. Blaise Pascal put this point rather well in his famous *Pensées,* where he says,

> All men seek happiness. This is without exception. Whatever different means they employ, they all tend to this end...the will never takes the least step but to this object. This is the motive of every action of every man, even of those who hang themselves. (Section vii, no. 425)

This concept will be considered more fully in the Conclusion below, as part of an in-depth discussion of the meaning of the term, 'morality'. This point will also figure in my discussion of Economics: you might say that nobody ever does anything unless they think that they are going to profit by it. It is this assumption, indeed, that underpins our entire free market economic system, as we have been seeing, rather to our cost, recently. Taken to extremes, it brings us to the currently fashionable economic creed of neoliberalism, which declares that, 'There is no such thing as society'. A corrective is badly needed here, as we will see in the Economics chapter below. It seems that the profit motive is hard wired into the human psyche, but because human beings are infinitely varied, everyone's conception of what constitutes 'profit' is also varied. That of the drug addict will be very different from that of the hedge fund manager, for example, although both are addicts in their way. In fact, it could be argued that even love is nothing more than a purely selfish interest taken in another person or thing for the sake of the pleasure that they have to offer you. As Confucius once noted, 'Can there be a love that does not make demands of its object?' '*Aber Gott im Himmel, was ist das?!? Dieser Mann ist* as pessimistic as Schopenhauer, as cynical as Camus! I will read no more of this amoral rubbish! Into the bin with it!' But nay, nay. Soft, gentle reader: stay thy revengeful hand. Only hear me out, and all will yet be well. Things work out. Personally, I have always rated love very highly on my list of priorities. Remember too the observation made by Alexander Pope (1688-1744) in his very long work, *An Essay on Man* that was finally published in 1734. Towards the end of 'Epistle III' he notes,

> Self-love forsook the path it first pursued
> And found the private in the public good...
> Thus God and Nature linked the general frame,
> And bade self-love and social be the same. (Lines 281-2, 317-8)

Pope is talking about what we might call, 'enlightened self-interest' here. The basic selfishness of humankind is in fact a zero-sum game: it all comes out in the wash: it does not make us all monsters. We are still the same people that you see around you every day. One man's idea of 'profit' is not necessarily another's: people choose different routes to happiness. Surely it is through giving that we receive, by loving that we are loved, and in service to the community that we find our place. Some people derive great happiness from making others happy, a motivation that we should all aspire to, for surely those who bring happiness into the lives of others cannot keep it out of their own. The motivation may be selfish, but the *consequences* of people's actions are always of much greater significance than their *motivation* for those actions. I little thought at the time I first conceived those ideas how hideously perverted and misapplied they were later to be by the neoliberals, who drew mainly on the philosophy of Ayn Rand (1905-82).

Besides, this idea of the basic selfishness of man, like all my other early thoughts, of course turned out to be not so original after all. I later came to realise that many others had danced around the concept, while not perhaps stating it as bluntly as I do here. I might just mention in this context Epicurus of Samos (341-270 BC), Niccolò Machiavelli (1469-1527), Thomas Hobbes (1588-1679), Blaise Pascal (1623-62), David Hume (1711-66), Claude Helvétius (1715-71), and the economic theorists Bernard Mandeville (1670-1733) and Adam Smith (1723-90). Jeremy Bentham (1748-1832) and the Utilitarians also toyed with the idea in the nineteenth century, and by the twentieth century the study of the subject had been put onto a more scientific footing, under the heading of 'egoism'. The sub-categories of ethical egoism, rational egoism, and psychological egoism were distinguished by writers like Herbert Spencer (1820-1903), Ayn Rand (1905-82), and Derek Parfit (1942-2017). When it comes to academic Philosophy, it seems that there really is nothing new under the sun!

Of course, philosophers tend to over-analyse and rarefy their concepts to such an extent that they cease to have any meaningful existence at all. For a concept to have practical utility, you have to keep it simple. If you come across a philosophical tenet or scientific theory that is impossibly complicated, you must suspect that it is either,

(a) Completely wrong or
(b) Right, but completely irrelevant or
(c) Half right, but equally irrelevant

The man who stayed behind to fight a rearguard action gave his life as a ransom for many, and therefore deserves to be honoured with the honour that is due to him in the society that we humans have superimposed upon God's world. Self-sacrifice is the highest form of morality, according to our human system of values, and we live now in a world of human values. But these are not God's values, as will later become clear. Nevertheless, this story will have a happy ending, although getting there might take a bit of reaching. and a bit of grasping, and, for that matter, a bit of courage. We must be prepared to look the truth in the face, however ugly that face may be. We often find this hard to do. As T.S. Eliot observed in *Burnt Norton*, the first of his *Four Quartets*, 'human kind cannot bear very much reality' (lines 42-3). But I would argue that the face of truth is not all that ugly – rather more a face of...er...'character', perhaps. Well, some would say 'character-riddled' I suppose, but in my view it is a face that the wise man can learn to love. It will be noted that my tone throughout is one of cheerfulness and gratitude for what I believe to be very good reasons, as we shall see.

I would like to mention at this point that as an academic I have been used to writing scholarly pieces of work that have been heavily referenced and footnoted: indeed, sometimes the footnotes have taken up half of the page! But I want to avoid footnotes here for a number of reasons. First, they will be rather tedious for both the reader and for me as the writer. Since this is basically just a general survey for the general reader, written in what I hope is plain language, I don't want to spoil the fun for either of us: I hope to make this something of an entertaining read! I will, however, always make a point of sourcing the lengthier quotations in the text, and I will provide page numbers when I cite references from journals. This book is not intended for professional philosophers or great intellectuals, but only for the interested layman, who feels that a background knowledge of philosophers and Philosophy ought to have a place in the well-furnished mind.

Secondly, a certain proportion of what follows will be simply my own views, with which you may agree or agree not. Thirdly, this text is so replete with references that once again footnotes would take up half the page, or require frequent flipping to the back of the book. Fourthly, I have a precedent for this. Bertrand Russell himself in his monumental *History of Western Philosophy* (1946) produced a book that was very short on footnotes indeed: they were almost entirely absent. But finally, and most important, we now live in a new age of profound intellectual revolution. There is no longer any excuse for anyone of an enquiring mind to remain ignorant about anything. I refer of course to the near-miraculous powers of the internet, the modern-day Oracle of Delphi, which will surely change our world in the most profound of ways. I have used it myself in the writing of this book. Of course, not all of the information provided on the web is accurate, and ye sceptical historian must remain as suspicious of this source as of all the others, if not more so, but multiple entries are provided for each topic, and they can all be checked against external sources. I often came to feel, in the course of researching and writing this text over thirteen years, that I was supporting Amazon's book department single-handed, but I found the web to be an invaluable guide to the books that I needed to buy to help with this project. So what I suggest is this. Read me with your laptop, tablet or smart phone glowing by your side. If you doubt anything that I say, or want more information on a topic, check it out immediately with The Oracle. Nobody is infallible, but I have gone to a lot of trouble here to ensure that my factual statements will prove to be robust. The text that follows is packed with information that I have found to be very interesting and which, I hope, may also prove to be of interest to others. As once noted, 'It is impossible to open a book without learning something', and I will be very surprised if anyone, whatever their speciality, can read through this entire text without emerging a little the wiser. Dull would he be of soul indeed who cannot find at least something of interest in the pages that follow. If all else fails, readers might amuse themselves by playing 'spot the literary allusion' as they go through the text. Have you just missed one?

If my tone is sometimes donnish, I must apologise for that: long years of teaching have left their mark. You can take the teacher out of the classroom, but not the classroom out of the teacher! Forgive me too for doing all the talking: as a teacher, I used to employ the Socratic method in my seminars and tutorials, constantly questioning the students about the topic they were supposed to have studied for that week. I found this to be a splendid way of getting the old brainboxes creaking into action: something of a heuristic approach. The more I could get the students talking, and the less I said myself, the more I counted the tutorial a success. Of course, this didn't always work! But I would say to teachers everywhere, if you are learned, then wear your learning lightly, and keep a sense of humour. If readers can get through this entire text without at least one hearty belly-laugh, then I will have failed! There is always room for humour in every context. If there is one thing that philosophy ought to teach us, it is not to take ourselves too seriously, and not to take the world too seriously either: you'll never get out of it alive! Arrogance is the enemy of truth. But on the other hand, professionalism *should* be taken seriously, for its own sake.

While on the subject of teaching, I would like to mention here something that long years of teaching have taught me. It is, quite simply, that important points need to be stressed more than once. If readers note, therefore, that some points are reiterated in different locations, it should not be assumed that this is indicative of encroaching senile dementia on my part: the re-stressing is deliberate, in the interests of clarity at different points. Teachers should also try to guide their charges towards clarity of thought, and encourage them to care about their fellow men, as so many of our
great religious figures have taught us. There is a place for religion in the world, and in our lives, but religion does need to be kept firmly *in* its place, and not allowed to run out of control. It will be a recurrent theme of this treatise that religion makes a good servant, but a bad master. The same might be said of economic philosophies.

Having said that, however, I must admit that those philosophers whom I admire the most were all religious sceptics, or at best indifferent on religious questions. I have in particular four 'heroes' who are Baruch Spinoza (1632-77), Tomas Paine (1737-1809), Albert Einstein (1879-1955), and Karl Popper (1902-94). Spinoza and Paine in particular appealed to me because both were uncompromising rationalists like myself. These four will all receive more detailed treatment in the chapter devoted exclusively to them below. The good philosopher needs to be possessed of a rare combination of courage, self-confidence, and humility, always remembering that however strongly he may feel that he is right, the only thing he can ever know for sure is that he could be wrong. All too often, however, this courage can shade into foolhardiness, the self-confidence into arrogance, and the humility into unshakable conviction. Not even my four philosopher heroes are entirely innocent on those counts. No one is perfect, no one is ever completely right, and even my four 'heroes' are open to criticism, as I shall show below.

My four thinkers all appealed to me initially entirely on the grounds of their philosophies, but on later researching into their backgrounds I was surprised to discover how much they had in common. First, three of my four heroes were Jewish by descent: Thomas Paine was the only gentile in my quartet. Next, three out of four trained as craftsmen before they became famous as writers and philosophers: Spinoza was a lens grinder, Paine a stay maker, while Popper left school at 16 and became an apprentice cabinetmaker. He did not begin serious academic studies until he was 23. Only Einstein had anything like a conventional academic education, although even his was patchy and disrupted. Considered to be rather dim academically, his tutors gave him poor references. He was unable to get the teaching job that he had trained for, and began his working life as a Patent Office clerk, not getting a full-time academic post until he was over 30. Not one of them took the primrose path through an expensive private schooling and on to a top flight university: indeed, not one of them ever took a first degree at all, although Einstein and Popper both acquired teaching certificates, and were able to submit dissertations in later life which earned them doctorates. But all four did have one thing in common: they all displayed a healthy contempt for authority, and were more than ready to think for themselves. Indeed, Albert is on record as saying, 'God has punished me for my contempt for authority by making me an authority myself!', while Paine observed, 'I never quote: I always think'. All four were in fact very largely self-educated men. Spinoza and Einstein were both panentheists and determinists and therefore held an obvious appeal for me as kindred spirits, but Paine and Popper were most certainly neither. Popper in fact harboured a profound distrust of 'historicism', which he saw as a kind of determinism, while Paine was simply a deist, describing his religion as 'doing good'. He came close to pantheism, but in the end retained his belief in a personal God and an afterlife. A final point of similarity between them was that all four suffered struggle, hardship, and persecution over the course of their lifetimes. Indeed, Einstein and Popper were forced to flee for their lives from Nazi Germany. Although they gave us so much, not one of them died a wealthy man. In fact, Spinoza and Paine died in poverty. Einstein and Popper became full-time academics, and as I know well, academics never die rich! But we count ourselves fortunate in other ways.

Now why those four in particular? The good philosopher must be possessed of total scepticism, utter disrespect, and complete indifference to other people's opinion of him. His loyalty must be only to the truth as he sees it, even if this truth proves to be unpalatable to his audience. All four of my heroes possessed these qualities in large measure. Einstein was cordially detested by the Right, and Popper by the Left, while Spinoza and Paine were perfectly happy to be unpopular with everyone. Despite this, however, all four were great humanitarians. In the cases of Paine, Popper, and Einstein their humanitarianism was overt, manifest, and palpable. In the case of Spinoza, some reading between the lines is required, but he too was a great humanitarian, with a genuine concern for the wellbeing of mankind.

Philosophy tends to be regarded by most people as an impossibly elevated, ethereal, abstract, and intellectual study that they would prefer not to have anything to do with. As regards academic Philosophy as taught in university departments, they may have something of a point there, but I believe that academic philosophers insist upon too narrow a definition of their subject. I intend to treat it in a broader context here. In my view, 'philosophy' in its broader sense may be seen as intersecting with every other academic discipline, and with every aspect of life in general. I suspect that in fact most of us become philosophers by compulsion: we have to arrive at a view of the world that makes sense to us. In my case, I was never overly concerned about whether my views were right or wrong: I simply thought that you had to believe in *something* as a starting position, and then keep an open mind, being ready to change your opinions in the light of new knowledge or experiences. But my own speculations have led me to the conclusions that,

Truth is absolute, not relative.
Morality is absolute, not relative.
Reality (for the individual) is objective not subjective.
But happiness is subjective, not objective.

In the political and economic spheres I am a Centrist: fanaticism and extremism are always to be avoided. I believe that every successful economy must have a free enterprise capitalist system at its core, and in consequence we must be prepared to tolerate a degree of inequality as a result of this. The question is, of course, how much inequality is tolerable? I do not stand for making the rich poor, but I believe that the poor need to be made richer. I am reminded here of Karl Popper's dictum that we should strive not for the greatest happiness of the greatest number, but rather for the least misery of the greatest number. Moreover, the capitalism that we have should not be unbridled, 'let 'er rip' private capitalism: this form of capitalism has proved itself to be ultimately self-destructive twice in recent times, once in the 1930s and again in 2007-9. Capitalism, like religion, makes a good servant, but a bad master. It needs to be regulated, controlled, and harnessed so that it works for the benefit of the entire community, and not just for a fortunate few. Capitalism on its own is not enough: the state also has a role to play. I have not changed my political and economic views greatly over the course of a longish lifetime, but the world has lurched violently to the Right around me in economic terms so that I now appear to be a 'Lefty', although I would see myself more as a Centrist. Apart from the monarchy and the House of Lords, which I have always believed to be indefensible, I approved of the status quo in the 1960s and was seen as a conservative: in fact, I even voted Conservative in 1964. I remember infuriating the Marxists of those days by telling them that I believed capitalism to be based upon a sounder understanding of human nature than was Communism. But today's Conservative Party bears no resemblance to the party that I voted for in 1964 and so, without changing my views, I now appear as a radical in terms of my economic thought. Basically, however, I stand with Karl Popper as a pragmatist and a humanitarian.

Now 'truth' has of course proved to be a somewhat elusive commodity over the centuries, but even the highly sceptical Popper was not prepared to deny that absolute truth did exist, only that it was impossible to prove. Well, perhaps so, but being a simple fellow I apply just two criteria as tests for truth.

(a) Does it *work*? If so, I say that it is *true enough* to be going on with.
(b) Does it stand up to scientific examination? If so, I am prepared to accept it as being true *for the time being*. Life must go on after all.

Of course, there was nothing unusual about such speculations: in fact, everyone becomes a philosopher when they form their own view of the world and decide on their priorities in life. For most, money figures highly on their list of priorities, rather like Lionel Bart's Fagin in the musical *Oliver*, who opined,

In this life, one thing counts:
In the bank, large amounts!
Sums like these don't grow on trees,
You've got to pick a pocket or two,
Yooooo have gotta pick a pocket or two!

This was not a very commendable philosophy to be sure, but at least Fagin did have a clear philosophy: rather like that of today's bankers and hedge fund managers, as a matter of fact! Again like Fagin, they much prefer to pay no tax on their ill-gotten gains! But the point is that the kind of philosophy that you adopt can have a profound influence on your happiness in this life. In the Conclusion of this work I will expand on the importance of philosophy as a route to personal happiness. Jesus said, 'What shall it profit a man should he gain the whole world, but lose his own soul?' (Mark 8:36) I am not a Christian myself, but I very much get the point there, and find myself entirely in sympathy with the ethical teachings of Jesus. Philosophy is not to be dismissed: it can play a crucial role in our happiness and success both as societies and as individuals. Can such abstract concepts as 'happiness' and 'morality' ever be satisfactorily defined? Perhaps not, but it is the task of philosophy to try to do so,. and after we have heard what the philosophers have to say, definitions of both of these terms will be offered in the Conclusion to this work. And now, bearing in mind this broader definition of 'philosophy', let us see how it may be applied to other disciplines, and how it might indeed have shaped the development of our world. Giving the Herbert Spencer Lecture at Oxford in 1933, Albert Einstein said, in effect, ‘Everything should be made as simple as possible, but no simpler’. That sounds like good advice to me, so let’s apply Ockham’s razor to some of the fields mentioned above, and see where it gets us.

I On Religion

In any history of ideas, religion must occupy a prominent position, because it is in fact religious conceptions that have dominated most of the thought, and much of the lives, of most of humanity over most of recorded history. Therefore, although this treatise is essentially about philosophy, it seems appropriate to begin here with an examination of religion, because religions represented in fact the earliest forms of philosophy, the first attempts by mankind to understand the world and his own place within it. Professional philosophers may of course dismiss this contention, and indeed deny that any 'religion' can be seen as real 'philosophy' at all, being based, as so many religions are, upon myth and legend. But I will argue later that philosophers are taking an unduly blinkered view in this regard: we need to keep our eye on the ball here. It was Socrates (c470-399 BC) who first tried to explain to the people of Athens that the true role of philosophy was not to attempt an explanation of how the world worked (about which they knew nothing), nor to answer the question 'Why are we here?' (about which they knew equally little), nor even to understand the nature of the divine. Rather, said Socrates, philosophers should confine themselves to considering a more modest question, one to which they actually had some chance of providing a sensible answer. The question was, 'How should we live, both as individuals and as communities?' On this issue, religions have had a great deal to say, and on those grounds alone I would argue that no study of philosophy can be complete without a serious examination of the religious dimension in human thought through the ages.

Mankind has been described as, 'a worshipping animal', (*homo religiosus*) and this would appear to be self-evidently true. Every society in past history seems to have created some form of religion for itself. But why this ubiquitous urge to worship? There are three fairly obvious answers to this question. First, in a pre-scientific age, the world must have engendered a sense of wonder in any intelligent being who observed it: the beauty, the order, the regularity, the exquisite symmetry of even the tiniest creature, each one seemingly so well designed for survival in its own environment. Surely such wonderful architecture implied an intelligent Creator of enormous power and majesty.

Secondly, in early societies life was very uncertain: disease and death were never far away. People came to feel that their destinies were in the hands of forces beyond their control, a sentiment with which I would entirely agree! Famine, fire, disease, earthquakes, flood, and tempest were ever-present threats. Could these ills be afflictions sent by a wrathful God or gods? Perhaps they needed to be propitiated with worship and sacrifice. Yet some people were clearly more fortunate than others. Was this because they deserved to be? Were they the darlings of the gods? From such thoughts arose the idea of 'deserving', and from that a whole code of religious do's and don'ts.

Thirdly, there was the fear of death, and the hope of an afterlife to follow beyond the grave. Many ancient cultures practised ancestor worship, as though their forebears were still alive. The Greeks and Romans were very vague about the kind of afterlife that could be expected in the land of shades after Charon had ferried souls across the Styx, although they did believe that there existed Fields of Punishment for those who had slighted or insulted the gods, and the Elysian Fields for those of particular merit. But what happened to everyone else was unclear! The ancient Hebrews were even more unclear about the afterlife in 'Sheol' or the underworld, which they appear to have regarded as a kind of waiting room. With the exception of the Sadducees, they seemed to rest their hopes on some form of bodily resurrection on 'the last day', when everyone would be judged. Both faiths seemed to believe that God or the gods punished or rewarded men in this life rather than the next, but it is worth noting that even these faiths looked to an afterlife of some description. This applies also to Buddhism, usually described as a 'non-theistic' religion, where the afterlife takes the form of a series of reincarnations. Islam took up the Jewish idea of the Last Day, a general resurrection, and a final judgement on all, although those of special merit (notably those who died in *jihad*) did not have to wait, and could go straight to paradise!

But beyond this, even the most secular of us seem to experience a deeper need, the need to hold some kind of belief, to espouse some form of value system. In recent times, these instincts have taken the forms of what are often termed 'secular religions' such as Communism, Socialism, Fascism or, closer to home, liberalism, humanism, individualism, capitalism, and even that most touching faith of all, the belief that endless economic growth will set us on the road to paradise. Well, even the darkest of these creeds has something to be said for them. But they all illustrate a point that the wise king Solomon made long ago: 'Where there is no vision, the people perish'. (Proverbs 29:18) I should add at this point that all my biblical quotes will be taken from the King James translation of 1611, one of the finest works of English literature ever produced, but now abandoned by philistines in favour of prosaic modern versions.

But what sort of gods were worshipped? I think it would be true to say that in general we humans have created our gods in our own image. This is particularly true of the 'Abrahamic' religions, that is to say Judaism, Christianity, and Islam, all three of which trace their origins back to Abraham and his original covenant with God. All three regard Abraham as their spiritual, and indeed also their ancestral father, the progenitor of 'the people of God'. Jehovah, or Yahweh, was of course originally the exclusively Jewish God, and Jews have every right to feel rather aggrieved that He has been hijacked and taken over by later faiths, which now declare the Jews to be in grave theological error! All three, however, accept the Genesis account of creation, in theological terms at least, and so all three agree that God created man in His own image – 'in the image of God created He him', as Genesis tells us (1:27). In reality, of course, the Jews were creating God in *their* own image, because they could not imagine a higher life form than man to see Him as, and so their vision of God was a literal, physical image of a human being, very much like themselves, but endowed with supernatural powers. In this respect, the later Abrahamic religions have followed suit, accepting the Jewish view of God as being essentially a man, but an immortal and omnipotent one. The Persian poet Omar Khayyam (1048-1131), who was of course a Muslim, got away with some near-blasphemous statements when he hinted at this in his famous poem *The Rubaiyat*, where he wrote,

> Oh Thou, who man of baser earth dist make,
> And who with Eden didst devise the snake,
> For all the sin wherewith the face of man
> Is blackened, man's forgiveness give – and take!
>
> Listen again. One evening at the close
> Of Ramazan, ere the moon arose,
> In that old potter's shop I stood alone
> With the clay population round in rows.
>
> And strange to tell, amongst that earthen lot
> Some could articulate, while others not:
> And suddenly one more impatient cried,
> 'Who is the potter, pray, and who the pot?' (Verses 58-60)

There can scarcely have been a more blasphemous question that Khayyam, or any other monotheist, could have posed than that asked in verse 60. Indeed, the whole poem is blasphemous in tone, and yet at the time Omar went not only unstoned and uncrucified for it, but was actually celebrated in his day as a great Islamic sage! This was the challenging, probing, enquiring, and tolerant spirit of eleventh-century Islam, but later, what a sorry falling off was there. Today *The Rubaiyat* is, to put it mildly, out of favour in the entire Islamic world, not least in Khayyam's native Persia, present-day Iran. Later in the poem he extols the virtues of wine, while today the drinking of alcohol is a flogging offence under *Sharia* law. Islam was to change its whole approach towards free thinking and scholarship in the later middle ages.

A closely anthropomorphic view of their God or Gods was not, however, one taken by other faiths. As Xenophanes of Colophon (c.570-475 BC) once observed,

> The Ethiops say that their Gods are flat-nosed and black,
> While the Thracians say that theirs have blue eyes and red hair.
> Yet if cattle, or horses, or lions had hands and could draw
> And could sculpture like men, then the horses would draw their gods
> Like horses, and cattle like cattle, and each would then shape
> Bodies of gods in the likeness, each kind of its own.

(Translation from Karl R. Popper, *The Open Society* (2002 ed.) p. 510)

The ancient Egyptians and the Hindus created for themselves many gods that combined both animal and human features or, if basically human, were distinctly mutated, like the Hindu Vishnu, usually depicted with four arms. However, all these physical images of God or gods that mankind has conjured up for himself are interesting, but irrelevant. What really matters are the spiritual qualities, the value systems, and the emotional characteristics of all these gods that are now being worshipped around the world. Here, we find that they all have one thing in common – their values and their temperaments are, unsurprisingly enough, very much like our own or, to be more specific, very much like the temperaments of those peoples who were alive at the time that these gods were envisaged. They were dreamed up in an age when rulers were absolute and all powerful, when they expected unquestioning obedience from all their subjects. Such rulers were known as 'Oriental Despots', the products of the first agricultural societies. They revelled in praise and adulation, loving to be told how great and wonderful they were. Anyone who crossed them or displeased them in any way could expect terrible punishments: indeed, the more awful the punishments, the 'greater' the ruler was assumed to be. Hence the Judaic god, who handed down laws to his people, and who punished idolatry, disobedience, or bad behaviour primarily with wrathful vengeance in this world, and the Christian and Islamic gods who were believed to have prepared a hellish afterlife for those who had displeased them. In this way, the ancient gods were envisaged as being very much like the rulers of the time. In fact, many Roman emperors declared that they actually *were* gods. And so, these gods had of course very human traits. They were vain, jealous, vengeful, and capricious, like the gods of ancient Greece and Rome. They took sides in the conflicts of mortals, as in the Trojan War, and if they had any values at all, these were entirely the human values of the time.

But what if the real God is in fact nothing at all like a human being with human values and human foibles? What if He is not a person at all, but rather a process, an inevitable working out of His purposes? What if He is, in fact, The Great Nature of All Things or, quite simply, The Way Things Are, incorporating also, The Way Things Work? This is what we panentheists believe. For us, there is no such thing as the supernatural, or even the unnatural: if it exists at all, it must be natural, a part of God's creation. For us, there is only the natural that we understand, and the natural that we do not understand (yet). A 'miracle' is simply a highly improbable event that happens against all the laws of chance, but is still allowable within the laws of physics. We see God in Nature: we see God everywhere. A more detailed definition of panentheism will be provided in the Spinoza section below, but that outline will serve for the time being.

Now this panentheist God is certainly powerful. He really did create the heavens and the earth and all that therein is, and He really does determine the destinies of us all. We are truly entirely in God's hands. As the old song says, 'He's got the whole world in His hands'! This, indeed, is where panentheism ties up with determinism. I shall be going into the scientific proofs of determinism later in this treatise, but for now, let's ask a second question. The panentheist God is certainly powerful, but is He benevolent? A good question. Christian theologians have always found the problem of evil in the world to be very troubling, because they want to represent God as all powerful, *and* all good. Whence then, comes evil? Why doesn't God prevent it? Does this mean He is all good, but not all powerful? Or is He all-powerful but not all good? The Christians try to get around this conundrum by saying that indeed God *is* all powerful *and* all good, but he gave us free will, and so *we* are responsible for all the evil in the world. But this attempt to shift the blame onto us won't wash. Natural disasters such as famine, plagues, earthquakes, tsunamis, volcanic eruptions, floods, tornados etc. are hardly our fault, but cause great human suffering. Three of the Four Horsemen of the Apocalypse, Famine, Plague, and Death were agents of God. Only one, War, was an agent of man. The panentheist, on the other hand, has absolutely no difficulty in dealing with the problem of evil. He can state, quite categorically, that God is indeed all powerful, but *not* all good. However, He isn't all bad either. Let's try to sum Him up.

As a creator God, He has certainly done a good job from our point of view as far as this planet is concerned. But what sort of values does He have? Are they anything like *our* values? To answer that question, we must consider the world as it was before the arrival of *homo sapiens* upon the scene, a mere 250,000 years ago, although earlier hominid species such as *homo erectus* and *homo habilis* go back for almost two million years. But let's look back for some seven million years, to a time when all we humans shared just one common ancestor with today's anthropoid apes, a creature that was, of course, more ape than man. What sort of world did that creature inhabit, when God had the world all to Himself, without the interference of any human agency?

The world of seven million years ago was one of nature red in tooth and claw. The creatures of the time killed and ate one another simply to survive, following their pre-programmed survival instincts, and terms such as 'murder' or 'morality' had absolutely no application at the time. Neither had the term, 'justice'. Survival was very much a matter of luck. If you were in the wrong place at the wrong time, so much the worse for you, whether you 'deserved' to die or not. In short, our human values did not apply at all in the world that God had to himself. We might call this 'God's world' or, 'the real world'. Here, there was no justice, no morality, no mercy, and no exceptions: everyone, every gene-passing living thing, was condemned to death. God's concern was not with the survival of any individual, but only with the survival of the species as a whole. You might say that God was no respecter of persons, or of how a creature had behaved in its lifetime, since 'morality' had no meaning in those days. Today, of course, things are very different. Today we humans have inherited the earth, and we have superimposed our own invented value systems upon God's world, the real world. But this world, the real world, has not gone away – it is still there beneath the surface of our civilisation, and in the end it is the nature of this real world that must ultimately have the last word.

Now let us return to the nature of God. I remember once seeing a Jew debating with a Christian on television. With some exasperation, the Jew was trying to explain to the Christian why no man could ever be God. I remember his words well: 'Man is man, and God is God, and the two are entirely different things!' Well, I would certainly agree with that. The Jew, of course, was explaining his denial of the divinity of Christ, but I would take the argument rather further than that. I would say that God is nothing like man at all. Because men love to be praised, worshipped, and adored they assumed that God must be the same. Because men loved power, they assumed that God must be all-powerful. Because men were capable of pity, mercy, and compassion, and could be swayed to all of them by suitably grovelling entreaties, they assumed that God must be the same. Because they had devised their own codes of values and morality they assumed that God too must have his moral laws, which all were expected to obey. Well, I would agree that God is indeed all-powerful and has His laws, but not with the rest of those assumptions. The God that I see is completely above praise or blame, and so is utterly indifferent to both. Not only is He indifferent to flattery or pleadings, but also He knows nothing of justice, morality, or mercy. He is no respecter of persons. He doesn't much care about who you are or what you've done. 'Yer gonna git what yer gonna git, and that's that'. (I would say that's a fairly succinct summing up of my philosophy!) Your future was predetermined for you from the moment of your birth: indeed, from long before that. This means, of course, that strictly speaking you are responsible for nothing. Everything that you did was predetermined by the Great Nature of All Things: you were entirely in His hands, and had no choice in the matter.

But here's the rub. Because you do not live *only* in God's world, the real world, but also in the artificial world that we have superimposed upon God's reality, you will be *held* responsible for everything that you do by your fellow men. God does not judge us any more than he judged the animals before us. God understands that we are all as he made us. Only people judge: we only ever judge one another. This is no bad thing for, knowing this, it will influence the predetermined decisions that we make in specific cases, which will tend to make the world a better place for us all. To an extent, of course, the distinction that I am drawing here between God's world and man's world is therefore an artificial one. Man's world too is a part of God's creation, a part of His great plan. But I find the distinction a useful one to draw as an aid to understanding The Great Nature of All Things, for the following reason. 'The Lord will provide' is an oft-quoted saying. But will he? Well, yes and no, really. Say that you found yourself in God's world of seven million years ago. What would be provided for you? Where would you live? You might find a cave unoccupied by a fierce predator if you were very lucky, or perhaps a hollowed tree. No ready-made clothes, of course, and edible fruits, nuts, or roots might be in short supply. There might be some game to catch, if you could run fast enough. In fact, if you left it to God to provide, you would find yourself not at all well off. So God is not a great provider then? Well, yes and no, really. He does not provide directly, but He has given us the wherewithal to provide for ourselves, in terms of the intelligence, the physical ability, and the raw materials. But we can make far better use of all those assets as a *collective* than any one of us ever could as an individual. In the last analysis, we have only one another to rely on. God does not love us. God means to kill us all, and he will kill us all. But we should not blame Him for that: He had no choice. That was the only way that evolution could come about, the only means of allowing us to be here at all. Not even God has free will.

We have to understand that God has provided us with an incredibly improbable planet, as we will see in the Science section below, but that's all that He's going to do for us. If we want a better world than He left us, then it is entirely up to us now to build it for ourselves. Physically, this will involve a lot of hard work on our part, but most of this work has already been done, at least as far as the developed world is concerned. What we need to do now is pay more attention to our value systems, those created concepts of justice, morality, and compassion which do not apply in God's world, but which are very important to us in the superimposed world that we have created. There will be more about this in the Politics and Economics sections below, but personally I would say that what we need at the moment is a good deal less stress on 'efficiency' and considerably more stress on ecology and humanity if we want to build a better world for our children.

But will we build it? The problems that lie ahead for our species are formidable. The determinist would say that we have already been predestined to success or failure, according to the kind of creatures that we are. But here, I seem to be posing a conundrum, almost an oxymoron. What, God has decided our future, and yet it's up to us what kind of future it will be? Yes, exactly. There is no contradiction here. It might help if we examined the Calvinist view of predestination at this point. Jean Calvin (1509-64), the founder of Presbyterianism, based his views on the letters of St. Paul to the early Christian communities, especially Romans 8: 28-30, 1 Corinthians 2:7, and Ephesians 1: 4,5,11. The gist of these passages is that to some eternal life, and to some eternal death is preordained from 'before the foundations of the world'. Calvin was not a true determinist, for his 'predestination' extended only to the question of whether one was 'saved' or not. But if this vital issue had been predetermined, then surely it did not matter how anyone behaved in this world? Ah, but it did! For how did you *know* whether you were one of the 'elect' or not? Why, by their fruits ye shall know them, of course! If you *were* one of the chosen, then you would *behave* like one of the chosen. The drunken, adulterous, fornicating robber couldn't possibly be one of the elect, while the 'godly' man might well be. So it *did* still matter how you behaved.

In the same way, although our future as a species is predetermined, we cannot foresee what it will be. But we can get some indication of it by looking at the way we are behaving at the moment. We have to learn to distinguish between the predetermined and the unpredictable. Many things are unpredictable, especially in the quantum world (where some things are *totally* unpredictable) but all things are predetermined, even in the quantum world. What we have to grasp is that we have to examine our behaviour *now* if we want to make an accurate forecast of our likely predetermined future.

Am I optimistic? I would like to be. We are such an intelligent species: you'd think we would be capable of working things out. I don't want to sound like an Old Testament prophet here – well, specifically Jeremiah, I suppose – but I am worried, because the challenges facing us at the moment are formidable indeed, as will be spelled out in the Conclusion below. For now, however, the important thing is to realise that we must not turn to God for help. What those touchingly insouciant Christians (and Muslims and Jews) have got to understand is the palpably obvious fact that, 'Quite frankly my dear, God doesn't give a damn', if I may paraphrase *Gone With the Wind.* But neither does he damn anyone: rather, he is totally indifferent. God doesn't care, only people care. We have only each other to rely upon. It really should not be necessary to have to point this out in the early twenty-first century, but it seems that it is. Volcano in Guatemala? 'Tough luck.' Genocide in Iraq? 'Don't blame me, pal.' Children dying from ebola in Liberia? 'It happens.' Tsunami in Japan? 'All part of the overall picture.' 116 primary school children killed by a sliding coal tip in Wales? 'Tough luck!' When people say 'God help them' of those in a desperate situation, what they mean is, 'There's virtually no hope for them'. We are a very small part of His overall plan, and the universe was not designed especially for us. We are simply an incidental and highly improbable by-product that turned up along the way. If our entire species were to be wiped from the face of the Earth, God would simply shrug, and the universe would roll steadily on its way. Indeed, all the other life forms on this planet would be left a good deal better off! So you might say that I belong to The Church of God the Utterly Indifferent. But this is not a doctrine of despair, as I shall later try to show. Your predetermined future as an individual may well prove to be a very happy one, in which case you should be profoundly grateful. God obviously *isn't* 'all good', but He isn't all bad either. The point is that we cannot rely on God for help, because God doesn't give a damn: we have only each other. If we are not prepared to love one another, to care for one another, and to provide for one another, then our future will be bleak indeed.

This chapter is not intended to be a review of the world's religions, past and present, but it might, at this point, be worth looking at the world's 'big four' to see whether they have anything in common. In ascending order of number of adherents these are Buddhism, Hinduism, Islam, and Judaeo-Christianity. I say 'Judaeo-Christianity' because my King James Bible is 2,558 pages long. Of those only 365, or rather less than 14.3% of the whole, are devoted to the New Testament. Clearly, the Christians have adopted Judaic theology almost wholesale, and have simply bolted JC onto the end of it! In a way, this is rather odd, for the message of the New Testament is very different from that of the Old: the two texts make uneasy bedfellows.

But what, if anything, do all these different faiths have in common? Well, they all enjoin good, socially acceptable behaviour on the part of their adherents, in the belief that this will secure for them a better place in one form of afterlife or another. This applies even to Buddhism, whose adherents deny the existence of an individual soul. Nevertheless, a mystical, transformed manifestation of 'the self' may progress upwards in a hierarchy of reincarnations which may ultimately allow this manifestation to join the '*anagamis*', or non-returners, because here the highest level of existence will have been reached. The Hindus take a more straightforward view of reincarnation, believing in the existence of an immortal 'atman' or soul, which may reincarnate through progressively higher levels of existence until finally attaining unity with the cosmic spirit Brahman, or Paramatman, under different versions of Hinduism. Christianity and Islam also offer rewards to the virtuous in an afterlife or at the Day of Judgement, and this is fine. anything that encourages people to behave in socially acceptable ways, even if for the wrong reasons, can only contribute to the general good. It will be a recurrent theme of this treatise that the *consequences* of people's actions are of far greater importance than their *motivation* for them. It is better to do the right thing for the wrong reasons than not to do the right thing at all. In saying this, I am flatly contradicting the view of Immanuel Kant as put forward in his *Critique of Pure Reason* (1996 ed.) pp. 422-9, where he argues that in fact the motivations for our actions are more important than their consequences. We should do the right thing simply because it is the right thing to do, and not because we hope for a heavenly reward in return for our efforts. We should always be motivated by the highest of moral principles, as established by reason, his famous, 'categorical imperative'. Of course, it would always be *preferable* to do the right things for the *right* reasons, and that is why getting at the truth is so important. Until we have established what is true, we cannot make what is best right. If you premise your conclusions upon false assumptions, the consequences for you may be seriously adverse. That is why religion makes a good servant, but a bad master. As for an afterlife, I have little time for the promises of religions, but the nature of the space-time continuum may offer us a kind of immortality, as we shall see in the Einstein section below.

This brings us to a consideration of some of the other features that these faiths share in common. They all believe in prayer or worship or meditation of one kind or another, in large groups or individually. They all have their pilgrimages to sacred shrines like Mecca, Lourdes, the Wailing Wall in Jerusalem, the Tooth of the Buddha in Sri Lanka, and innumerable Hindu shrines. They all enjoin some form of self-denial, such as fasting, giving up pleasures for Lent, or giving away large sums to charity. Again, these things are all worthy enough practices in themselves, but clearly they can all be overdone by the fanatical believer. It has driven some to bankruptcy, to monasticism, or to becoming wandering ascetics, like John the Baptist.

So what is the judgement of history upon religion? How does the balance sheet pan out? In so far as religions have encouraged moral and socially acceptable behaviour among their followers, this is to be cited to their credit. Religious belief has also inspired great works of art, in painting, sculpture, architecture, literature, and music, too numerous to mention here, but well known to us all. A further interesting point in favour of religion was put forward by the philosopher William James (1842-1910), who was the brother of the novelist Henry James (1843-1916) but also a very considerable figure in his own right. During the pragmatic phase of his thought, he seemed to suggest that religion could be seen as useful, and therefore valuable, if it brought some kind of spiritual comfort, however delusional, to its adherents. There is considerable controversy over just what James was actually saying here, and perhaps this point should be more fairly associated with the later thought of the psychologist Carl Jung (1875-1961), but this argument deserves to be taken seriously. God grant us our illusions. We clutch them to our bosoms: we wrap them around our psyches like blankets warmed before the fire: we need them to survive. It is a part of being human.

There are, therefore, those three points to be made in favour of religion. But what should we put on the debit side of the balance? First, while religious belief may have brought comfort to some, it has brought anguish to others by enjoining impossibly high standards of behaviour, backed by the threat of hellfire for those who fall short of the prescribed requirements for salvation. Too many people have trembled through life, constantly being made aware of their own 'sinfulness'. But to my mind, the greatest charge to be laid against religion is its sheer wastefulness – waste of prayer, waste of worship, waste of sacrifice, waste of material resources, and above all waste of thought. Just think of all those temples, shrines, pagodas, mosques, statues, Nazca lines, churches, monasteries, priories, and cathedrals that have been built all over the world. Today we can look back and say, 'thank God that they were', because now we have all those wonderful structures to enjoy. Artistically impressive yes, but at the time they consumed enormous amounts of scarce resources that could have been far better expended on practical projects that could have been of real benefit to the people of the time. I know that happiness is subjective, but come on – this is completely over the top! However, those people did at least make sacrifices to build for posterity, leaving us a rich legacy of beautiful parish churches and soaring cathedrals. They had convictions, while today we have only opinions. But opinions do not build cathedrals on that scale. By comparison, what are we leaving to posterity? The answer is a soaring national debt, and hospitals crippled by PFI schemes, all because our politicians think it is clever to look good for the moment at the expense of posterity. We ought to be ashamed of ourselves.

Nevertheless, the charge sheet against religion remains a heavy one. The waste of *thought* is another aspect which needs to be taken into consideration. While people were thinking about their gods, they were prevented from thinking about anything else, and the spirit of intellectual enquiry was stifled. Perhaps the most tragic example of this is seen in the fate of early-modern Islam. From about 800 to 1500 AD the Arabs moved far ahead of Christian Europe in intellectual terms, leading the way in mathematics, medicine, architecture, astronomy, geography, engineering, hygiene, poetry, and philosophy. Today we use Arabic numerals, and many of our naked-eye stars bear the common names given to them by Arab astronomers, as Aldebaran (the follower), Altair (the flying eagle), Rigel (foot of the giant), and Vega (the falling eagle). They produced poets like Omar Khayyam (1048-1131) Ibn al-Farid (1181-1235) and Muhammad Rumi (1207-1273), philosophers like Abu al Fida (1273-1331), Ibn Khaldun (1332-1406), and Ibn Alhazen (965-1040), claimed by some to be the father of the scientific method. Ibn Rushd (1126-1198), a remarkable polymath, was better known in the West as Averroes. The University of Al Karaouineat at Fez in Morocco, founded in 859, is recognised as the oldest degree-granting institution in the world. So fastidious about hygiene were the Arabs that in 851 an Arabian trader in China was shocked to notice what he considered to be a dirty Chinese habit. He wrote that the Chinese were, 'not careful about cleanliness, for they do not wash themselves with water when they have done their necessities, but only wipe themselves with paper'. (Needham, J., *Science and Civilization in China* Vol. V (1985) p. 123) The Chinese had been the first to perfect a form of paper making by around 100 AD, and had evidently found multiple uses for their new product.

It was the Arabs who preserved the learning of classical Greece and Rome while Barbarian Europe of the Dark Ages was forgetting it. Innumerable classical texts have survived only because Arabic translations were made of them. During the Christian Crusades of the eleventh to thirteenth centuries, the European invaders appeared as crude, unwashed barbarians beside the sophistication of their Muslim opponents. When the crusaders won a battle, they eagerly dismounted to seize the swords of their fallen foes, because Damascus steel was then the finest in the Western World. But slowly, Islamic thought came to dominate the minds of the Arabs. The torch of learning passed to the Ottoman Turks, and then sputtered out even there. Why think about anything else, when the only thing that mattered was one's eternal salvation? The Islamic world sank into a kind of torpor, nestling snugly, but inertly, in the bosom of Allah, forgetting all that they had learned. It was one of the saddest examples of intellectual decline in history.

Of course Christianity also has a lot to answer for here, dominating European thought almost to the exclusion of all else during the Middle Ages, and opposing scientific advance in the early-modern period. But just as the torch of secular learning was sputtering out in Islam, in Christian Europe it was beginning to blaze more brightly there than ever before with an artistic renaissance, a religious reformation, and the first stirrings of a scientific revolution, the beginnings of a sustained enlightenment that continues to this day. Open-mindedness is essential to intellectual progress, and of course religion closes minds. It is this waste of precious thought that is to be regretted even more than the waste of material resources.

But the most tragic waste of all is surely warfare. Nobody ever 'wins' a war: *everybody* loses. Here, of course, religion is again culpable, having inspired innumerable 'wars of religion'. The origin of these can be traced far back into the mists of time. The wars of the Mesopotamian city-states between 2000 and 3000 BC seem to have included religious elements, and the Israelite conquest of Canaan that we read of in the Book of Joshua could also be seen as a religious war. Archaeologists have dated a great battle at Jericho to about 1500 BC. But the era of large-scale religious wars was surely most clearly ushered in with the Islamic conquest of the Middle East in the seventh and eighth centuries AD. There was no doubt about the religious nature of those wars, and they were soon to be followed by many others. The Crusades are another obvious example, as were the Hussite Wars in Bohemia (1420-1431). The Reformation in Europe of course ushered in a whole new series of terrible religious wars in the sixteenth and seventeenth centuries, the worst of these being the Thirty Years War in Europe from 1618 to 1648. The 1715 and 1745 Jacobite rebellions in Scotland were inspired largely by religious factors, as were the many wars in Ireland that followed the Reformation. The sorry list could be extended almost indefinitely, but the point hardly needs to be laboured. Obviously religion has been a major cause of warfare in the past, and even today continues to be a terrible cause of conflict in the Middle East. As Blaise Pascal observed in his *Pensées*, posthumously published in 1670, 'Men never commit evil so completely and so cheerfully as when they do it from religious conviction'. (Section XIV No. 895) History bears this out, as witness the St. Bartholomew's Day massacre of 1572, when Protestant Huguenots were slaughtered on the streets of Paris by Catholics, or the Drogheda and Wexford massacres of September 1649 when Cromwell's Protestant troops slew Catholics in Ireland. On both occasions, men, women, and children were butchered indiscriminately.

The charge sheet against religion would therefore seem to be a heavy one: a cause of anxiety, a waste of resources, waste of time, waste of thought, and a cause of warfare. But perhaps we should remember that political elements were also a factor in these conflicts, and it was not so much religion itself that caused the wars as extreme religious intolerance and fanaticism. This proves once again that religion can be a good thing in moderation, but it needs to be kept in its place. Religion makes a good servant, but a bad master, a point recently proved yet again by the fanatical behaviour so-called 'Islamic State' supporters in Iraq and Syria.

Christianity is, by nominal number of adherents, the world's most widely followed faith, and the predominant religion of the western world. Perhaps, therefore, it deserves some detailed consideration here. So how does it appear through a historian's eyes? It is not too difficult for historians to strip away the mythology and get down to the true wonder of the Christian story. We historians are of course rather obsessive about sources, and here our sources for the Judaeo-Christian faith are to be found primarily in the Bible. But which Bible? As far as the Old Testament is concerned, the various Christian sects have different views on which old Jewish writings should be included in their canon. The Catholic Old Testament includes books that have been rejected by the Protestants, while the Greek and Russian Orthodox Churches, the Syriac, Coptic, and Ethiopic Churches include more books which have been rejected as apocryphal by both Catholics and Protestants! There is, however, more agreement on the New Testament canon. At the Synod of Hippo in 393 AD the basic framework of our Western Bible was agreed upon, and St. Jerome of Stridon (347-420 AD) spent most of his life producing the first Latin translation of our western Bible, the Vulgate. This translation, however, marked the first parting of the ways between eastern and western Christianity, as the Eastern Greek Orthodox Churches produced translations, and canonical collections, of their own. These differences grew into the so-called 'Great Schism' of 1054, when the cleavage between the eastern Greek and western Latin churches became more formalised. The Catholic Church effectively confirmed the Vulgate as orthodox during the long sessions of the Council of Trent, held between 1545 and 1563.

Catholics and Protestants now agree on the 27 books that make up the New Testament, although these were by no means the only 'gospels' that were produced. Jesus obviously caused a great stir during his ministry, and many people wrote about him after his death. Dozens of 'gospels' exist that were never accepted into the official biblical canon, and fragments of many more, now lost, may still be seen. In fact, every conceivable thing has been said about Jesus since his death. Some said that he was married, some said that he had children, some said that he was gay, and some that he was married *and* gay. Some said that he was mad, some called him a traitor to Israel for not leading the people against the Romans, as a Messiah was expected to do. Some called him a prophet, and some said that he was a god, and decided to worship him. There are nine 'Gnostic' gospels and four Jewish-Christian gospels that were never accepted into the Western canon, alleged 'childhood gospels' purporting to describe the childhood of Christ, and fragments have been found of many more 'lost gospels'. Even the earlier editions of our own King James Bible of 1611 at first included an appendix of 'Apocrypha', giving a nod in the direction of these more dubious works, but this appendix was dropped in the later eighteenth century. So what are we left with? Naturally, it was only those gospels most flattering to Jesus that were finally included in the official canon.

If we confine ourselves to the 27 books of the New Testament alone, we must ask the historian's first question, 'Who wrote them?' Here we meet with immediate disappointment. The only author about whom we know anything at all is Paul of Tarsus (c5-c67 AD), and we cannot even be sure of all our facts here. However, 14 of the 27 books of the New Testament are at least attributed to Paul, although only seven of his 14 letters are now believed to be genuinely by his hand. When it comes to the four canonical gospels, Mathew, Mark, Luke, and John, we have no idea who wrote them at all. The authors were given the names of apostles as a convention only. The second century traditional belief that Mark the Evangelist, companion and helpmeet to Peter, who was probably illiterate, wrote the earliest synoptic gospel, has now been discredited. After much research and computer-aided textual analysis, Bible scholars have been able to establish only the chronological order in which they were written, which was, Mark, Matthew, Luke, and John. They have also established that whoever wrote the Gospel of Luke also wrote the Acts of the Apostles, and whoever wrote the Gospel of John also wrote the Book of Revelation. But it seems that even the earliest of the synoptic gospels, Mark, was written some 30 to 40 years after the death of Christ, and that all four canonical gospels were written by people who had never actually met Jesus, and who were writing on the basis of hearsay evidence only. This, of course, undermines their historical credibility, because the historian's second question is, 'How well qualified is this writer as an authority on his subject? Does he really know what he's talking about?'

The best qualified of all the New Testament writers was undoubtedly St. Paul. His Epistles are the earliest of all the Christian writings that have come down to us, pre-dating even the Gospel of Mark. Paul too never met Jesus before his death, but he did do the next best thing, meeting with two of the original twelve apostles, including Peter, the most prominent member of the group. In his Epistle to the Galatians, a letter that is undoubtedly from Paul's own hand, he writes, 'Then after three years I went up to Jerusalem to see Peter, and abode with him fifteen days. But other of the apostles saw I none, save James, the Lord's brother.' (Galatians I, 18-19) It is interesting to speculate on a timeline here. After the crucifixion, it would have taken a few years for the Christians to grow in numbers sufficiently to come to the notice of the Jewish authorities as a troublesome, heretical sect of Judaism. Saul of Tarsus, a prominent Pharisee, was then appointed to head up the movement against the heretics. In Galatians I:13 he writes that, 'beyond measure I persecuted the church of God, and wasted it'. Presumably he must have spent a year or two as a persecutor, in the process meeting many Christians and learning of their beliefs, before his dramatic conversion, when he took the name of Paul. It is interesting to note, however, that in none of his letters, not even in those now believed to be forgeries, does Paul mention the dramatic events alleged to have occurred on the Damascus road as described in Acts 9: 3-19. Had these events really happened, we must assume that Paul's letters would have made frequent reference to them, but he never mentions any such episode. In I Corinthians 3-7 he lists all those alleged to have seen Jesus after his resurrection, and then adds in a rather cryptic verse 8, 'And last of all was he seen by me also, as of one born out of due time.' In the original Greek text the term used is έκτρωμα, which means clearly enough a premature birth, a birth at the wrong time. Paul is probably saying here that he had been born at the wrong time to have allowed him to meet Jesus in the flesh, but he felt as though he had met him in spirit.

Paul tells us that he spent three years preaching to the heathens in 'Arabia' (Galatians I:16-17), before travelling to Jerusalem to meet Peter and James. He then seems to have travelled all over Asia Minor, visiting and founding Christian churches, to which he subsequently wrote encouraging letters. It is possible that the earliest of these dated to only ten or fifteen years after the crucifixion. Paul was writing before the New Testament had been drawn up, and had only the spirit of Jesus' teachings to guide him, as had been reported to him by others. But he did have the Old Testament, and his letters are heavy on Old Testament morality, only lightly interspersed with references to Jesus. Paul saw no contradiction between being both a Christian *and* a Jew: this distinction was to arise only later.

Paul is worthy of special consideration, because his authentic letters were the earliest and most reliable of all the New Testament writings. Moreover, at least we have some idea of who he was! But we know that none of the NT writers had ever met Jesus or heard him preach, and they were biased in favour of Christianity to the point of fanaticism. These facts must make the entire New Testament suspect as source material in the eyes of a historian. Even the very name 'Jesus Christ' was probably not the original birth name of Jesus as given to him by his parents, but rather a soubriquet, a nickname given to him by his followers and taken up by the gospel writers. 'Jesus' means 'he who saves', and 'Christ' refers to someone who has been anointed, as Jews expected their Messiah to be. 'Messiah' also means 'the anointed one', and the early Christians, being Jews, were desperate to prove that Jesus was indeed the long-awaited Messiah prophesised in the Old Testament. The real birth name of Jesus might well have been Zacchaeus-bar-Joseph, or something similar.

But when all the evidence has been sifted, there seems to be little doubt that Jesus was a real historical figure who caused a considerable stir in his lifetime: many people wrote about him after his death. But what is the likely truth? Historians do not have too much difficulty in stripping away the mythology from his story. Was Joseph a carpenter? He is described in the Koine Greek in which the New Testament was written as a τέκτων (Matthew 13:55) which means simply an unspecified craftsman, but carpenter is the usual translation. As a carpenter's son, Jesus would have been trained in his father's trade, rather than receiving a formal education. Reading and writing were for the scribes and the Pharisees like St. Paul, and the doctors of the law: what need had a carpenter's son for literacy? The account given in Luke 4:16-20 of Jesus reading in the synagogue is probably apocryphal. Books, or rather scrolls of parchment at that time, were hand-written, expensive, and not to be found in the households of manual workers. But Jesus would have become well versed in scripture from his weekly attendance at the local synagogue, and could probably recite passages of scripture from memory.

The Catholic Church would like us to believe that Jesus was the only child of Mary, but the New Testament writers make it clear that he had both brothers and sisters, although he may have been the eldest child. (Mark 6:3, Matthew 13:55-6) He would have been born in Nazareth, not Bethlehem, and no miraculous signs would have marked his birth. We may be sure that there were no angels, no shepherds, no star, no manger, and most certainly no three kings who of orient were! The North Koreans claim that the birth of Kim Jong-il was also marked by celestial wonders! The Romans were not fools: if they wanted to tax people or count them, they would have taxed or counted them where they stood. They would not have had people running around all over Palestine to 'the city of their fathers' just to be taxed or counted. In any case, making a return would have been the job of the head of household only: wives would have had nothing to do with it. There would certainly have been no need to inflict an 80-mile donkey ride on a nine-months-pregnant woman. But the first Christian evangelists were of course Jews, like Peter, Paul, and the Gospel writers. They were desperate to sell Judaism and Christianity together as a package deal, and in this they were very successful. They wanted to prove that Jesus was in fact the long-expected Jewish Messiah, as foretold in the books of the Old Testament. These declared that the Messiah would be born in Bethlehem, and that he would be of the House of David. (II Samuel 7: 12-16, Micah 5:2). St. Luke even went to the trouble of inventing a spurious genealogy for Jesus, tracing his male line through David back to Adam! (Luke 3:23-38) In addition, the gospel writers had to somehow place the birth of Jesus in Bethlehem, even although everyone knew that he was Jesus of Nazareth. Hence the preposterous invention of the nativity story by the gospel writers. Moreover, we may be sure that if Jesus was of the 'House of David' at all, he would be no more so than many thousands of others were so many generations after David's prolific life. Mainstream Judaism, of course, would have none of it. Many passages from the Old Testament had led them to look for a grand military and political figure from a royal house, who would conquer all their enemies and restore the greatness of Israel. Jesus did not fill their bill at all. I have always been suspicious about Isaiah 9:6 which reads,

For unto us a child is born, unto us a son is given: and the government shall be upon his shoulder: and his name shall be called Wonderful, Counsellor, The Mighty God, the Everlasting Father, The Prince of Peace.

This is a beautiful passage, so memorably set to music in Handel's *Messiah*, but surely the Jews were strict monotheists, who would never have dreamed of calling any of their worldly leaders 'The Mighty God', however wise and victorious those leaders may have been. Surely their expected Messiah, 'the anointed one', was supposed to be a king, not a god? However, my Hebrew was not up to challenging the passage in its original, so I was forced to wait for the internet to come to my aid. Sure enough, the text above is a deliberate Christian mistranslation of the original Hebrew, in an attempt to justify their assigning of divine status to Christ. Just type into your search engine 'How to interpret Isaiah 9:6' for some splendid pieces of biblical hermeneutics. The Jews themselves, of course, would have none of all this. The early Christian leaders soon realised that if they hoped for mass conversions, they would have to turn to the less well informed Gentiles.

If the early life of Jesus followed the normal course for the times, then soon after puberty, Jesus would have been married off to a wife chosen by his parents, in compliance with their duty according to the prevailing customs. If so, the marriage was probably an unhappy one, since Jesus was clearly a man of strong opinions, and perhaps even gay, as some such as Peter Tatchell have recently suggested, although some of those who wrote about Jesus did claim that he had children. We should remember that none of the wives or children of the apostles are ever mentioned either in the canonical texts, although it is inconceivable that they should all have been bachelors. Rather, they too would have been married off soon after puberty as the custom of the times required. But in those days, women and children hardly counted at all, and so were rarely mentioned. The gospel of Matthew that relates the story of the miraculous multiplication of loaves and fishes states, 'And they that had eaten were about five thousand men, besides women and children'. (14:21) The latter groups literally 'did not count'! Of course, the gospel writers had good reason not to mention the wives and children of the apostles, who were abandoned when they set off to follow Jesus. 'Eternal life, eh? Oh yeah! I'll have some of that! So long, suckers! You can look after yourselves!' Yes, that wouldn't have sounded very good at all.

The man who changed the life of Jesus was evidently his cousin, John the Baptist, whom Jesus had met and greatly admired. After John's execution,

Jesus took on his mantle, and became a wandering preacher, perhaps only too glad of an excuse to escape from his wife! He was more likely in his twenties than in his thirties at this point. How long did his ministry last? Three years? Two years? One year? We do not know. We do know, however, that he called disciples to follow with him, mostly poor and illiterate men like himself, who would also have been married off at a very young age. No source tells us what their wives and children thought of their departure to follow Jesus. The next episode of Jesus' life that rings true was his overturning of the tables of the money changers at the Temple in Jerusalem, driving away the sacrificial beasts. This outrageous behaviour by an upstart, illiterate, holier-than-thou carpenter from Nazareth was more than the Jewish authorities could bear. It was they who had Jesus crucified by Pilate. This part of the story also rings true.

As for the rest, we must of course be sceptical of the 'miracles': suffice to say that the blind are often not entirely blind, and the lame not entirely lame, while the placebo effect is known to be very powerful. It is interesting to note that as the chronological order of the gospels proceeds, so the scale of the 'miracles' worked by Jesus increases. For example, only the latest canonical gospel, that of John, mentions the raising of Lazarus, surely the most spectacular raising of the dead of all. Evidently, some doubts had been expressed concerning others that Jesus had 'raised'. Had they really been dead in the first place? But there could be no doubt about Lazarus since, 'By this time he stinketh, for he hath been dead four days.' (John 11:39). It is interesting to note that none of the other gospel writers thought of mentioning this most spectacular raising of all, although they do describe other 'raisings' performed by Jesus.

The story of the woman taken in adultery is also told only in John. As a historian, I must suspect that this story too is factually apocryphal, but what a moving image it conjures up as, one by one, the stones dropped from their hands, and they all turned, and slunk away. When they had all gone, Jesus said (allegedly), 'Woman, where are those thine accusers? Hath no man condemned thee?' She said, 'No man, Lord.' And Jesus said unto her, 'Neither then do I condemn thee: go thy way, and sin no more.' (John 8:10-11) What a beautiful story. Factually, it probably never happened, but spiritually it is entirely in keeping with the teaching of Jesus, relating just the kind of thing that he *might* have said. This indeed is a general trend of all the four gospels. As they proceed in chronological order they decrease in historical credibility, but increase in spiritual impact. When it comes to the Resurrection, I find it interesting that Mary Magdalene and the disciples did not at first recognise their risen Lord, although no one could have known him better than they. Could it be that a fringe follower of Jesus, perhaps from Galilee, who physically resembled him, had decided to impersonate his great hero for a time, until the fraud was detected, and he suddenly had to make himself scarce?

In short, no historian could ever regard the gospels as reliable source material. All of the New Testament writers, even Paul, were relying on hearsay accounts of the life of Jesus, and the trouble with an oral tradition is that the tales told tend to be elaborated on with the telling, especially when the tellers have their own agenda, as the Christian writers clearly had. But when all the fiction has been sifted out, what probably reliable information remains? There can be little doubt that early in the first century AD a man to whom his followers gave the name of Jesus Christ lived, travelled, and preached. Eventually he overreached himself, and was in consequence crucified. Is that all that there is to be said? I think not, for it is here that we come to the real miracle of the Christian story, which even the most hard-nosed of historians cannot deny. It seems indisputable that here was a man who never led an army: never held a political office: never wrote a book: was poor and uneducated: and yet became one of the most famous and influential figures who has ever lived, exercising a profound influence upon our history and the shaping of our world. The influence of Christianity has not always been benign, but the faith he founded has certainly been influential! So how did Jesus do it? Well, he walked, and he talked: that was all. I would suggest that this makes what he had to say worth listening to. His teaching was nothing like what might have been expected from a man of those times, heavily influenced by the mores of his day. Jesus thought for himself. His teaching was so novel, so revolutionary, so startlingly, dazzlingly, different that he made a great impact at the time, and his legacy is still strongly evident in the Christian world of today. For example, we read in Matthew 18:21-2,

> Then came Peter to him and said, Lord, how oft shall my brother sin against me, and I forgive him? Till seven times? Jesus saith unto him, I say not unto thee until seven times: but until seventy times seven.

This was in total contradiction of the Old Testament directive, 'An eye for an eye, and a tooth for a tooth'. (Exodus 21:24)

We must remember, however, that Jesus did not establish Christianity entirely on his own. He may have started the ball rolling, but others then picked up the ball and ran with it, others who *were* educated, and who *did* write books. The founding of a major religion is always a team effort. Christianity could never have become established without the efforts of Peter, Paul, and many others like them, including the writers of the four accepted gospels, whoever they were. It has even been argued by some that St. Paul and the gospel writers did more to establish the Christian religion than Jesus himself. Since these people have left us our only sources, we can never be sure how many of the words of Jesus were actually spoken by Jesus, and how many were words put into his mouth by later New Testament writers. For example, the injunction, 'Be not overcome of evil, but overcome evil with good' sounds like just the sort of thing that Jesus might have said. But Jesus did not say it: St. Paul did. (Romans 12:21)

It does seem, however, that the spirit of Jesus' teaching has indeed been well captured by all the New Testament writers. It seems clear enough that Jesus preached a doctrine of peace, love, forgiveness, inclusiveness, and non-violence. The Jesus written about in the NT reached out to everyone, defying the exclusiveness of Jewish traditions – centurions, Samaritans, Cannanites, tax collectors, publicans and sinners, lepers, and yes, even women, even Samaritan women, even women taken in adultery. No one was beyond the reach of Jesus' love. St. Paul captured this spirit of tolerance and inclusiveness very well when he wrote in Galatians 3:28, 'There is neither Jew nor Greek, there is neither bond nor free, there is neither male nor female, for ye are all one in Christ Jesus'. Indeed, women did preach and played an important role in the very early Christian churches, before the patriarchal traditions of the times once more asserted themselves. We also hear from Jesus a timely warning about the perils of 'filthy lucre' and obsession with material possessions. 'For what shall it profit a man should he gain the whole world, but lose his own soul?' (Mark 8:36) Jesus laid great stress on extending relief to the poor and disabled for, 'Inasmuch as ye have done it unto one of these, the least of my brethren, ye have done it unto me' (Matthew 25:40). When Jesus said, 'The meek shall inherit the Earth' (Matthew 5:5) people must have thought him mad in an age when the brutal Roman Empire ruled the world by the sword. How could the meek ever inherit the Earth? But by God, He was right! The meek *shall* inherit the Earth, or there ain't gonna be no earth to inherit! Well, not by us anyway. Worth listening to? I should say so. Never mind the mythology, listen to the message! If only people had listened a little better! For centuries they have paid lip-service to the teachings of Jesus, and then have behaved as though he had never been born. As Ralph Waldo Emerson (1803-1882) once observed, 'Every Stoic was a Stoic, but in Christendom, where is the Christian?' What a good servant to humanity this faith might have been, if only people had followed Jesus more faithfully. Christians should be recognised not so much for what they believe as by how they behave. If we had all followed Jesus more closely it might indeed have brought us salvation, but in this world rather than the next. In this light, I recognise Christianity as a being a genuine philosophy, for it tries to answer the question, 'How should we live?' For me, this is the central question that every philosophy ought to ask. Here, Christianity has undoubtedly provided its own answer which, despite our backslidings, has proved to be a very influential one in the shaping of our world. I am not a Christian myself because I very much agree with the insistence of the Muslims and the Jews that no man can ever be God, and too much of the New Testament is not historically reliable. But I very much approve of the Christian ethic, as we all surely should.

The second most widely followed religion in the world is that of Islam, which is assuming an ever-greater significance in our modern world, and indeed in our own country. The minarets are rising in every major British city,

Muslim faith schools may be seen, and Muslims now form a significant minority of our own population. Islamic militancy is on the march in the Middle East and Africa, where Islamic terrorism of one form or another makes frequent news. Despite this, however, the Christians of my acquaintance, and non-believers too, seem to know very little about Islam. This is regrettable, so I think that a few words about the Muslim faith might be not inappropriate here. If you are a Christian who already knows all about it, then I must apologise for boring you: but in that case, you will be a very exceptional Christian indeed. I have never yet met a Christian who could tell me even what The Five Pillars of Islam are. The worrying implication of this is that the Moslems probably know as little about our faith as we do about theirs.

We might begin by looking at the life of the founder of the faith, Abu al-Qasim Muhammad (c. 570-632). Muhammad was born in Mecca, probably in the year 570 AD, into the Banu Hashim clan of the tribe of Quraysh, a powerful Meccan tribe who were able to afford Muhammad some protection in the later years of his life. Orphaned at the age of six, Muhammad was raised first by his paternal grandfather for two years, then on his death by his uncle, Abu Talib, the leader of the Banu Hashim clan. His uncle was a merchant who traded to Syria and the Middle East, and Muhammad accompanied him on his journeys from his teenage years, as an apprentice merchant himself. Having no parents to marry him off, and busy travelling while he learned the merchant's trade, Muhammad married late in life for the times, at the age of 25. In 595 he married Khadijah, a wealthy, forty-year-old widow, a marriage which gave him some financial security. From an early age Muhammad had acquired a reputation as an upright and honest man, so much so that in 605 he was called upon to resolve a potentially explosive dispute that had arisen amongst the clans of Mecca. Even in pre-Islamic times Mecca had been a place of pilgrimage to a sacred shrine of pagan gods, the Ka'aba, surrounded by some 360 idols, each representing a separate tribal deity. Set into the wall of the Ka'aba was the sacred Black Stone, a lump of volcanic rock. Its origins are unknown and pre-Islamic, but in Islamic tradition it had fallen from heaven to direct Adam and Eve to a holy spot where a shrine was to be raised. In 605, however, the sacred Black Stone had been removed from its shrine so that the Ka'aba could be repaired. But disputes had arisen between the clans over which one should have the honour of restoring the Black Stone to its place in the repaired Ka'aba. Tradition has it that Muhammad, appealed to as a just man, resolved the dispute by placing the stone on a blanket, the four corners of which were carried by representatives of the four main clans, thus satisfying the honour of all. They carried the stone to its shrine, and Muhammad himself set it in place.

By this time Muhammad had himself become a merchant, trading to Syria and beyond. There he would have come into contact with both Christians and Jews, but mainly, it would seem, with Jews because the Koran makes it clear that Muhammad knew much more about the Old Testament than the New. Indeed, his knowledge and understanding of Christianity seem to have been almost non-existent. He had no grasp of the Trinity, seeming to believe that Christians worshipped the Jewish God, Jesus, and his mother Mary as three separate gods. Although the Koran often mentions Jesus, it makes no detailed references to the teachings of Christ at all. On the other hand, it does show considerable familiarity with the old Jewish texts. The central message imbibed from these was that of strict monotheism. In his earlier life Muhammad had been content to worship the pagan deities of Arabia, but his experiences in the Levant seem to have inclined him towards monotheistic ways of thought, and he took to spending long periods of time in isolated locations, deep in prayer and meditation. It was during one of these sessions, believed to be at the Cave of Hira on the mountain Jabal al-Nour that, according to Islamic tradition, the angel Gabriel appeared to Muhammad, and began to dictate the Koran to him in the year 610 AD, when Muhammad was 40. According to the *hadith* of Sahih al-Bukhari, regarded in Islam as a most reliable account of Muhammad's life, the Prophet was at first told by Gabriel not to listen, but rather to 'read'. Muhammad replied, 'I do not know how to read.' (Bukhari 1:1:3) The first words of Gabriel to Muhammad are recorded in the Koran, chapter (sura) 96, verses (ayat) 1-3).

Troubled by these visions, Muhammad at first kept them to himself, and it was not until 613 that he began to preach. His message was one of strict monotheism, and allegiance to Allah, the one true God, whom Muhammad associated with the Jewish Jehovah. His preaching, however, made him unpopular with the Meccans, who feared that his teaching would undermine their profitable position as holders of the leading shrine of the pagan gods. At first ridiculed, Muhammad slowly began to gather followers for his new faith, and as he increased the intensity of his teaching against idolatry he became ever more unpopular, even with his own tribe, the Quraysh, who were the guardians of the shrine. In 615 Muhammad had to recommend to his followers that they should flee for protection to the Christian Emperor of Ethiopia. Muhammad himself remained in Mecca but, desperate to regain the support of his tribe, he acknowledged three of their pagan goddesses as true daughters of Allah. This acknowledgement seems to have effected a reconciliation, for Muhammad's followers returned later that year, only to discover that in the meanwhile Muhammad had retracted his verses on the goddesses. Gabriel had warned him that these had been whispered to him by the devil himself, and they became known as, 'The Satanic Verses'. It was of course his book of this title that got Salman Rushdi into so much trouble. The episode is also referred to as 'The Story of the Cranes'.

In 619, known as 'the year of sorrows' Muhammad's first wife died, and so too did his uncle and protector, Abu Talib, who had been head of the Banu Hashim clan. The new clan leader was opposed to Muhammad, and withdrew clan protection from him, placing his life in danger. Muhammad left Mecca and travelled Arabia, seeking a new protector, but without success. On returning to Mecca he was warned of a plan to assassinate him and so, gathering his followers, he migrated to the oasis city of Medina some 200 miles to the north of Mecca, in June, 622. This migration is known as the *Hijra*, and the Moslem calendar dates from this event. Muhammad and his followers were quite well received in Medina, partly because the Medinans were jealous of the privileged position of Mecca, and hoped that Muhammad's new religion might divert attention away from the great pagan shrine there. In addition, there had been feuding between the clans of Medina, and Muhammad was welcomed as an outsider who might be able to mediate between them. In 622 he was instrumental in pulling together the Constitution of Medina, a legal code that at last enabled the clans to live peacefully together, and also allowed Jews and Christians to live under their own laws as 'People of the Book' (the Bible). Many in Medina converted to his new faith, making Medina in effect the first Islamic state. Almost inevitably, Mecca came to be seen as the enemy, and in 623 Muhammad began to lead raids on Meccan camel caravans. These raids developed into open warfare, which culminated with the conquest of Mecca in 629. When Muhammad entered the city he ordered the destruction of all the pagan idols there, but re-dedicated the Ka'aba to his own new religion. Mecca therefore continued to be a place of pilgrimage, much to the chagrin of the Medinans! In the last years of his life Muhammad extended his conquests across the whole of the Arabian Peninsula, converting it into the first Islamic empire by the time of his death in 632.

Because Muhammad had spent so much of his later years after 610 in struggle, conflict, and warfare, the idea of *jihad* or 'holy war' assumed a position of great importance in his life. This doctrine of holy war was continued under Muhammad's successors, the Caliphs, or rulers of the Islamic empire. This was swiftly extended in the hundred years after 632 to stretch from Spain to India and beyond. This was despite civil wars within the Islamic community itself over leadership issues. Some believed that only the direct male descendants of Muhammad through his daughter Fatimah should serve as rulers or *imam*, while others thought that Caliphs should be elected, or win their right to rule by the sword. At the civil war Battle of Karbala in 680 AD Husayn, the grandson of Muhammad, and many of his Shia followers were slain. This marked the final irreconcilable division between these two views. Those favouring rule by descent came to be known as Shia or Shiites, with the others known as Sunni. This division of Islam into two distinct sects persists to this day. There are some doctrinal differences between them, but both agree on the basic tenets of Islam.

We know much more about the life of Muhammad than we do about the life of Christ, because we have two detailed sets of sources to draw on. These are the *sirah, sirat,* or *seerah* (all three spellings are used in the West) and the *hadith*. Both exist in various versions, but the most reliable *sirah* is thought to be that of Hassan ibn Thabit (d. 674) an Arabian poet and one of the *sahaba* or companions of Muhammad. The *seerah* are simply factual reports, giving details of military campaigns, political treaties, letters to foreign rulers, the appointment of officials, and a few of the formal speeches of Muhammad, including his last, the Farewell Pilgrimage speech. The *seerah* were written by named eye witnesses who were alive at the time those events took place, and this lends them a substantial degree of historical credibility. The *hadith* too are based on the accounts of named eye witnesses who were the assumed companions of Muhammad during his lifetime, including the accounts of his third wife, Aisha. This lends historical credibility to the *hadith* as well, although these accounts were transmitted orally for some 100 to 200 years before being compiled into recognised editions. Unlike the *seerah*, the *hadith* adopt a distinctly moral tone, concentrating on the words and deeds of The Prophet with a view to establishing religious doctrine and a basis for Islamic law, the *Sharia*. As with the Christian gospels, numerous *hadith* were produced, but only a few versions have been accepted by Islam as reliable. The Sunni accept six versions of the *hadith*, but the Shiites only four. Both agree, however, that the most reliable *hadith* is the collection compiled by Sahih al-Bukhari (d. 870), who completed his compilation in 846 AD. This *hadith* is now available in English and Arabic on the internet, and all of the following *hadith* quotations are taken from it.

The collection consists of nine volumes with 93 chapters or books in all, and 7,068 verses, or separate accounts of the words and deeds of Muhammad, many of which are multiple accounts of the same events or sayings. The *hadith* relate the words and deeds of Muhammad, the *sunnah*, just as the gospels relate the words and deeds of Christ. The *hadith*, however, command more respect as accurate historical accounts than do the gospels, which were written by men who had never met Jesus. The *hadith* purport to be the eye-witness accounts of those who were actually present at the time, carefully preserved and collected by later scholars like al-Bukhari. They are remarkably detailed, and often attested to by more than one witness. For example, al-Bukhari Vol. 8 Book 82 Nos. 809 and 825 give two accounts of the same event from different eye witnesses. A Jew and Jewess were brought to Muhammad, accused of committing adultery. Jews in conquered lands were allowed to live under their own laws, and so Muhammad ordered that the Torah should be brought, and one of his literate followers, Ibn Salam, read from it. The penalty prescribed was *rajam*, stoning to death. 'And so', narrates Abdullah bin Umar in No. 825, 'they were stoned, and I saw the man bending over the woman so as to protect her from the stones'. The fact that they contain such touching and minute details as these from eye-witnesses to events lend great credibility to the *hadith* as historical sources. Moreover, the *hadith* gain further credibility from the fact that they attribute no working of miracles to Muhammad. Some suspicions must remain about both the *hadith* and the gospels, however. Both have been carefully selected from numerous accounts, and we can never be entirely sure just how far these really depict the words and deeds of Muhammad or Jesus, and how far they were inventions, or elaborations, devised by those who wrote about them. But just as the gospels convey the spirit of Jesus' teaching very well, so the *Hadith* do the same for the spirit of Mohammed's message. On reading the Koran and the *Hadith*, and comparing them with the Old and New Testaments, one point emerges very clearly. While the teaching of Jesus was very much ahead of its time, the teaching of Muhammad, like the content of the Old Testament, was very much *of* its time. This was a time of violence, warfare, slaughter, torture, blood feuds, patriarchy, and the subjection of women, so we should not be surprised that the Koran and the *hadith* make frequent references to all these things, for they were an accepted part of The Prophet's daily life. The astonishing thing is the teaching of Jesus, which was truly revolutionary, and far ahead of its time.

For example, Muhammad showed no mercy to the 'enemies of Islam', and was especially hard on apostates, those who turned away from Islam after embracing it. Sahih al-Bukhari's *hadith* Vol. 8, Book 82, verses 794-7 gives four separate, but agreeing accounts of the people of the tribe of Ukl or Uraina, who had embraced Islam and had been helped by Muhammad. However, they turned renegade, renouncing the faith, killing Muhammad's camel master, and stealing his camels. Muhammad ordered their pursuit and capture, and when they were brought before him, Muhammad directed that their eyes should be put out with red-hot irons, that they should each lose one hand and one foot, and that they should then be left to die of thirst in the desert. This may seem rather harsh, but such were the practices of the time, and Muhammad had no patience with apostates! Although the Koran does not specifically prescribe the death penalty for Muslim apostates, the *hadith* clearly do, and in fact the death penalty for apostasy may still be applied today in Saudi Arabia, Iran, Afghanistan, and Pakistan under *sharia* law. Equally severely, 8:82:803-42 makes it clear that stoning to death should be the punishment for adultery for both sexes, while 3:48:817 prescribes 100 lashes for pre-marital sex, a punishment frequently recommended elsewhere as well for other crimes, such as drinking alcohol. Again this may seem harsh, but plenty of sex was allowed within marriage. The Prophet himself took 13 wives, nine of whom were still living at the time of his death. Probably his third wife, Aisha, was the most important, for many of the *sunnah* are allegedly based on her accounts. In 7:62:64-5 of al-Bukhari we learn that Muhammad married Aisha when she was six, and consummated the marriage when she was nine. 7:72:715 makes it clear that Muhammad found wife beating to be entirely acceptable, but of course English law also allowed this until the early twentieth century. Men were expected to control and discipline their wives and concubines, and the plural is used advisedly here, because in Muhammad's day they were apparently allowed unlimited numbers of both! In 1:6:301 Muhammad states bluntly that 'women are deficient in intelligence and religion' and in 3:48: 826 he again refers to 'the deficiency of woman's mind'. Therefore, women should never be allowed to serve as head of state, and in *sharia* courts the testimony of one man is to be considered worth that of two women. This was, of course, very convenient for rapists, who could simply deny any such charge brought against them by a woman, and be believed. 8:81:764-793 prescribes flogging as a punishment for alcohol consumption, and the amputation of a hand for theft. 4:52:41-301 are passages all about *jihad,* that is 'holy war' and the merits of slaughtering unbelievers. 4:52:44 reads, 'A man came to Allah's Apostle and said, "Instruct me in such a deed as equals *jihad* in reward." He replied, "I do not find such a deed."' The nine volumes of this *hadith* also give directions on every other aspect of Islamic life, including pilgrimage, fasting, bathing, business dealings, wills, inheritance, charitable giving, blood money, marriage, and divorce. Many of its accounts have been incorporated into *sharia* law.

Apart from the fact that both claimed to be prophets, and both were illiterate, Jesus and Muhammad had very little in common. Unlike Jesus, Muhammad *did* lead armies, *did* hold high political office, *did* dictate a book, and *did* make himself very rich (one-fifth of all booty was to go to Muhammad). In addition, he enjoyed many wives and concubines, and advocated violence, slaughter, and terror as a means of spreading his faith. Jesus, on the other hand, advocated self-sacrifice, non-violence, and the setting of examples as a means of spreading Christianity. Muhammad's ordering of the immediate stoning to death of all those guilty of adultery should be compared with Christ's treatment of the woman taken in adultery as described in the Gospel of John, 8:1-11.

But the most important book in Islam is of course the Koran, believed by Muslims to be not the word of Muhammad, but the word of God himself, as dictated to Muhammad by the angel Gabriel. Muhammad's revelations began in late 609 or early 610, but at first he kept them to himself, only later beginning to preach and gather followers around him. Muhammad himself was, by his own admission illiterate, but some of his followers, such as Hassan ibn Thabit (d. 674) were literate, and they began to note down the utterings of the Prophet when he entered a trance state and began to pronounce his verses. As was the case with the literate followers of Jesus, Muhammad could never have established his religion without the help of those scribes. None of these followers ever noticed the presence of the angel Gabriel, but they were often taken by surprise when Muhammad suddenly fell into a trance state and began to utter his rather incoherent verses. These were therefore hastily jotted down on anything that came to hand at the time, including stones, palm fronds, pieces of bark, and the skeletal shoulder blades of dead camels. This detritus was later swept together, and fair copies were made of it piecemeal onto parchment.

After Muhammad's death his successors as rulers of the Islamic empire were known as Caliphs. Soon after the Prophet's demise the first Caliph Abu

Bakr (d. 634) ordered all of these manuscripts to be incorporated into one volume under the direction of Zayd ibn Thabit (d.655), who should not be confused with Hassan ibn Thabit (d.674). Zayd used all of the surviving parchments, and also the testimony of the *sahaba*, the companions and followers of Muhammad, who had memorised many of his verses. Copies were made of this compilation, but in 650 the third Caliph, Uthman ibn Affan (d. 656) noticed that differences were beginning to creep in between successive copies. He therefore ordered one, definitive, standard copy to be prepared by a committee headed by Zayd. Earlier copies were destroyed, and this 652 edition has remains the standard version of the Koran still in use today. It is interesting to notice that this was compiled only 20 years after the death of Mohammad, and was based on the testimony of those who had actually met the Prophet and had heard him preaching and reciting his verses. Therefore, between the *sirat*, the *hadith*, and the Koran, we can be much more sure that the related words and deeds of Muhammad really were his words and deeds than we can be of the words and deeds of Jesus, as related by the gospels.

The Koran is divided into 114 chapters or *sura*, beginning with the longest and ending with the shortest *sura*. Each *sura* is divided into verses or *ayat*, with 6,236 verses in all. They are not, therefore, recorded in the chronological order of their utterance by Muhammad. The earliest *sura* is thought to be number 96, 'The Embryo'. The Koran begins, however, with The Prologue, an exception to the general rule that shorter *sura* are placed last in order, for The Prologue consists of only seven short, one-line *ayat*. However, it is the most quoted *sura* in the Koran, recited at nearly every prayer meeting. It begins, 'All praise be to Allah, Lord of all the worlds, most beneficient, ever merciful, King of the Day of Judgement. You alone do we worship, and to You alone do we turn for help...' My own copy of the Koran runs to 561 pages.

In terms of content, the Koran is rambling, repetitive, and in some places self-contradictory, as might be expected from the piecemeal way in which it was recorded and compiled. For example, there are conflicting accounts of how much goods should be worth before a man's hand was amputated for their theft, and conflicting references to Christians, who are sometimes described as friends, and sometimes as enemies. But the main message in the Koran relates to monotheism: worship is to be reserved for Allah alone. There is also a great deal of eschatology, that is doctrine about the end of the world and a 'Day of Judgement' when all will be resurrected to face their Maker. Roughly a third of the Koran harps on this theme, and on the joys of paradise which may be expected by the just. Paradise is a garden fed by crystal streams where exquisite food and drink are available, as are the services of numerous 'handmaidens' who are described as 'full breasted' and 'doe-eyed'. The services they are to provide are not specified, but needless to say paradise seems to have been designed primarily for men! On the other hand, the torments of hell for infidels and the unjust are also vividly described at some length. In *sura* 4, *ayat* 36, God says, 'And those who disbelieve our revelations shall be cast into hell, and when their skin is burned and scorched away we shall give them a new skin, that they may go on tasting the agony of punishment.' If you are not a Muslim, then this means *you*.

The Koran contains many references to Old Testament figures such as Moses, Noah, Abraham, and Jonah, and also some 25 references to Jesus, although these are not detailed, and are mostly critical, as in *sura* 5 *ayat* 72-7 which begins, 'They are surely infidels who say, "God is the Christ, son of Mary"...Whosoever associates a compeer with God will have Paradise denied to him by God, and his abode shall be Hell...Disbelievers are they surely who say, "God is the third of the trinity"'. But on the other hand, Jesus is accepted as a genuine prophet along with the Old Testament figures. All have delivered authentic messages from God, but Muhammad's revelations are the summation and culmination of all prophecy, the final word of God. The Koran, however, is ambiguous in what it has to say about Jews and Christians, the 'People of the Book', that is the Old and New Testaments. *Sura* 5 *ayat* 51 says, 'Oh believers, do not hold Jews and Christians as your allies. They are allies of one another, and anyone who makes them his friend is surely one of them, and God does not guide the unjust'. 8:39 adds, 'and fight with them until there is no more unbelief: religion should be only for Allah'.

All this seems clear enough, but 5:69 states, 'All those who believe, and the Jews and the Sabians and the Christians, in fact anyone who believes in God and the Last Day and performs good deeds will have nothing to fear or regret', while 5:82 adds, 'the closest in love to the faithful are the people who say, "We are the followers of Christ"'. These contradictory statements, and a highly ambiguous attitude towards Jews and Christians, pervade the whole of the Koran.

However, there is no self-contradiction about the importance of *jihad*, or holy war. Early on in the Koran 2:216 declares, 'Fighting is prescribed for you, and you dislike it. But it is possible that you dislike a thing that is good for you, and like a thing that is bad for you.' 4:76 states, 'Those who believe fight in the way of God, and those who do not fight only for the powers of evil.' 4:95 warns, 'Not equal are those who sit at home and receive no hurt with those who strive and fight in the cause of Allah with their goods and their persons.' This warning is repeated in 9:20 with, 'Those who believe and have left their homes and striven with their wealth and lives in Allah's way are of much greater worth in Allah's sight'. Moreover, this warfare is to be waged with utter ruthlessness. 5:33 reads, 'The punishment of those who make war against Allah and his messenger is that they should be murdered or crucified or their hands and feet cut off on opposite sides, or they should be imprisoned'. But imprisonment is just an afterthought. 8:67 declares, 'It is not for a Prophet that he should have prisoners of war until he has made a great slaughter in the land'. 17:16 adds, 'And when We wish to destroy a town, We destroy it with utter destruction'. 4:23 is all about incest, and prohibited degrees of relationship. But 4:24 adds, 'Also forbidden to you are married women, unless they are captives of war'. In other words, it's open season on the wives and daughters of all those who 'fight against Allah', and there was, of course, plenty of fighting to be done. This attitude towards women captives in occupied territories has recently been pursued by the Islamic State set up in Iraq and Syria. Captured women were sold at public slave auctions, and passed from hand to hand for what amounted to gang rape. But this behaviour is sanctioned by the Koran, 4:24.

There is so much about *jihad* as ruthless warfare, slaughter, pillage, and rapine in the Koran that even the Muslims themselves have become embarrassed by it. They have therefore devised the doctrine of 'The Greater Jihad' and 'The Lesser Jihad'. They claim that when the term *jihad* is used it often relates to an inward and spiritual struggle against the tendencies towards lax behaviour and unbelief within oneself, 'The Greater Jihad' and only in the latter sense to actual physical warfare, 'The Lesser Jihad'. But there seems to be little doubt about what Allah means when he talks about *jihad*. In context, it can mean only physical warfare. 48:16 once more directs the faithful to engage in *jihad*, but 48:17 adds, 'It is not binding upon the blind, the lame, or the ill to follow this command'. Evidently, therefore, the command can be only to physical warfare, since even the blind and lame could engage in a spiritual struggle.

Both the Koran and the *hadith* lay great emphasis on the importance of *jihad*, which is not surprising, in view of the fact that after his 610 conversion Muhammad spent most of the rest of his life in struggle or conflict of one form or another. As the years went by, this increasingly took the form of physical warfare. His followers had literally to fight for their faith, and this fighting did not end with Muhammad's death in 632. On the contrary, within the next 100 years Islam was spread by the sword over a far greater area than Muhammad himself had ever conquered. Knowing how the Koran exalts *jihad*, and condemns those who sit idly at home when there is a holy war to be fought, helps us to understand those young Muslims who recently have left Britain and gone to Iraq and Syria to fight in the conflicts there on the side, as they believe, of true Islam. Such warriors are known as *mujaheddin*, and if they die in *jihad* they are promised immediate entry to Paradise. (Presumably everyone else has to wait for the resurrection and judgement on the Last Day.)

It is young men like these who have recently been responsible for some terrible acts of terrorism in the West, such as the very public murder and beheading of Lee Rigby on the streets of London in May, 2013, and the massacre of journalists at the offices of Charlie Hebdo in Paris on January 7, 2015, and the even more terrible Paris massacres of November 13 in the same year. The London Bridge slaughter by vehicle followed in 2017. But these

Islamists are the exception. All the Muslims that I have ever met have been decent, responsible, law-abiding citizens, playing vital roles within our society. Where would our National Health Service be without its Muslim doctors and nurses? Indeed, the families of those who have gone to fight are usually very upset to discover what has happened to their loved ones. Some have even reported their departure to the police, knowing that their children might be jailed on their return to Britain. The sad truth remains, however, that if you have inclinations towards extreme religious intolerance, the use of violence to promote your beliefs, the slaughter of 'infidels', the subjection of women, polygamy, or grooming for child sex like the gangs of Rochdale, Rotherham, Oxford, Huddersfield, and Derby, then you can find justification for all these things in the Koran and the *hadith*. Had not The Prophet himself married a six-year-old, and consummated the marriage when she was nine? The *hadith* say he did, so that must be all right then. Fortunately, most Muslims apply common sense and do not take their faith beyond the bounds of what is reasonable in a twenty-first century society. They understand that the Koran and the *hadith* were written in times that espoused very different values from those of our own today. The problem arises when some Islamists choose to take their faith too literally. I get the impression that many Muslims live in genuine fear and terror of the wrath of their god. In Christianity today fanaticism is rare, but in Islam it is all too common. Islam can make a good servant, but obviously it can also make a very bad master. We saw Islam at its worst in the so-called 'Islamic State' or caliphate which in 2016 occupied large swathes of Iraq and Syria, where the Koran was taken too literally by fanatics.

So, with regard to what we might call normal or everyday Islam as practised in Britain and abroad, what do we find? We could begin by looking at 'The Five Pillars of Islam', which are core beliefs. The first is acceptance of the view that there is no god but Allah, and that Muhammad is his prophet: the *Shahadah*. The second is the obligation to pray five times a day: the *Salat*. The third is the obligation for the better off to give alms to the poor: the *Zakat*. The fourth is an obligation to fast for a month each year, the *Sawm*, during *Ramadan*, the ninth and most holy month of the Moslem calendar. This is a moveable feast, or rather famine, which lasts for 29 or 30 days according to the phases of the moon. Since the Islamic lunar calendar year is 10 to 11 days shorter than the solar year and includes no intercalation, *Ramadan* migrates through the seasons. But the injunction to fast for 30 'days' is strictly interpreted. Muhammad said nothing about the nights! So all the eating is done before sunrise and after sunset on each day of the 'fast', and many groups are exempted from fasting at all. The fifth pillar is the obligation on all who can afford it to make the pilgrimage to Mecca at least once in a lifetime: the *Hajj*. Panentheists of course would say that Allah is not listening to the *Shahadah* or the *Salat* and is not watching to see who observes the *Sawm* at *Ramadan* or the *Hajj*: only the *Zakat* would have merit in their eyes. But the *Zakat* is very important, for it ensures that the poor, the elderly, and the ill are always properly looked after within an Islamic society. As Karen Armstrong explains in her book, *Islam: a Short History* (2000),

> Social justice was, therefore, the crucial virtue of Islam. Muslims were commanded as their first duty to build a community (*ummah*) characterised by practical compassion, in which there was a fair distribution of wealth. This was far more important than any doctrinal teaching about God. In fact, the Quran has a negative view of theological speculation, which it calls *zannah*, self-indulgent whimsy about ineffable matters that nobody can ascertain one way or the other. It seemed pointless to argue about such abstruse dogmas: far more important was the effort (*jihad*) to live in the way that God had intended for human beings. The political and social welfare of the *ummah* would have sacramental value for Muslims. (pp. 5-6)

In Saudi Arabia, for example, while there are certainly great disparities of wealth, every care is taken to ensure that all Saudi citizens are adequately provided for, with none left in poverty. Islam has something to teach Christendom in this regard, for Muslim communities offer genuine mutual support. Islam also has its own legal code, known as *Sharia* Law. This is not strictly adhered to in all Muslim countries, but is acknowledged to some extent in most of their legal systems. It is based first of all on the Koran, and secondly on the *hadith,* the records of Muhammad's words and deeds during his lifetime, known as *sunnahs*. A third pillar of *Sharia* is the *ijma*, the consensus view of historical and contemporary Muslim jurists. The fourth pillar is the appeal to analogical reasoning or *qiyas*, what westerners would call case law. *Sharia* law, where it is fully accepted, regulates every aspect of Muslim life, religious, social, economic, and political, as in present day Saudi Arabia and Iran. Among its more commendable recommendations are bans on gambling, and the taking of drugs or alcohol.

Islam is fundamentally a religion of equality (except, of course, for equality between men and women). From the outset it has been non-racist (another lesson for Christendom) recognising the equality of all Muslims before God. It has no priestly cast with special sacerdotal powers, recognising, with the Protestants, 'the priesthood of all believers'. For each individual God is 'closer to you than your jugular vein'. However, some are clearly more learned in theology and the law than others, and their learning is recognised in Islam, giving them leadership status. The *imam* is a prayer leader, usually learned in theology, but he may simply be chosen by the congregation for his moral and spiritual qualities, for in Islam moral behaviour is valued above learning. The better educated are known as *mullahs*, many of whom would be *huffaz*, that is those who have memorised the entire Koran. The *mullahs* are usually the preachers at Friday prayers, although any believer may take on this role. Those who are most learned in both theology and Islamic law are known as *mufti* in the Sunni branch of Islam, or *ayatollahs* in the Shiite tradition. Their pronouncements on legal matters are known as a *fatawah*, a judicial decision that carries great weight, although it is not necessarily binding on all Muslims.

There are today three main Moslem sects, the Sunni, the Shiite, and the Ibadi, this last being a very small but distinct sect, forming 75% of the population of Oman. The Sunnis are by far the overall majority, making up some 80% to 90% of the whole, depending upon definitions. The Shiites are found mostly in Iran, where Shiism is the state religion, and Iraq where they are the majority, although substantial numbers may also be found in Pakistan, India, Yemen, and Turkey. All Muslims accept one version of the Koran, which is believed to be the direct word of God, delivered through his prophet, Mohammed, and all accept at least four versions of the *hadith*.

In comparing the two faiths, the moral superiority of the teachings of Jesus becomes apparent. His message was one of peace, love, inclusiveness, self-sacrifice, toleration, and forgiveness. Jesus did not advocate the mass slaughter or persecution of anyone. But in Islam, although Allah is always referred to as 'the merciful', there is little mercy to be found. The Koran and the *hadith* speak mainly of harsh judgements and severe punishments in this world and the next. Islam is not a religion of peace, because it glorifies *jihad* and martyrdom in holy war, and the slaughtering of *kuffars*, non-believers, since worship should be for Allah alone. It is not a religion of toleration, although 'People of the Book', that is Jews and Christians, did receive marginally more toleration than others. In conquered lands they were treated merely as second-class citizens. Nor is Islam a religion that accords equal status to men and women. In consequence, with Christianity it is possible to be a socially good Christian while also being a theologically good Christian, like the people of many churches, who put themselves out to do so much good work for their communities, and who are tolerant of all. With Islam, however, those who live in Christian communities can be socially good Muslims only by being theologically bad Muslims, that is by not taking the injunctions of the Koran and the *hadith* too seriously. It is the terrorists, the *jihadists*, and the martyrs who can claim to be the truly 'good' Muslims, while condemning those who 'sit idly at home' when there is a holy war to be fought. Such a war was of course the struggle recently waged in Syria and Iraq by 'Islamic State', whose *jihadists* were seen as being proponents of the true faith by extremists. Since they were being opposed by Christians, this justified terrorism in their eyes. But again it must be stressed that *jihadists* and terrorists are very much the exception in Muslim communities. Most Muslims live responsibly and peacefully within Christian societies, while observing their own traditions, which are socially admirable within their own communities. Muslims and Christians can live happily together, as was touchingly illustrated on December 14, 2017, when a commemorative service was held for the victims of the Grenfell Tower fire, many of whom were Muslims, exactly six months after the disaster. The service was held in St. Paul's Cathedral, and there Christians and Muslims stood side by side and wept together, all religious differences forgotten, and only the basic values of our common humanity remembered.

There is one more interesting comparison that can be made between Islam and Christianity. Islam was at first spread by warfare and the sword, and only later by the spiritual power of its message, as in Indonesia, where 87% of the population are Muslims today. But in Christendom, the reverse was the case. Christianity was spread at first in an entirely non-violent way, relying on the sacrifices of Jesus' followers and the spiritual power of his teaching. Far from imposing their faith on others by violence, the early Christians themselves underwent great sufferings, and frequently martyrdom, to spread their faith. St. Paul who, tradition has it, was martyred in Rome under Nero, related some of the hardships he had endured in earlier years in II Corinthians 11:23-7. Speaking of other Judaeo-Christian missionaries he writes,

> Are they ministers of Christ? (I speak as a fool) I am more: in labours more abundant, in stripes above measure, in prisons more frequent, near deaths oft. Of the Jews five times received I forty stripes save one. Thrice was I beaten with rods, once was I stoned, thrice I suffered shipwreck: a night and a day I have been in the deep. In journeying often, in perils of waters, in perils of robbers, in perils by my own countrymen, in perils by the heathen, in perils in the city, in perils in the wilderness, in perils on the sea, in perils among false brethren: in weariness and painfulness, in watchings often, in hunger and thirst, in fastings often, in cold and nakedness....

It is very understandable why so many post-Reformation sects have tried to get back to the purity and simplicity of the early days of Christianity. But later, it was Christianity that was spread by the sword. The Crusades were only a harbinger of things to come. In the early-modern period the Christians of Europe burst out of their own continent and went a-conquering and a-colonising all over the world, first in the Americas, then in Asia, then in Africa and Australia. They took their religion with them, and imposed it on native peoples, sometimes with great violence and cruelty, as in Central America. It is mainly thanks to that great wave of European imperialism and colonisation that Christianity is today the most widely professed religion in the world.

Those of a secular turn of mind would, of course, be surprised to hear that the desert visions of an illiterate Arab camel-driver could be accepted as the voice of God, but we should remember that Jesus too had been poor and illiterate. Moreover, there can be no doubt that the ideas of Muhammad have profoundly shaped our world in the past, and are increasingly shaping it in the present. According to the Pew Research Centre, Islam is now the world's fastest growing religion, and will overtake Christianity in terms of adherents by 2050.

Besides, stranger things have happened. To take just one example (there are many others) we might consider the short and inglorious career of one Joseph Smith (1805-1844), the founder of the Mormon Church. Smith claimed that in 1823, when he was just 18, an angel called Moroni had appeared to him and told him of the existence of a set of golden plates which happened to be buried quite near his home at Palmyra in New York state. These were inscribed with esoteric knowledge in a text which Smith described as 'Reformed Egyptian', a script never heard of by any scholars of the Ancient World. Nor did Smith explain just what the 'Reformed Egyptians' were supposed to have been doing on the North American continent thousands of years ago. However, Smith could decipher the golden plates with the help of two 'seer stones', clearly a half-baked version of the 'philosopher's stone', which were also buried conveniently close by. Using the stones, Smith allegedly translated the plates, and from them produced The Book of Mormon in 1830, which is still to this day the basis of the Mormon faith. The angel then took back the plates and the seer stones which, conveniently, are no longer available for inspection, although Smith did persuade eight of his followers to swear that they had actually seen the plates before they disappeared. In 1826 Smith had been prosecuted as a fraudulent 'treasure finder', and in 1832 he was tarred and feathered by an indignant mob, outraged at the tenets of Smith's new faith, which allowed unlimited polygamy to himself and his followers. Shortly afterwards the Bank of Mormon which Smith had founded failed spectacularly, after Smith had enriched himself. Despite all this, Smith managed to gather numerous followers for his new faith, although it wasn't long before they fell out among themselves. In 1844 Smith was indicted on charges of perjury, polygamy, incitement to riot, and treason. While remanded in custody at Carthage, Illinois, a mob broke into the jail and shot Smith several times as he tried to escape through a window. His murderers were all later acquitted by a jury which clearly believed that Smith had richly deserved to be shot. Despite this, under its second president Brigham Young (1801-1877) Smith's church went from strength to strength. Young took 55 wives, and banned all persons of African descent from its priesthood.

To my mind, Smith bears all the hallmarks of a classic fraudster, and yet the 'religion' that he founded still exists today as a wealthy and powerful church with a world-wide reach and a splendid headquarters at Salt Lake City in Utah. It was Adolph Hitler in *Mein Kampf (1924)* who first noted that people will more readily believe a big lie than a small one (Vol. I chpt. X p. 150 in Ford pdf), a trait of human nature later to be exploited by Donald Trump. I must admit to being seriously alarmed by the evident fact that so many people, even today, are still ready to believe whatever they are told on the basis of no credible evidence whatsoever. But since so many people obviously *are* prepared to believe whatever they are told, histories such as that of Joseph Smith sometimes tempt me to found my own church. I would call it, 'The Church of the Fairies at the Bottom of My Garden'. Its holy text would consist of the eye-witness accounts of those who had actually met and spoken with the fairies (those who had been literally 'away with the fairies') just as Joseph Smith had met and spoken with the angel Moroni, so that my church would be based on foundations as sound as his. Every successful religion needs a book behind it, even if it is only the Book of Mormon, so that the precious revelations of the fairies would be recorded in the sacred text of the faith, *Fairyword.* That famous faked 1917 photograph of two little girls watching fairies I would insist was genuine. I would claim that the fairies are angry with us because not enough people believe in them, and that everything that goes wrong in the world is the result of 'fairy curses'. The only way to save ourselves is to turn to faith in the fairies and listen to what they have to tell us. Just as members of other creeds feel an obligation to wear burqas, or turbans, or big black bushy beards, so good Fairylanders would feel obliged to wear diaphanous, transparent plastic wings on their backs as a sign of their faith, for true believers would be admitted to Fairyland on their deaths, and become airy sprites themselves, to enjoy eternal life in the foliage at the bottom of people's gardens. On the other hand, non-believers would descend to a dark nether world, where they would be chased by hob-goblins through all eternity. Charitable and tax exempt status would of course be claimed for my new *bona fide* church and just as the Christian Church and Smith collected tithes from their followers, so the founder of the C.F.B.M.G. too would collect tithes from the faithful, which would of course remain with him as head of the church for...er... safekeeping. Oh, and both Muhammad and Smith also believed in polygamy, so I would of course require full and free access to female church members at all times, so that I could render any one of them 'truly blessèd' whenever I felt like it. I have no doubt that my new faith would quickly gain adherents. That church would be no less credible than the beliefs of many other sects that flourish around the world today. In 2022 The Flat Earth Society still exists. Their website may be visited at *www.theflatearthsociety.org*.

I must further say that the idea of the Christian heaven also seems to me to be a totally preposterous concept, and not at all like the kind of place in which anyone would want to end up. Have you Christians ever really thought that one through? Can you imagine the scene?

St. Francis of Assisi (1181-1226) meets St. Thomas Aquinas (1225-1274) in the Christian Heaven: A Short Play

The scene: St. Thomas is sitting disconsolately on a cloud, surveying the Heavenly Host. In the background is a small crowd, continually waving their hands in the air and bowing down before three figures. The central figure, seated slightly higher, is richly attired, with long white hair and a beard. At his right hand sits a younger man with long black hair and a beard. On his left is a figure draped in a white sheet with two eyeholes cut in it. A halo on a stick is propped above its head. The three figures are nodding and waving graciously in acknowledgement of all the adulation, after much the same fashion as that of our own beloved royal family. Heavenly music plays, and carbon dioxide smoke rolls across the stage. Enter St. Francis.

St. F. Tommy! Is that you? I haven't seen you for centuries!
St. T. (Despondently) Oh, hello Frankie.
St. F. How the devil are you?
St. T. (Somewhat testily, being of a scholastic turn of mind) How am I? Why I'm absolutely fine of course, just the same as everybody else up here! That was a bit of a damn silly question wasn't it?
St. F. (Chastened) Oh, er, yes I suppose it was, really. Anyway, what've you been doing lately?
St. T. Me? Oh, I've been praising my Saviour all the day long. How about you?
St. F. Yup, me too. Got any plans for tomorrow?
St. T. Oh, pretty much the same sort of thing, really. Well, there's not a lot else to do up here, is there?
St. F. You're not wrong there T.A. You'd think He'd get fed up with listening to us, or perhaps even find us something just a little bit more constructive to do.
St. T. Well, what else *can* we do? These wonderful transfigured bodies of ours don't need any food or drink, so dinner parties are out. You can't even have a friend round for a cup of tea. It had to be that way, of course – you can't have crapping in Heaven with all those people below. And because nobody does any work up here, there's no need for any training or education. It gets me down that thinkers like me are out of a job.
St. F. That's true. Up here all hearts are open, all desires known, and from us no secrets are hid. Down on earth we could see things only through a glass darkly, but up here face to face. So, now that all has been revealed to us, no more striving for knowledge, no mysteries to ponder, no more thrill of making new inventions and discoveries…
St. T. Yes, there are no goals to achieve, no ambitions to fulfil, no difficulties to overcome…I'd love to have been able to figure out quantum gravity for myself…
St. F. It's the animals that I miss most: since they have no souls, they can't follow us to heaven, but…well…I used to preach to the birds, you know. They were better company than the people up here. Who needs you? This lot just drift around on cloud nine as though they were all high on drugs or something. Back on earth, where people needed each other for all sorts of reasons, I used to feel that I was doing some good in the world, but now…
St. T. Well, relationships up here have got to be pretty impersonal, haven't they? Since our transfigured bodies are immortal, there's no need for reproduction, so there's no sex, and neither marriage nor giving in marriage in our Father's kingdom. No wonder everybody up here looks sex starved.
St. F. It's all a bit depressing, really – are you sure we weren't promised tennis courts, swimming pools, room service…?
St. T. (Wearily) No, no, nothing like that: just prayer and praising all men raising, worshipping God Most High. We have to be continually expressing our gratitude for being here, you see.

St. F. Yes, nothing to do but sing praises all day, like that lot over there. Just look at them, the Whole Company of Heaven, all in unison, and waving their arms about like there's no tomorrow.
St. T. Well, there *is* no tomorrow up here is there? Just one long continual today. Remember, these wonderful transfigured bodies of ours don't need any sleep either.
St. F. Ugh! Er…yeah, that's true. This place isn't exactly Paradise, is it?
St. T. It is, actually.
St. F. Oh well yes, technically, but…um…you don't think there might have been some kind of ghastly administrative error, do you, and that we're really in Hell?
St. T. (With a weary sigh) No, this is Heaven all right. It's exactly what we were told to expect. And when I think of how I bust a gut making sure I'd get in here…
St. F. Well, it's just that…you know…I often wonder whether I'm really cut out for this place... I sometimes feel that I might as well be dead.
St. T. You are, actually.
St. F. Huh! If only!
St. T. Well, I know how you feel. I hear they have newspapers down on earth these days…with crosswords…the lucky bastards…and if I have to listen to one more bar of that goddamn harp music…
St. F. But the Big Fella – how long did He say we'd be stuck here for?
St. T. Well, I have heard that when we've been here ten thousand years (bright shining as the sun) we've no less days to sing God's praise than when we first begun.
St. F. Oh dear, that sounds a bit like…forever…
St. T. Yes, I'm afraid it does rather, doesn't it…

(They stare desperately at each other for a few seconds: then, in unison…)
St. T., St. F. ARRRRRRRGH! (They flee from the stage, screaming and tearing their hair out. Curtain)

But comfort ye, my people. God, the real God, isn't going to let that happen to you. He can be very cruel, but he couldn't possibly be *that* cruel. What, an eternity in a place like that? Heaven forbid. Place your trust in the Lord: He knows what is best for you. Change is the first law of this universe, and so we, as individuals, should not expect an eternal anything. The small minority who are still sincere Christians in this land will be offended by that play, but as George Orwell once observed, 'If freedom means anything at all, it must mean the freedom to tell people things that they do not want to hear'. Freedom of speech must include the right to offend, and to be offended. Personally, I am not only offended by the beliefs of some religions that I see around the world, but also seriously alarmed by them. If some people are prepared to believe in *that* sort of thing, then what else are they prepared to believe? What is our reason for?

Having said all that, however, it would ill behove me if, having condemned religious fanaticism, I were then to adopt a fanatical anti-religious stance myself. That would simply reduce me to the fanatics' level. Instead, I remember the wise words of my mentor, Spinoza: 'Odium nunquam potest esse bono' (Hatred can never be good) from his *Ethics*, Part IV, Proposition 45. As it happens, my wife enjoys church going, and likes to have me by her side, so I attend our local Methodist church on most Sundays. It saddens me to see one half of a partnership attending church while their wife or husband refuses to join them 'on principle'. People are more important than principles. She knows my views, but I attend for her sake, and even put my money where my mouth isn't, with a regular (and sizable) weekly subscription! (Ouch! That was my wife's idea!) 'Where your treasure is, there will your heart be also' say the little yellow subscription envelopes. Yeah, well, they would say that, wouldn't they?

I try to explain to anyone at church who asks that I am in fact a panentheist, but they just go glassy-eyed and drift away. Nobody seems to hold it against me, which is as it should be. Live and let live is what I say. The people at our church do not talk about their faith, but they do practise it, doing a lot of good, charitable work in our community, in which I have become involved myself. This experience has led me to suspect that Kant was wrong, and that consequences are of greater importance than motivations. But I sometimes wonder whether they are good people because they are Christians, or whether they are Christians because they are good people? I rather suspect it is the latter. I am tempted to the conclusion that it is fine for everyone to have a religion, so long as nobody believes too strongly in it, since it is not so much the religion itself as religious extremism that causes the problems.

However, sadly, our congregation is elderly, with nearly all of us over 70, and no young people are joining the church. In twenty years or so we will all be gone, and something beautiful will have been lost forever. But for now my wife is no fanatic either, and is gracious enough to admit that she could be wrong, and so I return the compliment, as every good philosopher should. We can all be wrong: arrogance is the enemy of truth. On this basis, we continue to live together in happy amity: we recently celebrated our 58th wedding anniversary! People are more important than principles: if we could all just grasp that, this world might be a happier place. In any case, as soon as I cross the threshold of our church I cannot help entering into the spirit of things: I love the beautiful cadences of the King James Bible, and the Wesleyan hymns, and the good fellowship that the church affords. I find that I too am waving an arm in the air, and pointing to the sky:

Thine be the glory, risen, conquering Son,
Endless is the victory Thou o'er death hast won!

In order to understand the religious emotion, you have to experience it. But I also came to understand what George Orwell said about the two minutes hate in *1984*: 'it was impossible to avoid joining in'. How easily can we slip into doublethink! I know what I believe, but I also understand completely how they feel. The Christian ethic too very much appeals to me. I am not a Christian myself because I reject the supernatural elements of the faith, but it does seem to me that some of the best advice ever given on how we should live together came from the lips of JC.

It hardly needs to be stressed here just how great an influence on the shaping of our world the teachings of Jesus and Muhammad have exerted in the past, but it should not be forgotten how important religious thought remains in our world of today. The Middle East of our times has become the Balkans of the twenty-first century, the cauldron, the flashpoint, from which a broader conflagration may arise, and religion plays a key role in the conflicts there.

Finally, since Christians always seem to be unduly concerned about death and their prospects in an 'afterlife', this may be a good point at which to address that topic, and to explain why the philosopher remains totally unconcerned about the prospect of death. There are several good reasons for this. First, let's hear from one of them, Epicurus of Samos (341-270 BC), who observed that, 'When we are, death is not, and when death is, we are not'. So, why worry? Put another way, you spent the first 13.8 billion years of the life of this universe in a state of nonexistence, and that didn't bother you at all, now did it? Very soon now on the cosmic timescale you will be spending the next 13.8 billion years in an identical state, but that will bother you equally little, now won't it? Nonexistence is your natural and normal state: that which you call life is merely a brief and anomalous interlude, an island in the sea of eternity. So why worry? For the individual death is not a problem, death is a solution – a solution to all problems. Rather, problems arise for those who are left behind.

Secondly, we should all feel extremely grateful for death, because without it, none of us would be here. Without it, there would have been no evolution to evolve us into the creatures that we are today. There is no other way in which God could have arranged things, given His own laws. Put your trust in the Lord. How many billions of more primitive creatures than ourselves had to live and die before us? Indeed, if any of our human ancestors had been immortal, there would have been no need for us at all! And just how many ancestors did you have? You can work this out quite easily: 2,4,8,16, etc. By the time you have gone back 23 generations, you had 8,388,603 ancestors, more than the estimated population of the British Isles at that time, whether we allow 20 years or 25 years to a generation, and millions more than that if we go back further. Every one of those ancestors had to live long enough to reproduce, no mean achievement for those times, just so that you, specifically and exclusively you, and nobody else, could be here. The odds against your existence were staggering: what a miracle. And I have not yet even begun to tell you what a highly improbable planet God has provided for us! (See Science chapter below)

Thirdly, we should remember that life is not a gift, it is only a loan, and a loan that must be repaid. We have only borrowed from the universe those elements that compose our bodies, and the universe wants them back. 'The wages of life is death', as St. Paul might have said. That's the deal. But it is a loan on the most favourable of terms. Millions and millions of our ancestors had to live and die, most of them in poverty and misery, just so that we could be here, at this time and in this place, to enjoy much better lives than any of them could ever have dreamed of. In return, we have to die only once. What a bargain! Yet you Christians expect eternal life *as well*?!? What arrogance: what presumption: what ingratitude. The Lord giveth, and the Lord taketh away: blessèd be the name of the Lord.

Fourthly, we all have a duty to die in order to make way for generations yet to come: a version of that intergenerational social contract that was recognised by Edmund Burke. We owe it as a debt of gratitude to our ancestors, and as an obligation to our descendents, so that they in turn might enjoy the miraculous gift of life, which is all the more precious for being transitory. Our indifferent God means to kill us all, and He will kill us all. But instead of being resentful of the fact of death, we should all feel eternally grateful for the miraculous gift of life, and should cultivate Spinoza's *amor intellectualis Dei*, of which more below. We all owe God a death: we should yield it to Him graciously.

II On Philosophy

Although this treatise is basically about the influence of Philosophy upon history, and how it can help us to live happier lives as individuals and as societies, we all have good reasons to be sceptical about Philosophy and philosophers. Below I will list just five of these reasons, by way of suggesting that Philosophy needs to be cut down to size if it is ever going to serve any useful purpose. It is easy to understand why Philosophy is not a subject that most people want to have anything to do with. This lack of interest is tinged with contempt: the popular assumption seems to be that the whole subject is just too abstract and remote to have any bearing on real life. I have some sympathy with that point of view. Even the philosophers themselves have warned us to approach the subject with a degree of scepticism. Blaise Pascal (1623-62) declared, 'To make light of philosophy is to be a true philosopher' (*Pensée*, Sect. I no. 4), and Cicero warned, 'There is nothing so absurd that it has not been said by some philosopher' (*De Divinations* ii, 58). Karl Popper too made a very good point when he wrote in *The Open Society and its Enemies*(2011 ed.).

> For some reason philosophers have kept around themselves, even in our own day, something of the atmosphere of the magician. Philosophy is considered as a strange and abstruse kind of thing, dealing with those mysteries with which religion deals, but not in a way that can be 'revealed unto babes' or to common people: it is considered to be too profound for that, and to be the religion and theology of the intellectuals, of the learned and wise. (p. 245)

Indeed, in this chapter I would like to propose once again a redefinition of the term 'philosophy' itself. I was first emboldened to do this whilst looking to see what the World Wide Web had to say about the subject. Here, we find that two of the most authoritative sources available are the Internet Encyclopaedia of Philosophy, and the Stanford Encyclopedia of Philosophy. The former, however, does not recognise Albert Einstein, Karl Marx, or Thomas Paine as being philosophers at all, although it does accept that the Einstein-Podolsky-Rosen Argument might legitimately be seen as a piece of genuine 'philosophy'. The Stanford Encyclopedia, on the other hand, does recognise all three as being authentic 'philosophers', although Einstein is recognised only as a 'philosopher of science', and Adam Smith only as a 'moral and political philosopher', playing down almost to vanishing point Einstein's role as a scientist, and Smith's role as an economic thinker. What are we to make of this? If philosophers cannot agree even on who was or was not a philosopher, or what he was a philosopher of, does not this suggest that they are unclear about even the meaning of the term 'philosophy' itself? This finding has emboldened me to put forward my own, wider definition of 'philosophy', which means, after all, simply 'a love of wisdom', without specifying what kind of wisdom. If we are to fully understand just how ideas have shaped our world, then to my mind, religious thought, economic thought, and scientific thought should all be recognised as legitimate forms of philosophy, as I will argue more fully below.

All of us have very good reasons not to allow ourselves to be intimidated by Philosophy, and not to show any undue respect for philosophers: as we shall see, they show very little respect for each other! Philosophy needs to be seized firmly by the scruff of the neck and given a good shake in an attempt to dislodge from it all the dross that it has accumulated over the last two-and–a-half millennia or so. It is very important to remember that philosophers all enjoy one great advantage over the rest of us: they do not have to be right (and in fact are usually wrong): they need only to be interesting, and thought provoking. How much can they get away with? Well, suffice to say that artistic licence and poetic licence pale into insignificance beside the latitude allowed to philosophical licence! This is a *very* important point, which I will have occasion to make again in context below. So, what's wrong with academic philosophy? Quite a lot, really. Let us consider five specific charges against it.

(a) Philosophers Make Things Needlessly Complicated

In his very revealing book, *23 Things They Don't Tell You about Capitalism* (Penguin, 2011) the Cambridge economist Ha-Joon Chang makes an interesting point when he says, 'Ninety-five per cent of Economics is common sense, and even for the remaining five per cent the essential reasoning, if not all the technical details, can be explained in plain terms.' (p. xviii). Well, I am not so sure that this really applies to Economics, but it is rather more apposite for Philosophy. Any piece of philosophy worth knowing about ought to be capable of expression in short and pithy terms, readily comprehensible to all. I can do no better here than to quote Karl Popper once again.

> Every intellectual has a very special responsibility. He has the privilege and the opportunity of studying. In return, he owes it to his fellow men (or 'to society') to represent the results of his study as simply, clearly, and modestly as he can. The worst thing that intellectuals can do – the cardinal sin – is to try to set themselves up as great prophets vis-à-vis their fellow men and to impress them with puzzling philosophies. Anyone who cannot speak simply and clearly should say nothing, and continue to work until he can do so. ('Against Big Words' in P.A. Schlipp (ed.) *The Philosophy of Karl Popper* Vol. I (1974) p. 83)

But what do we find? To listen to Aristotle in his *Nicomachean Ethics* going on and on and on about his definition of 'virtue' is enough to put anyone off Philosophy for life, as are the protracted attempts by Plato to define 'justice' in *The Republic* (neither discussion gets us anywhere)! Nor will anyone be encouraged by trying to follow through the reasoning of Gottfried Leibniz (or is it Dr. Pangloss?) as he tries to explain why 'everything happens for the best in the best of all possible worlds' in his *Théodicée* of 1710. And as for listening to Immanuel Kant labouring the distinction between 'analytic' and 'synthetic' statements in his *Critique of Pure Reason* of 1781, don't even think about it! This is not to say that Kant makes no points of interest: he is generally recognised as the greatest philosopher of the eighteenth century: his views on epistemology, determinism, morality, and the limitations of rationality certainly deserve to be taken seriously. But he was even worse than Spinoza when it came to labouring his ideas to death. By 1783, only two years after the publication of his *Critique*, it had become clear that almost nobody could understand it because of his convoluted and needlessly involved form of expression. He was forced to bring out a second and shorter version of his masterwork, usually referred to as the *Prolegomena*, but even this shortened and 'clarified' version remained incomprehensible to most of his readership. At last, in 1787, he produced a substantially revised edition of the original work, which was certainly an improvement in terms of clarity of exposition, but still pretty heavy going. Like Spinoza, he seemed to see some merit in excessively refining his thought, thereby elevating basically simple concepts into the realm of incomprehensibility. Jacques Derrida (1930-2004) provides another case in point, seemingly working hard to make his readers work hard to understand what are basically simple concepts. No wonder so many people want nothing to do with philosophy! The point I want to make here is that any piece of philosophy worth knowing about must be readily comprehensible in plain terms, and practically applicable to real life. Such pieces do exist, but you have to sift through a great deal of chaff to find the wheat. Philosophy needs to be cut down to size if it is to be of any practical use to anyone.

(b) Philosophers Use Big Words

Like Karl Popper, quoted above, I am all for clarity of expression, but the use of some 'big words' is, I fear, unavoidable when dealing with Philosophy. Many people have been put off the subject when they found that philosophers bandied about big words like 'ontology', 'epistemology', 'empiricism', 'phenomenology', and 'structuralism', terms that most people have never heard of. But these words are not so difficult to understand. Ontology deals with the nature of reality or being, from the ancient Greek root 'οντ', 'οντως', that is to say 'ont', or 'ontos', being or reality. Before the dawning of the scientific age, philosophers spent a great deal of time pondering this question, and wondering whether they could trust the evidence presented to them by their senses. Of course, they were working in complete ignorance of today's knowledge of cosmology, evolution, the earth sciences, and the material sciences, so they didn't get very far with their speculations, although one or two of them did hit on elements of truth by chance, like the pre-Socratic Democritus with his atomic theory. They seemed to be obsessed with the idea that there must be a further, higher reality beyond the one that we can perceive. Plato, for example, believed that our world was only a shadow of the perfect reality of things, which existed in a higher realm beyond our perceptions. Such a conception will be familiar to those of a religious persuasion: heaven, perhaps, or an abode of bliss for departed souls? Obviously this idea has a long pedigree, and is still with us today. However, evidence for the existence of this other realm is in short supply, and so modern philosophers tend to dismiss it as mere wishful thinking. The real world, that we can see, and hear, and feel, is quite wonderful enough, so wonderful in fact that it is very understandable that a pre-scientific age should have posited the existence of creator gods and ideal realms, especially since their own lives were often so hard and brutal. For my part, I am content to believe that the real world, as revealed to us by our senses and by modern science, is the only one that we have, and that this life is the only one that we will enjoy. But what a great privilege it is to have even this, as we shall see.

Epistemology derives from the ancient Greek word 'ἐπιστήμη', that is to say, 'episteme', which means 'knowledge'. Once again, philosophers have spent a great deal of time on pondering the nature of knowledge, wondering about the limitations imposed on us by our bodily senses and mental capacities. Are there things that we can never know because of these limitations? Well, it seems to me that if there are such things, it is hardly our fault if we don't know about them, given the limitations of our capacities. Moreover, if they do exist, what sort of bearing do they have on our lives? If they have no perceptible bearing on them, do they matter? It seems to me that if our senses did not give us an accurate view of the realities around us, we would not have survived as a species. But it is quite true that our natural senses cannot provide us with a *complete* picture of reality. Our eyes, for example, can detect only a small portion of the electromagnetic spectrum, and our ears cannot detect infrasound or ultrasound. However, here our intellects come to the rescue, enabling us to build instruments that *can* detect these different wavelengths, and so artificially extend our perceptions into such fields as radio astronomy. In a similar way, although we still cannot see atoms, we can be very sure that they must be there because we have a huge body of instrumental and experimental evidence to attest to their existence. And so, our intellects have enabled us to see beyond the immediate evidence of our senses, just as the great rationalist philosophers, René Descartes (1596-1650), Baruch Spinoza (1632-77), and Gottfried Leibnitz (1646-1714) argued long ago that they could, although we have not used our reason in quite the way that they envisaged! Rationalists like Descartes believed that we could begin from indubitable first principles as a foundation, like his own famous *cogito, ergo sum*, (I think, therefore I am) and from there construct an entire edifice of truth by reason alone. But such a structure would inevitably be very shaky, increasingly unstable as it rose. The use of our reason has indeed helped us to understand the material world, but indirectly, and not by the direct use of reason alone.

In questions of epistemology, the classic opponents of the rationalists have been seen as being the empiricists, and empiricism has traditionally been set against rationalism as a contrasting form of philosophy. The term, 'empiricism' again derives from an ancient Greek word 'ἐμπειρία', that is to say 'empiria', which means experience. Far from distrusting the evidence of their senses, the great empiricists like John Locke (1632-1704), George Berkeley (1685-1753), David Hume (1711-76), and Edmund Burke (1729-97), insisted that the *only* evidence which should be used was that obtained from our senses! While admitting that this evidence might be incomplete or even misleading, the empiricists argued that it was the best evidence that we could get, and that any subsequent conclusions to be drawn must be based, *a priori*, on the observations provided by our senses. Well, this seems reasonable enough, and was in keeping with the new scientific methods which were gaining credence at the time, but some philosophers, such as Immanuel Kant (1724-1804) in his famous work, *A Critique of Pure Reason* (1781) still insisted that our senses gave us only a partial or shadowy impression of the true nature of things, a sort of Neo-Platonist point of view.

Despite the title of his treatise, however, Kant's attack was aimed more at the empiricists than at the rationalists. Our observation of an object was a mere *phenomenon*, while the true reality of objects was their '*noumenon*', a term that he had himself invented from the Greek word 'νομος', or 'nomos', which means 'a dwelling place'. Kant, of course, wrote in German, and this term is also used in its German form as '*ding-an-sich'* or, 'thing in itself'. Taking this approach, it might be thought that Kant would be seen as the father of 'phenomenology', but philosophers do not recognise him as such. Rather, they see phenomenology as a fairly modern movement, developed in the early years of the twentieth century by Edmund Gustav Husserl (1859-1938). Husserl was Jewish by descent but was born in Moravia, which was then a part of the Austrian empire. His 'phenomenology' aimed at creating conditions for the objective study of topics usually regarded as subjective, such as judgement, perceptions, and emotions. Well, I'm sorry, but to me all this fatuous speculation is just a big waste of time. I am perfectly prepared to accept the evidence of our senses, especially when augmented by our instruments and experiments, as providing us with an accurate enough guide to the nature of reality. Although I am ready to admit that we still haven't got the whole picture, I do think that we have more than enough to be going on with. Incidentally, I wouldn't worry about either phenomenology or structuralism if I were you: both are entirely useless concepts, invented by philosophers simply to give themselves something to do.

However, when it comes to limitations on what we can know, philosophers have raised a different kind of question, which relates to our mental capacities. Perhaps we are incapable of comprehending some aspects of reality, because our minds are not equal to the task? This was another proposition put forward by Kant. Well, this is of course quite a different question from that of the reliability of our senses, and one that requires much more serious consideration. I would say that this possibility cannot be ruled out, but let us look at the empirical evidence collected on this question so far. As science has progressed, our minds have been able to embrace some truly staggering concepts, like the nature of the space-time continuum, general relativity, and quantum mechanics, even although all of these subjects have been well outside the realm of our everyday experience. Arguing, therefore, from the particular to the general, a process that philosophers call 'induction', I would say that the evidence existing so far would suggest that there are no aspects of reality that our minds are incapable of grasping. But the philosophers go even further than this in their arguments. Even if we are able to understand the whole of external reality, will we ever be able to fully understand ourselves? Is a mind capable of knowing and understanding itself? Again, Kant thought not. This is certainly a most interesting and challenging question, and once again we cannot yet give a completely certain answer to it, but I would say that the answer is, 'yes'. Indeed, far from doubting our mental capacities, I would say that the full potential of the human brain has not yet been completely realised. Can some people really foretell the future? Is telepathy possible? What about remote sensing, as used by the C.I.A. with people like Yuri Geller? What about the remarkable mental abilities of those with autistic conditions? What about the strange results of 'near death' experiences? There is much still to be explored here, but I rather suspect that, when it comes to realising the full potential of our mental capacities, we still have much to discover.

So where does all this leave us on the subjects of ontology and epistemology? When it comes to ontology, I do think that it is rather important to know how things really are, i.e. the true nature of reality. That is because we base many of our decisions upon this concept. Now if you premise your conclusions upon false assumptions, the consequences for you could be seriously adverse. This is why I find an over-commitment to one religion or another to be very saddening. It seems to me it is overwhelmingly probable that, for our purposes, this world is the only one that there is, and this life is the only one that we are going to get, and that therefore we should start our reasoning from there. But when it comes to epistemology I would advise readers not to worry unduly about it. Perhaps we never can know absolutely everything, but does this really matter to our everyday experiences? The important thing is to know *enough* to enable us to lead happy and fulfilled lives, and I would venture to suggest that here, the glass is substantially more than half full. Yes, we do need to approach both ontology and epistemology with a degree of humility, but when it comes to *how much* we can know, I would say that this is not the proper question to ask. We can know *enough*. As the immortal Jimmy 'Schnozzle' Durante (1893-1980) once so trenchantly opined, 'It's whatcha do wid whatcha got dat really counts!', as profound an observation as any ever made by the self-styled philosophers, and who better than Jimmy to have made it? Here was a man from the lower east side of New York who had an ugly face, a gravelly voice, and no more than a mediocre talent as a piano player, yet from these unpromising attributes he forged an international reputation as an entertainer. 'Out of the mouths of babes', indeed. Come to think of it, JC didn't begin with many advantages either!

Someone else who forged a very successful career as a singer even although he couldn't sing was Bob Dylan. Can you imagine him singing the Duke of Mantua in *Rigoletto*? He was quite good on guitar and harmonica to be sure, but his real strength lay in the fact that although he had no great singing voice he *was* a very considerable poet, and he made the most of that. It was the lyrics of his songs that made them attractive. Listen to a verse from *Mr. Tambourine Man*:

> Then take me disappearin' through the smoke rings of my mind
> Down the foggy ruins of time, far past the frozen leaves,
> The haunted, frightened trees, out to the windy beach
> Far beyond the twisted reach of crazy sorrow...
> Yes, to dance beneath the diamond sky with one hand wavin' free
> Silhouetted by the sea, circled by the circus sands
> With all memory and fate driven deep beneath the waves
> Let me forget about today until tomorrow.
>
> Hey! Mr. Tambourine Man, play a song for me:
> I'm not sleepy, and there ain't no place I'm going to:
> Hey! Mr. Tambourine Man play a song for me
> In that jingle jangle morning I'll come following you.

Bob must have been having a trying time when he wrote that one, but he was so good at expressing how he felt. I am strongly reminded here of *The Rubaiyat of Omar Khayyam*: both are songs of despair. Both poets are seeking an escape from situations that they found to be intolerable, one through wine and the other through song, but neither route will lead them anywhere. It is of course impossible to play a song upon a tambourine! In October, 2016 Bob Dylan was awarded the Nobel Prize for Literature, which surprised some, but in my view was quite well deserved. At the very least, it was refreshing to see how broad-minded the Nobel Literature Committee could be.

On the topic of long words used by philosophers, however, I must add here a special warning about epistemology. Of all branches of philosophy, this is the most involved, convoluted, and fatuous. Those writing about it invariably sink deeper and deeper into the quagmire of this subject, taking us all around the mulberry bush, and usually concluding that we can never really 'know' anything about anything at all! Their speculations remind me of nothing so much as the flight of the mythical Oozlum bird, which allegedly flies round and round in ever-diminishing circles until it finally disappears up its own anus. When philosophers turn to epistemology, it is time to put the book down, or to skip a chapter: that way madness lies. Two of my philosopher heroes, Einstein and Paine, wisely avoided the topic, but Spinoza could not resist wandering into the swamp, while Popper fell headlong into the mire.

(c) Philosophers Can't Agree

Many people find it difficult to take a discipline seriously when so many of its practitioners contradict one another, and when almost all of them seem to have a different and unique point of view to put forward. One is left with the inescapable impression that they cannot all be right, and indeed that it seems highly probable that most of them will be wrong! We can see, for example, that the empiricists don't agree with the rationalists, and the phenomenologists don't agree with the empiricists, while the logical positivists don't quite agree with any of them! But it gets even worse than that: many individual philosophers have even managed to disagree with themselves!

One of the major German thinkers of the Romantic period, Friedrich Schelling (1775-1854) was greatly celebrated in his lifetime as 'the philosopher of nature' but his views on this subject changed so radically from those of his earlier years that he became an embarrassment to himself, and stopped publishing altogether at the age of only 35! This kind of inconsistency has also been seen in philosophers of the twentieth century, some of whose views changed so radically over their lifetimes that they almost seem to have become different philosophers, with their work divided by scholars into 'earlier' and 'later' phases. Thus we have 'the early Heidegger' whose work should be distinguished from that of 'the late Heidegger', and 'the early Wittgenstein', whose ideas came to be seen as badly flawed by 'the later Wittgenstein'. Yet both retain their status as towering figures of twentieth-century thought. Martin Heidegger (1889-1976) is best known for his classic work, *Being and Time* (1927), widely regarded as the bible of twentieth-century existentialism. However, his last major publication, *What is Philosophy?* (1956) scarcely seems to have been written by an existentialist at all! In the same way, Ludwig Wittgenstein (1889-1951) published his first master work at the age of only 32 with his *Tractatus Logico-Philosophicus* (1921), introducing the world to linguistic philosophy. His last published work, however, appeared only after his death, the *Philosophical Investigations* of 1953, in which we see him correcting the 'oversights' of his earlier book. Indeed, some might say that he admitted here that his 1921 work was entirely mistaken!

Another leading philosopher whose approach changed several times during a very long life was Bertrand Russell (1872-1970). Russell himself recognised this in his last word on the subject, *My Philosophical Development* (1959). In this book he traces his thought from mathematical logic to analytic philosophy, and on to logical positivism and then linguistic philosophy. To this last field he made a major contribution, and was instrumental in fathering the whole approach, yet towards the end of his life he declared himself 'dumfounded' that anyone could consider it an adequate conception of philosophy! I beg to differ with him on this point, and indeed philosophers of the twenty-first century continue to be concerned with the logical analysis of formulations in language as they surely must, for language is the vehicle of philosophical thought.

Finally, Jean-Paul Sartre (1905-1980) provides yet another example of the inconsistent philosopher. He began his writing under the influence of the Austrian philosopher Edmund Husserl (1859-1938), who developed and refined the concept of phenomenology, but then fell increasingly under the influence of Martin Heidegger (1889-1976) and existentialist thought. Finally, the ideas of Georg Friedrich Hegel (1770-1831) and Karl Marx (1818-1883) dominated the last years of Sartre's life, and he began writing what was intended to be a monumental work, *A Critique of Dialectical Reason*, which was aimed at reconciling existentialism with Marxism. This was surely the most fatuous philosophical essay ever attempted, for Sartre equated 'Marxism' with the kind of Communism then being practised in the Soviet Union, obstinately defending Stalinism. This creed was, of course, completely irreconcilable with existentialism, which stressed individualism, with the heroic individual forming his own values, charting his own way in life, and 'creating himself' without regard to the mores of the society around him, while Marxism as practised in Russia actually demanded a uniformity of belief from all its adherents, and the suppression of individuality. The futility of his task seems to have dawned upon even Sartre at last, for he left the work unfinished, publishing just a single volume of it in 1960, although his notes for a second volume were published in 1985, after his death. Although his name appears in every Encyclopaedia and Dictionary of Philosophy Sartre was not, therefore, an original thinker, but rather a populariser of the ideas of others. This he did so successfully, in large measure through his novels, that he became more famous in his own lifetime than most of those whose ideas he had championed, with the exception, of course, of Marx. For example, he usurped the title, 'Prophet of Existentialism' from those who had done all the original thinking on the subject, namely Søren Kirkegaard (1813-1855), Friedrich Nietzsche (1844-1900), and Martin Heidegger (1889-1976). Indeed, at the end of his life Sartre admitted that he had exaggerated the extent to which any individual could opt out of the society in which he lived. Sartre was, however, a rather good novelist, being offered the Nobel Prize for Literature in 1964 which, remarkably, he turned down. His first novel, *La Nausée* (Nausea) was one of his best. He should have stuck to novel writing. Personally, I would not award him any prizes for philosophy!

(d) Philosophers Can Be Dangerous

What hope is there then, for this benighted study, whose exponents not only disagree with each other, but also often cannot even agree with themselves? Nor is this the end of philosophical inconsistencies. Even in the instances of those philosophers who have maintained a loyalty to a single set of beliefs in their lifetimes, it has often happened that their ideas have been re-interpreted, or misinterpreted after their deaths by subsequent 'followers', who have deliberately perverted their views for their own ends. For example, Søren Kierkegaard (1813-55), the founding father of existentialism, was a deeply religious and spiritual thinker, in the tradition of the Danish Lutheran Church. He stressed the importance of the individual as the supreme moral entity, and the importance of decisions made by the individual, because it is through the choices that we make that we create our lives and become ourselves. His concern, however, was with the individual soul, and the eventual union of this soul with God through making the 'correct' choices in our lifetimes. He would have been dismayed to find that in the twentieth century his disciples had split into two camps, the Christian Existentialists and the Humanist Existentialists with the latter group, by far the larger, thoroughly agreeing with the importance of individual decision making, but wanting no truck with God at all!

Kierkegaard was, in large measure, reacting against the views of Hegel, who had envisaged the individual as being subsumed into great waves of evolutionary development, and swept along by the tide of history to an inevitable destiny. Indeed, this great nineteenth-century German philosopher Georg Wilhelm Hegel (1770-1831) provides us with another good case in point. Hegel was an enormously influential figure, whose ideas dominated German philosophical thought in the middle years of the nineteenth century. He was the first of the great philosophers to stress a historical dimension in his thought, seeing all things as being in a process of inevitable change and development. But Hegel was not a materialist: he saw this process as applying primarily to the moral and spiritual development of humankind which, through an ongoing process of conflict (thesis, antithesis) would eventually resolve itself into a synthesis which would embrace elements of both former views, but would contain within itself the seeds of future conflict. This process would continue until at last the ideal society would be achieved, through a synthesis of ideas. Hegel was an ardent idealist, and envisaged an organic society in which every individual was a harmoniously functioning part of the whole, freely serving the interest of a totality very much greater than himself. Hegel saw this condition as being one of 'freedom' for the individual, who could find himself and his true happiness only as a functioning part of the organic state. Here, we may detect echoes of Confucianism, and of the theory of 'the general will', most famously propounded by Jean-Jacques Rousseau (1712-1778) in his treatise, *Du Contrat Social* (The Social Contract) of 1762. The general will was actually the will of every individual within a society, whether they realised it or not. In consequence, the state had a duty to enforce conformity, to bend the individual will to the general will, to 'force them to be free'. Those terrible words have echoed down the corridors of time, finding new expression in the Communist and Fascist dictatorships of the twentieth century. Hegel himself was enormously influential, not only in nineteenth-century Germany, but subsequently in twentieth-century Europe, thanks to the ways in which his followers developed and interpreted his philosophy. Scholars divide them into the 'Left Hegelians' and the 'Right Hegelians'. Very broadly speaking, the Left Hegelians developed through Karl Marx and John Stuart Mill into Socialists and Communists, while the Right Hegelians developed through Darwin and Nietzsche into Fascists and Nazis. Many people have been surprised to discover that Hegel was the intellectual grandfather of both Communism and Fascism, which superficially appear to be two very different creeds, ideologies that did indeed come into violent conflict in the middle years of the twentieth century. Yet what they both had in common was the idea of the powerful, all-embracing, all-consuming organic state, which had every right to demand total loyalty and self-sacrifice from its citizens. Hegel was in fact an appalling statist, a worshipper of state power, and a Christian to boot! This comes out most clearly in his *Philosophy of Law*, first published in 1821. I should warn readers at this point that this work is commonly mistranslated as *The Philosophy of Right*. This is because Hegel called it *Grundlinien Der Philosophie des Rechts*, and *recht* in German can mean both right and law, but sounds more like 'right' to an English ear. However, in context *Law* is the better translation, as used by Karl Popper, a native German speaker. In his *Philosophy of Law* (1833 ed.) Hegel criticises Rousseau's *Social Contract* because he, 'reduces the union of individuals in the state to a contract, and therefore to something based on their arbitrary wills, their opinion, and their capriciously given express consent; and by abstract reasoning proceeds to draw the logical inferences which destroy the absolutely divine principles of the State, together with its majesty and absolute authority...the state takes priority over the individual, whose supreme duty is to be a member of the State...the march of God in the world – that is what the State is.' (Section 258)

He later adds,

> The state is the actuality of concrete freedom. (Section 260)
>
> If states disagree, the matter can be settled only by war. (Section 334)

Hegel maintained these grandiose views of the 'State' until the end of his life. And what was the embodiment of this divine 'State'? Why, none other than the near-absolute monarchy of Prussia, which Hegel served at that time as a paid civil servant! In 1830 and 1831 he gave a series of lectures at the University of Berlin on the *History of Philosophy*. These were published posthumously as a book in 1837, where we read,

> All the worth which the human being possesses – all spiritual reality, he possesses only through the State...The State is the Divine idea as it exists on earth...we must therefore worship the State as the manifestation of the Divine on earth. (p. 54)

Nothing must be considered higher and more sacred than good will towards the state...sacrifice on behalf of the state is the substantial tie between the state and its members. (p. 469)

Surely no power-crazed dictator could ever hope to discover a more convivial philosophy! There is much to be wary of in Hegel's thought, but it does include one redeeming feature. In his *Lectures on the History of Philosophy* (1896 English edition, Vol. III, Chpt. 1, p. 283) Hegel declared, 'One is either a Spinozist or not a philosopher at all.' Well said Wilhelm, and amen to that!

In the strongly statist tone of Hegel's writings, we may clearly see the Hegelian roots of both Communism and Fascism. And yet Karl Marx himself was no statist, and would have been appalled to see how his teachings have been perverted by the likes of Joseph Stalin and Kim Jong-un. Marx himself decried jingoistic nationalism and war-mongering nation states: his cry was, 'Workers *of the world* unite!' Marx in fact envisaged the eventual 'withering away' of the state, as people came to realise that they could live in peace and harmony and with mutual support without it: an impossible dream perhaps, but certainly not Stalinism! Even before his death in 1883 Marx had lived long enough to lament the perversion of his doctrines by his 'followers'. Engles reported him as saying in that year, 'ce qu'il ya de certain que moi, je ne suis pas Marxiste.' (If there is one thing that is certain it is that me, I am not a Marxist). Marx made this comment in French because he was referring to the so-called 'Marxist' policies of the *Parti Ouvrier Français* that had been founded in 1880 by Jules Guesde and Paul Lafargue, even although the latter was Marx's own son-in law! How quickly can doctrines be distorted!

In the same way, Friedrich Nietzsche (1844-1900) was far more of an early existentialist than a proto-fascist. True, he preached 'the death of God' and 'the coming of the superman', but this new man was simply an individual who recognised that the current Judaeo-Christian values by which Europe then lived were outdated, and irrelevant for the new times. This new individual thought for himself, created his own values, 'made himself', and 'dared to be free'. This would inevitably bring him into conflict with others, but this conflict was a good, indeed an inevitable thing. The stronger man, the stronger philosophy, would win out. The influence of Darwinism is evident here. In his most famous work, *Thus Spake Zarathustra,* published between 1883 and 1891, Nietzsche spoke of 'the will to power', and had no sympathy for the weak, since it was only through conflict that progress could be made. Under his system, great leaders like Napoleon would naturally emerge, the very embodiment of his concept of '*der Übermensch'*, 'the superman'. One can see how this philosophy might have appealed to proto-fascists. Mussolini, the founder of Fascism, read Nietzsche extensively, and Hitler admired him too, presenting Mussolini with a collection of Nietzsche's complete works at their historic meeting on the Brenner Pass in 1938. But Nietzsche was neither a statist nor a nationalist, and certainly not a militarist. He admired the French, who were at that time the enemies of Germany, and he also admired the Jews. Of the Germans themselves Nietzsche had a very low opinion, trying to claim (unsuccessfully) that he himself came from Polish stock! In 1889 he published *Twilight of the Idols*, a long philosophical work. Section VIII is headed, 'What Germans Lack'. Here we read,

What the German spirit might be – who has not had his melancholy ideas about that? But this people has deliberately made itself stupid, for nearly a millennium: nowhere have the two great European narcotics, alcohol and Christianity, been abused more dissolutely! (p. 2)

In another famous work, *Beyond Good and Evil* (1886) Nietzsche says,

I have never met a German yet who was well disposed towards the Jews...heaven have mercy on European understanding if ever one wanted to remove from it Jewish intelligence...Germany should expel anti-Semitic screamers from the country. (p. 198)

In *The Gay Science* (1882) he adds,

Europe owes the Jews no small thanks for making people think more logically, and for establishing cleanlier intellectual habits. (p. 348)

Nietzsche would have been as appalled as Marx at the behaviour of his so-called followers. He was no Nazi.

Another philosopher who has been sadly misused by his acolytes of the present day is Adam Smith (1723-1790). He must be turning in his grave to see how his name has been taken in vain by the proponents of that regrettable economic philosophy which is politely termed 'neoliberalism'. Members of the so-called Adam Smith Institute should remember that Smith began his career as a Professor of Moral Philosophy at the University of Glasgow, and that he was in his time regarded as being a philosopher rather than an economist. He is famous not only for *The Wealth of Nations*, but also for an earlier great work, *The Theory of Moral Sentiments*, published in 1759. According to his biographer John Rae, Smith regarded this, rather than *The Wealth of Nations*, as being his masterwork. Within this book, I would direct the attention of the neoliberals to Part I, Section I, Chapters 1 and 2, 'Of Sympathy' and, 'Of Pleasure and Mutual Sympathy', sections which the neoliberals prefer to ignore when they invoke the name of Adam Smith. In reality, Smith understood very well that it is more important to run an efficient society than an efficient economy, and that this would require some degree of state participation in the economy, particularly in the field of legislation. There will be more to say about Adam Smith in the Economics chapter below.

We have, therefore, good reasons to be sceptical about philosophy and philosophers. But Nietzsche had a point when he said that controversy and conflict can lead to progress. Today, while we are still far from having achieved a Hegelian synthesis, at least we do now understand a good deal more about political systems, economic principles, and the workings of our material world than we did 300 years ago, thanks to the arguments and disagreements of philosophers in these fields over hundreds of years. However, I would not agree with the over-optimistic views of Francis Fukuyama, who spoke of *The End of History and the Last Man* in his 1992 book of that title. Here he claimed that Western-style liberal democracies with capitalist economies would eventually be adopted worldwide, just because of the collapse of the Soviet Union in 1991. This is still far from being the case. China, for example, one of the world's largest economies, still has a political system that is far from being entirely democratic, and an economic system that is far from being entirely based on private capital. Meanwhile, in many Third World countries regimes that pose as democracies simply remain in fact the same old corrupt oligarchies. Even here in the West we are still in need of political and economic reforms to our present systems, but it cannot be denied that some progress has been made in these fields. Philosophers have built upon each other, learned from each other, fed upon each other in ways that have left us a rich heritage of understanding of our world and of ourselves, as we shall see later in this treatise. So perhaps we should forgive them their inconsistencies: perhaps these were an inevitable route to the heritage that we enjoy today.

e) Philosophers Are Blinkered and Arrogant

Speaking as a layman, it has struck me that academic philosophers have been a rather exclusive bunch, taking an unduly narrow view of their discipline. We should bear in mind that Philosophy sets out above all to answer the question, 'How should we live?' Therefore, just as there are many different aspects to life, so there should be many different aspects to Philosophy, reflecting the complexity of life itself. For example, while it is true that some scientists and a few theologians have been admitted to the hallowed ranks, and accepted as *bona fide* philosophers by the self-styled authorities in this discipline, their numbers are few, and one gets the impression that they have been admitted with reluctance, as though no mere scientist or religious thinker, whatever his merits, could ever be a true 'philosopher'. When it comes to science, Newton and Einstein are usually admitted to this exclusive club, but equally brilliant and influential scientists like James Clark Maxwell (1831-79), Charles Darwin (1809-1882), and Gregor Mendel (1822-84) are usually ignored in surveys of Western Philosophy. It often seems as though philosophers not only have their own vocabulary and their own language but also their own rather narrow and exclusive conception of what 'philosophy' actually is. Having admitted that the scientific method can be seen as a form of philosophy, and celebrating some early scientists such as Bacon and Newton, philosophers seem to think that they have given a sufficient nod in the direction of the scientists, and thereafter proceed to ignore them until the arrival of Einstein who, they are somewhat grudgingly prepared to admit, did make one or two points that might be accepted as being 'philosophical'! The field of ontology, what used to be called 'natural philosophy' in Newton's day, is of course best left to the scientists these days, but the *conclusions* delivered by the scientists ought to be of the greatest interest to philosophers everywhere. But more on this in the Science section below.

Religious thinkers too are generally given very short shrift in our histories of Western Philosophy. St. Augustine (354-430) gets a look in because of his interest in Platonism, and so does Thomas Aquinas (1225-74) because of his attempts to 'baptise' Aristotle, but while religious *commentators* like these are recognised as philosophers by the genre, religious *founders* themselves are always ruled out as *bona fide* philosophers. This is unfortunate, because it seems to me that these people have a lot to say on the key question of how we should live, which surely ought to be the main concern of all philosophers. Nor can it be denied that religious thinkers have had a profound influence in the shaping our histories.

Let us look first at the thoughts of Zhongni Kong Qiu (551-479 BC), who was better known by his honorific title of 'Kong Fuzi' (Master Kong), which in its anglicised version has become 'Confucius'. Unlike Jesus and Muhammad Confucius was certainly literate, working as a civil servant in the ancient Chinese state of Lu, which covered much the same area as present-day Shantung province. Here he rose to the office of Minister for Crime during the difficult 'Spring and Autumn Period' which immediately preceded the 'Period of the Warring States'. Scholars still dispute the extent to which Confucius had a hand in writing or editing the famous *Four Books* and *Five Classics* which formed the basis of Chinese traditions, philosophy, and law for many centuries, but there is general agreement that the third of the *Four Books,* the *Analects*, is very largely Confucius' own work. Like Muhammad, however, Confucius had many disciples and followers who noted down his sayings so that, as is also the case with Jesus and the Gospels, we can never be entirely sure just how much of the *Analects* is pure Confucius and how far words were put into his mouth by later writers and editors. However, as with Jesus and Muhammad, the spirit of his teaching comes through clearly enough. Indeed, one of his most striking sayings from the *Analects* closely echoes the words of Jesus.

> What you do not want done to yourself, do not do to others...love your neighbour as yourself...forgive your enemy, be reconciled to him, give him assistance, invoke God on his behalf. Book XV:23

In fact, this so-called 'golden rule' crops up in one form or another in many other religions as well, including Judaism, Hinduism, Buddhism, Taoism,

Islam, and Zoroastrianism. It sounds rather like a piece of philosophy to me. But here are some other sayings of Confucius, taken from his *Analects.*

> You cannot open a book without learning something.

> Without knowing the power of words, it is impossible to know men.

> The man who asks a question is a fool for a moment: the man who does not ask is a fool for life.

> A gem cannot be polished without friction, nor a man without trials.

> Learning without thought is labour lost: thought without learning is dangerous.

> Choose a job that you love, and you will never have to work a day in your life.

> In a country well governed, poverty is something to be ashamed of: in a country badly governed, wealth is something to be ashamed of.

> To meet with and listen to the wicked is already the beginning of wickedness.

I find much food for thought in these and many of the other sayings of Master Kong, and many applications of them to the present day in, say, the unfortunate friendships forged by Prince Andrew, or the way Russia is presently governed. But the point is that Confucius was a serious political thinker, much exercised by the question of how to achieve a peaceful, just, and harmonious society. In *The Great Learning*, one of the famous *Four Books* attributed to Confucius, he wrote,

> If the people are ruled by laws, and conformity imposed on them by punishments, they will seek to avoid the punishments, but will have no sense of shame. However, if they are led by virtue, and conformity instilled into them by the rules of propriety, they will develop a sense of shame, and will become good. (Book XVII:25)

This idea of appealing to man's better nature by instilling a sense of shame into wrongdoers is an interesting one, which finds an echo in the teaching of St. Paul.

> If thine enemy hunger, feed him: if he thirst, give him drink, for in so doing thou shalt heap coals of fire upon his head. (Romans 12:20)

An interesting idea indeed, although it rather presupposes that everyone *has* a better nature that can be appealed to! Confucius may have been right or wrong, but he was a contender, a heavyweight philosopher and political thinker. Why then is he so largely ignored in general histories of philosophy? I fear this is simply because he bears the taint of being religious. True, it is much disputed whether Confucianism really is a 'religion', but he does often mention

God, the afterlife, and heaven, and this seems to be enough to rule him out as a serious philosopher in the eyes of this subject's aficionados.

The same could be said of the sayings of Siddhartha Guatama Buddha, better known as simply 'the Buddha'. His dates are uncertain, but most modern scholars now agree that he died in or around the year 400 BC, at the age of roughly 80. His place of birth is also uncertain, but seems to have been either Nepal or north-eastern India. By tradition, he died at Kushinagar in Uttar Pradesh. Hard evidence on the life of the Buddha is scarce, but in his lifetime he clearly made a great impact, for his sayings have been preserved and entire ways of life and attitudes of thought have been built around his teaching.

Essentially, the Buddha taught that a man's happiness lies not in the things that he has, but in the things that he can do without. I have a lot of sympathy for this point of view, but I would add that in addition we should also cultivate a sense of grateful appreciation for the things that we *do* have. Here follow some of the sayings of the Buddha.

Three things cannot be long hidden: the sun, the moon, and the truth.

Just as a candle cannot burn without fire, men cannot live without a spiritual life.

To keep the body in good health is a duty: otherwise we shall not be able to keep our minds strong and clear. Without health life is not life: it is only a state of languor and suffering, an image of death.

Holding on to anger is like grasping a hot coal with the intention of throwing it at someone else: you are the one who gets burned.

We are what we think: all that we are arises from our thoughts. With our thoughts, we make our world.

To be idle is a short road to death, and to be diligent is a way to life: foolish people are idle, wise people are diligent.

Whatever words we utter should be chosen with care, for people will hear them and be influenced by them for good or ill.

I could add at this point some of the wise sayings of Muhammad and Jesus as well, but I think that the point has been sufficiently made. Neither of these great religious figures ever finds their way into books on Philosophy either: their association with religion rules them out. True, the eastern religions do get a look into the western philosophical canon through the works of Arthur Schopenhauer (1788-1860), but as in the cases of Augustine and Aquinas it is the commentator who is celebrated rather than the original founders themselves.

Both scientific and religious thinkers are, therefore, given short shrift by professional philosophers. While they are not entirely ignored, they are given very little consideration. But speaking as an economic historian, I am even more dismayed by the fact that economic thinkers too tend to be denied entry into their rather exclusive club by this blinkered crew! Today, the great importance of economic thought is widely recognised, but philosophers do not seem to have yet caught up with the times! Is greed good? Does 'trickle down' really work? How much wealth inequality should a society tolerate? Is inequality a drag on economic growth? As something of an economist myself, I can give categorical answers to those four questions. They are, 'no', 'no', 'less', and 'yes'. These are not just my views: economists everywhere are rapidly approaching a consensus of agreement on all of those points. At last they are all singing from the same hymn sheet, but unfortunately our plutocratic ruling classes are not listening to them. Therefore the answers to our economic ills are not economic answers, since they have already been given, but rather they are political answers, which will enable the economic answers to be implemented. Some suggestions for political reform will be made in the Conclusion below.

Surely all those economic issues have a crucial bearing on the question, 'How should we live?' Since their inception in 1901 the famous Nobel Prizes have been awarded each year to those who have made an outstanding contribution in the fields of Physics, Chemistry, Medicine, Literature, and the promotion of world peace. In 1969, however, an award was also given in a new field for the first time. This was the grandly titled, 'Nobel Memorial Prize in Economic Sciences'. Those possessed of a passing knowledge of the subject might balk at the association of the term 'science' with Economics (some say that God invented economists to make weather forecasters look good) but the institution of the new prize was an indication of the world's growing awareness of the importance of economic thought. Nobel himself had not recognised it, however, and as Ha-Joon Chang reminds us,

> Incidentally, the prize is not a *real* Nobel prize but a prize given by the Swedish Central Bank 'in memory of Alfred Nobel'. As a matter of fact, several years ago the Nobel family even threatened to deny the prize the use of their ancestor's name, as it had been mostly given to free-market economists of whom Alfred Nobel would not have approved. (*23 Things They Don't Tell You About Capitalism* (2010) p. 170)

Those disapproved of included Friedrich Hayek, who won the prize in 1974, and Milton Friedman, who won it in 1976. Nobel obviously had a social conscience. Some two-thirds of the Economics prizes awarded so far have gone to English-speaking writers from Britain, America, and Canada. This is not surprising, because the British were among the first Europeans in the field with serious economic thought. I am therefore doubly offended by the refusal of professional philosophers to admit economic thought into their fold, firstly as an economic historian, and secondly as a Briton. I must illustrate this point here by reference to some of the great economic thinkers that Britain has produced.

We could begin with Sir Thomas Smith (1513-77), the Essex man who has a good claim to being the first truly modern economic thinker in the world. Some would award this title to the great Islamic scholar Ibn Khaldun of Tunisia (1332-1406), but in my opinion Smith displayed a better grasp of the essentials, and did not find it necessary to bring in theology. We also produced Thomas Munn (1571-1641), the high priest of mercantilism, Sir William Petty (1623-87), John Locke (1632-1704), Charles Davenant (1656-1714), Bernard Mandeville (1670-1733), John Law (1671-1729), Adam Smith (1723-90), Jeremy Bentham (1748-1832), Thomas Malthus (1766-1834), David Ricardo (1772-1823), James Mill (1773-1836), John Stewart Mill (1806-73), Walter Bagehot (1826-77), Alfred Marshall (1842-1924), John Hobson (1858-1940), Arthur Pigou (1877-1959), John Maynard Keynes (1883-1946), Joan Robinson (1903-83), John Hicks (1904-89) and we could also perhaps even lay claim to Friedrich August von Hayek (1899-1992) who, although born in Austria, became a British citizen by choice in 1938, and found that his heart was English. In an interview given shortly before his death in 1992 Hayek declared,

> Neither on my early visit to the United States nor during my later stay there, or still later in Germany did I feel that I really belonged there. English ways of life seemed so naturally to accord with all my instincts and dispositions that, if it had not been for very special circumstances, I should never have wished to leave the country again. (S.Kresge & L. Wenar (eds.) *Hayek on Hayek;: An Autobiographical Dialogue* (1994) p. 86)

In the second half of the twentieth century we lost our leadership in economic thought to the USA., but we have a history to be proud of. Hayek, in addition to being one of the most influential economic thinkers of the twentieth century, was also a very considerable philosopher, and I find it surprising that surveys of philosophical thought usually ignore him, presumably because he is tainted by being an economist. But perhaps even more outrageous was the remark made by Bryan Magee in his very popular survey, *The Story of Philosophy* (1998). On p.178 he declares,

> It can confidently be claimed for Nietzsche that he had more influence on European writers of the front rank than any other philosopher after Karl Marx – *if indeed Marx can satisfactorily be thought of as a philosopher.* (My italics)

To say this of the philosopher who clearly had a greater influence on the history of the twentieth century than any other is something that I find astonishing. Moreover, Magee is a man who was thanked for his advice by the great Karl Popper himself on the Acknowledgements page of the fourth edition of his monumental work, *The Open Society and its Enemies,* which came out in 1961. I see this as a very good illustration of the extent to which any taint of economic considerations in their thought tends to disqualify writers from the title of 'philosopher' in the eyes of the philosophical establishment. Karl Marx (1818-1883) most certainly *was* a philosopher: he had studied the subject at the universities of Bonn and Berlin, and was influenced by Hegelian thought. After having studied Greek and Latin at the Friedrich Wilhelm Gymnasium at Trier from 1830 to 1835 he later became an accomplished classicist and a polyglot. His doctoral thesis, successfully submitted to the University of Jena in 1841 was on, *The Difference between the Democritean and Epicurean Philosophy of Nature.*

The above statement by Magee might be described as arrogant and dismissive, but it is certainly not the only statement of that kind to have been made by philosophers. In general they display a rather poor opinion of 'the mass' of mankind in general, and usually a rather poor opinion of other philosophers as well, believing that only they themselves have at last discovered 'the truth'. But this generalisation is less true of three of my four philosopher heroes. Thomas Paine was certainly arrogant, but he avoided epistemology entirely, while Einstein and Popper were both very cautious in their approach to 'truth' which is indeed one of the reasons why they are my heroes, but Spinoza provides a classic case in point. In his *Tractatus Theologico-Politicus* Spinoza begins with a thirty-page Introduction which he calls, 'The Scope and Purpose of This Work'. It is devoted entirely to a denigration of mankind in general, which is depicted as ignorant, prejudiced, superstitious, credulous, easily led, and governed by their passions rather than by their reason. On the last two pages of this Introduction he sums up his views in one of his final paragraphs:

> I know that the matters I handle here will be of interest to persons of philosophic and enquiring minds. To others indeed I do not recommend this Treatise, there being nothing in it which I could hope would by any possibility give them pleasure: for I know full well how pertinaciously those prejudices stick in the mind which have been embraced by it as a kind of religion. I know too that it is impossible to divest the vulgar mind of superstition and puerile fear. I know, in fact, that by the vulgar constancy is accounted contumacy, and that they are never governed by reason, but always moved to praise or blame by impulse or passion. I invite not the vulgar, therefore, nor those whose minds like theirs are full of prejudices, to the perusal of this book. I would much rather they neglected it entirely than, by misconstruing its purpose and contents after the fashion usual with them, that they prove troublesome.

He concludes his Introduction by displaying a glimmer of humility.

> I know that I am a man and liable to err, but I have taken pains not to err, and I have been especially solicitous so to express myself that all that I have written should be found in harmony with the laws of my country, and with piety and good manners.

However, on closer inspection this passage might be translated as, 'I know I might be wrong, but in fact I'm not'! Of course, to set oneself up as a philosopher at all does indeed require a high degree of self-confidence, but how easily can this self-confidence shade into arrogance. Some philosophers indeed have noted this quality in themselves. Thomas Hobbes dedicated the 1651 edition of his great work *Leviathan* to Sir Francis Godolphin (1605-67), and towards the end of his dedication he concludes, in a rather sheepish way, by saying to his patron, 'If you find my labour generally decried, you may be pleased to excuse yourself, and say that I am a man that loves his own opinions, and think true all that I say.'

In addition, of course, philosophers tend to display a rather low opinion of one another! Just a few examples will have to serve as illustrations here, but they could be multiplied. Spinoza himself begins the first chapter of his *Tractatus Politicus* (also sometimes called the Introduction) with a sweeping attack on all earlier philosophers because they have all failed to understand human nature!

> For they have conceived of men not as they are, but as they themselves would like them to be. Hence it has come to pass that instead of ethics they have generally written satire, and that they have never conceived a theory of politics which could be turned to use, but something that might be seen as a chimera, or might have been formed in Utopia, or in that golden age of the poets when, to be sure, there was least need of it.

But of course he, the great Spinoza, was just about to put everybody right once and for all on that one! However, Spinoza himself was later to come under savage attack from Nietzsche, who also dismissed all other philosophers at the same time. They all needed to be put right by the great man himself. In *Beyond Good and Evil* (1886) Nietzsche declares in Section 5 of Chapter 1,

> Philosophers all pose as though their real opinions had been discovered and attained through the self-evolving of a cold, pure, divinely indifferent dialect...whereas in fact a prejudiced proposition, idea, or 'suggestion' which is generally their heart's desire abstracted and refined, is defined by them with arguments sought out after the event...for example the hocus-pocus in mathematical form by means of which Spinoza has as it were clad his philosophy in mail and mask – in fact, the 'love of *his* wisdom', to translate the term fairly and squarely – in order thereby to strike terror at once into the heart of the assailant who should dare to cast a glance on that invincible maiden, that Pallas Athene! How much of personal timidity and vulnerability does this mask of a sickly recluse betray!

We find similar sentiments being expressed by Ludwig Wittgenstein in his *Tractatus Logico-Philosophicus* of 1921. Its title was meant to reflect not so much a tribute to Spinoza's *Tractatus Theologico-Politicus* as an implied correction to it! In his Proposition 4.003 Wittgenstein declares,

> Most of the propositions and questions to be found in philosophical works are not false, but nonsensical. Consequently, we cannot give any answers to questions such as these, but can only point out that they are nonsensical. Most of the propositions and

questions of philosophers arise from their failure to understand the logic of their language.

Once again therefore, nearly everyone before him had been wrong, but now he, the great Wittgenstein, was about to put everybody right! Karl Popper joined in this general condemnation of other philosophers, declaring on the occasion of his 90th birthday party,

> I think so badly of philosophy that I don't like to talk about it...I do not want to say anything bad about my dear colleagues, but the profession of teacher of philosophy is a ridiculous one. We don't need a thousand trained, and badly trained, philosophers – it is very silly. Actually most of them have nothing to say. (*Intellectus*, Vol.23 (July-September, 1992), p. 2.

I find this arrogant streak that so many philosophers display to be rather depressing, for arrogance closes minds, and makes it less likely that worthwhile conclusions will be arrived at. It is of course entirely wrong to make a sweeping dismissal of all the thought that has gone before, however sure of your own opinions you may be. While it is quite true that a good deal of nonsense has indeed been written, every philosopher of note has had at least *something* interesting to say, and there is much to be learned from a general survey of their views.

A Case *For* Philosophy: the Ancient Greeks

So, is there anything left to be said for this confused and blinkered discipline? Can any good thing come out of Philosophy? I clearly have no illusions about the subject, but despite my strictures as listed above, I believe that it can. Indeed, history teaches us that it has been first religious thought, and then political thought, then scientific thought, and finally economic thought that have been instrumental in shaping the modern world that we see around us today. Scientific and engineering achievements have indeed helped us to massively increase our output of material wealth over the last 200 years, but when it comes to how to use and how to distribute all this wealth, philosophy still has a great deal to teach us.

In the Western World, it might be said that serious philosophical thought began with the ancient Greeks. It is not my intention to produce yet another history of philosophical thought here, but I would like to single out just a few of the ancient philosophers for special mention, and just a few elements of their thought that have particularly resonated with me. I have already mentioned Confucianism and Buddhism, which certainly sound a lot like philosophies in my opinion, but it must also be acknowledged that something very remarkable in the history of thought began to emerge in the ancient Greek world from 600 BC onwards. We should, perhaps, more strictly speak of the Hellenic world, for the Greeks of the time called themselves 'Hellenes'. This world extended far beyond present-day Greece, stretching from the southern shores of the Black Sea and the western coast of present-day Turkey to southern Italy and Sicily, and included Cyprus, Crete, and parts of North Africa, for the Greeks were great seafarers and colonisers. It was from this widespread community that the first great philosophical thinkers of the Western World emerged from about 600 BC. Their name is legion, for they are many, and what is remarkable about them is that they tried to understand the nature of reality in purely rational, logical, and secular terms, without simply shrugging their shoulders and putting it all down to creator gods. To the best of my knowledge, nowhere else in the world did this happen at such an early date, and this makes the Hellenic world of the time both unique and remarkable. Some of the better known of these philosophers were Thales of Miletus, Heraclitus of Ephesus, Pythagoras of Samos, Parmenides ofElea, Democritus of Abdera in Thrace, and Anaxagoras (c.510-428 BC) of Clazomenae on the eastern coast of the Aegean Sea, who became the first great Athenian philosopher.

Interestingly, all of these early Greek philosophers are known collectively as 'the pre-Socratics'. What then, was so significant about the thought of Socrates of Athens (c470-399 BC)? Why is he seen as a pivotal figure? The answer is that prior to Socrates, all of the other Greek philosophers had been primarily ontologists, that is to say they had speculated about the nature of reality, and about how the world worked. But Socrates came along and told them that they had been asking the wrong questions. The question that philosophers should really have been asking was the much more important and appropriate one of, 'How should we live, both as individuals and as communities?' This recommendation was highly appropriate at the time, for philosophers then knew practically nothing about ontology, but it is even more appropriate in our own day, when ontology can safely be left to the scientists, who really are extremely good at it. 'How should we live?' was the proper question for philosophy to be asking, and it was moreover one to which there was some prospect of finding an answer. In my opinion, it was Socrates who set philosophy onto its proper course. He pointed out that all the speculations of earlier philosophers about how the world worked were just that – speculations. Nobody actually *knew* anything. Socrates admitted that this applied to himself as well. When the oracle at Delphi named Socrates as the wisest of all the Greeks, Socrates assumed that this meant that he alone knew that he knew nothing! This applied even to what he had called the key question, namely, 'How should we live?' However, Socrates did at least set about trying to find the answer to this question, by asking others for their opinions on important issues such as, 'What is justice?', What is morality?', 'What is piety?', 'What is courage?' Significantly, however, none of his questions related to the natural world: they concentrated rather on human behaviour and human emotions, probing for an answer to the question, 'How should we live?' In quizzing his fellow Athenians in this way Socrates was being disingenuous. He knew full well that nobody, including himself, really knew the answers to these questions, but he sought to bring home to people the full extent of their own ignorance. He showed his contemporaries just how much these topics needed to be thought about and how, even if an answer was reached in the form of a consensus, this answer itself should always remain open to question.

Today, this open-mindedness about the ultimate nature of truth is an established part of the scientific method, a lasting legacy of Socrates' thought. In his own day, however, although Socrates aroused a lot of interest, he was not popular with everybody, especially with the ruling class of Athens, who disliked his probing and questioning. They saw him as a disruptive influence, and a threat to law and order. At last the authorities arrested him on charges of atheism, and corruption of the young. Socrates was condemned to drink the hemlock, a fatal poison. He could have saved his life by fleeing from Athens, but he chose to stay, believing that everyone should be subject to the law of the land. Reflecting on the sad death of Socrates, I am reminded here of the contemporary colloquialism, 'Everybody hates a smartarse', as JC was also to find out later, the hard way! In my opinion, however, it was Socrates who set Philosophy on its right and proper course, and made Athens the leading centre of Greek philosophical thought for generations to come.

Present at and an eye-witness to the very public death of Socrates in 399 BC was a young Plato of Athens (c428-c348 BC), who was then aged about 30. He was a great admirer of Socrates, and did much to spread his fame and his thought. In addition, among his many other achievements, Plato was the first philosopher to see man as a political animal (ζωον πολιτικον), speculating on the nature of the ideal state in his most famous work, *The Republic,* written around 380 BC. Although it was Aristotle who first actually coined the phrase, 'Man is a political animal', this assumption is clearly implied in *The Republic.* My own copy of this great masterpiece is the Penguin Classics edition of 1961, translated by H.D.P. Lee, which I bought in that year for just five shillings. The pages are battered and yellowing now, but my views on the work have not changed over the last half century. One has to admire the towering intellect of the man, and his ideas were later to be well received in an age of absolutism and Christianity, but in my opinion Plato has little to say to modern times. This is hardly surprising in view of the mores of those times in which he lived. Indeed, his influence upon political thought down the ages has been, in my view, a baleful one, and I would classify him as a dangerous philosopher. There are many aspects to Plato's philosophy, but in political terms the Plato who emerges from the *Republic* and the *Laws*, despite his obviously good intentions, appears to me as too much of an organic statist, with a predilection for eugenics.

His most famous pupil, however, was Aristotle of Stagira (384-322 BC) who was drawn to Athens at the age of 17 to study at the Academy which Plato had founded there. Aristotle later founded a school of his own in Athens, which he called the Lyceum. I find the views of Aristotle to be more acceptable, partly because he did not show the same obsessive fear of 'corruption of the soul' which had so concerned Socrates and Plato. They seemed to associate this terrible fate with not being true to oneself. Again, I cannot agree here. It seems to me that Adolph Hitler was entirely true to himself as, for that matter, was Vlad the Impaler. Nor do I admire Aristotle for the breadth of his interests, and his speculations on the nature of things, but I do admire him for two elements in his thought. The first of these was his introduction of the idea of 'the golden mean'. Socrates had baffled people by asking them such questions as, 'What is courage?', 'What is generosity?', and 'What is self-respect?'. Socrates himself had not tried to answer these questions, but had sought only to stimulate discussion about them, and to show people that they did not really understand as much as they thought they did. Aristotle, however, *did* attempt to answer them, with his doctrine of 'the golden mean', spelled out in his *Nicomachean Ethics*, written around 340 BC. According to this, courage is the mean between cowardice and foolhardiness, generosity the mean between profligacy and meanness, and self-respect the happy medium between vanity and grovelling self-abasement. In other words, Aristotle preached moderation in all things, wise advice for his own and all subsequent ages. In his other famous work, the *Politics*, Aristotle provided a much more subtle and in-depth analysis of political structures than had Plato in his *Republic*, recognising different constitutional frameworks, and proposing a division of powers within government, although this division was to be on class lines rather than our modern idea of a division of powers by function of government into the executive, legislative, and judicial branches. He also advocated the supremacy of law, but he too had little time for individualism, liberalism, or human rights. Like Plato he was authoritarian in his approach, approved of slavery, and was a racist, regarding all non-Greeks as inferior barbarians, and indeed as 'slaves by nature'. Therefore I would argue that Aristotle too has only a limited amount to say to modern times on political issues, but we will look again at both of these great philosophers in the section on Karl Popper below.

After the passing of Plato and Aristotle, four distinct and competing schools of philosophy emerged as dominant in the Greek world for the last 300 years of the pre-Christian era. The four groups were known as the Sceptics, the Stoics, the Cynics, and the Epicureans. The first three schools were the products of collective and evolutionary thought, but the last school was very much the creation of a single thinker after whom the school was named, Epicurus of Samos (341-270 BC). The thought of these four schools is well worthy of some detailed consideration, because when it comes to the question of how we should live as individuals, it could be argued that between them they gave the Western World nearly all the philosophy that was worth having.

Scepticism as a philosophy had been originated by Pyrrho of Elis (c360-270 BC), but it was his pupil Timon of Phlius (320-230 BC) who lent real intellectual credibility to the school. His successor as the leading Sceptic was Arcesilaus of Pitane (315-240 BC), who took over the management of Plato's Academy in Athens, which then remained in the hands of the Sceptics for the next 200 years. The Sceptics really were sceptical, arguing that certainty about anything cannot be established by argument, demonstration, or proof, since every 'proof' itself rests on unproven premises, and every argument can be met by a counter argument. This may sound like a doctrine of despair, but twentieth-century logic, science, and even mathematics eventually came round to accepting the Sceptics' point of view. Today, this is not seen as a doctrine of despair, but rather as 'a healthy scepticism', an admission that everything we think we know at the moment must remain open to question and challenge, accepted only as the best approximation to the truth that we have for the time being. But Scepticism does not mean that we should believe in nothing. The Scottish philosopher David Hume (1711-76) was basically a Sceptic, but he injected a dose of Gaelic common sense into the philosophy by stating that while indeed we cannot be absolutely sure about anything, yet we are still obliged to make choices in life, and it seems clear enough that some things are more likely to be true than others, so we must make our choices, decide what we are going to believe for now, and proceed on that basis. The Sceptics were therefore well ahead of their time, and made a lasting and very valuable contribution to philosophical thought. They pointed out to us all the dangers of arrogance and dogmatism. The good philosopher, like the good scientist, and indeed the good historian, must be possessed of a due degree of humility.

The Cynics, on the other hand, were not really 'cynical' in the modern understanding of the word. This term acquired its pejorative overtones only in the early years of the nineteenth century as representing someone who was inclined to a disbelief in the sincerity or goodness of human motives and actions. The first Cynics were in fact more ascetics than 'cynics', eager to renounce the values of the world. The early Cynics owned no property, and rejected the common desires for money, fame, power, or reputation. Instead they lived on the streets and wore rags or nothing at all, wandering and preaching. They believed that they were living in accordance with nature as understood by human reason, which was the only path to true virtue. The aim was to thereby achieve happiness by freedom from suffering, since it was a common belief at the time that the only requirement for happiness was the achievement of this ἀρετή (arête), or virtue.

This philosophy might sound rather like Buddhism, but in fact it seems to have owed more to the ascetic traditions of Hinduism, as discovered by Alexander the Great (356-323 BC) and his men at the eastern limit of their drive into India. There they encountered the gymnosophists, or naked philosophers, who clearly made a great impression on the Greeks as men who had renounced all worldly pleasures and possessions in pursuit of 'virtue'.

But the alleged founder of the Cynic school, in so far as being credited with giving it a name, was Antisthenes of Athens (c445-365BC) a student and keen admirer of Socrates, who was present at the great man's execution. He was a contemporary of Plato, with whom he disagreed, attacking him in his writings. Antisthenes is credited with giving the school its name by teaching at the Cynosarges (κυνοσαργες) gymnasium in Athens, which translates as 'the place of the white dog'. In Greek κύων (cyon) means dog, and the genitive form, 'of a dog' is κυνος, while κυνικος, pronounced cynikos, means dog-like, and hence the 'Cynics'. However, it is also possible that their name was applied to the Cynics only at a later date as a term of abuse, because they lived like dogs, and like dogs they were shameless in their behaviour, going out of their way to flout normal social conventions. But Antisthenes himself was hardly an archetypical Cynic. It is true that he taught the merits of poverty as part of the path to virtue, and believed that we should not allow ourselves to be distracted from this path by the worldly pursuit of wealth, fame, or power. Instead we should try to acquire 'virtue' by living in accordance with nature, as revealed to us by the use of reason. Nor should we care about the opinions held of us by others: indeed, to be held in ill-repute was a positive merit. Was not Socrates so held in his time?

However, while he lived an austere and virtuous life, Antisthenes did at least wear clothes and lived in a conventional house. It is rather his follower Diogenes (c412-c323 BC) of Sinope on the southern coast of the Black Sea who is seen to be the archetypical Cynic. Diogenes certainly visited Athens, and may have been tutored by Antisthenes, although some scholars doubt whether the two men actually met. What is beyond doubt, however, is the fact that Diogenes was strongly influenced by the teachings of Antisthenes, and took them to what might be described as their logical conclusions, going naked, begging in the streets, and living in a large earthenware pot. He went out of his way to outrage public decency, and followed his master in baiting Plato, often interrupting his lectures. In return Plato called him 'a Socrates gone mad', but he was treated with respect by the citizens of Athens, and other Greek cities, who admired the extremes to which he was prepared to go in his pursuit of 'virtue' . He is said to have wandered the streets of the city carrying a lighted lantern in broad daylight, saying that he was trying to find an honest man in Athens.

Two famous legends about Diogenes have him meeting Alexander the Great at Corinth, as the philosopher was resting in the sun. When Alexander approached and asked whether there was anything he could do for him, Diogenes replied, 'Yes, stand out of my sunlight'. Delighted by this reply, Alexander is said to have exclaimed, 'If I were not Alexander, I would wish to be Diogenes!' To which Diogenes returned, 'And if I were not Diogenes, I too would wish to be Diogenes.' Another version of the story of their meeting has Diogenes pondering a pile of bones when Alexander approached him. When asked what he was doing, he replied, 'I am searching for the bones of your father, but I cannot distinguish them from those of a slave.' Diogenes certainly had no time for social distinctions, nor for national pride. When asked where he came from, he replied that he was a 'cosmopolitan', a citizen of the world. Although they flouted social conventions, challenging even state laws, the Cynics were not 'drop outs', but very much in the world, publicly teaching their views and practising what they preached, openly demonstrating their conception of the path to virtue.

Diogenes in his turn had a famous follower, Crates of Thebes (c365-c285 BC), who is said to have renounced a large fortune to move to Athens and study under Diogenes. Again the closeness of the relationship between the two men has been disputed, but Crates certainly became a Cynic, begging on the streets of Athens and having no home of his own. However, he was less austere than Diogenes, allegedly wearing a cloak and carrying a large wallet or shoulder-bag with a few possessions. He did not go out of his way to outrage public decency as Diogenes had done, and he was prepared to accept hospitality in people's homes. He was said to have been a man of good cheer, and again unlike Diogenes, he married. His wife was Hipparchia of Maroneia (c350-c280 BC), a remarkable woman of a good family who also gave up everything to join Crates, begging with him on the streets of Athens. Their relationship was exceptional for the times as being one of complete equality, and Hipparchia was indeed a respected philosopher in her own right, leaving behind some philosophical tracts of her own.

Crates in his turn had another famous student, Zeno of Citium in Cyprus (c334-c262 BC), who is credited with founding the Stoic school of philosophy. Zeno is said to have been a merchant who suffered shipwreck on the Greek coast, and so found his way to Athens, where he was much impressed by the teaching of Socrates, as recorded by Plato. When he asked where he could find such a man as Socrates in the Athens of his day, Crates was pointed out to him. Zeno then began to study under Crates, but he also attended lectures by other Athenian philosophers of the time, such as Stilpo, Philo, Xenocrates, and Polemo. Zeno led an ascetic life in Athens, partly because he was by nature a sombre and austere man, but also in deference to his first teacher, Crates. However, his natural dignity restrained him from the worst excesses of the Cynic lifestyle, and he even ended his days in a house of his own! Zeno was, therefore, not quite a Cynic, although obviously respectful of their philosophy. However, although he is credited with originating the creed, he was not quite a Stoic either, as the term later came to be understood, for his teaching was considerably extended by later writers, who gave Stoicism its final form. What Zeno did do, however, was to give the creed its name.

After studying under several philosophers for many years, Zeno eventually began to teach himself, lecturing in the open air as was the custom of the time, at around 300 BC. Zeno chose as his 'pitch' the Στοά Ποικίλη, or painted porch, located in the colonnade of the Agora, the market place in Athens. His followers were at first called Zenonians, but later Stoics, after the Stoa Poikile where they congregated. Zeno himself was a pantheist, following Antisthenes in declaring that there was only one god, whom he associated with nature as revealed by reason. But this 'nature' was more The Great Nature of All Things, which the Greeks called λόγος, logos, The Word. An interesting term, 'logos'. My Greek dictionary gives no fewer than 52 different definitions of 'The Word', the longest single definition in the book. Seeing that this really is an all-encompassing term helps us to understand its use in the opening lines of St. John's gospel: 'In the beginning was the Word, and the Word was with God, and the Word was God.' The term used here in the Koine Greek in which the New Testament was written was λόγος, logos. This reflects the Stoic view of the universe as a living, purposeful totality, following its own laws, which could be understood through the exercise of reason. Chronologically, St. John's gospel was the last of the four canonical gospels to be written, at a time when Stoicism was a well-established creed among the educated. The early Christian writers indeed borrowed other words from the Stoics as well, employing their terms in the use of such words as 'virtue', 'spirit', and 'conscience'. But Stoicism and Christianity also shared certain concepts. They both believed that their creed gave them an inner freedom from the external events that surrounded them, a kind of incorruptibility of the soul. They both believed that their creeds enabled them to establish a deeper understanding of God or the universe, so that they could form a closer and better relationship with Him or it. They were both suspicious of attachment to worldly possessions as a path to happiness, and although they both preached brotherly love, they both acknowledged an innate depravity, a persistent evil, in the mass of humankind. Both believed that the baser emotions such as lust, anger, envy, and greed should be suppressed or redirected, so as to achieve 'virtue', ἀρετή, or spiritual purity. It would not be surprising if at some future date we were to discover that some of the presently anonymous gospel writers had been influenced by Stoic thought.

Living in accordance with nature, as understood by reason, was a central tenet of Stoic philosophy. Logic was therefore very important to Stoicism, and the next major contribution to the creed was made by Chrysippus of Soli in Cilicia, who lived from about 279 to about 206 BC. He developed a system of propositional logic, intended to promote a better understanding of the workings of the universe and humanity's role within it. So important was his contribution that he is regarded as the second founder of Stoicism. In later antiquity the doctrine was refined, and indeed finally defined, by some of its most famous practitioners, such as the Roman statesmen Marcus Tullius Cicero (106 BC -44 BC) and Lucius Annaeus Seneca (c4 BC-65 AD) in a number of treatises. On the other hand, an important contribution to Stoic thought was also made by Epictetus of Hierapolis in Phrygia (present day Turkey), who lived from 55 to

135 AD, and spent most of his life as a slave in Rome! But the most famous of all the Stoics was surely the Emperor Marcus Aurelius (121-180 AD) who, towards the end of his life, wrote his famous *Meditations*, a classic exposition of Stoic philosophy that ran to twelve books.

The Stoics were pantheists and determinists of a sort, thus stealing two of my 'original' ideas and publicising them 2,000 years before I was born! Naturally this makes me well disposed towards their philosophy, but I must say they seem to have been a rather dour and miserable bunch, more fatalists than determinists, expecting the worst to happen, and trying to inure themselves against it. There are echoes of Buddhism and Cynicism here with the stress laid by the Stoics on never becoming too attached to anything or anyone. You should always be prepared to lose everything with equanimity, for no one knew what fate would bring. Epictetus said, 'Permit nothing to grow to you that may give you agony when it is torn away' (*Discourses iv.1.112*) and later, 'Freedom is secured not by the fulfilling of men's desires, but by the removal of desire.' (*Ibid. iv.1.175*). The Stoics also believed in the fundamental equality of all mankind, and urged kindness towards slaves, for as Seneca observed, 'He whom you call your slave sprang from the same stock, is smiled upon by the same skies, and on equal terms with yourself breathes, lives, and dies.' (*Moral Letters to Lucilius, 47*) He expanded on this point in his *De beneficiis* where Seneca declared,

> It is a mistake to imagine that slavery pervades a man's whole being; the better part of him is exempt from it. The body indeed is subjected, and in the power of a master, but the mind is independent, and indeed is so free and wild that it cannot be restrained even by this prison of the body, wherein it is confined. (III, 20)

This was a point later to be expanded upon by Spinoza. In this way, the Stoic philosophy represented a radical departure from the views of Plato and Aristotle, both of whom had believed that some people (especially non-Greeks) were 'slaves by nature', and marks the beginning of that very radical notion that perhaps, 'all men are created equal'.

The Stoics also preached mutual assistance and the brotherhood of men, but at the same time they seemed to expect very little from the generality of mankind. Marcus Aurelius wrote in his *Meditations*(Book II, part 1),

> Say to yourself in the early morning: I shall meet today ungrateful, violent, treacherous, envious, uncharitable men. All of these things have come upon them through ignorance of real good and ill...I can neither be harmed by any of them, for no man will involve me in wrong, nor can I be angry with my kinsman or hate him; for we have come into the world to work together...

The Stoics tried to build around themselves a kind of mental or spiritual fortress that would protect them from the ills of the world, and ensure the immunity of their personal 'virtue'. Within his self-created fortress the Stoic sage could dwell secure, with his precious 'virtue' intact. In the words of Epictetus a Stoic could be, 'ill and yet happy, in peril and yet happy, in exile and yet happy, in disgrace and yet happy, dying and yet happy'. However, if all else failed and the stalwart Stoic still found life to be intolerable, they allowed themselves a final remedy, a last way out, which was suicide. Not believing in a personal god who might be offended by such behaviour, the Stoics saw this as simply a rational course of action. But there was an element of snobbery here, which permeated the whole of Greek philosophical thought, going right back to the intellectualism of Socrates, as described by Plato. The Stoics, like all the other Greek philosophers, believed that only the sage (i.e. philosophers like themselves) was capable of achieving true 'virtue', and so happiness. There was not much hope for the uneducated mass of mankind! Plato magnified this assumption into the notion of the 'philosopher king', i.e. that only a certain class of men (and,remarkably, women too) had a 'natural' right to rule.

Stoicism indeed became the favoured philosophy of the ruling classes in later antiquity, to such an extent that Gilbert Murray could declare that, 'Nearly all the successors of Alexander the Great professed themselves to be Stoics.' (*The Stoic Philosophy* (1915) p. 25) I too find the Stoic philosophy an attractive one, although I can detect some flaws, and we will return to it again later in this treatise.

The last of the four post-Platonic schools of thought to emerge was Epicureanism. While the other three all evolved as time went on, Epicureanism remained remarkably self-consistent, in part because it was the creation of just one man, Epicurus of Samos (341-270 BC). As a young man Epicurus studied under Nausiphanes of Teos, who had himself been tutored by Pyrrho the Sceptic, although Nausiphanes was also a follower of Democritus, and had clearly been much influenced by his thought. As a pupil of Nausiphanes, Epicurus too was much influenced by the thought of Democritus, and became an atomist like him, although he did not adopt the determinist views of Democritus, who had believed that atoms followed predetermined paths, so that from any given situation there was only one possible outcome. Epicurus argued that atoms could swerve unexpectedly in their courses, and from that assumption developed a doctrine of free will. In 306 BC Epicurus moved to Athens, where he remained for the rest of his life. There he purchased a house, and established his own school of philosophy, teaching in The Garden (κήπος) of his home. Unlike the Stoics, however, who were named after the Stoa or porch where they met, the followers of Epicurus were not known as 'The Gardeners'! Instead they took the name of the founder of their philosophy, but The Garden nevertheless became a famous site, located about halfway between Plato's Academy and Zeno's Stoa.

Epicurus is at once one of the most interesting, and one of the most misunderstood of all the Greek philosophers. An inscription on the gate of his famous garden read, 'Stranger, here you will do well to tarry, for here our highest good is pleasure'. As a result, my Chambers Modern Dictionary defines 'epicurean' as, 'n. someone who enjoys pleasure and good living: adj. given to luxury or to the tastes of an epicure'. However, Epicurus himself seems to have taken a very idiosyncratic view of 'pleasure', one that was far removed from our modern conception of the term. From his surviving letters he seems to have been a vegetarian, living mainly on bread and water, supplemented from time to time with a little cheese. Wine was apparently off his menu. In his *Letter to Menoeceus* Epicurus wrote,

> When we say then that pleasure is the end and aim, we do not mean the pleasures of the prodigal or the pleasures of sensuality, as we are understood to do by some through ignorance, prejudice, or wilful misrepresentation. By pleasure we mean the absence of pain in the body and of trouble in the soul. It is not an unbroken succession of drinking bouts and of revelry, not sexual lust, not the enjoyment of fish and other delicacies of a luxurious table which produce a pleasant life: it is sober reasoning, searching out the grounds of every choice and avoidance and banishing those beliefs through which the greatest tumults take possession of the soul...wisdom is a more precious thing even than philosophy: from it spring all the other virtues, for it teaches that we cannot live pleasantly without living wisely, honourably, and justly; nor live honourably, wisely, and justly without living pleasantly. For the virtues have grown into one with a pleasant life, and a pleasant life is inseparable from them.

Epicurus never married, and was of the opinion that sex was a very bad thing. Among his sayings in an ancient text now preserved among the Vatican archives, Epicurus declares, 'sex is never beneficial, and you are very lucky if it does not do harm as well.' (*Vatican Sayings,* 51) Instead Epicurus prized friendships very highly, so long as these did not develop into sexual relationships which might cause 'perturbations of the soul'. Epicurus' idea of 'pleasure' was therefore a life of no women, no wine, and presumably no song either, the whole sustained mainly on a diet of bread and water! On examination therefore, he appears to have been more of an ascetic, more of a Cynic, more of a Buddhist, more of a monk than anyone that we would today describe as an 'epicurean'. In our own times we might better describe Epicurus as someone who sought tranquillity rather than positive happiness. He sought peace of mind through freedom from fear, freedom from pain, and freedom from desire. In fact, all desires should be regarded with suspicion. When one drank water, the pleasure came not from the drinking itself, but the attaining of freedom from the desire to drink. Yes, Epicurus really was a barrel of fun. Freedom from fear he called *ataraxia*, and freedom from pain *aponia*. His version of the golden rule was that we should cause no pain to others by our actions, and no pain to ourselves through the indulgence of unregulated desires. In fact, a man who far better fitted the description of someone whom we would today call an 'epicurean' was Aristippus of Cyrene in present-day Libya (c435-c356 BC). Aristippus was for a time a student of Socrates, but Plato believed him to have become a disgrace to his master because of the truly hedonistic lifestyle that he later adopted.

Epicurus was an out and out materialist. He had no belief in an immortal soul or an afterlife, declaring, 'Death is nothing to us, for when we are death is not, and when death is, we are not'. In this way, he freed himself from the fear of death. Nor did he fear divine retribution. He was probably an atheist, but to declare this openly would have been dangerous. Instead he acknowledged the existence of the gods as role models, perfect beings. However, they were far above the concerns of the world, and did not interest themselves in the affairs of men. Therefore, we should not fear divine retribution, for the gods neither rewarded the just nor punished the unjust. Here, I recognise in Epicurus a fellow member of the Church of God the Utterly Indifferent.

Another of Epicurus' maxims was the injunction to 'live unknown'. Unlike the Stoics who saw participation in public life as a duty, Epicurus believed that we should not seek power or fame, but rather be content to enjoy the small pleasures of life, such as friendship. This point too chimes with me. From my shooting days I learned that 'he who keeps a low profile makes a hard target', a maxim which, I later found, had a wider application in life. Like the Stoics and the Cynics Epicurus also believed in the fundamental equality of all men, but he took this maxim even further, admitting women as well as slaves to The Garden. This notion that not only were all *men* created equal, but that possibly even all *people* might be equal as well was truly revolutionary for the times. It added to the reputation of the Epicureans as hedonists, and made The Garden an imagined scene of sexual orgies. In reality of course, nothing was further from the minds of true Epicureans.

Epicurus therefore shared some beliefs in common with the Cynics and the Stoics. All three schools believed in the achieving of freedom from base desires as a route to *arête*, virtue, which in turn was the only route to happiness. All three schools prized wisdom above all, for wickedness derived from ignorance. If all men could be wise, then all men would be virtuous, and so happy, but unfortunately most men were not wise, and hence there was much wickedness and unhappiness in the world. This arose largely from greed for material possessions, lust for status and power, and an excessive readiness to indulge the passions, or desires. But the sage lived simply, content with bare necessities, controlled his passions, and curbed his desires. In this way, only the sage could achieve true virtue, living a moral and upright life, and so achieving happiness. All three schools could therefore be described as the heirs of Socrates, in that they all tried to provide answers to the questions that he had posed. But even the fourth school, the Sceptics, could also be included in this description. The Sceptics had taken nothing from Socrates except his scepticism, but the other three schools had taken up the challenge thrown down to them by this pivotal thinker, namely, 'How should we live?' This, Socrates had said, is the question that Philosophy *should* be asking. In their different ways, all three schools had set out to answer it, thereby well deserving their collective title of 'the post-Socratics'.

It seems to me that by the time of the fall of the Roman Empire in the West the Ancient World had taught us all that we need to know on the question of how we should live as individuals. Anicius Boethius (477-424), one of the last Roman senators was a Christian, but faced with dire circumstances towards the end of his life it was to the Greek philosophers that he turned for comfort in his best-known work, *The Consolation of Philosophy* (424). But when it comes to the question of how we should live as societies, as communities of fellow human beings, the ancients did not give us much advice that is of relevance to the modern world. Their political philosophy was rudimentary, and they knew nothing of the principles of economics, constitution building, or the discipline of sociology.

Margaret Thatcher of course famously said, 'There is no such thing as "society": there are only individuals'. But Margaret Thatcher was wrong. Even Jean Paul Sartre came to realise towards the end of his life that no one could fully isolate himself from the society of which he was a part. We humans are inherently social, the quintessential pack animals. We constitute indeed a superorganism: we are the termite mound, the beehive, the ant nest, the colony of coral, the community of naked mole rats writ large. We can achieve immensely more as an integrated society than any one of us ever could as an individual. It is indeed impossible to fully address the question of how we should live as individuals in isolation from the question of how we should live as societies, with the latter question by far the more difficult. But the question of how we should live as societies is a political question, which will be dealt with below in the chapter on Politics, where we shall hear from the philosophers again, but this time from more recent thinkers.

III Four Great Philosophers

My 'Four Greats' have been singled out for detailed consideration mainly for personal reasons: these are the four who speak most directly and personally to me. But each one may also be seen as a landmark figure in the history of Western thought. Spinoza and Paine were truly revolutionary figures, far ahead of their time, while Einstein and Popper were very much *of* their time, each one setting benchmarks for twentieth-century thought in their different ways. They are significant because the twentieth century has given us a great deal to think about in the political, economic, scientific, and ecological spheres. Today, in 2022, we badly need guidance for the century that lies ahead of us, for it will surely prove to be 'make or break' time for our species.

Baruch Spinoza (1632-77)

Spinoza came from a family of Sephardic Jews, originally from Portugal, where they had been forced to accept nominal conversion to Catholicism. In 1627, however, shortly before Spinoza's birth, his father Miguel had moved to Amsterdam, where he was allowed to resume his Sephardic faith under the relatively tolerant government of the United Provinces at that time. Baruch himself was therefore raised as a Jew and educated at the local *yeshiva*, a Jewish school specialising in the study of the Talmud and Torah. His father Miguel was a moderately successful merchant, importing tropical fruit for sale in Amsterdam. Baruch was evidently a star pupil at his *yeshiva*, and seen as a future rabbi, but on the death of his elder brother Isaac in 1649 he left his studies to help his father with the running of the family business. It was 1653 before he resumed his formal education on a part-time basis, and it was at this point that Baruch began to fall in with what the Catholic Church would describe as 'bad company'.

At the age of 20 Spinoza began to study Latin at the school of Franciscus van den Enden (1602-74), a Dutchman and a Christian, but a lapsed Jesuit and a bold freethinker. He was later to be described by his enemies as a Cartesian and an atheist, although we must suspect some exaggeration here. At any rate, in the 1660s his writings were progressively placed on the Catholic Church's Index of Banned Books, as Spinoza's were later to be also. In all probability it was van den Enden who introduced Spinoza to Cartesian thought. At the same time as studying with van den Enden Spinoza continued trying to run the family business with his father, but the latter's health was failing, and he died in 1654 when Spinoza was still just 21 years of age. Spinoza then worked with his younger brother Gabriel to keep the family business afloat, but neither man showed much aptitude for commerce. His father had accumulated debts, and the business began to decline. After a few months Spinoza moved in to board with van den Enden, and later began to teach at van den Enden's school, partly to generate an income to help with the importing business. Increasingly, however, he left its management to Gabriel in order to pursue his intellectual interests. He began to attend meetings of the Collegiants, a loose association of dissident Protestant sects which objected to the strict Calvinism that was the predominant creed in the Netherlands at that time. Their membership consisted mainly of Arminians and Anabaptists, but included an eclectic mix of other dissenting sects as well. What they all had in common, however, was a readiness to think for themselves on rational lines, and to challenge established authorities and dogmas. It was from this group, and by his own reading, that Spinoza began to learn about Christianity. Significantly perhaps, in 1655 Spinoza changed his name to the Latinised form of Benedictus de Spinoza.

Perhaps as a result of his association with the Collegiates, Spinoza then began to question the tenets of his own faith. He did not do this lightly, feeling that to question the faith was a betrayal of the proud Sephardic community of which he was a part. At last, however, Spinoza's dedication to truth proved stronger than his loyalty to the Jewish faith. One of the leading tenets of Judaism was the belief that Moses himself had written the first five books of the Bible, from Genesis to Deuteronomy, known as the Pentateuch, but Spinoza found it impossible to accept this. Spinoza's view was, of course, entirely correct. The Pentateuch always refers to Moses in the third person, and Deuteronomy 34:5-7 actually records the death of Moses, allegedly at the age of 120. The Pentateuch was clearly written long after the death of Moses, with the real author or authors representing Moses as a semi-mythical figure with supernatural powers. This was Spinoza's belief, and these views were fine to hold in private, but Spinoza carelessly aired them abroad, and even went on to question the Jewish conception of God. This was a recklessly incautious thing to do, even in the Netherlands, which was then the most religiously tolerant state in Europe. Early in 1656 Spinoza was attacked on the steps of the Amsterdam synagogue by a zealot crying, 'Heretic!' who slashed at Spinoza with a knife, tearing his cloak. Spinoza himself escaped unharmed, but he was badly shaken by the attack, and subsequently adopted as his motto the Latin term *caute*, which means 'cautiously'.

1656 indeed proved to be a momentous year in Spinoza's life. Shortly after the synagogue attack, Spinoza found himself in Amsterdam's municipal court, fighting a complicated suit that included a challenge from his sister Rebekah over the distribution of their mother's inheritance. Spinoza won his case, but then renounced his claim in his sister's favour. At the same time he essentially entered a plea of bankruptcy to escape the burden of his father's debts, and thereafter left the running of the family business increasingly to his brother Gabriel, while he devoted himself ever more closely to his studies. But this turning to the municipal court of Amsterdam had not pleased the Jewish authorities, who believed that family matters should be settled in a rabbinical court under Jewish law. Spinoza was already in bad odour with them because of his carelessly expressed heretical views, and they decided to make an example of Baruch. On July 27, 1656 the Talmud Torah of Amsterdam issued a decree of *herem* against Spinoza, which was a form of excommunication, and expulsion from the Jewish community. The *herem* stated that Spinoza was being expelled because of 'the abominable heresies which he uttered and taught, and his monstrous deeds'. Neither the heresies nor the deeds were specified, but we can gather a very good idea of the former from Spinoza's subsequent writings. These revealed not only his panentheism and determinism, but also his denial of the immortality of the soul, his belief that the Torah or Old Testament was unhistorical, and a suggestion that the Talmud, the body of Jewish law, should not be considered as binding on the Jews of his day. These were 'abominable heresies' indeed, and more than enough to get Spinoza excommunicated. The *herem* concluded with the order that, 'no one should communicate with him orally or in writing, or show him any favour, or stay with him under the same roof, or come within four ells of him, or read anything composed or written by him'.

According to his biographer Roger Scruton, Spinoza took his expulsion calmly. Scruton quotes him as saying, 'Very well: this does not force me to do anything that I would not have done of my own accord, had I not been afraid of a scandal.' (Scruton, R. *Spinoza* (2002) p. 10) Far from repenting, as he was expected to do, Spinoza wrote a letter to the elders of the synagogue justifying his position on intellectual grounds! This must have enraged them even further. The *herem* against Spinoza has never been rescinded and still stands to this day, despite a 2012 appeal from the Jews of Amsterdam to their chief rabbi to have it lifted. We should remember that in July 1656 the young Spinoza, born on November 24th 1632, was still only 23 years of age, and had few means of material support. What intellectual courage he showed, and how strong his convictions must have been.

Following the *herem*, the Amsterdam municipal authorities expelled Spinoza from the city at the urging not only of the rabbis but also of the powerful Calvinist clergy, who had also been highly offended by the views which Spinoza had so carelessly expressed. His close association with the Collegiants also offended them, because if there was one sentiment that all the members of this diverse group shared it was their anti-Calvinism! However, a few months later, after the fuss over his *herem* had died down, Spinoza returned to Amsterdam and lived there quietly and unnoticed, teaching himself how to grind lens for a living, and also giving a few private philosophy lessons. In 1660 he moved to Rijnsburg near Leiden, the headquarters of the Collegiants with whom he had remained in close contact, frequently attending their meetings. It says a great deal for the free-thinking spirit of this group that they were prepared to welcome Spinoza into their community, for a panentheist is not a Christian, as were the other members of the group, and Spinoza must have made his views clear enough. Such a tolerant circle of free thinkers could have existed in no other part of Europe but the Netherlands at that time. However, the United Provinces harboured Spinoza, just as they had harboured Descartes before him.

In 1663 Spinoza moved to Voorburg, and then on to The Hague in 1670, where he spent the rest of his life. During his final ten years Spinoza became increasingly interested in optics, manufacturing microscopes and telescopes as well as lenses, and writing a short essay on the rainbow. His earnings at this time were meagre, but from 1670-2 he enjoyed a small pension from Jan de Witt (1625-72), the republican Grand Pensionary of the Netherlands, until he and his brother Cornelis were murdered by royalist supporters of the Prince of Orange. His friends and admirers also rallied around, regularly making small contributions for his support. Spinoza himself lived very simply, an ascetic and monastic life. In 1673 he was offered the Chair of Philosophy at Heidelberg University, but turned the offer down, preferring to go his own way. Even his enemies were forced to admit that he lived a saintly life, practising the doctrines of benevolence and toleration that were the hallmarks of his philosophy. He was known to be unfailingly courteous to all. Spinoza never married, devoting himself entirely to study and writing during his last years at The Hague. He died there on February 20th 1677 while still only 44 years of age, and by his own choice was buried not in a Jewish cemetery, but in the Christian churchyard of Nieuwe Kerk at The Hague. In 1880 the good citizens of The Hague commissioned a handsome statue of Spinoza by the distinguished French sculptor Frédéric Hexamer (1847-1924) to stand near the house where he had lived on the Paviljoensgracht. During his lifetime Spinoza was despised and decried as 'an atheist and a Jew', but both appellations were unfair and untrue. By the time of his death Spinoza was, theologically speaking, much more of a deist than an atheist, and more of a Christian than a Jew. In one of his last letters to Henry Oldenburg of late November or early December 1675 Spinoza wrote,

> Lastly, to open my mind more clearly...I say that it is not entirely necessary to salvation to know Christ according to the flesh; but we must think far otherwise of the eternal son of God, who was the eternal wisdom of God, which has manifested itself in all things, more especially in the human mind, and most of all in Christ Jesus. For without this wisdom, no one can attain to a state of blessedness, inasmuch as it alone teaches what is true and what is false, what is good and what is evil. And since, as I have said, this wisdom was most manifest through Jesus Christ, his disciples, in so far as he had revealed it to them, preached it, and showed that they were able above all others to glory in that spirit of Christ. (Wolf, A. (ed.) *The Correspondenceof Spinoza* (1928) p. 344)

As regards the charge of atheism that was levelled against Spinoza, the whole of *The Ethics*, which many believe to be his greatest work, revolves around the idea of God, and an attempt to prove His existence by a series of logical propositions. Indeed, the German poet Novalis (1772-1801) described Spinoza as *ein gottrunkener mensch*, 'a God-intoxicated man'. After his *herem*, Spinoza never repented of his 'heresies', and never sought re-admission to the Jewish community. Rather he seems to have felt much more at home among his Christian friends, the Collegiants. Perhaps he was particularly taken by the verse in John 4:24: 'God is spirit, and they that worship him must worship him in spirit and in truth'. It is clear from his books and his correspondence that Spinoza was very impressed by the teachings of Jesus, although he never actually became a Christian since, as a panentheist, he could not accept the divinity of Christ. Indeed, he came to disapprove of all forms of organised religion, just as Thomas Paine was to do after him.

It is of course for his writings that Spinoza is famous. These were comparatively few, but they were both profound and influential. His major works were, in order of their completion,

A Short Treatise on God, Man, and his Well-Being (1660)
(Korte verhandeling van God, de mensch, en deszelfs welstand)

On the Improvement of the Understanding (1662)
(Tractatus de Intellectus Emendatione)

The Principles of Cartesian Philosophy (1663)
(Renati des Cartes Principia Philosophiae)

A Theological-Political Treatise (1670)
(Tractatus Theologico-Politicus)

The Ethics (1674)
(Ethica: Ordine Geometrico Demonstrata)

The Politics (unfinished in 1677)
(Tractatus Politicus)

A Compendium of Hebrew Grammar (unfinished in 1677)

R.H.M. Elwes (ed.), *The Correspondence of Benedict de Spinoza* (2009)

A. Wolf (ed.), *The Correspondence of Spinoza* (1928)

When it comes to citations from these works, the *Tractatus Theologico-Politicus* will be abbreviated to TTP, the *Tractatus Politicus* to TP, and the

Ethica to E. Figures will be used to refer to the chapters and sections of the TP and the E, while chapters and page numbers from an 1862 edition of the TTP (available on line) will refer to that work.

It is clear from these writings that Spinoza was heavily influenced by the thought of earlier and contemporary philosophers, notably Euclid (fl. 300BC), Archimedes (c287-212 BC), Aristotle (384-322 BC), the great Jewish scholar Moses Maimonides (1135-1204), Hugo Grotius (1583-1645) the Dutch jurist and international lawyer, Thomas Hobbes (1588-1679), René Descartes (1596-1650), the first of the great rationalists, and also Nicolo Machievelli (1469-1527), to whom he seems to give the benefit of the doubt. (See TP chpt. V sect. 7) However, Spinoza outdared them all, and made a contribution to modern thought that is uniquely his own. In his works Spinoza writes on God, on man, and on society but, in his relentless seeking for the truth as he sees it, Spinoza displays no illusions about any of them: he takes a rather stern view of all three. At the same time, however, he expresses the traditional philosopher's belief that only the sage can be truly happy, because only the sage can be truly wise, and so only the sage can be truly virtuous. Wickedness is not weakness, as Milton suggested, but rather ignorance. He is equally forthright in his views on the state, and what its proper function should be. In his writings Spinoza tends to repeat his views, continually elaborating on them rather than altering them, or even introducing fundamentally new concepts. Because of this overlapping, it might be more appropriate to consider Spinoza's views in order rather than his works in order, although these latter will first of all be referred to.

Spinoza's vision of God has been described by the American philosopher Charles Hartshorne (1897-2000) as 'classical pantheism', but there are some problems with this definition. The term 'pantheism' was first coined by the English Whig philosopher John Toland (1670-1722) in 1705, specifically to describe the theology of Spinoza who, he assumed, simply associated God with nature. However, in 1828 the new term 'panentheism' was coined by the German philosopher Karl Krause (1781-1832) to describe his own beliefs. There is a small but subtle distinction between the two views. The panentheist does indeed associate nature with God, and in his Latin texts Spinoza often uses the term *Deus sive Natura*, which means clearly enough 'God or Nature' with capital letters used for both terms. However, in November 1675 Spinoza wrote in one of his last letters to his good friend and regular correspondent Henry Oldenburg (Letter LXXIII),

> The supposition of some that I endeavour to prove in the Tractatus Theologico-Politicus the unity of God and Nature (meaning by the latter a certain mass or corporeal matter) is utterly erroneous. (Wolf ed., p.343)

For Spinoza therefore, God was indeed in nature but also much more than nature: nature was but an aspect, but a mode, but an attribute of God, who transcended nature, although He was immanent in the world. God the Process transcended God the Creation. The German philosopher Karl Jaspers (1883-1969) explained this distinction by stressing that for Spinoza God was *natura naturans*, that is 'Nature naturing' rather than *natura naturata* or 'nature natured', a point made by Spinoza himself in his *Ethics* Part I Proposition 29. Panentheism is therefore more than the simple nature worship that we might associate with the Lake Poets, Wordsworth, Coleridge, and Southey. A panentheist is most certainly not an atheist: rather he regards the world with reverence, with wonder, with awe, and with gratitude. My own early view that God was 'The Great Nature of All Things' included not only 'The Way Things Are' but also, 'The Way Things Work'. Together, although these are basically just the laws of physics, they can produce a whole that is much greater than the sum of its parts. This is known as, 'the phenomenon of emergent qualities', transcendent qualities if you like, which is nowhere better illustrated than in the case of the human body. Here we have a form which begins life consisting of half a gallon of water with a few handfuls of cheap chemicals thrown in, and yet, and yet...truly, what a wondrous piece of work is a man! Here is 'the phenomenon of emergent qualities' indeed. 'It's wotcha do wid wotcha got dat really counts!' This may be seen in the universe and all its works, which are clearly capable of producing miracles of improbability, including ourselves, in ways that may be regarded as little short of divine. The panentheist senses this quasi-divine element in all aspects of nature, and adopts a reverence towards it that is little short of worship. Perhaps it would be more accurate, therefore, to regard both Spinoza and myself as panentheists rather than pantheists.

Both creeds, however, see an abstract, impersonal, amoral, and deterministic God who is deaf to the pleadings of mortals, totally unconcerned with their behaviour, and nothing at all like the envisaged Judaeo-Christian deity. God has no free will, since it is supremely incumbent upon God to obey His own laws. Both deny the immortality of the soul, and have no expectation of an afterlife. In this Spinoza clearly breaks with Cartesian dualism, which sees a clear distinction between body and soul: for Spinoza, body and soul were one. Here, Spinoza is closer to the materialism of Thomas Hobbes.

To find that a man of the seventeenth century, before the terms 'pantheism' and 'panentheism' had even been coined, could take such a radically different view of God from that of either the Jews or the Christians, is little short of astonishing. Although the Stoics of classical times had been pantheists of a sort, the concept had remained very poorly understood in Christian Europe, either dismissed or confused with animism or polytheism. It took Spinoza to spell the concept out clearly, and to introduce an idea of God as creator and controller of the universe that even the most rational and logical of thinkers could accept.

However, these ideas were far ahead of their time, provoking outrage in Spinoza's day. Moreover, he did nothing to increase his popularity by going on to question the authenticity of the entire Old Testament, held to be sacred by both Jews and Christians. The full title of his *Tractatus Theologico-Politicus* goes on to read, 'A Critical Enquiry into the History, Purpose, and Authority of the Hebrew Scriptures, with the Right to Free Thought and Free Discussion Asserted, and Shown to be Not Only Consistent but Necessarily Bound Up with True Piety and Good Government'. Here, Spinoza views the Old Testament not as holy writ, nor even as accurate history, but rather as a mix of mythology, metaphor, and allegory designed to 'impress the minds of the masses with devotion'. He was the first to introduce biblical criticism as a serious academic subject, and to apply something of the historian's rigor to the factual content of the texts. In his analyses, however, he is always careful to distinguish 'true religion' from mere superstition.

Structurally, the *TTP* is much more about theology than about politics. Of its 20 chapters, the first 15 are concerned mainly with the Old Testament, although they include some references to Christ and to Christianity as well. Spinoza, however, denies the reality of miracles in both Testaments, and suggests that the laws of the ancient Hebrews should no longer be considered binding on modern Jews. Chapter 15 is transitional and historical, taking lessons in politics from 'the commonwealth of the Hebrews', Roman history, and the recent experiences of both Britain and Holland. It is only from chapter 16 that Spinoza turns his attention more fully to politics, although even there he continues to draw examples from Jewish history. Once again the full titles of his chapters are revealing. While chapter 15 is entitled, 'Theology Does Not Assist Reason, Nor Does Reason Aid Theology. Of the Grounds for Our Belief in the Authority of the Sacred Scriptures', there is something of a sea change to chapter 16, entitled, 'On the Foundations of a Commonwealth. On the Natural and Civil Rights of Individuals, and on the Rights of the Government or Ruling Authority'. Chapter 17 is headed, 'Individual Right is Never Wholly Abandoned to the Ruling Power in a State. Of the Hebrew Republic in Different Periods of its Existence, and of the Causes of Its Decline and Fall'. Chapter 18 is entitled, 'On Certain Political Axioms Derived from the Constitution of the Hebrew Republic and the History of the Jewish People', while the heading of chapter 19 reads, 'All Authority in Sacred Matters Rests Exclusively with the Civil Power, and Religious Worship Must Be in Harmony with the Institutions of the State if God is to be Rightly Obeyed'.

In declaring that the final say in religious matters should belong to the head of state rather than any ecclesiastical authority Spinoza was following the Erastian principle of *cuius regio, eius religio* (Let he who rules decide on religion) which had been agreed at the Peace of Augsburg in 1555 as a means of ending religious wars within the Holy Roman Empire. Under the 1579 Union of Utrecht that had formed the United Provinces, religious toleration had been declared within the Dutch Republic for Catholics, Jews, and dissenters of every kind. However, the great majority within the new rebel state, determined to break away from the Spanish empire, were strict, intolerant Calvinists. It had been this Presbyterian Church that had urged Spinoza's expulsion from Amsterdam in 1656. This had led Spinoza to believe that ecclesiastical authorities were more of a threat to free speech and free thought than were secular ones, for the former were more fanatical! This had been a factor in his siding with the strongly anti-Calvinist Collegiants.

Chapter 20, the final chapter, stresses one of the main points of the whole *Tractatus* with its heading, 'In a Free State Everyone is at Liberty to Think as He Pleases, and to Say What He Thinks'. Towards the end of this chapter Spinoza writes,

From the foundations of the commonwealth as already explained, it follows most obviously that its purpose is not dominion, nor the coercion of men by fear, nor that they should act at the arbitrary bidding of others: on the contrary, it is that everyone may be free from fear, that he may live securely, in so far as this is possible: that is to say that he may possess in the best sense his natural right to existence, and to the fruits of his industry. No, the object of the state is not to change men from rational beings into beasts or puppets, but to enable them to develop their minds and bodies in security, and to employ their reason unshackled, so that hatred, anger, deceit and strife should cease among its members. In fact, the true end and aim of the state is LIBERTY. (TTP 20/344)

To this one might add 'fraternity' as well, for in Spinoza's civil society men were to render each other mutual aid and support. Indeed, it could be argued that in his ideal commonwealth Spinoza would aspire to equality as well. In Chapter VII of his *Tractatus Politicus* Spinoza suggests in Section 20 that,

In order that the citizens may be as far as possible equal, which is the first necessity of a commonwealth, none but the descendants of a king should be thought of as noble.

Liberty, Equality, Fraternity: these are in fact that same triumvirate of leading ideals that were to be espoused during the French Revolution, more than one hundred years later. Spinoza's views on the role of the state stand in sharp contrast to those of Wilhelm Friedrich Hegel, outlined above.

But for a full understanding of Spinoza's political views the *Tractatus Theologico-Politicus* of 1670 must be read in conjunction with his last, unfinished work, the *Tractatus Politicus* which Spinoza was still in the process of writing at the time of his death in 1677. The work consists of only 11 chapters, the first of which is an Introduction, followed by four chapters on political science in general. The next two chapters deal with monarchy, and the following three with aristocracy. It is only in chapter 11, the last,, that Spinoza begins to deal with democracy.

It is impossible to summarise here every detail of Spinoza's political thought, but its main outlines emerge clearly enough from these two works. It becomes clear that Spinoza was both a republican and a democrat. He was such a strong supporter of the republican Jan de Witt that Spinoza's own life was in danger after an Orangist mob had murdered de Witt and his brother in 1672. Spinoza believed that governments could derive their just powers only from the consent of the governed. In Chapter VII, his second chapter on monarchy in the *Tractatus Politicus*,Spinoza declares in Section 25,

> And so it appears that no man succeeds the king by right but him whom the multitude wills to be successor...for the king's sword, or right derives in reality from the will of the multitude itself, or its strongest part, or else from the fact that men endowed with reason never so utterly abdicate their rights that they cease to be men, and are accounted as sheep.

Later, in discussing the foundations of the state, Spinoza adds in Section 26, 'It remains only to warn the reader that I am here conceiving of that monarchy which is instituted by a free multitude, for which alone these foundations can serve'. In Section 1 of the same chapter Spinoza had noted, 'It is in no way repugnant to experience for laws to be so firmly fixed that not even the king himself can abolish them'. Spinoza had borrowed from Grotius the idea of the supremacy of the rule of law, and he borrowed from Hobbes the idea of a social contract made between men to save themselves from 'the state of nature', or 'war of all against all', whereby they agreed to place themselves under one supreme authority which would keep the peace. He agreed with Hobbes that it was only within a civil society that men could achieve their highest fulfilment and true freedom, and that only by agreeing to a social contract could they bring this about. But he moved beyond Hobbes in declaring that once made, this contract was not unbreakable, as Hobbes had maintained. In Section 6 of chapter IV of his Political Treatise, Spinoza states,

> Contracts or laws whereby the multitude transfers its rights to one council or man should without doubt be broken when it is expedient for the general welfare to do so.

In general Spinoza is a great champion of the state as the upholder of civil society because of the benefits which only civil society can afford, to such an extent that some have seen him as a Hobbesian. But Spinoza did not see himself in that light. In a letter to Jarig Jelles dated June 2, 1674, he wrote,

> With regard to politics, the difference between Hobbes and myself about which you enquire consists in this, that I ever preserve the natural right intact, so that the supreme power in a state has no more right over a subject than is proportionate to the power by which it is superior to the subject. (*Correspondence*, Wolf ed., p. 269)

Spinoza spells out most clearly the differences between himself and Hobbes in the opening paragraphs of Chapter XVII of the TTP (pp.287-90). But wherein does the state's 'superior power' lie, since Spinoza had made it clear that governments derive their just power only from the consent of the governed (TP 2:17)? Spinoza suggests that a government is justified by its 'usefulness', that is by its ability to maintain a calm and orderly condition within its dominions, something that individuals in the state of nature would not have the power to guarantee for themselves. Therefore, when it comes to the social contract,

> From these premises we conclude that a contract can have no force save by reason of its usefulness: this taken away, the contract is at the same time cancelled, and made null and void. (TTP 16/274-5)

The 'power' of a state therefore rests entirely upon its ability to keep the people happy.

> Since the right of a commonwealth is determined by the collective power of a people, the greater the number of subjects who are given cause by a commonwealth to join in conspiracy against it, the more must its power and right be diminished. (TP 3:9)

If this were to happen, the people are not to blame, but rather responsibility must be 'laid at the door of the commonwealth'. (TP 5:3) It therefore becomes clear that in Spinoza's thought the power of the state is far from being absolute, but rather is conditional upon its good or 'useful' behaviour, its ability to persuade the people that its rule is in their interests. It would seem that the 'natural right' to which Spinoza referred in his letter to Jelles was in fact nothing less than a natural right of rebellion. This would be entirely in keeping with Spinoza's view of what he calls the *conatus*, the impulse of all men to preserve their own lives and best interests. On close examination, therefore, it would appear that Spinoza was in fact a proponent of resistance theory, albeit in a rather oblique, subtle, and low key way. It is unfortunate that, as with so many other of his very good ideas, Spinoza failed to spell this out clearly. Despite this, however, he may be said to have here anticipated Sydney and Locke, who were to write much more specifically on resistance theory just a few years later.

Spinoza makes it clear that he strongly disapproves of the idea of rule by one man, but instead favours a form of collective leadership, backed by a representative assembly. In the middle of Chapter 16 of his *Tractatus Theologico-Politicus*, on p. 277 of the 1862 translation, Spinoza declares,

> No one, as Seneca says, rules long who rules by violence. Further, absurdities are less to be expected in a democracy, for it is next to impossible that a majority of an assembly, especially if it be numerous, should yield to one foolish person, or agree to any foolish or pernicious thing.

However, if you must have a monarchy, as most states did at that time, Spinoza outlines in Chapter VI of his Political Treatise his ideas for the constitution of a monarchy. The king should not only rule under the law, but should also be advised and restrained by a very large elected council, which sounds very like the king's Great Council in England, i.e. a Parliament. As the chapter progresses, it becomes clear that this 'council' is in fact to be more powerful than the king! In Section 26, Spinoza goes on to suggest that a second 'council' should also be formed. 'For the administration of justice, another council is to be formed of jurists, whose business should be to decide suits, and punish criminals.' The section goes on to insist that these jurists must be strictly impartial and subject to no outside influences. This sounds very like an independent judiciary. In short, it could be argued that Spinoza here anticipates Montesquieu's doctrine of the separation and balancing of powers by almost a century, although he does not manage to put this idea over with anything like the same clarity and impact that Montesquieu was later able to achieve.

In a preceding chapter, Chapter II 'On Natural Right', Spinoza had declared in section 15,

> And so our conclusion is that natural right, which is special to the human race, can hardly be conceived except where men have general rights, and combine to defend the possession of the lands that they inhabit and cultivate, to protect themselves, to repel all violence, and to live according to the general judgement of all. For the more there are that combine together, the more right they collectively possess. And if this is why the schoolmen want to call man a social animal – I mean because men in the state of nature can hardly be independent – I have nothing to say against them.

This translation uses the term 'general judgement of all', but the Latin term that Spinoza himself uses here and elsewhere is in fact *mens una*, which means 'one mind', and could just as legitimately be translated as 'the general will'. Here it could be argued that he anticipates Rousseau. We are further reminded of Rousseau in what Spinoza has to say in section 2 of Chapter V.

> Now the quality of the state of any dominion is easily perceived from the end of the civil state, which end is nothing else but peace and security of life. And therefore that dominion is the best where men pass their lives in unity, and the laws are kept unbroken. For it is certain that seditions, wars, and contempt or breach of the laws are not so much to be imputed to the wickedness of the subjects, as to the bad state of a dominion. For men are not born fit for citizenship, but must be made so.

This statement chimes with what Rousseau had to say early in book IX of his *Confessions,* published in 1789.

> I had come to see that in the last analysis everything depends entirely upon politics, and that whatever men may do, no nation will ever be anything other than what the nature of its government may make it.

Here again, Spinoza anticipates Rousseau by about 100 years.

In section 10 of Chapter VI Spinoza looks to the defence of the state, which he believed was best ensured by a citizens' militia, and certainly not by a standing army maintained by the king. Here he declares,

> The militia must be formed out of citizens alone, none being exempt, and of no others. And therefore all are to be bound to have arms, and no one to be admitted into the number of the citizens until he has learned his drill, and promised to practice it at stated times in the year.

This statement resonates with the controversial Second Amendment to the Constitution of the United States, which reads,

> A well regulated militia being necessary to the security of a free state, the right of the people to keep and bear arms shall not be infringed.

The Americans of the time saw this amendment as a kind of ultimate guarantee against arbitrary government ever being established in their country. It was a wise precaution at the time. Unfortunately, in the last analysis Chairman Mao's dictum remains eternally true – political power does grow out of the barrel of a gun. Today, however, the Second Amendment has become much more of a liability than an asset.

A further point of interest emerges in section 12 of Chapter VI of his *Tractatus Politicus*. Here, Spinoza writes,

> The fields, and the whole soil, and, if it can be managed, the houses too should be public property, that is the property of him who holds the right of the commonwealth. And he should let them out at a yearly rent to the citizens, whether townsmen or countrymen, and with this exception let them all be free or exempt from every kind of taxation in time of peace.

One might ask here who then would be responsible for building the houses, and indeed whether the whole proposal was not just too ambitious to be practical. However, there were indeed later to be calls for the nationalisation of all the land in England, and the idea of making some kind of land tax the only form of taxation that should be imposed on citizens was also later to be given very serious consideration. It was an idea proposed by Thomas Paine in Part II of his famous work, *The Rights of Man*. Here, in Chapter 5 entitled 'Ways and Means of Improving the Condition of Europe', he advocates a single land tax as a means of defraying the expenses of government, paying down the national debt, and in effect establishing the first welfare state in England. This again on first reading sounds like a fanciful scheme, but Adam Smith in Book V of *The Wealth of Nations* (Chapter 2, Article 1) had noted in 1776 that,

> Ground rents are a still more proper subject of taxation than the rent of houses...Ground-rents and the ordinary rent of land are, therefore, perhaps the species of revenue which can best bear to have a peculiar tax imposed upon them.

Indeed, even the modern right-wing economist Milton Friedman (1912-2006) is on record as describing some form of land tax as 'the least bad tax'. But the strongest advocate of a single land tax which should be imposed in lieu of all other levies was undoubtedly the American political economist Henry George (1839-1897) with his 1879 book, *Progress and Poverty*. This made the economic concept of 'Georgism' a seriously taken part of the economic lexicon, and so it has remained from that day to this. Joseph Stiglitz (b. 1943), perhaps the world's greatest living economist, has taken up and enlarged upon these ideas with his own 'Henry George Theorem'. But we should remember that the first 'single taxer' was in fact Baruch Spinoza.

In fact, so complex and detailed is Spinoza's political thought that it is possible to see in him the forerunner of many later schools. For example, in both the *Tractatus Theologico-Politicus* and the *Tractatus Politicus* Spinoza often makes use of the Latin terms *utilis* and *utile,* both of which mean 'useful' to describe the proper function of the state. In his *Ethics* Chapter 4, Proposition XL Spinoza says, 'Whatsoever conduces to man's social life, or causes men to live together in harmony, is useful (*utile*) whereas whatsoever brings discord into a state is bad'. In context, he uses these terms to stress that the state exists to serve the people, and not the people the state, a mechanistic rather than an organic view of government. The state must be 'useful' to the people. But these Latin terms of course form the root of the English 'Utilitarianism', the creed of Bentham and Mill. It might be fanciful to find a precursor of this doctrine too in Spinoza, for as in the comparison with Montesquieu, where Spinoza does not clearly spell out the need for a separation and balancing of powers between executive, legislature, and judiciary although he implies this, so too in the case of 'Utilitarianism' Spinoza does not actually say that the state should exist to promote 'the greatest happiness of the greatest number', but clearly implies that this should be its proper function. Montesquieu and Bentham were both capable of expressing themselves with far greater clarity, but it could be argued that Spinoza had anticipated them both. Indeed, with his *Ethics* Spinoza is sometimes credited with anticipating Nietzsche and Freud as well, although these claims will require some examination. In fact, it is to Spinoza's *Ethics* that we should now turn.

Although it is generally considered to be his greatest work, *The Ethics* was published only in 1677, immediately after Spinoza's death, by a small group of his friends. The work was considered to be too dangerous to its author to be published during his lifetime, and it was very quickly placed on the Catholic Church's Index of Banned Books. The full Latin title of this work is, *Ethica: Ordine Geometrico Demonstrata*. Here, Spinoza sets out his ethical and metaphysical concepts in the form of geometrical propositions, which he purports to 'prove' with the same certainty with which geometrical theorems can be proved, such as Pythagoras' theory. He triumphantly concludes each 'proof' with the letters Q.E.D., which stand for the Latin term *Quod Erat Demonstrandum* which means, 'that which has been proved'. This of course was a rather ridiculous claim, and indeed a rather ridiculous way to set about the writing of philosophy. However, this was only the first of many later attempts by philosophers to put their study onto a 'scientific' footing, attempts that were all destined for inevitable failure, and for good reason, as we shall see later in this chapter. But proven or not, the propositions which Spinoza puts forward in his *Ethics* are to say the least interesting, and there are a great many of them – 207 in all, contained in just five chapters or Parts. As with the *Tractatus Theologico-Politicus* the titles of these sections are themselves of interest, and are cited below.

Part I: Concerning God
Part II: On the Nature and Origin of the Mind
Part III: On the Origin and Nature of the Emotions
Part IV: Of Human Bondage, or the Strength of the Emotions
Part V: Of the Power of the Understanding, or of Human Freedom

The title of Part IV, 'Of Human Bondage', was taken up by W. Somerset Maugham in 1915 as the title for one of his novels.

Although Spinoza is one of my philosopher heroes, I would be the first to admit that he is an extremely irritating and frustrating sort of fellow. His works contain a plethora of really good ideas which were far ahead of their time, but they are very badly expressed, in stilted Latin which was obviously not Spinoza's native tongue. Moreover, not only does he express his ideas very badly but he then goes on to over-elaborate them and complicate them to such an extent that the brilliance of his original vision is obscured. As I noted above in Chapter 2, this is a very common failing of many philosophers. Nowhere is this better illustrated than in his *Ethics*. For example, while I would entirely agree with his panentheistic conception of God, he cannot simply say that God is 'The Great Nature of All Things', which incorporates both 'The Way Things Are' and 'The Way Things Work': oh dear me no! Instead he has to muddy the waters with unhelpful concepts such as 'substance', 'attributes', 'modes', and 'essences' which are entirely irrelevant to the case and do absolutely nothing to help us to understand what he is saying, but simply distract us from his central idea. Nevertheless, it emerges clearly enough that Spinoza's conception of God was entirely revolutionary for its time, and completely unacceptable to all versions of the Christian and Jewish faiths of his day.

Like a good panentheist, Spinoza envisioned an impersonal, abstract, and amoral God, who knew nothing of justice or mercy, and was totally unconcerned with the doings of mankind. In Proposition 19 of Chapter V of the *Ethics*, Spinoza famously states, 'He who loves God cannot endeavour to bring it about that God should love him in return.' (*Qui Deum amat, conari non potest ut Deus ipsum contra amet.*) And yet, says Spinoza, we should love God, but in a particular way that Spinoza calls the *amor intellectualis Dei*, the intellectual love of God. We should love Him not for what we want to receive from Him, but rather for what we have already received from Him, as the creator and sustainer of mankind.

As noted earlier, it is extremely difficult to be a panentheist without also being a determinist, once the full implications of panentheism are completely grasped. Spinoza did grasp this point, arguing that free will was an illusion. In Proposition 48 of Chapter II of the *Ethics*, Spinoza declares,

> In the mind there is no absolute or free will, but rather the mind is determined to wish this or that by a cause, which has also been determined by another cause, and this last by another cause, and so on to infinity.

This principle of causation, of an endless chain of cause and effect can also be applied to all the events that occur in the universe, until we get right back to a prime cause which, in this universe at least, is believed to be the Big Bang. This event created not only all of matter and all of energy but also of all of space and all of time, these latter two being in fact one, the 'space-time continuum'. In this way, all of time, past, present, and future, was created at a single moment, together with all of space. These are difficult concepts to grasp, but will be explained more fully in the Einstein section below.

In treating of mankind, Spinoza at first seems to be a rather harsh critic, declaring that men are credulous, led by their passions rather than their reason, and are in particular prone to foolish and superstitious beliefs. Spinoza begins his *Tractatus Theologico-Politicus* with an Introduction headed, 'The Scope and Purpose of this Work'. In his opening paragraph he begins with a sweeping condemnation of mankind.

> Did men always act with understanding and discretion, or were fortune always propitious, they would never be the slaves of superstition. But as they frequently fall into straits and difficulties, and find no counsel in themselves, as they mostly strive without measure for the questionable favours of fortune, and in their vain aspirations after these are often tossed miserably between hope and fear, so is their spirit commonly disposed to credulity. The mind besieged by doubt indeed is easily swayed by every impulse, more especially when wavering between hope and fear, as in other moods it is but too apt to be self-sufficient and presumptuous. No one, I imagine, can be ignorant of these things, though I believe that few know themselves: for whoever has lived in the world must assuredly have seen that in prosperity the mass of mankind, however ill informed, seem to themselves so full of wisdom that they deem it an insult should anyone presume to offer them advice; while in adversity they seem not to know where to turn, but seek counsel and countenance from everyone, and nothing can be suggested so vain, so unreasonable, so absurd, but they are inclined to follow it. (1862 ed., p. 19)

Later, on p. 290 of the 1862 edition, he launches into another swingeing attack upon the proclivities of humanity. It would appear from all this that Spinoza harboured a rather low opinion of mankind in general, but his is not the misanthropy of a Molière, a Swift, or a Flaubert. It later becomes clear that Spinoza believes the species to be redeemable. In Section 4 of Chapter I of his Political Treatise Spinoza famously declares that he has always striven, '*humanas actiones non ridere, non lugere, neque detestare, sed intelligere*' – 'not to laugh at the deeds of men, nor to weep over them, nor to hate them, but to understand them'. It is indeed this 'understanding', which Spinoza closely associates with the application of reason, that can elevate and transform mankind. As long as man is governed by his mindless passions, he is their slave, in a 'passive' state, in 'human bondage'. But if he can apply his reason to understand *why* he feels the emotions that he does, then he gains control over those emotions, and transforms himself from being their slave to being their master, moving from a 'passive' to an 'active' state, and so he achieves true freedom. It is in this sense that Spinoza has been seen by some as anticipating Freudian analysis by providing a metaphysical basis for Freud's dictum that, 'where there was id, there shall be ego' as the dark and primitive forces of the soul are banished by enlightenment. In Chapter 5 of his *Ethics*, which is entitled, 'Of the Power of the Understanding, or of Human Freedom', Spinoza declares in PropositionIII that, 'An emotion, which is a passion, ceases to be a passion as soon as we form a clear and distinct idea of it', adding as a corollary, 'The more an emotion becomes known to us, the more it falls within our power, and the less the mind is passive to it'. Here was an early form of cognitive behavioural therapy perhaps, some 300 years before its time!

This theme of self-empowerment through the application of reason and the achieving of understanding recurs again and again in Chapter 5 – one might almost say that man becomes superman, *der Übermensch* in a Nietzscheian sense. There are shades of Nietzsche too in Spinoza's use of the Latin term *conatus*. This may be variously translated as 'exertion', 'effort', 'impulse', or 'striving', but in the contexts in which Spinoza uses it, the term may also be translated as 'life force', or even 'will to power', *der Wille zur Macht*, a prominent concept in the philosophy of Nietzsche. Spinoza discusses the *conatus* in Propositions VI to IX of Chapter 3 in his Ethics.

A parallel with Nietzsche may also be seen in Spinoza's conceptions of good and evil, to which he denies an objective existence. Instead, says Spinoza, there are merely events, which we interpret as being good or evil in accordance with their effects upon us: in other words, 'good' and 'evil' are purely subjective concepts. However, Spinoza is speaking here only about *fortuito occursi*, that is events which happen to us. He remains strangely silent about deeds which we ourselves perpetrate.Spinoza discusses good and evil in the Preface to Chapter 4 of his Ethics, and defines the terms there in his Propositions I and II. Nietzsche, of course, was later to discuss these concepts in more depth in his own book, *Beyond Good and Evil* (1886). Indeed, to see Spinoza as a precursor of Nietzsche can hardly be regarded as fanciful, since he was recognised as such by Nietzsche himself! In later life Nietzsche had some harsh things to say about Spinoza, but on a postcard to his friend Franz Overbeck dated July 30, 1881, Nietzsche wrote,

> I am utterly amazed, utterly enchanted! I have a precursor, and what a precursor! I hardly knew Spinoza: that I should have turned to him just now was inspired by 'instinct'. Not only is his major inclination like mine – namely to use all knowledge to the most powerful effect – but in five main points of his doctrine I recognise myself. This most unusual and loneliest thinker is closest to me precisely in these matters: he denies the freedom of the will, teleology, the moral world order, the unegoistic, and evil. Even although the divergences are admittedly tremendous, they are due more to the differences in time, culture, and science. *In summa* my loneliness which, as on very high mountains, often made it hard for me to breathe and make my blood course, is now at least a twosomeness. Strange! (Cited in W. Kaufmann, *The Portable Nietzsche* (1954) p. 92

Indeed, so fecund is the thought of Spinoza that he may even be seen as a precursor of Isaac Newton (1642-1727)! As a Corollary to Proposition XIII in Chapter 2 of his *Ethics*, Spinoza writes,

> Hence it follows that a body in motion remains in motion until it is brought to a state of rest by some outside influence, and a body at rest remains at rest until acted upon by some outside force.

This observation is so astonishingly similar to Newton's First Law of Motion as defined in his *Principia* of 1687 that one might almost suspect that Newton had stolen the idea from Spinoza! Later, as Axiom II of the same Proposition, Spinoza observes,

> When a body in motion impinges on another body at rest which it is unable to move, it recoils in order to continue its motion, and the angle made between the line of motion in the recoil and the plane of the body at rest, whereupon the moving body has impinged, will be equal to the angle formed by the line of motion of incidence and the same plane.

There are echoes here of Newton's *Opticks* of 1704, where he observes, much more succinctly, that the angle of incidence of light equals the angle of reflection.

The French philosopher Giles Deleuze (1925-1995) described Spinoza as 'the prince of philosophers', but for me he is rather 'the philosopher's philosopher', not only because he can be identified as the precursor of so many later thinkers, not only because he showed how far pure rationalism might take a philosopher, but also because he over-elaborates on basically simple and very sound ideas, obscuring them behind a web of superfluous verbiage. This, I have found, is what so many other philosophers also love to do, apparently seeing some merit in deliberate over-elaboration, believing that this will make them sound more profound. Hence they recognise in Spinoza a kindred spirit. His *Ethics*, for example, is scarcely about what we would recognise as ethical concepts at all – indeed, he denies the objective reality of good and evil altogether, and makes no effort to define 'morality'. Rather he writes here about metaphysics, epistemology, and psychology. Indeed, his *Ethics* is more of an ethnology, a study of mankind.

Spinoza had great difficulty with the term 'morality' because he saw God as being fundamentally amoral, and he therefore tended to dismiss the term 'morality' altogether, avoiding any serious discussion of the concept. Indeed, in God's world, the real world before mankind appeared on the scene, there was no morality, no objective 'good' or 'evil'. If a lion caught a gazelle, then this was a good thing from the lion's point of view, but a bad thing from the gazelle's point of view, both views entirely subjective. Therefore, a clear definition of the term 'morality' is not to be found in any of Spinoza's works, certainly not in *The Ethics*. God's world is indeed amoral, but Spinoza seems to overlook the fact that we humans have superimposed our own world of artificial concepts and values upon God's reality. For us, terms such as justice, mercy, kindness, and morality have a very real meaning, and a very real value. It is a pity that Spinoza did not show more appreciation of this fact, and try give us his own understanding of these terms. He concentrates on explaining for us the natures of God and of man, but has little to say about man's created world of concepts. The man who pressed Spinoza hardest in this area was one of his correspondents, William van Blyenbergh (1632-96), a grain dealer from Dordrecht and a staunch Calvinist. He argued that surely there *was* an objective difference between good and evil, between moral and immoral behaviour. The two men exchanged four letters each between December 1664 and June 1665, but they were eternally at cross purposes, since Spinoza wrote as a philosopher, and Blyenbergh as a theologian. In addition, they had entirely different conceptions of God. However, Blyenbergh did succeed in at last cornering Spinoza in letter XXIII of the Wolf edition of *The Correspondence of Spinoza* (1928), dated March 13, 1665. On p. 192 Spinoza finally concedes that,

> If you then ask whether the thief and the righteous are equally perfect and blessed, I answer No....And if the question is this, whether men who slay and men who give alms are not equally good or perfect, I again say no.

However, these concessions hardly amounted to a succinct definition of morality. Like the rest of us, Spinoza was not without his faults. If it took 200 years for his philosophy to be fully appreciated, then in my opinion Spinoza had no one to blame for that but himself. He should have expressed his thoughts much more cogently than he did. Nevertheless, I find both his theological and political positions to be entirely sound, although I harbour some doubts about the value of his metaphysics and epistemology. I do so on the grounds of my belief that any worthwhile philosophy must be *useful*, in the sense that it is capable of making a genuine contribution to the happiness of humankind, and I rather doubt that Spinoza's speculations in these latter fields do so. With his epistemology in particular, he allows his arrogance to run away with him. For those who would like to follow his thoughts in these areas, however, I would recommend 'Spinoza's Modal Metaphysics' by Samuel Newlands in *The Stanford Encyclopaedia of Philosophy* (Winter 2013 edition), and 'Benedict de Spinoza: Epistemology' by Nels Dockstader in *The Internet Encyclopaedia of Philosophy* (September, 2009). Both works are available online under 'Spinoza'.

Despite my misgivings in those areas, however, overall I hold Spinoza in the highest esteem. What astonishing prescience, what tremendous intellectual courage, what dazzling originality of thought. Here was contempt for authority writ large. It was easy enough for me, as a man of the free-thinking, tolerant twentieth century with all its scientific knowledge available to us, to reach conclusions that moved me towards panentheism and determinism. But for a man of the uninformed and highly intolerant seventeenth century to have reached similar conclusions some 350 years earlier was little short of astonishing. Like Nietzsche, I find in Spinoza a kindred spirit, and like Nietzsche I reach out a grateful hand to him.

Thomas Paine (1737-1809)

The second of my philosopher heroes also showed great intellectual courage, and great originality of thought. Thomas Paine was a Norfolk man, born in the village of Thetford in the south-west of the county. His father Joseph was a Quaker and a craftsman, a maker of stay ropes for sailing ships. Thomas received a good basic education at Thetford Grammar School, a medieval foundation which the village was fortunate to possess. It is still operational as an independent school to this day, and the building in which Paine studied may still be seen in the village. He left school at 13, however, and became an apprentice to his father, who had forbidden him to learn Latin at the Grammar School on the grounds that it was used by the Catholic Church, and was therefore 'popish'! In his late teens he briefly served a turn as a deckhand on a privateer, but soon decided that a life at sea was not for him!

Paine's enemies, of whom there were many, claimed that he had been a maker of whalebone stays for ladies' corsets, but this was untrue. In fact the stay ropes manufactured by his father were the thick hawsers designed to give fore and aft support to the masts of sailing ships. They were distinguished from the thinner shrouds, which gave lateral support to the masts and were usually webbing rigged. They were made of hemp, and weatherproofed with pine tar, both commodities mainly imported from the Baltic states at this time. Eighteenth-century Norfolk was a maritime county with a long coastline. It was also the birth county of Horatio Nelson (1758-1805), a close contemporary of

Paine. In those pre-industrial times Norfolk was one of England's most populous counties, and Norwich was the country's second city after London. Thetford was a good way from the sea, but in those days of poor roads and no railways, water transport was key, by rivers, canals, or the coasting trade. Joseph could send his wares via the Little Ouse and Great Ouse rivers downstream to what was then the major port of King's Lynne on the Wash. However, the temptation to slur Paine as a corset maker was too strong for his enemies to resist. In 1793 the cartoonist James Gillray satirised Paine by depicting the figure of Britannia desperately clinging to a tree while Paine, with one foot on her rump, pulled tight the draw strings on a very uncomfortable looking corset! The caption below read, 'Fashion Before Ease, or a Good Constitution Sacrificed for a Fantastical Form'. In reality, Paine completed his apprenticeship and became a master stay-maker, setting up his own business at Sandwich in Kent in 1759. This business soon failed, however, and after a rather chequered career as a schoolmaster, tobacco shop keeper, and excise officer, by 1774 Paine found himself bankrupt and newly separated from his second wife, née Elizabeth Ollive.

At this low point in his fortunes, however, Paine had a stroke of luck. Through his excise work Paine had become acquainted with George Lewis Scott (1708-80), a diplomat, man of letters, and Commissioner of Excise. In September 1774 Scott introduced him to Benjamin Franklin (1706-90), who was nearing the end of his current stay in England before returning to America. Franklin was favourably impressed by Paine, and suggested to him that he should emigrate to America, supplying him with a letter of recommendation. Accordingly, Paine set sail for Philadelphia in October, arriving there on November 30, 1774. He was lucky to have survived the voyage. The ship's water supply was contaminated, and five of the passengers had died of typhoid during the crossing. Paine himself was so ill on his arrival at Philadelphia that he had to be carried off the ship, and also came close to death. However, he was met at Philadelphia by Franklin's personal physician, who nursed him back to health over a period of six weeks. Soon after his recovery Paine registered himself as a citizen of Pennsylvania, and in January 1775 took a job as co-editor of *The Pennsylvania Magazine*, a post he held with some success. Paine had a natural talent as a writer, with one influential pamphlet already to his credit, *The Case of the Officers of Excise*, which had been published in 1772 as a plea for better pay and working conditions for the officers. One of the articles that he wrote for *The Pennsylvania Magazine* soon after becoming an editor was entitled, 'African Slavery in America', a scathing attack on the whole institution. Slavery was ubiquitous in all 13 American colonies at that time, but Pennsylvania was the first to turn against the practice, introducing its first piece of anti-slavery legislation in 1780. This was just as well for Paine: in the southern states, his article might well have got him lynched!

At this point, fate took a hand in elevating Paine to his place in history. No sooner had he settled into his new life and work in Philadelphia than the American Revolutionary War broke out with the first armed clashes at Lexington and Concord on April 19, 1775. Once the fighting had begun Paine immediately felt himself in sympathy with the rebels, and wrote in support of American independence in *The Pennsylvania Magazine*. However, this did not make him universally popular. The consensus of historical opinion is that there was no majority in favour of independence when the war broke out. Estimates are obviously difficult, but perhaps at best only about one third of the population of the colonies at that time was firmly in favour of independence, with another third of the people just as firmly against the idea. The final third were undecided, and not firmly committed either way. Some sources, however, have estimated that the truly 'patriot' party represented as few as only 20% of the American population in 1775. Moreover, the war did not go well for the rebels in its first year, and it seemed that America's bid for independence would fail. The Canadian territories stayed loyal to the Crown, and the rebels were faced with fighting not only the formidable British army and navy, but also the Indian tribes that the British had encouraged to revolt, in addition to American loyalists, dubbed 'Tories', who took up arms to oppose the cause of independence. At that point, however, Paine weighed into the conflict with one of the most influential pamphlets ever written, one that was instrumental in turning the tide of history and ensuring that American independence would, after all, be won at that point in time.

His pamphlet was, of course, the famous *Common Sense*, which he first published anonymously in January, 1776. In this pamphlet Paine argued strongly for independence, pilloried George III, and ridiculed the idea of monarchy, decrying the corrupt and unfair nature of the British Government. The opening lines of this pamphlet struck a chord with me. Paine wrote,

Some writers have so confounded society with government as to leave little or no distinction between them; whereas they are not only different, but have different origins. Society is produced by our wants, and government by our wickedness; the former promotes our happiness *positively* by uniting our affections, the latter *negatively* by restraining our vices. The one encourages intercourse, the other creates distinctions. The first is a patron, the last a punisher.

We see here the germ of an old-established American idea, namely, 'That government governs best which governs least'. Now in the eighteenth century this would have been true, especially of the government of Britain at that time, which was a clear enough kleptocracy, supporting a system that robbed the common people through the imposition of rents, tithes, tariffs, consumption taxes, excise duties, and a host of other levies. The monies so raised went mostly into the pockets of a very small ruling class. This class misused their power to maintain enormous disparities of wealth in the land, doing little or nothing to improve the lot of the common people. Less of *that* kind of government would indeed have been a good idea. But now, the case is altered. Today we face a new class of robber barons in the form of the bankers, the plutocrats, and the giant corporations, the new kleptocrats, who exercise far too much self-interested power. Today our only hope is for *more* government, firm, fair, and truly democratic government that will enforce the necessary regulations, and introduce a sensible taxation policy. Unfortunately, as we see only too clearly, our present governments have conspicuously failed in their obvious duty.

A similar situation applied in eighteenth-century Britain, but Paine held out to Americans a vision of what they might become as an independent state. His vision was not just of a new country, but of a whole new world, a world of republican virtue, complete religious freedom for all, and genuine democracy, the kind of state which, at that time, existed nowhere else in the world. In the Appendix to his second edition Paine wrote,

> Should an independency be brought about...we have every opportunity and every encouragement now before us to form the noblest, purest constitution on the face of the earth. We have it in our power to begin the world over again. A situation similar to the present hath not happened since the days of Noah until now. The birthday of a new world is at hand, and a race of men perhaps as numerous as all Europe contains, may receive their portion of freedom from the events of a few months...

He concluded the third section of his work with this stirring appeal:

> O ye that love mankind! Ye that dare oppose not only tyranny, but the tyrant, stand forth! Every spot of the old world is overrun with oppression. Freedom hath been hunted round the globe. Asia and Africa have long expelled her – Europe regards her like a stranger, and England hath given her warning to depart. O receive the fugitive, and prepare in time an asylum for mankind.

Common Sense was nothing if not tendentious. It was rather unfair to describe George III as a 'tyrant' in the sense that his contemporaries Louis XVI of France (1754-93) or Catherine the Great of Russia (1729-96) had been tyrants in their absolutist states. Moreover, Britain had made genuine efforts to redress the grievances of the colonists, repealing the unpopular Stamp Act of 1765 in the following year, and rescinding nearly all of the Townsend duties on American trade that had been imposed in 1770. In 1774 the British Prime Minister, Lord North (1732-92) offered to impose no taxation of any kind upon the colonies if they would agree to make a fixed contribution towards the cost of their defence by the British army and navy. But this offer was rejected: the patriots, who had by that time seized control of the colonial governments, were not to be appeased.

However, it is also true that in the 1770s George III (1738-1820), with the support of his Prime Minister Lord North, had been making efforts to revive those powers of the Crown that had lain dormant ever since the Hanoverian succession of 1714. His efforts greatly displeased the 'auxiliaries', the political nation that had been used to having everything their own way since the Glorious Revolution of 1688-9. On April 6, 1780, John Dunning (1731-1783) was prompted to stand up in the House of Commons and make his famous declaration that, 'The influence of the Crown has increased, is increasing, and ought to be diminished'. George's efforts in this direction had been just enough to allow him to be satirised as a 'tyrant', but the Crown was soon beaten back to its 'proper' place in the unwritten British Constitution.

This was the background to the quarrel, but Paine of course, had no intention of providing an impartial view of events. He had set out only to write a rousing piece of propaganda, and as this his pamphlet was a runaway success. The initial printing ran to 100,000 copies but subsequently, with pirated editions, some half a million copies were produced in the first year alone. The population of the 13 colonies at that time was roughly two and a half million, most of whom were literate, for the puritanical Americans had always taken education seriously, so that all could read the Bible. For those who were not literate, copies of Paine's pamphlet were read out in taverns and at public meetings, so that very few Americans were left who had not read or heard his words. The original pamphlet ran to only 48 pages, but Paine brought out second and third editions, each one longer than the last, with the longest edition running to 77 pages. In proportion to the size of the population at that time, Paine's pamphlet ranks as the best-selling publication in American history. This fact is all the more remarkable when we remember that Paine was a man who had received only an elementary education to the age of 13, before going out to work as an apprentice. In 1776 he was 39 years of age, and his reading (he claimed) had not extended far beyond the Bible, although he did also know a little history, and had very decided views of his own on politics. Fortuitously, however, Paine turned these very weaknesses into strengths. There were no classical allusions in this work, nor references to Locke, Montesquieu, or Rousseau: Paine wrote in plain language for the plain man, intending to involve in politics those who had never thought it their place to be involved before, for the colonies at that time were still far from universal manhood suffrage. The whole tone of his work was, as its title suggested, one of *Common Sense*, and his aim was to rouse the entire American populous.

In that aim, the pamphlet was a resounding success. The undecided were swung over to side with the rebels, and by the end of 1777 a clear majority had come to favour independence, while the 'Tories' were in full retreat. But Paine did not rest satisfied with *Common Sense*. He followed up this first pamphlet with a whole series, under the generic heading of *The American Crisis.* There were 18 of these pamphlets in all with 13 published in 1776 and 1777, and the remainder between 1777 and 1783. The first pamphlet began with the ringing words,

> These are the times that try men's souls. The summer soldier and the sunshine patriot will, in this crisis, shrink from the service of his country; but he that stands by it now deserves the love and thanks of man and woman. Tyranny, like hell, is not easily conquered, yet we have this consolation with us; that the harder the conflict, the more glorious the triumph. What we obtain too cheap, we esteem too lightly: it is dearness only that gives everything its value. Heaven knows how to put a proper price upon its goods, and it would be strange indeed if so celestial an article as freedom should not be highly rated.

This pamphlet was read to his troops by General George Washington (1732-99) immediately before his dramatic crossing of the Delaware River in the dead of winter near the end of 1776. Morale in the American army had been low following a series of defeats by the British, but Paine's words rallied and inspired Washington's men. After a nine-mile march they surprised a force of 3,000 of George III's Hessian soldiers at Trenton in New Jersey on December 26th, and won a resounding victory, capturing nearly all of the German troops. The victory had been small but pivotal because of its effect on army moral, and recruitment for the rebel army took a sharp upturn from that point onwards.

But Paine did not limit his support for independence to writing alone. He also joined the Continental Army, serving as an aide to the very successful general Nathanael Greene (1742-86) in the early years of the war. In 1777 he became Secretary of the Congressional Committee on Foreign Affairs, and in March 1781 he accompanied Colonel John Laurens (1754-1782) on a crucial mission to France. There they joined Benjamin Franklin (1706-90) who was then serving as an American chargé d'affaires to France in pleading for French support in their war of independence. The mission was highly successful. Still smarting from their defeat by the British in the Seven Years War of 1756-63, the French welcomed the chance to weaken and humiliate their old enemy by depriving her of her most prized colonial possession. They agreed to supply the Americans with a gift of six million livres in silver, and a loan of ten million more for their war chest. Even more significantly, France agreed to lend the colonists the full support of their West Indies fleet, and provided a battalion of 7,800 French Troops to support the Continental Army. As a result, Washington was able to muster a Franco-American force of 19,000 men to confront General Cornwallis, who was holding the port of Yorktown in East Virginia at the mouth of Chesapeake Bay with some 9,000 troops in October, 1781. Cornwallis had counted on the British Navy to evacuate him if American pressure on his position became too great, but a French fleet of 31 warships under de Grasse and Barras gained temporary control of Chesapeake Bay, cutting off his retreat. Cornwallis found himself surrounded by land and sea, outnumbered, cut off from supplies and reinforcements, and unable to retreat. After a few days of fighting, the heavily outnumbered Cornwallis was forced to surrender his entire army. When the British Prime Minister Lord North heard the news of the Yorktown defeat, he is reported to have exclaimed, 'My God, it is all over!' So indeed it proved. Their Yorktown victory effectively ended the Revolutionary War in America's favour, although sporadic fighting continued until the Treaty of Paris formally concluded the war in September, 1783. In the meanwhile, Paine had also helped to organise the Bank of North America to raise money for the patriot army. During the war Paine had refused all remuneration for his services, even waiving the royalties he might have received for *Common Sense*, to ensure its widest possible circulation. However, after the war, in 1784, Congress presented Paine with $3,000 in recognition of his services, and he was also given a small estate at New Rochelle in New York state, plus a modest pension.

There can be no doubt about Paine's right to be counted among the Founding Fathers of the American republic, for despite his humble origins he cut a not incongruous figure among their numbers. Only James Madison and Thomas Jefferson among the Founders could be counted as American aristocracy, being substantial landowners and slave owners, with others such as Benjamin Franklin, Alexander Hamilton, and John Adams coming from comparatively humble backgrounds. Even George Washington and James Monroe came from families that were at best only middle class. However, this did not prevent Washington, Adams, and Monroe from later serving as Presidents of the United States of America. In view of his key role in swinging American opinion in 1776, and the part he played in winning that French support which was so crucial to the Yorktown victory of 1781, it might even be claimed that Paine made a greater contribution to the success of the American Revolution than any other individual.

John Adams (1735-1826), a Founding Father of the new republic who served as Washington's Vice-president from 1789 to 1797, and as President himself from 1797 to 1801, is often quoted as saying, 'Without the pen of the author of *Common Sense*, the sword of Washington would have been raised in vain'. This quotation may well have been misattributed, for Adams hated Paine, but certainly he once complained indignantly in a letter to Thomas Jefferson (1743-1826) that, 'History is to ascribe the American Revolution to Thomas Paine!' (Quoted in C. Nelson, *Thomas Paine: His Life, His Time, and the Birth of Modern Nations* (2007) p. 93) Certainly Adams was hardly an admirer of Paine, disparaging him for his deistic religious views, his advocacy of universal manhood suffrage, and his lack of formal education. However, in 1805 after Paine had played a major role in the French as well as the American Revolution, and had shaken Britain with his *Rights of Man*, *Agrarian Justice*, and *Age of Reason*, Adams was forced to admit, 'I know not whether any man in the world has had more influence on its inhabitants or affairs for the last thirty years than Tom Paine', adding with deliberate irony, 'Call it then, the age of Paine!' (Quoted in D.F. Hawke, *Paine* (1974) p. 7)

There was some truth in Adams' words: *Common Sense* was not the end of Paine's role in history, but only the beginning. Shortly after the colonies had finally won their independence under the 1783 Treaty of Paris, Paine was to find a new cause to champion with the outbreak of the French Revolution in 1789. In 1787 Paine had returned to England, hoping to raise money for the construction of new type of bridge which he had designed. This proved to be a difficult task, but Paine was greatly cheered in 1789 to see the outbreak of revolution across the channel in France, believing it to be the first sign of the importation of American ideals into Europe. Paine made all haste to join the revolutionaries in France, and to support their cause, writing eagerly to George Washington on October 16, 1789, 'A share in two revolutions is living to some purpose!' He was greatly chagrined, therefore, to read the pamphlet *Reflections on the Revolution in France*, written by the Anglo-Irish politician Edmund Burke (1729-1797), published in November, 1790. Burke had himself been prompted to write this famous treatise in response to a sermon that had been printed by the Rev. Richard Price (1723-91), entitled, *A Discourse on the Love of Our Country*, published just one year earlier in November, 1789. In this work Price had warmly welcomed the French Revolution, likening it to England's Glorious Revolution of a hundred years earlier, and expecting from it similar benefits for France. Price indeed may be credited with igniting the famous 'French Revolution Controversy' which raged on for years in Britain, producing a blizzard of tracts, and sharply divided opinions. It is indeed a tribute to the extent of freedom of the press in England at this time that the airing of so many radical views was allowed.

Price is usually described as being a nonconformist clergyman, which sounds innocuous enough, but he was in fact very nonconforming indeed, belonging to that sect known as the Unitarians. This group denied the divinity of Christ, and so could scarcely be described as Christians at all! Nevertheless, they were accorded freedom of worship under the Toleration Act of 1689, and freedom of expression for their views, although they were still denied many civil liberties that were available only to Anglicans, including the right to study at a university or hold a political office. Price had been born at Tynton in Glamorganshire to a Welsh minister who was himself a Unitarian. As was so often the case in Britain, dating from the time of the Civil Wars, religious radicals were frequently found to be political radicals as well, and this was also true in Price's case. He had been a keen supporter of American independence, writing in 1776 the pamphlet, *Observations on the Nature of Civil Liberty, the Principles of Government, and the Justice and Policy of the War with America.* This tract was enormously popular in England, selling more than 150,000 copies in a year. Some of these found their way to America, although they had nothing like the same circulation there as Paine's *Common Sense*. He wrote a second pamphlet in support of the colonists in 1777, earning for himself the gratitude of America's Founding Fathers. In 1781 Yale College awarded Price the honorary degree of Doctor of Laws. The only other recipient of such an honour in that year had been George Washington. Dr. Price then confirmed his place in the affections of Americans with a final tract, *Observations on the Importance of the American Revolution, and the Means of Rendering it a Benefit to the World* in 1784.

Unlike Thomas Paine, Price was a more normal example of the intellectual of the times, having received an excellent education at various dissenting academies up to the age of 21 since, as a dissenter, he had been denied entry to England's Anglican universities. He earned his living as a preacher, holding the post of minister at Newington Green Meeting House in London for many years. He was also a prodigious writer on many topics, including theology, finance, morality, metaphysics, politics, and demography. In 1767 he was awarded the honorary degree of D.D. by the University of Aberdeen, and in 1769 a second D.D. from the University of Glasgow. No Anglican university would ever have honoured Price in this way, but Presbyterianism was the established religion in Scotland. However, he was also granted the Freedom of the City of London, and elected a Fellow of the Royal Society in 1765. Price moved in intellectual circles, like the informal dining club called by Benjamin Franklin 'The Club of Honest Whigs'. He was also a member of the 'Bowood Circle', a group of liberal intellectuals who met at Bowood House, Lord Shelburne's seat in Wiltshire. Price's own home at Newington Green was also a meeting place for all the liberal intellectuals of the day. Among those entertained there were John Howard the prison reformer, Mary Woolstonecraft, Adam Smith, Joseph Priestly, James Burgh, David Hume, and the Americans Thomas Jefferson, John Adams, Benjamin Franklin, and Thomas Paine, who was by then an American citizen. Leading politicians such as Earl Stanhope, Pitt the Younger, Lord Lyttleton, and Charles James Fox were also occasional visitors. Price was also a member of the radical Society for Constitutional Information, and the London Revolution Society. This latter was less alarming than its name suggested, since it existed only to commemorate the Glorious Revolution of 1688-9, and the benefits that had followed from it. Like Paine, Price typified the daring and radical political thought that was abroad in England at that time, mainly amongst the dissenting community.

One prominent figure who came to strongly disapprove of Richard Price and all his circle was, however, Edmund Burke (1729-97). He too deserves an extended mention at this point, because Burke is seen by history as the leading political opponent of Tom Paine and all his works, the classic exponent of the conservative point of view. The polemical battle between these two leading figures dominated the final years of the eighteenth century. Burke had been born in Dublin of old Irish stock. His father had been born and raised as a Catholic, but seems to have converted to Anglicanism in 1722 to further his career as a solicitor. Burke's mother remained a Catholic all her life, as did his sister Juliana. Burke himself, however, followed his father into the Anglican faith. In 1744 he entered Trinity College Dublin where he studied Classics, graduating in 1748 from an institution which, at that time, did not award degrees to Catholics or Dissenters. His father intended him for the law, and in 1750 could afford to send him to the Middle Temple in London to begin legal studies. Burke, however, soon tired of the law, and decided instead to pursue a career as a writer and a politician. As a writer Burke enjoyed some success, among other things founding the *Annual Register* in 1758, a journal in which various contributors commented on the political events of the previous year.

Burke's great ambition, however, was to play a part in political life himself. For a man in his position, this meant acquiring a patron. In 1760 he was introduced to William Gerard Hamilton (1729-96), who had been an English MP since 1755. In 1761 Hamilton was also elected to the Irish Parliament as MP for Killybegs, and then became chief secretary to Lord Halifax, the Lord Lieutenant of Ireland. From 1763-8 he served as Ireland's Chancellor of the Exchequer. In 1761 Burke went with Hamilton to Ireland as his private secretary, holding the post for four years. His great opportunity came in 1765, however, when he secured the post of private secretary to the liberal Whig statesman Charles, Marquis of Rockingham (1730-1782) who was then serving as Prime Minister. Thanks to Rockingham's influence, Burke was able at last to enter Parliament in 1765, sitting for the pocket borough of Wendover in Buckinghamshire, which was controlled by Lord Fermanagh, a close political ally of Rockingham. In 1769, using borrowed money supplied mostly by Rockingham, Burke bought a small, 600 acre estate for himself, Gregories, near Beaconsfield in Buckinghamshire. Burke was then able to pose as a country gentleman and member of the ruling class, although he was never able to repay the money he had borrowed for his estate.

Burke began his political career as a liberal Whig in the Rockingham tradition, urging conciliation with the American colonies, opposing the political pretentions of George III, and arguing for free trade and Catholic emancipation, so that Catholics could enjoy full civil rights. In 1774 Burke was elected MP for Bristol, a large constituency and not a pocket borough, which he won in a fair fight. However, he lost his Bristol seat at the elections of 1780, and for the rest of his parliamentary career to 1794 sat for the borough of Malton in Yorkshire, another pocket borough under the control of the Rockinghams. The reason for Burke's loss of his Bristol seat is interesting. In 1774 in his published *Speech to the Electors of Bristol at the Conclusion of the Poll* Burke put his cards on the table. After admitting that an MP should, in all cases, prefer the interests of his constituents above his own, Burke then went on to say,

> But his unbiased opinion, his mature judgement, his enlightened conscience, he ought not to sacrifice to you, to any man, or to any set of men living. These he does not derive from your pleasure; no, nor from the law and the constitution. They are a trust from Providence, for the abuse of which he is deeply answerable. Your

representative owes you not his industry only, but his judgement; and he betrays, instead of serving you, if he sacrifices it to your opinion.

There are several points of interest to note about these lines. First, it should be noted that Burke made this statement only *after* the poll had been held, and he was safely elected. It might have been more honest of him to have put his cards on the table *before* the vote was held. Secondly, these lines perfectly sum up Burke's attitude to democracy: the hoi polloi were not to be trusted: they needed to be led by their 'betters'. Unlike Paine, Burke was not a true democrat at all, or even a believer in representative democracy. The above lines make it clear that he thought he should answer to God rather than his constituents, who had apparently elected him just so that he could do exactly as he pleased, according to the lights of his 'conscience'. In 1778 Burke spoke in Parliament in support of free trade with his beloved Ireland, and in favour of Catholic Emancipation. The electors of Bristol, a port which enjoyed privileges under the existing arrangements, begged him to change his mind, but Burke refused, saying,

> If, from this conduct, I shall forfeit their suffrages at an ensuing election, it will stand on record as an example to future representatives of the Commons of England, that one man at least had dared to resist the desires of his constituents when his judgement assured him they were wrong. (J. Prior, *Life of Burke* (1854) 5th ed. p. 175)

In one light this might be seen as Burke taking a 'principled stand', knowing it would probably cost him his Bristol seat at the next election. On the other hand, Burke must also have known that should this happen, the Rockingham clan would soon provide him with another pocket or rotten borough to sit for, so that he would be no worse off. This is indeed what happened, and Burke sat for the pocket borough of Malton for the rest of his parliamentary career. In another light, this was a shameful dereliction of duty on Burke's part, and a selfish indulgence of his own pro-Irish sentiments. The notion that governments derive their just powers from the consent of the governed does not appear to have been in his lexicon.

The acid test of Burke's views, however, came with the outbreak of the French Revolution in 1789. Paine, who was at that time in England, welcomed the Revolution, as the first sign of the spread of American principles to the European continent. Burke, however, instinctively recoiled from the violence and radicalism of the changes in France, and was prompted to take up his pen by the pro-Revolution writings of English radicals, notably Richard Price. Burke's greatest fear was that French Revolutionary principles might take root in England. The first fruits of these thoughts was his famous *Reflections on the Revolution in France*, published in November 1790. Pompous, arrogant, overweeningly ambitious, and a chancer, there was little to commend in the character of Burke. He was in addition a besotted worshiper of monarchy and the titled. One of the most quoted passages from his *Reflections* relates to the queen of France.

It is now sixteen or seventeen years since I saw the queen of France, then the dauphiness, at Versailles; and surely never lighted on this orb, which she hardly seemed to touch, a more delightful vision. I saw her just above the horizon, decorating and cheering the elevated sphere she had just begun to move in – glittering like the morning star, full of life, and splendour, and joy. Oh, what a revolution! And what a heart must I have to contemplate without emotion that elevation and that fall!...little did I dream that I should have lived to see such disasters fallen upon her in a nation of gallant men, in a nation of men of honour and of cavaliers. I had thought ten thousand swords must have leaped from their scabbards to avenge even a look that threatened her with insult! But the age of chivalry is gone. That of sophisters, economists, and calculators has succeeded, and the glory of Europe is extinguished forever. Never, never more shall we behold that generous loyalty to rank and sex, that proud submission, that dignified obedience, that subordination of the heart which kept alive, even in servitude itself, the spirit of an exalted freedom. (Penguin edition (1969) pp. 169-70)

The queen whom he eulogised here was of course, none other than Marie (let them eat cake) Antoinette. Thomas Paine. On the other hand, was utterly contemptuous of hereditary monarchy, declaring that the country which accepted it laid itself open to rule by 'an infant, an imbecile, an invalid, or a lunatic'. In the Chapter 'Of Monarchy and Hereditary Succession' in *Common Sense* he had noted,

One of the strongest *natural* proofs of the folly of hereditary right in kings is that nature disapproves it: otherwise she would not so frequently turn it into ridicule by giving mankind *an ass for a lion*. (Gutenberg e-text, para. 40)

Despite Burke's rather unpalatable character, however, and his disgustingly sycophantic worship of monarchy and aristocracy, his *Reflections* must be taken seriously as a statement of the conservative case. In his championing of the British government of 1790, Burke was attempting to defend the indefensible. The regime was in fact a shameless kleptocracy, and Paine had no difficulty at all in pointing this out very clearly, winning his debate with Burke on that score hands down. But Burke had a canny political instinct which had helped him to make his way in the world, and his apprehensions about the future course of the French Revolution proved to be well justified. He foresaw that by too rapidly abandoning all the political and social structures of their past, the French risked a descent into political instability that might border upon anarchy, result in large-scale bloodshed, and end with the emergence of a dictator whose rule could prove to be more tyrannical than that of the monarchy which they had just deposed. With the rise of first Robespierre and then Napoleon, his prophesies proved to be entirely correct. His warnings against too hastily abandoning all the well-established traditions of a long past were well founded. The stream of political development should not be too violently disrupted in its course. History teaches us that revolutions and violent coups are usually followed by the emergence of some frightful dictator or other: Cromwell, Robespierre, Napoleon, Stalin, Hitler, Mao Zedong, Pol Pot, etc. The value of political stability, based upon the general acceptance of long-standing political traditions, is not to be underestimated. This point was appreciated even by Paine himself. In Part II of his *Rights of Man* Paine wrote,

> When a nation changes its opinions and habits of thinking, it is no longer to be governed as before; but it would not only be wrong, but bad policy to attempt by force what ought to be accomplished by reason. Rebellion consists in forcibly opposing the general will of a nation, whether by a party or by a government. There ought, therefore, to be in every nation a method of occasionally ascertaining the state of public opinion with respect to government...It may be considered as an honour to the animal faculties of man to obtain redress by courage and danger, but it is far greater honour to the rational faculties to accomplish the same object by reason, accommodation, and general consent. (Pelican ed., 1971, pp. 287, 292)

Ever the humanitarian, although Paine strongly advocated the abolition of the monarchy, he wished no ill to the person of the king himself. He believed that the day of abolition could not be far off, but that,

> When such a time, from the general opinion of the nation shall arrive, that the honourable and liberal method would be to make a handsome present in fee simple to the person, whoever he may be, that shall then be in the monarchical office, and for him to retire to the enjoyment of private life, possessing his share of general rights and privileges, and to be no more accountable to the public for his time and his conduct than any other citizen. (ibid., p. 292)

The undesirability of violent revolution leading to over-hasty radical political change was one of the very few points on which Burke and Paine found themselves in agreement. No doubt Paine was dismayed and disappointed to witness the later course of the French Revolution, although he never fully committed his feelings on this to writing.

Burke also introduced an interesting new view of the social contract, which had figured so prominently in the writings of political thinkers ever since the days of Hobbes. In the *Reflections* he wrote,

> Society is indeed a contract...It is a partnership in all science; a partnership in all art; a partnership in every virtue, and in all perfection. As the ends of such a partnership cannot be obtained in many generations, it becomes a partnership not only between those who are living, but between those who are living, those who are dead, and those who are to be born. (Penguin edition, 1969, pp.194-5)

We owe a debt of gratitude and respect to the achievements of those who have gone before us, and we have a duty of obligation to those who will come after us, to hand on to them an acceptable inheritance. These obligations do not rule out the possibility of changes being made, but they must be made wisely and cautiously, so as to preserve the best of our present inheritance for future generations. This is a point of view that deserves to be taken seriously.

By the end of 1791, well before war between Britain and France had been declared, Burke foresaw ideological warfare on a new and terrible scale sweeping across Europe. In a letter to a Member of the National Assembly dated November 1791, Burke wrote,

> The hell-hounds of war on all sides will be uncoupled and unmuzzled. The new school of murder and barbarism, set up in Paris, having destroyed (so far as in it lies) all the other manners and principles which have hitherto civilised Europe, will destroy also the mode of civilised war, which more than anything else has distinguished the Christian world. (E.J. Payne (ed.), *Burke: Select Works* Vol. II (1875) p. 543)

The term 'civilised war' is of course an oxymoron, but in so far as it went this prophecy too proved to be correct, with the long series of Revolutionary and Napoleonic Wars which plagued Europe from 1792 to 1815.

Burke followed up his 1790 *Reflections* with a further tract, published in its final form in September, 1791 entitled, *An Appeal from the New to the Old Whigs*. This tract essentially repeated all of the arguments and warnings about the French Revolution of his earlier work, but in addition it reflected a very real and growing division of opinion within the Whig party. With the worst excesses of the French Revolution still to come, most Whigs still looked with favour upon the changes in France, likening them to their own 'Glorious Revolution' of 1688-9. Burke's criticisms at that time were premature, and made him unpopular with a majority of his own party, who saw him as something of an apostate, who had betrayed Whig principles. The Prime Minister at that time was William Pitt the Younger (1759-1806), in office from December 19, 1783 to January 1, 1801. He called himself an 'Independent Whig', but was in reality the king's man, kept in office by George III despite numerous defeats in the Commons. Pitt, his party, and George III himself had thoroughly approved of Burke's *Reflections*, while the leader of the Whig majority in the Commons, Charles James Fox (1749-1806), had just as strongly disapproved of the work. Burke broke openly and acrimoniously with Fox in the summer of 1791, effectively leaving his party, then in opposition to the Pitt government, which was in effect more of a Tory party at that time. At first few of the 'Old Whigs' sympathised with Burke, but as the French Revolution became increasingly violent and radical, and after warfare between Britain and France had broken out in 1793, more and more of them drifted over to Pitt's side. The old Whig party was permanently shattered, and was forced to reconstitute itself in the early years of the nineteenth century.

For all its merits, however, Burke's *Reflections* was essentially a powerful piece of propaganda in favour of the status quo, which suited Burke very well at the time. Recognising its tendentious tone Paine, himself an inveterate polemicist, rose to the challenge. His reply, the *Rights of Man*, became one of the classics of British political thought.

Burke's *Reflections* had been published in November, 1790, and Paine's reply had followed swiftly, with his *Rights of Man* being published in two parts, Part I appearing in March 1791, and Part II in February, 1792. The dating of these publications is significant, for the work was subtitled, *An Answer to Mr. Burke's Attack on the French Revolution.* In February 1792 the worst excesses of the French Revolution, including the September Massacres of that year, still lay in the future. Britain and France were not yet at war, France was still nominally a monarchy, and the time of mass executions and the Terror still lay ahead: it was far easier at that time to defend the Revolution than it subsequently became. But as we now know, Burke's pessimism about the French Revolution proved to be far better founded than Paine's optimism. Burke was later to display even more far-sighted prescience when he warned the British government that their Irish policies would eventually lead to the loss of Ireland, just as they had lost America.

As noted in discussing the American Constitution, I am rather sceptical about this concept of 'natural rights'. For me, 'natural rights' can exist only in the state of nature where, as Hobbes says, a man's only 'natural' right was in fact,

> ...to use his own power, as he wills himself, for the preservation of his own Nature; that is to say of his own life; and consequently of doing anything which, in his own judgement and reason, he shall conceive to be the aptest means thereunto. (Leviathan I, xiv)

In other words, he has only such 'natural right' as his own power allows him to claim for himself: it is, in short, not a *right*, but rather a *power*. In the 'state of nature' there is no such thing as 'natural rights' but only natural powers. In his *Tractatus Politicus* Spinoza basically agreed with Hobbes' view of the state of nature and 'natural' rights. (Chpt. 2, section 15) This distinction between *rights* and *powers* is a most important one to grasp. For example, freedom of thought has been seen by many philosophers as an inalienable natural right. The Stoics were certainly prepared to concede this right even to slaves. Seneca the Younger wrote,

> It is a mistake to imagine that slavery pervades a man's whole being: the better part of him is exempted from it: the body indeed is subjected and in the power of a master, but the mind is independent, and indeed is so free and wild that it cannot be restrained even by this prison of the body, wherein it is confined. (De Beneficiis, III, 20)

The Stoics rejected the thought of Plato and Aristotle, who believed that some men were 'natural' slaves. Instead the Stoics, like the Epicurians, believed in the fundamental equality of all men. Indeed, one of the leading Stoic philosophers, Epictatus of Hierapolis (c55-135 AD) was himself a slave! No lack of free thought there!

But in reality this freedom is a natural *right* only because everyone has the *power* to exercise freedom of thought under any circumstances whatsoever, simply because it is extremely difficult to deprive anyone of this *power*. However, sadly, this has not prevented many regimes from attempting to do just that nevertheless. Under the Catholic Inquisition, Fascism, Nazism, and Communism, every effort was made to stamp out freedom of thought. These regimes assumed that nobody had a *right* to any such thing. Everyone was supposed to believe that those regimes were absolutely faultless and wonderful – or else! Sadly, we still see such a regime in operation today in North Korea, and increasingly in China. This raises another, and rather sinister point. When men surrender their natural rights, or rather powers, which they enjoyed in the state of nature to one supreme authority under the social contract, they might find themselves in danger of losing *all* their rights and *all* their powers as well, since mighty Leviathan is then in a position to overpower every individual. The social contract can in fact be very threatening indeed. Mankind submits himself to being allowed only those 'rights' which Leviathan sees fit to grant him, and these may be precious few. It is important to understand that no rights in civil society can ever be seen as being 'natural': in reality, they are all manufactured and granted by the state. We have only those 'rights' which we invent and allow to each other.

To be realistic, therefore, no civil rights should ever be regarded as being 'natural' or 'inalienable', but rather only as highly desirable. These rights might be granted by a benevolent Leviathan, but equally they could be withheld by a malevolent one. In modern times Locke famously described these 'natural' or 'inalienable' rights as being those to 'life, liberty, and property'. But these claims were fraudulent. Even in Locke's envisaged commonwealth, the state could still deprive men of their lives, liberty, and property under the terms of the law laid down by the state itself. These so-called 'rights' were therefore not 'inalienable' at all – they could be violated at will by the state. The social contract can in fact be very threatening indeed, and before anyone signs up to it, its terms should be very carefully examined.

Having said all that, however, it is clearly highly *desirable* that every state should extend as many rights and freedoms as possible to all its citizens, while bearing in mind that every right and freedom may always be withdrawn from any individual under the terms of the law, so that none of these highly desirable rights is in fact 'inalienable'.

Thomas Paine had very clear ideas on which rights were in fact highly desirable and which should under normal circumstances be accorded to all. He thoroughly approved of the *Declaration of the Rights of Man and of Citizens* which was finally adopted by the National Constituent Assembly of France on August 26, 1789, and incorporated the entire *Declaration* into Part I of his *Rights of Man*. (Pelican ed., 1971, pp. 132-4.) There were 17 articles in all to the *Declaration*, but Paine considered the first three articles to be of the greatest importance, claiming that all of the other articles followed naturally as corollaries of these first three. He reproduced these articles again on p. 166.

I. Men are born and always continue free and equal in respect of their rights. Civil distinctions, therefore, can be founded only on public utility.
II. The end of all political associations is the preservation of the natural and inalienable rights of man; and these rights are liberty, property, security, and resistance to oppression.
III. The Nation is essentially the source of all sovereignty; nor can any INDIVIDUAL or ANY BODY OF MEN be entitled to any authority which is not expressly derived from it.

The 17 articles of the *Declaration* bore some similarity to the American Bill of Rights which was being drawn up at the same time, and was finally appended to the U.S. constitution in December 1791. Indeed, the *Declaration* had been drawn up mainly by the Marquis de Lafayette (1757-1834) with the help of Thomas Jefferson (1743-1826) who was based in France at that time. However, the situation differed from the American case in that this Bill of Rights had come first, with an intended constitution based on it to follow. Article XVI added, 'Every community in which a separation of powers and a security of rights is not provided for needs a constitution'.

Seen in France as a good friend and supporter of the Revolution, Paine had been granted honorary French citizenship on August 26th 1792, along with George Washington, Alexander Hamilton, James Madison, and Joseph Priestly. He was elected to the newly established National Convention in September, 1792 as member for the Pas-de-Calais district, despite knowing only a few words of French. He left England to take up his seat in late September, arriving just two weeks after the notorious massacres of September 3-7, when all the prisoners in French jails who were suspected of anti-revolution sympathies were summarily executed. Paine was never to see his native land again. After spending ten years in France playing a part in the revolutionary politics of the day, he returned to America, finally dying in New York city in 1809. Paine had been looking forward to helping with the framing of a new constitution for France, but events were to take a sinister turn. In the Convention Paine sided with the more moderate Girondists against Robespierre and the 'Montagnards', later to be the basis of the Jacobin party, voting for the establishment of a republic in France, but voting against the execution of the king. Paine had several reasons for doing this. As a natural humanitarian he recoiled from the needless taking of life, but further he could not forget the invaluable assistance which Louis XVI's France had rendered to America in its struggle for independence. Without this French help, the whole American enterprise might well have failed. Finally, he knew well what damage would be done to the reputation of the revolutionaries in Europe if they could be decried as regicides.

Unfortunately for Paine, however, it was the radicals' star which was in the ascendant. The Girondists lost support, foreign delegates were expelled from the Convention, and in December 1793 Paine himself was arrested as a suspected royalist, and imprisoned in the Luxembourg, a former palace. There was a fine irony here: few men held the institution of monarchy in greater contempt than did Thomas Paine! However, his position had become more parlous after February 1st, 1793 when France had declared war on Britain. Paine then became doubly suspect as both a royalist after the execution of Louis XVI in January, and as an enemy alien, possibly a spy, despite his claim to be an American citizen. He was in fact marked out for trial and probable execution himself in July 1794 along with many hundreds of other suspected 'reactionaries' and was saved, according to many accounts, only by a curious stroke of chance. The door of his cell opened outwards, and cell doors were often left open to allow prisoners to receive visitors or go out for exercise, since the Luxembourg itself was very secure. The jailor had been given the names of those destined for trial, and told to chalk a mark on their cell doors so that they could be collected later for yet another mass slaughter. However, on marking out day the door of Paine's cell happened to be open, and swung back against the outside wall of his cell. The jailor, perhaps drunk at the time, therefore carelessly marked the inside of Paine's cell door instead of the outside. On collection day, Paine's cell door happened to be closed, with its fatal mark visible only from the inside, and so Paine was saved!

Now this is a pretty tale indeed, told by Paine himself in his personal papers, but it had clearly been related to him by a third party long after his release from prison. He mentions it for the first time only in 1802, in a letter printed in Washington's *National Intelligencer*, a pro-Democrat paper, for December 29th. At the time of his arraignment Paine had no idea of what was taking place. In his letter to Washington of July 30, 1796 he states that on the fateful night,

> A violent fever which had nearly terminated my existence was, I believe, the circumstance that preserved it. I was not in a condition to be removed, or to know of what was passing, or of what had passed, for more than a month. It makes a blank in my remembrance of life. The first thing I was informed of was the fall of Robespierre.

It seems more likely that this was the real reason for Paine's survival. Those being executed by the Committee of Public Safety at that time were first of all put through a brief show trial to prove their 'guilt', thus giving the process a semblance of legality, and Paine was clearly too ill to stand trial. He was probably unconscious at the time, and expected to die at any moment. Had he been named as one of those arraigned for trial, it would have taken more than a misplaced chalk mark on his door to save him, and he clearly had been so arraigned. It was well known who Paine was, and where he was. Found among Robespierre's papers after his fall, and in Robespierre's own hand, was a brief instruction regarding Paine, which he quoted with great bitterness in the *Intelligencer* letter of 1802 cited above. By this time Paine had come to believe that Robespierre had been acting on the direct instructions of Washington himself, because of Paine's anti-Federalist views. He wrote,

> When Robespierre had me seized in the night and imprisoned in the Luxembourg (where I remained eleven months) he assigned no reason for it. But when he proposed bringing me to the tribunal, which was like sending me at once to the scaffold, he then assigned a reason, and the reason was, for the interests of America as well as of France. 'Demander que Thomas Paine soit decreté d'accusation, pour l'interérèt de l'Amerique autant que de la France'. The words are in his own handwriting, and reported to the Convention by the committee appointed to examine his papers, and are printed in their report, with this reflection added to them, 'Why Thomas Paine more than another? Because he contributed to the liberty of both worlds'. There must have been a coalition in sentiment, if not in fact, between the Terrorists of America and the Terrorists of France, and Robespierre must have known it, or he could not have had the idea of putting America into the bill of accusation against me. Yet these men, these Terrorists of the new world, who were waiting in the devotion of their hearts for the joyful news of my destruction, are the same banditti who are now bellowing in all the hacknied language of hacknied hypocricy, about humanity, and piety, and often about something they call infidelity, and they finish with the chorus of Crucify him, crucify him.

As with his first voyage to America, which had nearly proved fatal, Paine had had another lucky escape, both from death by fever, and death by guillotine! Nevertheless, Paine spent nearly a year incarcerated in the Luxembourg, from December 1793 to November 1794 while the violence of the French Revolution raged around him outside his prison walls. The more moderate Girondists, with whom Paine had sided, continued to lose support, and on June 10, 1793 the radical Jacobins gained control of the Committee of Public Safety. On September 6 Robespierre, the leader of the Jacobins, instituted his notorious 'Reign of Terror', during which thousands more were executed. On October 16, Marie Antoinette was guillotined, and on October 31, 21 Girondist deputies followed her to the scaffold. The Terror lasted until the Thermidorian Reaction of July 27-8 in 1794. In this Robespierre was arrested and himself guillotined without trial, together with his leading supporters on the Committee of Public Safety. This marked the end of Jacobin power, with the Jacobin Club itself being closed down on November 11. Only then was Paine released (actually on November 4) partly due to the urging of James Monroe (1758-1831) who was at that time American Minister to France, but later the fifth President of the United States. During his incarceration, however, Paine had become both surprised and resentful of the fact that Washington's administration had made no representations to the French government to have him released: Monroe had apparently acted on his own initiative. George

Washington was then serving as President of the United States, and during the Revolutionary War Paine had come to regard him as a personal friend, dedicating Part I of *The Rights of Man* to him. After his release Paine wrote to him twice in 1795, asking him to explain his neglect of an old friend who had lain in danger of his life, but twice Washington sent no reply. Finally, puzzled and hurt, Paine decided to publish an open letter to Washington dated July 30, 1796 expressing his bitterness and resentment. It was a very lengthy letter indeed, criticising Washington as both a military commander and a political leader. It ran to some 64 pages (available online) but it came to be remembered only for its last few lines, which read,

> If there is sense enough left in the heart to call a blush into the cheek, the Washington Administration must be ashamed to appear. And as to you Sir, treacherous in private friendship (for so you have been to me, and that in the day of danger) and a hypocrite in public life, the world will be puzzled to decide whether you are an apostate or an imposter; whether you have abandoned good principles, or whether you ever had any.

It was this libelling of a national hero, together with the notoriety of his *Age of Reason*, that was later to make Paine very unpopular in America. By denigrating Washington, Paine was also denigrating every American who idolised him as a national hero, and that meant virtually every American.

In 1795 Paine was re-admitted into the Convention in France, and continued to play a part in the ongoing Revolution. He was one of only three deputies to vote against the instituting of the new constitution of 1795, on the grounds that it did not allow for universal manhood suffrage, as had its two predecessors.

There was another fine irony in the fact that Paine had almost been executed by the Jacobins, because in most regards Paine was actually a Jacobin himself! He had differed with them only over the execution of the king, but he shared their conception of popular sovereignty and representative democracy in its most extreme, republican form, being a virulent opponent of monarchy.
He believed that all just power derived only from the consent of the people, and advocated universal manhood suffrage, exactly what the Jacobins themselves favoured. Again like them he believed that the state should work for the abolition of poverty among its people, and encourage a redistribution of property to bring this about. Finally, like them he believed in complete religious freedom for all, with full civil rights for all creeds. His religious views were basically deistic, like theirs with their 'Cult of the Supreme Being', which also included a belief in an afterlife, a conviction shared by Paine himself. In short, the problem lies rather in finding those ways in which Paine was *not* a Jacobin! We can say only that he did not share their bloodlust.

Paine had made his political views clear in Part I of his *Rights of Man* which had been published in March, 1791, but these views were not very different from those of Richard Price, Joseph Priestly, or any of the other republican radicals of late eighteenth-century England. It was only in Part II of his most famous work , published in February 1792, that Paine revealed himself to be also a deep thinker upon social and economic issues, to an extent that took him beyond the standard radicalism of his time. Part II consisted of five chapters. The first chapter was headed, 'Of Society and Civilisation' where Paine basically agreed with Locke's conception of the 'state of nature' as being a state of peace rather than of war. Like Locke, he argues that men should not fear a temporary breakdown of government, since society can function very well on its own without a government. He declared,

> The landholder, the farmer, the manufacturer, the merchant, the tradesman, and every occupation prospers by the aid which each receives from the other, and from the whole. Common interest regulates their concerns, and forms their law; and these laws, which common usage ordains, have a greater influence than the laws of government. In fine, society performs for itself almost everything which is ascribed to government. (*Rights of Man*, Pelican ed., 1971, p. 185)

In Chapter 2, 'Of the Origin of the Present Old Governments' Paine decries the ancient 'Norman yoke'. He writes,

> It could have been no difficult thing, in the early and solitary ages of the world, while the chief employment of men was that of attending flocks and herds, for a banditti of ruffians to overrun a country, and lay it under contributions. Their power being thus established, the chief of the band contrived to lose the name of Robber in that of Monarch; and hence the origin of Monarchy and Kings...What at first was plunder assumed the foster name of revenue; and the power originally usurped, they affected to inherit. (Ibid., pp.190-1)

The kleptocratic nature of all the regimes in Europe up to that point in time was clearly recognised by Paine here. In Chapter 3, 'Of the Old and New Systems of Government' he compares representative democracy with hereditary monarchy, to the great detriment of the latter, pointing out how much lower taxes are in republican America than in monarchical England. In Chapter 4, 'Of Constitutions', he declares that,

> A constitution is not the act of a government, but of a people constituting a government; and government without a constitution is power without a right. (Ibid., p. 207)

Paine denied that Britain had a constitution at all, because there was no existing written document to testify to that fact, as in America. The clear implication was that the then government of Britain was illegitimate. This was enough to get Paine arraigned on a charge of seditious libel, for which he was tried in his absence just after his departure for France in September, 1792. This was yet another lucky escape for Paine, for he was found guilty, and would have faced at least a long term of imprisonment had he remained in England. It was only in Chapter 5, however, entitled, 'Ways and Means of Improving the Condition of Europe, Interspersed with Miscellaneous Observations' that Paine turned his attention to social and economic matters. This was by far the longest chapter in Part II, taking up half of that section on its own. It was this chapter, more than any other part of Paine's writings, that revealed him to be a man of dazzling originality of thought, far ahead of his time. It is here, in two significant passages, that he summarises his political creed.

> Whatever the form or constitution of government may be, it ought to have no other object than the *general* happiness. When, instead of this, it operates to create and increase wretchedness in any of the parts of society, it is on a wrong system, and reformation is necessary. (Ibid., p.232)

> When it shall be said in any country of the world, my poor are happy; my jails are empty of prisoners, my streets of beggars; the aged are not in want, the taxes are not oppressive; the rational world is my friend, because I am the friend of its happiness: when these things can be said, then may that country boast its constitution and its government. (Ibid., p. 286)

It should be noted at this point that Paine had always strenuously renounced the title of 'intellectual'. He boasted of his lack of reading, claiming that he had, 'never read Locke, nor even held the work in my hand', and that, 'I neither read books nor studied other people's opinions. I thought for myself'. (Ibid., pp. 13, 241) We are reminded here of Mark Antony's somewhat disingenuous claim, 'I am no orator as Brutus is, but just a plain, blunt man'. The truth is, however, that although Paine denied the title of intellectual, he moved in intellectual circles. He was an opinionated man, and revelled in debate with his intellectual peers. While working as an excise officer at Lewes in Sussex he had joined the Headstrong Club, a political discussion group which met at the White Horse Inn, close to his lodgings. Later, between 1787 and 1792 he became a member of the Johnson Circle, attending several of the famous 'dinners' hosted by Joseph Johnson (1738-1809) the London bookseller and publisher. The fare was notoriously meagre, but his guests attended not for the food, but rather for the quality of discussion available with the likes of Joseph Priestley, Erasmus Darwin, Mary Wollstonecraft, Horne Tooke, and John Howard. Benjamin Franklin had introduced Paine to his own favourite discussion group, which he had affectionately dubbed, 'The Club of Honest Whigs'. This group met fortnightly on Thursdays at various London coffee houses, where the topics discussed were more broadly philosophical than specifically political. It was here if anywhere that Paine would have learned of the works of Spinoza. Paine was also known to have attended social evenings hosted by Richard Price (1723-91) where he could have met Adam Smith, David Hume, and Charles James Fox. Paine was the good friend of Maurice de Talleyrand (1754-1838), the French aristocrat who played a key role in the early stages of the French Revolution, and to whom he dedicated Part II of his *Rights of Man*. It is inconceivable that Paine could have moved in such circles as these and yet learned nothing of Locke, Montesquieu, Rousseau, and perhaps even Bentham. He may never have read their books, but he could certainly have become familiar with their ideas. Indeed, in his *Rights of Man* he specifically mentions Voltaire, Montesquieu, Rousseau, de Quesnay, and Turgot by name. (Ibid., p. 116) It is also inconceivable that he could have lived in France for ten years, from 1792 to 1802, without learning at least something of the language.

Returning now to Chapter 5 in Part II of the *Rights of Man*, it was here that Paine staked his strongest claim to being a thinker far ahead of his time by proposing a plan for what would have been the first welfare state in the world, had his proposals been taken up. The chapter deals first of all with war and trade, contrasting the naturally peaceful and ordered state of civil society with the international anarchy, where governments behave as though they were in a Hobbesian state of nature, with no 'rights' beyond what their own powers could win for them. He points out how badly war disrupts trade, and how it increases taxes. Optimistically, however, he blames kings and courts for the international anarchy, suggesting that if all states were democratic republics, wars would cease. It is clear from this section that Paine was familiar with such concepts as 'the state of nature' and 'the social contract'. He goes on to criticise municipal corporations and guilds as restrictive to trade, reflecting here the ideas of Adam Smith and the Physiocrats. He then attacks the House of Lords, asking,

> What pillar of security does the landed interest require more than any other interest in the state, or what right has it to a distinct and separate representation from the general interest of a nation? The only use to be made of this power (and which it has always made) is to ward off taxes from itself, and throw the burden upon such articles of consumption by which itself would be least affected. (Ibid., p. 246)

Paine then goes on to adduce ample evidence in proof of this charge by referring to the recently published *History of the Public Revenue of the British Empire* by Sir John Sinclair (1754-1835), a Scottish baronet. Sir John was totally obsessed with statistics, and was indeed the first person to use the word 'statistics' in the English language. Between 1791 and 1799 he compiled the massive *Statistical Account of Scotland* in 21 volumes! This was the same Sir John who was also President of the first Board of Agriculture between 1793 and 1822, with Arthur Young (1741-1820) serving as Secretary to the Board. Between them they compiled the splendid *County Reports to the Board of Agriculture*, an invaluable source for social and economic historians. Sinclair's *History of the Revenue* was first published in 1785, but in his obsessive way he continually updated it, thereby providing another invaluable source, but this time for political historians.

Using Sinclair's figures, Paine was able to show that during the later Middle Ages the total amount of taxation levied on the country had actually decreased, from about £200,000 p.a. in 1166 to only £100,000 in 1466. By 1566 this sum had risen to £500,000 p.a., and by 1666 to £1,800,000. We should remember, however, that the years from 1500 to 1650 were a period of secular inflation, when the general level of prices rose nearly six fold, which somewhat reduced the burden in real terms. From 1650 to 1750, on the other hand, there was a slight decline in price levels, after which time inflation set in once again. On its own, however, this was nowhere nearly enough to account for the £17,000,000 in taxation which Paine found was being levied in 1791! Even more significantly, however, Paine was able to show that the great bulk of this new taxation was now being paid by the mass of the population, while the taxation levied on landowners had not increased at all since a specific land tax had first been introduced in 1692. Paine claimed that Sinclair had assessed the 'land tax' paid in 1646 at £2,473,499 (Ibid., p. 247) but this figure is spurious: its precise accuracy alone is enough to arouse suspicion, but in addition this sum is in fact larger than the whole national revenue for 1666, according to Paine's own figures! What can be said with some accuracy, however, is that the specific land tax instituted in 1692 brought in about £2,000,000 p.a. at that time, roughly the same amount as in 1788. In the 1690s this sum represented about 35% of England's national revenue, but because it remained fixed it declined as a proportion of total revenue, to about 17% in the 1790s 'notwithstanding the rentals are in many instances doubled since that period', as Paine noted. As an agricultural historian myself, I can testify to the accuracy of that statement. By the 1820s the land tax was returning only 11% of the national revenue. (M. Pearsall, *The Land Tax, 1692*-1963 (1966) p. 16) Meanwhile, the level of consumption taxes thrown upon the mass of the population had steadily increased. Paine traced the beginning of this scurrilous exercise in self-interest by the ruling class back to the Restoration of 1660, writing,

> As an instance of it screening itself, it is necessary only to look back to the first establishment of the excise laws, at what is called the Restoration, or the coming of Charles II. The aristocratical interest then in power commuted the feudal services itself was under by laying a tax on beer brewed for *sale*; that is, they compounded with Charles for an exemption from those services for themselves and their heirs, by a tax to be paid by other people. The aristocracy do not purchase beer brewed for sale, but brew their own beer free of the duty, and if any commutation at that time were necessary, it ought to have been at the expense of those for whom the exemptions from those services were intended; instead of which it was thrown onto an entirely different class of men. (Ibid., p.276)

Paine specifically mentions here the aristocracy of the House of Lords, but his condemnation applied equally to the landed gentry who filled the House of Commons, and who also brewed their own beer. Using Sinclair, he was then able to present a breakdown of all the sources of taxation revenue in the year 1788 as a table, reproduced below together with his following comment.

Land tax
£1,950,000
Customs
3,789,274
Excise(including old and new malt)
6,751,727
Stamps
1,278,214
Miscellaneous taxes and incidents
1,803,755
£15,572,970

Since the year 1788 upwards of one million of new taxes have been laid on, besides the produce from the lotteries; and as the taxes have in general been more productive since than before, the amount may be taken, in round numbers, at £17,000,000. N.B. The expense of collection and the drawbacks, which together amount to nearly two millions, are paid out of the gross amount; and the above is the net sum paid into the exchequer. (Ibid., p. 255)

While the precise accuracy of Paine's figures may be suspect, the general trend of taxation policy in the eighteenth century emerges clearly enough. Whenever 'new taxes were laid on' it was always consumption taxes like the excise, paid by the mass of the population, that were increased, and never the land tax. Paine estimated that approximately one quarter of a working man's wages went to pay the taxes on articles of consumption. (Ibid., p. 233) This was hardly surprising, given the structure of British government at that time. The ruling class was essentially the landed class, and they governed entirely in their own interests. The greatest landowners filled the House of Lords, but it was the landed gentry who filled the House of Commons, and those gentry who were not MPs ruled the countryside in more direct ways, as Lord Lieutenants, Sheriffs, and Justices of the Peace. The aristocracy and gentry held about three-quarters of all the land in England in 1790, with the Crown, Church, and small freeholders owning the other quarter between them, although as heads of families, the gentry and aristocracy numbered fewer than one percent of the whole population. This small number of individuals not only owned most of the land of England, but also wielded the political influence which ensured that both houses of Parliament would represent nobody's interests other than their own. As a class, they maintained their landed and political preponderance mainly through the system of primogeniture, whereby only the eldest son inherited the estate, with his siblings being provided for in various parsimonious ways, preferably by appointment to some sinecure office paid for out of the public purse. In this way, the preponderançe of property ownership was maintained in just a few hands.

This system of primogeniture, with its associated concentration of political power, was one of Paine's main targets in his *Rights of Man*. Speaking of the House of Lords he wrote,

> As a combination, it can always throw a considerable portion of taxes from itself; and as an hereditary house, accountable to nobody, it resembles a rotten borough, whose consent is to be courted by interest. There are but few of its members who are not in some mode or other participators or disposers of the public money. One turns a candle-holder or a lord in waiting, another a lord of the bed-chamber, a groom of the stole, or any insignificant nominal office to which a salary is annexed, paid out of the public taxes, and which avoids the direct appearance of corruption. Such situations are derogatory to the character of man; and where they can be submitted to, no honour can reside.
>
> To all these are to be added the numerous dependents, the long list of younger branches and distant relations, who are to be provided for at the public expense: in short, were an estimation to be made of the charge of aristocracy to a nation, it will be found nearly equal to that of supporting the poor. The duke of Richmond alone (and there are cases similar to his) takes away as much for himself as would maintain two thousand poor and aged persons. (Ibid., p. 250)

The whole cost of the poor rate in England was estimated by Paine to be about £2,000,000 p.a. However, this was not a national but a local tax, set by town corporations or JPs, so once again the landed classes sheltered themselves. As Paine noted,

> Their residences, whether in town or country, are not mixed with the habitations of the poor. They live apart from distress, and the expense of relieving it. It is in manufacturing towns and labouring villages that those burdens press the heaviest; in many of which it is one class of poor supporting another. (Ibid., p. 247)

Paine boldly proposed a scheme that would completely reverse the existing situation. Firstly, the poor should be supported not from local, but from national taxation, and secondly, this national tax should be raised entirely from landed property, or more specifically from the rent received from landed property. As noted above, leading economists from Adam Smith to Milton Friedman have agreed that this is the least damaging form of taxation in terms of its being a hindrance to national economic growth. It was first recommended by Spinoza, as noted above. This taxation would be progressive, so that the largest estates paid the heaviest taxes. Paine's tax would be imposed in addition to the existing land tax, and designed in such a way that the tax on estates returning more than £23,000 p.a. in rent became prohibitive. The idea here was to undermine the custom of primogeniture by forcing the division of large estates into smaller units so as to avoid the worst burdens of his progressive tax. Paine produced numerous tables to show how his scheme would work, saying of the last one,

According to this table, an estate cannot produce more than £12,370 per year clear of the land tax and the progressive tax, and therefore the dividing of such estates will follow as a matter of family interest. An estate of £23,000 a year, divided into five estates of four thousand each and one of three, will be charged only £1,129 in all, *which is but five per cent*, but if held by one possessor will be charged £10,630. (Ibid., p. 278)

He made it clear that primogeniture was one of the main targets of his scheme, declaring,

But the chief object of this progressive tax (besides the justice of rendering taxes more equal than they are) is, as already stated, to extirpate the overgrown influence arising from the unnatural law of primogeniture, and which is one of the principle sources of corruption at elections...let it be sufficient to remedy the evil by putting them in a condition of descending again to the community, by the quiet means of apportioning them among all the heirs and heiresses of those families. This will be the more necessary, because hitherto the aristocracy have quartered their younger children and connections upon the public in useless posts, places, and offices, which when abolished will leave them destitute, unless the law of primogeniture be also abolished or superseded. (Ibid., pp.276-7)

The interesting words to note from the above extract lie in the phrase 'by the quiet means'. Paine was already opposed to the idea of violent revolution even in 1792, *before* the French Revolution had embarked upon its violent and bloodstained phase. He did believe in a redistribution of property, but not by confiscation or by violent means. Notice too his concern that the younger sons should not be left destitute, even although they belonged to a class that he despised. As noted above he believed that even deposed kings should be treated kindly. Paine's humanitarianism emerges clearly here.

Of course, Paine was envisaging his progressive tax as being imposed under a republican form of government, where the monarchy and the House of Lords had been abolished, and replaced by a representative assembly, elected by universal manhood suffrage. Given the times in which he was writing, this was as much of a pipe dream as Plato's *Republic,* or Sir Thomas More's *Utopia*. We need not, therefore concern ourselves overmuch with the accuracy of the figures that Paine presented. He claimed, for example, that a republican government in peacetime could be run for no more than £500,000 p.a., exclusive of the cost of armed forces, and that the returns from his land taxes alone would allow for the abolition of all existing taxes, including the house tax, window tax, poor rates, and all existing consumption taxes. But most remarkably of all, the money so raised should be used to set up the world's first welfare state! The interesting point is not the accuracy of his figures, but rather the idea behind them, and how his money raised was to be spent. He summed this up under 14 points, and here we should allow Paine to speak for himself.

1. Abolition of two million poor rates.

2. Provision for 252,000 poor families, at the rate of four pounds per head for each child under fourteen years of age which, with the addition of £250,000 p.a. provides also education for one million and thirty thousand children.
3. Annuity of six pounds each for all poor persons, decayed tradesmen, or others (suppose 70,000) of the age of fifty years, and until sixty.
4. Annuity of ten pounds each for life for all poor persons, decayed tradesmen and others (suppose 70,000) of the age of sixty years.
5. Donation of 20 shillings each for 50,000 births.
6. Donation of 20 shillings each for 20,000 marriages.
7. Allowance of £20,000 for the funeral expenses of persons travelling for work, and dying at a distance from their friends.
8. Employment at all times for the casual poor in the cities of London and Westminster.
9. Abolition of the tax on houses and windows.
10. Allowance of three shillings per week for life to 15,000 disbanded soldiers, and a proportionable allowance to the officers of the disbanded corps.
11. Increase in pay to the remaining soldiers of £19,500 annually.
12. The same allowance to the disbanded navy, and the same increase of pay as to the army.
13. Abolition of the commutation tax (a tax on consumption).
14. Plan of a progressive tax, operating to extirpate the unjust and unnatural law of primogeniture, and the vicious influence of the aristocratical system. (Ibid., pp.280-1)

The scale of the relief that would have been afforded to the poor of England by this scheme may be imagined, but Paine's ideas were a good century and a half ahead of their time. They reveal him, however, to have been a great humanitarian, in the same mould as his close contemporary, Jeremy Bentham.

Paine went on to suggest a related but simplified social welfare scheme for France with another influential pamphlet, his *Agrarian Justice*, published in the winter of 1795 and addressed to 'The Legislature and the Executive Directory of the French Republic', although he added in his dedication,

The plan contained in this work is not adapted for any particular country alone: the principle upon which it is based is general.

He did, however, in that same dedication, specifically rebuke the French for failing to maintain universal manhood suffrage in their 1795 constitution. He also criticised them by implication for failing to include any element of social welfare into that same constitution. A pdf version of *Agrarian Justice,* edited by Thomas Piketty is available on line. It is just 20 pages long, and the citations below come from it. Here, Paine made the bold suggestion that every French citizen, male or female, should be gifted by the state with fifteen pounds each, or its equivalent in the currency of the day, when they reached the age of 21. He pointed out that,

When a young couple begin the world, the difference is exceedingly great whether they begin with nothing or with fifteen pounds apiece. With this aid they could buy a cow, and implements to cultivate a few acres of land; and instead of becoming burdens upon society, which is always the case where children are produced faster than they can be fed, would be put in the way of becoming useful and profitable citizens. (p. 16)

He also proposed that everyone, regardless of wealth or income, should be provided with an old-age pension of ten pounds a year or its equivalent, on reaching the age of fifty, which was a good age for the times. He assumed, optimistically perhaps, that those too wealthy to need such assistance would throw their share back into the general fund. However, if they fell into hardship later, they could draw their arrears. He explained,

It is not a charity but a right, not bounty but justice, that I am pleading for. The present state of civilization is as odious as it is unjust. It is absolutely the opposite of what it should be, and it is necessary that a revolution should be made in it. The contrast of affluence and wretchedness continually meeting and offending the eye is like dead and living bodies chained together. Though I care as little about riches as any man, I am a friend to riches because they are capable of good. I care not how affluent some may be, provided that none be miserable in consequence of it. (p.15)

Statements such as the above indicate that Paine was no socialist. He believed in capitalism and free enterprise, but he was arguing here for modified capitalism, or what you might call, 'capitalism with a human face'. He argued that, in the 'state of nature' such as the Indians of North America still enjoyed at that time, land had been the common property of all. Only 'civilisation' had made it private property, held in grossly unequal shares. Just as Rousseau had been impressed to see Swiss peasants effortlessly settling their affairs by conclave under the village oak tree, so Paine had been very impressed by the lives of the North American Indians he had seen. He admired their egalitarian society, their ability to live in harmony with nature, and the way they governed themselves by direct democracy in small groups. He pointed out that,

The life of an Indian is a continual holiday compared with the poor of Europe; and on the other hand it appears to be abject when compared to the rich. Civilisation therefore, or that which is so called, has operated two ways, to make one part of society more affluent, and the other more wretched, than would have been the lot of either in a natural state...the first principle of civilisation ought to have been, and ought still to be, that the condition of every person born into the world after a state of civilisation commences, ought not to be worse than if he had been born before that period. (p. 7)

There are strong echoes of Rousseau here. But Paine then went on to say it followed that,

Every proprietor, therefore, of cultivated land, owes to the community a *ground rent* (for I know of no better term to express the idea) for the land which he holds, and it is from this ground rent that the fund proposed in this plan is to issue. (p. 8)

Paine's 'ground rent' was, however, to take the form of an inheritance tax, to be paid when the land passed from one generation to the next, averaging ten per cent of the value of the estate. This value was to include personal as well as real property, because,

All accumulation, therefore, of personal property beyond what a man's own hands produce, is derived to him by living in society, and he owes on every principle of justice, of gratitude, and of civilization, a part of that accumulation back again to society from whence the whole came. (p. 18)

If only some of the very wealthy in our twenty-first century society would heed those words! Paine argued that very few would be the losers from such a scheme, since the wealthy could easily afford to pay the inheritance tax, while,

I do not suppose that more than one family in ten in any of the countries of Europe has, when the head of the family dies, a clear property left of five hundred pounds sterling. To all such the plan is advantageous. The property would pay fifty pounds into the fund, and if there were only two children under age they would receive fifteen pounds each (thirty pounds) on coming of age, and be entitled to ten pounds a year after fifty. It is from the overgrown acquisition of property that the fund will support itself...(p. 17)

The wealthy should not object to paying this tax, but rather should see it as a kind of insurance against the threat of violent revolution, which might lose them *all* their land. The provision of social justice for all would be the best guarantee against any such eventuality.

It is necessary as well for the protection of property as for the sake of justice and humanity to form a system that, whilst it preserves one part of society from wretchedness, shall secure the other from depredation. (p. 18)

Paine concluded his pamphlet with the kind of rhetorical flourish which showed that he had lost none of that literary flair that had inspired George Washington's men on the Delaware, and later at Valley Forge:

Already the conviction that government by representation is the true system of government is spreading itself fast in the world. The reasonableness of it can be seen by all. The justness of it makes itself felt even by its opposers. But when a system of civilization, growing out of that system of government shall be so organised that not a man or woman born in the Republic but shall inherit some means of beginning the world, and see before them the certainty of escaping the miseries that under other governments accompany old age, the revolution of France will have an advocate and an ally in the heart of all nations. An army of principles will penetrate where an army of soldiers cannot; it will succeed where diplomatic management would fail: it is neither the Rhine, the Channel, nor the ocean that can arrest its progress: it will march on to the horizon of the world, and it will conquer. (p. 20)

How true. Representative democracy, universal suffrage, and social welfare schemes were indeed later to spread all over the world: such is the power of ideas. But the process of assimilation of these ideals was a lengthy one, and indeed is still not complete. Here, Paine was at least 200 years ahead of his time. But his most remarkable proposition was surely the idea that the nation state owed some kind of duty of care to all its citizens, and that it was national, not local government, that should provide this care, out of a general taxation levied on all. Paine's 'welfare state' was surely the most revolutionary of all his proposals, and the first of its kind.

Just a year earlier, however, soon after his release from the Luxembourg in November, 1794, Paine had published Part I of the work that was to do his reputation more harm than any other. This was his notorious *Age of Reason*, which gave Paine's views on religion, and included an all-out attack on the authenticity of biblical accounts, on Christianity, and indeed on all forms of organised religion, both Christian and non-Christian. It was a very long work indeed, more than ten times as long as his *Agrarian Justice*, running to some 208 pages. In fact the writing of it stretched over several years, with Paine publishing Part II in October, 1795, and Part III only in 1807, just two years before his death on June 8th, 1809, making Part III the last of his major works to appear. Again, a complete 1880 edition of *The Age of Reason* is available on line in a pdf version, edited by Charles Bradlaugh, and page citations are taken from that edition.

Like *Agrarian Justice*, *The Age of Reason* was penned initially for the French nation, and French translations of both works appeared hard on the heels of his English versions. Paine was prompted to begin this work while he was serving as a deputy in France's National Convention in 1793, because he feared that under Robespierre and the Jacobins France was plunging headlong into atheism. Paine knew how damaging this would be to the reputation of the Revolution, but in addition it offended his own sentiments, for Paine was no atheist. Part I was evidently written in some haste, as it became clear that the Jacobins viewed Paine with increasing suspicion as a secret royalist and foreign spy. By the December of 1793 it had become clear that Paine would be arrested, and he hurried to finish Part I. He explained his position at the beginning of Part II.

> Conceiving this, that I had but a few days of liberty, I sat down and brought the work to a close as speedily as possible; and I had not finished it more than six hours in the state it has since appeared before a guard came there about three in the morning with an order, signed by the two Committees of Public Safety and Surety-General, for putting me in arrest as a foreigner, and conveyed me to the prison of the Luxembourg. I contrived, in my way there, to call on Joel Barlow, and I put the manuscript of the work into his hands, as more safe than in my possession in prison; and not knowing what might be the fate in France of either the writer or the work, I addressed it to the protection of the citizens of the United States. (Ibid., p. 55)

Joel Barlow (1754-1812) was an American poet, diplomat, and political thinker who was at that time stationed in France. The latest research has attributed to him the famous quote, 'Without the pen of Paine, the sword of Washington would have been wielded in vain', that has traditionally been attributed to John Adams, America's second president. (H.J. Kaye, *Thomas Paine and the Promise of America* (2006) p. 5) In fact, Adams hated Paine, and would have been the last man to praise him.

At the opening of Part I of *The Age of Reason* Paine initially explained his motivation for writing the work in tactful enough language on page one.

> The circumstance that has now taken place in France, of the total abolition of the whole order of priesthood, and of everything appertaining to compulsive systems of religion, and compulsive articles of faith, has not only precipitated my intention, but rendered a work of this kind exceedingly necessary, lest in the general wreck of superstition, of false systems of government, and false theology, we lose sight of morality, of humanity, and of the theology that is true.

Paine then went on, however, on the same page, to be far from tactful, writing,

> As several of my colleagues, and others of my fellow citizens of France, have given me the example of making their voluntary and individual professions of faith, I also will make mine; and I do this with all that sincerity and frankness with which the mind of man communicates with itself.
>
> I believe in one God, and no more, and I hope for happiness beyond this life.
>
> I believe in the equality of man; and I believe that religious duties consist in doing justice, loving mercy, and endeavouring to make our fellow creatures happy.
>
> But, lest it be supposed that I believe many other things in addition to these I shall, in the progress of this work, declare the things I do not believe, and my reasons for not believing them. (1880 edition, p. 1.)
>
> I do not believe in the creed professed by the Jewish church, by the Roman church, by the Greek church, by the Turkish church, by the Protestant church, nor by any other church that I know of. My own mind is my own church. All national institutions of churches, whether Jewish, Christian, or Turkish, appear to me no other than human inventions, set up to terrify and enslave mankind, and monopolise power and profit.
>
> I do not mean by this declaration to condemn those who believe otherwise; they have the same right to their belief as I have to mine. But it is necessary to the happiness of man that he be mentally faithful to himself. Infidelity does not consist in believing or in disbelieving, it consists in professing to believe what one does not believe. (Ibid., p. 2)

According to his own account, Paine's scepticism about established religions in general and Christianity in particular went back to his childhood. When he was 'about seven or eight years of age' he heard a sermon preached on the theme of salvation through belief in Jesus Christ. He wrote of his reaction to it,

After the sermon was ended, I went into the garden, and as I was going down the garden steps (for I perfectly recollect the spot) I revolted at the recollection of what I had heard, and thought to myself that it was making God Almighty act like a passionate man that killed his son when he could not revenge himself in any other way; and as I was sure a man would be hanged that did such a thing, I could not see for what purpose they preached such sermons. This was not one of those thoughts that had anything in it of childish levity; it was to me a serious reflection arising from the idea I had that God was too good to do such an action, and also too mighty to be under the necessity of doing it. I believe in the same manner to this moment; and I moreover believe that any system of religion that has anything in it that shocks the mind of a child cannot be a true system. (Ibid., p. 37)

However, it was Christianity as it was being currently practised that was Paine's target in the *Age of Reason* rather than the person of Christ himself. As a deist he denied the divinity of Christ and the idea that salvation could come only through Christ, but about Jesus himself he was fairly complimentary, as in the two passages below.

Nothing that is here said can apply, even with the most distant disrespect, to the *real* character of Jesus Christ. He was a virtuous and an amiable man. The morality that he preached and practised was of the most benevolent kind; and though similar systems of morality had been preached by Confucius, and by some of the Greek philosophers many years before; by the Quakers since; and by many good men in all ages, it has not been exceeded by any. (Ibid., p. 5)

That such a person as Jesus Christ existed, and that he was crucified, which was the mode of execution at that day, are historical relations strictly within the limits of probability. He preached most excellent morality and the equality of man; but he preached also against the corruption and avarice of the Jewish priests, and this brought upon him the hatred and vengeance of the whole order of priesthood. (Ibid., pp. 6-7)

The Christian church, on the other hand, was a different matter.

...with the assistance of some old stories the church has set up a system of religion very contradictory to the character of the person whose name it bears. It has set up a system of pomp and of revenue in pretended imitation of a person whose life was humility and poverty. (Ibid., p.19)

Paine then went on to dismiss all the scriptures as so much nonsense and mythology.

Whenever we read the obscene stories, the voluptuous debaucheries, the cruel and tortuous executions, the unrelenting vindictiveness, with which more than half the Bible is filled, it would be more consistent that we called it the word of a Demon than the word of God. It is a history of wickedness that has served to corrupt and brutalise mankind: and for my own part, I sincerely detest it, as I detest everything that is cruel. (Ibid., p. 12)

Where then, may we hear the authentic word of God? Paine gives the pantheist's answer.

THE WORD OF GOD IS THE CREATION THAT WE BEHOLD, and it is in *this word*, which no human invention can counterfeit or alter, that God speaketh universally to man. (Ibid., p. 21)

It is only in the CREATION that all our ideas and conceptions of *a word of God* can unite...It preaches to all nations and to all worlds, and this *word of God* all that is necessary for man to know of God.

Do we want to contemplate his power? We see it in the immensity of the Creation. Do we want to contemplate his wisdom? We see it in the unchangeable order by which the incomprehensible whole is governed. Do we want to contemplate his munificence? We see it in the abundance with which he fills the earth. Do we want to contemplate his mercy? We see it in his not withholding that abundance, even from the unthankful. In fine, do we want to know what God is? Search not the book called the Scripture, which any human hand might make, but the Scripture called the Creation. (Ibid., p. 22)

Those views brought Paine close to pantheism, but in the end he retained a belief in a personal God and an afterlife. On pages 26-7 there are echoes of Spinoza in what Paine has to say about geometry, and he does in fact mention Spinoza later on page 89. Paine then goes on to show a lively interest in science, mentioning Newton and Descartes, and relating how he bought 'a pair of globes' (presumably terrestrial and celestial) as soon as he could afford them, and later an orrery, a hand-cranked working model of the solar system. He adds that he,

...attended the philosophical lectures of Martin and Ferguson, and became afterwards acquainted with Dr. Bevis of the society called the Royal Society, then living in the Temple, and an excellent astronomer. (Ibid., p. 36)

He then goes on to extol the wonders of nature in this world as proof of God's existence, and concludes from his study of astronomy that,

The probability therefore is that each of those fixed stars is also a sun, round which another system of worlds or planets, though too remote for us to discover, performs its revolutions as our system of worlds does round our central sun. (Ibid., p. 36)

This was a very bold conclusion for the times, but it would now seem that in this as in so much else, Paine was once again entirely correct. Part I was only 53 pages long in the 1880 edition, and towards the end of it Paine provides a good summary of his deist-inspired philosophy.

That seeing as we daily do the goodness of God to all men, it is an example calling upon all men to practise the same towards each other, and consequently that everything of persecution and revenge between man and man, and everything of cruelty to animals, is a violation of moral duty. (Ibid., p. 53)

We hear echoes of Bentham here in Paine's remarkable humanitarianism, which extended not only to all mankind, but to all sentient creatures.

Part II begins on p. 54 of the 1880 edition, and early on Paine makes the remarkable confession that he wrote Part I without having a Bible to hand, but rather relying entirely on his own memory of scripture. Since Part I was written in France Paine might have been unable to lay hands on a Bible in English, but clearly he did not keep a personal copy that he carried with him. This could well have been because of his extremely low opinion of the Bible, an opinion that he makes abundantly clear in *The Age of Reason*. He did, however, have a Bible to hand for Part II, and as part of his reply to the many critics of his Part I, he writes,

> They will now find that I have furnished myself with a Bible and Testament, and I can say also that I have found them to be much worse books than I had conceived. If I have erred in anything in the former part of *The Age of Reason* it has been by speaking better of some parts of those books than they deserved. (Ibid., pp.56-7)

Paine has no difficulty in finding many passages in the Old Testament where the Jews are ordered to massacre their enemies, men, women, and children, sparing none. Paine writes,

> The Bible tells us that these assassinations were done *by the express command of God*. To believe, therefore the Bible to be true, we must *unbelieve* all our belief in the moral justice of God: for wherein could crying or smiling infants offend? And to read the Bible without horror, we must undo everything that is tender, sympathising, and benevolent in the heart of man. Speaking for myself, if I had no other evidence that the Bible is fabulous than the sacrifice I must make to believe that it is true, that alone would be sufficient to determine my choice. (Ibid., p. 58)

Paine quotes from Numbers 3:17-18, which relates to the aftermath of a great victory by the Israelites over the Midianites. The Israelite captains returned, expecting praise from Moses, but instead faced his wrath because they had been too merciful in sparing women and children from the carnage.

> 17 Now therefore kill every male among the little ones, and kill every woman that hath known a man by lying with him.
>
> 18 But all the women children, that have not known a man by lying with him, keep alive for yourselves.

It could well have been by hearing stories like that from the Old Testament that Muhammad was prompted to declare open season on all female captives of his own wars. (Koran 4:24) God obviously approved of such behaviour. However, Paine took a different view, writing,

Among the detestable villains that in any period of the world have disgraced the name of man, it is impossible to find a greater than Moses if this account be true. Here is an order to butcher the boys, to massacre the mothers, and to debauch the daughters. (Ibid., p. 69)

Paine continues in this vein for many pages: the Pentateuch was not written by Moses, nor the Book of Joshua by Joshua, the Old Testament is fabulous, fanciful, and unhistorical, the book of Job was not written by a Jew and does not belong in the canon at all, Solomon's Songs are 'amorous and foolish enough'; Isaiah 7:14 does not foretell the birth of Christ, the virgin birth is 'a fraud', etc. etc.

It would seem that Paine could hardly have been more inflammatory than he was up to this point, but on p. 114 of Part II he turns his attention to the New Testament, pointing out the contradictions that may be found in the Gospel accounts of the four evangelists. Paine correctly stated that the authors of all four books are unknown, and that they were all written long after the death of Jesus by people who had never met him. The resurrection and ascension are fraudulent and contrary to reason, many of Paul's epistles are forgeries (this is now believed to be true), and much of the story of Jesus is pure invention. The whole New Testament is dismissed out of hand.

Of all the systems of religion that ever were invented, there is none more derogatory to the Almighty, more unedifying to man, more repugnant to reason, and more contradictory in itself, than this thing called Christianity. Too absurd for belief, too impossible to conceive, and too inconsistent for practice, it renders the heart torpid, or produces only atheists or fanatics. (Ibid., p. 147)

He concludes Part II with this summary.

I have shown, in all the foregoing parts of this work, that the Bible and Testament are impositions and forgeries; and I leave the evidence I have produced in proof of it, to be refuted, if anyone can do it; and I leave the ideas that are suggested in the conclusion of the work to rest in the mind of the reader; certain as I am that when opinions are free, either in matters of government or religion, truth will finally and powerfully prevail. (Ibid., p. 152)

In his final conclusion above Paine was once again right, but it takes us a very long time to finally arrive at those correct conclusions, and in terms of our political and economic thought we still have a good way to go. Although Paine did not publish the third and final part of *The Age of Reason* until 1807, he had completed it by at least 1802, but delayed its publication on the advice of Thomas Jefferson, a fellow deist and personal friend. It was wise advice. Jefferson had probably hoped that Paine would not publish Part III at all! Paine was already in enough trouble over Parts I and II, which had badly damaged his reputation and credibility in both Britain and America. By 1799 alone more than 50 indignant replies to Parts I and II had already been published, and refutations continued to appear until at least 1812. The most celebrated of these was one of the earliest, *An Apology for the Bible in a Series of Letters to Thomas Paine* (1796). This was penned by Richard Watson (1737-1816) then Bishop of Landaff, but erstwhile Regius Professor of Theology at Cambridge University. It consisted of ten letters in all, and the whole document is available online. It demonstrates that, despite the devastating criticisms launched by Paine, the Christians were still capable of coming back with counter arguments in defence of the Bible.

Paine's decision to press ahead with the publication of Part III, against the advice of his friend Jefferson, was an act of reckless bravado on his part. Paine was utterly convinced that he and he alone could see the truth of things, and that he had a sacred duty to share these truths with the world. To be fair, Paine indeed usually *was* right, but it would also be true to say that his arrogance knew no bounds.

Part III, which begins on p. 153 of the 1880 edition, is headed, 'To the Ministers and Preachers of all Denominations of Religion'. It is once again as offensive to Christians as Paine can make it. He writes,

> One set of preachers make salvation to consist in believing. They tell their congregations that if they believe in Christ, their sins shall be forgiven. This, in the first place, is an encouragement to sin, in a similar manner as when a prodigal young fellow is told his father will pay all his debts, he runs into debt the faster, and becomes the more extravagant. Daddy, he says, pays all, and on he goes. Just so in the other case, Christ pays all, and on goes the sinner.

After this provocative introduction, Paine then goes on to provide us with 'An Essay on Dreams', since dreams of one form or another figure so prominently in both the Old and New Testaments. On dreams Paine quotes the opening of Chapter 34 of Ecclesiasticus, now considered to be part of the Apocrypha and no longer included in Protestant Bibles.

> Vain hopes delude the senseless, and dreams give wings to a fool's fancy. Paying heed to dreams is like clutching at a shadow, or chasing the wind.

On p. 161 Paine turns to, 'An Examination of the Passages in the New Testament'. This section is devoted almost entirely to showing that all the so-called prophesies relating to the coming of Christ in the Old Testament did not relate to the coming of Christ at all! Paine was on strong ground here, for the first Christians were in fact simply heretical Jews, desperate to prove that Jesus really was their long-awaited Messiah prophesised in the Old Testament, and they were quite prepared to interpret, or re-interpret, or distort, many OT passages to suit their aims. The section concludes with another paean of praise for the cult of deism, celebrating the creation as the only true word of God. It is here that Paine draws on support from the writings of Conyers Middleton. The section ends on p. 206 with this extremely provocative declaration, spelled out in capital letters.

> HE THAT BELIEVES IN THE STORY OF CHRIST IS AN INFIDEL TO GOD.

Paine then indulges himself in a short section headed, 'Contradictory Doctrines between Matthew and Mark', before concluding on quite a different tack with, 'Private Thoughts of a Future State'. Here again Paine has views that are entirely his own, writing,

> My own opinion is that those whose lives have been spent in doing good and endeavouring to make their fellow-mortals happy – for this is the only way in which we can serve God – will be happy hereafter; and that the very wicked will meet with some punishment. But those who are neither good nor bad, or are not too insignificant for notice, will be dropped entirely. (Ibid., p. 208)

This highly enigmatic statement badly needed elucidation, but Paine provides us with none. Instead he concludes Part III with a small paean of self praise, simply saying of the above passage,

> This is my opinion. It is consistent with my idea of God's justice, and with the reason that God has given me, and I gratefully know that he has given me a large share of that divine gift. (Ibid., p. 208)

Surely no other man alive at that time could have done quite such a thorough hatchet job on both the Old and the New Testaments as Thomas Paine. None would have possessed that rare combination of the courage, the inclination, and the ability to do so. As Paine himself observed at the opening of Part III,

> It is the duty of every man, as far as his ability extends, to detect and expose delusion and error. But nature has not given to everyone a talent for that purpose; and among those to whom such a talent is given, there is often a want of a disposition or of the courage to do it. (*ibid.*, p. 152)

But Paine of course went too far. As with *Common* Sense, he made no attempt to present a fair and balanced appraisal, but sought only to write a rousing piece of propaganda. Speaking of the Old Testament, he declared, 'For my own part, I do not believe there is one word of historical truth in the whole book'. (Ibid., p. 179) He deliberately set out to shock, hoping in this way to jolt people out of their complacency, and force them to think. In reality, however, the Old Testament, although heavily laced with mythology and many historical inaccuracies, is not *entirely* unhistorical. There probably was an 'Egyptian captivity' and a 'Babylonian captivity' when at least a portion of the Jewish people were carried off to slavery in Egypt and Babylon. Joshua was probably a real historical figure, and there probably was a great battle at Jericho in his time. Paine himself seemed to acknowledge some historical truth in the Old Testament when he accepted that,

> On the death of Solomon the Jewish nation split into two monarchies, one called the kingdom of Judah, the capital of which was Jerusalem, the other the kingdom of Israel, the capital of which was Samaria. The kingdom of Judah followed the line of David, and the kingdom of Israel that of Saul; and these two rival monarchies frequently carried on fierce wars with each other. (Ibid, p. 163)

As for the New Testament, although it too contains its share of mythology, as observed above in the chapter on Religion, Jesus did not become one of the most famous and influential people in the history of the world by saying nothing of any importance. Paine went out of his way in *The Age of Reason* to be as offensive as possible to all Christians, but sought to justify his approach in the following terms:

> In writing upon this, as on every other subject, I speak a language full and intelligible. I deal not in hints and intimations. I have several reasons for this. First, that I may be clearly understood. Secondly, that it may be seen that I am in earnest; and thirdly because it is an affront to truth to treat falsehood with complaisance. (Ibid., p. 196)

Indeed, it was this very ability 'to be clearly understood' that made Paine so dangerous in the eyes of the Establishment of the day. His book was issued in pamphlet form, one section at a time, at a very low cost which most people, even of modest means could afford, and again Paine waived all royalties to keep its cost down. Neither Bible criticism nor deism were new ideas in themselves, but hitherto writings on such matters had appeared only in ponderous, expensive tomes which had been read only by the wealthy and highly educated.

The cult of deism, in one form or another, could be traced back as far as the days of Arius of Alexandria (c250-336 AD), and the so-called 'Arian controversy'. Was Jesus actually God in another form? Or was he divine although not God himself, but rather the creation of God? Or was he not divine at all? This controversy raged between the Council of Nicaea of 325 to the Council of Constantinople in 381, with the Roman Church eventually settling on the Trinitarian view which has been generally accepted by most Christians ever since. With the Reformation of the sixteenth century, however, many heresies emerged, with some sects breaking away from the Roman Catholic Church altogether. One such heretic was Fausto Sozzini (1539-1604), an Italian theologian from Siena, who rejected the concept of the Trinity, and denied the divinity of Christ. His doctrine became known as Socinianism, and gave rise to the Unitarian sects that emerged in Poland, England, and elsewhere in the Europe of the seventeenth century. By the early eighteenth century deism had found several intellectual supporters in England, including Matthew Tindal

(1657-1733), John Toland (1670-1722), Peter Annet (1693-1769), and Conyers Middleton (1683-1750) who was quoted extensively by Paine in Part III of *The Age of Reason*. Nor was trenchant Bible criticism a new departure: Spinoza had done as much in his *Tractatus Theologico-Politicus*. But Paine was seen as being more dangerous than any of them, because he put his subversive ideas, both religious and political, into the hands of the masses, written in 'vulgar' language that they could readily understand.

By moving first to France and then to America Paine kept himself out of the hands of the British authorities, but those who printed and distributed his works were savagely punished, notably during the sedition and treason trials of 1792-4. However, persecution of Paine's publishers continued for long after this. One celebrated case was that of Richard Carlile (1790-1843) who was prosecuted for blasphemy and seditious libel after publishing Paine's complete works in 1818. He was found guilty, and remained in prison from 1818 to 1825.

In *The Rights of Man* Paine wrote, 'I followed exactly what my heart dictated. I neither read books, nor studied other people's opinions. I thought for myself.' (p. 241) This may have been true at the time, but of all Paine's works, there is none that more clearly gives the lie to his claim that he was an unread man, who simply thought for himself, than *The Age of Reason*. Here Paine refers to a plethora of ancient and modern writers including Homer, Herodotus, Josephus, Aesop, Euclid, Addison, Defoe, Cervantes, Swift, Middleton, and even Spinoza. Paine may have been comparatively unread when writing *Common Sense*, but certainly not by the time he had completed *The Age of Reason*.

Had Paine never written *The Age of Reason* he might simply have become the object of unqualified admiration in three countries and two continents as a great political, social, and economic thinker. But the Christians could never forgive him for rubbing their noses in the fact that, integral to their faith, they were required to believe 'six impossible things before breakfast', and indeed a good deal more than six. For them, his merits were totally eclipsed by his blasphemy and disrespect for established religions. In puritanical, Bible-thumping America this led the majority to forget all of his services to political thought and the American Revolution, and to remember only his views on theology. John Adams (1735-1826) who served as American President from 1797 to 1801, wrote to Benjamin Waterhouse in a letter dated October 29th 1805,

> I am willing you should call this the Age of Frivolity as you do, and would not object if you had named it the Age of Folly, Vice, Frenzy, Brutality, Daemons, Buonapart, Tom Paine, or the Age of the Burning Brand from the Bottomless Pit, or anything but *The Age of Reason*. I know not whether any man in the world has had more influence on its inhabitants or affairs for the last thirty years than Tom Paine.

There can be no severer satyr on the age. For such a mongrel between pig and puppy, begotten by a wild boar on a bitch wolf, never before in any age of the world was suffered by the poltroonery of mankind, to run through such a career of mischief. Call it then the Age of Paine. (Quoted in J. Fruchtman, *The Political Philosophy of Thomas Paine* (2009) p.3)

Paine later came to be admired by many prominent Americans, including Abraham Lincoln, Mark Twain, and Thomas Edison, but others were still decrying him even in the early twentieth century. In 1888 in his *Life of Governor Morris* Theodore Roosevelt (1858-1919), who served as President of the United States from 1901 to 1909, famously described Paine as 'a filthy little atheist'. Over the next 30 years he had to endure numerous calls from various quarters to retract his libel, but he consistently refused to do so. In 1918, in a series of letters to William van der Weyde (available online) he was at last persuaded to a partial retraction, but only with great reluctance.

Throughout his writings we can detect in Paine a lively interest in science and in economics. Whenever possible Paine always tried to quantify in so far as he was able to do so. In 1796 he published a short pamphlet entitled, *The Decline and Fall of the English System of Finance* which was concerned with the rapidly increasing public debt of Britain, the rising inflation, and the issuing of paper money. Paine firmly believed in 'sound money' for both Britain and America, and predicted that the British system of finance would eventually collapse under the strain of war. In later years, his fears appeared to be well founded. In 1815, after two decades of war, the British national debt exceeded 200% of GDP, a figure higher than any ever reached before. Yet remarkably, Britain survived this crisis, thanks to an unprecedented rate of economic growth as the Industrial Revolution took off after 1815. But perhaps Paine's words on the importance of sound money were eventually heeded however, for Britain returned to the gold standard in 1821.

Although Paine during his lifetime had enjoyed citizenship in three countries, he felt a special allegiance to none. He saw himself as being detached from nationalism, just as he was detached from any form of established religion: in his own mind, he owed allegiance to nothing but the truth as he saw it. He declared in Part II of *The Rights of Man*, 'My country is the world, and my religion is to do good'. (Pelican edition, (1971) p. 250) Just how thoroughly Paine felt himself to be detached from national allegiances was well illustrated in 1797 when he met Napoleon, who was then nothing more than a successful French general, commander of the Army of Italy. Paine discussed with him a plan for the invasion of England, and in December 1797 wrote a pamphlet with the threatening title, *Observations on the Construction and Operation of Navies with a plan for an Invasion of England and the Final Overthrow of the English Government*. This in part reflected Paine's despair at the fact that the English people had failed to follow the examples of America and France, and had shown no signs of rising against their obviously corrupt and self-interested government. Instead, they had allowed their nationalism to dominate their feelings after the outbreak of war with France in 1793. Although Paine had earlier expressed his distaste for violent revolutions (*Rights of Man*, Pelican ed. (1971) pp. 278, 292) he was not a pacifist, and was coming to the view that the power of the landed classes in England was so firmly entrenched that only a violent revolution or a foreign invasion could overthrow it. This was certainly true in 1797. It took another century and a half to break that power completely, and even in 2020 we see it returning in another form, as will be explained below. If it came to a choice between nationalism and the principles in which Paine believed, there was no doubt where his allegiance would lie.

This point was further illustrated in 1798 when, while still in France, Paine wrote an article for *Le Bien Informé* advising the French government on how best to conquer America! This was little more than a petulant gesture from Paine, reflecting his disgust with John Adams, who was then President of the United States. Paine believed that Adams, a Federalist, had betrayed the principles of both the American and French Revolutions. He disapproved of the American constitution's establishing of a one-man executive, believing that this smacked too much of monarchy. He also decried its failure to impose universal manhood suffrage upon all the states, instead leaving each one to draw up its own franchise. None opted for universal suffrage, and of course the constitution had done nothing to abolish slavery in America. He was also suspicious of the centralising, anti-democratic tendencies of Washington, Adams, and the Federalists, and their preference for a hierarchical social and political system, fearing that they would simply resurrect another version of the Old World in the New. Adams felt a reciprocal revulsion for Paine, seeing him as a dangerous radical and a force for instability: the two men hated one another. It was only after Adams had ended his term and the Democratic-Republicans, led by Paine's friend and fellow deist Thomas Jefferson (1743-1826) had come to power in 1801, that Paine felt able to go back to America. Although a deist, Jefferson very wisely kept his views to himself and attended Christian services, but Paine was sure that Jefferson would uphold 'republican principles'.

Great landowner and slave owner though he was, Jefferson himself announced that his intention was to engineer 'a second American Revolution', and he immediately set about dismantling everything that the Federalists had stood for, reversing the trend towards strong, centralised government. He repealed three of the four Alien and Sedition Acts passed by the Federalists in 1798, believing these to be a threat to the freedom of the press. The American historian Joyce Appleby tells us that,

> The thoroughness with which Jefferson exorcised from the government the influence of his opponents still astounds. He removed a whole cohort of young Federalists from civil and military offices; he eliminated domestic taxes; he substantially reduced the national debt; he shrank the size of the bureaucracy despite

> the nation's growth in population and territory; he hastened the conveyance of land in the public domain to ordinary farmers; and he replaced Federalist formality with a nonchalance in matters of etiquette that gave daily proof that he was a practising democrat. Not a symbol, a civil servant, or a presidential initiative escaped his consideration as a tool in dismantling the 'energetic' and elitist government of his predecessor. (D. Rubel (ed.), *Days of Destiny* (2001) p. 95)

Jefferson's two successors in the office of president, James Madison and James Monroe, were both men of Jefferson's mind, so that by 1825 'Jeffersonian democracy', what you might call 'grass roots' or 'bottom up' democracy, had become a firmly established part of the American political tradition.

In October, 1802 Paine returned to America at Jefferson's request to live in the state of New York, on his 277 acre farmstead at New Rochelle in Westchester County which a grateful America had gifted to him in 1784. Once there Paine had yet one more last, great service to render to his adopted country. When the opportunity arose in 1803, he urged his friend Jefferson, then President, to proceed with the Louisiana Purchase of land from France, in the teeth of Federalist opposition to the proposal. Using his knowledge of France, Paine wrote to Jefferson on Christmas Day 1802, informing him that Napoleon was desperately short of funds, and would be ready to do a deal, explaining that,

> The French Treasury is not only empty, but the government has consumed by anticipation a great part of the next year's revenue. A monied proposal will, I believe, be attended to.

Jefferson then overruled the constitutional objections of the Federalists, and proceeded to negotiate. In April 1803 Napoleon did indeed agree to the sale, and by December of that year the purchase was complete. Originally French, the Louisiana Territory had been ceded to Spain in 1762, but Napoleon had succeeded in wresting it back to French control in 1800. It was a huge territory, consisting of the whole of the Mississippi-Missouri basin, an area so vast that it doubled the size of the young republic at a stroke. This huge territory was acquired for the relatively trifling sum of fifteen million dollars, surely one of the greatest bargains in history: the land was purchased for just under three cents per acre.

Between 1803 and 1805 Jefferson often invited his old friend to dinners at the White House that were also attended by leading politicians. This was a courageous gesture, for Paine was widely unpopular in America at the time. Not to put too fine a point upon it, after the publication of Part II of his *Age of Reason* in 1795, and his open *Letter to George Washington* in 1796, Paine's name was mud in America. Even Jefferson's own daughters, Mary and Martha, mindful of *The Age of Reason*, were at first appalled at the prospect of receiving 'a Godless atheist' under their roof. They refused to meet Paine, and urged their father to rescind his invitation. But Jefferson replied with dignity, 'Thomas Paine is too well entitled to the hospitality of every American not to cheerfully receive mine'. His daughters later softened their views on Paine, but others were shocked by Jefferson's generosity. William Plumer, a Federalist senator from New Hampshire, noted with dismay that at dinner Paine sat next to the President, talking to him 'with the familiarity of an intimate and an equal'. (J. Keane, *Tom Paine: a Political Life* (1995) p. 470) Although no conclusive evidence has ever been found to prove this as fact, it seems quite likely that both men were Freemasons. At some time between 1803 and 1805 Paine had written *An Essay on the Origin of Freemasonry*, although it was not published until 1810. The deistic theology of the society, and its emphasis on the equality and brotherhood of all men, would have appealed to both Jefferson and Paine, and would account for the familiarity between them. It was true that even 'Jeffersonian democracy' was not radical enough for Paine, since it still allowed slavery and had not established universal manhood suffrage across the country, but Paine blamed the American Constitution for this rather than Jefferson himself. In Paine's eyes, Jefferson could do no wrong, and the feeling was mutual.

The family de Bonneville was to play a prominent role in Thomas Paine's last years. Nicholas de Bonneville (1760-1828) was a printer, bookseller, journalist, writer, and revolutionary. He shared many of the same beliefs as Paine, and the two became fast friends. From 1797 to 1802 Paine boarded with him, his wife, and family in Paris, and became godfather to their three sons, Benjamin, Louis, and Thomas. All went well until 1800, when Nicholas was briefly jailed for libelling Napoleon by likening him to Oliver Cromwell, a comparison which was, in fact, very apt. On his release he found that his printing presses and bookshop had been destroyed, leaving him destitute and under heavy suspicion. He was forced to withdraw from Paris and take refuge with his father in the family home at Evreux in Normandy, where police surveillance kept him under virtual house arrest. Paine then took responsibility for looking after the family in Paris, relying on his own small means. Life was difficult for all of them, however, and when Jefferson invited Paine to return to America, he decided to accept the invitation in the hope of being able to provide a better living for the family on his own small estate there. He could not, of course, abandon Marguerite de Bonneville (1767-1846) and her children, so he took them with him on his voyage to America. The plan was that Nicholas would join them as soon as he could escape from house arrest. However, in the event Nicholas was not able to do this until the fall of Napoleon in 1814.

At New Rochelle Marguerite kept house for Paine, while Paine paid for the education of her children. But life remained difficult for all of them; it was not easy to make a living from the smallholding. In 1808 Paine was forced to sell most of his land for ready cash. In addition his health was deteriorating. New Rochelle lay in the south of Westchester County, just a few miles north of the city of New York, and as his condition deteriorated, Paine moved to the city to be cared for by friends. He ended his days there on June 8th 1809 in Greenwich Village, at 59 Grove Street, where Marguerite Bonneville nursed him in his last illness. Marguerite was a radical feminist who, in the absence of her husband, had reverted to her maiden name of Brazier, which has caused confusion for some historians. In his will Paine left the remainder of his land and wealth to Marguerite and her children.

Also in his will Paine, who had been raised as a Quaker, asked to be buried in the Quaker churchyard at New Rochelle, but the local Quakers denied him his wish. He was instead buried under a walnut tree on his own farm. He had earlier been spitefully denied a vote at New Rochelle as well, on the grounds that he was not a properly registered citizen there. So died Thomas Paine, impoverished, despised, and neglected in the country that he had served so well. In the last analysis, it had been his arrogance that had brought him down, with his insistence on publishing *The Age of Reason* as soon as it was completed. From his point of view as a deist, he was entirely right in what he said, but from the point of view of his own best interests, he was entirely wrong to have it published during his lifetime. He should have taken a leaf from Jefferson's book, and made sure that the work was published only after his death. But Paine's arrogance, and his allegiance to nothing but what he saw as being the truth, were his downfall. His funeral cortège consisted of just six mourners, Marguerite and her two surviving sons, two grateful Negroes, and one Quaker who had attended out of Christian charity. America forgot its heavy debt to Thomas Paine, but the world has not forgotten him. More than anyone else of his time, Paine had the courage to speak truth unto power, reckless with regard to the consequences for himself, and his views on the politics and religion of his day were essentially correct.

Like Spinoza, Paine remained completely untrammelled by the mores of his time. He too thought for himself, and went wherever his reasoning took him. Moreover, just as Paine had boasted of his lack of book-learning, so too he was also proud to boast of his poverty, but in this latter case with far more justification. Paine was emphatically not for sale, and he wanted the world to know it, making a point of not enriching himself. After castigating members of the House of Lords for their selfishness and greed in his *Rights of Man*, Paine went on to declare,

> In stating these matters, I speak an open and disinterested language, dictated by no passion but that of humanity. To me, who have not only refused offers because I thought them improper, but have declined rewards I might with reputation have accepted, it is no wonder that meanness and imposition appear disgustful. Independence is my happiness, and I view things as they are, without regard to place or person. (Pelican ed. (1971) p. 250)

His adopted country of America was the first to conform closely to Paine's political and religious ideals, but over the following 200 years many more countries all around the world were to follow in America's footsteps. Monarchies and aristocracies were abolished, free speech and religious toleration were accepted, republics were set up, slavery was abolished, representative governments were established, and universal voting suffrage, for women as well as men, was gradually adopted. Most nations have also followed America's lead by drawing up written constitutions for themselves, and most have also provided welfare benefits for their citizens. In so far as Paine had advocated all of these measures (except votes for women, to which he would surely not have been opposed) it could be argued that his influence has been immense. Ironically, however, Paine's native land of Britain was one of the slowest to embrace these progressive measures. Even today we are still burdened with a monarchy and House of Lords, and Britain still has no clear, written constitution.

Even more than Carlyle's Robespierre, Paine was in fact 'the sea-green incorruptible' or, if you like, a Robespierre with a human face, unshakable in his convictions, but constant in his humanity. Wolfe Tone (1763-98), the Irish revolutionary leader, met Paine in 1797, when again a plan to invade England was discussed, and had this to say about him in his journal entry for March 3rd.

> I have been lately introduced to the famous Thomas Paine, and like him very well. He is vain beyond all belief, but he has reason to be vain, and for my part I forgive him. He has done wonders for the cause of liberty, both in America and Europe, and I believe him to be conscientiously an honest man. (T. W. Tone, *Memoirs of Theobald Wolfe Tone* (1827) p. 172.

But perhaps we should leave the last word on Paine to H.N. Brailsford (1873-1958) the left-wing journalist, who wrote of him,

> The neglected pioneer of one revolution, the honoured victim of another, brave to the point of folly, and as humane as he was brave, no man in his generation preached republican virtue in better English, nor lived it with a finer disregard for self. (cited in A. J. Ayer, *Thomas Paine* (1988) p. 188)

Albert Einstein, 1879-1955

Albert Einstein must be one of the best documented and most written about persons in the history of the world. Under the terms of his will, Einstein left to the Hebrew University of Jerusalem all of his personal papers and the copyright to them in 1955, but since that time, as more material has come to light, it has been added to the collection. The archive now runs to some 55,000 items, many of them letters in Einstein's own hand, and many of the letters that were written to him. The University has been very generous in making this material available to scholars, and is now in the process of digitalising much of the archive and making it available online. In consequence, although no one has ever counted up all of the books and articles that have been written about Einstein during his life and after his death, they too must run to many thousands. Why then, is there any need to say anything more about him? Well, in the first place Einstein is one of my philosopher heroes, whose scientific work has lent credibility to my philosophical beliefs, and in the second place I have my own particular perspective on Einstein to present. My argument here is that Einstein was not nearly so great a physicist as has been generally assumed, but that he was a much greater philosopher than he is usually given credit for. He was in many ways a flawed human being, but he was very human, a great humanitarian, and a profoundly interesting personality. The most recent definitive biography of Einstein, drawing on the latest available archive material, has been Walter Isaacson's *Einstein: His Life and Universe* (2007). It is a fine piece of work, on the whole very fair to Einstein, but I still feel that Isaacson, a fellow Jew and not a scientist himself, has somewhat overplayed Einstein's prowess as a physicist, as I shall try to prove below.

In 2005 Nigel Rodgers and Mel Thompson jointly authored a book with the intriguing title of, *Philosophers Behaving Badly*. Despite the levity of the title, it is a scholarly and revealing piece of work, featuring the usual suspects: Rousseau, Russell, and Sartre mainly because of their colourful sex lives, Wittgenstein and Heidegger because of character flaws, and a few others. Einstein was not included in their gallery, but perhaps he might have been. Albert was born on March 14, 1879 at Ulm in Wurttemberg, then within the post-1871 German Empire, but in 1880 the family moved to Munich where his father, who was an electrical engineer, set up a company to manufacture electrical equipment that operated on direct current. Einstein's parents, Hermann and Pauline, were both Ashkenazi Jews, but they were non-observant, and quite happy for Albert to attend a Catholic elementary school from the ages of five to eight. He was then transferred to the Luitpold Gymnasium in Munich, where he was intended to finish his primary and secondary education. In 1894, however, when Albert was only fifteen, Hermann found that direct current electrical devices, for which his factory was geared, was rapidly going out of fashion in favour of the more efficient alternating current. After failing to secure a major contract in that year, he was forced to close his factory, and the family moved to Italy, eventually settling in Pavia. After staying on in Munich for a few months to finish that year's schooling, Albert joined his family in Pavia in December, 1894. The following year, at the age of sixteen, Albert sat the entrance examinations for the Swiss Federal Polytechnic in Zurich, a German-speaking part of Switzerland. He failed this entrance exam, despite gaining high marks in maths and physics, and so enrolled at the Argovian Cantonal School in nearby Aarau to the west of Zurich, another gymnasium, again in a German-speaking part of Switzerland, to complete his secondary education in 1895-6. While staying in Aarau he lodged with the family of Professor Jost Winteler, and fell in love with

Winteler's daughter Marie. This was the beginning of a long-term connection between the two families, for Einstein's sister Maja later married Winteler's son Paul, while his close friend Michele Besso married a Winteler daughter, Anna.

In January 1896, with his family's approval, Einstein renounced his German citizenship in order to avoid a spell as an army conscript, a wise move. Later, in February 1901 Einstein took Swiss citizenship, but managed to evade military service in that country as well on the rather dubious medical grounds of 'varicose veins and flat feet'! In September 1896 he passed the Swiss Matura, a certificate of secondary education. Einstein took 13 subjects, getting high grades in 9 of them, including maths, physics, and geometry. Significantly, he also gained a high grade in Italian. It may be that his parents were Italian speakers, for they had no qualms about moving to Pavia and working there. While still only 17, Einstein was then accepted at the Zurich Polytechnic to begin a four-year course for a maths and physics teaching diploma. He left his first love Marie behind, but found that on the maths and physics diploma course there were only ten students, one of whom was Meliva Maric (1875-1948), a Serbian girl and the only woman taking those subjects. Einstein soon found that Meliva, like himself, was interested in extra-curricular physics, on which they read books and had discussions together. It has been suggested that Meliva might even have helped Einstein with the writing of some of his famous 1905 papers, but this seems unlikely, as her mathematical skills were probably not up to it. In 1900, at the end of their four-year course, Einstein was awarded his teaching diploma, but Meliva failed the examination due to her poor grades in maths. She was later to fail the exam for a second time. However, their extra-curricular reading and discussions must have been of inestimable value to Einstein, for they probably took him to the cutting edge of the physics of his day. Moreover, by 1900 their friendship had warmed into love, and Einstein began an affair with Meliva. In 1901 she became pregnant, and returned to the home of her parents at Novi Sad in northern Serbia to have the child early in 1902. It was a daughter, christened Lieserl, but no record survives to say what became of her. It is assumed that she either died in infancy or went for adoption, taking another name. Einstein probably never saw his daughter. There are shades here of Rousseau's treatment of his own illegitimate children!

However, Einstein and Meliva married in January 1903, and in May 1904 their first son, Hans Albert, was born at Bern. Their second son, Eduard, was born in July, 1910 at Zurich. By this time, however, the Einsteins' marriage was in trouble. Meliva had recently discovered that Einstein had been trying to form a relationship with his married cousin Elsa Lowenthal (1876-1936). At the same time Albert had kept in touch with his first love Marie Winteler, writing to her in 1910 while Meliva was pregnant, 'I think about you with heartfelt love every spare minute, and am so unhappy as only a man can be', speaking of his 'misguided love' for Mileva and his 'missed life' with Marie. At this stage, therefore, Einstein was not just two-timing Meliva, but actually three-timing her! Later, things got worse. During the Easter of 1912 while visiting Elsa in Berlin, Einstein rather ungraciously made a play for her sister, Paula. He later apologised to Elsa for this, excusing himself by explaining that Paula had been, 'young, a female, and complaisant'. (Isaacson's translation, p. 173). He evidently felt that this constituted a sufficient excuse. I have not been able to trace this letter in the original German, but I suspect that the term Einstein used to describe Paula would have been *willfahren*, which may indeed be translated as 'complaisant', but is more usually and more accurately translated as 'compliant'! Einstein did in fact begin an affair with Elsa in 1912, while she was still married to Max Lowenthal (1864-1914).

Einstein was clearly a passionate and emotional man who genuinely imagined himself to be in love on numerous occasions, but found it impossible to form a lasting and meaningful relationship with any woman for any period of time. Despite his surviving passionate letters to Meliva from their early days and their two sons, he had clearly grown tired of her by 1912. Einstein demanded a divorce, but Meliva refused to agree. Finally, in July 1914, Albert drew up a set of rules for Meliva that he told her she must abide by if she insisted on their continuing to live together. They were presented in a very cold and clinical fashion. There was to be no sex between them, and further,

A. You must make sure:

That my clothes and laundry are kept in good order and repair.
That I receive three meals regularly in my room.
That my bedroom and office are always kept neat, in particular that the desk is available to me alone.

B. You renounce all personal relations with me as far as maintaining them is not absolutely required for social reasons. Specifically you do without:

My sitting at home with you.
My going out or travelling with you.

C. In your relations with me you commit yourself explicitly to adhering to the following points:

You are neither to expect intimacy from me nor to reproach me in any way.
You must desist immediately from addressing me if I request it.
You must leave my bedroom or office immediately without protest if I so request.
You commit yourself not to disparage me either in word or deed in front of my children. (Isaacson, pp.185-6)

Meliva did put up with these terms for a while, but in June, 1915 she finally left Einstein, taking her two sons with her. They were divorced on February 14,

1919, after having lived apart for some years. Einstein then married Elsa on June 2, 1919, but not before he had first proposed to Elsa's twenty-year-old daughter, Ilse! A remarkable letter has recently come to light, dated May 25, 1918, written by Ilse to her close friend George Nicolai, a medical doctor. Scrawled across the top in large letters is the plea, 'Please destroy this letter immediately after reading it'. But Nicolai did not destroy it, and now it has found its way into the Einstein archive, and is available online. The letter reveals that Einstein had proposed to Ilse the day before, while still technically married to Mileva, and officially engaged to Elsa. Ilse had immediately told her mother of the proposal, and Elsa had nobly offered to release Einstein from his engagement to her and allow him to marry Ilse, if that would make Ilse happy. But Ilse was confused and upset, writing to Nicolai, 'I know that A. Loves me very much, more perhaps than any man ever will: he told me so himself yesterday...It will seem peculiar to you that I, a silly little thing of twenty, should have to decide on such a serious matter: I can hardly believe it myself, and feel very unhappy doing so...Help me!' (Online at 'Einstein, Confused in Love and Sometimes Physics') But Ilse was herself no innocent, having already had an affair with Nicolai. (Isaacson, p. 244)

Einstein was already a distinguished scientist with an obviously bright future ahead of him, but Ilse saw him more as a father figure than as a lover (he was twice Ilse's age) and eventually decided to reject his proposal. Baulked of his designs on the daughter, Einstein had to settle for marrying her mother instead, which of course gave him continuing access to the daughter! Elsa, who was by then a widow, can have had no illusions about what kind of man she was marrying. She wrote in a letter to a friend, 'Such a genius should be irreproachable in every respect: but nature does not behave this way. Where she gives extravagantly, she takes away extravagantly'. By this of course she meant that all of Einstein's talent had been bestowed on his scientific side, leaving very little left for his skill in personal relationships! But she carefully preserved all of his early love letters to her in a folder, sadly labelled, 'Especially Beautiful Letters from Better Days'. (Isaacson, p. 363)

Less than four years after marrying Elsa, Einstein began an affair with his secretary, Bette Neumann, and a string of mistresses followed: an Estella, a Margarete, two called Toni, and an Ethel. In some cases, Einstein did not even bother to conceal these affairs from his wife, declaring that he did not believe men and women to be naturally monogamous. The long-suffering Elsa died at last from heart and kidney problems in December, 1936, aged only 60. Einstein seems to have been genuinely upset by her death, and he never married again. The succession of mistresses continued, however, with some overlapping. One of them, Margarita Konenkova, was later discovered to have been a Russian spy, although this did not come to light until 1998. (Isaacson, pp. 436, 503) The last of these mistresses was Johanna Fantova (1901-81), a librarian 22 years his junior, who stayed with Einstein to the end of his life in 1955. Many of his letters, poems, and cartoons to Johanna are now preserved in the Einstein archive.

Philosophers Behaving Badly? I think that Einstein might just have merited a place in the book. His personal life suggests that he had a devious streak, and was perhaps less than entirely honest. This may be of some relevance when it comes to considering his scientific side. In later life Einstein did not scruple to accept all the credit for an achievement that was far from being entirely his own work, as we shall see.

After graduating from the Zurich Polytechnic in 1900 with his teaching qualification Einstein spent two years searching for a teaching post, but without success. His final grades had been mediocre, barely a pass, and his teachers had thought him lazy, disrespectful, and rather dim, declining to give him good references. Einstein was obliged to survive for two years on temporary teaching posts and some private tuition work. However, at the Zurich Polytechnic Einstein had become friendly with Marcel Grossman (1878-1936), a pure mathematician who was kind enough to lend Einstein his splendid mathematical lecture notes, since Einstein himself had been remiss at lecture attendance. In later life Einstein was often to get by with a little help from his friends, and sometimes with more than a little! In this instance it was Grossmann's father who recommended Einstein for a job at the Swiss Patent Office in Bern, since it seemed unlikely that he would ever find a secure teaching post, and Meliva's pregnancy had made the quest for a permanent job more urgent. Einstein was appointed as a probationary junior clerk, grade III, at the Patent Office in June, 1902. Meanwhile Grossmann had found a teaching post immediately, and in 1902 earned a doctorate from the University of Zurich.

Einstein was to remain working at the Patent Office in Bern for just over seven years, from June 1902 to July 1909. He was, therefore, still working there on March 14, his 30th birthday. He had, however, managed to earn his own PhD in 1905, and in 1908 he had been offered a position as a *privatdozent* at the University of Bern. This was a form of apprentice lectureship, purely a teaching job and not a faculty position with a fixed salary. He did receive some fees from his students, but these were not enough to support a family, so Einstein was obliged to continue working at the Patent Office. In July 1909, however, he was at last offered the post of *professor extraordinarius* at the University of Zurich. As such Einstein had to teach for several hours a week and supervise Ph.D. students, but the salary did enable him to become a full-time academic, and he was at last able to leave the Patent Office.

Einstein's rise from this point was meteoric. In April 1911 he was offered the post of *professor ordinarius* at the University of Prague, a decided step up, and in July 1912 Einstein became a full Professor of Theoretical Physics at the

Zurich Polytechnic, with a little help from Grossmann. In 1914 he was appointed to the very prestigious post of Director of the Kaiser Wilhelm Institute for Physics in Berlin where he remained until 1932, also holding a professorship at the Humboldt University of Berlin. He became a member of the Prussian Academy of Sciences, and in 1916 was made President of the German Physical Society. Here was a meteoric rise indeed for a man who, just a few years earlier, had been a humble clerk, second class from 1906, at the Bern Patent Office! How had this come about?

Einstein had received a little help from his friends. This had begun with his reading and discussions on extra-curricular Physics with Meliva. Then in 1902 Einstein, together with two friends, Conrad Habicht and Maurice Slovine, set up a discussion group which they grandly entitled, 'The Olympia Academy'. The group was later to include Marcel Grossmann, Michele Besso, Paul Ehrenfest, Janos Plesch, and Stephen Wise. Most of the group's members were of Jewish descent. Once again their discussions dealt with the latest ideas in physics, especially with the work of Henri Poincaré, but also embraced literature and philosophy. Einstein was particularly impressed by the works of Spinoza, Hume, and Kant. Moreover, he evidently found his work at the Patent Office to be not too demanding! Einstein had found plenty of time for the reading of Physics journals, as well as discussing the latest ideas with his friends. Thanks to this self-education, Einstein was able to begin to contribute to those journals himself. By the end of 1905, while still a Patent Office clerk grade three, he had published no fewer than 31 articles and reviews in the *Annalen der Physik* and the *Beiblätter zu den Annalen der Physik*, a review journal, of which 23 were on the subject of thermodynamics. Most of these items however, 21 in all, were simply reviews of other people's work, including items in French, Italian, and English.

At this stage it appeared that Einstein was set to specialise in the field of thermodynamics, and this would have been understandable, for the laws of thermodynamics are of fundamental importance to many branches of science. Thermodynamics deals with heat and temperature, and their relationship to energy and work. The importance of these relationships was first grasped by the inventors of early steam engines, the Englishmen, Thomas Savery (1650-1715), Thomas Newcomen (1664-1729), and James Watt (1736-1819), a Scot who spent most of his life in England. All three engines burned coal, but they were extremely inefficient, with the Newcomen engine converting only one per cent of the heat produced by the burning coal into useful work. The only advantages offered by these early engines was the fact that they could be kept running for 24 hours a day, and so could drain mine shafts in circumstances that would have made this difficult or impossible for direct human labour. The Watt engine, with its separate condenser for steam and later use of rotary motion, doubled the efficiency of the Newcomen engine, but still converted only two per cent of its required heat into work. By comparison the internal combustion engines of modern cars are about 25 per cent efficient, with still a lot of heat wasted, but they are light and transportable. Coal-fired power stations are nearly 50 per cent efficient, and steam-cooled combined cycle gas turbine engines can reach 60 per cent efficiency.

Because of the practical importance of thermodynamics, the subject came to be closely studied and subjected to measurement by a number of leading scientists, including Sadi Carnot (1796-1832), James Joule (1818-89), Rudolph Clausius (1822-88), James Clerk Maxwell (1831-79), Ludwig Boltzmann (1844-1906), and William Thomson, better known as Lord Kelvin (1824-1907). By the end of the nineteenth century three key laws of thermodynamics had been established. The First Law related to the conservation of energy, stating that energy, like matter which is a form of energy, could be neither created nor destroyed, but could only ever change its form or its distribution in space. The Big Bang has provided our universe with all the energy that it is ever going to get.

The Second Law of thermodynamics, in its basic form simply states that heat cannot spontaneously flow from a colder body to a warmer body. The adverb 'spontaneously' is significant here, since heat can be forced to flow from a colder body to a warmer one through the use of a cleverly devised heat pump, and the input of a good deal of energy. This is how refrigeration works. But this of course requires human intervention, and does not occur in nature. This sounds very simple, but the implications of this law are profound, for its implication is that heat always flows from a warmer location to a colder location. But heat is a form of energy, which means that concentrations of heat or energy will always tend to disperse into their cooler surroundings, referred to as a 'heat sink'. Now the point is that concentrated, contained heat is use*ful*, because it can be harnessed to perform work, while dispersed heat is use*less*, because it cannot be recovered from the environment without the application of more energy than could be recovered from the dispersed heat. But this dissipation of heat from a concentrated to a dispersed state is characteristic of the entire universe, which began as a very hot and concentrated Big Bang, and has been steadily cooling and dispersing ever since as the universe expanded. The early universe was in a state of uniformity when the whole thing was just a hot plasma of ionised matter and energy, a state of uniformity which represented order of a sort. However, as this plasma cooled into distinct matter and energy it became more disordered in form, and as various types of stars and planets coalesced, more disordered still. This disorder is known by scientists as entropy, and the Second Law states that the entropy of any closed system must always increase with time. The universe as a whole is regarded as a closed system, because it was provided with all the energy it was ever going to get at the time of the Big Bang. But within it, individual entities such as our planet may be regarded as open systems. Within an open system entropy may be driven into reverse by the input of external energy from the environment, such as sunlight, and highly ordered structures such as living things may emerge, but only at the cost of increasing the overall entropy, or heat dispersal, of the universe as a whole. This is still consistent with the second law of thermodynamics, which states that the overall entropy of a closed system must always increase. It is in fact the Second Law that gives direction to the arrow of time, and introduces the principle of irreversibility into nature. A hen's egg is highly ordered, but once it is scrambled it cannot, in any practical sense, be unscrambled.

The Third Law of thermodynamics declares that as the temperature of a system approaches absolute zero, all processes cease and the entropy of the system approaches a minimum value. If there is no change, there can be no disorder, for the system is uniform throughout in a condition of stasis. However, a temperature of absolute zero, believed to be -273.15 degrees Celsius or zero degrees Kelvin (zero degrees Celsius = 273.15 Kelvin) is very difficult to reach, even with the most powerful heat pumps. In his book on thermodynamics, *Four Laws That Drive the Universe* (2007), Peter Atkins tells us that the lowest temperature obtained so far is 0.000,000,000,1 degrees Kelvin (p. 111). The current thinking in this field suggests that extremely high and extremely low temperatures may be effectively the same in terms of producing minimum entropy, since in a totally uniform system no work may be done by the transfer of heat. This is known as the Recurrence Theorem, first put forward by Henri Poincaré (1854-1912) in 1890, and given mathematical credibility by Constantin Carathéodory (1873-1950), using measure theory, in 1919. It suggests that certain systems will, after a long but finite period of time, return to a state very close to their initial state in terms of their entropy. It may be that this will be the pattern of development for our universe if it ends in the deep cold of a heat death, as seems increasingly likely. It would then be moving from one state of very low entropy with the Big Bang to another state of very low entropy with the 'Big Freeze' despite the fact that entropy, i.e. disorder, was increasing between those two stages. This would mean that the Second Law of Thermodynamics would in fact be thrown into reverse in the last stages of the universe. Initially our universe was all heat and energy, in a state of high uniformity and low entropy, but without a heat sink for the thermal energy to flow into, no work could be performed, and no matter could emerge, because no change could take place. It was all heat, but with no heat sink. In its last days, however, it seems likely that our universe will be all heat sink with no heat! The amount of heat/energy in the universe will still be exactly the same as at the time of the Big Bang, but because of the continuing expansion of the universe over trillions of years this heat will then be dissipated over such a vast volume that there will be very little available for any individual part, so that the whole will near a temperature of absolute zero. Therefore, once again there will be high uniformity and low entropy, but again no creative work can be performed, since no heat will be able to flow, bringing an effective end to time.

Although there are in fact four fundamental laws of thermodynamics, there is no 'Fourth Law of Thermodynamics'! This seeming paradox results from the fact that in the early twentieth century scientists decided that there were actually four basic laws of thermodynamics, and not three. But they also believed that the fourth law that they had decided upon was more fundamental than the other three, and so should really have been called the First Law. By that time, however, a vast body of literature had already been produced referring to the First and Second Laws, so that to change the nomenclature at that point would have been too confusing. The new law was therefore bizarrely dubbed the Zeroth Law! It states that if two systems are both in thermal equilibrium with a third, then they are also in thermal equilibrium with each other. This self-evident fact might be thought to be too obvious to be graced with the status of a law, but it is certainly true, and the point is that this law offers an empirical definition of temperature, and therefore a justification for the construction of practical thermometers. The Zeroth Law is in fact crucial for the measurement of heat, and therefore arguably more fundamental than the other three laws.

Personally, I have always felt that equating entropy only with 'disorder' rather demeans the term. It comes from the Greek εν, 'in' and τρόπος, meaning 'turn' or 'change', so increasing entropy implies a dynamic system in which change is happening. Yes, it implies an overall decrease in uniformity, but within this decrease in uniformity, complexity and creativity can arise as a part of the variety associated with increasing entropy. As noted above, within an 'open' system such as is the case with our planet entropy, in its sense of disorder, may be driven into reverse with the aid of an input of external energy, such as that of the sun. In an open system, entropy may be locally diminished so long as this is at the cost of increasing the overall entropy of the universe as a whole, thus preserving the integrity of the second law. Even solar systems represent order of a sort, though of far less complexity than life forms. Increasing entropy implies change, but not necessarily increasing disorder when it comes to individual open systems. As noted earlier, change is life, while stasis is death. Animal life is totally dependent on a process of continual change, not only from the point of view of evolution, but also with regard to the life processes of the animals themselves. Increasing entropy can, therefore, incorporate a process of creativity within itself, which may produce highly ordered entities like ourselves within the context of an increasingly disordered universe. Rather, therefore, than seeing increasing entropy only as a running down, it could also be seen as a building up, a working out of God's purposes for His universe. (I speak as a panentheist here.) It was this ability of life within an open system to locally reverse the second law which so fascinated Erwin Schrödinger in his book, *What is Life?* (1944). Not only can life create order out of chaos, but also increasingly complex order over time, seemingly 'remembering' each step of this growing complexity as it is achieved.

Schrödinger could not understand how this was done, but we now know that it was achieved through the medium of DNA. This will be more fully explained in the Science chapter below. But it seems to me that there is something of a contradiction here. If growing 'entropy' is defined as the steady dispersal of heat from a highly concentrated and potentially useful state where it can be harnessed to perform work to a widely dissipated and useless state where it cannot be, then yes, the second law will apply to the end of time. But 'entropy' is also often also defined in terms of increasing disorder, that is a lack of uniformity. If so, then surely this can apply only up to a certain point in the history of the universe. In its last days the universe must move back to a state of near uniformity again, when all the stars have burned out, the black dwarfs have crumbled to dust, the black holes have evaporated, heat/energy is so widely dispersed that no work can be done, and only a uniform cold and darkness pervade the universe. But we will look at 'entropy' again in the Science chapter below.

Einstein's early fascination with the laws of thermodynamics, reflected in the fact that 23 of his first 31 articles and reviews dealt with this topic, is therefore entirely understandable, in view of the central importance of the subject in the realm of science. In 1905, however, we notice something of a change of direction, although Einstein's new interests were not unrelated to thermodynamics. This was Einstein's so-called *annus mirabilis* year, during which he produced four remarkable papers in quick succession between March 18th and September 27th, all of them appearing in the *Annalen der Physik* (Series 4), Vols. 17 and 18. In order of publication they were,

'On a Heuristic Point of View Concerning the Production and Transformation of Light' (Series 4 Vol. 17) pp.132-48

'On the Movement of Small Particles Suspended in Stationary Liquids Required by the Molecular-Kinetic Theory of Heat' (Series 4 Vol. 17) pp. 549-60

'On the Electrodynamics of Moving bodies' (Series 4, Vol. 17) pp. 891-921

'Does the Inertia of a Body Depend upon its Energy Content?' (Series 4, Vol. 18) pp. 639-641

In the first of these papers, Einstein turned to the theory that light might be transmitted as a series of small quanta of energy rather than as waves. This was not an entirely new idea. As long ago as 1704 Isaac Newton had suggested in his *Opticks* that the physical behaviour of light was due to its 'corpuscular' nature as small particles. In 1900 Max Planck had already surmised that black body radiation, that is thermal radiation emitted from a body mainly in the infra red range of the spectrum, could be seen as being quantised, that is emitted in discreet units, and Einstein acknowledged Planck's work. But in his own paper Einstein extended this theory to light of all wavelengths, suggesting that it too could be seen as being emitted in discrete quanta, despite earlier strong experimental evidence, dating back to 1801 and the famous 'double-slit' experiment of Thomas Young (1773-1829), and the equations of James Clerk Maxwell (1831-79) in the 1860's, which seemed to prove conclusively that light in fact propagated as a wave. Einstein also dealt here with the phenomenon of the photo-electric effect, whereby light of a sufficiently short wavelength falling upon a metal surface could produce cathode rays, by driving electrons from the metal at the points of impact of the light quanta. The light energy, which could be in the form of ultra violet or gamma radiation with a neutral electric charge, was thereby transformed into beta radiation, or cathode rays, (free electrons) with a negative electric charge. Einstein noted that this photo-electric effect was dependent not on the intensity, but only upon the wavelength of the incident light. These points had already been made by Philipp Lenard (1862-1947) who had been working on cathode rays since 1888, and was awarded the Nobel Prize for his achievements in this field in 1905. But Einstein suggested that the constant of proportionality between the frequency of the incident light and the kinetic energy of the electrons emitted might be equal to Planck's constant. This was a figure that had been arrived at by Max Planck just five years earlier, based on a series of careful experiments and calculations, and published in a 1900 edition of the *Annalen der Physik*. Planck had defined it as the energy of a quantum of electromagnetic radiation divided by its frequency. It was a very small figure indeed, a measure of energy equivalent to 6.626070041 x 10-34 joule-seconds, or 4.135667662 x 10-15 electron volts. These were measures of energy appropriate to the atomic and sub-atomic world of quantum physics. The energy equivalent of one quantum of light, which later came to be called a photon, could therefore be expressed as E=hf. 'h' came to be the universally accepted symbol for Planck's constant, and 'f' stood for the frequency of the light, so that the higher its frequency, the greater its energy. Einstein's suggestion about the kinetic energy levels of the emitted electrons was later proved to be correct experimentally in 1914 by the American physicist Robert Andrews Millikan (1868-1952). In fact Millikan was awarded the Nobel Prize in 1923 for his ingenious experimental work in this field, which not only precisely defined the photo-electrical effect, but also enabled him to obtain a more accurate measurement of Plank's constant, a figure that is of fundamental importance in physics. Ironically, in December of the previous year Einstein had also been awarded the Nobel Prize, mainly for his 'discovery' of the law of the photo-electric effect, even although he had only hypothesised about its possible existence. This was in contradiction of the Nobel Committee's understanding at that time that the prize could not be awarded for theoretical work, but only for some confirmed form of 'discovery or invention', as Alfred Nobel had stipulated in his will.

Einstein was not the first to use the term 'quanta'. Planck had already spoken of energy being emitted in discrete units with respect to black body radiation, and Philipp Lenard (1862-1947) had already used the term 'quanta' as measures of energy of the electrons emitted from metals as a result of the photoelectric effect, and had noted the relationship between wavelengths and energy levels. Einstein was, however, the first to apply the term 'quanta' to those ingoing energy packets of light which were finally dubbed 'photons' in 1926 by Gilbert Lewis (1875-1946), and the term was generally accepted by the Physics community in the following year. In his 1905 paper Einstein fully acknowledged all the work of his predecessors in the field, including Maxwell, Planck, Wien, Boltzmann, Stark, Drude, Stokes, and Lenard. It might be argued that Einstein had simply 'joined the dots' here and drawn a logical conclusion from work that had been done by others, but his paper reflected his very wide reading in this field, and the suggestion that all electro-magnetic radiation might be regarded as a stream of particles rather than as a series of waves was a truly revolutionary one for the time. However, Einstein actually proved nothing with his paper: he merely suggested a possibility.

Einstein's second 1905 paper also appeared in Vol. 17 of the *Annalen*, with the title, 'On the movement of Small Particles Suspended in Stationary Liquids Required by the Molecular-Kinetic Theory of Heat' (pp. 549-60) This interesting phenomenon had been noticed as long ago as the days of Titus Lucretius Carus (99-55 BC), the Roman poet and philosopher, in his long poem *De Rerum Natura*, 'On the Nature of Things'. He had surmised even then that it lent support to the atomic theory of Democritus (c. 460-370 BC). However, in modern times the observation is usually credited to Robert Brown (1773-1858), a Scottish botanist, who wrote on it in 1827, so that it became known as Brownian motion. In his paper Einstein drew on the molecular kinetic theory of heat and the kinetic theory of gases, which suggested that a heated gas expanded because extra kinetic energy was imparted to its individual molecules, which then struck more forcefully against the walls of its container. Applying this theory to liquids, Einstein suggested that microscopically visible particles might be seen to be continually jostled by random collisions with the molecules of the liquid, which were themselves in continual motion. Using statistical mechanics, a formulation that had been devised by Ludwig Boltzmann (1844-1906) and most clearly expounded by the American mathematical physicist J. Willard Gibbs (1839-1903) in 1902, Einstein derived expressions for the mean squared displacement of the particles, which gave a figure for the number of molecules in a given volume, and hence a way to actually count atoms. This was a challenging concept at a time when atoms and molecules were being regarded as useful concepts, but physicists and chemists were still debating their actual reality! Indeed the wretched Boltzmann, a great philosopher as well as a physicist who had made an enormous contribution to the science of thermodynamics and had been a strong advocate of atomic theory, hanged himself in 1906 because so many of his colleagues refused to believe in atoms! It is remarkable to reflect that only 40 years later the atomic structure of matter was so well understood that chemists had drawn up the periodic table of elements, and physicists had built the atomic bomb. Only a few years after that, Watson and Crick were able to unravel the molecular structure of DNA, opening a whole new chapter in genetic studies, and indeed in the science of biology itself. Again, however, Einstein was a theorist and not an experimentalist. The suggestions put forward in this 1905 paper were confirmed experimentally a few years later by the French physicist Jean Baptiste Perrin (1870-1942). Perrin was awarded the Nobel Prize in Physics for this work in 1926. Thanks to the work of Einstein and Perrin, by 1913 even the most die-hard disbelievers in the reality of atoms, like Georg Helm (1851-1923) and Wilhelm Ostwald (1853-1932), had surrendered their positions, although in 1897 even the great Ernst Mach (1838-1916) had publically declared, 'I do not believe that atoms exist!'. By 1913 in his book *Les Atomes* Perrin was able to conclude it with the words,

> The atomic theory has triumphed. Until recently still numerous, its adversaries, at last overcome, now renounce one after the other their misgivings, which were for so long both legitimate and undeniably useful.

But note that it was Perrin, not Einstein, who was awarded the Nobel Prize for his work on proving the existence of atoms, because Perrin's work had afforded experimental proof, while Einstein's paper had merely put forward theoretical suggestions.

Einstein's third paper, 'On the Electrodynamics of Moving Bodies', again appeared in Vol. 17 of the *Annalen*, on pages 891 to 921, making it the longest of his four famous articles. This paper referred to the work of only five other scientists, Newton, Maxwell, Hertz, Doppler, and Lorentz, but in fact a good deal of work in this field, which came to be known as that of special relativity, had already been done by others as well, notably Henri Poincaré (1854-1912), George FitzGerald (1851-1901), and Joseph Larmor (1857-1942). Also highly relevant to this field was the Michelson-Morley Experiment, which had first been carried out in 1887 by Albert Michelson (1852-1931) and Edward Morley (1838-1923) in Cleveland, Ohio. It was designed to detect the motion of the Earth through the imagined 'luminiferous aether', that very fine medium which was thought, at that time, to conduct light waves. However, this and many subsequent experiments completely failed to detect any trace of this imagined medium.

Einstein therefore proposed in this paper (quite correctly) that the 'luminiferous aether' did not in fact exist, and that another means would have to be found to reconcile Newtonian mechanics with Maxwell's equations of electromagnetism, which seemed to prove that light was in fact just another wave form of electromagnetic radiation. In this paper Einstein argued that the only thing in the universe that was constant relative to all frames of reference was the speed of light in a vacuum, which remained constant to all observers, regardless of the motion or direction of the light source. This speed had been estimated as early as 1676 by the Danish astronomer Olaus Rømer (1644-1710), who had observed the eclipses of the moons of Jupiter by Jupiter itself as the Earth either approached or moved away from that planet. He had estimated a speed of 140,000 miles per second, or about 220,000 kilometres per second, less than today's figure of 186,000 miles per second or 299,792 kilometres per second, but at least in the right ball park! The French physicist Marie Alfred Cornu (1841-1902) established a figure very close to today's in 1875 by using rapidly rotating mirrors. Einstein argued that Newtonian mechanics were applicable only to objects travelling at a negligible proportion of the speed of light relative to an observer. At near light speeds the observer would witness a length contraction of the moving object, an increase in its relativistic mass, and a time dilation effect. Even the simultaneity of two events, which would appear the same to two stationary observers, would be different at relativistic speeds – the faster one travelled through space, the slower one would travel through time relative to a stationary observer. This theory destroyed the notion of a universal time which applied everywhere, as Newton had believed, replacing it with the idea of time that is dependent on a reference frame and spatial position. In other words, space and time must be viewed as a unity, the space-time continuum, and the only invariant interval between events is the space-time interval.

This theory predicted the famous 'twins paradox', whereby one twin leaves Earth in a spaceship that reaches near light speed, and finds on his return that his twin is then much older than he is, because for the spacefaring twin, time has slowed relative to the passing of time on Earth. Specifically, if a spaceship were to be built that could accelerate continuously at one g (9.81 m/s^2), after one year it would reach 77% of light speed. If an astronaut were to travel on at that acceleration (decelerating from the half-way point) to an object 165 light years from Earth on a 20-year round trip (five years accelerating and five years decelerating twice), he would find on his return that 335 Earth years had passed, while he himself had become only 20 years older. Longer trips at higher accelerations would lead to even more marked time dilation effects, which would seem to rule out the possibility of manned spaceflight to distant stars with planets even within our own galaxy, which is 100,000 light years across. These postulates remained mere theories until the building of the Large Hadron Collider mentioned below in the Science chapter. This machine actually could accelerate particles up to very near light speed, and it was proved both that their mass increased, and that their survival times were greatly extended at these velocities due to the time dilation effect.

Special relativity also postulated that as the speed of an accelerating body increased it would gain kinetic energy, and so mass, until light speed was neared. At that point its mass would be so great that an infinite amount of energy would be required to accelerate it any further, so that the speed of light was, in effect, a universal cosmic speed limit. It is therefore impossible for matter *or information* to travel faster than light. This second proviso is crucial, because since time and speed are so closely related in special relativity, an object travelling faster than light could in theory travel into its own past, and by the same token information could be transmitted from the future to the past. This would violate the law of causality, which states that the cause of an event must always precede the event itself in time. But *special* relativity is called 'special' because it applies only in the special case where the curvature of space-time due to gravity is negligible. In order to incorporate the effects of gravity into his theory, Einstein had to devise the theory of *general* relativity later, in 1915. By the same token, Newtonian mechanics might be said to apply only in those 'special' cases when objects are moving at speeds which are a negligible proportion of light speed, and in relatively weak gravitational fields. Under these conditions Newtonian mechanics give very nearly entirely accurate forecasts, but not quite, as was noted from the apparent anomalies in the orbit of Mercury in Einstein's time.

The fourth and last of Einstein's *annus mirabilis* papers also appeared in the *Annalen*, but this time in Volume 18 for September 27, 1905 on pages 639-41. This made it the shortest of Einstein's 'famous four', in part because its conclusions had already been implied in Einstein's relativity paper, and he was simply spelling out these conclusions more clearly in these last three pages, as Einstein explained in his introduction. He titled the article, 'Does the Inertia of a Body Depend Upon its Energy Content?' This was a rather curious way of wording the title: Einstein did not use the term 'mass', but in this context 'inertia' may be taken as the equivalent of mass. The use of a question mark in the title is also significant, suggesting that the idea of the equivalence of mass and energy had already been put forward by others, as indeed it had. In this paper Einstein acknowledged the previous work of James Clerk Maxwell and Heinrich Hertz, but not the work of others who had already built on their findings. In fact the equivalence of mass and energy had already been implied by the work of other physicists, including that of James Clerk Maxwell as early as 1865, by J.J. Thomson in 1881, by Oliver Heaviside in 1889, and of course by the work on relativity done by Lorentz, Fitzgerald, and Poincaré in the 1890s. Friedrich Hasenohrl (1874-1915) was groping towards the correct formula in two papers published in the *Annalen der Physik* which Einstein could hardly have failed to have read. The first, in Series 4 Vol. 15 pp. 344-70 appeared in 1904, and the second, with a correction, in Vol. 16, pp. 589-92. In these Hasenohrl (not mentioned by Isaacson) first derived the formula $E=3/8\ mc^2$, correcting this to $E=\frac{3}{4}\ mc^2$ in 1905, with 'c' by this time representing the speed of light. But he was clearly moving in the right direction, and both papers appeared before even the first of Einstein's *annus mirabilis* works.

Even more remarkably, a little-known Italian physicist and geologist (not mentioned by Isaacson) Olinto de Pretto (1857-1921) had come even closer to the correct formula in a 62-page article published in the *Atti del Reale Istituto Veneto di Scienze Lettere ed Arti* (*The Proceedings of the Royal Venetian Institute of Science, Letters, and Arts*)Vol. 63, which appeared on November 29, 1903. Einstein was fluent in Italian, and his attention may have been drawn to this article by his Swiss-Italian friend, Michele Besso. Like Hasenohrl, de Pretto (also not mentioned by Isaacson) did not get the maths quite right, declaring that $E=\frac{1}{2}mc^2$, but both men clearly understood the relationship between mass and energy, and that the ratio between them had something to do with c^2. Although this relationship had been implicit in the work of many previous scientists, including James Clerk Maxwell, nobody had wanted to believe it, because the calculations suggested that the amount of energy contained in every gram of matter was just too much to be believable. In fact de Pretto himself found it difficult to believe his own calculations, writing in his 1903 article,

> To what astonishing result has our reasoning brought us? Nobody would easily admit that, stored in a latent state in any kilogram of matter, completely concealed from all our investigations, hides such a sum of energy, equivalent to the amount that can be produced by burning millions and millions of kilograms of coal! The idea would be adjudged crazy. (p. 459)

But Einstein himself also found it difficult to believe that such a relationship could exist: hence the question mark at the end of the last of his *annus mirabilis* papers. In September 1905 he wrote to his friend Conrad Habicht,

> The relativity principle, together with Maxwell's equations, requires that mass be a direct measure of the energy contained in a body. Therefore light carries mass with it. With the case of radium, there should be a noticeable reduction of mass. The thought is amusing and seductive, but for all I know the good Lord might be laughing at the whole matter and might have been leading me up the garden path! (Isaacson, p. 138)

Einstein was being slightly inaccurate here. Photons of course carry no mass, but they do carry energy which may be seen as equivalent, and the emission of radiation may be an indication that the mass of a body is being reduced by changes within it. However, the radioactive decay of radium is so slow that no scales of the time could have noted a reduction in its mass within a reasonable time span. Moreover, Einstein did not actually present in his 1905 paper the famous equation $E=mc^2$. Like Hasenohrl and de Pretto, he did not get it quite right. What he did say, however, in the conclusion to this article was,

> If a body gives off the energy L in the form of radiation, its mass diminishes by L/V^2...the energy being measured in ergs, and the mass in grams. (p. 641)

This sounds a long way from the famous $E=mc^2$ with which Einstein is credited, but this was partly due to the odd nomenclature that he used here. He was using L to represent energy, and V to represent the speed, or velocity, of light. If we simply turn the equation around a bit so as to express it differently while introducing the term 'm' for mass, then we may say that $L=mV^2$. Now here Einstein had used L to represent energy in the form of radiant energy, but in 1912 he crossed this out in a manuscript and replaced it with the more common E. This was because in 1911the German physicist Max von Laue (1879-1960) had by then pointed out that Einstein's radiant energy could be generalised to include all forms of energy. Einstein had earlier replaced his V with c, which had become accepted by then as the common symbol for light speed. So his equation finally emerged as $E=mc^2$ in 1912, with a little help from von Laue. In other words, for any given quantity of mass at rest relative to an observer, that stationary mass represents its inertial mass multiplied by the speed of light squared in terms of its energy equivalent.

But why should the speed of light be squared? Surely this is a ridiculous concept, indicating an enormous speed which could never possibly be reached in reality, since c itself is the cosmic speed limit? The answer is of course that c^2 is simply a mathematical construct, introduced to bring the two sides of the equation into balance. This was necessary because there is an implied squared factor within the symbol E. Einstein measured his energy in ergs, and one erg represents the unit of energy expended when one dyne moves through a distance of one centimetre. But a dyne is a unit of force which produces an acceleration of one centimetre per second every second on a mass of one gram, which is to say that it produces an acceleration rate of one second per second, or one second squared on that mass. This is where the squared element comes into the left-hand side of the equation, requiring a squared factor on the right-hand side to bring the equation into balance.

Of course the above is merely an oversimplification of the full subtlety and implications of $E=mc^2$. As noted above, de Pretto covered 62 pages with calculations to justify his 'astonishing result', while Brian Cox and Jeff Forshaw have written a whole book attempting to explain, *Why does $E=mc^2$?*(2009). On p.143 they remind us that this equation applies only to a body at rest. For a body in motion relative to an observer the full equation should read $E=mc^2 + \frac{1}{2}mv^2$, where v is the speed of motion, adding kinetic energy to the body in question. This is why our astronaught, mentioned above, although he accelerates away from earth at only one g continuously and so feels only earth gravity, would soon reach 77% of light speed relative to an observer on earth, and so would experience a mass increase and time dilation effect relative to the earthbound observer. As noted above, on his round trip he would in fact have aged by only 20 years while 335 years had passed on earth.

As noted in the Science chapter below, matter may be viewed as simply a concentrated form of energy, mainly because it is held together by the strong nuclear force, which binds quarks to quarks, protons to protons, and protons to neutrons within atomic nuclei, and the electromagnetic force, which keeps electrons in their orbits around those nuclei. These forces are unfamiliar to most of us, but gravity is familiar to us all, and can seem to be quite a strong force on some occasions! However, if the force of gravity is taken to be one, then the electromagnetic force is by comparison 10^{36} times stronger, while the strong nuclear force is roughly 100 times stronger than that again! Therefore, when matter is broken apart in nuclear explosions, enormous amounts of energy are released, although in a fission explosion only a small amount of matter is actually converted into energy, the rest being blown away by the power of the blast. The Hiroshima bomb, for example, converted only 0.7 grams of uranium into pure energy: on average, nuclear fission releases only about 0.1% of all the energy in the atoms involved, and nuclear fusion only about one per cent. But this is still a ten-fold increase over fission, which is why the hydrogen bomb gives you, 'a bigger bang for your buck'. The only way to convert a kilogramme of matter into pure energy is to combine it with a kilogramme of antimatter, in which case the two will mutually annihilate into photons. Indeed, so ponderous a process is fusion when it comes to converting matter into energy that Cox and Forshaw, in their book mentioned above, tell us that the sun is, kilogram for kilogram, 5,000 times less efficient at producing energy than is the human body! (p. 172) The sun is currently powered by the fusion of hydrogen into helium, and for every kilogramme of its mass produces only 1/5000 of a watt of power on average. This is because fusion takes place only deep in the heart of the sun, a region occupying only a small percentage of its total volume and mass. The outer plasma layers are indeed very hot, but not because they generate any energy. They are heated only from the radiation generated by fusion in the relatively small core. The human body, on the other hand, while it generates energy only by chemical rather than nuclear reactions, employs its whole body mass for energy production. This means that, kilogramme for kilogramme, for every kilogramme of body mass, the human body generates rather more than one watt of power per kilogramme, or 5,000 times as much as the sun! A watt is a unit of power that generates energy at the rate of one joule per second, or 60 joules a minute, or 3,600 joules in a watt-hour. A kilowatt-hour, familiar to us all on our electricity bills, is of course 1,000 times this amount.

We should also remember, however, that in addition to his famous four papers, Einstein had also managed to write and present his PhD thesis in 1905! It was entitled, 'A New Way to Determine Molecular Dimensions', and was the basis of the second of his *annus mirabilis* papers, which has been explained more fully above. This thesis is available on line in the original German, complete with official stamps, seals, and introductory material, where it may be seen that the text itself is only 17 pages long, and includes only one footnote reference to another published work! The thesis is dated April 30, 1905, but of course if such a paper were to be submitted today for a science PhD, it would be regarded as a joke! However, in 1905 Einstein's examiners, Professor A. Kleiner and Professor H. Burkhardt of the University of Zurich, which examined PhD degrees for the Zurich Polytechnic, were pleased to award him a PhD for it.

This thesis is also available in English, but only in its published form as it appeared as a paper in the *Annalen der Physik* Series 4 Vol. 19 (1906) pp. 289-306. Here it is again only 17 pages long, with only one footnote reference, and as usual it is a theoretical work, based entirely on mathematical calculations, and making a number of provisos and assumptions: Einstein was not a hands-on experimentalist. However, this published version did include an added on supplement referring to experimental work that had recently been done in this field by Landolt, Bornstein, Thovert, and Hosking. Their work showed that although Einstein's methodology for calculating molecular dimensions had been sound, the many provisos and assumptions that he had been forced to make in the absence of hard experimental evidence had left his final calculations very wide of the mark. What Einstein had been trying to do in effect was to establish a figure for Avogadro's Number, a postulate which had been put forward in 1811by the Italian physicist Amedeo Avogadro (1776-1856). It represented the number of atoms or molecules to be found in one mole of any gas, which is a volume of 22.4 litres at standard temperature and pressure. A mole is one of the seven standard SI units of measurement, and therefore of fundamental importance. (The other six are the metre, the kilogram, the second, the ampere, the kelvin, and the candela.) Einstein's initial calculations led him to suggest firstly a number of 3.3x1023, but later new experimental evidence that he was able to draw on enabled him to revise his figure to 6.56x1023, much closer to today's accepted number of 6.022x1023. His revised article appeared in the *Annalen der Physik* for 1911 entitled, 'Correction to my Paper: A New Determination of Molecular Dimensions' (Series 4 Vol. 35 pp. 679-694)

We have to remember that all this remarkable work of 1905 had been done not by an established academic, nor even by a recognised scientist, but by a junior Patent Office clerk, class III! Einstein was not promoted to class II until 1906. Even then, he was still expected to work at the Patent Office for eight hours a day, six days a week. How had all this been possible? There are some who claim that it was not possible at all, and that Einstein had simply plagiarised the work of others. Type into your search engine 'Einstein a plagiarist?' and a plethora of items will appear referring to books and articles which lay this charge at Einstein's door. One of the most forceful is Christopher Jon Bjerknes' *Albert Einstein: The Incorrigible Plagiarist* (2002). There is a note of hysteria, anti-Semitism, and fanatical hatred of Einstein in many of these charges, but at the same time there is some truth behind them.

One of the most interesting of these can be read online at www.biblebelievers.org.au/einstein.htm. The 'Believers' are clearly a rabidly right-wing, anti-Semitic sect of Christian fundamentalists, but with regard to all the work that had already been done by others on Einstein's *annus mirabilis* topics before 1905, what the 'Believers' have to say is essentially true. Einstein was obviously very well read in the journal literature of the time, in French, Italian, and English as well as German, as was shown by the many reviews that he wrote for the *Beiblätter*, and it was a little dishonest of him not to mention all the work on relativity that had already been done by the most famous physicist of the day Henri Poincaré (1854-1912), of which Einstein could not have been unaware. Nor did he mention the work of the Irishmen George Fitzgerald (1851-1901) and Joseph Larmor (1857-1942) in this field, and he glossed over with hardly a mention the vital work on relativity done by the Dutchman Hendrick Lorentz (1853-1928). Every scientist draws on the work of his predecessors, but the honest scientist will fully acknowledge their contribution to his own work. In fact, in 1904 Lorentz had already published 'Electromagnetic Phenomena in a System Moving with Any Velocity Smaller Than That of Light' in the *Proceedings of the Royal Netherlands Society of Arts and Sciences* Vol. 6 pp. 809-31. (Not mentioned by Isaacson) Here Lorentz had presented a series of equations that came to be known as the 'Lorentz transformations'. These transformations are key to the whole theory, but to this day they are still referred to as 'Lorentz transformations', and not 'Einstein transformations'. These described mathematically the increase of mass, the contraction of length, and the relative slowing of time for a body moving at near light speed. Working with the Irishman George Fitzgerald they had already calculated the length shortening effect, which was known as the 'Lorentz-Fitzgerald contraction' by 1900. In fact, the whole theory of special relativity was so entirely ripe for elucidation in 1905 that it would certainly have become generally accepted at about this time even if Einstein had never been born. Indeed, special relativity was initially known as the Lorentz-Einstein theory, and Einstein himself admitted towards the end of his life, in 1953, 'For me personally, he (Lorentz) meant more than all the others I have met in my lifetime'. (Isaacson, p. 166) Essentially, Einstein had presented a conceptual, 'top down' approach to explaining special relativity, but Lorentz had already contributed the harder slog of a 'bottom up' approach, working from first principles and providing mathematical formulations. Both approaches are valid, but Lorentz had published his paper first. Einstein had every reason to be very grateful to Lorentz, who could easily have bitterly resented this intrusion into his field by a Patent Office clerk, and could have accused Einstein of plagiarism. In fact he did not, displaying the same generosity of spirit that was later to be shown to Einstein by David Hilbert, who worked with him on the theory of general relativity. On those two occasions Einstein had been fortunate, but Philipp Lenard was to adopt a less generous attitude, as we shall see. One of Einstein's less well known quotations appears in Times Newspapers' little book, *Great Quotations* (2020) p. 92. He said, 'The secret of creativity is knowing how to hide your sources'.

In short, none of Einstein's *annus mirabilis* papers dealt with concepts that were entirely original, and none was based on experimental research done by Einstein himself. The best that can be said for them is that they may have slightly advanced some of the theoretical concepts associated with those four topics at the time. However, on the basis of these modest achievements Einstein is credited, in the eyes of the world, with 'discovering' photons and the photo-electric effect, originating quantum theory, proving the existence of atoms, devising the theory of special relativity entirely on his own, and being the first to realise that $E=mc^2$. How could such distortions of historical truth have come about? This is something that perhaps historians can understand better than most. The answer may be derived in part from the fact that most historians of science have been scientists, and not historians. It is a very convenient shorthand to simply speak of 'Einstein's' theory of special relativity', and 'Einstein's' discovery that $E=mc^2$'. Most science writers do not have the time or the space to spell out the full truth. A second explanation lies in the fact that society seems to have a need for heroes, and if real ones cannot be found, then they have to be invented. These heroes must be invincible and infallible – Superman, Wonderwoman, the Pope, the Queen, Adolph Hitler, anyone will do, but we must have our heroes to admire. Einstein was one of those who benefitted from this syndrome.

Between 1906 and the end of 1915 a great variety of articles on scientific topics in various journals continued to flow from Einstein's pen, 75 in all, although 13 of them had been co-authored with other scientists, usually those who had been better at practical experiments or mathematics than Einstein himself. These papers had covered a great variety of topics, mostly harking back to his earlier work on photons, thermodynamics, statistical mechanics, and relativity. But from the time of the completion of his paper on special relativity of 1905, Einstein had been troubled by the fact that his theory had taken no account of gravity, and he had begun to dream of a 'super theory' which would incorporate the force of gravity into a general theory of relativity that could explain completely the interrelationship between time, space, matter, energy, and velocity.

Einstein's first sally into the field of general relativity appeared in the *Jahrbuch der Radioaktivitat* for 1907, Vol. 4, pp. 411-62. This was a very tentative sally, and a correction to his maths had to be issued in Vol. 5, pp. 98-9. In Vol. 4 Einstein had once again asserted (p.443) in effect that $E=mc^2$, but again had not presented the magic formula in precisely those terms, still treating energy only as L, that is radiant energy. This paper was highly significant, however, because it marked Einstein's first serious approach to the enterprise that would obsess him for the next eight years, the quest for a general theory of relativity.

In this quest, Einstein was burdened with something of a handicap. General relativity could be understood and explained only in mathematical terms, but Einstein was, by his own admission, not very good at maths. Even on the day before he died, Einstein was still lamenting, 'If only I had more mathematics!' (Isaacson, p. 542) In 2002 Alice Calaprice published a charming little collection under the title, *Dear Professor Einstein: Albert Einstein's Letters to and from Children*. In 1943 a little girl of nine called Barbara wrote to Einstein saying that she found maths very difficult. Einstein replied to her, 'Don't worry about experiencing difficulties with maths. I can assure you that my own problems have been even more serious!' (p. 140)Indeed, he had always relied heavily on his friend Marcel Grossmann for assistance in that department, even from their earliest days together as students at the Zurich Polytechnic. Here, Einstein had often not bothered to attend maths lectures at all, but Grossman had generously lent him the excellent notes that he had taken while attending them. In their final examination, while Grossmann had achieved a perfect score of 6 on the maths papers, Einstein had scored only 4.25, just barely passing. Einstein himself was fully aware of his deficiency in that department. In 1905 he wrote to friends of Meliva in Serbia, only half jokingly, 'I need my wife: she solves all the mathematical problems for me!' (Isaacson, p. 136) In reality, however, it is likely that Meliva only checked over his figures and proof read his papers for him, since she was even worse at maths than Einstein himself, having failed the subject twice at the Zurich Polytechnic.

One of Einstein's former tutors at the Polytechnic, Herman Minkowski (1864-1909), also of Jewish descent, had been eagerly following developments in relativity theory for many years, absorbing the work of Poincaré, Lorentz, Fitzgerald, and Einstein. But Minkowski was a far better mathematician than Einstein, and the close friend of David Hilbert, the leading mathematician of the day, who had credited him with mathematical prowess equal to his own. Minkowski quickly grasped an implication of special relativity that Einstein had evidently missed, namely that, if the theory held good, then space and time could no longer be considered as separate entities, but only as a four-dimensional whole, the space-time continuum. Minkowski devised an eloquent mathematical expression to illustrate this concept, and presented his findings to the 80th Assembly of German Natural Scientists and Physicians, held on September 21, 1908, in Berlin. He opened his paper with the famous and oft-quoted words,

> The views of space and time which I wish to lay before you have sprung from the soil of experimental physics, and therein lies their strength. They are radical. Henceforth space by itself, and time by itself are doomed to fade away into mere shadows, and only a kind of union of the two will preserve an independent reality.

Not only had Einstein missed this point, but he failed to grasp it even after Minkowski had explained it! He dismissed Minkowski's work as 'a mathematical trick' and 'superfluous learnedness', joking to his friends, 'Since the mathematicians have grabbed hold of the theory of relativity, I myself no longer understand it!' (Isaacson, p. 133) This came as no surprise to Minkowski, who had attempted to teach Einstein maths at the Zurich Polytechnic. He declared that Einstein's reputation as a physicist had, 'come as a tremendous surprise to me, for in his student days Einstein had been a lazy dog. He never bothered about mathematics at all'. (Isaacson, p. 132) Sadly, Minkowski died of peritonitis in January, 1909, allegedly saying, 'What a pity that I have to die in the age of relativity's development'. (Isaacson, p. 133) Had he lived, we might well today have been speaking of 'Minkowski's theory of general relativity', delivered rather sooner than Einstein's version.

Not only was Einstein incapable of devising new mathematical techniques for himself, but he was incapable even of recognising those mathematical formulae which had already been devised, and which could be of assistance to him in his work on general relativity. But fortunately his friend Grossmann was an expert in differential geometry and tensor calculus, introducing Einstein to the pioneering work on absolute differential calculus then being done by the Italians Gregorio Ricci-Curbasto (1853-1925) and Tullio Levi-Civita (1873-1941). Einstein began a correspondence with Levi-Civita, who was later able to point out to Einstein some errors that he had made in his use of tensor calculus in his relativity theories. Einstein wrote to him with gratitude saying, 'I admire the elegance of your methods of calculation: it must be a fine thing to ride through those fields upon the horse of true mathematics, while the likes of us have to make our way laboriously on foot'. (Wikipedia entry on Levi-Civita) Levi-Civita was also Jewish, and the two men corresponded in Italian.

It would be no exaggeration to say that Grossmann mentored Einstein throughout his entire early career. In 1912 it was Grossmann who helped to conduct the negotiations to bring Einstein back as a Professor of Theoretical Physics at the Zurich Polytechnic. But at that time Einstein felt that he had been getting nowhere in wrestling with the major problem of his career, how to elucidate a general theory of relativity. Once again he turned to Grossmann for help. 'Grossmann, you've got to help me or I will go crazy', he wrote in 1912. (Isaacson, p. 193) By this time Einstein had experienced something of a change of heart with regard to his attitude towards mathematics. Isaacson writes of him,

Until then, Einstein's scientific success had been based on his special talent for sniffing out the underlying physical principles of nature. He had left to others the task, which to him seemed less exalted, of finding the best mathematical expressions of those principles...But by 1912 Einstein had come to appreciate that maths could be a tool for discovering – and not merely describing – nature's laws. Maths was nature's playbook. (p. 193)

This was very true. God is indeed a mathematician, and a very good one. 'Subtle is the Lord', as Einstein later put it. Breakthroughs like the general theory of relativity help us to understand the mind of God. As recently as 1908 Einstein had been sneering at mathematicians like Minkowski, but on October 29, 1912 he wrote to the physicist Arnold Sommerfeld, 'I have gained enormous respect for mathematics, whose more subtle parts I considered until now, in my ignorance, as pure luxury'. (Isaacson, p. 193) Einstein's intellectual strength lay not in his mathematical abilities, but rather in his ability to conceptualise. Once he had grasped the implications of Minkowski's space-time continuum, he began to envisage it as indeed continuous, but not even. Rather, it would be locally warped or twisted by heavy concentrations of matter, which would generate strong gravitational fields. Lorentz had already demonstrated mathematically how an accelerating body would experience a relativistic increase in mass and a time dilation effect. Einstein felt sure that gravity and acceleration were equivalent, and that therefore a powerful gravitational field would also have a locally distorting effect upon space and time relative to an outside observer. This was the essential difference between special and general relativity, for the latter took account of gravity as well as acceleration, but Einstein was unable to represent this in mathematical terms.

Grossmann's response to Einstein's desperate plea was that he should turn to the theorems of Riemannian (non Euclidian) geometry, which could be used to describe not only curved, but also arbitrarily curving surfaces. These concepts had been pioneered by the work of Bernhard Riemann (1826-66), the German physicist who rose to become head of the Mathematics Department at the very prestigious University of Gottingen. He had been the first to suggest using dimensions higher than merely three or four in order to describe physical reality. For this he had devised and employed a device known as a metric tensor, always now denoted as $g_{\mu\nu}$. It had 16 components, ten of them independent of each other, and it could be used to define and describe a distance in curved, four-dimensional space-time. His introduction to these concepts fired Einstein with a new zeal, and he redoubled his efforts to discover genuinely covariant equations to support a theory of general relativity.

Grossmann continued to work with Einstein through to 1913, when the two men jointly produced their breakthrough paper, 'An Outline of a Generalised Theory of Relativity and of a Theory of Gravitation' in the *Zeitschrift für Mathematik und Physic* Vol. 62, pp. 225-261. The work appeared in two sections, with the mathematical section written by Grossmann. Einstein referred to this paper as his 'Entwurf', which means design or blueprint from the German *entwerfen*, a sketch or draft, indicating that these were only preliminary propositions. The mathematics had come from Grossmann, but the imagination and vision had come from Einstein. Einstein soon realised, however, that their 'Entwurf' fell short of a complete theory of general relativity, because its equations were not universally covariant, that is applicable to matter in all forms of motion, and to space-time under all degrees of curvature. Technically speaking, his equations were not covariant under a transformation that uniformly rotated the coordinate axes. This flaw was pointed out to him by his old friend from their 'Olympia Academy' days, Michele Besso (1873-1955). This realisation drove Einstein to despair, and deflected him from the path of metric tensors, which had in fact taken Grossmann and Einstein closer to a correct solution than they had realised at the time.

Therefore, Einstein was still far from a satisfactory final solution when, in late June 1915, he was invited to the University of Gottingen by David Hilbert (1862-1943) to give a one week series of lectures on his theory. Einstein gave four lectures in all, but found the experience to be rather embarrassing. With each lecture, he was obliged to correct the errors of the previous one! But his host was fascinated by what Einstein had to say. From 1895 to 1930 David Hilbert served as Professor of Mathematics at Gottingen, and under his leadership the university had acquired its reputation as the preeminent institution in the mathematical world. Hilbert himself was probably the greatest of all the brilliant mathematicians who lectured there. On hearing that one of his students was leaving to study poetry instead, Hilbert declared, 'Good. He did not have the imagination for mathematics!' Although he had always been a pure mathematician, by 1912 Hilbert was turning his interest increasingly to the field of physics, even employing a physics tutor for himself in that year. He soon came to believe, however, that physicists were somewhat deficient when it came to their mathematical abilities. He described their approach to the subject as 'sloppy' and 'ugly', and joked that, 'Physics is too hard for physicists', implying that the necessary mathematics was generally beyond them. He collaborated with his colleague Richard Courant (1888-1972) in writing a book with the title, *Methods of Mathematical Physics* which was first published in 1924, designed explicitly to help physicists to understand key mathematical concepts. Although the whole book was written by Courant, he cited Hilbert as co-author because the book included so many of Hilbert's mathematical formulations. Sadly, soon after this, the mathematics department of Gottingen University was totally destroyed by the Nazis. Most of its leading lights had been Jewish, but those academics were expelled from their posts. The expulsions were carried through by Bernhard Rust (1883-1945), the fanatical and unbalanced Nazi Minister for Education and Culture. In 1934 he found himself seated next to Hilbert at a banquet, and asked him whether his mathematics department had suffered from the expulsion of its Jews. 'Suffered?', Hilbert replied, 'It no longer exists, does it!' (Wikipedia entry on Hilbert)

By 1915 Hilbert was on the lookout for interesting problems in physics to tackle, and on hearing Einstein's lectures he became fascinated by his quest for a theory of general relativity, and began to work on the problem himself. Einstein was at first delighted and flattered by Hilbert's interest, and by his swift grasping of the principles involved. The two men exchanged a lively correspondence in the summer and autumn of 1915, sparking ideas off each other. It is debatable whether Einstein helped Hilbert more with the concepts or Hilbert helped Einstein more with the maths, but by the October of 1915 Einstein had become worried that, by pursuing a purely mathematical strategy which concentrated only on finding covariant equations, Hilbert was pulling ahead of him, and would be the first to produce a coherent formula that would give mathematical expression to a general theory of relativity. He complained at this point that Hilbert was trying to 'nostrify' his theory, that is to claim joint credit for finally arriving at the correct solutions. (Isaacson, p. 221) Einstein therefore changed tack, and decided to concentrate entirely on a mathematical approach himself. By the middle of November 1915 he felt confident enough of his new formulations to employ them in trying to account for the anomalous perihelion of the orbit of Mercury, which could not be explained by Newton's laws of motion. Einstein had already tried to explain the anomaly with an earlier calculation produced in conjunction with his friend Besso, but that attempt had failed. This time however, to Einstein's delight, his formula predicted with complete accuracy the degree of anomaly in Mercury's perihelion – 43 arc-seconds per century. The anomaly had been caused by Mercury's closeness to the sun, the tremendous mass of which had warped space-time in its immediate vicinity more strongly than in the rest of the solar system. Einstein wrote, 'I was beside myself with joyous excitement...The results on Mercury's perihelion movement fills me with great satisfaction. How helpful to us is astronomy's pedantic accuracy, which I used to secretly ridicule!' (Isaacson, p. 218) By November 25, with a few more additions, Einstein was able to present to the Prussian Academy of Sciences in Berlin his final lecture on general relativity which he entitled, 'The Field Equations of Gravitation', a set of covariant equations which entirely supported his general theory of relativity.

However, on November 16 Hilbert had already delivered a lecture of his own at Gottingen, giving his version of the field equations, and on November 20 he submitted this lecture as an article to a Gottingen science journal, giving it the rather grandiose title of, 'The Foundations of Physics'. He had sent Einstein a copy of this lecture which Einstein had received on November 18, just as he was putting the finishing touches to his own momentous lecture of November 25. However, Hilbert later slightly revised these equations on the following December 16, to bring them more into line with Einstein's version. It had in fact been a photo finish between the two men. Over the previous few months they had assisted each other, and it seems pointless to argue over any 'priority dispute'. Nevertheless such a dispute does exist, not only over

Einstein's claim to be the sole originator of the general relativity equations, but also over his claim to have been the first to explain special relativity. (Type in 'Relativity Priority Dispute' for a full discussion.)

In any case, Einstein should never have worried about Hilbert trying to steal his thunder. The latter was not only a mathematical genius, but also a perfect gentleman. In contrast to Einstein's colourful sex life, the rather staid Hilbert had managed to marry only one wife and to produce only one (legitimate) child over a long lifetime. He had been looking about for an interesting physics problem to solve in the summer of 1915, and his attention had been caught by the challenge of general relativity. Hilbert had simply been amusing himself by racing with Einstein to produce a viable set of field equations to support the theory. He recognised that Einstein had been sweating blood over his pet project for the previous eight years, and had never had any intention of snatching the prize from under Einstein's nose. The famous tag about genius being 1% inspiration and 99% perspiration has been attributed to Thomas Edison, and Einstein had provided a classic case in point. Indeed, he did not hesitate to apply the quotation to himself, after it appeared in the September 1932 edition of *Harper's Monthly Magazine*, with its attribution to Edison.

In the event Hilbert was the soul of graciousness and generosity, always referring to the field equations as, 'Einstein's theory of general relativity' and 'the magnificent theory of general relativity established by Dr. Einstein'. Gottingen University was at that time the world's leading mathematical centre, and Hilbert is reported to have said, 'Every boy on the streets of Gottingen understands more about four-dimensional geometry than Einstein, yet in spite of that Einstein did the work and not the mathematicians'. (Isaacson, p. 222) This equitable settlement between Hilbert and Einstein stands in agreeable contrast to the unseemly spat between Gottfried Leibnitz (1646-1714) and Isaac Newton (1642-1727) over which of them had first invented 'the calculus'. Newton had been obliged to devise this new mathematical formulation in order to set out his laws of gravity.

However, it might also be said that, from a standing start in the July of 1915 once Einstein had explained the problem to him, Hilbert had managed to produce over the following five months equations that Einstein had been struggling to formulate over the previous eight years without perfecting them. Moreover Hilbert had done this with the assistance of nobody except Einstein himself. By contrast, Einstein had needed a lot of help over those eight years, from the work of Poincaré and Lorentz, from Grossman, from Besso, the equations of Minkowski, and finally from Hilbert. In addition we should remember that neither Einstein nor Grossmann nor Hilbert would have been able to produce the required covariant equations without the earlier tensor calculus formulations inspired by Carl Gauss (1777-1855), devised by

Bernhard Riemann (1826-1866), and elaborated upon by the Italian mathematician Gregorio Ricci-Curbasto (1853-1925). By 1915 there was no need to devise any new mathematics for the equations of general relativity – the mathematical tools for the job lay ready to hand, but Einstein had needed others to point this out to him. Unlike Newton, Einstein did not have to invent any new formulations. In one of its many condensed forms, Einstein's field equations may be denoted as,

$$R_{\mu\nu} - \frac{1}{2} R g_{\mu\nu} + \Lambda g_{\mu\nu} = \frac{8\pi G}{c^4} \times T_{\mu\nu}$$

Here, $R_{\mu\nu}$ is the Ricci curvature tensor, referring to the formulations of Ricci-Curbasto, R is the scalar curvature referring to the work of Riemann, $g_{\mu\nu}$ is the metric tensor, Λ (lambda) is Einstein's cosmological constant, G is Newton's gravitational constant, c is the speed of light in a vacuum as first measured with near accuracy by Marie Alfred Cornu (1841-1902) in 1875, and $T_{\mu\nu}$ is the stress-energy tensor, which makes allowance for the velocity of objects travelling through space. The only original term inserted by Einstein was Λ (lambda), his 'cosmological constant' designed to keep the universe in a steady state, for so it was believed to be until the discoveries of Edwin Hubble (1889-1953) in 1929, who proved that the universe was in fact expanding. After this discovery, Einstein then called his cosmological constant, 'My greatest blunder', assuming that the outward momentum of this expansion was sufficient to counter the effects of gravity, so that no separate anti-gravitational force was needed. But as will be explained in the Science chapter below, the significance of Einstein's Λ has been re-assessed since 1998. With a lot of help, Einstein had reached his goal at last, but this was due not so much to his 'genius' as to his knack of knowing who to ask for help, and to his persistence, a dogged determination to see the project through to the end, despite his many setbacks. But after all that, Isaacson still has the gall to refer to, 'the development of relativity theory, which was largely the product of one man working in near solitary splendor'! (p. 326) What a travesty of historical accuracy! His pro-Einstein bias becomes evident here. Brian Cox and Jeff Forshaw, who were not even professional historians, presented a much sounder perspective on Einstein in their book *Why Does E=mc²?* (2010)when they wrote,

> Relativity was not the work of one man, although in a book about relativity this can sometimes appear to be the case. Einstein was undoubtedly...led to his radical revision of space and time by the curiosity and skill of many. (pp.239-40)

But what does general relativity mean to us in everyday life? Very little really, because it applies noticeably only in the presence of very strong gravitational fields. It has an application for satellite navigation instruments, because clocks on satellites in orbit will run slightly faster than clocks on the surface of the earth, since the earthbound clocks are subject to a stronger gravitational field. The difference is small, but enough to produce serious navigational errors over time unless the satellite clocks are adjusted to run more slowly, bringing them into line with earthbound timepieces. However, this effect had already been predicted by the theory of special relativity. Essentially, all that the theory of general relativity did was to explain (in theory) the effects of gravity upon the theory of special relativity, which latter might be regarded as much the more practically important of the two, even although its development and presentation attracted far less public attention.

The philosophical implications of special and general relativity are, however, profound, indeed mind-blowing, because they spell out the relationship between time, space, matter, gravity, and velocity. To put this in lay terms, we might begin by asking, 'What is time?' Put as baldly as this, it sounds like a very difficult question, but if we turn it around a bit and ask instead, 'Well, what creates time for us?' then the question becomes easier to answer. Obviously our conception of time is created by matter changing its form and its position in space. We have no other way of measuring time. Time then, for the individual observer, is the fool of matter? Yes. But matter is the fool of gravity, so is time also the fool of gravity? Again the answer is yes. Strong gravitational fields slow time. But these fields are themselves created by matter, and so everything is interconnected in a cosmic dance. Matter generates gravity, telling space-time how to curve, and warped space-time affects matter, telling it how to move. Matter and energy are equivalent, gravity and acceleration are equivalent, and space and time are interrelated. The faster you travel through space, the slower you travel through time relative to a stationary observer, and the stronger the gravitational field in which you find yourself, the slower will time pass for you relative to an observer in a weaker gravitational field. For example, it may be that every black hole is in fact exploding, but because of their massive gravity, time in their vicinity has slowed so much that to us they appear stable!

We have already had to get used to the idea that matter and energy are in fact just different aspects of the same thing, and Minkowski has shown us that time and space are similarly related. The implications of the space-time continuum are that both time and space are just that – continuous. Neither 'flows': both just *are*. We have had to get used to the idea that all of matter, all of energy, and all of space were created at the Big Bang. More difficult to grasp is the idea that all of *time* was also created in that event. That is *all* time, past, present, *and* future, in accordance with the law of causality, and the second law of thermodynamics. Time does not 'flow', it just *is* and we move through it, living out our inevitable destinies.

This is not just the wishful thinking of a convinced determinist like myself, but a scientific fact. Of all the many science books that I have read in the last few years, I found that the most helpful for understanding the implications of general relativity was, *The Fabric of the Cosmos: Space, Time, and the Texture of Reality* (2004) by Brian Randolph Greene, a Professor of Theoretical Physics at Columbia University in New York City. On p. 139 he explains,

> Events, regardless of when they happen from any particular perspective, just *are*. They all exist. They eternally occupy their particular point in spacetime. There is no flow. If you were having a great time at the stroke of midnight on New Year's Eve 1999, you still are, since that is just one immutable location in spacetime. It is tough to accept this description, since our worldview so forcefully distinguishes between past, present, and future. But if we stare intently at the familiar temporal scheme and confront it with the cold hard facts of modern physics, its only place of refuge seems to lie within the human mind.

This is a difficult concept to grasp indeed, but as so often happens, the poets got there first in presenting a difficult concept clearly. Brian Greene wrote in 2004, but T.S. Eliot's *Four Quartets* were penned in 1943. I must here quote once again the opening lines of *Burnt Norton*, the first of these.

> Time present and time past
> Are both perhaps present in time future,
> And time future contained in time past.
> If all time is eternally present
> All time is unredeemable.
> What might have been is an abstraction
> Remaining a perpetual possibility
> Only in a world of speculation.

Everyone understands how utterly impossible it is to reach a hand back into the past and change what has been.

> The moving finger writes, and having writ,
> Moves on: not all thy piety nor wit
> Shall lure it back to cancel half a line,
> Nor all thy tears wash out a word of it.
> (*The Rubaiyat of Omar Khayyam,* verse 51)

Why, therefore, is it so difficult to realise that it is equally impossible to reach a hand forward into the future and change what will be?

Between pages 132 and 139 of his book, in a section headed, 'The Persistent Illusion of Past, Present, and Future', Greene tries to explain the link between time, space, and motion with the aid of a number of diagrams representing 'time slices' to assist the layman in understanding his points. Over vast distances of space-time, the effects of relative motion on time-shift are magnified. This may be described as the 'scissors' effect. Imagine a pair of scissors the handles of which are just the normal length and normal distance from their fulcrum, but the blades of which are enormously long. Therefore, just a small separation of the handles will result in a wide separation of the blade tips. Greene asks us to imagine a Star Wars character, Chewbacca the Wookiee, situated on a planet ten billion light-years from Earth. So long as Chewie remains stationary relative to you, your 'now' will coincide with his. But his relative motion, and relative time-shift, will be magnified by distance. Greene writes,

> By using the equations of special relativity we can calculate how different your *nows* will become. If Chewie moves away from you at about ten miles per hour, the events on Earth that belong on his new now-list are events that happened about 150 years ago, according to you!...If he moved towards you at the same speed, his *now* would coincide with what you would call 150 years into the future!...Similarly, there are things about our future, such as who will win the presidential election in the year 2100, that seem completely open: more than likely, the candidates for that election haven't even been born, much less decided to run for office. But if Chewie walks towards earth at about 6.4 miles per hour, his now-slice – his conception of what exists, his conception of what has happened – *will* include the selection of the first president of the twenty-second century. Something that seems completely undecided to us is something that, for him, has already happened. (pp. 136-7)

Now obviously, Chewie could not walk into your future unless your future was already there for him to walk into, just as your past is already there. But Chewie cannot influence any of these events, because any signal that he sends will take ten billion years to reach us! This is the meaning of *all* of time being simply there, simply present, just as all of space is simply there, simply present, with each observer's 'time slice', his concept of 'now', being just as valid as anyone else's, all created at the same instant by the Big Bang. On p. 139 Greene quotes from a letter written by Einstein to his friend Michele Besso, where Einstein wrote, 'For we convinced physicists, the distinction between past, present, and future is only an illusion, however persistent'.

There is some comfort to be drawn from these conceptions, however. 'If all time is eternally present', as T.S. Eliot said, this means that, because you existed, you have your place within the space-time continuum forever: no power on Earth or in heaven can change the fact that once you *were*. From the perspective of someone, somewhere, moving in another part of the universe therefore, you are eternally alive, and that is a kind of immortality. Your presence will endure for as long as the space-time continuum endures, that is, at least for the lifetime of this universe.

The scientific community, which had been little enough impressed by Einstein's *annus mirabilis* papers, pricked up its ears on the news about general relativity. In late 1915 Einstein published his four lectures on general relativity which he had delivered to the Prussian Academy of Sciences in their Journal, *Preussische Akademie der Wissenschaften Sitzungsberichte* (Proceedings of the Prussian Academy of Sciences), but only the last of these included his final and workable field equations. On March 20, 1916, however, he published a very long and definitive account of his new theory in the much more widely read *Annalen der Physik* (Series 4, Vol. 49, pp. 769-822), and it was this which fully brought it to the attention of the scientific world. This final version had been honed and polished by the elegant formulations of Hilbert, which he had borrowed from Hilbert's papers, although they simply supported the calculations which Einstein had already made less elegantly and marginally earlier to reach his own conclusions. Einstein then took a further step to ensure the widest publicity for his new theory by publishing a book for lay readers in that same year with the title, *Relativity: The Special and General Theory* (1916). It was published in English in 1920, and subsequently in many other languages as well.

Those who could understand it were mightily impressed, but was there any practical experiment which might be carried out to support these wonderful theories? One obvious way presented itself. If the theory was correct, then among other things the great mass of the sun would produce a gravitational field strong enough to warp space-time in its immediate vicinity to a noticeable extent. This would mean that starlight passing close to the sun would be bent around it, displacing the apparent position of stars close to the sun's rim. However, the brightness of the sun made it impossible, under normal circumstances, to observe stars near to its rim as the sun crossed the sky. But a solar eclipse would change these normal circumstances since the moon was, very conveniently, just close enough to Earth to blot out the sun completely over parts of the Earth during a total eclipse, casting a thin trail of darkness across the sunlit side of the world. Within this corridor, for a short period of time, starlight passing close to the sun actually *could* be observed, and the apparent displacement of the stars from their normal position in the sky measured. Using his new theory, Einstein calculated that the degree of displacement would approximate to 1.7 arc-seconds. In fact, Newton had already predicted a small deflection of starlight as it passed close to the sun, but only to half the extent of Einstein's estimate, some 0.86 arc-seconds. Although Newton believed in a 'corpuscular' theory of light, i.e. that it came in small packages, he also believed that these 'corpuscles' would cause small ripples in the ether as they passed through it, which would cause light to be deflected as it passed large bodies. The question now was, which theory would be proved correct? But we must first understand what a very small angle of deflection we are talking about here. There are 360 degrees in a circle, so that each degree subtends quite a small angle in itself. Each degree is divided into 60 minutes for measurement purposes, and each minute into 60 seconds. One arc-second, therefore, represents only 1/3,600th of a degree, a very tiny angle indeed. But the difference between Newton's predicted deflection and Einstein's was less than one arc-second.

As it happened, the next total eclipse was due on May 29, 1919 when the theory could be tested, but at this point politics took a hand in the practice of science. The man who was determined to test the theory in 1919 was Sir Arthur Eddington (1882-1944), Britain's leading astronomer, who was knighted for his services to astronomy in 1930. He planned to photograph the eclipse from two different points on the Earth's surface, but unfortunately the shadow path of this particular eclipse would lie almost entirely over the Atlantic Ocean! Eddington therefore sent one team to northern Brazil, while he himself set up his cameras on the tiny island of Principe, a Portuguese colony just off the west coast of Africa, near the equator. The resulting photographs, however, provided far from conclusive evidence. On the day Eddington suffered from passing clouds over Principe, while the Brazilian team found that the heat of the Amazonian jungle had distorted their telescopes, resulting in fuzzy images. Nevertheless, both teams agreed that *some* form of light deflection had been observed, but within a wide range of error. This was hardly surprising. The angular distinction that they were trying to measure was roughly that subtended between the base line and the hypotenuse of a right-angle triangle whose vertical side was one inch high, and whose base line extended for one mile! The equipment of the day was simply not up to the task. Photographs of the teams at work show them using small refracting telescopes that were completely inadequate for the job. However, by discounting the Brazil results completely, and juggling furiously with his own measurements, Eddington was at last able to come up with an average deflection of 1.7 arc-seconds, matching Einstein's prediction.

Science this was not. Eddington had in fact set out with a prior determination to prove Einstein's theory correct. Eddington was one of the few people who completely understood general relativity, and had concluded that the theory was 'too beautiful to be wrong'. Moreover, Eddington, like Einstein, was a pacifist, an element of his Quaker faith. Both men had opposed and denounced the recent war as folly, and now Eddington was eager to bind up its wounds, bring people together again, and restore a good relationship between Britain and Germany. What better way than for a British Christian astronomer to confirm the theory of a German Jewish physicist? On this occasion, Eddington allowed his political principles to override his scientific integrity. The general public was convinced by Eddington's findings, but the scientific community knew full well that Eddington's 'confirmation' of relativity theory was hardly worth the paper it was written on. As it happened of course, his instinctive feeling for the accuracy of the theory was later proved to be entirely justified, but not on this occasion.

In any case, Einstein was in no mood to accept a negative result from the observations. When Eddington's triumphant telegram reached him, he was with a graduate student, to whom he showed the message. The student congratulated him warmly, but Einstein feigned indifference. 'I *knew* the theory was correct', he told her. 'But what if the observations had disproved it?' she asked. 'In that case', Einstein replied, 'I would have felt sorry for the dear Lord. The theory is correct'. Max Planck also congratulated Einstein, by letter. Einstein modestly wrote back, 'The intimate union between the beautiful, the true, and the real has again been proved'. (Isaacson, pp. 259-60)

The astronomical community, well aware of the limitations of Eddington's instruments, remained sceptical of his findings, but Eddington was one of their leading lights, and nobody openly challenged him. This was good enough for the world's press when news of the eclipse results was finally made public in November, 1919. 'REVOLUTION IN SCIENCE', shouted *The Times* of London on November 7. 'NEWTONIAN IDEAS OVERTHROWN'. 'Newtonian Ideas Very Slightly Modified' might have been a more accurate form of reportage. At tiny fractions of light speed and in weak gravitational fields, including those of the planets, Newtonian mechanics serves perfectly well. In fact it was Newtonian mechanics that were relied upon to send men to the moon, and to guide satellites around the planets in later decades. Even the carefully measured anomalous perihelion of Mercury had varied from Newtonian predictions by only 43 arc-seconds per century. This does not detract from the validity of relativity theory under more extreme conditions, but in fact general relativity, unlike special relativity, has very few practical applications in our everyday lives. While it is true that general relativity theory overthrew Newton's ideas of absolute time and absolute space, this had already been done by Minkowski in 1908, and Einstein had incorporated Minkowski's calculations into his own work.

Nevertheless, the newspaper headlines in that November of 1919 catapulted Einstein to world fame, as the press in other countries took up the story. Einstein's reputation as a genius was made, and was to stay with him for the rest of his life. Whilst he feigned annoyance and impatience with all the ballyhoo, Einstein did not go out of his way to avoid the consequences of his fame. He regularly gave public lectures and interviews to the press, and he knew how to play to the gallery with charm and wit. Isaacson writes of him,

> Einstein's response to adulation was as complex as that of the cosmos to gravity. He was attracted and repelled by the cameras, loved publicity and loved to complain about it. His love-hate relationship with fame and reporters might seem unusual until one reflects on how similar it was to the mix of enjoyment, amusement, aversion and annoyance that so many other famous people have felt. (p. 269)

The next milestone in Einstein's life was his receipt of the Nobel Prize for Physics in 1922, but this was not so straightforward a matter as might appear on the surface. In the first place, Einstein had already signed away his rights to the prize money even before he had received the prize! In January 1918 Einstein's wife Meliva was still obstinately refusing to grant him a divorce, despite the harsh terms that he had imposed upon her. Desperate to be free to marry Elsa (or her daughter) Einstein therefore in that month made Meliva an offer she could not refuse. If she would agree to divorce, Einstein would raise her annual stipend immediately from 6,000 to 9,000 German marks a year, and in addition, if he ever won the Nobel Prize, then the cash value of the honour would be paid to her in full, although some would remain in a trust for their sons. At that time, the prize was worth 135,000 Swedish Krona, or 225,000 German marks, some 37 times her existing income of 6,000 marks p.a. For Meliva, the offer was a gamble, but too good for her to turn down. She agreed to a divorce. In 1922 the prize was worth only 121,572 Swedish Krona, about 32,250 American dollars, but this when the German mark was beginning its long decline into hyperinflation. This sum was still about ten times the annual salary of a professor at that time. (Isaacson, p. 316) As he had agreed, Einstein payed all the money to Meliva and their sons.

But there was a further unusual aspect to Einstein's award. In his will, which had set up the prize, Alfred Nobel had specified that it should be awarded for 'the most important discovery or invention' of that particular year. But it could be argued, and indeed it was argued at the time, that Einstein had neither discovered nor invented anything. His work had been entirely theoretical, and even his theories had not been proven to the satisfaction of members of the scientific community. Anyone who knew just how narrow an angle was subtended by one half of an arc-second, which was all of them, knew that Eddington's measurements could not be trusted, and even the alleged anomalous perihelion of Mercury lay within the range of observational error. But on the other hand, by 1922 Einstein was probably the most famous scientist in the world. Amongst the general public, nobody understood his theory of general relativity, and very few had even heard of his *annus mirabilis* papers, but everyone assumed that his general theory must be a very clever one indeed, and that therefore Einstein must be a genius. In 1921 he had, with Elsa, embarked on a triumphal visit to America. On April 4, he headed a motorcade that had been arranged for him in New York city, standing up in the back of an open-topped Ford to acknowledge the cheers of the crowd. By 1922, as Isaacson wrote, 'His lack of a prize had begun to reflect more negatively on the Nobel than on Einstein'. (p. 313) A further embarrassment for the Nobel Committee had been the fact that in 1921 the Physics Prize had been awarded to nobody, on the grounds that no candidates of sufficient merit had been available! This had been a kind of left-handed swipe at Einstein, but by 1922 it had redounded upon the Committee's heads. What was to be done?

At last, galloping to the rescue, came a Swedish theoretical physicist, Carl Wilhelm Oseen (1879-1944), who joined the Nobel Physics Committee in 1922. Realising that it would be extremely difficult to justify awarding the Prize to Einstein for his general theory since in 1922 it remained just an unproven theory in the eyes of the scientific community (in fact he never was awarded the Prize for this) Oseen suggested taking a different tack. He argued that in fact Einstein *had* 'discovered' something – a *law*. In his 1905 paper on the photo-electric effect, Einstein had suggested that the constant of proportionality between the frequency of the incident light and the kinetic energy of the emitted electrons might be equal to Planck's constant. This was regarded at the time as nothing more than an interesting theoretical idea, but it was later proved to be correct by the careful experimental work of the American physicist Robert Andrews Millikan (1868-1952), who was awarded the Nobel Prize for this achievement in 1923. For his 1905 paper Einstein, who was not an experimentalist himself, had drawn heavily on the experimental findings on the photo-electric effect that had been discovered by Philipp Lenard (1862-1947), who had been studying the phenomenon since 1888, and who won the Nobel Prize for this work in 1905. Lenard rather resented this intrusion by a Patent Office clerk into his field, and felt that Einstein had hitched a free ride on all his years of labour. He was later to oppose Einstein's nomination for the Nobel Prize, and later still he became a fervent Nazi supporter and anti-Semite. Indeed, there can be little doubt that Einstein's few theoretical suggestions in this field had been completely overshadowed by the many years of solid experimental work on the topic put in by Lenard and Millikan. Einstein's 1905 suggestion had been a frail enough straw to hang a Nobel Prize upon, but the Physics Committee clutched at it gratefully.

It is in fact with relation to Lenard that Isaacson again allows his pro-Einstein bias to slip out. On p. 98 of this classic biography Isaacson relates how Einstein referred to 'what he graciously called Lenard's "pioneering work" on the photoelectric effect'. The use of the adverb 'graciously' was entirely inappropriate here, as was the use of inverted commas around 'pioneering work'. Lenard's work in this field most certainly *had* been pioneering, and most ingenious too in the originality of the experiments that he had devised, so there was nothing 'gracious' about Einstein's acknowledgement of that fact – he was simply stating the truth. Lenard's 1905 Nobel Prize had been well deserved. We are reminded here of how Isaacson had also 'forgotten' to mention the previous work on the formula $E=Mc^2$ that had already been done by Hasenohrl and de Pretto prior to Einstein's 1905 paper, and how he had also 'forgotten' to mention the key article on special relativity that had been published by Lorentz in 1904 in the *Proceedings of the Royal Netherlands Society of Arts and Sciences* referred to above. This paper had essentially already explained all the basic principles of special relativity, and had expressed them in mathematical terms.

In the event, in September 1922 the Nobel Committee decided to give Einstein the unawarded Prize for 1921, while Niels Bohr (1885-1962) was given the 1922 Prize for his work on quantum mechanics. The presentation ceremony was held that December, but Einstein could not attend in person because he was travelling in Japan at the time. Einstein's official citation declared that the Prize had been awarded for, 'his services to theoretical physics, and especially for his discovery of the law of the photoelectrical effect'. Now of course Einstein had not 'discovered' this law at all, any more than Democritus had 'discovered' atoms 2,400 years earlier simply because he had suggested that they might exist. A law is not 'discovered' until it is proven, and as noted above, the law of the photoelectric effect was proved to exist only by the careful experimental work carried out by Robert Millikan in 1914. However, this ruse satisfied the consciences of the desperate Nobel Physics Committee. Shamelessly, they then went on to award Millikan himself the 1923 Physics prize for his discovery of exactly the same effect! So an interesting question still remains as to whether Einstein would ever have been awarded a Nobel Prize for that 1905 paper if he had remained a Patent Office clerk, and had published nothing more after that date. Almost certainly his photoelectric paper would have been completely forgotten about, or at best relegated to a footnote in the history of science. It would certainly *not* have won a Nobel Prize. Einstein's success had owed a lot to the hype and publicity that had surrounded his name, and had elevated him to a status as a physicist which Einstein himself acknowledged he did not deserve. (Isaacson, pp. 268-9, 273) In fact, Einstein never was awarded any prizes for his theory of general relativity, because at the time of his death in 1955 there was still no way of proving its validity. The entire scientific community knew that Eddington's 'proof' of 1919 was entirely unreliable, and in 1955 the space age had not yet begun. There were no satellites in orbit, and no Large Hadron Collider at CERN, which was later to provide conclusive proof of the validity of relativity theory.

In short, Einstein the physicist might be regarded as something of a one-hit pop star, whose reputation was grotesquely overblown by the media. The one important concept that he could claim as being entirely his own was the theory of general relativity, although even this had been merely an extension of special relativity, which had scarcely been Einstein's own original idea. Even to derive those field equations he had needed a lot of help from his friends, as we have seen. His formulation of this theory was the high point of Einstein's career: he was never to produce its like again. As noted above, he was made director of the Kaiser Wilhelm Institute for Physics and professor at the Humboldt University of Berlin in 1914, and remained there until 1932. By that time, however, the rise of the Nazi party, and growing anti-Semitism in Germany, forced Einstein to consider moving abroad. In December 1930 and December 1931 he had made two further visits to America, and had developed a strong affection for the country. In January 1931 he had very publically attended the first screening of *City Lights* with its star, Charlie Chaplin, a fellow pacifist. .From December 1932 to March 1933 he visited America again. On his return he docked at Antwerp on March 28, and stayed in Belgium until July 21. He then crossed the Channel for a short stay in England until October 9th.

By 1933, with Hitler in power, Einstein was facing expulsion from his university post, together with all other Jewish academics. In April 1933 the

Nazis produced a photograph album showing alleged 'enemies of the state'. Einstein's picture was included, with some derogatory comments about him beneath, and the caption 'Not yet hanged'.(Clark, R.W. *Einstein. The Life and Times* (1996) p. 443) It was rumoured that a bounty worth $5,000 had been placed on his head. (Isaacson, p. 410) It was clearly time to flee from Germany: it was bad enough that Einstein was a Jew, but in addition he had made no secret of his anti-Nazi views while in America. Had he stayed Einstein would have been rounded up, and almost certainly murdered, as were millions of his fellow Jews. Einstein had already been in negotiation for a post at Princeton in 1932, and took up their offer in 1933. But on his way to America, in July to October of that year, Einstein stopped off in England to accept the hospitality of his friend Commander Oliver Locker-Lampson. (McLaren, S. *Saving Einstein* (2021) pp. 108-161). In September he stayed at Lampson's holiday cottage on Roughton Heath near Cromer, where Lampson provided an armed guard for his protection. A plaque on the wall of the New Inn at Roughton records Einstein's visit there, and a photograph of Einstein outside Locker-Lampson's rough hut, complete with his two armed guards, appears on Einstein's Wikipedia entry. While at Roughton Einstein posed to have a bust made of himself in clay by the distinguished sculptor Jacob Epstein. This bust may now be seen in bronze at the Tate Gallery. Legend has it that Einstein visited Sheringham beach in that September of 1933. A painting of Einstein enjoying a cup of tea adorns the wall of Trendies' Beachside Café on the promenade.

In 1932 Abraham Flexner had been sent to Berlin by the Institute for Advanced Study at Princeton, New Jersey with orders to negotiate with Einstein about a possible research post there, and he was to be surprised by Einstein's modesty. Well aware of his overblown reputation, and of the fact that there were many better physicists in the world than himself, Einstein made no great demands. Isaacson writes,

> Flexner asked Einstein how much he would expect to make. 'About $3,000', Einstein tentatively suggested. Flexner looked surprised. 'Oh', Einstein hastened to add, 'could I live on less?' Flexner was amused. He had more, not less in mind. (p. 397)

In the event, with no prompting from Einstein, a sum of $15,000 p.a. was agreed upon. However, Einstein was most insistent on one further stipulation. Mindful of his deficiency in the mathematics department, in 1929 Einstein had hired an Austrian mathematician, Walther Mayer (1887-1948), a fellow Jew, to act as his mathematical assistant. Einstein referred to him as 'the calculator' (Isaacson, p. 363), and found his services to be indispensible. Einstein was insistent that, if he came to the Institute, then a position there must also be provided for Mayer, so that they could continue to work together. The Institute baulked at this, but eventually it was agreed, and Mayer became an associate in mathematics there. The pair took up their posts at Princeton in October, 1933.

But although Einstein and Mayer remained at Princeton for the rest of their lives, the Institute never really got the value for money from them that had been hoped for.

Under the terms of his engagement, Einstein was to be given no teaching or administrative duties, but was to be left free to pursue his own lines of research and speculation in theoretical physics. Unfortunately, however, from this point onwards Einstein was to become obsessed with the hunting of a chimera, in the form of his imagined 'unified field theory'. This was an attempt to prove that gravity and electromagnetism were in fact simply different aspects of the same force, which could be represented in a series of field equations. Even today, no such 'unified field theory' exists, and with the discovery of gravitational waves in 2016, it now seems increasingly likely that gravity is in fact mediated by a gauge boson, the elusive 'graviton' that will be discussed in the Science chapter below, although it has not yet been clearly isolated. The electromagnetic force is of course mediated by photons, which suggests that the two are in fact distinct and separate forces. However, even on the last day of his life, Einstein was still struggling to produce a viable 'unified field' theory. On p. 543 Isaacson reproduces the last equation that Einstein ever wrote on the day he died, still trying to find a viable formula for his pet theory. Einstein's persistence, his dogged determination to see a project through, which had served him so well in his quest for a theory of general relativity, had worked against him in this instance, distracting him from other avenues that he might have more profitably explored.

There was one other field of enquiry, however, that did arouse Einstein's interest. This was the new science of quantum mechanics. In 1905, when Einstein had taken up Planck's theme of black body radiation being emitted as quanta, and Lenard's theme of cathode rays also being quantised, and had extended this idea to a suggestion that light rays might be quantised as well, he had little realised what a Pandora's box he had been helping to open. Ever since 1803, when Thomas Young (1773-1829) had reported on the results of his first slit screen experiments, it had been assumed that light propagated as a wave. Light shone through the slits showed up on a screen beyond demonstrating a clear interference pattern, which was indicative of waves interfering with each other. In 1865 James Clerk Maxwell (1831-1879) had published a paper showing that light was just another form of electromagnetic radiation, propagating as waves. In 1900 Max Planck (1858-1947) had shown that the energy carried by these electromagnetic waves was equivalent to the frequency of the wave multiplied by Planck's constant, which is now represented by the symbol h. Clearly, only a wave can have a frequency, so that appeared to be that: light, and indeed all forms of electromagnetic radiation, clearly propagated as waves. But by 1905, through the work of Planck, Lenard, and Einstein, a new theory was beginning to emerge, which would be dubbed 'quantum theory'.

According to this new theory electromagnetic radiation, although it propagated as waves, could also be seen as emanating from a single point and impacting at a single point as discrete bundles of energy, dubbed 'quanta'. In other words, it appeared to possess a wave-particle duality! On the face of things, this was clearly impossible. A wave emanates from a point and then propagates outwards as an ever-expanding sphere in three dimensions. A particle, on the other hand, emanates from a point and then moves in a straight line (or a curved line through curved space-time) from point A to point B. The two forms of propagation are clearly entirely different things! The plot thickened in 1924 when the French physicist Louis de Broglie (1892-1987) suggested in his PhD thesis that, if a wave can behave like a particle, should not a particle then be able to behave like a wave? This was soon proved to be the case. Protons, electrons, large atoms, and even molecules fired through the classic slit screen also showed an interference pattern on an impact field beyond the screen, exactly like photons. Yet these material particles obviously were *not* waves! What could this mean?

Using the law of the photoelectric effect established by Millikan, de Broglie was able to show that the wavelength associated with an electron (or any other particle) would be equal to Planck's constant divided by the particle's momentum, that is its mass times its velocity. Planck's constant is measured in joule-seconds as a quantum of energy, in fact the minimum quantum of energy that can exist. As noted above, it is a very tiny figure indeed, 6.626 x 10^{-34} joule-seconds. This means that, as far as the quantum world is concerned, size really does matter! As the size of an object increases, its wavelength diminishes, until the point is soon reached, at the size of a few molecules and above, when the diffraction pattern will begin to fade, steadily merging into just two clearly defined lines, and eventually disappearing altogether. Rather, the effect will be as though machine gun bullets were fired through the two slits, and only two distinct lines will appear on the impact field. In other words, the larger particles will behave exactly like classical objects, with no wave properties. In theory even an object as large as a cricket ball would still have a very short wavelength, but in practice this would be far too tiny to measure, and would have no practical significance in the classical world.

As far as atomic and sub-atomic objects were concerned, however, the propagation problem still remained. Wave or particle? Max Born (1882-1970), a German Jewish physicist, came to the rescue by suggesting in 1922 that perhaps these 'matter waves' were not real waves at all, but only 'probability waves', giving an indication of where the particle *might* be found at any point in time. This idea was given a mathematically credible foundation by the Austrian physicist Erwin Schrodinger (1887-1961) who, in 1926, published his famous wave equation, which gave a statistical basis to the probability of the particle being found at any point along its wave front. His work instituted the wave mechanics approach to quantum theory, but since it dealt only with the *probability* of a quantum particle being found at any one location, it still did not resolve the quantum uncertainty problem.

At the same time another brilliant young physicist, the German Werner Karl Heisenberg (1901-1976) was adopting a quite different mathematical approach to the wave-particle conundrum which came to be known as matrix mechanics. He focused his studies on electrons, as undoubted matter particles with a known mass, and began by measuring the wavelengths of the spectral lines of the radiation emitted by electrons as they lost energy. His matrix mechanics approach was later shown to be entirely compatible with, and indeed equivalent to, Schrodinger's wave equation model. However, in 1927 Heisenberg moved more deeply into the subject by declaring that neither form of quantum mechanics would allow us to establish both the precise position of a particle, such as a moving electron, and its precise momentum at the same time. The more accurately one property was measured, the less accurately could be the other, since the very act of observing affects the observation. This dictum became known as the 'Heisenberg uncertainty principle', and took its place with the 'Pauli exclusion principle', explained in the Science chapter below, as one of the cornerstones of modern physics. But Heisenberg went even further than that, to claim that an electron did not have *any* definite position or velocity at all until we observed it. This is a feature of our universe, he said, and not merely some defect in our measuring or observing abilities. This was radical stuff indeed. It implied that there was no objective reality at all beyond our own ability to observe, or perhaps even create, that reality. In addition, Heisenberg's principle and other features of quantum mechanics undermined the notion that the universe obeyed strict causal laws. Instead, chance, indeterminacy, and probability took the place of certainty.

As a convinced determinist, Einstein was very upset by these conclusions. The theories of special and general relativity implied determinism, with the future as real as the past, even for quantum particles, all within the framework of the space-time continuum. To this day, therefore, it is still argued that the two central pillars of modern physics, relativity and quantum mechanics, are fundamentally irreconcilable. Einstein wrote to Heisenberg in June 1927 expressing his misgivings, but Heisenberg wrote back declaring firmly, 'I believe that indeterminacy, that is the nonvalidity of rigorous causality, is a necessary feature of our universe'. Einstein never accepted this premise. He stuck to his belief in an objective reality, rooted in certainty, which existed whether or not we could observe it. In 1931 Einstein collaborated with J.J. Thomson and Max Planck to edit a festschrift to Maxwell, in which he declared, 'Belief in an external world, independent of the perceiving subject, is the basis of all natural science.' (*James Clerk Maxwell, a Commemorative Volume*, p. 73) But other quantum physicists of the time supported Heisenberg. Niels Bohr (1885-1962) the Danish physicist, had done fundamental work on the structure of the atom, showing how electron orbits around a nucleus could be boosted to higher energy levels by absorbing photons. It was he who coined the phrase, 'a quantum leap' as the electrons moved up from one orbit to another. He won the Nobel Prize for his work on atomic structures in 1922. But he entirely supported Heisenberg's philosophy, declaring, 'It is wrong to think that the task of physics is to find out how nature *is*. Physics concerns only what we can *say* about nature'. (Isaacson, p. 333) Philosophy, in particular the philosophy of science, was beginning to merge with physics.

As time went on, the experimental evidence in support of quantum mechanical theories continued to mount. For example, a radioactive substance will decay over time by emitting alpha particles as alpha radiation, or electrons as beta radiation, also known as cathode rays. But it is impossible to predict, even in principle either when such an emission will take place, or the path that the emitted electron will take. Einstein lamented this conclusion, writing in a letter to Max Born dated April 29, 1924, 'I find the idea quite intolerable that an electron should choose *of its own free will* not only its moment to jump off but also its direction. In that case I would rather be a cobbler, or even an employee of a gaming house, than a physicist'. He later confided to Niels Bohr, 'If all this is true, then it means the end of physics'. (Isaacson, p. 325)

Einstein spent the next few years trying to poke holes in quantum theory, seeking to undermine its credibility. His chief opponent in this quest was always Niels Bohr, and a battle royal ensued between them, although they remained good personal friends. Through it all, the citadel of quantum mechanics resisted Einstein's every attempt to undermine it, but both sides learned a great deal from their exchanges. The American astrophysicist John Archibald Wheeler (1911-2008), who first coined the terms 'black hole' and 'wormhole', declared that, 'In all the history of human thought, there is no greater dialogue than that which took place over the years between Niels Bohr and Albert Einstein about the meaning of the quantum'. (Isaacson, p. 325) Was there an objective reality that existed whether or not we could ever observe it? Were there laws that restored strict causality to phenomena that seemed inherently random? Was everything in the universe predetermined? Einstein had first expressed his famous dictum, 'God does not play dice' in a letter to Max Born dated December 4, 1926, and he continually stressed this point to Bohr. At last, in a fit of exasperation, Bohr snapped back, 'Einstein, stop telling God what to do!' (Isaacson, p. 326)

Eventually Einstein was forced to admit that experimental evidence did indeed support the existence of quantum mechanical effects, so he changed tack somewhat on the issue. Yes, he admitted, quantum mechanics did indeed provide a plausible explanation of reality, but it was an *incomplete* explanation. By 1935, even his loyal 'calculator', Walther Mayer, had tired of Einstein's quixotic attempts to assault what seemed to be the impregnable fortress of quantum mechanics, and declined to give him any further assistance on the subject. Einstein therefore turned instead to other friends for help. These were Nathan Rosen (1909-1995) a young fellow at the Institute, and Boris Podolsky (1896-1966), an old friend from Einstein's Caltech days, who was then also working at the Institute for Advance Studies. Both men were Jewish, but Podolsky was later revealed to have been a Soviet spy! The result of their collaboration was a brief four-page article published in May, 1935 in the *Physical Review*, Series 2, Vol. 47, pp. 777-80, with the title, 'Can the Quantum-mechanical Description of Physical Reality be Considered Complete?' This was the celebrated Einstein-Podolsky-Rosen Paper, usually referred to as the EPR paper, or sometimes as the EPR paradox. This published English version was written by Podolsky, because although Einstein had been able to read English from an early age, he had always experienced some difficulty when it came to speaking and writing in the language. Most of the mathematics had been done by Rosen, indeed rather overdone in the view of Einstein, who complained that the central point of the paper had been obscured beneath a superfluity of mathematics. The central idea had of course come from Einstein. It concerned the fate of entangled quantum particles that have collided or merged in some way but have then flown off in opposite directions, and therefore have properties that are correlated. By measuring the position of the first particle P, we can determine precisely the position of the second particle Q, 'without in any way disturbing the second particle'. Further, we can do the same for the momentum of particle P. 'In accordance with our criterion for reality, in the first case we must consider the measurements of P as being elements of reality, in which case the projected measurements of Q must also represent elements of reality'. (For example, if P has spin up, then Q must have spin down.) In other words, at any moment the second particle, which we have not observed, has a position that is real and a momentum that is real. These two properties are features of reality that quantum mechanics had declared could not be measured simultaneously, and therefore quantum mechanics' description of reality was not complete.

It took Bohr more than six weeks to hit back with a paper of his own. Yes, he admitted, there was no question of a mechanical disturbance to system Q. This was an important concession. Until then, the disturbance caused by a measurement had been part of Bohr's physical explanation of quantum uncertainty. However, he went on to say, the EPR experiment did not allow for the measuring of both the precise position *and* the precise momentum of particle Q *at the same moment*, so therefore Heisenberg's uncertainty principle remained unviolated. But Einstein continued to argue that other fundamental principles *had* been violated by quantum entanglement, namely those of locality and separability. According to Bohr's 'Copenhagen school' of quantum mechanics, a quantum particle propagates as a wave, which does not resolve itself into a particle until it is observed. The act of observation forces the 'collapse of the wave function', and so calls into creation the particle itself. It is our observation which creates a specific reality. This would imply that by forcing particle P to assume specific qualities such as a momentum or spin up, you would instantaneously be forcing corresponding qualities on particle Q. This would constitute instantaneous 'spooky action at a distance', thus violating the cosmic speed limit, c.

Personally, I have never found this argument to be convincing. Consideration of this so-called EPR paradox later gave rise to quantum information theory and to Bell's theorem, named after John Stewart Bell (1928-1990). In a BBC radio interview of 1985, Bell had this to say:

> There is a way to escape the inference of superluminal speeds and spooky action at a distance. But it involves absolute determinism in the universe, the complete absence of free will. Suppose the world is superdeterministic, with not just inanimate nature running on behind-the-scenes clockwork, but with our behaviour, including our belief that we are free to choose to do one experiment rather than another, absolutely predetermined, including the 'decision' by the experimenter to carry out one set of measurements rather than another, the difficulty disappears. There is no need for a faster-than-light signal to tell particle A what measurement has been carried out on particle B, because the universe, including particle A, already 'knows' what that measurement, and its outcome will be. (Wikipedia, Bell's Theorem)

This is very close to my own position, in so far as I am indeed a 'superdeterminist'. It is nonsense to say that we 'create' objective reality by observing it. As Einstein demanded of Heisenberg in 1928, 'Are you trying to tell me that the moon is not there unless I look at it?' Of course there is no reality *for us* until we observe it, but that reality was, is, there all the time whether we observe it or not. The act of observation simply makes it real *for us*. Entangled particle A was *already* predestined to be spin up (or spin down) *before we observed it* and therefore entangled particle B was *already* spin down (or up). Neither particle was forced to adopt any particular property by our observations. There was no 'spooky action at a distance'. We were simply able to establish for ourselves the characteristics of entangled particle B by observing those of entangled particle A. It is more realistic to regard all quantum entities as being primarily particles, but particles with wave-like features. Each particle has, however, predetermined characteristics of its own whether we observe them or not.

Quantum mechanics preaches that until we observe it, a quantum particle has no particular position at all: it is in a 'superposition' of states. By virtue of its wave function, it can be quite literally in two places at once. A single photon (or electron) fired at a slit screen appears to actually passes through *both* slits like a true wave, bifurcating into two beyond the slits, and interfering with itself! Only when it is 'observed' by the impact screen does it resolve itself into a single location, but only ever onto one specific point. Well, that is the quantum explanation of reality, but is it complete, or even entirely accurate?

Einstein was never happy with the implications of quantum mechanics, and he did manage to find for himself one ally amongst the quantum physicists. That man was Erwin Schrodinger (1887-1961), an Austrian physicist from Vienna who had, at one time, hoped to become a philosopher, but had discovered that Austria already had more than enough philosophers at that time! Having trained as a physicist, he was therefore obliged to remain with that profession. He took up the suggestion made by Max Born (1882-1970) in 1922 that perhaps quantum 'waves' were not really physical waves as we usually understand them but, as noted above, were merely *probabilit* waves, which gave an indication of where the quantum particle *might* be at any point in time. Working from this basis, he was able to devise, in 1926, the Schrodinger wave equation which could predict the most likely position of a quantum particle along its wave front at any point in time, its *eigenwert*, or 'own value' probability. Technically speaking, it is a linear partial differential equation, representing the wave function by the Greek letter psi (Ψ), but it is also entirely compatible with Heisenberg's matrix mechanics The Schrodinger equation became central to all applications of quantum mechanics, including quantum field theory, which combined special relativity with quantum mechanics.

Schrodinger was awarded the Nobel Prize for his work in this field in 1933. However, his equation still did not resolve the quantum uncertainty problem, and like Einstein Schrodinger was never happy with the probability interpretation of quantum mechanics, declaring in 1937, 'I don't like it, and I'm sorry I ever had anything to do with it'. (Wikipedia entry, Schrodinger) This attitude made him the natural philosophical ally of Einstein, and he even joined Einstein in his quest for a unified field theory which would unite electromagnetism with gravity, though of course both men failed in their efforts. But Schrodinger congratulated Einstein on his EPR paper of 1935, being no less keen than Einstein himself to undermine some of the basic implications of quantum mechanics. One of these was the assumption that a quantum particle is in no particular place at all until it is observed. According to Bohr's Copenhagen school, it is this observation which causes a collapse of the wave function, so that the quantum particle decoheres into one specific location. Until then it is in a 'superposition' of locations as a wave, and can theoretically be in two places at once. In other words, particles have no specific reality until they are observed: it is the observation which calls them into being. But this would introduce an element of subjectivity into the nature of reality. It was Schrodinger who coined the terms 'superposition' and 'quantum entanglement' in relation to this conundrum.

This weird state of 'superposition' might apply to tiny particles in the quantum world, but did this have any relevance for the macroscopic, classical world? Schrodinger thought not, and in 1935, inspired by the EPR paper, he devised a thought experiment to prove his point which involved a cat in a box. In consequence, 'Schrodinger's cat' has become the most famous feline in history! In the box with the cat was a slightly radioactive substance which might or might not decay within a given period of time, releasing, say, an alpha particle. Also in the box was a detector which would register this, and would activate a device which would smash a phial of cyanide, killing the cat. Did this mean that until we opened the box to make an observation the poor cat existed in a superposition of states, being both alive and dead at the same time? Schrodinger devised this thought experiment to illustrate how ridiculous such an assumption would be, but he was dismayed to discover that some of his colleagues, convinced that reality was called into existence by observation, replied, 'Yes Erwin, you are quite right, the cat *would* be in a superposition of states!' This of course is nonsense. There is nothing special about the human retina. In this case the 'observation' was made by the detector, which collapsed the wave function, and was either activated or not. It is completely impossible for a large classical object like a cat to be in a superposition of states. The cat would be always *either* alive *or* dead whether we observed it or not. Although *for us* it would be in an indeterminate state until we opened the box. It would never be in a 'superposition' of states in reality. It is always our *perception* of reality that is changed by observation, never reality itself. Reality remains objective, not subjective. Nevertheless decades of heated debate followed on the fate of Schrodinger's poor cat, because the thought experiment had raised so many fundamental questions about the implications of quantum mechanics.

But in my opinion, both Einstein and Schrodinger were unduly concerned about quantum uncertainty, for the simple reason that the quantum world is one thing, while the macroscopic, classical world in which we live is entirely another. While it is true, as de Broglie showed, that all matter does indeed have a wavelength, as the size of matter particles increases their wavelength diminishes until, at the scale of just a few molecules, it becomes negligible for all intents and purposes, and its mysterious quantum ability to 'superposition' vanishes. Even a cricket ball thrown at 90 mph does have a wavelength of sorts, but this wavelength is some 10-34 metres, less than the diameter of a proton, and entirely negligible for all practical purposes. As objects increase in size their calculated wavelength decreases, until it becomes shorter than the Planck length, and so entirely insignificant. With the diminishing of wavelength, the possibility of quantum uncertainty also diminishes. One might say that the smaller an entity is the less predictable its behaviour, but the larger an entity becomes the more predictable its behaviour, the more subject to the laws of classical physics, which are entirely deterministic for all practical purposes.

Under highly contrived circumstances, such as those of Schrodinger's thought experiment, or perhaps within the quantum computers of the future, the quantum world can be forced to impinge and interact with the classical world in which we live, but this does not happen in nature. In reality the wave function of even tiny particles is collapsed almost immediately by contact with its surroundings, including air molecules, so that even tiny particles instantly assume definite positions. While it is true that the timing of the decay of individual atoms in a radioactive substance cannot be predicted, yet even out of this seeming chaos a kind of order emerges. Over the radioactive lifetime of the substance, a very definite number of atoms will decay over a specific time period. This period is known as the half-life of the substance, the time taken for half of the atoms to decay, and is so precise that it can be used as a dating technique, as in the case of radioactive carbon 14, which has a half-life of 5,730 years within a small margin of error, and so may be used for dating organic remains. After another 5,730 years half of the remaining carbon 14 atoms will have decayed, and so on. This illustrates an important point. Quantum particles exist in their trillions and trillions. While *individually* their behaviour may not be predictable, collectively, en masse, their behaviour *does* become predictable.

It is true that some mysteries about quantum mechanics remain. For example, we cannot yet predict when any one atom of a radioactive substance will 'choose' to decay, although this may simply be a reflection of our present levels of ignorance. It is also true that particles which are so small that their size is a reasonable proportion of their wavelength also have a seeming 'choice' over just where they will decohere, which also cannot be predicted. It was factors like these which led Richard Feynman (1918-1988), one of the greatest quantum physicists of the twentieth century, to make his famous declaration, 'Anyone who says that he understands quantum mechanics does not understand quantum mechanics!' While it is therefore possible to agree with Einstein that quantum theory is incomplete, surely it is more important to stress that in terms of the everyday world, it is *irrelevant*! Quantum objects larger than a few molecules, like ourselves, have a wavelength that is so short that they have no practical choice about where they will decohere. In that state, they then become subject to the laws of classical physics for all practical intents and purposes. For example, quantum physics tells us that if you open a box of matches and place one match beside the open box, there is an unimaginally tiny, *but non-zero* chance that the match will jump back into the box. However, you would have to wait for longer than the predicted life of the universe to have a fifty-fifty chance of witnessing that event. *This* is the relevance of quantum uncertainty in the real world under normal conditions. Technically it does exist, but for all practical intents and purposes it does not. I would say, therefore, that Einstein's concerns about quantum mechanics undermining his beloved determinism were misplaced. It does nothing to undermine my own belief in determinism. I would say that even the behaviour of individual quantum particles, although still at this point in time unpredictable, is nevertheless predetermined. It may be that the quantum superposition effect will be harnessed in the near future in quantum computers, but even then it will be harnessed in predictable ways. An unpredictable computer would not be of much use to anyone!

Obviously Einstein was worthy of detailed consideration here because his career intersected with so many key developments in twentieth-century science, developments which were of great significance for philosophical thought. But the main intention of my argument here is to show that Einstein was, and still is, overrated as a physicist, but underrated as a philosopher. His overblown reputation as a physicist was recognised by Einstein himself, when he wrote in July, 1921, giving his first impressions of the USA.,

> The cult of individual personalities is always, in my view, unjustified. To be sure, nature distributes her gifts variously among her children. But there are plenty of the well-endowed ones too, thank God, and I am firmly convinced that most of them live quiet, unregarded lives. It strikes me as unfair, and even in bad taste, to select a few for boundless admiration, attributing superhuman powers of mind and character to them. This has been my fate, and the contrast between the popular estimate of my achievements and the reality is simply grotesque. The consciousness of this extraordinary state of affairs would be unbearable but for one great consoling thought: it is a welcome symptom in an age which is commonly denounced as materialistic, that it makes heroes of men whose ambitions lie wholly in the intellectual and moral sphere. (*The World as I See It,* (2002 ed.), p. 40.)

Note Einstein's mentioning of 'the moral sphere' in the quotation above. There will be more on this point below but first, let us begin with the physics side of my argument. I have already shown, with the information above, how Einstein came to be overrated as a physicist, but I will briefly recap.

In the first place, Einstein never carried out a single practical, hands-on experiment which actually discovered something new in his whole career. He was entirely a theoretical physicist. He did collaborate with others on some papers that did involve practical experiments, but those experiments had always been carried out by the other parties. Many scientists were happy to have Einstein's name attached to their 'joint' papers, but in every case the experimental and mathematical work in them had been done by others, and many were completely written by the other parties, as with the celebrated EPR paper. Now because he was entirely a theoretical physicist, it was rather important that Einstein should have been extremely good at maths, but by his own admission, as shown above, Einstein was not. Hilbert, Minkowski, even Grossman and Besso were entirely out of his league. Einstein's genius lay not in his mathematical ability, but rather in his genius for knowing who to ask to help him with his maths, and all four of the above did so. In his collaborative papers with others especially, it was common for the mathematical sections to be written entirely by the other contributors, as with Grossman in the case of their *Entwurf* paper, and Rosen in their EPR paper. If ever anyone 'got by with a little help from his friends' that man was Albert Einstein.

It could also be argued that Einstein never had a wholly original idea in his life. All of his papers were based on the ideas of others, which he simply worked on and took a little further with some unproven theoretical suggestions of his own. This applied particularly to his 1905 papers. It was only *after* his triumph with general relativity that it came to be assumed that he had been the sole progenitor of special relativity as well. This was far from true, but if Poincaré, Lorentz, and Fitzgerald noticed this, they politely stood back and said nothing about it, displaying the same generosity of spirit as had Hilbert. The only one who ever openly showed any resentment over the way Einstein had commandeered his ideas was Philipp Lenard, who bitterly opposed Einstein's nomination for the Nobel Prize. Einstein came closest to originality with the theory of general relativity, but even this was simply an extension of special relativity, which had certainly not been Einstein's original idea, as shown above. In fact, special relativity was of much greater practical and scientific significance than general relativity, although it received much less publicity. Even here, Einstein failed to grasp its full implications with regard to the space-time continuum, failing to understand it (by his own admission) even after Minkowski had explained it to him in mathematical terms. Indeed, this failure to understand the implications of his own work extended to other fields. In 1916 he rejected a paper sent to him by Karl Schwarzschild (1873-1916) which suggested that, according to general relativity, black holes might exist, and even in 1939 he was still claiming that, 'these Schwarzschild singularities do not exist in physical reality'. (Isaacson, pp. 250-1) In 1934 he denied that atomic energy, an atomic bomb, or even the splitting of the atom would ever be possible. (Isaacson, p. 469) In fact Hans C. Ohanian managed to fill a whole book on the theme of *Einstein's Mistakes: the Human Failings of Genius* (2009), where he enlarges on 23 specific mistakes made by Einstein.

In reality, Einstein was very much a one-hit pop star. His reputation rested entirely on the theory of general relativity which, as shown above, had been very much a collective achievement, rather than emerging solely from the mind of one outstanding genius. It had been Einstein's dogged persistence, and his talent for knowing where to turn for help, that had finally brought the theory to fruition. He was never to achieve its like again. Instead he wasted most of the rest of his career on two quixotic quests: his attempts to deny the reality of quantum effects even in the face of mounting experimental evidence, and his equally futile attempt to devise a unified field theory, which obsessed him to the end of his life, but ended in failure. As early as December 1919 Einstein noted to his friend Heinrich Zangger, 'With fame I become more and more stupid, which of course is a very common phenomenon.' (Isaacson, p. 272) A great physicist? This is rather questionable. Even Einstein's Nobel Prize was a bit of a fiddle, as shown above. Einstein was certainly *a* physicist, certainly a scientist, but he was not in the same league as Maxwell, Rutherford, Poincaré, Thomson, Lorentz, Bohr, Heisenberg, or Dirac. Rather, Einstein was a man who benefitted from, and still enjoys, an overblown reputation as a physicist.

Having said all that, however, I am not anti-Einstein. Indeed, he is one of my philosopher heroes, and I was disappointed to discover that, as a physicist, he was rather less than he is usually represented in the textbooks. I had to report this only because, as a historian, my first allegiance must be to the truth. A bit of a cheat in his love life, and a bit of a fraud in his professional life, Einstein was something of a flawed human being. But this made him very human: who amongst us is fit to cast the first stone? Through it all, he kept a keen, self-deprecating sense of humour, never believing in his own myth, but always a cheerful and convivial companion. Moreover, Einstein was not *just* a physicist. He was also a musician, talented on the violin and competent on the piano. Music played an important part in his life: sometimes, when invited to give a speech, he would surprise his audience by giving them a violin recital instead! (Isaacson, p. 272) He was particularly fond of Mozart and Bach. Einstein was also a linguist, fluent in German and Italian, and competent in French and English, although he always had most difficulty with this last, which was odd, since English and German are often said to be 'sister' languages. In his spare time he was a yachtsman, with a small sailboat of his own, and he enjoyed country walks.

More importantly, however, Einstein became, in later life, a political campaigner, and a deep thinker on social, economic, philosophical, and racial issues. While, over the course of his lifetime, he published over 300 scientific works as books (15 books, nearly all different takes on relativity), chapters in the books of others, and articles, he also published some 150 non-scientific works on philosophy, religion, and the affairs of the day. Many of these were later collected into books under his name as author, such as, *Essays in Humanism* (1950), *Ideas and Opinions* (1954), and *The World as I See It* (1956). All three of these books, and some others on Einstein too, rest on my shelves. Of these latter, the most revealing of Einstein's views is Max Jammer's *Einstein and Religion* (1999), although my own copy is the 2002 paperback edition. No one who reads these books can doubt for a moment that Einstein was indeed a philosopher, and a considerable one. But of them all, I was most taken, most moved, by the opening paragraphs of Einstein's 'The World as I See It', which is in fact just a short essay which begins the collection under that title, but originally was only five pages long. As I read it, I felt the same tingling of the spine, the same rising of the hairs on the back of my neck, that I had first felt on reading of the thoughts of Spinoza, as I came to realise how closely his views paralleled my own. Because I found them so moving, and so revealing of Einstein the philosopher, I feel obliged to quote those two paragraphs here.

> What an extraordinary situation is that of us mortals! Each of us is here for a brief sojourn; for what purpose he knows not, though he sometimes thinks he feels it. But from the point of view of daily life, without going deeper, we exist for our fellow-men – in the first place for those on whose smiles and welfare our happiness

depends, and next for all those unknown to us personally with whose destinies we are bound up by the tie of sympathy. A hundred times every day I remind myself that my inner and outer life depend on the labours of other men, living and dead, and that I must exert myself in order to give in the same measure as I have received and am still receiving. I am strongly drawn to the simple life and am often oppressed by the feeling that I am engrossing an unnecessary amount of the labour of my fellow-men. I regard class differences as contrary to justice and, in the last resort, based on force. I also consider that plain living is good for everybody, physically and mentally.

In human freedom in the philosophical sense I am definitely a disbeliever. Everybody acts not only under external compulsion but also in accordance with inner necessity. Schopenhauer's saying, that 'a man can do as he will, but not will as he will', has been an inspiration to me from my youth up, and a continual consolation and unfailing well-spring of patience in the face of the hardships of life, my own and others. This feeling mercifully mitigates the sense of responsibility which so easily becomes paralysing, and prevents us from taking ourselves and other people too seriously; it conduces to a view of life in which humour, above all, has its due place. (2006 ed., pp. 3-4)

I am so entirely in agreement with those sentiments that I could have written them myself: indeed, careful readers of this book will note that in various places I actually have, albeit in different words. But Einstein was not just a theoretical philosopher: he actually practised what he preached. On discovering the plight of coloured races in the America of the 1930s, Einstein announced, 'I do not intend to remain silent on this issue'. As someone who had suffered from racial discrimination himself, Einstein's sympathies were entirely with the coloured races of America. He actively campaigned for racial equality, and took up the cause of blacks wrongly accused of crimes in the southern states, such as that of the Scottsboro Boys, wrongly accused of rape in 1930s Alabama. Such interventions, of course, made Einstein extremely unpopular with the southern rednecks of his day. To them, Einstein was nothing but 'a nigger-loving Jew Boy', and they would have lynched him as readily as the Nazis. Einstein very wisely always stayed north of the Mason-Dixon line, but even there discrimination existed. In 1937 the black contralto, Marian Anderson, came to Princeton to give a concert, but the Nassau Inn refused her a room, maintaining a 'no blacks' policy. So Einstein welcomed her into his own home on Mercer Street, where she was to stay on all subsequent visits to Princeton. (Isaacson, p. 445)

Einstein also became a Zionist, actively campaigning for a Jewish homeland (but not necessarily a state) in the British protectorate of Palestine, which covered the former territories of Judea and Samaria, the ancient Jewish homelands before the Jewish Diaspora, which had followed from their two failed rebellions against their Roman masters in 70 AD and 135 AD. Under the Balfour Declaration of November 1917, the British declared themselves to be in favour of the establishment in Palestine of a national homeland for the Jewish people, providing that, 'nothing shall be done which may prejudice the civil and religious rights of existing non-Jewish communities in Palestine'.

Einstein, though a Zionist, entirely sympathised with this proviso. In 1929 he wrote to the then Jewish leader Chaim Weizmann to warn that, 'Should we be unable to find a way to honest co-operation and honest pacts with the Arabs, then we have learned absolutely nothing during our 2,000 years of suffering'. He also warned his Zionist friends that unless an accommodation with the Palestinian Arabs could be found, the struggle would haunt them in decades to come. How prophetic his words were to prove.

From an early age, Einstein had also been against strident nationalism and mindless militarism. He carefully avoided military service himself, and became a pacifist. Like so many others, Einstein was horrified by the tragedy and waste of the First World War. Within six months of its outbreak in 1914 Einstein was writing to friends giving it as his opinion that the only alternative to eternal warfare was the setting up of some form of supranational authority which could arbitrate on all international disputes. (Isaacson, p.209) Such a body, thought Einstein, should hold a monopoly of military power, so that its decisions could be enforced. This of course implied voluntary world disarmament as a first step! Einstein's friends, such as Robert Oppenheimer, later warned him that his plan was Utopian, and hopelessly idealistic, but after 1945 Einstein advocated it with renewed vigour. Isaacson wrote of him,

> For the remaining ten years of his life his passion for advocating a unified governing structure for the globe would rival that for finding a unified field theory that could govern all the forces of nature. Although distinct in most ways, both quests reflected his instinct for transcendent order. In addition, both would display Einstein's willingness to be a nonconformist, to be serenely secure in challenging prevailing attitudes. (p. 488)

Einstein believed that rampant nationalism was a major factor as a cause of war, and he strongly disapproved of it. Over the course of his life he was happy to live for a time in Germany, or Italy, or Switzerland, or in America, becoming, like Thomas Paine, a real *citoyen du monde*. In 1901 Einstein had acquired Swiss citizenship, partly as a ruse to avoid military service, and he retained this for the rest of his life. For a time, he accepted his native German citizenship as well, but on March 28, 1933, on seeing the rise of Nazism, Einstein renounced his German citizenship in disgust, handing in his passport at the German consulate in Brussels. He was never to see his native land again. However, just a few years later, on October 1, 1940, Einstein eagerly and proudly adopted American citizenship. When asked if he would renounce all other loyalties, he joyously declared that he 'would even renounce my cherished sailboat' if that should prove necessary. (Isaacson, p. 479) There were aspects of American society that Einstein disapproved of – its racism, the great disparities of wealth between rich and poor, its lack of anything resembling an adequate welfare state – but these defects were more than compensated for in Einstein's mind by what America *did* have to offer, something that Einstein prized above all else. That was America's tolerance of freedom of thought, freedom of speech, and all forms of nonconformist belief. As Isaacson wrote,

> For Einstein, creativity required being willing not to conform. That required nurturing free minds and free spirits, which in turn required a spirit of tolerance. And the underpinning of tolerance was humility – the belief that no one had the right to impose ideas and beliefs on others. (p. 550)

In America, people could be as critical as they liked about the government, in speech, in print, and even over the airwaves, and nobody dreamed of imprisoning them for their views. This contrasted sharply with the situation in Hitler's Germany, Stalin's Russia, and Mussolini's Italy. For this reason Einstein was opposed to both fascism and communism, although he felt some sympathy with the latter, because he believed that it was genuinely attempting to improve the lot of the mass of the Russian people.

In political terms, Einstein was definitely a man of the left, a champion of both socialism and pacifism, actively campaigning for both during most of his life. But could both ends be achieved together? Einstein thought not. In March, 1931 Einstein attended a pacifist rally organised by the War Resisters' League in New York. There he met the socialist leader Norman Thomas, who tried to convince Einstein that pacifism could work only within the context of world socialism, and that therefore it was more important to establish socialism first. But Einstein disagreed, saying, 'It is easier to win people over to pacifism than to socialism. We should work first for pacifism, and only later for socialism.' (Isaacson, p. 375) Einstein saw war as being a greater evil than capitalism. The latter may condemn people to poverty, misery, unemployment, and debt, but at least it leaves them alive!

Both before and after the Second World War, Einstein remained an ardent pacifist, regarding war as the greatest of follies. One of his last actions in the year of his death, 1955, was to sign with Bertrand Russell *The Russell-Einstein Manifesto,* a document calling for nuclear disarmament, which was also signed by a number of prominent scientists and intellectuals of the time. But during the Second World War itself, as the full evil of Nazism emerged, especially in the nature of Hitler's 'final solution' to the 'Jewish problem', even Einstein was forced to admit that there was justification for armed opposition to Hitler's regime. When America joined the war in December, 1941, Einstein raised no objections. In an interview given to the *New York Times* on December 30, 1941, Einstein said,

> In the twenties, when no dictatorships existed, I advocated that refusing to go to war would make war improper. But as soon as coercive conditions appeared in certain nations, I felt that it would weaken the less aggressive nations vis-à-vis the more aggressive ones.

One is reminded here of the retort attributed to the economist John Maynard Keynes (1883-1946) when a detractor accused him of inconsistency. He replied, 'When the facts change, I change my mind. What do you do, sir?' Indeed, the horrors of the Second World War turned Einstein savagely against *all* Germans, and not just the Nazis. He never forgave the Aryan intellectuals of Germany for not only failing to oppose Hitler, but in fact actively supporting his regime in many cases. He held the whole German people guilty of Nazism. Indeed, we must ask ourselves, supposing that Hitler had called an election just after the fall of France in June 1940, how many Aryan Germans would *not* have voted for Hitler? Indeed, despite the view of Einstein's hero Spinoza that 'Odium nunquam potest esse bono' (*Ethics,* Pt. 4 Prop. 45) (Hatred can never be good) he ignored this warning with respect to Germans, coming very close to hatred for them. In the summer of 1942 he wrote to his friend Otto Juliusburger,

> Because of their wretched traditions, the Germans are so evil that it will be very difficult to remedy the situation by sensible, not to say humane means. I hope that by the end of the war they will largely kill themselves off, with the kindly help of God. (Alice Calaprice (ed.) *The Ultimate Quotable Einstein* (2011) p. 169

In 1944, referring to the Warsaw Ghetto uprising, Einstein wrote,

> The Germans as an entire people are responsible for these mass murders, and must be punished as a people...Behind the Nazi Party stand the German people, who elected Hitler after he had in his book and in his speeches made his shameful intentions clear beyond the possibility of any misunderstanding. (*ibid.*, p. 169)

At the same time Einstein was proud to be a Jew, and proud of the Jewish heritage, as he had every right to be. He wrote in August 1933, 'The pursuit of knowledge for its own sake, an almost fanatical love of justice, and the desire for personal independence – these are the features of the Jewish tradition which make me thank my lucky stars that I belong to it.' Later, in November 1938, he added, 'The Jews as a group may be powerless, but the sum of the achievements of their individual members is everywhere considerable and telling, even though these achievements were made in the face of obstacles.' (*ibid.* pp. 210, 213) Einstein was, in every other respect, a fervent anti-racist, as opposed to racial distinctions as he was to class distinctions. However, his attitude towards the Germans and his Zionism were just enough to provoke a book from Christopher Bjerknes entitled, *Albert Einstein, the Incorrigible Racist* (2016). It is largely nonsense from beginning to end, but as with the charges against Einstein of the Bible Believers, there is just a grain of truth in it.

It was in fact Einstein's contempt for the Nazi regime that prompted him to take part in a project that he would never otherwise have sponsored. In 1939 two refugee Hungarian physicists who had fled from the threat of Nazism in Europe realised that it might be possible to build an atomic bomb. They were

Leo Szilard (1898-1964) and Eugene Wigner (1902-95), who were both then living in America. The key raw material required for the bomb would be uranium, which was then being mined in the Belgian Congo. But the two physicists realised that, if the Nazis were to occupy Belgium, then they would control the uranium supplies. The neutron had been discovered in 1932, and the Germans were known to be already carrying out fission experiments. The two physicists were very alarmed by the thought that Germany might be the first country to develop an atomic weapon, and they felt that America should be warned of the danger, but how should this be done? Who would listen to a pair of obscure Hungarian refugees? But Szilard was an old colleague of Einstein's from their Berlin days in the 1920s, and in July 1939 Szilard and Wigner sought him out to explain their fears to him. Nuclear physics was not Einstein's strong suit, but when they had explained to him how two units of'enriched' uranium,high in the more fissile isotope U235, could be suddenly brought together to reach a 'critical mass', Einstein soon grasped their point. The highly reactive U235 released neutrons, and since neutrons had no electric charge, they were not repelled by either the negative charge of an atom's electron shell, nor by the positive charge of the nucleus, which they could therefore smash into, releasing more neutrons in the case of uranium 235, initiating a chain reaction that could split more atoms, releasing an enormous amount of energy. Einstein was alarmed, exclaiming, 'I never thought of that!' (Isaacson, p. 472) The three men decided to recruit another Hungarian refugee physicist, Edward Teller (1908-2003) who was a nuclear expert, to help them formulate a case. Teller did not actually sign their subsequent letter, but he advised on its contents. Finally they appealed to Alexander Sachs (1893-1973), a banker with Lehman Brothers and a personal friend of President Roosevelt. Sachs, like Teller, was Jewish, and he agreed to help the physicists by delivering a letter signed by all three of them, by hand and in person, to the President himself. This meant that three out of the five collaborators on that momentous letter were Jewish. Sachs finally got an interview with Roosevelt on October 11, 1939, just a month after the outbreak of the Second World War and, on reading the letter signed by Szilard, Wigner, and Einstein, the President immediately agreed that action should be taken. Fission research had already begun in America, but the result of Roosevelt's decision was the massive Manhattan Project, which produced the first workable atomic bomb in July,1945. The project was headed by Robert Oppenheimer (1904-67), another Jewish physicist, and several other refugee Jewish scientists also worked on the project. Hitler could not have raised up for himself a more dangerous set of enemies, not only in Germany itself, but around the world.

There was a strange irony here. Einstein, the passionate anti-war campaigner, had played a key role in launching a project that led to atomic weapons, since his signature on the letter was instrumental in persuading Roosevelt that it ought to be taken seriously. In reality, of course, Einstein knew comparatively little about nuclear physics, and had never dreamed of a chain reaction, yet his signature on that letter gave rise to another Einstein myth, namely that he had been 'the father of the atomic bomb'. In fact, however, Einstein had nothing more to do with the Manhattan Project, and after the war, when it became clear that Germany had been nowhere near to developing an atomic weapon, he bitterly regretted his involvement with that momentous letter to Roosevelt. He declared in an interview with *Newsweek* magazine, published on March 10, 1947, 'Had I known that the Germans would not succeed in producing an atomic bomb, I never would have lifted a finger.' (*ibid.,* p. 275)

After the war, Einstein reverted to his pacifist stance, campaigning more desperately than ever for world peace, guaranteed by some form of supra-national authority. He also championed socialism as an economic system, and here, Einstein was unambiguously very left-wing indeed, referring to capitalism as 'the predatory phase of human development'. His famous article, 'Why Socialism?' appeared in the first edition of a new socialist journal, *The Monthly Review* for May, 1949, but it is reproduced on pages 1-10 of the Einstein collection, *Essays in Humanism* (1978 ed.), and I refer to those pages here. Einstein claimed that capitalism was causing a deterioration of the human spirit, writing,

> All human beings, whatever their position in society, are suffering from this process of deterioration. Unknowingly prisoners of their own egotism, they feel insecure, lonely, and deprived of the naive, simple, and unsophisticated enjoyment of life. Man can find meaning in life, short and perilous as it is, only through devoting himself to society. The economic anarchy of capitalist society as it exists today is, in my opinion, the real source of this evil. (p. 6)

On the next page Einstein wrote,

> Private capital tends to become concentrated in few hands, partly because of competition among the capitalists, and partly because technological development and the increasing division of labour encourage the formation of larger units of production at the expense of smaller ones. The result of these developments is an oligarchy of private capital, the enormous power of which cannot be effectively checked even by a democratically organised political society. This is true because the members of legislative bodies are selected by political parties which are largely financed or otherwise influenced by private capitalists who, for all practical purposes, separate the electorate from the legislature. The consequence is that the representatives of the people do not in fact sufficiently protect the interests of the underprivileged sections of the population. Moreover, under existing conditions, private capitalists inevitably control, directly or indirectly, the main sources of information (press, radio, education). It is thus extremely difficult, and indeed in most cases quite impossible, for the individual citizen to come to objective conclusions and to make intelligent use of his political rights. (pp. 7-8)

How little have things changed in 70 years. Einstein could here have been writing about our own times. Later he added,

> The profit motive, in conjunction with competition among capitalists, is responsible for an instability in the accumulation and utilisation of capital which leads to increasingly severe depressions. Unlimited competition leads to a huge waste of labour, and to that crippling of the social consciousness of individuals that I mentioned earlier. This crippling of individuals I consider the worst evil of capitalism. Our whole educational system suffers from this evil. An exaggerated competitive attitude is inculcated into the student, who is trained to worship acquisitive success as a preparation for his future career.
>
> I am convinced there is only one way to eliminate these grave evils, namely through the establishment of a socialist economy, accompanied by an educational system which would be orientated towards social goals. In such an economy the means of production are owned by society itself, and are utilised in a planned fashion. A planned economy, which adjusts production to the needs of the community, would distribute the work to be done amongst all those able to work and would guarantee a livelihood to every man, woman, and child. The education of the individual, in addition to promoting his own innate abilities, would attempt to develop in him a sense of responsibility for his fellow men in place of the glorification of power and success in our present society. (pp. 8-9)

However, mindful of the evils of Stalin's communism, with its totalitarianism and overweening bureaucracy, Einstein concluded by adding,

> Nevertheless, it is necessary to remember that a planned economy is not yet socialism. A planned economy as such may be accompanied by the complete enslavement of the individual...Clarity about the aims and problems of socialism is of the greatest significance in our age of transition. Since, under present circumstances, free and unhindered discussion of these problems has come under a powerful taboo, I consider the foundation of this magazine to be an important public service. (p. 10)

The magazine was of course *The Monthly Review,* and the 'powerful taboo' to which Einstein referred was in fact McCarthyism, named after Senator Joseph McCarthy (1908-57), who led the rather paranoid witch-hunt against suspected Communist subversives in America between 1947 and 1956. This was the period known as the Second Red Scare, since America had gone through a similar First Red Scare between 1917 and 1920 following the emergence of Communism in Russia. McCarthy was supported in his investigations by J. Edgar Hoover (1895-1972), who was at that time head of the FBI. Thousands of Americans were wrongly accused of disloyalty during this period, losing their jobs and even suffering imprisonment, on grounds later declared to be unconstitutional and illegal. Einstein himself came under heavy suspicion, with the FBI holding a large file on him, but he was never actively persecuted, perhaps because of his age and celebrity. Nevertheless, Einstein was bitterly disappointed to see America lapsing into this kind of behaviour, a land which he had believed to prize free thought and freedom of expression. It took some courage to publish his article on socialism in 1949, but Einstein did it as a deliberate act of defiance, careless of the potential consequences for himself. Even in 1939, had Einstein wanted to join the Manhattan Project, he would not have been allowed to do so on security grounds, because of his already known socialist, pacifist, anti-racial, and internationalist views. The FBI had some grounds for suspicion. Einstein was certainly very left wing, and one of his colleagues, Boris Podolsky of the EPR paper, and one of his mistresses, Margarita Kokenkova, were both later discovered to have been Soviet spies!

Einstein had derived his views in part from a deep study of philosophy, which had fascinated him throughout his life. He too had his philosopher heroes, who were Baruch Spinoza (1632-77), David Hume (1711-1776), Immanuel Kant (1724-1804), Arthur Schopenhauer (1788-1860), and Ernst Mach (1838-1916). Mach was a Moravian physicist and philosopher, best known for his experiments with supersonic projectiles, who gives his name to airspeeds, as Mach 1, Mach 2, etc. with Mach 1 being the speed of sound. As a philosopher of science he was an empiricist, refusing to believe in anything that could not be seen and directly measured. This led him to announce in 1897, 'I do not believe that atoms exist!' Einstein was inspired by the empiricism of Hume and Mach in his early career, but later began to believe that they were mistaken after he came to appreciate the power of mathematical analysis and prediction.

One of Einstein's most attractive features was his humility: he was always ready to admit that our understanding of the universe was not complete. In conversation with Alfred Kerr in 1927 Einstein declared,

> Try to penetrate with our limited means the secrets of nature and you will find that, behind all the discernable concatenations, there remains something subtle, intangible, and inexplicable. Veneration for this force beyond anything that we can comprehend is my religion. To that extent I am, in point of fact, religious. (Cited in Calaprice, op. cit. p.324)

In 1936, in a letter to Phyllis Wright, he was more specific.

> A spirit is manifest in the laws of the universe – a spirit vastly superior to that of man, one in the face of which we with our modest powers must feel humble. In this way the pursuit of science leads to a religious feeling of a special sort. (Cited in Isaacson, op. cit. p. 551)

But Einstein's views on religion and morality had also been strongly influenced by his philosophical studies. He believed in what he called 'cosmic religion', which corresponded very closely to the panentheism of Spinoza. On November 11, 1930 Einstein published an article in the *New York Times Magazine* with the title, 'Religion and Science', where he declared,

The beginnings of cosmic religious feeling already appear in earlier stages of development – e.g. in many of the Psalms of David and in some of the Prophets. Buddhism, as we have learnt from the wonderful writings of Schopenhauer especially, contains a much stronger element of it. The religious geniuses of all ages have been distinguished by this kind of religious feeling, which knows no dogma and no God conceived in man's image, so that there can be no Church whose central teachings are based on it. Hence it is precisely among the heretics of every age that we find men who were filled with the highest kind of religious feeling and were in many cases regarded by their contemporaries as atheists, sometimes also as saints. Looked at in this light, men like Democritus, Francis of Assisi, and Spinoza are closely akin to one another...

You will hardly find one among the profounder sort of scientific minds without a peculiar religious feeling of his own. But it is different from the religion of the naive man. For the latter, God is a being from whose care one hopes to benefit and whose punishment one fears; a sublimation of a feeling similar to that of a child for its father, a being with whom one stands to some extent in a personal relationship, however deeply it may be tinged with awe. But the scientist is possessed by the sense of universal causation. The future, to him, is every whit as necessary and determined as the past. There is nothing divine about morality: it is a purely human affair. His religious feeling takes the form of a rapturous amazement at the harmony of natural law, which reveals an intelligence of such superiority that, compared with it, all the systematic thinking and acting of human beings is an utterly insignificant reflection. This feeling is the guiding principle of his life and work, in so far as he succeeds in keeping himself from the shackles of selfish desire. It is beyond question closely akin to that which has possessed the religious geniuses of all ages...A man's ethical behaviour should be based effectually on sympathy, education, and social ties and needs. Man would indeed be in a poor way if he had to be restrained by fear of punishment and hope of reward after death. (pp. 2-3)

There are echoes here of Kant's 'categorical imperative' with which I do not entirely agree but again, in every other respect I could have written the above passage myself, since it so entirely reflects my own views. For Einstein, there was no essential conflict between science and religion; for him, they could be seen as very much the same thing, but divorced from ethical considerations, which he believed fell very much within the purely human sphere.

Einstein was a remarkable all-rounder. He was of course keenly interested in science, but he was not *just* a physicist. Although he never believed in his own myth, he was happy to use his celebrity to campaign for socialism, pacifism, Zionism, internationalism, world government, and racial equality. He had always also been very interested in philosophy from his earliest days at the 'Olympia Academy', where Hume was discussed with Mach, and Cervantes with Poincaré. In his private life he was a musician, a linguist, a yachtsman, and a country walker with a keen appreciation of nature. Surprisingly, he was also a cartoonist and a poet, as revealed in his many surviving letters to his mistresses. He was even moved to write a poem about Spinoza in 1920, *Zu Spinozas Ethik*. Because of the many very bad English translations of this poem that abound, we get the impression that Einstein was a bad poet. For instance, the first and last verses of that poem are usually translated as,

How much do I love this noble man,
More than I can say with words.
I fear though he'll remain alone,
With a holy halo of his own.

You'd think his example would show us
What this teaching can give mankind,
Trust not to the comforting facade,
One must be born sublime.

But in the original German it sounds much better.

Wie lieb ich diesen edlen Mann
Mehr al sich mit Worten sagen kann.
Doch feurcht' ich, dass er bleibt allein
Mit seinem strahlenden Heiligenschein.

Du denkst sein Beispiel zeigt uns eben
Was diese Lehre den Menschen kann geben.
Vertraue nicht dem troestlichen Schein:
Zum Erhabenen muss man geboren sein.

You need not know much German to be able to see that the German version *does* actually rhyme *and* scan!

Einstein died on April 18, 1955, just a month after his lifelong friend and collaborator the Swiss-Italian Michele Besso (1873-1955). Einstein wrote to Besso's family, 'He has departed from this strange world a little ahead of me. That means nothing. For us physicists, the distinction between past, present, and future is only a stubborn illusion'. Einstein had introduced Besso to his future wife, Anna Winteler, and commented in his letter that Besso had, 'succeeded in living in harmony with a woman, an undertaking in which I twice failed rather miserably'. (Isaacson, p. 540)

No other scientist of the twentieth century, or indeed any other century, ever involved himself so deeply in the affairs of his time, or wrote so widely on topics not directly connected with his scientific speciality. I cannot go into every aspect of Einstein's thought here, but I can recommend the paperback edition of C. Seelig (ed.) *Ideas and Opinions by Albert Einstein* (2005) based on Einstein's own *Mein Weltbild*. The book consists entirely of Einstein's writings in his own words. Also very revealing is Alice Calaprice's book, *The Ultimate Quotable Einstein* (2011). You cannot fill a thick volume with quotations from someone who has nothing of importance to say. His writings show Einstein to have been a deep thinker on social, economic, political, and religious issues, and reveal his keen interest in philosophy and philosophers. Moreover, Einstein thought to some purpose about issues that were of immediate relevance to his day, wisely avoiding the quagmire of epistemology into which so many philosophers have sunk without trace, leaving only a few bubbles on the surface to mark the point of their demise. Einstein treated his women badly and was a little too left-wing for me, while his hopes for a world government and world peace were obviously unrealistic, at least for our stage of human development. But his ideals were a reflection of his strong humanitarianism, and in all other respects I find little to disagree with, and much to admire, in Einstein's approach to life and philosophical outlook, so that for me he is and will remain a great philosopher, albeit an underrated one. No doubt professional, academic philosophers will sneer at Einstein's wise words, dismissing them as not 'proper' philosophy at all because Einstein eschewed complexity, and the convoluted forms of expression so beloved by those 'professionals'. But that is not my view.

Karl Popper (1902-1994)

Sir Karl Raimund Popper, CH, FRS, FBA, died in 1994 bedecked with more honours than those of any other twentieth-century philosopher: certainly more than Einstein's, and perhaps more than those of any philosopher who has ever lived. From Britain he received a knighthood in 1965, and was made a Companion of Honour in 1982. He was also elected as a Fellow of both the Royal Society and the British Academy. This in itself was a remarkable achievement, since that Royal Society was none other than The Royal Society of London for Improving Natural Knowledge, mentioned in the Science Chapter below. It was founded in 1660, and is the world's oldest, and arguably most prestigious scientific society. To be elected as a Fellow of this society is one of the highest accolades that can be awarded to any British scientist, short of a Nobel Prize. But Popper was also elected as a Fellow of the Arts equivalent of the Royal Society, which is the British Academy. The British Academy was founded much later, but also by royal charter, in 1902. Its purpose is to recognise and support outstanding achievement in the humanities and social sciences, such as history, literature, economics, sociology, music, the performing arts, and philosophy. To be elected as an FBA is one of the highest honours that can be awarded to an Arts man, and the Academy has an exclusive membership of only 900 in the early twenty-first century. But the point here is that one spends one's life *either* as a scientist aspiring to become an FRS at the end of a very distinguished career, *or* one spends a lifetime in the Arts, hoping one day to become an FBA. I know of no other case of a philosopher (or anyone else) achieving *both* distinctions, although this may be simply a reflection of my ignorance. Even C.P. Snow (1905-1980) who was both a novelist and a scientist, who was made a CBE and a peer of the realm, and who did his best to bridge the gap between *The Two Cultures* with his 1959 lectures and book of that title, failed to be elected as either an FRS or an FBA. Even Bertrand Russell was elected only as an FRS, a well-deserved honour because he was a very considerable mathematician. He was not elected as an FBA as well, despite his many influential writings, although Russell did enjoy the consolation of receiving the Nobel Prize for Literature in 1950. However, like Einstein's, Russell's Nobel Prize had been something of a fiddle. It was awarded, 'in recognition of his varied and significant writings in which he champions humanitarian ideals and freedom of thought'. So on those grounds it would seem that Popper, who had done exactly the same thing, might quite possibly have been awarded the Nobel Prize for Literature as well! Conversely, if Russell had been considered enough of an Arts man to have won the Nobel Prize for Literature, it is surprising that he did not become an FBA as well. It may have been that Russell's private life and religious beliefs were factors here. However, Russell's prize was a bit of a fiddle because the terms of Nobel's will made it quite clear that the literature prize was to be awarded for *creative* writing, that is novels, short stories, poetry, and the like, not for philosophical or political writings. Russell of course never wrote a novel or a short story in his life. There is in fact no Nobel Prize for philosophy. Jean-Paul Sartre and Albert Camus were both awarded the literature prize, but only because both were novelists as well as philosophers. Russell's Nobel Prize was, like Einstein's, more of an attempt by the Nobel committee to bask in the reflected glory of the recipient.

Austria, his native land, awarded Popper the Austrian Decoration for Science and Art in 1980, and the Grand Decoration of Honour in Gold for Services to the Republic of Austria in 1986. Vienna awarded him its Prize for the Humanities in 1965 and its Ring of Honour in 1983. Germany weighed in with its Grand Cross with Star and Sash of the Order of Merit, and the Otto Hahn Peace Medal. Even Japan joined the party, awarding Popper the Kyoto Prize in Arts and Philosophy in 1992. The above is by no means a comprehensive list of all the honours showered upon Popper, but only a representative sample. To judge from his honours list, one might conclude that Popper was the most distinguished philosopher of the twentieth century. How had Popper managed to accumulate such a basketful of honours and, more importantly, had he deserved them? In their book *Rethinking Popper* (2009) R.S. Cohen and Z. Parusniková (eds.) launch what is intended to be a eulogy of Popper on page one of their Introduction, writing,

> Karl Popper was a radically influential philosopher of the last century, ever questioning, stimulating, inventive, rational and humane, always curious, always critical. Almost every aspect of human existence was within his range, in principle and recurrently in practice, and open to his sharp and unremitting questioning. Epistemology, logic, political economy and social theory, the history of ideas, scientific method, the relationship between body and mind, on and on...he was a thoughtful gadfly to all. (p. 1)

A gadfly, however, is an ephemeral and irritating insect that lives by sucking the blood of others. Moreover, he who sets out to be a jack of all trades runs the risk, if not of becoming the master of none, then at least of becoming something less than a master of some of them.

There is often an element of chance, not to say farce, when it comes to the awarding of honours. (The OBE has been said to stand for 'Other Buggers' Efforts'!) Russell, for example, received far fewer honours than Popper although he had much the better mind of the two because he was an avowed atheist and believer in free love and open marriages, practising what he preached. He was therefore regarded as not quite respectable by the Establishment of the day, while Popper had remained entirely blameless in those regards. Indeed, both Russell and Einstein had displayed just a little too much independence of thought to be entirely acceptable to their respective Establishments. Moreover, Popper flattered the Western world, declaring it to possess the best of all available systems, and everyone likes to be flattered. He wrote in his essay collection, *All Life is Problem Solving,*

> We live in a simply wonderful world, and here in the West we have created the best social system there has ever been...we have achieved far more than any of us (myself, for example) ever hoped. (2001 ed., p. 111)

Conformity pays! In addition Popper happened to move in Old World circles where honours proliferated, while Einstein, for example, had moved to republican America, which had always been chary of awarding marks of distinction to its citizens. The USA created no knights or peers or Companions of Honour, and it had no Royal Society or British Academy. As a result, the luckless Einstein was actually showered with more commemorative honours after his death than he had ever received in his lifetime! But what were they worth? The cynical view of the honours system was expressed by Napoleon Bonaparte, who observed, 'By such baubles men are ruled'. However, there was in addition one more reason for Popper's cavalcade of honours, which will become clear later in this section.

But what of Popper himself? He was born in Vienna on July 28, 1902, as the youngest of three children: he had two elder sisters, Dora and Annie. The Popper family was middle-class and relatively well off, much as Einstein's had been, but again as in Einstein's case, no special provisions were made for Popper's education: both men simply attended their local gymnasium. Karl's father Simon was a lawyer with his own law firm, and also a Doctor of Law who lectured part-time at the University of Vienna, so that Popper was brought up in a scholarly atmosphere, with access to his father's large private library. The family was entirely Jewish by descent, but had officially converted to Lutheranism just before Karl was born in an attempt to assimilate into gentile society. Popper therefore received a Christian baptism, but he never forgot his Jewish heritage.

It was perhaps because of his scholarly home background that Popper was moved to leave school at the age of 16, disgusted by the slow progress in learning that was being made by his class. Instead, he began to attend lectures at the University of Vienna on an informal basis, choosing topics that interested him. These included mathematics, physics, philosophy, psychology, and the history of music. Again like Einstein, Popper was a great music lover, although he never mastered an instrument, despite his mother Jenny (1864-1938) being a talented amateur pianist. As a child he had a few violin and piano lessons, but did not get far with either instrument. He tried to persevere with the piano, but never learned to play well. At this stage of his life Popper became increasingly left wing, joining the Association of Socialist School Students at the age of 17, and later the Social Democratic Workers' Party of Austria, a clearly Marxist organisation. However, his disillusionment with Marxism began on June 15, 1919. On that day Popper was demonstrating with a small Marxist crowd outside a prison on Vienna's Hörlgasse against the imprisonment of some members of the Workers' Party. Fearing that the group was about attempt a jailbreak for them, the local police opened fire, shooting dead one of the demonstrators and injuring seven more, although all were unarmed. This was shocking enough, but what alarmed Popper even more was the way in which the party celebrated the victims as martyrs, fully accepting that violence and casualties would be necessary if they were to attain their ends. This prompted Popper to think more deeply about the full implications of Marxism, and he began to doubt its intellectual basis. His disillusionment with Marxism was to prove permanent: he was later to describe its doctrines as examples of 'historicism'.

Unlike the saintly Spinoza, the courageous and self-denying Paine, or the charming, urbane, and self-effacing Einstein, Popper was possessed of a personality that few found to be attractive. Abrasive, dour, and melancholic, in later life he was to become obsessed with his studies, sparing time for little else. His workaholic attitude imposed a great strain on both himself and his wife, Josefine Anna Henninger (1906-1985), whom he married in 1930. Popper never learned how to type, so this task was left to Josefine, who acted as his amanuensis throughout her life. They had met at the Pedagogical Institute in 1925, where both were studying. Popper freely acknowledged the enormous contribution she had made to the furthering of his career, writing of her,

> She was one of my fellow students, and was to become one of the severest judges of my work. Her part in it ever since has been at least as strenuous as my own. Indeed, without her much of it would never have been done at all. (*Unended Quest* (1977 ed.), p. 73)

Josefine would have preferred Popper to devote his spare time to skiing or mountain climbing, sports which they both enjoyed, but she sacrificed her wishes to his. Together they made a conscious decision never to have children, perhaps because Popper feared that they might take up too much time. He was later to describe his choice as, 'perhaps a cowardly, but in a way a right decision'. However, Popper did have one redeeming feature: like Paine and Einstein, he was a genuine humanitarian, with a real concern for the wellbeing of his fellow men. This concern showed itself in his early life, when he was much moved by the poverty and destitution that he saw on the streets of Vienna at that time. His enduring humanitarianism was to emerge again in all of his later writings on political themes. In this respect, he followed in his father's footsteps. Simon Popper (1856-1932) had worked with two organisations that had offered shelter and food to the homeless of Vienna, one of which had in 1908 sheltered a destitute 19-year-old by the name of Adolph Hitler!

The First World War ended in November 1918 with Austria on the losing side. This brought more poverty and ruin to the streets of Vienna. Among the victims was the Popper family, with Simon losing most of their savings in the financial chaos that had followed the war. Trying not to be a burden to his parents, Popper therefore left home early in 1920, and tried to earn his own living. Associating himself very much with the working-class poor of the time, Popper first of all worked as a road mender, but found the manual labour to be too strenuous for him. He next began an apprenticeship as a cabinetmaker. His aim at that time was to start a daycare facility for poor children, and he believed that an ability to make furniture would be an advantage in that context. In his autobiographical work, *Unended Quest (1977 ed.)* Popper wrote of this phase of his life,

> If I thought of a future, I dreamed of one day founding a school in which young people could learn without boredom, and would be stimulated to pose problems and discuss them; a school in which no unwanted answers to unasked questions would have to be listened to; in which one did not study only for the sake of passing examinations. (p. 40)

In 1924 he qualified as a journeyman, but never became a master cabinetmaker. Popper's philanthropic instincts were very clear at this stage of his life: during his apprenticeship he did voluntary work in one of Alfred Adler's clinics for disturbed children. He was beginning to feel a vocation for teaching at this point, but specifically for the teaching of children. In 1922 he registered formally at the University of Vienna and began to study for a certificate which would allow him to teach school at elementary level. He obtained this in 1924, and began work at an after-school care club for socially disadvantaged children. In 1925 he joined the newly founded Pedagogical Institute in Vienna, where he continued with his studies of philosophy and psychology. At the same time he registered as a research student at the University of Vienna under the supervision of Karl Bühler (1879-1963) and in 1928 obtained a doctorate in psychology with his dissertation, 'The Question of Method in Cognitive Psychology'. As in Einstein's case, it was not necessary in German-speaking lands at that time to have a first degree before embarking on doctoral work. However, as Einstein's case demonstrated, the dissertation presented did not have to be the very demanding piece of work that would be required today. In 1929 Popper obtained a certificate which allowed him to teach general science at secondary school level, covering maths, physics, chemistry, and biology (*All Life is Problem Solving* (2001 ed.) p. 151). He took up a teaching post in Vienna in 1930. It was in that year too that he married Josefine Henninger, whom he had met while studying at the Pedagogical Institute five years earlier.

It was at this point in Popper's life that his workaholic obsession set in. While teaching full-time during the day, he began to use his evenings and weekends to work on his first book, an epistemological work which he entitled, *The Two Fundamental Problems in the Theory of Knowledge*. This title was meant to reflect Schopenhauer's work of 1841, *The Two Fundamental Problems of Ethics*. In his own book Popper identified the problems of induction and of the line of demarcation between science and non-science as being the two basic problems in the theory of knowledge. Popper later claimed that his motives for writing this book were political and personal: that he had foreseen the rise of Nazism in Germany, and an eventual Anschluss between Germany and Austria. This would make it necessary for Popper to find a job abroad, because of his Jewish background. At that time he feared only persecution and the loss of his post, something that did indeed happen to Jewish teachers and academics under Nazism. However, he could not have foreseen just how vicious this persecution was to become. Under the insane Nazi racial laws the possession of just *one* Jewish grandparent was enough to qualify you for the gas chambers, and Popper was entirely Jewish by descent: his Lutheran baptism would have been no defence. But was Popper's hard work entirely due to his political foresight, or more motivated by his desire to obtain an academic post for its own sake? It may be noted that while Popper never lost his vocation for teaching, he gradually developed a desire to teach at higher and higher levels.

Popper's *Two Fundamental Problems* developed into a lengthy two-volume work, a shortened version of which was eventually published in German as *Logik der Forschung* (*The Logic of Scientific Discovery*) in 1934, and in English in 1959. This book was essentially a summary of his *Two Fundamental Problems,* which is now available in full as an English translation of 2008. As soon as this volume was completed, Popper immediately began to work on his next major publication, *The Poverty of Historicism*. His theme this time was much more political than scientific, for it was basically an attack on the so-called 'scientific method' which had become fashionable in the social sciences, and on the idea that political and social developments were predictable and inevitable. Although Marx was very little mentioned in this work, it was widely taken to be a thinly veiled attack on Marxism. It was first of all published in 1944 and 1945 as a series of articles in *Econometrica*, a British Journal of

Economics which is still publishing today. The work appeared as a book in 1957.

While working on this book Popper was also desperately brushing up his schoolboy English, hoping for an academic post in an English-speaking country. After several unsuccessful applications, Popper at last managed to secure the academic position of lecturer in philosophy at Canterbury University College, a constituent body of the University of New Zealand at Christchurch, the largest city on New Zealand's South Island. Popper took up this appointment in October 1937, and so had just been able to escape from Vienna before the German-Austrian Anschluss of March, 1938. He was to remain at Christchurch until 1946, and it was while there that Popper began work on his second, and probably best known book, *The Open Society and its Enemies.* Popper again claimed a political motivation for this piece of work, writing in the preface to its 1950 edition, 'The final decision to write it was made in March, 1938, on the day I received news of the invasion of Austria'. He was later to refer to *The Open Society* as 'my war work', by which he meant, 'my contribution to the defeat of Hitler'. The first edition of the book was published in 1943, and earned Popper a promotion to senior lecturer. But his promotion had been hard won, at the cost of imposing a rather miserable existence upon both himself and his wife, who liked to be called, 'Hennie'. Ernst Gombrich (1909-2001) the art historian, was a friend of the Poppers from their Vienna days. Like Karl, he was Austrian and of Jewish descent, and like Karl he too moved to England, adopted citizenship, was knighted, and lived to be 92. He was instrumental in helping to get *The Open Society* published, and they corresponded extensively while Karl was in New Zealand. In the 2011 Routledge Classics paperback edition of *The Open Society,*Gombrich included a preface recounting his memories. Here he quotes from a letter that he received from Hennie, dated May 4, 1943, which described the Poppers' life at Christchurch.

> It gets frightfully dry, and the raising of vegetables is not easy. I try hard in the little time I have, and from October to March we eat only 'homegrown' vegetables, mainly peas, beans, potatoes, carrots, spinach, silverbeet, lettuce, and tomatoes. It is really never quite sufficient, but we have to make the best of it. The rest of the year we live chiefly on a carrot and rice diet for economy's sake. Karl's salary was never adequate, and is now less so than ever...During term-time Karl can only work at the weekends, but during the summer holidays he worked literally 24 hours a day. For the last three or four months he was in a state of almost complete exhaustion: he hardly went to bed because he could not sleep...Karl finished just two days before College started again. On both days which remained from our 'holiday' we went to the sea and ate as many ice creams as we could! (pp xx-xxi)

As someone who has had to live on a junior lecturer's pay myself, I can heartily endorse Hennie's comments on their finances! The letter was written in

German, but 'homegrown' was inserted in English. In a later letter, dated October 24, 1944, Hennie wrote to Ernst,

> I am the worst possible typist, and the more distance I gain from the last nightmare years of typing, the less I can understand how on earth I managed it.

Gombrich then added a comment of his own:

> I very much doubt that Karl ever touched a keyboard. He left it to Hennie, in what she described as the nightmare years, to type and retype countless versions and revisions. Not that Karl was not utterly devoted to her. He suffered agonies when she was ill. But he was convinced that the importance of his work had always to override his own comfort, that of Hennie, and possibly also my own, as the future was to show. (pp. xxi)

Popper himself suffered from recurrent ill-health in those years, and a bad relationship with his head of department at Christchurch. In addition to all these hardships, Popper also had to struggle with the wartime paper shortage, never knowing from one month to the next whether he would have enough paper for his writing and Hennie's typing. That they managed to produce a work of such quality under these circumstances is a great tribute to both of them. The book was published at last in 1945, but only after several rejections and by dint of herculean efforts on the part of Gombrich and Friedrich Hayek (1899-1992), the economist and philosopher who had also been born in Vienna, but had later taken out British citizenship, in 1938. Hayek's views were very similar to Popper's, and the two remained friends for life. The book was little regarded at the time, but is now considered to have been one of the great works of twentieth-century political thought. Perhaps there is hope for us all!

In 1946 Popper was appointed to the post of reader in logic and scientific method at the London School of Economics, and moved to England where he was to remain for the rest of his life, with only a short break in Austria in 1985 to 1986, owing to the death of his wife, Josefine (Hennie). Popper took out British citizenship, and in 1949 he was appointed as Professor of Logic and Scientific Method at the University of London, remaining in this post until his official retirement in 1969. This was by no means the end of Popper's academic career, however, for after settling down at Kenley, now in the London Borough of Croydon, he continued to write and to lecture for another 25 years, until his death in 1994.

Popper's best known pieces of work were his two political publications, *The Poverty of Historicism* and *The Open Society and its Enemies*. But Popper always regarded himself as being primarily a philosopher of science. After those two well-known books he never wrote another coherent volume on political issues, although some of his lectures on these themes were later published as collections in separate volumes. As his first priority, he remained obsessed with his conception of 'the scientific method' throughout his life. Sadly, speculations in this field inevitably dragged him into the swamp of epistemology, from which few philosophers have ever emerged with honour. Indeed, I find it difficult think of any at all. As explained in the Philosophy chapter above, we have several good reasons for being sceptical about all forms of philosophy, but for centuries epistemology has proved to be the most futile of all fields of speculation. However, any form of 'philosophy of science' must also be suspect. In view of the dazzling success of twentieth-century science, I feel that it is rather presumptuous for any mere philosopher to intrude into the field with advice to scientists as to how they should define or practise their profession. I cannot help suspecting that twentieth-century science would have achieved precisely the same level of dazzling success even if Popper and all the other members of his philosopher tribe had never been born. A genius might be described as someone who points out the obvious that was not obvious until he pointed it out. Into this category I would place Baruch Spinoza, Tom Paine, and Charles Darwin. On the publication of *The Origin of Species* in 1859, how many of Darwin's fellow naturalists must have clapped a hand to their foreheads and cried, 'Of Course! It seems so obvious now! Why didn't *I* think of that?' Indeed, one of Darwin's close contemporaries, Alfred Russell Wallace (1823-1913), already *had* thought of that, and had corresponded with Darwin on the subject, prompting Darwin to publish his own views in 1859. Evolution by natural selection was an idea whose time had come: the genie was out of the bottle, and our world has never been quite the same again.

On the other hand, the buffoon might be described as someone who points out the obvious that was already obvious, and then congratulates himself on having been very clever indeed. I rather fear that when it comes to his scientific thought, Popper falls into this latter category. For me, his so-called 'philosophy of science' per se is an unhappy mix of the obvious and the mistaken. Very few scientists ever admitted that Popper's philosophy had been of any help to them at all. Nearly all of them simply ignored Popper and continued to practise their science in the same very sensible and successful ways that they always had. But Popper's philosopher colleagues, most of whom knew very little about science, were more easily impressed.

For me, Popper is a philosopher hero not because of his contributions to the philosophy of science, but because of his political thought, and it is on this aspect of his career that I would like to concentrate. However, since Popper's 'philosophy of science' did earn him a Fellowship of the Royal Society, I must first of all say something in support of my contention that it is as a political philosopher, and not as a philosopher of science, that Popper deserves to be celebrated.

Let us begin by considering Popper's first piece of published work, *The Two Fundamental Problems of the Theory of Knowledge*, completed in 1933 and now available in full as a 2008 translation, but published in 1934 in a much shortened version as *The Logic of Scientific Discovery.* Popper described the 'two fundamental problems' as being the use of induction in science, and the problem of demarcation between a science and a non-science. However, for most people this latter 'problem' is not and never has been a problem at all. That is why universities divide their faculties into Faculties of Science and Faculties of Arts, or of Humanities. The sciences are those studies which concern the natural world, what used to be called ontology, while the Arts relate to those studies which concern human behaviour and human emotions. The sciences include mathematics, the queen of sciences, which is employed in all the rest, cosmology, physics, chemistry, biochemistry, biology (botany and zoology), geography, geology, geophysics, and palaeontology. Medicine too is generally regarded as a science these days which is a fair enough description, although human behaviour and emotions can also have a bearing on health. But on the borderline between science and the humanities lies psychiatry, which would like to regard itself as a branch of medicine and therefore a science, but also has a great deal to do with human behaviour and human emotions, involving talking as well as drug therapies. Studies which concern themselves entirely with human behaviour and human emotions are known as the Arts, or more specifically as the humanities. These include psychology, philosophy, literature, history, politics, economics, theology, sociology, and anthropology, which might be defined as historical sociology. Some aspects of these studies may be subjected to statistical analysis, but not on a scale sufficient to turn them into sciences: few things are more unpredictable than human behaviour, or more irrational than human emotions! Also clearly in the camp of non-sciences are music, together with the visual and the performing arts. All of these concern themselves with human behaviour and human emotions rather than with the natural world. However, this clear and obvious distinction was evidently not clear enough for Popper, who felt that he had to come up with his own distinction between a science and a non-science, and then explain it to everyone else.

I must here quote from Popper's intellectual autobiography, *Unended Quest* (1977 ed.), because with regard to the above point, the passage describes Popper's 'eureka moment'. In 1919 he attended a lecture by Albert Einstein on general relativity, and wrote of it,

> But what impressed me most was Einstein's own clear statement that he would regard his theory as untenable if it should fail certain tests. Thus he wrote, for example: 'If the redshift of spectral lines due to the gravitational potential should not exist, then the general theory of relativity will be untenable'. Here was an attitude utterly different from the dogmatic attitude of Marx, Freud, Adler, and even more so that of their followers. Einstein was looking for crucial experiments whose agreement with his predictions would by no means establish his theory; while a disagreement, as he was the first to stress, would show his theory to be untenable.

This, I felt, was the true scientific attitude. It was utterly different from the dogmatic attitude which constantly claimed to find 'verifications' for its favourite theories. Thus I arrived, at the end of 1919, at the conclusion that the scientific attitude was the critical attitude, which did not look for verifications, but for crucial tests; tests which could *refute* the theory tested, though they could never establish it. (p. 38)

Leaving aside the question of whether Einstein used those actual words, Popper was, at that point in time, just 17 years old, but he never changed his view on the crucial importance of falsifiability, and continued to dine out on it for the rest of his life. If a theory cannot be falsified by some crucial test or piece of evidence, he declared, then it cannot be regarded as a *scientific* theory. However, what does not seem to have occurred to the young Popper at the time, nor even to the older Popper much later, was the obvious fact that by making the statement above Einstein, in common with all the other scientists of his day, was already very well aware of the importance of falsification as an aspect of the experimental method, and was already ranking it above verification in significance. They hardly needed to have this very obvious piece of methodology pointed out to them by a philosopher whose own qualifications in science had not extended beyond those required of a secondary school teacher.

The experimental method itself is of course the cornerstone of modern science, dating back to at least the seventeenth century, and arguably perhaps to the days of the Franciscan Friar Roger Bacon (1220-1292), or even to Aristotle. Moreover, Popper's overreliance on the criterion of falsification led him to some rather ridiculous conclusions: it would imply, for example, that Marxism was 'scientific', because it made predictions that could be falsified by experience, while Darwinism was 'unscientific', because its conclusions could not be falsified. However, by continually insisting that Marxism was in fact *not* scientific, Popper flew in the face of his own criterion. Moreover, even at the age of 75 Popper was still adhering to his curious view of evolution, writing in the 1977 edition of *Unended Quest*,'I have come to the conclusion that Darwinism is not a testable scientific theory, but a *metaphysical research programme'*. (p.168) But the first edition of *Unended Quest* had come out in 1974, and Popper was to change his mind on this point in 1978, perhaps in reaction to the outcry which his views had provoked. In the journal *Dialectica* Vol. 32 (1978) he declared, 'I have changed my mind about the testability and logical status of the theory of natural selection, and I am glad to have an opportunity to make a recantation.' (p. 339) Popper was quite right to do this even although, as he correctly pointed out, there was no test that could conclusively *disprove* the theory of evolution, and so Darwinism was therefore *not* falsifiable. Sometimes the purely inductive evidence in favour of a theory becomes so overwhelming that it may legitimately be accepted as proven, at least for the time being. But this was not the only problem with his criterion of falsification. I cannot go into all the details here, but they are well aired in the Popper entry of the *Internet Encyclopedia of Philosophy*, readily available to all online, under the heading, 'Criticisms of Falsificationism', and in the *Stanford Encyclopaedia of Philosophy* on Popper under 'Critical Evaluation', also available online. Those who wade through those entries will soon understand my reluctance to go into any further details here, but the Stanford Encyclopaedia concludes, 'falsificationism, for all its apparent merits, fares no better in the final analysis than verificationism'.

Popper was, however, quite correct to be highly sceptical of the psychoanalytical methods then being practised by Sigmund Freud, Alfred Adler, and all their followers. Essentially their theories could be twisted or amended in such ways as to allow them to account for any form of psychotic behaviour whatsoever, and so they remained unfalsifiable under all circumstances. A theory which purports to explain everything, argued Popper, in fact explains nothing. But the fact that psychoanalysis is an art form which deals exclusively with human behaviour and human emotions was evidently lost on Popper. It can make no pretensions to being a science. The more serious charge to be laid against Freud, Adler, et al. was, however, not that they were unscientific (they could hardly have been anything else) but rather that they often actually harmed their patients. A recent book by Fredrick Crews, *Freud: The Making of an Illusion* (2017) launches a devastating attack upon Freud, criticising both his methods and his motives.

As noted above, Popper's early interests were entirely in teaching and psychology, leading him to do voluntary work at one of Adler's clinics for children in the early 1920s. His 1928 doctoral thesis was on a psychological theme, 'The Question of Method in Cognitive Psychology'. It was only in 1929, after he had obtained his teaching qualification in general science (covering maths, physics, chemistry, and biology) that Popper turned his attention to the philosophy of science. The result of this change of tack was the eventual publication of his first book, *The Logic of Scientific Discovery* (1934), written in German as *Logik der Forschung*. This volume is now available online in its English version of 1959, and makes for as tedious a piece of reading as anyone could ever have the misfortune to come across. It includes such pearls of wisdom as, 'We do not know: we can only guess'. (2005 ed., p. 278) But this nihilistic position is taking scepticism too far, especially with regard to science. David Hilbert (1862-1943), the leading mathematician of his day, who was instrumental in helping Einstein to formulate a successful version of his theory of general relativity, would have none of this doctrine of despair. In response to the Latin tag, 'Ignoramus et ignorabimus' (We do not know, we shall not know) coined by Emil du Bois-Reymond (1818-96), Hilbert had carved upon his tombstone, '*Wir müssen wissen. Wir werden wissen.*' (We must know. We will know). At the end of his text Popper appends a letter which he had received from Einstein in 1935 regarding a thought experiment which Popper had proposed. Einstein is faultlessly tactful and courteous in his reply, but as Popper noted in his introduction to it, the letter, 'briefly and decisively disposes of my imaginary experiment in section 77 of the book'. In this volume Popper sinks very quickly into the quagmire of epistemology, from which there is never any rational escape. Essentially, however, he expands on the themes of his earlier, at that time unpublished work, *The Two Fundamental Problems in the Theory of Knowledge*. The 'two fundamental problems' were those of demarcation between a science and a non-science, dealt with above, and the so-called 'problem' of induction.

Philosophers are careful to recognise the distinction between 'induction' and 'deduction'. Induction, in logic, means reasoning from the particular to the general. The example usually given is, 'All the swans that I have ever seen are white. Therefore all swans are white.' But this assumption may be falsified by the discovery of just one black swan. This did in fact happen in 1697, when the Dutch sea captain Willem de Vlamingh (1640-1698) and his crew were the first Europeans to see black swans on the appropriately named Swan River in Western Australia. The point here is that no number of confirming observations can certify the absolute truth of a general assumption, while just one counter-observation can nullify it. Deduction, on the other hand, means reasoning from the general to the particular, the reverse of induction. The example usually given here is, 'All men are mortal. Socrates is a man. Therefore Socrates is mortal'. This would appear to make deduction the more reliable form of reasoning, but it is dependent upon the assumption that some generalisations can be established beyond any reasonable doubt. The mortality of all humankind would seem to fall into this category, but in the minds of philosophers, very few other general assumptions do!

Induction as an infallible means of establishing absolute truth is therefore a straw man, very easily knocked down. Its fallibility had already been pointed out two centuries earlier by David Hume in his *Treatise of Human Nature* (1739) Book I, Part III, section VI. This does not mean, however, that induction is a completely useless instrument to employ in the quest for scientific truth. A large number of supporting observations might legitimately be regarded as corroborating evidence for a theory, even although they could not be said to conclusively prove it, as in the case of evolution theory. It is in fact true that all swans native to the northern hemisphere actually *are* white. But here we are beginning to splash our toes in the swamp of epistemology, which is to be avoided at all costs.

Another very questionable piece of 'philosophy of science' put forward by Popper was his contention that speculation precedes observation. In 1994, just before his death, Popper produced a collection of his lectures and articles as a book in German with the title, *Alles Leben ist Problemlösen* or, *All Life is Problem Solving*. Here he declared,

> The old theory of science taught, and still teaches, that the starting point for science is our sense perception or sensory observation. This sounds at first thoroughly

reasonable and persuasive, but it is fundamentally wrong. One can easily show this by stating the thesis: *without a problem, no observation*. (2001 ed., p. 6)

Notice that Popper speaks here of 'the old theory of science'. He believed, of course, that he had entirely redefined the 'theory of science' with his great thoughts, which everyone now accepted. He boasted that he would say to his lecture classes, 'Observe', and note their looks of dismay. 'But what should we observe?' 'Exactly', Popper would reply. 'We observe only those things which strike us as problematic. A speculation always precedes the observation.' This was not a new idea: Popper had stolen it from Auguste Comte, but it was just as wrong in Comte's day as in Popper's. In fact, Popper was rather obsessed with the idea of problem solving. Indeed, On p. 3 of the 2001 English edition he declares, 'The natural as well as the social sciences always start from *problems*, from the fact that something inspires *amazement* in us, as the Greek philosophers used to say'.

I would not agree with this contention that speculation precedes observation, and that only those things which amaze us are observed: science does not work that way. Scientists are interested in every aspect of the natural world, whether it has presented them with a 'problem' or not. They have explored the depths of the deep oceans not because there was any 'problem' with them, but rather for the same reason that mountain climbers climb mountains – 'because they are there'. Scientists are interested in every aspect of reality, whether they see them as problems or not. However, Popper later went on to claim that by making his dogmatic statement, 'without a problem, no observation' he had undermined the whole traditional approach to empiricism as being the basis of the scientific method. Empiricism assumes that knowledge can be gained only through *first* observation and experimentation, followed by observing the results of the experiment. On p. 72 of the 2001 edition, however, he modestly declares that, 'I have, I believe, refuted classical empiricism'! This was an absurd claim.

But how do we know that a problem is a problem in the first place? Here I must bring in another distinction in logic that is made by both scientists and philosophers, namely the difference between *a priori* and *a posteriori* knowledge. *A priori*, as the name suggests, is knowledge already possessed prior to reasoning from it. It might be described as self-evident knowledge, or generally believed knowledge, or even instinctive knowledge. *A posteriori* knowledge on the other hand, is knowledge derived from logical deductions that have been drawn from *a priori* knowledge, that is to say conclusions that have been reached by reasoning or by observation, or by experimentation, thereby extending the knowledge that we possess. But how much of our knowledge should we regard as being *a priori*, and how much *a posteriori*? Here Popper refers to Kant's *Critique of Pure Reason*, declaring,

> In Kant, knowledge *a priori* means knowledge that we possess *prior* to sense observation, and knowledge *a posteriori* means knowledge that we possess *posterior* to sense observation, or after observation...Kant himself uses his term *a priori* to mean, in addition, knowledge that is not merely prior to observation but also *'a priori valid'*; by which he means necessarily or certainly true. Of course, I shall not follow him in this since I am stressing the uncertain and conjectural character of all our knowledge. (op. cit. p. 69)

Here Popper falls headlong into the swamp of epistemology. Epistemologists always end up disappearing into the inevitable aperture by concluding that we can never know anything for certain. Popper then goes on to examine further Kant's distinction between *a priori* and *a posteriori* knowledge and proceeds to announce,

> But I am going much further than Kant. I think that, say, 99 per cent of the knowledge of all organisms is inborn and incorporated in our biochemical constitution. And I think that 99 per cent of the knowledge taken by Kant to be *a posteriori* and to be '*data'* that are 'given' to us through our senses is, in fact, not *a posteriori* but *a priori*. For our senses can serve us (as Kant himself saw) only with yes-and-no answers to our own questions; questions that we conceive, and ask, *a priori*; and questions that sometimes are very elaborate. Moreover, even the yes-and-no answers have to be *interpreted* by us – interpreted in the light of our *a priori* preconceived ideas. And, of course, they are often *misinterpreted*. Thus, all our knowledge is hypothetical. (op. cit. p. 70)

It is statements like this which make you despair of academic philosophy in general, and epistemology in particular. To suggest that 99% of our knowledge is *a priori* is ridiculous. There are shades of Plato's *Meno* here, but really we ought to know better than that by now. Moreover, as noted above, our knowledge is *not* hypothetical if it can be scientifically tested, and on being applied, it actually *works*. It does not need to be complete, or even entirely correct, rather like Newtonian mechanics, so long as it does the job required of it. Newtonian mechanics were employed to send men to the moon, and robot probes to the planets.

The above quotations were taken from a lecture given by Popper in 1989, and then incorporated into his collection, *All Life is Problem Solving*. The lecture was entitled, 'Towards an Evolutionary Theory of Knowledge', and in it Popper argues that our knowledge grows by continually subjecting our theories to rigorous critical testing, and discarding those that fail the tests by being conclusively falsified, so that only our 'fittest' theories survive. Well yes, of course – this is called the experimental method in that 'philosophy of science' at which Popper claimed to be an expert. But did we really need to have such an obvious methodology pointed out to us by Karl Popper? It was already generally accepted by the scientific community that a theory which could be neither proved nor disproved remained just that: a theory and nothing more. It was for this reason that Einstein was not awarded his Nobel Prize for the theory of general relativity. It became possible to prove the validity of the theory only with the coming of the Space Age and the Large Hadron Collider at CERN after Einstein's death.

The whole notion of the 'philosophy of science' as a distinct study dates only from the middle years of the twentieth century. Before that it was just 'science'. The new 'philosophy' emerged from a school of thought known as logical positivism, or sometimes logical empiricism, popular in the 1920s and 1930s, which was an attempt by a group of philosophers led by the Vienna Circle to jump aboard the scientific bandwagon, and use 'scientific' methods to prove their philosophical concepts beyond any reasonable doubt. That attempt was a resounding failure, which was hardly surprising. But in fact this attempt had been going on ever since the experimental method had emerged clearly in the seventeenth century. As noted above, Spinoza tried to use geometric formulations to prove the truth of his axioms, and David Hume published in 1739, *A Treatise of Human Nature: Being an Attempt to Introduce the Experimental Method of Reasoning into Moral Subjects.* All of their attempts failed of course, since philosophy is not and never will be a scientific subject. Logical positivism soon collapsed under the weight of its own internal inconsistencies. In 1967 the Australian philosopher John Passmore (1914-2004) writing in P. Edwards (ed.) *The Encyclopedia of Philosophy* Vol. 5 pp. 52-7 explained these inconsistencies very well, and was able to conclude, 'Logical positivism, then, is dead, or as dead as a philosophical movement ever becomes'. But just as logical positivism was crumbling in the middle years of the twentieth century, a small band of despairing philosophers came up with a new idea. 'Very well then.' They said. 'If we cannot make a science out of philosophy, then we will make a philosophy out of science!' Leading the charge was Karl Popper. This was *faute de mieux* indeed, a desperate attempt to associate the very questionable success of their own discipline with the dazzling success of mid-twentieth century science, which had clearly aroused the jealousy of those philosophers. Unfortunately, however, this involved them in trying to explain science to the scientists, which cast them in a rather ridiculous light.

In his entry on logical positivism cited above in which Passmore charts the decline and fall of this particular philosophy, he scarcely mentions Popper at all, simply noting in the opening lines that Popper was not a full member of the Vienna Circle of logical positivists. This is certainly true. The logical positivists favoured a technique known as verificationism, a form of inductive empiricism, while Popper stood their methodology on its head by preferring falsifiability as his key criterion. The logical positivists had attempted to use 'scientific' methods to separate sense from nonsense in philosophy, while Popper's more modest aim had been simply to distinguish science from non-science, rather than to attack logical positivism as such. In his autobiographical work *Unended Quest* (1977 ed.) however, Popper includes a chapter entitled,

'Who Killed Logical Positivism?' And who was responsible for this dazzling intellectual feat? Why, it was none other than lil' old Karl Raimund Popper himself! 'I fear that I must admit responsibility', Popper declares modestly. (op. cit. p. 88) We are reminded here of Popper's reference to 'the old theory of science' on p.6, implying that he, the great Karl Popper, had redefined science itself by such means as his simple statement, 'without a problem, no observation'. When it came to his reputation as a philosopher of science Popper, unlike Einstein, came to believe in his own myth, and proceeded to make pompous and increasingly ill-founded pronouncements on the subject.

Popper plays the role of the typical epistemologist with his insistence that all knowledge is merely conjectural and hypothetical – we can never be absolutely certain about anything. This doctrine of despair has something to be said for it in relation to Arts subjects such as political theory, economics, and sociology, but is entirely wrong with respect to Science, in which field we *can* be absolutely certain about some phenomena. If we really know nothing about electricity, then how have we been able to harness it so effectively to serve our needs? If we really know nothing about atomic energy, then how have we been able to build nuclear power stations? To take just one more specific and concrete example, although there are many others in Science, we do know with absolute certainty that the compound water is composed of the two elements hydrogen and oxygen, gases at room temperature and sea-level pressures. Water, a liquid under these conditions, may be decomposed into its constituent elements by the process of electrolysis. If the two resulting gases are then trapped in a sealed chamber and a spark introduced to them, the resulting explosive reaction will yield water again as a condensate. Chemists know even the specific shape and properties of the water molecule, and can thereby explain why all snowflakes are basically hexagonal in shape, and why beautiful frost patterns can appear on frozen window panes. But Popper extends his claim that *all* knowledge is conjectural to the Sciences. I quote here from his collection of essays and lectures, *All Life is Problem Solving* (2001 ed.).

> *So-called scientific knowledge is not knowledge*, for it consists only of conjectures or hypotheses – even if some have gone through the cross-fire of ingenious tests. In short, we do not know, we guess. Although *scientific knowledge* is not knowledge, it is the best we have in this field. I call it conjectural knowledge – more or less to console people who want certain knowledge and think they cannot do without it. (p. 37)

Indeed, we *cannot* do without it. Without certain scientific knowledge, our modern world could not exist. For a so-called 'philosopher of science' to make such dismissive and patronising statements about scientific learning is outrageous. Later on he adds,

> Those of us who are scientists ought to be a little more modest and, above all, less dogmatic. Otherwise science will fall by the wayside. (p. 43)

So, Popper is a fully fledged 'scientist', is he? Moreover, unless scientists stop being arrogant enough to suggest that they might know what they are talking about, science will 'fall by the wayside', will it? First of all, scientists *do* know what they are talking about, and they can actually *prove* that they know, unlike philosophers. Moreover, to suggest that science could ever 'fall by the wayside' in this modern world of ours would be an absurd statement coming from anyone at all, but to hear it coming from a *soi-disant* 'philosopher of science' is simply grotesque.

As noted in my Philosophy chapter above, philosophers do not have to be right (and usually are not) they need only to be interesting. But with his pronouncements on the 'philosophy of science' Popper got away with murder. Not that his views passed without criticism, as the many online entries on Popper will show – but what a nerve he had to present them in the first place, and how remarkable that he could even be celebrated for them in some quarters. I can only suppose that philosophers have been wrong so often that nobody really expects them to be right any more. Poetic licence and artistic licence pale into insignificance beside the latitude allowed to philosophical licence! Having frequently remarked in his writings that the terms 'science' and 'scientist' were both open to a variety of definitions, Popper then went on to have no hesitation in claiming that he had redefined 'science', and to have no hesitation in describing himself as a 'scientist'!

Now if the claiming for one's self of achievements which were not one's own achievements at all is a hallmark of buffoonery, another is the claiming for oneself of a status to which one is not entitled. In his writings Popper often speaks imperiously of 'we scientists' or, 'those of us who are scientists' (e.g. *All Life is Problem Solving*, p. 43) and had the temerity to debate with Schrödinger, Einstein, and Bohr and to criticise Darwinism. But Popper could, by no stretch of the imagination, be described as a scientist himself. His formal scientific education had been rudimentary, he never carried out a scientific experiment in his life beyond those elementary ones required of a secondary school teacher, he had no great mathematical ability, and he never invented or discovered anything. Even his thought experiments got him nowhere. Popper was in fact a *philosopher of science*, which is quite a different thing from being a scientist. To know something about science is not to be a scientist. I too know a few things about science and the scientific method, and I too have secondary school qualifications in science, but I would never dream of calling myself a scientist on those grounds. Having spent a great deal of time complaining about 'pseudo-science', Popper completely failed to realise that a shining example of the pseudo-scientist was none other than Popper himself!

Indeed, even as a 'philosopher of science' Popper was, in my opinion, a very bad one. Others who made a contribution to what might be described as the philosophy of science in the late nineteenth and early twentieth centuries had at least been scientists themselves, and so had a much better idea of what they were talking about: men like Charles Sanders Peirce, Ludwig Boltzmann, Ernst Mach, Henri Poincaré, Albert Einstein, Niels Bohr, and Werner Heisenberg. Scientists of course continued to write on the philosophy of science after 1950, men like Thomas Kuhn (physics), Stephen Jay Gould (biology), Rudolph Carnap (maths and physics), and Richard Feynman (physics). But from the 1960s their ranks were swamped by a swelling tide of 'philosophers of science' who were purely philosophers. This new trend, this desperate determination to make a philosophy out of science, had been led by Karl Popper. In their collection of essays on scientific themes, *Scientific Metaphysics* (2013), James Ladyman and Don Ross (eds.) note, 'There has been a tendency for philosophers of science to regard Popper as something of an embarrassment' (p. 115), and his views have been described as 'wrongheaded'. But this is a commonplace amongst those philosophers of science who were purely philosophers: men like David Bloor, Barry Barnes, and Paul Feyerabend soon got lost in the fog of epistemology. This last produced books with titles such as, *Against Method* (1975) and *Farewell to Reason* (1987). He ended by concluding that there was no such thing as a philosophy of science, nor indeed any form of methodical scientific procedure at all, a classic example of the flight of the oozlum bird. The present sorry state of philosophers of science who are purely philosophers is well covered by Robert Nola in his book, *After Popper, Kuhn, and Feyerabend* (2001).

Popper described his approach to science as being one of *critical rationalism*. He declared,

> When I speak of reason or rationalism, all I mean is the conviction that we can *learn* through criticism of our mistakes and errors, especially through criticism by others, and eventually also through self-criticism. A rationalist is simply someone for whom it is more important to learn than to be proved right; someone who is willing to learn from others – not by simply taking over another's opinions, but by gladly allowing others to criticise his ideas and by gladly criticising the ideas of others. The emphasis here is on the idea of criticism or, to be more precise, *critical discussion*. The genuine rationalist does not think that he or anyone else is in possession of the truth, nor does he think that mere criticism as such helps us to achieve new ideas. But he does think that, in the sphere of ideas, only critical discussion can help us sort the wheat from the chaff. (*All Life is Problem Solving* (2001 ed.) p. 84

However, the Stanford Encyclopaedia of Philosophy is rather harsh on Popper in this regard, writing of him under Section 1 (Life),

> He combined a combative personality with a zeal for self-aggrandisement that did little to endear him to professional colleagues at a personal level...Popper was a somewhat paradoxical man, whose theoretic commitment to the primacy of rational criticism was counterpointed by a hostility towards anything that amounted to less than a total acceptance of his own thought. (Available online)

It is certainly true that Popper often defended his views robustly, as in his intellectual autobiography *Unended Quest*, in the preface to his, *Realism and the Aim of Science* (1956), again in his 1982 Introduction to an expanded edition under the same title, and in his essay, 'Replies to My Critics', which was included in P.A. Schlipp (ed.), *The Philosophy of Karl Popper* Vol. 2(1976). In this last Popper adopts a rather testy tone, writing, for example,

> It is not the goal to bless theories with claims of certainty or justification, but to eliminate errors in them. There are no such things as good, positive reasons, nor do we need them, but philosophers obviously cannot quite bring themselves to believe that this is my opinion, let alone that it is right. (p. 1043)

Popper also defended himself vigorously against the attacks of outraged Platonists, who had sprung to the defence of their hero, with a lengthy addenda to the 1961edition of his *Open Society*. (2011 ed., pp. 193-212)

How then, did Popper come to be elected as an F.R.S.? As noted above, the honours system is a curious business. In the Old World, once you had acquired enough honours, people tended to think that you must be very distinguished. Fame feeds upon itself. In Popper's case, the philosophers thought that he must be a great scientist, and the scientists thought that he must be a great philosopher, but only the scientists were right. As in the cases of Russell and Einstein, neither of whom really deserved their Nobel prizes under the terms of Nobel's will, appointing committees often wish to bask in the reflected glory of their appointees, and so bend the rules. In Establishment terms, Popper *was* distinguished, and the Fellows of the Royal Society obviously wanted to have him on board, despite his very dubious scientific credentials. Perhaps the Fellows wanted to show that they were not just a group of philistines, interested in nothing beyond their test tubes and calculations: 'Hey, look at us! We appreciate a *philosopher!'* But I cannot help wondering how many members of the Royal Society's nominating committee had ever ploughed through Popper's *Logic of Scientific Discovery*, or any other of his writings on the philosophy of science. They had probably been too busy out in the field practising real science themselves for any such indulgence. If it is true that philosophers usually do not know much about science, it is equally true that scientists usually do not know much about philosophy. *Nullius in Verba* is the motto of the Royal Society, but I suspect that there might have been some going on word-of-mouth evidence in Popper's case. On the other hand, however, Popper's election as an FBA was, I believe, well deserved. Indeed, Karl Popper *was* a great philosopher, just not a great philosopher of science.

When it comes to his political thought, Popper does not fit easily into any point along the ideological spectrum. Because of his adamant opposition to Marxism he is often regarded, especially by the Left, as a right-wing thinker, but Popper was opposed equally strongly to Fascism and Nazism. He was in fact something of a pragmatist, eschewing every 'ism' except humanitarianism.

He was very fond of quoting E.M. Forster's dictum, 'I do not believe in belief', and would certainly agree with Bertrand Russell's declaration, 'I would never die for my beliefs, because I know I could be wrong'. Popper believed that all knowledge was conjectural and hypothetical which, in the field of political and philosophical thought, is an entirely reasonable view to hold, although I do not believe that it applies to ontology, that is, the study of the natural world as distinct from its human inhabitants. In fact Popper did not deny the reality of absolute truth, just the reality of absolute certainty about absolute truth. But here we are in danger of veering into epistemology, so it is time to change tack.

Popper began his career as a political philosopher with his first book on the subject, *The Poverty of Historicism*. The title was intended to reflect one of Marx's early writings, *The Poverty of Philosophy* (1847), which in turn had alluded to Proudhon's *Philosophy of Poverty* (1846). The term 'historicism' was first coined by the German philosopher Karl Friedrich Schlegel (1772-1829) in 1811, but it remained a vague and controversial concept until Popper gave it substance in the middle years of the twentieth century. Under Popper's definition the term came to mean the idea that historical events are determined by natural laws (naturalism), the study of which would make it possible to predict the inevitable course of future developments. This is hardly a tenable concept in itself, but when belief in such laws assumes theological proportions, historicism can become extremely dangerous, leading to such convictions as the manifest destiny of an Aryan master race to rule the world, or the inevitable emergence of Communist societies on a global scale. Popper spells out the Aryan historicist myth in the 2001 edition of his collected essays, *All Life is Problem Solving*.

> In Germany, the nationalist or racist interpretation of history flourished between the Napoleonic Wars and the collapse of Hitler's Reich. Being fashionable even before Hitler, it created an intellectual atmosphere, a view of the world, without which Hitler would not have been possible. It is partly Napoleon, partly Hegel [Popper could have added the names of Darwin and Nietzsche here] whom we have to thank for this view of the world. History is seen as a struggle for dominance between nations and races in which the issue at stake is total extermination. (p. 106)

This was of course a tragic, disastrous, and utterly mistaken view of history. Popper dedicated his 1957 edition of *The Poverty of Historicism* to 'the memory of the countless men and women of all creeds or nations or races who fell victim to the Fascist and Communist beliefs in Inexorable Laws of Historical Destiny'.

The Poverty of Historicism, however, can be seen as merely a prelude, merely a dry run, merely an introduction to Popper's truly *magnum opus*, his 1945 publication, *The Open Society and its Enemies*, where all the themes addressed in his earlier book were greatly enlarged upon. Despite the dedication in *The Poverty of Historicism*, this book itself does not mention either Communism, Fascism, or Nazism by name, and refers to Plato, Hegel, and Marx only very briefly and in passing. It deals with the concept of 'historicism' entirely in the abstract, including, to my mind, rather too much in the way of metaphysics, epistemology, and dubious logic, although it also makes some good points. All of these are, however, repeated and greatly enlarged upon in his *Open* Society. *The Poverty* is quite a slim volume: my 1986 paperback edition runs to only 166 5"x8''pages. By contrast, my 2011 paperback edition of *The Open Society* runs to 755 6"x9" pages! It was in fact published as a two-volume work in 1945. But despite its small scale, *The Poverty* gave the world an expanded and clarified definition of 'historicism'. Popper said of it,

> I mean by 'historicism' an approach to the social sciences which assumes that *historical prediction* is their principle aim, and which assumes that this aim is attainable by discovering the 'rhythms' or the 'patterns', the 'laws' or the 'trends' that underlie the evolution of history. Since I am convinced that such historicist doctrines of method are at bottom responsible for the unsatisfactory state of the theoretical social sciences (other than economic theory) my presentation of these doctrines is certainly not unbiased. (*Poverty of Historicism,* (1986 ed.) p. 3

Although coined in1811 by Karl Schlegal, the early development of the term 'historicism' can be traced back to the work of the French philosopher Auguste Comte (1798-1857), who is seen as a seminal figure in many ways. He not only developed 'historicism' into a definable creed, but is also regarded as the progenitor of that 'logical positivism' which Popper claimed to have 'killed', with its attempts to introduce 'scientific' techniques into the study of philosophy. Comte's special field of interest was praxeology, that is the study of human planned behaviour, as distinct from reflexive or instinctive behaviour. His central concern was with human society, and he is credited with being the father of sociology. The term 'sociology' itself was originally coined as a neologism by Emmanuel Sieyès (1748-1836) in 1780, but it was Comte who gave the concept meaning by tracing the evolution of society through three distinct stages, which he called the theological, metaphysical, and positivist stages. The final, positivist stage was one in which society progressed by observation and deduction, testing all social theories by experimentation before proceeding. Because of this he has also been described as the first philosopher of science, although he never applied that title to himself. He did try, however, to apply scientific 'laws' to the evolution of societies, which would enable the skilled 'sociologist' to predict future developments. Comte's *magnum opus* was his *Cours de Philosophie Positive*, first published in Paris in 1835.

Similar ideas of 'inevitable' historical developments were also put forward by Wilhelm Hegel (1770-1831), Karl Marx (1818-1883), and Friedrich Nietzsche (1844-1900). Popper, of course, decried them all. As a philosopher he denied determinism, answering Einstein's, 'God does not play dice' by claiming that God liked to be surprised, finding that he had created a more ‘interesting’ universe that way! Popper devoted an entire book to his arguments on these lines, *The Open Universe: An Argument for Indeterminism*, first published in book form in 1982. This was followed up by his, *The Future is Open* in 1985. I of course would say that God does *not* like surprises, since he is the one in charge, but that he *does* like change: hence change as the first law of the universe. But although I am a convinced determinist myself, I entirely agree with Popper in his declaration that our future is unpredictable. As I have stressed before, we must learn to distinguish between the predetermined and the unpredictable. Many things are unpredictable for us in our present state of knowledge, but all things are predetermined. It is just that we are not, as yet, in any position to see into our own futures. As noted above, few things are more unpredictable than human behaviour, or more irrational than human emotions, and these will be the elements that will shape our future. To these factors Popper quite correctly added the fact that our past and present have been heavily influenced by scientific developments, and certainly our future will be too, but we have no reliable way of accurately foreseeing what these scientific developments will be. Forty years ago people expected to be enjoying flying cars by 2020, but nobody foresaw the coming impact of the internet.

Karl Popper was a great political philosopher because he defined for us ‘the open society’, a concept that was perhaps in need of some clarification. When he spoke of ‘the open society’, Popper had in mind primarily a society that was open to change, and *peaceful* change. Moreover, not only was it open to change, but it was actually *expected* to change, constantly evolving for the betterment of that society. Popper contrasted this ideal with what he called ‘The Closed Society’ which, on the contrary, was dedicated to the *avoidance* of change. He saw the open society as being necessarily a liberal democracy, where unpopular governments could be replaced peacefully, where the rule of law obtained, and where freedom of thought and freedom of speech would be not only tolerated, but actively encouraged. The closed society, on the other hand, he equated with totalitarian dictatorships, governed by small elites who were desperate to keep themselves in power, and who therefore wanted to *avoid* all change, and to suppress freedom of speech and thought. Here, Popper was thinking of the Communist, Fascist, and Nazi dictatorships that had characterised the period in which he was writing. Under such regimes the rule of law was undermined, freedom of thought and freedom of expression were ruthlessly suppressed, and the people were given no opportunity to change their governments peacefully, because free elections were not allowed. The goal of these governments was the *avoidance* of change, as far as was possible. But of course, in the fast-moving twentieth century, with information becoming ever more freely available, living standards rising, and scientific progress going on apace, regimes such as these tended to become unstable, even if they were not ended by military defeat. Nazism was defeated militarily in 1945, but Fascism lived on in Spain under General Franco until his death in 1975, and Communism lived on in the Soviet Union until 1989, only to collapse at last under the burden of its own restrictions. In China, a form of nominal Communism lives on into the twenty-first century, but since 1978, when Deng Xiaoping (1904-97) took power, a free market, private enterprise system has been introduced, a sector which now works in parallel with the centralised, Communist economy. Deng called his new hybrid system, 'socialism with Chinese characteristics', and it has delivered very rapid economic growth, and a rising living standard for all of China's people. Essentially, however, the Communist Party retains permanent dictatorial power in China, and so would be defined by Popper as a 'closed' society.

In his book *The Open Society* Popper sought out the philosophical roots of twentieth-century totalitarianism, and targeted in particular four philosophers of the past, Plato, Aristotle, Hegel, and Marx. All four had been major figures in the history of thought, but Popper wrote of them in the preface to his first edition of 1945,

> If in this book harsh words are spoken about some of the greatest among the intellectual leaders of mankind, my motive is not, I hope, the wish to belittle them. It springs rather from my conviction that, if our civilisation is to survive, we must break with the habit of deference to great men. Great men may make great mistakes, and as this book tries to show, some of the greatest leaders of the past supported the perennial attack on freedom and reason. Their influence, too rarely challenged, continues to mislead those on whose defence civilisation depends, and to divide them. The responsibility for this tragic and possibly fatal division becomes ours if we hesitate to be outspoken in our criticism of what admittedly is a part of our intellectual heritage. By our reluctance to criticise some of it, we may help to destroy it all. (2002 edition, p. xxxi)

With these words, Popper endears himself to me as a kindred spirit. As noted in my Introduction above, 'The acceptance of orthodoxy is the surrender of thought, and contempt for authority is the beginning of wisdom. It is only a beginning, but it is an essential start'. We must indeed break with the habit of deference to great men, because *great men may make great mistakes*, as can we all. Not even my four philosopher heroes are above criticism, as will be noted above. Popper himself observed,

> Leaders and prophets are looked for, so it is hardly surprising that leaders and prophets are found. But 'grown men do not need leaders', as H.G. Wells once said. And grown men ought to *know* that they do not need leaders. As for prophets, I believe in the duty of every intellectual to keep them at arm's length. (*All Life is Problem Solving* (2001 ed.), p. 85)

In his treatment of Plato, Popper criticises what he calls Plato's holism and his essentialism. By 'holism' Popper means Plato's tendency to view the state as a whole, as something that is greater than the sum of its parts. There is some sense in this view, but Plato then goes on to reason that therefore the interests of individuals should be made secondary to those of the state: in other words, the individual should serve the state, rather than the state serving the individual. This may be seen as an organic rather than a mechanistic view of the state. By 'essentialism', Popper referred to Plato's vision of the world of 'ideals' as distinct from the mere shadowy versions of these 'essences' which we see around us. Included in his 'essentialism' was Plato's vision of the ideal state, a perfect form which perhaps could never be achieved, but which should be striven for. As pointed out in the politics chapter below, Plato's 'ideal state' was distinctly hierarchical, with humankind carefully divided into the men of gold, of silver, of bronze or of iron, and finally we must assume of dross, for Athens had a large slave class, which Plato seemed to deem unworthy of mention. The 'men of gold' were the 'philosopher kings', for Plato believed in rule by the wise, a system which he called 'aristocracy'. For Popper, however, the idea of 'philosopher kings' was anathema. He wrote,

> What a monument to human smallness is this idea of the philosopher king! What a contrast between it and the simplicity and humaneness of Socrates, who warned the statesman against the danger of being dazzled by his own power, excellence, and wisdom, and who tried to teach him what matters most – that we are all frail human beings. What a decline from this world of irony and reason and truthfulness down to Plato's kingdom of the sage, whose magical powers raise him high above ordinary men; although not quite high enough to forego the use of lies, or to neglect the sorry trade of every shaman – the selling of spells, of breeding spells, in exchange for power over his fellow-men. (*Open Society*, 2011 ed., p. 146)

Plato had indeed spoken of 'the noble lie', which he seemed ready to accept as a propaganda device, to help keep the hoi polloi in order. But with this passage, Popper once again appeals to me very directly. As also noted elsewhere, unfortunately neither Superman nor Wonderwoman is available to lead and guide us – we always end up with no one but fallible human beings, not so very different from ourselves as our leaders. Popper therefore argued that the question we should ask is not, 'Who should rule?' but rather, 'How can we peacefully get rid of those who rule badly?' In his own words, we should, 'replace the question: *Who should rule?* by the new question: *How can we so organise political institutions that bad or incompetent rulers can be prevented from doing too much damage?*' (*ibid*, p.115) In Popper's view, this could be achieved only within the context of a liberal democracy, governed by the rule of law, where bad rulers could be peacefully voted out of office. He quoted Pericles, the leader of democratic Athens, on this point, who had observed that, 'Although only a few may originate a policy, we are all able to judge it.'(*ibid,* p. 177) So committed was Popper to democracy that he made no bones about it, declaring, 'You can choose whatever names you like for the two types of government. I personally prefer to call the type of government which can be removed without violence 'democracy', and the other 'tyranny'. (*Conjectures and Refutations* (2002 ed.) p. 464)

Plato, on the other hand, favoured an aristocracy, i.e. government by the wise, who would remain permanently in office. These 'wise' were to rule in a completely autocratic way: everyone must be taught to obey, and under no circumstances be allowed to think for themselves. There are shades of *1984* in this quotation from Plato's *Laws* which Popper cites on p. 99 of his *Open* Society:

> The greatest principle of all is that nobody, whether male or female, should be without a leader. Nor should the mind of anybody be habituated to letting him do anything at all on his own initiative; neither out of zeal, nor even playfully. But in war and in the midst of peace – to his leader he shall direct his eye and follow him faithfully. And even in the smallest matter he should stand under leadership. For example, he should get up, or move, or wash, or take his meals...only if he has been told to do so. In a word, he should teach his soul, by long habit, never to dream of acting independently, and to become utterly incapable of it. (*The* Laws, Article 942)

But Plato was a pessimist, fearing that all states had a tendency to decay from this 'ideal' rule by aristocracy to timocracy, that is rule by a warrior class. He had Sparta in mind at this point, but such a term could also be applied to feudal Europe or Japan. Timocracy in turn tended to decline into oligarchy, which means literally rule by a few, but Plato saw it as rule by the rich, what we would call a plutocracy. Here, we might think of feudalism being replaced by capitalism. But oligarchy would then degenerate into democracy. Plato took a very dim view of democracy, blaming democratic Athens under Pericles for first inciting and then losing the Peloponnesian war against Sparta, and for executing Socrates. Democracy he saw as being the most unstable, and almost the worst form of government, which would in its turn degenerate into the very worst form of government, which was tyranny. Plato detected this tendency to decay in all aspects of life, and therefore the aim of the state should be to prevent this decay from its ideal form, i.e. aristocracy, by preserving the status quo by all means possible. This meant, in Popper's view, the enforcement of a 'closed' society, one that was resistant to change, so that his 'philosopher kings' could remain permanently in charge. It seems here that Plato was betraying a certain admiration of Spartan society.

Popper equated the open society with 'civilization' and the closed society with 'tribalism'. But he conceded that there was something comforting and reassuring about living in a 'tribal' society, where everyone knew their place, where change was kept to a minimum, and where individualism was discouraged. Ancient Sparta was such a society, and it must have been easy for Popper to associate it with Nazi Germany, or Communist Russia. By contrast the open society was open to change, open to class mobility, open to new ideas. These could be disruptive and upsetting, imposing upon the open society what Popper called 'the strain of civilization'. It was under this strain that Athens had abandoned its experiment in democracy, and executed its wisest citizen, Socrates, for his disturbing influence. Yet while Sparta had been strong, stable, and militarily triumphant, it had produced no great writers or philosophers, in sharp contrast to the monumental intellectual achievements of Athens. In Popper's day, Nazi Germany too had become a cultural desert due, in no small measure, to the expulsion of its Jews. The 'strain of civilization' had been a productive one. Therefore, wrote Popper,

> This strain, this uneasiness, is a consequence of the breakdown of the closed society. It is still felt even in our own day, especially at times of social change. It is the strain created by the effort which life in an open and partially abstract society continually demands from us – by the endeavour to be rational, to forego at least some of our emotional social needs, to look after ourselves, and to accept responsibilities. We must, I believe, bear this strain as the price to be paid for every increase in knowledge, in reasonableness, in co-operation and in mutual help, and consequently in our chances of survival...it is the price we have to pay for being human. (*ibid*, p. 168)

Plato and Marx are undoubtedly Popper's major targets in *The Open Society*, where he devotes the first one-third of his text to attacks on Plato, and most of the rest to attacks on Marx. But Aristotle and Hegel also come in for criticism. Aristotle agreed with Plato in his classification of men into distinct grades of worthiness, and also approved of slavery, declaring that some men were 'slaves by nature'. These views did not endear him to Popper, but Aristotle at least did not share Plato's pessimism. Rather than seeing all things as having a tendency to decay, Aristotle saw them rather as evolving, growing up to their 'final cause', in the sense that an acorn's 'final cause' was an oak tree. His hope was that societies too would evolve, to achieve a perfect 'final form'. This doctrine is known as teleology, the idea of a recognisable, ascertainable, clearly determinable final end to a process of development, from the ancient Greek τέλος, (telos), which means 'end' or in this context, 'final cause'. But this notion of society or anything else evolving to an inevitable, predestined 'final cause' did not appeal to Popper: to him, it sounded too much like historicism. He insisted that the future was 'open' and unpredictable. The idea of a perfect, 'final cause' also smacked to Popper of Utopianism, another of his pet hates. Popper abhorred the idea of working to achieve a 'blueprint', a 'final cause', a perfect society. He declared that, 'Those who promise us paradise never succeed in creating anything but a hell'. He associated Utopianism with aestheticism and romanticism, writing in his *Open Society,*

> Aestheticism and radicalism must lead us to jettison reason, and to replace it by a desperate hope for political miracles. This irrational attitude, which springs from an intoxication with dreams of a beautiful world, is what I call Romanticism. It may seek its heavenly city in the past or in the future; it may preach 'back to nature' or 'forward to a world of peace and beauty'; but its appeal is always to our emotions rather than to reason. Even with the best intentions of making heaven on earth it only succeeds in making it a hell – that hell which man alone prepares for his fellow-men. (*ibid*, p. 157)

Wilhelm Friedrich Hegel (1770-1831) although much admired by Karl Marx, was of course not at all a materialist like Marx himself, but rather a philosophical idealist, hoping that man's moral qualities would steadily evolve through his envisaged pattern of thesis, antithesis, and eventually synthesis to produce a new and superior form of humanity. However, he also believed that this higher form of self-fulfilment could be achieved only within the context of the state, into which the individual was to be entirely subsumed. Popper therefore accused Hegel of historicism, and the championing of dictatorship and the closed society. As noted in the Philosophy chapter above, Hegel was indeed an appalling statist, worshiping the state as God on earth. But Popper seems to have overlooked here the importance of Hegel's introduction of the dialectic as a means for allowing the evolution of ideas. The term 'dialectic' comes from the Greek διά, 'dia' meaning through, and λεκτός, 'lectos', meaning 'that which is said': hence διάλεκτος, which means talking through our differences and our ideas in conversation. Popper had noted at the end of his *Open Society* that, 'the role of thought is to carry out revolutions by means of critical debates rather than by means of violence and warfare; it is in the great tradition of western rationalism to fight our battles with words rather than with swords.' (*ibid,* p. 510) Later Popper noted, 'The war of ideas is a Greek invention. It is one of the most important inventions ever made. Indeed, the possibility of fighting with words instead of fighting with swords is the very basis of our civilization, and especially of all its legal and parliamentary institutions.' (*Conjectures and Refutations* (2002 ed.), p. 501) And again, 'in the sphere of ideas, only critical discussion can help us sort the wheat from the chaff.' (*All Life is Problem Solving* (2001 ed.), p. 84) In view of these comments, it is surprising that Popper did not give Hegel more credit for introducing us to the idea of the dialectic. But Popper had only condemnation for Hegel, tracing his thought back to what he saw as its Platonic and Aristotelian roots. (*Open Society* (2011 ed.), pp. 219-241).

However, Arthur Schopenhauer (1788-1860) was a philosopher of whom Popper, like Einstein, *did* warmly approve, and so perhaps we may simply provide here Schopenhauer's view of Hegel, as he is quoted by Popper in his *Open Society*. The quotation is taken from the Preface to the second edition of Schopenhauer's *World as Will and Idea* (1844). This rousing piece of invective provides us not only with Popper's own view of Hegel, but also with a splendid example of the very poor opinion that philosophers usually hold of one another! For Schopenhauer, Hegel was nothing but the self-interested paid agent of the Prussian state, writing of him,

> Hegel, installed from above by the powers that be, as the certified Great Philosopher, was a flat-headed, insipid, nauseating, illiterate charlatan, who reached the pinnacle of audacity in scribbling together and dishing up the craziest mystifying nonsense. This nonsense has been noisily proclaimed as immortal wisdom by mercenary followers and readily accepted as such by all fools, who thus joined into as perfect a chorus of admiration as had ever been heard before. The extensive field of spiritual influence with which Hegel was furnished by those in power has enabled him to achieve the intellectual corruption of a whole generation...Philosophy, brought

afresh to repute by Kant...was soon to become a tool of interests; of state interests from above, of personal interests from below... The driving forces of this movement are, contrary to all these solemn airs and assertions, not ideal; they are very real purposes indeed, namely personal, official, clerical, political, in short material interests... Party interests are vehemently agitating the pens of so many pure lovers of wisdom...Truth is certainly the last thing they have in mind...Philosophy is misused, from the side of the state as a tool, from the other side as a means of gain...Who can really believe that truth also will thereby come to light, just as a by-product? *Governments make of philosophy a means of serving their state interests, and scholars make of it a trade.* (*Open Society*, pp. 247-8)

While we are on the subject of invective, it might be worth mentioning at this point that in addition to Plato, Aristotle, Hegel, and of course Marx, Popper had two other philosopher *bêtes noirs* in the forms of Martin Heidegger (1889-1976), and Ludwig Wittgenstein (1889-1951). Interviewed on the occasion of his 90th birthday, Popper said of the former that he was 'a swine', and added,

I appeal to the philosophers of all countries to unite and never again mention Heidegger or talk to another philosopher who defends Heidegger. This man was a devil. I mean, he behaved like a devil to his beloved teacher, and he has had a devilish influence on Germany. One has only to read Heidegger in the original to see what a swindler he was. His philosophy is merely empty verbiage put together in statements which are absolutely empty. (*Intellectus* Vol. 23 (July-Sept. 1992) p. 3.

It is certainly true that Heidegger supported Hitler during World War II, and betrayed his former teacher, Edmund Husserl (1859-1938), who was Jewish, by joining in the persecution of Jews in 1930s Germany. But Popper's other pet hate was Ludwig Wittgenstein, whose linguistic philosophy Popper saw as being abstruse, pointless, and utterly irrelevant to the times they were living in. The two men met for the first time on October 25th, 1946, just after Popper had been appointed as Reader in Logic and Scientific Method at the London School of Economics. The occasion was a meeting of the Cambridge University Moral Sciences Club, a venerable institution founded in 1878, which had been attended by all the great British philosophers over the years. On that evening, Bertrand Russell, Richard Braithwaite, Georg Kreisel, and Stephen Toulmin were also present. The meeting took place in room H3 of King's College Gibbs Building, an austere Palladian structure heated only by open coal fires in its rooms. The two men sat on opposite sides of the coal fire in H3, since Wittgenstein was chairing the meeting, and Popper was guest speaker. His paper was entitled, 'Are there philosophical problems?' Popper of course believed that such problems were real, while to Wittgenstein they were just linguistic puzzles. He grew increasingly irate as the paper went on, and began poking crossly at the coals in the hearth. When Popper had finished, Wittgenstein angrily demanded that Popper should give him an example of a moral principle, certain that he could reduce it to a mere linguistic puzzle very quickly. But in his irritation he had been waving the poker in Popper's face, so Popper replied, 'Thou shalt not threaten visiting speakers with hot pokers!'

Wittgenstein was so enraged by this reply that he threw the poker down and stormed out, leaving Braithwaite, whose room it was, to chair the meeting. The legend of 'Wittgenstein's poker' has since entered into the folklore of British philosophy.

But Popper's main target in his *Open Society* was of course Karl Marx. There were several reasons for this. First, Marx was a historicist, believing that history was following a predetermined and predictable path that only he, Karl Marx, could understand and explain. Secondly, Marx was a Utopianist, imagining that an ideal society would emerge at the end of this historical process. In his writings Popper repeatedly stressed that, 'Those who promise paradise on earth never deliver anything but a hell'. This was because, in Popper's view, Utopianists always had to work to a blueprint, with their imagined perfect society in mind. This not only implied the use of excessive state power, but also laid them open to 'the law of unintended consequences'. Popper believed that state planning never went entirely according to plan. He may have been thinking here of the great Soviet famine of 1932-3 which had been the direct result of the forced collectivisation of agriculture as part of the first Soviet five-year plan. This had involved the seizure of all land by the state, with those who resisted, notably the larger, wealthier peasants known as kulaks, being arrested, deported, or executed. This massive disruption to agricultural production had resulted in over three million famine deaths in the Ukraine, Northern Caucasus, Volga Region, and Kazakhstan. Popper was deeply opposed to the idea of granting too much power to the state, very understandably in view of the times he lived in. Stalin's Russia, Hitler's Germany, Mussolini's Italy, and Franco's Spain had all been totalitarian dictatorships. Popper viewed the 'dictatorship of the proletariat' as just another undesirable form of absolutism, pointing out that even in democracies, 'the people do not rule anywhere; it is always governments that rule (and unfortunately also bureaucrats or officials, who can be held accountable only with difficulty, if at all)'. (*All Life is Problem Solving* (2001 ed.), p. 93) He saw the 'dictatorship of the proletariat' as just another excuse for allowing a small, self-interested clique to seize and retain power. Popper believed that, of all the potential enemies of the open society, Marxism was the most dangerous, because it was the most seductive and the most persuasive. It therefore deserved to be the main focus of his attack.

In addition, Popper was against any sudden and violent revolutionary change, whether Marxist or otherwise, partly because of his fear of 'the law of unintended consequences'. There are echoes of Edmund Burke here. He was a gradualist, which for me is one of his most appealing features. He never invoked the spirit of Darwin to support his stance on this point, but he might well have done so, by arguing that slow and steady evolution can produce successively higher life forms, but that sudden genetic mutations are more likely to produce monsters. Popper never forgot how his colleagues, shot down around him on June 15, 1919, had been celebrated as martyrs by fellow Communists, who were quite clearly prepared to countenance the use of violence to bring about a radical revolution. This was enough to distance Popper from Communism for the rest of his life. However, he wrote in his autobiographical work *Unended Quest*,

I remained a socialist for several years, even after my rejection of Marxism; and if there could be such a thing as socialism combined with individual liberty, I would be a socialist still. For nothing could be better than living a modest, simple, and free life in an egalitarian society. It took some time before I recognised this as no more than a beautiful dream; that freedom is more important than equality; that the attempt to realise equality endangers freedom; and that, if freedom is lost, there will not even be equality among the unfree. (1977 ed., p. 36)

Popper also believed that the whole of *Das Kapital* had been devoted to criticising a system that no longer existed. He wrote in the first edition of his *Open Society*,

Laissez-faire has disappeared from the face of the earth, but it has not been replaced by a socialist or communist system as Marx understood it. Only in the Russian sixth of the earth do we find an economic system where, in accordance with Marx's prophecy, the means of production are owned by the state, whose political might however shows, in opposition to Marx's prophecy, no inclination to wither away. But all over the earth, organised political power has begun to perform far-reaching economic functions. *Unrestrained capitalism* has given way to a new historical period, to our own period of *political interventionism*, of economic interference by the state. Interventionism has assumed various forms...The development which led to this intervention started in Marx's own day, with British factory legislation. It made its first decisive advances with the introduction of the 48-hour week, and later with the introduction of unemployment insurance and other forms of social insurance. How utterly absurd it is to identify the economic system of the modern democracies with the system Marx called 'capitalism' can be seen at a glance. (2011 ed., p. 350)

At the time of his writing this was of course true, because China had not yet undergone its Communist Revolution, and capitalism in Western Europe was under strict state control. However, today's neoliberal plutocrats seem bent upon restoring the conditions of Victorian England almost in their entirety! Finally, Popper dismissed Marxism as mere soothsaying, with no claim to 'scientific' status whatsoever. In his *Conjectures and Refutations* he wrote,

It is a typical soothsayer's trick to predict things so vaguely that the predictions can hardly fail: that they become irrefutable. The Marxist theory of history, in spite of the serious efforts of some of its founders and followers, ultimately adopted this soothsaying practice. In some of its earlier formulations (for example in Marx's depiction of the character of the 'coming social revolution') their predictions were testable, and in fact falsified. Yet instead of accepting the refutations the followers of Marx re-interpreted both the theory and the evidence in order to make them agree. In this way they rescued the theory from refutation; but they did so at the price of adopting a device which made it irrefutable. They thus gave a 'conventionalist twist' to the theory; and by this stratagem they destroyed its much advertised claim to scientific status. (*ibid,* p. 49)

But in talking about science and the scientific method Popper was, as usual, on rather shaky ground. In fact, genuinely scientific theories have often needed modification in the light of later discoveries which have not invalidated the theory, but rather refined it. Quantum mechanical theory is a good case in point. It provides us with a basically correct view of the structure of matter, but the original theory did need to be refined in the light of subsequent discoveries, and of criticisms made of it by Einstein among others, yet it still retains its scientific status.

To some this may sound paradoxical, but Popper was very fond of paradoxes. He stressed first the paradox of tolerance. While declaring that tolerance was a good thing, yet there had to be limits to tolerance for 'If we extend unlimited tolerance even to those who are intolerant, if we are not prepared to defend a tolerant society against the onslaught of the intolerant, then the tolerant will be destroyed, and tolerance with them.' (*Open Society* (2011 ed.) p. 581) He also spoke of the paradox of freedom at several points. Freedom too was a good thing, but again there must be limits to freedom, for complete freedom in a society would allow the strong to bully the weak. Then there was too the paradox of peace: peace was worth fighting for! Those who begin wars do so because they believe they will gain more than they lose by war. Their potential opponents must therefore remain constantly vigilant, and well-armed, as a deterrent. He believed in the old adage, 'If you seek for peace, prepare for war'. Popper would not have wanted to admit this, but I detect here echoes of Aristotle's doctrine of the 'golden mean'. Yes, we must be tolerant, but not too tolerant. Yes, we must be free, but not too free. Yes, we must strive for peace, but not via a naive pacifism.

Popper was also fond of inversions. As noted above, he believed that the question should be not, 'who should rule' but rather, 'who should *not* rule, and how can we peacefully get rid of them?' Where the logical positivists had proposed verification as a criterion of the 'scientific', Popper had proposed falsification. Against the idea of Bentham and Mill that we should strive for 'the greatest happiness of the greatest number', Popper proposed that we should instead strive for 'the least misery of the greatest number'. He called this 'negative Utilitarianism', which tied in with his sister doctrine of 'piecemeal social engineering'. He considered these doctrines to be 'safer' than standard Utilitarianism, which smacked too much for him of state planning, authoritarianism, and threats to personal liberty. Instead of trying to make everyone happy, which sounded rather like Utopianism, Popper argued that the state should concentrate on reducing misery, specifically those miseries which were most obvious, and most open to relief first of all, in small, piecemeal steps. There was no 'moral equivalence' between happiness and suffering since,

> Human suffering makes a direct moral appeal, namely, the appeal for help, while there is no similar call to increase the happiness of a man who is doing well anyway. The Utilitarian formula 'maximise pleasure' assumes, in principle, a continuous pleasure-pain scale which allows us to treat degrees of pain as negative degrees of pleasure. But, from the moral point of view, pain cannot be outweighed by pleasure, and especially not one man's pain by another man's pleasure. Instead of the greatest happiness of the greatest number one should demand, more modestly, the least amount of avoidable suffering for all. (*ibid,* p. 602)

But this doctrine of piecemeal social engineering should be applied in the political sphere as well. Popper believed that constitutions too ought to be amended slowly, one piece at a time, so that each change could then be scrutinised critically and rationally, then discarded if it was found to be undesirable. He declared,

> The piecemeal engineer knows, like Socrates, how little he knows. He knows that we can learn only from our mistakes. Accordingly, he will make his way, step by step, carefully comparing the results expected with the results achieved, and always on the look-out for the unavoidable, unwanted consequences of any reform; and he will avoid undertaking reforms of a complexity and scope which will make it impossible for him to disentangle causes and effects, and to know what he is really doing. (*Poverty of Historicism* (1986 ed.) p. 67)

Once again we see him advocating an evolutionary rather than a revolutionary approach, embracing the principle of trial and error, in the best scientific tradition. Well, by their books ye shall know them. The painter, the sculptor, and the composer can all be ambiguous, and hide behind their art. But the writer, whether of fact or of fiction, has nowhere to hide: the writer gives everything away. 'Le style, c'est l'homme même.'

Because of his swingeing attack upon Marxism, generally accepted as being the most devastating and effective of the twentieth century, Popper tends to be regarded, especially by the Left, as a right-wing thinker. His reputation with the Left was not improved by the fact that, in 1947, he joined with Friedrich Hayek, Ludwig von Mises, and Milton Friedman in founding the Mount Pelerin Society. Those three are of course known as the high priests of unrestrained free enterprise, private capitalism, and indeed the founding fathers of neoliberalism. The Society was named after Mont Pèlerin, the Swiss resort where it first convened. But the Society was not quite the right-wing monster envisaged by the Left. Its 1947 *Statement of Aims* included the investigation of

> 'methods of re-establishing the rule of law and of assuring its development in such manner that individuals and groups are not in a position to encroach upon the freedom of others, and private rights are not allowed to become a basis of predatory power' and

'the possibility of establishing minimum standards by means not inimical to initiative and the functioning of the market'. Indeed, one aim was to examine, 'the principles and practice of a free society and to study the workings, virtues *and defects* of market-oriented economic systems.' (My italics)

Even so, Popper later distanced himself from the Society, feeling that its views had moved too far to the Right. While he was prepared to take a leaf from von Mises' book, arguing that only a free market system could efficiently balance supply and demand, delivering the goods that people actually wanted at competitive prices, his acceptance of free markets was not unconditional. From the very beginning, he had been aware of the dangers of unrestrained free enterprise private capitalism, without the safety net of a social welfare system. As a young man, he had seen its results on the streets of Vienna. Therefore, from the first edition of his *Open Society* he had written,

> Even if the state protects its citizens from being bullied by physical violence, it may defeat our ends by its failure to protect them from the misuse of economic power. In such a state, the economically strong is still free to bully one who is economically weak, and to rob him of his freedom. Under these circumstances, unlimited economic freedom can be just as self-defeating as unlimited physical freedom, and economic power may be nearly as dangerous as physical violence...the nature of the remedy is clear...We must construct social institutions, enforced by the power of the state, for the protection of the economically weak from the economically strong. The state must see to it that nobody need enter into an inequitable arrangement out of fear of starvation, or economic ruin.
>
> This of course means that the principle of non-intervention, of an unrestrained economic system, has to be given up. If we wish freedom to be safeguarded, then we must demand that the policy of unlimited economic freedom be replaced by the planned economic intervention of the state. We must demand that unrestrained *capitalism* give way to *economic interventionism*. (2011 ed., p. 333)

I am completely in agreement with those statements. Popper's prime concern was, like Spinoza's, with LIBERTY for the individual, and he was just as determined to defend this liberty from the capitalist Right as from the socialist Left. Poverty is, in fact, one of the greatest restraints upon personal freedom imaginable. But it was Popper's humanitarianism that trumped any shade of political belief. In an interview given just before his death in 1994 Popper is on record as saying,

> Well, I do believe that in a way one has to have a free market, but I also believe that to make a godhead out of the principle of the free market is nonsense. If we do not have a free market, then quite obviously the things that are being produced are not being produced for the consumer, really. The consumer can take it or leave it. His needs are not taken into account in the process of production. But all that is not of a fundamental importance. *Humanitarianism*, that is of fundamental importance.
>
> Traditionally, one of the main tasks of economics was to think of the problem of full employment. Since approximately 1965 economists have given up on that; I find it very wrong. It cannot be an insoluble problem. It may be difficult, but surely it is not

insoluble! Our first task is peace; our second task is to see that nobody be hungry; and the third task is fairly full employment. The fourth task is, of course, education. (Cited in Daniel Stedman Jones, *Masters of the Universe: Hayek, Friedman, and the Birth of Neoliberal Politics* (2014 ed.) p. 40)

What a voice of sanity, of moderation, and above all of humanitarianism was that of Karl Popper. How upset he would have been to see the original conception of neo-liberalism evolve into the reckless selfishness and greed, the 'let 'er rip' capitalism that brought about the great crash of 2008. By 1991 Popper had distanced himself from even the views of Friedrich Hayek who, in fact, was less of an ardent neoliberal than Ludwig von Mises or Milton Friedman. Writing in *All Life is Problem Solving* (2001 ed.) Popper declared,

It is perfectly true that some problems – air pollution, for example – may require special legislation. There are ideological worshipers of the so-called 'free market'...who think that such legislation limiting market freedom is a dangerous step down the road to serfdom. But that again is ideological nonsense. Forty-six years ago in the first edition of *The Open Society and Its Enemies*, I had already shown that a free market can exist only within a legal order created and guaranteed by the state. (p. 101)

This was the only point in his writings at which Popper even hinted at his disapproval of Hayek's *TheRoad to Serfdom* (1944), but this was only because he felt deeply indebted to Hayek who, with Gombrich, had made herculean efforts to get *The Open Society* published, and who had also been instrumental in securing for him a readership at the London School of Economics in 1946. Popper declared in his *Unended Quest* (1977) that Hayek had thereby 'saved my life' twice. (p. 120)

Finally, like my other three philosopher heroes, Popper too rejected established religions, but also denied the charge of atheism. All four had idiosyncratic religious views of their own. Popper was, in general, very modest about his own views on religion, and almost none of them appear in his writings. However, in a 1985 lecture he declared,

I am anything but an enemy of religion. My religion is the doctrine of the splendours of the world; of the freedom and creativity of wonderful human beings; of the terror and suffering of the despairing people we can help; of the extent of good and evil that has emerged in human history and keeps emerging over and over again; of the joyful message that we can prolong people's lives, especially those of women and children who have had the toughest life. I know nothing else. (*All Life is Problem Solving* (2001 ed.) p. 42).

The above extract is a translation from the original German in which the lecture was delivered and a rather bad translation in view of the clumsy style, but there are shades here of Tom Paine's 'religion of doing good'. Essentially, however, Popper had more of a religious sense than he wanted to admit. We get a clue to this in his *Unended Quest*, (p. 19), where he says of Spinoza's *Ethics*, 'It gave me a lifetime's dislike of theorising about God. Theology, I still think, is due to a lack of faith'. In 1969 he gave an interview to Edward Zerin on condition that it should be published only after his death. It finally appeared in the journal *Skeptic* Vol. 6 No.2 (1998) entitled, 'Karl Popper on God: The Lost Interview'. Here Popper admitted,

> I don't know whether God exists or not...some forms of atheism are arrogant and ignorant and should be rejected, but agnosticism – to admit that we don't know and to search – is all right...When I look at what I call the gift of life, I feel a gratitude which is in tune with some religious ideas of God. However, the moment I even speak of it, I am embarrassed that I may do something wrong to God in talking about God. (p. 32)

For Popper, his religious views were a very personal and private matter, about which he said very little in his published work. But such views as he did hold were in some ways similar to those of Einstein and Paine.

Essentially, in a century of mindless fanaticism, radical revolution, and violent extremism, Popper's was a voice of reason, of gradualism, and of moderation, the voice of a man who eschewed both extremes of the political spectrum. The only 'isms' in which he believed were pragmatism and humanitarianism. For me, this makes him a philosopher hero of his times. But Popper also has an important message for our own age which, as we shall see, has unfortunately fallen victim to a creed of economic extremism. Today, there is more need than ever to listen to his wise advice on balance and moderation.

IV On Science

We have already looked at thermodynamics, special and general relativity, and quantum mechanics in the Einstein section above: what might be described as the 'hard' sciences. But in this chapter we will be venturing into more speculative fields, and linking them more closely with philosophy. As noted in the Introduction above, Albert Einstein famously said, 'Science without religion is lame, religion without science is blind', one of his best known quotations. But he could more appropriately have said, '*Philosophy* without science is blind, science without *philosophy* is lame'. Linking the two in this way may seem odd, because while science is the road to truth, philosophy is, in my opinion, the road to happiness. These would appear to be two very different destinations for, as observed in the Introduction, 'reality is objective, but happiness is subjective'. However, it might also be said that, 'Until we know what is true, we cannot make what is best right'. In addition, simply acquiring a full understanding of the workings of this wonderful and highly improbable planet that we live upon ought in itself to make a substantial contribution to human happiness, in my opinion. There are indeed valuable links to be forged between science and philosophy, for the two disciplines have much to learn from each other, as I shall try to make clear in this section. It is surely very important for the philosopher to have a firm grasp of the nature of reality, or 'the way things are', for this might be viewed as *The Mind of God*, as the physicist Paul Davies argued in his 1992 book of that title. Nature has kept her secrets so well, and the truth is often so entirely counter-intuitive, especially in the realm of quantum mechanics, that it almost seems as though we were never meant to unravel those mysteries, but science has now taken us a very long way down the path of understanding, although of course many mysteries still remain.

However, having admitted this, some things are clearer than others. It is of course impossible to cover the whole field of Science, so the main purpose of this chapter will be to bring home a realization of just how lucky we are to be here at all, in this most improbable of universes, within a highly unusual solar system, and on this remarkably atypical planet, the like of which must be very rare in the galaxy. Moreover, if you live in the developed world at this particular point in time and as members of our particular species then you have been triply fortunate: a good fortune that ought to be appreciated. An awareness of all this highly improbable good fortune which has been heaped upon you should contribute substantially to your personal happiness.

Until about 200 years ago Science was regarded as just another branch of Philosophy. The earliest Greek philosophers, the 'pre-Socratics' such as Pythagoras, Heraclitus, Anaxagoras, and Democritus had concerned themselves almost exclusively with ontology, that is with speculations on the workings of the natural world, until Socrates (c470-399 BC) came along and did something to broaden their field of interest! But even 2,000 years later, in Britain Science was still referred to as 'Natural Philosophy', and our early scientists such as Robert Boyle (1627-91), Isaac Newton (1642-1727), and Joseph Priestley (1734-1804) called themselves 'natural philosophers'. Even Michael Faraday (1791-1867) would not have been offended if that title had been applied to him. The term 'scientist' was first used in print by the English philosopher and polymath William Whewell (1794-1866) in 1834, and only from that time did Science begin to be regarded as a separate and distinct field of study in its own right. Now it is hardly necessary to stress here just how much this particular branch of philosophical thought has done to change and shape our world and all, essentially, within the last 250 years or so, the mere blinking of an eye in terms of the long history of our species. It is not only scientific discoveries in themselves that have achieved this great feat, but also the *appliance* of Science. The pure scientist discovers what is, but the inventors and the engineers use those discoveries to create what has never been, and in this way a whole new world has been shaped for us. Truly, 'It's wotcha do wid wotcha got dat really counts', as Jimmy (Schnozzle) Durante once so trenchantly observed. Even more than changes to our material world, however, Science has radically re-shaped our conception of ourselves. Only 250 years ago nearly all Christians, Muslims, and Jews believed the Genesis creation story, and generally accepted the calculations made by Bishop James Usher (1581-1656) which seemed to 'prove' that the world had been created at precisely 6 p.m. on October 22, 4004 BC! Since that time, of course, our whole conception of ourselves, of our origins, of the planet we live upon, and of our place in the universe have been radically reshaped, and our lifestyles have changed accordingly.

The methodology of Science has already been referred to in the Introduction, but to briefly recap on its four stages these were, (a) Observation (b) Speculation (c) Experimentation (d) Validation/Refutation. If the speculation is not supported by experimental evidence, then the speculation is *wrong*. However, there is another route that Science sometimes takes in its eternal quest for truth, and it goes like this:

(a) Observation
(b) Speculation
(c) Calculation
(d) Consensus

In other words, it is sometimes impossible to conduct a repeatable experiment that would prove the speculation to be true. But on the basis of facts that *have* previously been proved to be true, it is possible to calculate what the outcome of that experiment would be. This applies in particular to the field of cosmology. Here we enter into the realm of theoretical physics, which some would argue is not true 'science' at all. The word 'science' derives from the Latin terms *scientia* (knowledge) from *scire* (to know). Strictly speaking, we do not ‘know’ anything at all until it has been proven by repeatable experimental evidence. A theory which can be neither proved nor disproved by such evidence remains just that, a theory and nothing more.

Nevertheless, the predictive power of mathematics is formidable. As examples, both gravitational waves and the Higgs boson were predicted mathematically decades before hard evidence was discovered to confirm their actual existence. We cannot recreate cosmic phenomena in the laboratory, but over the past hundred years science has discovered a great deal about particle physics and quantum mechanics, and the elements that exist here on earth are exactly the same as those to be found in deep space. It is therefore possible to calculate how they would behave under extreme conditions. For example, we cannot recreate in the laboratory a supernova explosion. However, we can say that such explosions do occur, albeit very rarely, because they are so violent that they can be observed even in distant galaxies. From our existing knowledge of the nature of matter and of astrophysics, we can be very sure that these extremely violent events mark the death throes of truly massive stars. However, we obviously cannot conduct a controlled experiment to prove this speculation to be correct! Nevertheless, calculations based upon our existing knowledge explain so perfectly what we have observed that no professional astronomer or astrophysicist doubts for a moment that the phenomena which we see do indeed result from the collapse of these very large stars. By the same token, no one has ever directly seen a black hole, or a super-dense neutron star, but based upon their calculations, all cosmologists agree that such entities must exist. Indeed, the ‘gravity waves’ recently discovered in 2016, 2017, and 2019 are thought to have emanated from the collisions of black holes or neutron stars in distant galaxies, objects which spiralled into each other, dragging the whole framework of the space-time continuum around with them as they circled inwards. These discoveries have been questioned, but mathematics support the idea that gravity waves must exist. Bearing in mind therefore that much of what scientists believe about our universe at the moment is based on calculation rather than experimentation, and so remains unproven, this chapter sets out to ask,

(a) How improbable is our universe?
(b) How unusual is our solar system?
(c) How unusual is our planet?
(d) How unusual is our sub-species?
(e) How secure is our future?

Our universe is currently believed to have come into existence some 13.8 billion years ago. Obviously we cannot create another universe in the laboratory, but observations and calculations now quite strongly support the ‘Big Bang’ theory, and there is a consensus of agreement on it, shared by nearly all scientists.

In the field of cosmology in particular, it is *quite probable* that many of our theories are true, even although we cannot yet conclusively *prove* them to be true by repeatable experiments. Indeed, it has been said that in science the problem has been not that too much trust has been reposed in theories and calculations, but rather that we have not trusted them enough! This point was well illustrated by Einstein's development of the theory of general relativity. His calculations told him clearly that the universe must be either expanding or contracting, but could not possibly be in a steady state. However, Einstein refused to believe his own calculations! This was because the consensus at that time favoured a steady-state universe, and Einstein believed the consensus rather than his own figures, adding a 'cosmological constant' to his calculations (the Greek capital L, lambda, rendered Λ) to keep his universe in a steady state. However, it was later shown by Edwin Hubble (1889-1953) in 1929 that the universe is in fact expanding, based upon the observed 'red shift' in the spectrum of light from distant galaxies which was taken to be a Doppler effect, implying that these galaxies were receding from us. Einstein then described his 'cosmological constant' as, 'my greatest blunder'. Ironically, however, the idea of a cosmological constant, still referred to as Einstein's Λ, has recently been revived with the discovery in 1998 that the expansion rate of the universe is actually accelerating. This is attributed to the recently proposed 'dark energy'. Its properties are still poorly understood, but it appears to act as a kind of negative gravity, which has not diluted with expansion, and so is causing the acceleration. Einstein could see that gravity pulled the universe in only one direction, inwards upon itself. If it was in fact stable, then some kind of anti-gravity force had to exist. It would now seem that this force *does* exist, in the form of dark energy. Perhaps Einstein's biggest mistake was to think that he had made a mistake! It seems that he did get things right, albeit for the wrong reasons, and his 'cosmological constant' is now associated with dark energy. The predictive power of calculation is certainly impressive.

Now whether this purely theoretical approach to our understanding of cosmology is really true 'science' or not remains a moot point, since the nature of massive black holes and supernovas cannot be proved by repeatable experiments. By the same token, their calculated properties cannot be disproved either, as all scientists will readily admit. Nevertheless, the power of calculation and prediction, based upon established facts, remains impressive, and a strong consensus of scientific opinion remains agreed upon both the causes and the properties of black holes and supernova, at least for the time being. So, let us turn now to the question of improbabilities.

(a) How Improbable is Our Universe?

Our own universe, we are told, had a clear beginning some 13.8 billion years ago, and is therefore still a very young universe. It will have its effective end trillions of years into the future when all the stars have burned themselves out, the black dwarfs have crumbled to dust, and even the black holes and neutron stars have radiated themselves away. There will be more on the life cycles of stars below, but the smallest red dwarf stars could have a main sequence lifespan of up to ten trillion years. When all the stars have gone our universe will then have reached a state of minimum entropy, eventually suffering 'heat death'. The early universe just after the Big Bang was all heat, but with no heat sink for this to flow into no work could be done, so the work of creation had to wait for the universe to expand. As it expanded and cooled stars and planets were formed and entropy (disorder) increased, allowing the work of creation to begin. But in the last days our universe will be all heat sink with no heat, so again no work will be done so no change can take place, thus bringing an end to time as we understand it. The universe will still contain precisely the same amount of heat/energy as before in accordance with the first law of thermodynamics, but the universe will have been expanding for trillions of years so that its heat/energy will then be very widely dispersed in a very cold, dark universe. But if entropy is defined as disorder in the sense of a lack of uniformity, the whole will then have returned to a state of very low entropy as a uniform sea of particles and photons. (I'm with Poincaré on this one!) Ours is still a very young universe, but the cosmologists tell us that although the stars are very hot, they are already so widely dispersed in the deep cold of outer space that the average temperature of the universe as a whole is already only 2.73 degrees Kelvin above absolute zero! Our own universe, therefore, will not last for an eternity. There is still some debate over just how it will end, but nearly all cosmologists agree that it *will* end. Brian Greene discusses a variety of less plausible possibilities in his recent book, *Until the End of Time* (2020), but here he strays too far from his remit as a scientist to include a good deal of superfluous verbiage.

Neither is the universe infinite. The Big Bang yielded eventually not only all of energy and all of matter, but also all of space and all of time – the space-time continuum of our own universe. Interestingly, although nothing *within* our universe can travel faster than light, the space-time continuum itself *can* expand faster than light, and has already done so in its earliest inflationary phase, or so we are told. This means that we will never be able to see to the edges of our own bubble universe, because that edge is now receding from us faster than the speed of light. Nevertheless, our universe *does* have such an edge, and therefore is not infinite in extent. The cosmologists tell us that, like the surface of our planet, the universe is finite, but unbounded. They believe that gravity has so curved the space-time continuum that anyone who travels in an entirely straight line (as he sees it) will eventually arrive back at his starting point, but will never reach the 'edge' of the universe, just as such a traveller on Earth would never reach the 'end' of the world, but could find himself back at his starting point. All of these statements represent of course mere theories based upon calculations, but such is the current consensus among cosmologists.

Where then, do infinity and eternity lie? Logic demands that they must exist somewhere, and mathematical calculations support this contention. But if not in our own universe, they can lie only outside our universe in that element which contains the multiverse, which must constitute eternity and infinity. It is often asked, 'If our universe is expanding, then what is it expanding into?' The answer can only be infinity, which is large enough to accommodate even our maximally expanded universe, which will of course by definition occupy only an infinitely small proportion of that infinity. But there will also be room there for other bubble universes as well, which presumably came into existence in much the same way that ours did, perhaps by a chance quantum fluctuation which gave rise to a phase transition from a prior state of pure energy. Some cosmologists tell us that if it can be proved that the amount of negative energy in the universe exactly balances its positive energy, then the sum total of its mass/energy is zero, and we could have had literally a universe from nothing! Such are the conclusions that may be reached through calculations, as demonstrated by L.M. Krauss (at some length) in his book, *A Universe from Nothing* (2012).

I will readily concede that when it comes to the multiverse, God does indeed play dice. Of course we cannot yet be sure of just what sparked off our own Big Bang, but the probability is that it was not a unique event. It is more likely that other bubble universes are being created all the time, perhaps 'budding off' from existing universes, but each one with only a limited life expectation. Indeed, some of their life spans, we may assume, will be much shorter than that of our own universe. The continual births, life spans, and deaths of all those universes could have been going on from everlasting to everlasting, thus constituting eternity. But all this, of course, is mere theory and speculation.

Let us return now to the claim made above that our own universe is a very improbable one indeed. This claim can be easily supported. First of all we can examine the assumed inflationary phase that followed the initiation of our Big Bang, the phase indeed which is more properly described as the Big Bang itself. This theory of 'inflationary cosmology' is closely associated with the name of Alan Guth (b.1947), the American physicist and cosmologist, who first gave the theory mathematical credibility in 1980. After such a violent event, the expanding explosion could have moved at any speed at all. Had this expansion been too fast, matter would have flown apart so rapidly that stars and galaxies could not have formed. If the expansion had been too slow, then gravity would soon have pulled all matter back together again into a 'Big Crunch', and our universe would have had only a short life span. The speed of the expansion had to be just right to allow our present universe to form. Just how fast was it? The calculations of cosmologists tell them that between 10^{-36} and 10^{-32} seconds after the Big Bang the universe expanded by a factor of 10^{25} (ten trillion trillion times), a rate considerably in excess of the speed of light.

How could this have happened? To explain their figures cosmologists have envisaged the existence of an as yet undiscovered hypothetical particle dubbed an 'inflaton'. This would be a scalar boson which created an 'inflaton field' rather as the recently discovered Higgs boson generates a Higgs field which permeates the whole of space. Already our credulity is stretched to its limits, but cosmologists tell us that this kind of inflation would have been necessary to account for the even distribution of matter, on the largest of scales, within our universe. Moreover, how much latitude was there for error in the pace of this inflation? The scientists tell us that if the rate of expansion had varied by so much as one part in 10^{60}, then the universe as we know it could not have formed. The pace had to be correct, therefore, to an incredible degree of precision in order to achieve a sustainable critical density of the universe! This is already, therefore, a very high level of improbability, verging upon the unbelievable. But John Gribbin and Martin Rees in their book, *Cosmic Coincidences* (1991) assure us that this 10^{60} figure is 'the most accurately determined number in the whole of physics'. (p. 26) Have the scientists got their figures wrong? Could there be some law of physics, as yet undiscovered, that dictated this degree of precision? Could most Big Bangs have resulted in a series of 'Big Crunches' until one of the ensuing re-explosions got it just right? Probably not. More likely, in an infinite number of universes, one simply had to get it right eventually at the first attempt, assuming that the Big Bang theory is correct at all.

So we have first of all the miracle of a highly improbable critical density for our expanding early universe. Once matter formed, its distribution within this critical density was very even thanks to that assumed inflation, but, crucially, not entirely even. It was just slightly 'lumpy', with density concentrations at the level of some fifty parts per million. Again this seems to have been just right. At greater variations of 'lumpiness' (so the scientists tell us) a superabundance of black holes would have resulted, and at lesser levels there would have been very few stars, and probably no galaxies. How wide were the allowable parameters of this 'lumpiness'? The astrophysicists have given us slightly varying figures, but all agree that the parameters were very narrow indeed. The precise level of 'lumpiness' in the early universe may be measured by local variations in the strength of the cosmic microwave background radiation, believed to be a kind of 'echo' of the Big Bang. These variations are seen as being expanded 'quantum jitters', suggesting a sub-atomic origin for our universe. They are slight, but just enough to have allowed stars and galaxies to form. This then is the story that most scientists are telling us about the origin of our universe, which is referred to as the Standard Model of Cosmology. However, we must remember that it is based on theory, speculation, and calculation, and has not been proved by repeatable experiment. Some scientists argue that the theory is completely wrong, that there was no 'Big Bang', and that our universe is actually much older than 13.8

billion years! A series of articles putting forward this case may be read online at http://msp.warwick.ac.uk/~cpr/paradigm/.

In many ways, the currently accepted Standard Model of Cosmology is certainly suspect. Based on the observed rotational speeds of galaxies for example, the Standard Model concludes that there is much more matter in and around these galaxies than can be seen, which has been dubbed 'dark matter'. In fact, the cosmologists now tell us that there is much more of this 'dark matter' in our universe than the normal, visible matter with which we are all familiar. It seems our universe is composed of only 4% 'normal' matter, 23% dark matter, and 73% dark energy, mentioned above as the mysterious force believed to be accelerating the expansion of the universe. Matter and energy are of course equivalent, under the famous formula $E= mc^2$, which tells us that matter is simply a highly concentrated form of energy. On the basis of calculations, there would seem to be good reasons for believing in these proportions, as explained at some length by Richard Panek in his book, *The 4% Universe* (2011).

Once again, however, these figures are hard to believe. They are based on observations of distant spiral galaxies, all of which revolve around a central star cluster. Stars on the outer fringes of these galaxies should be revolving at a much slower speed than stars near the galactic core, but their speed is seen to be higher than expected. This could be the result of invisible 'dark matter' situated above and below their plane of revolution, which prevents them from spinning away. But it has also been suggested that the allegedly anomalous revolution rates of galactic fringes could be the result of 'inertial frame-dragging', as the huge mass of the galaxy drags the whole space-time continuum around with it, thus dispensing with the need for any additional 'dark matter' at all. However, the overall distribution of galaxies on the largest of scales also suggests that they are being acted upon by some form of matter which exercises a gravitational effect, but which is invisible. Our problem is that this matter neither absorbs nor reflects light, and so we cannot see it. It is detectable only via its gravitational effects on matter that we *can* see.

By the same token, the Doppler effect which cosmologists rely upon so heavily might not be a Doppler effect at all over vast distances, but again due to gravitational influences, or a stretching of the space-time framework on an inter-galactic scale. This would weaken the case for a more rapidly expanding universe, and the existence of 'dark energy', currently assumed to be causing an acceleration in this rate of expansion. Dark energy, if it exists, would be mediated by a scalar boson similar to the Higgs boson, which permeates the whole of space. Such a field would not dilute with the expansion of the universe, while 'dark matter' would do so. This would account for the accelerating rate in the expansion of the universe. Ian Stewart in his book, *17 Equations that Changed the World* (2012) therefore notes that,

Cosmic counter-theories which question the current Standard Model, may well be wrong, but the fascinating point is that you can retain Einstein's field equations unchanged, dispense with dark matter, dark energy, and inflation, and *still* get behaviour reasonably like all of those puzzling observations. So whatever the theory's fate, it suggests that cosmologists should consider more imaginative cosmological models before resorting to new and otherwise unsupported physics. Dark matter, dark energy, inflation, each requiring radical new physics that no one has observed...In science, even one *deus ex machina* raises eyebrows. Three would be considered intolerable in anything other than cosmology...imagine what would happen if a biologist explained life by some unobservable 'life field', let alone suggesting that a new kind of 'vital matter' and a new kind of 'vital energy' were also necessary – while providing no evidence that any of them existed! (pp. 241-2)

Truly, arrogance is the enemy of truth, and when it comes to theories that cannot be proved by repeatable experiments, it behoves us all to keep an open mind. Dark matter and dark energy might one day come to be seen as myths of the early twenty-first century. Personally, I find the current Standard Model of Cosmology to be rather suspect. Perhaps the heretical views referred to above are correct, or perhaps neither theory is correct. More elaborate theories, such as 'M' theory and 'brane' theories are classic examples of very complex speculations which, whether right or wrong, cannot be conclusively proved. The jury is still out on these great cosmological questions, but since the Standard Model is currently the generally accepted view, let's go with that one for now.

Next, however, we must look at the structure and properties of 'normal' matter itself, where science is on much firmer ground, because here science *does* rely on repeatable experiments. The matter that we are familiar with of course consists of protons with a positive electrical charge, electrons with a negative electrical charge, and neutrons with no electrical charge. The mass of the proton is almost 2,000 times that of the electron (938 MeV against 0.51 MeV) and yet the negative electrical charge carried by the tiny electron precisely balances the positive electrical charge of the much more massive proton: this fact is all that gives atoms their stability. How improbable is that? Yet these are indisputable facts, proved by repeatable experiments. The atoms that they form consist mainly of empty space, since the electron clouds orbit their proton nuclei at relatively large distances. If the nucleus were the size of a golf ball, the nearest electron shell would be one kilometre away! Even atoms of lead consist of 99.9999 per cent empty space by volume. It is only because the negative charges of the electron shells on individual atoms repel each other that the normal matter which we see and feel gives the appearance of solidity. It is in fact the feather-light electrons that resist our pressure when we try to squeeze most solid lumps of matter.

At the temperatures and pressure that prevail on the surface of our planet these particles exist in combination to form the chemical elements familiar to us all, but at high temperatures such as those inside the sun their velocities are increased, their atomic structure is torn apart, and they exist as separate charged particles known as ions. Matter in this state is in fact a plasma. At high altitudes on our own planet, between 50 and 1,000 kilometres, a plasma may also be found in that region of the atmosphere known as the ionosphere. Here the air is so thin that its constituent atoms can be torn apart by incoming ionising radiation from the sun in the form of ultraviolet and x-rays, and separate charged particles, protons and electrons, may exist for some time as ions before finding a partner of the opposite charge with which they can recombine.

However, a substance known as antimatter can also exist in our universe, in which the protons have a negative charge (antiprotons) and the electrons a positive charge (positrons). When matter and antimatter meet, they mutually annihilate each other, converting their matter into pure energy, and releasing that energy as photons. Now in very violent events, such as the atom smashing that takes place in the Large Hadron Collider at CERN, equal amounts of matter and antimatter are always produced, with the two forms mutually annihilating into photons and other particles. The Big Bang was, we are told, another such violent event, producing equal numbers of particles and anti-particles in a process known as charge conjugation parity, or CP for short. These particles then proceeded to annihilate each other into pure energy. How then, did any matter survive at all? Why does our universe not consist simply of pure energy, perhaps that 'dark energy', whose nature is still baffling the cosmologists?

The answer lies in the composition of the atoms themselves. We now know that protons and neutrons are composed of two of the six fundamental particles called quarks. There are only six of them, affectionately named as the up, down, top, bottom, strange, and charmed quarks. For reasons too complicated to go into, six varieties of quark (but no fewer than six) allow for CP symmetry violation, usually known as CP asymmetry. Thanks to this CP asymmetry, for roughly every billion particles of antimatter created in the Big Bang, one billion and one particles of matter were also created, to form our visible universe. But although the existence of six quarks *allows* for CP asymmetry, it does not *require* it. There also had to be a stage in the early universe when energy and matter were in a state of non-equilibrium, and there also had to exist a mechanism for transmuting quarks and positrons (which are both fundamental particles) into each other. Miraculously, both of these conditions also applied, or so the scientists tell us. (See M. Malary, *Our Improbable Universe* (2004), pp. 26-30) In effect, they are heaping monumental improbability upon monumental improbability, until the story they are telling becomes less convincing than the fairytale of Goldilocks and the Three Bears! In fact in 2006 Paul Davies published a book entitled, *The Goldilocks Enigma: Why is the Universe Just Right for Life?* The title was appropriate because, like

Baby Bear's porridge, our universe appears to be 'just right' - a 'Goldilocks Universe' indeed!

But the remarkable coincidences continue. In his article, 'The Fine Tuning of Nature's Laws' which appeared in Issue No. 47, the Fall 2015 edition of the American scientific journal *The New Atlantis*, Luke A. Barnes tells us that the masses of each of the six quarks also have to be exactly right in order for matter to produce the chemistry that we see in our universe. As it happens, of course, they are. The masses of the up and down quarks, the lightest of the six, seem to be particularly crucial, for these are the only two stable quarks, with protons consisting of two ups and a down, and neutrons of two downs and an up. But Barnes continues,

However, we can calculate all the ways the universe could be disastrously ill-suited for life if the masses of these particles were different. For example, if the down quark's mass were just 2.6x10-26 grams or more, then adios periodic table! There would be just one chemical element and no chemical compounds, in stark contrast to the approximately 60 million known chemical compounds in our universe. With even smaller adjustments to these masses, we can make universes in which the only stable element is hydrogen-like. Once again, kiss your chemistry textbook goodbye, as we would be left with one type of atom and one chemical reaction. If the up quark weighed 2.4x10-26 grams, things would be even worse – a universe of only neutrons, with no elements, no atoms, and no chemistry whatsoever. The universe we happen to have is so surprising under the Standard Model because the fundamental particles of which atoms are composed are, in the words of cosmologist Leonard Susskind, 'absurdly light' compared to the range of possible masses that the particles described by the Standard Model could have. The range that avoids complexity-obliterating disasters is extremely small. (p.89)
(Available online at www.thenewatlantis.com/publications/number-47-fall-2015)

While we are on the subject of crucial masses, it seems that the mass of the neutron is also a critical factor when it comes to the life of stars. A neutron consists of a positively charged proton which has absorbed a negatively charged electron, giving it no electrical charge of its own. But mysteriously, in the case of the neutron, the whole becomes greater than the sum of its parts. If we look at the relative masses of these three particles we find that if the neutron mass is taken as 1.0, then the proton mass is 0.9986235 in proportion, and the electron mass 0.0005439. It will be seen that these two latter figures do not quite add up to 1.0. The shortfall is very small, only the mass of an antineutrino, but highly significant, because it is only this additional mass that makes isolated neutrons unstable. As Michael Mallary tells us in his book, *Our Improbable Universe* (2004),

Heavyweight neutrons are required for long-lived stars. If the mass of a neutron were less than that of a proton plus an electron, then the Big Bang would have produced a profusion of very heavy elements. There would be no lack of chemicals in that alternate universe. However, all hydrogen would be in a form that would burn rapidly in stars. Therefore, all stars would be short-lived. The fact that neutrons are heavier (than a proton plus an electron) depends on details of sub-nuclear physics. If they were 0.1% lighter than they are, there would be no long-lived stars in our universe. (p. 8)

So it seems that we are once again here only by the skin of our teeth, this time thanks to that 0.1%! The form of hydrogen to which Mallary is referring here is known as 'heavy hydrogen' or deuterium. This is a stable isotope of hydrogen with a nucleus that consists of one proton and one neutron. These are still circled by just one electron, since only the positive proton needs to be balanced by a negative electric charge. All elements have their isotopes, which is simply their normal atomic structure (which is, strictly speaking, an isotope itself) with extra neutrons attached, having been captured on impact. Each element has its atomic number, which is simply the number of protons in its nucleus: but its atomic weight, or atomic mass, can vary from isotope to isotope according to the number of neutrons attached (or sometimes detached). For example 'normal' carbon has six protons and six neutrons, existing as carbon 12. But it also has two isotopes, carbon 13 and carbon 14, with one and two extra neutrons in the nucleus. Both isotopes are rare on earth, with carbon 14 found in 'normal' carbon at only one part per trillion. But carbon 14 is radioactive, with a half-life of roughly 5,750 years, and so can be used for the radio-carbon dating of ancient organic remains.

As matter condensed out of the very hot plasma generated by the Big Bang, we are told that protons and neutrons emerged in equal numbers. However, neutrons are stable only when bound up with protons. In their free state, they have a half-life of only a few minutes before they decay into a proton, an electron, and an antineutrino. This meant that most neutrons in fact decayed before they had a chance to combine with a proton, and actually produced a surplus of protons and electrons by their decay. This in turn meant that deuterium in fact became a very rare form of hydrogen, constituting only about .02% of all hydrogen. But neutrons decay only because they have that very slightly higher mass than protons. If they had possessed a smaller mass they would have been as stable as protons, and would have had time to combine with nearly all of them. This would have meant that nearly all hydrogen would have existed as deuterium. Most of our familiar chemistry would still have been possible under this arrangement, but in the heart of stars the heavier deuterium would have combined into helium at a very much faster rate. Helium is composed of two neutrons, two protons, and two electrons, so that two deuterium atoms could easily combine into a new form as helium. This would have produced stars with a lifespan that was too short to allow for the evolution of star-dependent life forms on their daughter planets. Fortunately for us, however, 'normal' hydrogen, without that extra neutron, is much more 'slow burning'! So here is yet another instance of highly improbable 'fine tuning' (to 0.1%) for which we should be very grateful.

All of the matter in the universe is held together by just four fundamental forces. These are gravity, electromagnetism, the strong nuclear force, and the weak nuclear force. Gravity is the most familiar force of these four, but it is also the most mysterious. Gravitational waves were finally detected for the first time only in February, 2016, a century after Einstein had predicted their existence in his General Theory of Relativity. They had been generated by the collision of two large black holes, or perhaps two neutron stars, which had spiralled into each other in a galaxy 1.3 billion light years away. The existence of waves in a vacuum suggests that gravity should be mediated by a force-carrying particle known as a gauge boson. In the case of gravity, this boson has not yet been discovered, and is proving to be even more difficult to trace than the elusive Higgs boson! However, in theory it should have zero charge, zero mass, spin 2, and propagate at the speed of light. If such a particle ever were discovered, it would be reasonable to assume that it was a 'graviton', the postulated carrier of the gravitational force. But the electromagnetic force is much better understood. It is carried by the massless photon, which keeps electrons in orbit around atomic nuclei, and also carries light waves, which are a form of electromagnetic radiation. The strong nuclear force holds quarks together inside atoms, and also binds protons and neutrons together. It is mediated by a vector gauge boson known as a gluon, for obvious reasons. The gluon is also massless, but unlike the gravitational and electromagnetic forces, which can operate over vast distances, the strong nuclear force is very short-range, acting only over sub-atomic distances. However, it is the strongest known force in the universe. It is 137 times stronger than the electromagnetic force, and roughly 10^{39} times stronger than the gravitational force! The weak nuclear force allows for the radioactive decay of unstable compounds via, for example, beta radiation, that is the emission of an electron and an antineutrino. The weak force is 10^{7} times weaker than the strong force, and also operates only over atomic distances, mediated by two heavy bosons, christened W and Z. But the strength relationship of the two forces is again crucial. The current Astronomer Royal Martin Rees has estimated that a change in the relative strengths of the weak and strong forces by just one part in 10,000 would have made supernova explosions impossible. These explosions are crucial for producing and dispersing the heavier elements which go to form planets. (Rees, M. 'Large Numbers and Ratios in Astrophysics and Cosmology' *Philosophical Transactions of the Royal Society* Vol. 310 Issue 1512 (Dec. 1983) p. 317).

Examples of these 'fine tunings' could be multiplied, but the point has been sufficiently well made. So what do scientists make of this astonishingly improbable string of cosmic coincidences which have made our particular universe possible? Some have been very impressed indeed. For example, Professor Sir Fred Hoyle (1915-2001) a very distinguished scientist, had this to say in his article, 'The Universe: Past and Present Reflections' which appeared in the *Annual Review of Astronomy and Astrophysics* Vol. 20 No. 16 (1982).

Some super-calculating intellect must have designed the properties of the carbon atom, otherwise the chance of my finding such an atom through the blind forces of nature would be less than one part in 10^{40000}... A common sense interpretation of the facts suggests that a superintellect has monkeyed with physics as well as with chemistry and biology, and that there are no blind forces worth speaking about in nature... The numbers one calculates from the facts seem to me so overwhelming as to put this conclusion almost beyond question. (pp. 1, 16) (Available online)

Hoyle is here suggesting that some kind of intelligent life form designed it all: but I don't buy into that, for a number of reasons. First we must remember that the concept of the multiverse, with all its implications, had not yet come to prominence in 1982, and Hoyle had not fully taken these implications into account. Here, Hoyle's use of the term 'monkeyed' is rather appropriate, for it resonates with the oft-quoted analogy of an infinite number of immortal monkeys banging away at random on the keys of an infinite number of typewriters for eternity. Would one of them eventually write the complete works of Shakespeare? The answer is, of course he would. This is not just a probability, but a certainty. Such are the implications of infinity and eternity. No superintelligence is needed: just the implacable laws of chance. By the same token, there is no universe within the multiverse so improbable as to be impossible, even our own. Incidentally, the complete works of Shakespeare *have* in fact been written which, in the context of the universe, is hardly any less miraculous than the monkeys having done it.

Secondly, if a superintelligence did design the universe, then it certainly wasted a lot of effort. Why bother? The most interesting thing in the universe for an intelligent life form is us, or similarly intelligent life forms. But they must be extremely rare, and in the earlier life of the universe they could not have existed at all, for reasons that will be spelled out later. Nearly all of the universe is totally unsuited for the evolution of any kind of advanced life whatsoever: what a waste of effort! Not very 'intelligent', I would say. This 'intelligence' must have created a vast universe that on the whole was pretty boring, with very little life in it as far as we can see, and even less intelligent life. Moreover, if the idea was to design beings like us, this 'intelligence' was in no hurry to meet us. It took over 13 billion years for us to turn up!

Thirdly, if a superintelligence had designed it all just so that it could create creatures like us, you'd think that it would have taken better care of us when we finally arrived. In fact, however, the human race has suffered from a pretty miserable existence for most of its time on this planet. History supports my long-held contention that 'God doesn't give a damn'.

However, having said that, there are many scientists who agree with Professor Sir Fred Hoyle and not with me. If you want to read what they have to say, just type into your search engine 'Quotes from Scientists Regarding Design of the Universe'. At www.godandscience.org/apologetics/quotes.html

There you will find 27 quotes and 27 footnote references for them in the item that appears, but surprisingly two of them are not to works by scientists at all. Those two were of particular interest to me, because both works were by scholars who were colleagues of mine at the University of Reading. Footnote No. 1 referred to a work by Professor Sir James Clarke Holt (1922-2014), who later became Professor of Medieval History at the University of Cambridge. From 1970 to 1978, however, he was my Head of Department at Reading. His article was entitled, 'Science Resurrects God', and it appeared in the British edition of *The Wall Street Journal* for December 24, 1997. Footnote 26 refers to an interview with Professor Antony Flew (1923-2010) who was Head of the Philosophy Department at Reading from 1973 to 1983. I knew them both well. To their colleagues they were simply Tony and Jim, and I knew that neither of them had any time for religion in the 1970s. In fact, Tony prided himself on his atheism. However, by 1997 Jim had obviously been impressed by all that 'fine tuning' that he had been reading about, while Tony later changed his mind completely! In 2007 he co-authored a book with Roy A. Varghese entitled, *There is a God: How the World's Most Notorious Atheist Changed His Mind.* Richard Dawkins would probably challenge him for a claim to that title, but again, it was the fine-tuning arguments that seem to have swayed Professor Flew.

Debate on this issue still rages, but both sides of it get a good airing in two works in particular. In 2011 Victor Stenger published a book with the title, *The Fallacy of Fine Tuning: Why the Universe is Not Designed for Us*. His case was answered almost immediately by Luke A. Barnes in his article, 'The Fine-Tuning of the Universe for Intelligent Life' which appeared in *Publications of the Astronomical Society of Australia* Vol. 29 (June 11, 2012) pp. 529-564. This article is available online.

My own view of course is that yes, the universe is indeed 'fine-tuned', but by accident and not by design. Now let us have a look at the history of our own universe, as it is currently seen by cosmologists. Perhaps I should more properly say the *relevant* history, for I shall concentrate on only a few key points that have philosophical relevance. Our universe is of course composed of elementary particles in combination. I should perhaps explain what these elementary particles are, since the unravelling of particle physics must count as one of mankind's greatest intellectual achievements of the twentieth century.

In 1941 the poet, playwright, and broadcaster Henry Reed (1914-86) was called up for military service, and in 1942 he wrote a poem called, 'The Naming of Parts'. The parts referred to were those of a rifle, which he was being taught how to use. I quote here from the second verse:

> This is the lower sling swivel. And this
> Is the upper sling swivel, whose use you will see
> When you are given your slings. And this is the piling swivel,

Which in your case you have not got. The branches
Hold in the gardens their silent, eloquent gestures
Which in our case, we have not got.

He was illustrating, of course, the tedious vacuity of military life, but sometimes the naming of parts really is necessary, because scientists like to define their terms very precisely, and so do philosophers. I therefore feel obliged to name a few parts here, with apologies if the following section is rather tedious.

Physicists divide elementary particles into two fundamental categories, namely fermions and bosons. Fermions were named after the very distinguished Italian physicist Enrico Fermi (1901-1954) by his equally distinguished colleague Paul Dirac (1902-84), an Englishman but of a French family. Dirac also named the boson, after the Indian physicist and polymath Satyendra Nath Bose (1894-1974). Essentially fermions are matter particles, while bosons are force-carrying particles. Fermions in turn are sub-divided into hadrons and leptons. Hadrons are not named after anyone, but take their name from the Greek ἁδρός (hadros) meaning 'stout' or 'thick', while leptons get their name from the Greek word λεπτος (leptos) meaning 'small' or 'thin'. Hadrons in their turn are divided into baryons and mesons. Both are composed of quarks, but mesons consist of a quark and an antiquark, which instantly annihilate each other. Short-lived particles like these result only from atom smashing in the Large Hadron Collider at CERN, or from cosmic ray strikes. The important hadrons are the stable baryons, composed of three quarks as mentioned above, essentially the protons and neutrons. There are six leptons - electrons, muons, and taus, each with its associated neutrino, but the most important one is the electron, which has the least mass of the three. The heavier muons and taus quickly decay into electrons and their associated neutrinos. Only the electron is stable, although an independent electron neutrino also exists. The neutrino was named by Enrico Fermi, and means 'little neutral one' in Italian, because it has no electrical charge. Neutrinos also have almost no mass, estimated to be roughly 10,000 times lighter than electrons. They are not affected by the strong nuclear force nor the electro-magnetic force, but are affected by the weak nuclear force at very short range, and very slightly by gravity. These ghostly particles pass through the nearly empty matter of normal atoms almost totally undetected. Uncounted trillions pour out of the sun every day, and most pass completely through the earth. Their detection was a master stroke of modern physics, and completed the list of what might be called the matter particles. Or at least, so it was thought at the time. The nature of 'dark matter' still remains to be discovered, assuming that it actually exists. Favoured suspect at the moment is the WIMP, or weakly interacting massive particle. Desperate efforts to prove its existence, in the same way that neutrinos were eventually proved to exist, are currently being made.

Bosons are the other category of elementary particles, and they obey a different set of rules from the fermions. They are the force-carrying particles, the photon, which carries the electro-magnetic force, the gluon, which carries the strong nuclear force, and the W and Z bosons which carry the weak nuclear force. The postulated graviton, if it were ever to be discovered, would carry the gravitational force. Photons and gluons are massless, as would be the hypothetical graviton, but the W and Z bosons do have mass. Bosons have different 'spin' properties from fermions. Both particles have a 'spin', but this is a difficult term to explain, because it is not a simple spin like that of the earth on its axis. It is, however, a kind of angular momentum, and its velocity is measured by 'spin numbers'. Bosons have full integer spin, that is, 0,1,2, while fermions have half-integer spin, that is ½, 3/2, 5/2. Although it is so difficult to explain, the spin number of particles can be crucial in determining their quantum state. For example, helium nuclei consist of two protons and two neutrons, both fermions with half-integer spin numbers. But in combination they can cancel one another out, giving the whole nucleus an overall spin of zero. This places it in the boson category, and helium nuclei can in fact act as bosons in the case of alpha radiation. This occurs with the decay of radioactive substances such as plutonium, when helium nuclei are ejected at high speed as radiation, made possible by the wave-particle duality of atomic and sub-atomic particles, the great mystery at the heart of quantum mechanics.

Another distinction between the two classes of particles is that many bosons can simultaneously occupy the same quantum state, as photons in a laser, for example, while fermions cannot occupy the same quantum state. Fermions obey the Pauli exclusion principle, named after the Austrian physicist Wolfgang Pauli (1900-58) who first observed the phenomenon. It means that no two electrons can occupy the same orbits (unless they have different spin numbers), nor any two baryons the same spatial volume. It is this principle that gives matter its solidity, but under extreme gravitational pressure the Pauli principle can break down, as in white dwarf stars, neutron stars, and black holes. The compressed matter in these objects is then known as degenerate matter. Finally, the behaviour of bosons is governed by a set of rules known as Bose-Einstein statistics, while fermions behave in accordance with Fermi-Dirac statistics, but we need not go into that!

The four bosons mentioned above are actually gauge bosons: that is, they carry a force from one point to another. The Higgs boson, however, whose existence was confirmed only in July 2012, is a scalar boson which creates a Higgs field that permeates the whole of space. It is believed that it is the movement of fermions and the two heavy bosons through this field that gives these objects mass. The Higgs boson is the only scalar boson so far discovered, although the hypothetical inflaton, believed to have caused the faster-than-light expansion of the universe after the Big Bang, would be another example of a scalar, whole-field boson if it is ever isolated. Current thinking, however, suggests that the 'inflaton' had a limited lifespan, and so is no longer available for discovery. But on the other hand, it may not have had a limited lifespan, and be in fact that mysterious 'dark energy' now causing an acceleration in the expansion of the universe!

But how did the production of all this matter and energy begin? I should perhaps say here that physicists believe there to be a minimum period of time in our universe, and a minimum length. This latter is known as the Planck length after Max Planck (1848-1947), the very distinguished German physicist, and father of quantum theory. It is roughly 1.6×10^{-35} metres, or about 10^{-20} times the size of a proton. This is adjudged to be the smallest possible measure of length with any meaning. The Planck time is measured as the time taken for light in a vacuum to cross the Planck length, which is about 10^{-43} seconds. Neither measure is absolutely precise because of the difficulty of measuring the Planck length, but the measurements are of this order of magnitude. It is believed that at its inception our universe could not have been smaller than the Planck length, nor have appeared more rapidly than within the Planck time, but the precise scale of its earliest phase is unknown. At this level of concentration of energy and matter the known laws of physics break down in what is called a singularity. However, at only 10^{-11} seconds after the moment of creation the picture becomes clearer, since particle energies had by that time dropped to levels that can be replicated in the Large Hadron Collider at CERN in Switzerland, the largest scientific instrument ever built, with its 27 kilometre ring of superconducting magnets. These steer the hadrons on their course, accelerate them to near light speed in opposite directions, and then smash them into each other. As a result of these experiments, physicists believe that they can reconstruct the earliest moments of our universe with considerable accuracy. Their findings suggest that at this time the universe consisted of a quark-gluon plasma with particles moving at near light speed due to the very high temperature. At about 10^{-6} seconds, quarks, anti-quarks, and gluons combined to form the major baryons, protons and neutrons, as matter and anti-matter, and the great mutual annihilation followed, with only about one in a billion matter particles surviving to form our visible universe. A similar process occurred at about one second for electrons and positrons. A few minutes into the exponential expansion that our universe was experiencing in its earliest phase, its temperature had fallen to about one billion degrees Kelvin, and some of the unstable neutrons that had survived to that point began to combine with protons to form the universe's first deuterium and helium nuclei. The deuterium, however, was very rare, since most protons remained uncombined as hydrogen nuclei, or linked to combine into helium nuclei.

At this stage the density of the matter particles was so great that the photons which had been formed in the mass annihilation could not radiate through it without being blocked by matter particles almost immediately. This meant that for the first 380,000 years of its existence the universe was just a dark mass of ionised matter and energy. This in turn makes the term, 'Big Bang' sound like a misnomer! First, at its inception, it really wasn't very big at all. Secondly, there was no bang, for a bang is of course a sound, and there were no air waves to carry it. Thirdly, there was no flash either, for the universe remained opaque for 380,000 years! By this stage, however, the temperature had fallen far enough to allow the surviving electrons to combine with the protons and neutrons to form the first atoms. This condensation out of the ionised plasma and continuing expansion of matter at last allowed photons to radiate freely through it, matter decoupled from radiation and, as God would say, 'Let there be light'! This 'first light' can still be detected today in the form of the cosmic microwave background radiation. The photons that formed it were initially highly energetic, mostly of very short wavelength, but the subsequent expansion of the space-time continuum stretched them over billions of years, so that most now register in the microwave range of the spectrum. But although the universe had become transparent to light, it was not of a wavelength that our eyes could recognise, and so the history of the universe from 380,000 years of age to about 500 million years of age is known as the Cosmic Dark Ages.

The first atoms to emerge from the plasma fog were mostly those of hydrogen, the simplest and lightest element consisting of one proton and one electron (c.75%), and helium consisting of two protons, two neutrons, and two electrons (c. 25%), with less than 1% of other atoms, such as deuterium, lithium, and beryllium. But these measurements are by mass. In numerical terms, only about six or seven per cent of all atoms were helium, because helium has four times the mass of hydrogen. Even today, our universe still consists overwhelmingly of hydrogen and helium because most stars consist mainly of hydrogen. Our own sun constitutes more than 99.86% of the mass of our solar system, and is c75% hydrogen by mass, with c25% helium, and less than 0.1% other elements. It is only tiny scraps of heavier elements like these in orbit around it that form the planets, making up (with hydrogen and helium) 0.14% of the mass of the solar system. 99% of this mass is accounted for by the four gas giant planets between them. In these terms, our Earth is a tiny and insignificant orbiting scrap indeed.

Lithium is the third lightest element, consisting of three protons, three neutrons, and three electrons. Because of the very slight unevenness in the distribution of these atoms, as reflected in the cosmic microwave background radiation, gravity was able to accentuate these slight concentrations, and pull the atoms together into gas clouds. These clouds adopted a spiral motion, pulling in still more matter at an increasing rate. At the heart of the spiraling disc, where the concentration of matter was greatest, proto-stars began to form. When the concentration became high enough, and gravity strong enough, hydrogen in the proto-star began to fuse into helium, releasing tremendous energy. The first stars ignited, and began to shine. There is still debate over the timing of the appearance of the first stars, but the earliest may have begun to form just 250-350 million years after the Big Bang. Oddly, although these were the first stars, they are known as population III stars because, although they were the first to form, they were the last to be observed. This is because such stars no longer exist in our present galaxy, and can be seen only in very distant, and therefore very old galaxies, whose light has taken billions of years to reach us. Even these observations are not conclusive, and the existence of population III stars remains conjectural, based on calculations. However, these calculations seem logical enough. In the early universe with its denser concentration of hydrogen and helium, the first stars were probably very large, perhaps 100-300 times the mass of our sun. These massive stars would have quickly exhausted their hydrogen fuel (because of their powerful gravity) in a process of stellar nucleosynthesis and would have exploded as supernovae, seeding the universe with the first heavy elements. But because such massive stars all had very short life spans, none have survived to this day in our galaxy.

Star 'populations' are in fact graded by the metal content of the stars. The oldest stars in our galaxy, known as population II, have a very low proportion of metallic elements in their compositions. This can be established by spectral analysis of the light emitted by these stars, and by the same means it can be shown that population I stars, like our own sun, are young and comparatively metal-rich. This is because they formed from clouds of dust and gas thrown out by the life-cycles of much older stars as they ejected planetary nebulae into the interstellar medium, or ended as supernovae. But confusingly, astronomers describe as 'metals' any content of stars that is not hydrogen or helium, and even 'metal rich' stars still consist almost entirely of those elements, with never more than one per cent of their mass as 'metals'.

The life cycles of these stars is of course crucial, for it was the stars that converted the primordial elements left by the Big Bang, hydrogen and helium, into the many elements that we find in the world around us today, and which have made our existence possible, although these vital elements constitute less than one half of one per cent of all the visible mass of the universe. We are, therefore, all star children, not quite such stuff as dreams are made on, but certainly made of stardust. The formation of these elements within stars, known as stellar nucleosynthesis, proceeds in distinct stages, with the lightest elements being fused into progressively heavier ones. How far this process goes depends on the mass of the star: when it comes to stellar astrophysics, size really does matter! Basically, however, each fusion reduces the total mass of the matter involved, as this is radiated away as photon energy, since mass and energy are equivalent. Each successive stage of fusion produces less energy than the one before it however, and the fusion processes proceed at increasing rates. First, enormous heat and pressure inside stars fuses ionised hydrogen nuclei into helium nuclei, a process that is well understood, releasing the energy that we see in the hydrogen bomb. Next, two helium nuclei, alpha particles, each with two protons and two neutrons, are fused to form a beryllium 8 nucleus, with four protons and four neutrons. If a further helium nucleus were then to fuse with the beryllium, a carbon 12 nucleus would result. But here there was a problem. Beryllium in a stable state exists only as its isotope beryllium 9, with one extra neutron, or beryllium 10 with two extra neutrons and a half-life of 1.39 million years. Beryllium 8 is highly unstable, with a half-life of only 10^{-17} seconds, and more likely to be smashed apart by the impact of an alpha particle than to fuse with it. Scientists were baffled, because according to their calculations stars should spend their lives creating helium and beryllium in an endless cycle, but no heavier elements at all! This was known as the 'beryllium bottleneck' problem. Yet stars clearly did create carbon and other elements – but how? The baffled scientists had been assuming the existence of a carbon nucleus in its lowest energy or 'ground' state. It was Professor Fred Hoyle who came up with a solution, suggesting in 1954 that a carbon nucleus might exist in an 'excited' state with a higher 'resonance' if it had absorbed energy from a star's magnetic field or a gamma ray strike. This might create a form of carbon nucleus with an energy level that would resonate perfectly with that of a combined helium and beryllium nucleus becoming carbon 12*, making it more likely that the two *would* in fact fuse into a carbon nucleus in this higher energy state. The carbon nucleus could then transition down into its stable ground state again by the loss of a gamma ray photon. Resonance levels are measured in MeV (millions of electron volts) and carbon in its normal ground state has a resonance of 7.3367 MeV. Hoyle proposed an 'excited' state of carbon, with a resonance of 7.65 MeV or thereabouts. This level was later proved to exist by experiment, and was just 4% above the level required to match the resonance of a beryllium-helium pairing. But the extra energy required for the beryllium-helium pairing came from the kinetic energy released by the impact of the helium nucleus, producing a perfect resonance match, and making it much more likely that beryllium and helium nuclei *would* in fact fuse into an 'excited' carbon nucleus, which would then transition down to its ground state. The 'beryllium bottleneck' problem was solved. But the point here is that it was extremely unlikely that a resonance of the carbon nucleus would exist at exactly this frequency, at exactly the right level. Hoyle arrived at his figure by calculation, on the grounds that it *had* to exist, otherwise *we* could not exist, a process described as 'anthropic reasoning'. Hoyle was so astounded by his own discovery, however, by the existence of such a highly improbable carbon resonance, that he made his statement about a 'superintelligence' designing everything, which has been quoted above.

When it comes to the next stage in the process of stellar nucleosynthesis, a carbon 12 and helium 4 molecule meet, and would fuse into a normal oxygen 16 molecule if there was an appropriate resonance. But the nearest required oxygen 16 resonance has one per cent *less* energy than a helium 4 plus carbon 12 pairing, and this one per cent is enough to ensure that a mutual resonance does not occur. This time, the added kinetic energy of the incoming particles is of no help. As John Gribbin and Martin Rees say in their book *Cosmic Coincidences* (1991), 'There is no way that kinetic energy could *subtract* rather than add the difference, so the trick simply would not have worked.' (p.246) If that oxygen resonance level had varied by just one per cent, then virtually all the carbon made inside stars would have been fused into oxygen, and then most of that into heavier elements. That crucial one per cent was all that ensured that the precious carbon, once formed, would survive in large enough quantities to allow carbon-based life to emerge, for although a carbon phase in this cycle was crucial, carbon itself would have been very rare in the universe, at about 0.01% of its present level, and carbon-based life forms like ourselves could not have existed. In the same way, a beryllium phase in the creation of carbon was crucial, but beryllium itself in the form of its stable isotopes Beryllium 9 and 10, is now a very rare find. Out of the 94 naturally occurring elements, it is the 56th most abundant, down among the rare earths! Carbon came within one per cent of suffering the same fate! The very fine tuning of the resonances of both carbon and oxygen have proved to be crucial to the enabling of our existence, ensuring that both elements exist in sufficient quantities in our universe. This is yet another astonishing 'cosmic coincidence' that is barely credible, yet proved beyond doubt by repeatable experiments. No wonder Hoyle was impressed, giving the odds against that specific carbon nucleus resonance existing as 10^{40000} to one against in his quotation above. But how he arrived at that figure he does not say. Personally, I suspect it is exaggerated. Nuclear resonances are quantized, like musical notes on a harmonic scale, and this reduces the options available for any one system. The odds against a match may still be high, but not as high as Hoyle suggested. Personally, I find it more surprising that the incoming kinetic energy contribution was just exactly right for producing the required resonance for the production of carbon atoms.

Oxygen is of course created in stars but at a much slower rate without that crucial resonance, later in a star's life cycle, deeper in its interior, and mainly from the breakdown of neon 20. Of course these two remarkable 'fine tunings' were not the only 'cosmic coincidences' noted by Gribbin and Rees, who manage to fill an entire book with similar examples! It seems that very slight changes to any one of a vast number of our crucial constants – the masses of the quarks, the charge on the electron, the relative strengths of the four fundamental forces, etc. etc. – would have made it impossible for a universe such as ours to exist. Change just any *one* of those vital parameters (or several others) to any significant degree and the whole shemozzle immediately collapses into a heap of dust and ashes, or so the scientists tell us. It seems that we have been blessed with a very highly improbable universe indeed!

Beyond carbon, different nuclear fusion processes occur in stars of different sizes. Stars that are larger than about 1.3 solar masses can utilise a carbon-nitrogen-oxygen cycle, but a proton-proton chain is more important in stars of one solar mass or less. Details of these processes need not concern us, but essentially lighter elements are progressively fused into heavier ones, reducing the total mass of the star and releasing energy with each transition as photons. Within our own galaxy this process has produced a 'top ten' list of the most abundant elements. These are, in order, hydrogen, helium, oxygen, carbon, neon, iron, nitrogen, silicon, magnesium, and sulphur. The final stage of this process is the fusing of silicon 28 into iron 56, for at this stage the fusion process must stop. This is because iron, which weighs in at No. 26 on the periodic table, is the first element that cannot be forced to release energy by the fusion process. What happens after that depends entirely on the size of the star. The smaller a star is, the longer a life it will have, but the fewer heavy elements it will produce. The larger the star, the shorter its life, but the more heavy elements it will yield.

The relative abundance of the most common elements in the universe looks promising at first glance, as far as the chances for life are concerned. Oxygen, the third most abundant element, of course combines with hydrogen to form H2O, and water does seem to be abundant in the galaxy, as witnessed by our own solar system's Inner and Outer Oort Clouds and the Kuiper Belt, which are believed to be the sources of water-bearing meteors and comets. It is thought that infalling objects from these trans-Neptunian regions must have brought water to the inner planets in the early life of the solar system. But Earth's own rocks also contained water, which condensed out as steam as the planet cooled from its molten state. Even Mercury received water in this way, which is still present as ice in the deep craters at its poles, where sunlight never penetrates. In addition of course, oxygen is known to be essential to the life processes of all advanced life forms on earth. Only single-celled microbes can survive in anaerobic conditions, and it is difficult to imagine which other gas could have been used by advanced life forms to fuel their chemical processes, since no other element in the universe is both so highly reactive and so abundant as oxygen. Meanwhile, carbon, the fourth most abundant element, is also the most sociable, a real party animal, just loving to pair up with a host of other elements to form compounds, far more in fact than those of any other element. This is because the carbon atom is tetravalent, with four electrons available on its outer shell, ready to form covalent chemical bonds with a wide range of other elements. Carbon is of course an essential component of RNA, DNA, and ATP, all atomic structures that appear to be essential for all known life forms. Some of the basic ingredients for life are therefore readily available in the universe, but the right conditions to allow for the emergence of advanced life are in much shorter supply, as we shall see. Within our own solar system advanced life has certainly emerged here on Earth, but should we expect this to happen within other solar systems as well?

(b) How Unusual is Our Solar System?

In the lead article of *Scientific American* for May, 2016, 'Born of Chaos' Konstantin Batygin, Gregory Laughlin, and Alessandro Morbidelli argue that our solar system is unusual. Their claims are perhaps premature, since they based them on the evidence of the few thousand exoplanets that were then known to exist, and by their own admission these hardly yet formed an adequate database for comparisons. So far, they suggest that our system is an unusually stable one. But certain unusual features of our solar system are undeniable. First, there is the size of our sun, believed to be larger than 95 per cent of the stars in the galaxy. It therefore hosts a larger than usual family of planets, moons, and minor planets. Secondly, our sun occupies a rather unusually isolated position in the galaxy, 27,000 light years from the galactic centre, placing it closer to the edge of our galaxy than to the massive star cluster that lies at its heart. Here we are located on a spur at the inner edge of the Orion-Cygnus spiral arm, but 20,000 light years above the plane of rotation of the galaxy, looking out into the gap that separates us from the Carina-Sagittarius arm, which is closer to the galactic centre. This comparatively isolated position is in fact advantageous, for a position within a dense star cluster carries its dangers. Nearby stars can perturb planetary orbits, and the larger the cluster the greater the danger of large stars reaching the supernova stage of their evolution, with disastrous consequences for their galactic neighbourhood.

Even the neutron star remnants of supernova explosions can still be a threat as they drift through space, because some of these stars develop into magnetars with enormously strong magnetic fields and a slower rate of rotation than normal neutron stars. These magnetars can experience 'starquakes', which disrupt the surface of the star and release enormous amounts of deadly gamma radiation. These bursts are powerful enough to sterilize all exposed life forms on the surface of a planet within almost 1,000 light years of the emission. It is only since we have had gamma-ray detecting satellites in orbit that these burst have been recorded and traced to their sources. On August 27, 1998 a burst was detected from a magnetar 20,000 light years away that sent detection instruments off the scale and required them to be shut down. This radiation penetrated to within 30 miles of the Earth's surface before dissipating in the atmosphere. On June 4, 2002 multiple bursts were detected from a source 18,000 light years away, with over 80 emissions recorded in just four hours. These multiple bursts are particularly dangerous to nearby planets, for as the planet rotates a greater proportion of its surface is exposed to the deadly rays. On December 27, 2004 the strongest burst ever was detected from a magnetar 50,000 light years away, that is to say on the other side of the galaxy. But as with the other two bursts, this one too sent instruments off the scale, and required them to be shut down. In short, there is no such thing as 'good' stellar neighbours so far as advanced life forms are concerned. Even without supernovas and magnetars, ordinary stars produce cosmic rays from solar flares, ionised protons and electrons together with neutrons and alpha particles, all travelling at near light speed, and harmful to all exposed life forms. Fortunately Earth's thick atmosphere and powerful magnetic field protect us from the worst effects of these rays, but not all planets are so well defended. As far as advanced surface-dwelling life forms are concerned, there is no doubt that isolation is the best policy, and we have been very fortunate in the location of our own sun. But this is not the only piece of good fortune that we have enjoyed.

It is now well known that stars are the stellar furnaces in which all of the elements that constitute our planet were forged, but in the 1920s this fact was no more than a controversial proposition. It was first put forward by Sir Arthur Eddington (1882-1944), one of the greatest astronomers of the twentieth century. It was argued by his opponents that the temperature within stars would never be high enough to fuse one element into another, so that the elements must have been present from the beginning of the universe. But Eddington replied eloquently to his detractors in his 1926 book, *The Internal Constitution of Stars*, where he declared, 'We do not argue with the critic who urges that the stars are not hot enough for this process; we tell him to go and find a hotter place!' (p. 301)

However, it must be added that not all stars produce all elements, so it is important to distinguish between them. In addition, some stars are more suitable for hosting families of planets than others, in particular planets that might support life. It is therefore important to recognise the different categories of stars. Astronomers categorise them into seven groups, according to their size, brightness, and surface temperatures. The first four categories are the largest and brightest blue stars, with masses of 1.7 to 60 times that of the sun, and surface temperatures of 6,000 to over 25,000 degrees Kelvin, dubbed star types O, B, A, and F. Only the largest, type O stars are termed 'giants', and 'supergiants' with stars of up to 20 solar masses still called 'dwarfs'! These very large stars are too short-lived to allow advanced life forms to develop on their planets, but they do play a crucial role by contributing the heavier elements into the interstellar medium at the end of their lives, for they end as supernovas. The remaining three categories, dubbed star types G, K, and M, are respectively the yellow dwarf stars like our own sun, the orange dwarfs, and the red dwarfs, of which more below.

The smallest so-called 'stars' can be just over two Jupiter masses, so that Jupiter itself, a gas giant consisting mainly of hydrogen and helium, may be seen as a kind of 'failed star'. Between two Jupiter masses and about 8% of the sun's mass such 'stars' are known as brown dwarfs, which do not shine in the visible spectrum, but radiate in the infrared range, owing to the gravitational heating of the gasses that compose them. Stars that have between 9% and 45% of the sun's mass are true stars, fusing hydrogen into helium, but at a very slow rate because of their smaller mass and lower gravity. Such stars are known as red dwarfs, M types, with a surface temperature of less than 4,000 degrees Kelvin. It is believed that these are the most enduring stars in the universe, with a potential lifespan of trillions of years. They are also believed to be the most common stars, at least in our galaxy, where they have been estimated to comprise at least 75% of all stars. The next size category up are known as orange dwarfs, K types, with between 45% and 80% of the sun's mass and a surface temperature of 4,000 to 5,200 degrees Kelvin. These stars do not have the trillion-year life spans of the red dwarfs, but they do have a longer life expectancy than our own sun, at an estimated 15 to 30 billion years, and they are thought to be three to four times as numerous as G types. Our own sun belongs to this next size category, the yellow dwarfs, G types, which range in size from 0.8 to 1.2 solar masses, and have surface temperatures of 5,300 to 6,000 degrees Kelvin, but can expect a main sequence life span of only about 10 billion years. Our own sun is roughly half way through its main sequence life cycle. Larger stars have a sharply reducing life expectancy. At 1.5 solar masses it drops to 3 billion years, at three solar masses to 370 million years, and at ten solar masses to just 32 million years, far too short a span to allow life to evolve on any planets around them. At 60 solar masses a star can last for only three million years before exploding as a supernova.

Our own sun is therefore one of the largest stars in the galaxy with a life span long enough to allow advanced life to evolve on its planets, since it took some four billion years for intelligent life to emerge on earth. An estimated 95% of the stars in our galaxy are thought to be smaller than our sun. Larger stars than this are quite rare, with those of more than 20 solar masses known as blue giants or blue-white super giants because of their very high surface temperatures of 10,000 degrees Kelvin or more. However, these stars are too short-lived to allow advanced life to develop on any planets that might surround them. Our sun therefore falls within that quite narrow range of the 2% of stars that are massive enough to host a large family of planets, but still sufficiently small to enjoy a lifespan long enough to allow advanced life to emerge within their solar system. Once again, therefore, we see the 'Goldilocks' phenomenon in action – our star appears to be 'just right'!

Stars are absolutely crucial to the existence of life in our universe, for two reasons. First, it is stars that forge all the elements of which life is composed out of the primordial hydrogen and helium of the Big Bang. Secondly, it is stars that must then sustain any advanced life that does develop on the surface of any planets that surround them. Not all stars synthesise heavier elements from hydrogen and helium, however. Brown dwarfs, which are scarcely stars at all, are of no use for this function, while the red dwarfs will simply carry on burning hydrogen into helium for trillions of years, but produce no heavier elements. It is the orange dwarf and yellow dwarf stars with masses of 45% to 120% of our sun's mass that contribute some of the heavier elements to the interstellar medium at the end of their lives. As long as stars are happily fusing hydrogen into helium they are known as ‘main sequence’ stars, because this is the stage in which stars spend most of their lives. During this phase the stars are in hydrostatic equilibrium, with the radiation pressure exerted by fusion at their cores exactly balancing the gravitational effects of the star’s mass, so that stars like our sun can continue in a stable state for billions of years. It is only in star cores, usually some 20-25 % of a star’s diameter, that fusion takes place. The rest of the star generates no heat of its own, but is simply a surging mass of plasma heated by rising convection currents and photon radiation from the core. Eventually, however, stars larger than red dwarfs exhaust their supply of hydrogen, and once the process of fusion into helium at the core ceases, gravity preponderates over radiation and compresses the star, reducing its diameter. Core temperatures rise with the contraction, so that the helium there begins to fuse into beryllium and carbon. It is the energy generated by this helium fusion process that causes the hydrogen and helium-depleted shell to expand outwards to many times its original size, but now at a lower temperature and density. Such stars are then known as red giants and can continue in this phase for up to a billion years. It is believed that this will be the fate of our sun, which will expand beyond the present orbits of Mercury and Venus, and probably vaporise the surface of Earth. When helium in the core depletes and fusion stops, the star shrinks again until a new helium shell reaches the core. When this helium ignites via fusion, the outer layers of the star are blown off in great clouds of gas and dust to form what is called a planetary nebula, or a circumstellar envelope. The larger the star the more of the slightly heavier elements it is likely to have produced from core fusion processes, most notably carbon, oxygen, neon, nitrogen, and magnesium. Some astronomers believe that long-chain hydrocarbons, the fundamental building blocks of life, may form in these envelopes. Lucy Ziurys has argued in a distinguished American journal that,

> The circumstellar envelopes of evolved stars are among the most remarkable chemical laboratories in the universe. These envelopes are created by extensive mass loss in the later stages of stellar evolution, caused by thermal pulses in the star interior and radiation pressure on dust. Because of the low temperature of the central star, and the long-time scales for mass loss, molecules and dust form in the envelope, and are then gently blown into the interstellar medium. The material lost from such envelopes is thought to account for nearly 80% (by mass) of the interstellar medium. (www.pnas.org/content/103/33/12274.full)
> Proceedings of the National Academy of Sciences of the United States of America Vol. 103 No. 33 (May 2006) *The Chemistry in Circumstellar Envelopes of Evolved Stars* p. 12,274

Once their outer layers have been fully dispersed, all that remains of the red giant is a very small, very dense electron degenerate star known as a white dwarf, usually composed of very high temperature carbon and oxygen. Just one cubic centimetre of this highly compressed matter would weigh one metric tonne on Earth, since the electrons in these stars have been forced by gravity out of their normal orbits and closer to their atomic nuclei, creating a very dense, electron degenerate form of matter. A white dwarf glows only by its stored thermal energy, since it does not generate any energy of its own. It therefore eventually cools to become an inert black dwarf.

Stars of ten solar masses or more usually end their lives as supernovas, while large stars of up to ten solar masses can produce more of the heavier elements, developing onion-like layers at their cores with progressive levels of hydrogen, helium, carbon, neon, oxygen, silicone, and finally iron at the heart of their cores, as the lighter elements are progressively fused into heavier ones. Once iron is reached, however, the process comes to a stop. This is because the nucleus of the iron atom is so tightly bound that it cannot be forced to *yield* energy by a fusion process. However, in the perfect storm that is a supernova explosion, which produces very high velocity particles, intense neutron bombardment, and gamma ray strikes, iron may be transmuted into heavier elements by the application of *outside* energies. These larger stars too may blow off their outer layers and end as white and then black dwarfs, producing no elements heavier than iron, provided that their white dwarf remnant is smaller than the Chandrasekhar limit, named after the Indian astronomer who calculated it, Subrahmanyan Chandrasekhar (1910-1995). This limit is about 1.44 solar masses. Beyond this mass the electron degeneracy pressure that sustains the very dense and heavy white dwarfs is overcome by the star's gravity, and it suffers a catastrophic collapse into a neutron star, with its electrons forced into its protons to form neutrons. This solid mass of neutrons is known as baryon degenerate matter, one cubic centimetre of which would weigh 100 million metric tonnes on Earth. While the atomic matter that is familiar to us consists of 99.9999 per cent empty space, neutron stars contain no empty space at all, but are just one solid mass of neutrons! The very strong gravity of those neutron stars prevents their neutrons from decaying as they would in free space. This explosive collapse yields a supernova, releasing energy levels so high that iron and other elements are fused into each other, producing all of the heavier naturally occurring elements up to plutonium. In the case of the largest stars, after they explode, the supernova remnant may indeed be a black hole rather than a neutron star.

The above very brief summary describes only one form, or rather type, of supernova explosion, but the others need not concern us. The main point to grasp here is that *only* supernova explosions (or, very rarely, the collision of neutron stars) can produce elements heavier than iron. Is that gold you are wearing on your finger? There is in effect only one force in the universe powerful enough to have created it. That gold can have been forged only in the raging inferno of a supernova explosion. It is explosions of this kind that have contributed the other 20% of heavier elements, those beyond iron, into the interstellar medium. Most of these are now found in stardust, the remains of population III stars. This dust shows up clearly as dark bands when our galaxy is viewed edge on, and much of it will coalesce into new stars and planets. The fact that our Earth contains all the heavier elements in its crust suggests that our sun and its surrounding planets in fact condensed from a giant cloud of dust and gas that was the remains of at least one, and possibly two supernova explosions. These would have been much more common in the early universe, with its much higher proportion of very large Population III stars, all of which must have ended as supernovas.

We must now return to our own solar system, and the question of how typical or otherwise our system is. We have already noted that our sun is a rather unusual star, situated in an unusually isolated part of the galaxy. It is larger than 95% of all stars, and so may be assumed to host a larger family of planets than most. Fewer than 1% of stars in our galaxy today end their lives as supernovas, so our sun falls just short of the size category that will supernova, instead ending its life as first a red giant and then a white dwarf after a 'main sequence' (hydrogen-burning) lifespan of about 10 billion years. Our sun is therefore one of the largest stars with a lifespan long enough to allow advanced life to evolve on its planets. At only 1.5 solar masses the main sequence lifespan of a star falls to just 3 billion years, which would not have allowed us to evolve at all. Our sun is also unusual in that it is a lone star, and not part of a binary or triple star system. c.85% of the stars in our galaxy in fact belong to such systems. Now, are multiple star systems more or less likely to harbour planets capable of supporting life? This is a difficult question, because the answer depends very much on the nature of the binary or multiple system. An ideal arrangement would be two K type orange dwarf stars both with 45% to 80% of the sun's mass in a relatively close, say 30 day, orbit around each other. Planets could then orbit the stars' common centre of gravity, the barycentre, and perhaps enjoy a wider habitable zone than is provided by our own sun. But this configuration would be unusual. Most binary and triple systems contain stars of different sizes and different stages of development, in a wide range of orbits around each other. Most multiple systems would in fact make life very difficult for orbiting planets. If one of a binary pair is a dense white dwarf star, for instance, it might begin to 'steal' solar matter from a close companion until its mass exceeded the Chandrasekhar limit, and it went supernova. In most cases, planets would be unlikely to be able to sustain stable orbits around multiple star systems. In my opinion, we should count ourselves very fortunate that our planet orbits one of the 15% of stars that is simply a large, single, uncomplicated entity! The odds were against this and yet, for us, it has happened.

But at least 75% of stars in our galaxy are thought to be red dwarfs, M types, with 9% to 45% of the sun's mass. Could single red dwarfs harbour life-supporting planets? Perhaps the larger ones could, but their habitable zones would have to be much closer to the parent star than is the case with our sun. In August 2016 the existence of a planet in orbit around Proxima Centauri, our nearest star just 4.24 light years away, was confirmed. Unsurprisingly, Proxima Centauri is a red dwarf star like most stars in the galaxy, but it is small even by red dwarf standards, at only 12% of the sun's mass. It has a predicted main sequence lifespan of 2.5 trillion years. The discovered planet has 1.3 times the mass of Earth, and orbits at a distance that would allow liquid water to exist on the planet's surface, if it has any. But this puts the planet in a very close orbit around its star, only seven million kilometres away as compared with Earth's 146 million kilometre distance from our sun. The newly found planet, Proxima Centauri B, orbits its star every 11.2 Earth days. This raises the danger of so-called 'tidal lock', where the gravitational pull of a close star slows or stops the planet's rotation, as has happened with Mercury in our own system, and with our own moon in orbit around the Earth. This of course would be a great handicap for the development of life, although it might not rule out the possibility entirely. A more serious threat, however, would be the intense ultraviolet and x-ray radiation which would continually lash the planet from its very close star, some 400 times more intense than that which our Earth receives from its sun. If the planet does not rotate, as seems very probable, then its dark side would be intensely cold, while its sun side would be permanently exposed to deadly radiation. It is not yet known whether the new-found planet has any atmosphere at all, or any water on its surface, but in my view it is an unlikely candidate as a life supporter.

In fact, however, it is single K type orange dwarf stars, just a little smaller than our sun at up to 0.8 solar masses, that may provide the best hope for alien life in our galaxy. These are thought to be some three times more numerous than G class stars like our sun, and they have longer life spans as main sequence stars, some 15 to 30 billion years, more than twice the lifespan of our sun on average. This of course provides more time for advanced life forms to develop. Again, however, it is only the small minority of *single* orange dwarf stars that would provide ideal conditions, with habitable zones far enough away from the parent star to avoid tidal lock. In short, it would seem that our solar system is a very unusual one, and that we have been very fortunate in both its size and in its position within the galaxy: a 'Goldilocks' system once again.

(c) How Unusual is Our Planet?

So, if we consider just that minority of star systems that might support a stable family of planets, what are the chances of life developing on any one of them? We have only the example of our own solar system to examine here, since we still know almost nothing about the exoplanets so far discovered around other stars. Our own large star hosts a family of just eight planets, now that Pluto has been officially discounted. How many of the eight harbour life, even microbial life? Only one, as far as we know for certain. Mercury and Venus are too hot, Mars is too cold, dry, and airless, while all the rest are gas giants with turbulent atmospheres and enormous pressures on their small, rocky cores. The dense clouds that surround them might host some kinds of primitive life forms as microbes, but that seems unlikely. Certainly only one of the eight, our own Earth, hosts advanced life forms. Most of our solar system therefore is not life-friendly at all, and ours is quite a large system. It would appear that, in order to support advanced life, a planet must be possessed of a number of very special characteristics indeed. What should these be? Many have been outlined for us in a book by Peter Ward and Donald Brownlee, *Rare Earth: Why Complex Life is Uncommon in the Universe* (2004).

It is generally agreed that any life-hosting planets must occupy the so-called 'habitable zone' around their stars. The usual meaning of this term is the AHZ, that is the 'animal habitable zone', although it is now recognized that the MHZ, that is the 'microbe habitable zone', may extend much further, and include any planets or moons that once harboured liquid water, or which still have water beneath an icy surface, provided that volcanism is or was also present. In both cases, however, liquid water must exist or have existed on or near the surface of the planet or moon, since as far as we know a liquid water environment is essential to abiogenesis, that is the emergence of life from non-living chemicals. We know that here on Earth life began in our oceans, and indeed it is difficult to imagine how life could have begun anywhere else in the absence of water. But what else is required? In my opinion, the vital second factor is volcanism. As research progresses, it begins to look increasingly likely that life originated on earth around 'black smokers', small undersea active volcanoes known as hydrothermal vents. These are usually to be found at the junctions of tectonic plates, especially those that are moving apart from each other, creating a 'tear' in the Earth's crust. Sea water that has leaked into these fissures seeps down towards the hot magma layer below Earth's crust, where it becomes superheated, expands, and begins to rise, bringing up a host of dissolved chemicals from the crust with it. But because these vents are found only deep in the oceans, it has not been possible to study them closely until recently, with the aid of modern technology. It was almost certainly these hydrothermal vents, some of which are 'white smokers' with a different chemical composition, that produced the first primitive self-replicating organisms on our planet. This conclusion may be reached by a series of logical steps.

(a) It is obvious that life on this planet originated in the sea, and not on the dry land. The evidence of palaeontology to this effect is overwhelming.

(b) But if in the sea, then whereabouts in the sea? Is it likely that just the right combination of chemicals could happen to drift together in the open ocean? Even on our improbable planet, this possibility seems to be too remote to deserve serious consideration.

(c) But if not on the open seas, then where else? Surely somewhere beneath the oceans there must have existed a series of natural chemical laboratories of considerable complexity. Where might these be found?

(d) Hydrothermal vents can provide a complete answer to these questions. Here, these undersea geysers continually erupt a rich mixture of chemical elements into the surrounding ocean, building pillars of chemical deposits which even today host colonies of both the most primitive and some more advanced life forms. These might be described as the 'smoking gun' evidence of where life originated on our planet.

(e) These vents provide the ideal conditions for the emergence of organic chemicals and eventually primitive life, because they provide not only a rich mix of chemicals with heat as a catalyst, but crucially also a series of *gradients*, in temperature, pressure, and acidity levels. Gradients allow energy flows, and energy flows provide the potential for creativity. These include pH gradients when what was then a slightly acid ocean contacted with alkaline rock formations producing proton gradients, and thus the generation of electricity. In the 2017 paperback edition of his book, *Forces of Nature*, Brian Cox eloquently explains how it was those proton gradients which were the most crucial of all, because they allowed the natural process of proton flows to be first harnessed, and then mimicked by the first living cells, enabling them to manufacture adenosine triphosphate or ATP, crucial for transporting stored energy around the organism. (pp. 173-5) ATP, like DNA (deoxyribonucleic acid) is essential to every living creature, and must therefore have existed at a very early stage in the evolution of life. The first living organism, preceding even the bacteria and archaea into which it diverged, has been dubbed by palaeobiologists LUCA, standing for Last Universal Common Ancestor, the predecessor of all life on Earth, both plant and animal. But even LUCA would have needed ATP. This molecule too is composed of just the five basic elements, hydrogen, carbon, oxygen, nitrogen, and phosphorous.

(f) One of the great problems facing abiogenesis researchers is the fact that you can't have a cell without a membrane to surround it, but you can't have a membrane without a cell. So which came first, the chicken or the egg? Again hydrothermal vents can provide the answer in the form of spongiform rocks and chemical deposits formed by gas bubbles which emerged from the vents while those materials were in a molten state. These small cavities, partially eroded, could have provided the first artificial 'membranes' within which organic chemistry could have done its work. It seems more likely that the 'cell' came first, in its spongiform womb, as an energy-consuming, self-replicating entity, perhaps expanding into adjacent cavities, and that an organic membrane later developed around it, allowing the cell mobility.

(g) To those who doubt that the environment around hydrothermal vents produced the first life on earth, I would roughly paraphrase Sir Arthur Eddington by saying, 'If you know of a more likely place, go to it'. But remember that it must be somewhere in the oceans, because we know for certain that this is where life first began. That fact rather reduces the options, I would say.

(h) Despite the ideal environment for abiogenesis provided by hydrothermal vents some, like Professor Hoyle, would argue that the odds against just the right organic chemicals coming together by chance still remain astronomically high. This is true, but we must remember that the early earth was more volcanically active than it is today, and probably produced more hydrothermal vents than we find in our modern oceans (although they are still very numerous today). Hoyle would probably have argued that his 'superintelligence' must have got down there to 'monkey' with the laws of chemistry and biology to produce the first living things. But no supernatural ingredient was necessary: the ordinary laws of chance could have done the trick. All known living organisms including most viruses of course store their genetic information in the form of DNA, deoxyribonucleic acid, which in turn consists of four bases, cytosine, guanine, adenine, and thymine (C,G,A,T). But each of these bases is composed of just four common elements in slightly different combinations. These are hydrogen, oxygen, nitrogen, and carbon. The famous double helix structure of the DNA molecule is linked together by the addition of a fifth element, phosphorous, which forms the phosphate-deoxyribose backbone linking the four bases. The ordering of those four bases are the letters that spell out the genome of each living organism. This miraculous molecule can unwind into two separate strands, with each strand then forming a perfect replica of itself. Left on its own, DNA is extremely stable, and a highly reliable transmitter of information from generation to generation: on average, it makes only one mistake per billion letters with each reproduction. There are just over three billion base pairs in the human genome, but of course there is rather more to evolution than this! DNA may be damaged by the ingestion of toxic substances or by natural radiation, some from the Earth itself, but most from cosmic ray strikes, which continually bombard our bodies. These can cause changes to germ cells. Most of these changes are harmful, but some can produce beneficial effects in offspring, and natural selection takes things from there to ensure that evolution progresses.

The simpler nucleic acid RNA (ribonucleic acid), which probably formed earlier than DNA. consists of just a single strand of molecules, often folded back upon itself and used in cells to convey genetic information. If properly folded, RNA molecules could function as both gene and enzyme, producing a primitive reproductive system. (P. Nurse, *What is Life?* (2021) pp. 204-5) But RNA is also composed of just the same four basic elements, hydrogen, oxygen, nitrogen, and carbon. In RNA the thymine base is replaced by uracil, but this base too is composed of just the same four elements, linked by a phosphate backbone. It was therefore just a case of juggling these five elements into the correct positions to produce a self-replicating compound that might have nestled in a cavity of spongiform rock initially. Still not an easy juggling trick, but many, many hydrothermal vents over half a billion years might well have pulled it off. These vents were more numerous in the early earth, which was covered almost entirely by water.

(i) Finally, we have the principle of 'anthropic reasoning', which was first introduced by Professor Hoyle himself when he argued that a highly improbable resonance of carbon simply *had* to exist, otherwise *we* could not exist. His theory proved to be correct. By the same token, abiogenesis *must* have occurred on Earth, otherwise we could not be here. Some argue that 'life spores' might have drifted in from outer space, but that theory sounds ridiculous to me. It would have been difficult enough for life to emerge even from the ideal environment of a hydrothermal vent. I cannot imagine it originating anywhere else.

What we have above is a theory of abiogenesis. But could this theory be tested experimentally? In fact this would be very difficult. At great expense, a piece of laboratory equipment could be built that would duplicate the environment of *a* hydrothermal vent: the great pressures, temperatures, chemical mixes, gradients, spongiform cavities, etc., but this would represent only *one* kind of hydrothermal vent. In reality they were highly varied and extremely numerous on the early Earth. In addition, they had about half a billion years or so to do their work, rather longer than is practical for a laboratory experiment! If that one man-made vent did *not* produce life from inorganic matter, that would not disprove the above theory. However, Brian Cox tells us that a group of scientists led by Nick Lane at University College London is currently attempting to carry out just such an experiment. (*Forces of Nature* (2017) p. 180)

There might, on the other hand, be another way to prove the above theory to be correct, if our technology one day allows us to make very close studies of hydrothermal vents. What, should our good Mother Earth that gave us birth and nurtured us now prove to be a barren womb? I think not. Our hydrothermal vents are still very numerous and very active. It is surely quite likely that abiogenesis is still taking place within some of them, and more LUCAs are still being produced Indeed, it seems likely that there is only one way in which

LUCA can form, either here or on other planets: it must form under anaerobic conditions within a hydrothermal vent. Because of the great difficulty in accessing these vents for close study a very advanced technology would be called for to observe this process, but such technology might one day become available.

Now if the key requirements for abiogenesis are liquid water plus undersea volcanism, might these conditions exist anywhere else in our solar system? The other planets do not look very promising, but Jupiter's moon Europa and Saturn's moon Enceladus are both ice covered, and probably have oceans of liquid water beneath their surfaces. If there is active volcanism on their rocky cores then they too might host primitive life, but we have as yet no firm evidence for either the volcanism or life forms beneath the ice. However, astronomers are now very sure that oceans of liquid water once existed on Mars three billion years ago, when its atmosphere was much thicker than it is today. Mars was also definitely volcanic: the largest extinct volcano in the solar system, Olympus Mons, is to be found on Mars. This means that hydrothermal vents must also have existed on the Red Planet, probably for a long enough period of time to allow abiogenesis to have occurred there in much the same way as happened on Earth. When we are able to explore Mars and study it in great detail, there is a fair chance that we will find either Martian microbes that have evolved to survive in today's harsher conditions, or at least fossil evidence of the fact that microbes once existed. The presence of seasonal methane gas on Mars suggests that the planet might harbour subterranean microbes quite similar to our own archaea, which are also methane-producing. If firm evidence of life on Mars, either past or present, ever is found then this will suggest that our theories about abiogenesis on Earth are correct. But if no such evidence is found, that will suggest that our miracle planet is unique indeed.

Any planet or moon that possesses the essential attributes of liquid water oceans and undersea volcanism might possibly harbour or have harboured simple life forms, and on this basis microbial life might be widespread in the galaxy. Indeed, some have suggested that Earth might have been 'seeded' with microbial life from Mars. It is true that meteors from Mars do land on Earth: one was discovered in Antarctica in 1984 containing a shape that might have been a fossil microbe. But the odds are against any such 'seeding' by live microbes. The microbes in question must have first of all survived the heat and shock of being blasted off Mars by the impact of an incoming body, so violently that they reached escape velocity. They would then have had to survive many years, probably centuries in orbit enduring the harsh cold and ionising radiation of deep space. Then they would need to have survived the heat of entering our atmosphere, and the impact of landing. Finally they would then need to have found an environment on landing that was close enough to the one they had left to allow them to flourish. Not a very likely scenario, I would suggest.

But obviously neither Europa nor Enceladus nor Mars is capable of hosting advanced mammalian life, and this is probably true of our galaxy in general: microbial life might perhaps be common, but more advanced life forms like ourselves are probably very rare: perhaps unique. Even here on Earth with its 4.5 billion-year history it was only within the last billion years that multicellular organisms became common, and only within the last 600,000 years or so that animal life emerged. For nearly 3.5 billion years all life had been unicellular.

Here on our own planet, if our Earth had remained the kind of water world that it was initially, some three to four billion years ago, evolution could never have progressed beyond the fishes. For advanced life forms to develop, a planet must possess not only liquid water oceans and volcanism, but also dry land onto which some forms of sea life might migrate. This is because survival on land is much more difficult than survival in water, requiring the evolution of animal life forms with advanced features to cope with the harsher environment. When astronomers talk of the 'habitable zones' for planets around stars they now distinguish between the MHZ (Microbial Habitable Zone) and the AHZ (Animal Habitable Zone). The latter is, of course, much narrower than the former, although it also depends to some extent upon the greenhouse gas content of a planet's atmosphere. Our planet would in fact be judged by alien astronomers to lie *outside* the AHZ, too far from its sun to allow for liquid water to exist on its surface. But Earth's greenhouse gasses make all the difference, raising its surface temperature to entirely life-friendly levels, and allowing water to exist in liquid form.

We now know that, once it has been created in water by volcanism, microbial life can rapidly evolve to survive in the harshest of environments. Such microbes are known collectively as extremophiles, and they have been found living in Antarctic ice, in the boiling springs of Yellowstone National Park, at the high temperatures and pressures of 3.5 kilometres below ground level, in solid sedimentary rock, and even in the basaltic rock of the Columbia River basin in the state of Washington. These last amazing microbes were found to be manufacturing their own organic compounds, using carbon and hydrogen taken directly from hydrogen gas and carbon dioxide dissolved in the rock. Because they are capable of producing organic material from inorganic compounds, such organisms are known as autotropes. These microbes were in fact not bacteria, but rather archaea. These account for most of the extremophiles, and since the advent of genetic analysis are now known to be members of an entirely different taxonomic group from the bacteria. Some of these specialists can survive without sunlight, without oxygen, and even without organic nutrients.

It now seems clear that, once created in hydrothermal vents, the archaea and bacteria can rapidly spread, evolve, and adapt to every conceivable environment on Earth. These simple, single-celled organisms are in fact the most successful and prolific life forms on the planet, estimated to form a biomass as large as that of all plants and animals combined. Even the human body hosts as many microbial cells as human cells. (P. Nurse, *What is Life?* (2021) p.11) Because of their wide dispersal in many different environments, these life forms could in fact survive any cataclysm, short of the disintegration of the planetary surface itself! But their amazing potential for survival depends entirely on their simplicity, and hence ability to evolve rapidly and adapt to new conditions. Once life had evolved to the multicellural stage about one billion years ago, it immediately began to become more vulnerable, and once the first animals evolved some 600,000 years ago, they were more vulnerable still, like the unfortunate dinosaurs, and indeed like more than 99 per cent of all the species that have ever lived on the Earth, but are now believed to be extinct. Increasing vulnerability is the price paid for increasing complexity and we placental mammals, as the most advanced life forms, are also the most vulnerable of all. Unlike the bacteria and archaea, many of which are extremophiles, we mammals are all so-called mesophiles. We can tolerate only a small and moderate range of temperatures and pressures. We are much more at nature's mercy than were our simple, single-celled ancestors. Therefore, advanced animal life can flourish only on a planet that is possessed of some very unusual characteristics indeed, but fortunately for us, Earth *is* such a planet, capable of playing host to an incredibly wide variety of life forms. We have been very fortunate indeed.

In 2006 the distinguished physicist Paul Davies (b. 1946) published a book with the intriguing title, *The Goldilocks Enigma: Why is the Universe Just Right for Life?* referred to above. The title is indeed fascinating, but also misleading. Certainly the structure of the universe makes life *possible*, as witnessed by our own existence, but that is not to say that it makes life *easy*. In fact very nearly 100 per cent of the universe is entirely unsuited for the evolution or survival of advanced mammalian life forms like ourselves. Within our own solar system, for example, we now know for a certainty that only one planet, our own, hosts advanced life forms: but Earth constitutes rather less than 0.001 per cent by mass of even our own solar system, which is very favourably located within the galaxy, orbiting a very favourable sun. Even here, it is only within the thin film of life that constitutes our biosphere that we can find an environment suitable for our survival, a film which itself constitutes only a small fraction of one per cent of Earth's mass. Even here, some 70% of our planet is water covered, while we are land dwellers, and by no means all of even the land surface is ideally suited for us. We should all take time to reflect on just how lucky we have been to have found this incredibly freakish little niche in the galaxy, which is all that makes our existence possible. How many other solar systems play host to an Earth-like planet at all? In all probability very few, for the location and history of our own planet reveal it to be highly exceptional in many ways. For much of the twentieth century, it was assumed that ours was just an ordinary planet orbiting an ordinary star in an ordinary part of the galaxy. Today, however, we now know that all three of those assumptions were entirely incorrect.

But why is our particular planet so exceptional within our own solar system, and probably also within our quadrant of the galaxy? This is because very exceptional circumstances were associated with its formation. There is still some debate about the details, but the consensus of scientific opinion now is that when the proto-Earth was still very young, only some 30 to 50 million years after it first coalesced into a molten sphere of matter, it was impacted by a very large, Mars-sized object, probably another proto-planet that had formed in roughly the same orbit as Earth. This impactor has been christened Theia, who in Greek mythology was a Titan, the mother of Selene, the moon goddess, because it is believed that this impact gave birth to our moon. The impactor theory is supported by the fact that moons are rare among the inner planets. Mercury and Venus have none, and Mars has only two tiny objects of irregular shape in orbit around it that are probably captured asteroids. Theia struck Earth a blow that was glancing, but still direct enough to first merge and then disperse the matter of the two proto-planets. After performing an elaborate ballet of dispersal and reformation, the matter of the two planetoids accreted mainly to the more massive of the two original bodies, which was Earth. Although our moon has just over one quarter of the diameter of Earth, it has only two per cent of Earth's volume and, remarkably, only 1.2 per cent of Earth's mass. This is because it was the bulk of the *heavier* elements, notably iron, nickel, uranium, and thorium that accreted to Earth, the larger of the two planetoids, after their collision.

The dispersed debris of the collision went into Earth orbit, where it eventually coalesced into our moon. However, this dispersed material consisted mainly of the lighter, crustal material of Earth. Now that moon rocks have been analysed we know that the isotopic composition of the crust of the moon is almost exactly identical to the crust of the Earth, suggesting a common origin for both. But overall the moon has an average density of only 3.342 kilograms per cubic meter, while that of the Earth is 5.515 kilograms per cubic meter, making our planet in fact the densest in the solar system. This is probably because Earth was able to 'steal' more than its fair share of heavy elements from Theia, leaving our moon with a markedly depleted nickel-iron core. Nevertheless, Theia was a generous contributor of heavy elements to the Earth, for despite its lavish provision to us, our moon still remains the second densest major moon in the solar system, exceeded in this regard only by Jupiter's satellite Io.

The formation of our unusually large single satellite was crucial to the development of life on Earth for several reasons. First, it is believed that the glancing blow struck by Theia sent the Earth into a rapid spin, that helped to disperse its crustal material, leaving the heavier core behind. Scientists have calculated that when the moon first assumed its final form it was in orbit only 15,000 miles from our planet's surface, as compared with today's distance of 238,855 miles on average. The moon is still receding from Earth at the rate of about four centimetres per year. Calculations also suggest that the impact of Theia left Earth spinning so rapidly that a day would have been only five hours long! This rapid rotation rate, combined with the nearness of the moon, would have meant that enormous tides, land tides as well as water tides, must have swept Earth's surface for a few millions of years, although the scientists tell us that in those early days the moon retreated quite quickly from its very close orbit. Those high tides would hardly have been conducive to the development of life, but in the longer term life on Earth was to owe a great debt to our unusual moon. It is now officially the largest moon in the solar system relative to the size of its planet, since tiny Pluto with only one-sixth of the mass of our moon and its own large moon Charon, have now been denied full planetary status and have been demoted to count only as a 'Kuiper Belt objects'.

Our moon therefore imparted an unusually rapid rotation rate to our planet which, while it may have been detrimental to life's chances at first, was later to prove a great boon, for this rate steadily slowed, and yet ensured that the entire planet continued to receive equal amounts of solar radiation. By contrast Venus rotates only once in every 243 Earth days, and Mercury hardly rotates at all, with a full Mercurian day occurring only once in every two Mercurian years! Because of its method of formation the moon revolves around the Earth very close to Earth's equatorial plane, and it of course revolves in the same direction as the rotation of the Earth, that is anticlockwise as seen from over the north pole. Because of this it has been moving slowly but steadily *away* from the Earth for billions of years as tidal and gravitational forces have absorbed energy and allowed the moon to move away. However, had the moon gone into a retrograde orbit, counter to the direction of the Earth's rotation, these forces would have been reversed, and the moon would have drawn steadily *closer*, eventually colliding with Earth! This kind of collision course is the fate which awaits Neptune's moon Triton, probably a captured planetoid, currently in retrograde orbit around the giant planet. In fact, however, our moon is no threat to us, and at the moment provides the very useful service of maintaining the Earth's obliquity, that is the tilt of its axis relative to the plane of its revolution around the sun, within remarkably constant limits.

The tilt of Earth's axis has remained remarkably close to just 23 degrees for at least hundreds of millions of years, and probably for much longer than that, causing marked seasonal changes of climate in the higher latitudes of our planet as first its north pole and then its south pole are tilted towards the sun in the course of one annual revolution. But without the gravitational pull of our moon, this angle of tilt would have varied erratically in response to the gravitational pulls of the sun and Jupiter, and Earth's tilt angle could have varied by as much as 90 degrees, causing chaotic and disastrous levels of climate change! This severe tilting has indeed already happened in the case of Uranus, which rolls around its very long orbit with one pole pointed towards the sun and the other in perpetual darkness for half a Uranian year. This extraordinary angle of tilt might perhaps have been caused by the collision with Uranus of a smaller planet. It is believed that Mars too, without a large moon to stabilise it, has experienced changes to its obliquity of 45 degrees or more over billions of years. Had our moon been smaller or further away, or if Jupiter had been larger or closer, or if Earth had been closer to the sun, the moon's beneficial influence would have been weakened, but as with so much else on our 'Goldilocks' planet, the present arrangements seem to be 'just right' for the creation of a comparatively stable climatic regime on Earth. In fact the position of Jupiter within our allegedly unusual solar system has also been highly beneficial for the inner planets, for this giant world has acted as a kind of sentinel, sweeping up stray comets, asteroids, and other pieces of space debris that might otherwise have entered Earth-crossing orbits, as with the Shoemaker-Levy comet which struck Jupiter in 1994.

In addition to our invaluable moon, Theia made an even more significant contribution to our planet in the form of a generous supply of heavy metals which accrued to Earth's core. These lent mass and density to our planet which allowed it to retain an atmosphere thicker than might have been expected for a planet of Earth's size. More importantly these heavy metals included not only iron and nickel but also radioactive uranium 238, thorium 232, and potassium 40. It was the slow radioactive decay of these elements which generated enough heat to keep the outer iron core of the Earth molten long after it would otherwise have cooled. Radioactive decay now contributes 80 per cent of the heat required to keep the outer core molten, with only 20 per cent as residual heat from Earth's original formation. The diameter of Earth at the equator is 12,756 kilometres, or very nearly 8,000 miles. At its centre lies a solid iron-nickel core at a temperature of around 6,000 degrees Kelvin, higher than that of the surface of the sun. It is only the great gravitational pressure at the centre of the Earth that prevents this core from melting. It is 2,556 kilometres in diameter, only one-fifth that of the Earth. Surrounding it is a mantle of liquid iron 5,780 kilometres in diameter, nearly half that of the whole Earth. Because the temperature of this liquid iron is higher near the solid core than further away from it, convection currents are set up and these, together with some friction between the solid and liquid iron cores, produce a dynamo effect which generates Earth's strong magnetic field. This field deflects the solar wind and other ionised particle from outer space, which in turn protects Earth's atmosphere from 'sputtering', by which solar radiation slowly strips away the upper layers of a planet's atmosphere.

Of the four rocky inner planets, only Earth has this strong magnetic field. In the cases of Mercury, Venus, and Mars their magnetic fields are entirely negligible, and provide no protection from the solar wind. This has stripped Mercury and Mars of their atmospheres, and is having the same effect on Venus, but Venus still retains an atmosphere because there it is so thick and heavy that sputtering has progressed much more slowly. There is now no water on Venus, and because of the strong greenhouse effect of its atmosphere, the surface temperature of the planet is 465 degrees Celsius, hot enough to melt lead and zinc. The atmosphere of Venus is 96.5 per cent carbon dioxide, with most of the rest sulphur dioxide, two heavy gases which together have 93 times the mass of Earth's atmosphere, producing a surface pressure 92 times greater. Unlike Venus, however, Earth desperately needed that strong magnetic field to protect its much lighter and thinner atmosphere from the sputtering effect.

But Earth also possesses another, and even more important unique feature, which it owes also to the contribution of Theia. On our planet, its long, linear chains of mountains provide conclusive evidence that here on Earth, and only on Earth, a process of plate tectonics is in operation. The Earth's lithosphere, (from the Greek λίθος, stone) that is its crust and upper mantle, is not a continuously uniform layer, but rather is broken up into a number of moving plates, basically seven large plates and ten smaller ones. The continental lithosphere is composed mainly of lighter rocks such as granites and feldspars with a high silicon content, while the ocean floors usually consist of denser, basaltic rocks. Just below the lithosphere lies the asthenosphere (from the Greek άσθενής, weak) which is indeed weaker than the lithosphere, and lies at the top of Earth's molten iron mantle, which in turn surrounds its iron-nickel core. The asthenosphere is not actually liquid, but is a so-called 'visco-elastic solid', which is capable of slow movement, carrying the plates of the lithosphere with it, piggy-back style. The energy to power this movement again comes essentially from those crucial heavy, radioactive elements which were in part stolen from Theia, the uranium, thorium, and potassium 40. It is mainly heat from the radioactive decay of these elements which sets up convection currents in the asthenosphere surrounding the liquid iron mantle of Earth, and this moves the surface plates. The asthenosphere consists of molten silicate rocks which are viscous, and capable of generating slow convection currents. The moving plates allow heat to escape from the liquid iron mantle more readily, and it is this escaping heat which, by cooling the surface of the mantel relative to its deeper layers, keeps the mantel's convection currents moving. All these beneficial developments may be traced back to our collision with Theia, but how common within solar systems can such collisions be? We cannot answer this question yet, but the extreme axial tilt of Uranus, its thin rings and its many moons, suggest that Uranus too may have collided with another protoplanet early in its history

.

The idea that continents could float around the globe on their tectonic plates was first proposed by the German geophysicist Alfred Wegener (1880-1930) in 1912, but the theory was originally considered to be so outrageous that it was not generally accepted. Only in the 1960s did mounting evidence prove that Wegener had in fact been entirely right. We now know that over billions of years these drifting plates have formed our land masses into single supercontinents, which have then broken up into separate continents, only to reform into a single supercontinent again. The supercontinent of Rodinia is thought to have formed about one billion years ago, and broken up into eight parts 600 million years ago. These parts then later reassembled into the supercontinent of Pangaea some 300 million years ago, only to begin to disperse again into our present pattern of continents some 175 million years ago. The plates are, of course, still drifting in the present day.

Those tectonic plate movements become most evident at the plate boundaries, and these boundaries are of essentially three types. First there are divergent boundaries, where two plates tear apart from each other, in effect by the creation of new plate material formed by convected, upwelling magma from the asthenosphere. These lines of upwelling magma are known as ‘ridges’, with the classic example being the Mid-Atlantic Ridge which runs almost from pole to pole beneath the Atlantic Ocean, and is steadily driving North and South America further and further away from Europe and Africa. All along this ridge are found the famous black and white ‘smokers’, the volcanic undersea hydrothermal vents, providing the kind of environment in which life probably originated. Next there are transform boundaries, where plates are neither created nor destroyed, but merely grind slowly past each other along ‘transform faults’. These are likely to be dangerous earthquake zones, as with the notorious San Andreas fault line, where the Pacific Plate is slowly grinding northwards past the North American Plate along the coast of California. Thirdly, there are convergent boundaries where two plates slide towards each other to create either a subduction zone, with one plate sliding underneath another, or a continental collision. In this latter case neither plate is subducted, but instead mountain chains are thrown up, such as the Alps, caused by the northward movement of the African plate against the Eurasian plate, and the Himalayas, formed by the northward movement of the Indian plate against the Eurasian plate. Geopaleontologists tell us that the Indian plate whizzed across the Indian Ocean from the southern hemisphere at the astonishing speed of six inches a year, a very high rate for plate movements. When it impacted with the Eurasion plate, it threw up the highest mountains in the world.

It is these convergent boundaries which are the most interesting, because it is here that mountain chains are formed on land, and deep trenches are formed beneath the oceans. Along the lines of ocean to continent subduction the dense oceanic lithosphere plunges beneath the less dense continental crust, but again mountain chains are formed as the crust crumples. The Andes range in South

America and the Cascade mountains in the western United States are example of mountains formed in this way. As the downward moving plate descends into the asthenosphere an ocean trench forms, and as the subducted plate is heated it releases its more volatile constituents, mainly water from hydrated minerals, into the surrounding mantle. It is this water which lowers the melting point of the mantle material above the subducting slab, causing it to melt, with resulting volcanism in the mountain chains. It has been estimated that at the present time Earth has roughly 56,000 kilometres of divergent ridges and only about 36,000 kilometres of subduction lines, but subduction takes place more rapidly on average than divergence.

It has been argued that the movement of Earth's tectonic plates has played a crucial role in the evolution of Earth's climate. This is because these movements can serve to either increase or diminish the amount of carbon dioxide gas in Earth's atmosphere, in accordance with how much volcanism they engender. Despite all the concern shown recently about mankind's growing contribution of carbon dioxide to our atmosphere, it remains true that most of this output still comes from natural sources, such as the oceans and volcanoes. Even extinct volcanoes are still producing CO_2 because the gas continues to permeate upwards from the depths through the lithosphere. Tectonic movements therefore *add* to CO_2 emissions when they lead to increased volcanism, but they can also serve to *remove* CO_2 from the atmosphere when they create additional land surfaces through mountain building. This is because atmospheric carbon dioxide readily combines with calcium and silicates in the Earth's crust to produce calcium carbonate and silicon dioxide ($CaSiO_3 + CO_2 = CaCO_3 + SiO_2$) thus 'locking away' excess carbon dioxide from the atmosphere. Photosynthesizing plants, of course, perform the same function, but of the two processes it is believed that the 'silicon sink' is the more important. It has been argued, therefore, that plate tectonics, by regulating CO_2 levels, act as a kind of global thermostat, keeping Earth's surface temperature at a level which allows liquid water to exist for long periods of time, and in fact keeping temperatures within that very narrow range (between 5 and 40 degrees centigrade on average) which makes life comfortable for very sensitive and vulnerable mammalian life forms like ourselves. As CO_2 levels in the atmosphere increase, temperatures rise, there is more evaporation from the seas, and rainfall increases. This increases erosion rates over land, exposing ever new silicate surfaces to react with CO_2, thus drawing it out of the air again. But then less carbon dioxide in the atmosphere means a reduced greenhouse effect, so temperatures fall again, reducing rainfall and erosion, so allowing a fresh build-up of CO_2, which raises temperatures once more. This theory of a 'carbon cycle' is a rather elaborate one, but it could well be true, drawing support from the fate of Venus. Here was a planet with volcanism, which indeed is still going on today, but with no plate tectonics. As a result, CO_2 simply built up in its atmosphere until temperatures rose to their present levels, making life on the planet unsustainable. But why is Earth the only planet in the solar system to have plate tectonics, as evidenced by its mountain chains? We must return once again to the assumed collision of the early Earth with the smaller planet Theia, which robbed the impactor of its heavy and radioactive elements. This left Earth as the densest planet in the solar system, with more than its fair share of these heavy elements. This kept its internal temperature high and its magma plastic, allowing it to move tectonic plates on its surface through convection currents. It also produced Earth's strong magnetic field. It seems that no other planet in our system had such a unique history, and therefore none of these unique characteristics.

On the whole, plate tectonics seem to have played a vital role in promoting the development of life on Earth, for a number of reasons. Some four billion years ago, when the young Earth had first cooled sufficiently to allow the steam in its atmosphere to condense into liquid water, the planet became in fact a water world, with only a few volcanic islands protruding above the waves. Only 0.05% of Earth's mass is made up by water, but this is enough to cover the entire globe with an ocean 2.7 kilometres deep if the surface of the Earth were absolutely smooth. In fact, however, the average depth of our present oceans is 3.7 kilometres, because plate tectonics has gouged out deep trenches in its bed such as the Marianas Trench between Japan and Papua New Guinea, which is 11 kilometres deep in places. Tectonics has also thrown up land surfaces, reducing the area of the oceans and so increasing their depth. Without these surface movements, Earth would have remained the water world that it was for the first one-and-one-half billion years of its existence. In the following half billion years, however, there seems to have been a sharp increase in continental formation, so that at two billion years of age, some two-and-a-half billion years ago, Earth already had two-thirds of its present land surface. This surface area then continued to increase steadily until the present day. This of course was crucial for the development of more advanced life forms, since in an entirely water world evolution would not have progressed beyond the fishes.

Much has been made in recent years of the threat posed to our planet by global warming, and the risk of a runaway greenhouse effect setting in as the amount of CO2 in our atmosphere increases. The theory is that more CO2 raises temperatures, which cause more evaporation from the seas, putting more water vapour into the atmosphere. But water vapour is the most effective greenhouse gas, leading to further greenhouse heating, leading to more evaporation, in a fatal, self-sustaining cycle. In fact, however, the geologists tell us that over the course of Earth's long history we have actually been more at risk of a runaway icehouse effect! The average temperature on the surface of the moon is -18 degrees centigrade, and this would be the average surface temperature of the Earth as well if we relied upon unaided solar heating. This would be low enough to leave us as an ice ball world, like Jupiter's moon Europa, or Saturn's Enceladus. It is only the greenhouse gasses in our atmosphere which, by absorbing and re-emitting some solar radiation back to

Earth's surface, have kept our average temperature up to 14 degrees centigrade, 32 degrees higher than might have been expected.

However, those gasses make up only a tiny proportion of our total atmosphere, with CO_2 taking up only .04% by volume at the present time. If we consider purely dry air, it consists of 78.09% nitrogen, 20.95% oxygen, and 0.92% argon, adding up to 99.96% of the entire atmosphere. However, none of these is a greenhouse gas, because none is made up of three or more atoms. It is only the slightly heavier gasses in our atmosphere, consisting of three atoms or more that produce a greenhouse effect: for example carbon dioxide (CO_2) and ozone (O_3), each with three atoms, and methane (CH_4) with five atoms. However, today methane is a rare trace gas, making up only .00017% of our atmosphere. This is too low a concentration to have any significant warming effect, but it is perhaps worth mentioning at this point another gas which *did* have a very significant effect, even at very low concentrations. It was one of a family of man-made gasses that were developed in the 1930s known as chlorofluorocarbons. These consisted basically of one carbon atom bound with three chlorine atoms and one fluorine atom. They were non-flammable, and so were widely used in refrigeration and as a spray can propellant. Although these are heavy gases, some drifted up on air currents to reach the Earth's ozone layer, where they were broken down by solar radiation to produce free chlorine. This chlorine reacted with the ozone, O_3, 'stealing' one of its oxygen molecules to form ClO. But free oxygen ions up there in the ionosphere were then able to 'steal' back the oxygen from the chlorine to form O_2, leaving the chlorine atom free to destroy another O_3 atom in an endless progression. In effect, free chlorine in the ionosphere threatened to convert all of our precious ozone into oxygen, which would have offered no shielding effect against the sun's ultraviolet radiation. Fortunately this effect was discovered in time, and chlorofluorocarbons were banned in 1996, but it will now take some decades for the ozone layer to fully recover. How easily can humankind upset nature's delicate balance.

In addition, we must remember that the composition of our atmosphere changes with altitude, and we have so far been speaking only of dry air at sea level. Ozone, for example is barely traceable at sea level at all, making up only 0.3 parts per million of our atmosphere overall, but in the stratosphere, at an altitude of 20 to 30 kilometres, this concentration rises to ten parts per million, still very low, but enough to shield Earth's surface from harmful ultraviolet radiation from the sun. This layer was thicker in the past, but it remains effective today, still shielding land-based life forms from potentially lethal short-wave radiation. Water vapour content too varies with altitude, constituting only 0.4% of our atmosphere overall, but more like one per cent near sea level. This is very significant, because water vapour (H_2O) with its three atoms is in fact the most effective greenhouse gas. At present carbon dioxide makes up only .04% of our atmosphere. However, if we allow this gas to increase to excessive levels Earth's surface temperature will rise, causing evaporation from the seas to increase, and it is the threat of rising water vapour in our atmosphere that concerns climate scientists, who fear that this might be the direct cause of a runaway greenhouse effect. At what point this runaway effect might set in is still a matter of debate, but we do know that since 1880 the proportion of CO_2 in our atmosphere has increased from .028% to .04%, evidently causing an average temperature rise of 0.8 degrees centigrade across the planet. Climate is, therefore, apparently very sensitive to quite small changes in the greenhouse gas content of our atmosphere.

Having said that, however, evidence suggests that over its very long history Earth has never experienced a runaway greenhouse effect, while it *has* experienced runaway icehouse effects. Scientists define an Ice Age as being one when ice is present at both poles, and by that definition we are still living through an Ice Age at the present moment. This is the Quaternary Ice Age, which began 2,588,000 years ago and is still going on. Amidst all this talk of global warming it is easy to forget that we are in fact living through an Ice Age, when carbon dioxide levels in our atmosphere have been unusually low, and global average temperatures have also reached an unusually low point in terms of the last half billion years of Earth history. (See Table A below) During the recent Holocene Glaciation, the land on which our house is now built was under the ice. I look out of my study window onto a steeply rising wooded hill, the north side of the Holt-Cromer Ridge, a terminal moraine that was left behind by the last retreat of the ice sheets from this part of Norfolk only 12,000 years ago. For the last 2.5 million years the glaciers have been regularly advancing and retreating over northern Europe in cycles of roughly 26,000 years. These have been linked with the so-called Milankovitch cycles, which relate to the Earth's orbital eccentricity, axial tilt, and precession. This link is still controversial, but if Earth runs true to its form of the last two million years, the glaciers will return! We are currently experiencing a merciful interglacial, but perhaps we should not take this interlude for granted: perhaps we should be grateful that CO_2 levels in our atmosphere are now rising. Just why the ice sheets from the poles have regularly advanced and retreated for the last two million years is still not fully understood, and it may be that we will need higher carbon dioxide levels to prevent a return of the glaciers. Our planet desperately needs its warming blanket of greenhouse gasses, for without them average global temperatures would plunge to -18 degrees centigrade, the same as those on the moon, prompting the return of a total glaciation.

Drifting continents play a key role in climate change. Land masses over or around both poles make it more likely that they will become ice covered, as they become cut off from warming ocean currents. Growing ice sheets over the poles reflect more of the sun's radiation back into space, and if this effect is combined with a reduction in volcanic activity, causing a fall in atmospheric

CO2 levels, a major Ice Age, perhaps even a Snowball Earth, may result, as has certainly happened in the past.

Palaeoclimatologists tell us that over the last 500 million years Earth has enjoyed a 'greenhouse' condition for 80% of the time, but never a runaway greenhouse effect, although global temperatures have sometimes reached very high levels, as in the Paleozoic Era some 368 million years ago, and again just 55 million years ago in the Eocene epoch, when global temperatures appear to have soared by five to eight degrees centigrade in just 20,000 years. There was no ice at either pole, and palm trees could have grown in the arctic, but there was no catastrophic greenhouse effect. On the other hand, we *have* experienced at least two 'Snowball Earth' periods, when ice covered all or nearly all of the planet. The first of these episodes took place between 2.4 and 2.1 billion years ago, and has been linked to the oxygenation of Earth's atmosphere. The second near total glaciation also stretched over millions of years, from about 750 to 580 million years ago, but even a partial glaciation similar to the last, which ended only 12,000 years ago, would be disastrous enough. Further discussion of man's effects on our climate appears in the Economics chapter below.

(d) How Unusual is Our Sub-species?

Even on this most life-friendly of planets, survival can sometimes be a matter of chance for the life forms that inhabit it, as witnessed by the many mass extinction events that our world has experienced. The first of these was known as the Great Oxygenation Event, or sometimes as the Oxygen Catastrophe or Oxygen Holocaust. This is because the first organisms to emerge on Earth nearly four billion years ago were anaerobic, that is to say they originated in an oxygen-free environment, probably in the deep oceans around hydrothermal vents, and so found oxygen to be poisonous when it began to build up in a free form on Earth. This is not surprising. Oxygen is a highly reactive and corrosive element, and in gaseous form should be as poisonous to most life forms as chlorine is to us. Only organisms that have evolved to tolerate this dangerous gas can survive in an oxygen-rich environment. Once free oxygen began to form as a gas in our atmosphere and to dissolve in our oceans, it proved to be toxic to most of the bacteria and archaea then in existence. The slaughter was not total, however, for oxygenation took place slowly enough for some of the microbial life then in existence to evolve and adapt to the changing conditions. Oxygenation levels were at first highest at the surface of the oceans, but later increasingly high at lower depths as well, giving time for adaptation to take place. In addition some species, especially the archaeans, were able to discover anaerobic niches for themselves where they have managed to survive to this day.

But where did this free oxygen come from? The culprits seem to have been an advanced form of bacteria which had learned to live in multi-cellular colonies, and had floated to the ocean surface. There they developed an ability to photosynthesize, using sunlight as an energy source to generate nutrients. Like plants, they then discharged free oxygen as a waste product of this process. These specialists were known as cyanobacteria. They were prokaryotes, simple single-celled organisms with no internal membrane-bound organelles such as chloroplasts. Instead photosynthesis took place in the membranes of these cells, also known as cytoplasmic membranes. Cyanobacteria probably first evolved some three billion years ago, but at first the oxygen they produced was absorbed by dissolved iron and organic material in the oceans, and by rock minerals on the land surface. It might be said that during this era the Earth 'rusted': as a result, most of the metals mined from the Earth's crust today occur in the form of their oxides!

These processes kept oxygen levels in Earth's atmosphere down to under five per cent, but this was substantially more than the virtually zero oxygen content of Earth's original atmosphere, which seems to have consisted mainly of carbon dioxide, ammonia, and methane. It is interesting to note that these are all powerful greenhouse gasses, but even they did not produce an irreversible runaway greenhouse effect on our planet. However, even this quite small rise in the oxygen content of our atmosphere *did* have a profound effect, since the free oxygen reacted with atmospheric methane to produce carbon dioxide and water (CH4 + 2O2 = CO2 + 2H2O). This process increased the carbon dioxide content of the atmosphere, but reduced the proportion of methane, which is approximately 30 times more effective as a greenhouse gas than carbon dioxide. At the same time our sun was radiating less strongly at that time than it is today: it is believed that our sun is now some 30 per cent brighter and stronger than it was at the time of its formation since as it steadily fuses its hydrogen into helium its density increases, intensifying pressure at the sun's core. This in turn accelerates the pace of helium production, in a positive feedback loop. It is thought that our sun grows roughly 10% hotter every billion years. Those two factors of a cooler sun and a weaker greenhouse gas envelope some two billion years ago were enough to allow a dramatic cooling of the Earth's surface, and bring on the first great Ice Age, known as the Huronian Glaciation. This is because evidence of its existence was first detected in the Lake Huron region of Canada. It seems likely that between 2.4 and 2.1 billion years ago ice cover extended to the equator, producing the first age of a 'Snowball Earth'. During those 300 million years, Earth must have been the brightest planet in the solar system! Beneath the ice, however, some bacteria and archaea continued to survive in their watery environment, especially around the many hydrothermal vents. It is thought that this Ice Age was eventually brought to an end by continuing volcanic activity, with volcanoes erupting through the ice and finally contributing so many greenhouse gasses into the atmosphere that Earth's surface temperature rose again. We must remember that with a total ice cover there would have been no exposed land to provide a 'silicon sink' for CO2, and neither would there have been any of today's photosynthesising plants to absorb this gas, and so volcanoes, piercing the ice sheet, were able to steadily build up greenhouse gasses, including methane, in the atmosphere, with no counterbalancing factors. But some cyanobacteria had survived beneath the ice, and as the glaciers retreated oxygen levels in our atmosphere rose again as the cyanobacteria once more flourished, and Earth's 'oxygen sinks' became saturated. The first primitive plants invaded the land about 435 million years ago, evolving from algae that had drifted ashore, and as they developed photosynthesis via chloroplasts, oxygen levels rose sharply, to peak at about 35% towards the end of the Carboniferous period, some 300 million years ago, before declining once more to today's level of 21%.

A second era of very low temperatures appears to have occurred between 750 and 580 million years ago, when there were perhaps four periods of very heavy glaciations, each lasting about ten million years. During these times ice sheets stretched to the equator, greatly increasing Earth's albedo, that is its reflectivity, so that most solar radiation reaching the planet was reflected back into space. Temperatures fell to as low as -50 degrees centigrade. This prolonged ice age was probably triggered by a thinning of greenhouse gasses caused by a period of reduced volcanic activity, which was in turn due to the pattern of tectonic plate movements at that time. Again, however, renewed volcanic activity eventually brought this great Ice Age to an end.

Its long history would suggest that Earth seems to have a built-in immunity to runaway greenhouse effects, but not to runaway icehouse effects. Given this fact, the greatest danger posed by today's global warming would seem to be a consequent rise in sea levels. To date, between 1880 and 2015, global mean sea level has risen by about 23 centimeters or nine inches. Many of today's great cities were originally great ports, built at sea level before it was known that continents drifted, that Ice Ages came and went, and that sea levels rose and fell. How threatened are they now by global warming? Between 2005 and 2010 a spate of articles appeared in learned journals which tried to predict average world temperatures and the extent of sea level rise by the year 2100. Their estimates varied, but were not too alarming, predicting on average a rise of about one meter in the next 100 years. Most of this rise, 70-75%, was expected to result from the thermal expansion of the oceans, and the rest from melting glaciers and shrinkage of the arctic ice cap. Remarkably, however, there was a consensus of agreement that over the same timescale the Antarctic ice cap would actually grow, and some researchers predicted that sea level rises would in fact level off by 2050. As ever, opinions differed on climate forecasting. Rises of this order are serious enough, but manageable. In a worst case scenario sea defences could be built around vulnerable cities. This would be expensive, but cheaper than abandoning them to the waves! In fact, this process has already begun with the construction of sea defences in Holland, and the building of the Thames Flood Barrier to protect London in 1984. Another threat might be acidification of the oceans, since carbon dioxide dissolves in water to form carbonic acid. However, so far acidification has been slight, moving the pH level of our oceans only from 8.2 to 8.1 since 1880. The pH scale ranges from 0 to 14, with 7 indicating pH neutrality, 6 a slight acidity, and 8 a slight alkalinity. On the whole therefore, global warming is likely to prove to be more of a regional disaster, especially for some low-lying parts of the world like Bangladesh and the Maldives Islands, than the harbinger of a global doomsday. But that development would be serious enough.

The story of life's emergence and progress on our planet has been a strange, eventful history indeed since the emergence of LUCA. The composition of the early ocean was rather different from that of our present oceans, but it is nevertheless quite possible that LUCA, or something very like it, is still being engendered around hydrothermal vents today, since these have not yet been subjected to very close scrutiny, owing to the technical difficulties of accessing them in the very deep ocean. There is still great uncertainty surrounding life's early stages, but it would seem that soon after its formation around four billion years ago, LUCA diversified into the two domains of archaea and bacteria. Both organisms were prokaryotes, simple membrane-bound bags of DNA. These single-celled life forms had no separate membrane-bound nucleus to contain their DNA, nor any other membrane-bound internal organelles of any kind, such as mitochondria or chloroplasts. They reproduced by simple cell division (mitosis) which normally produced clones, but they were still able to evolve through chance mutations, and by lateral gene transfer through external cell membranes. These processes were sufficient to give rise to a very wide variety of both bacteria and archaea, and it seems likely that some of these became predatory, ingesting other prokaryotes as a source of nutrition in a process known as phagocytosis. Because of genetic similarities, it seems more likely that we are descended from predatory archaeans rather than predatory bacteria. Eventually, instead of digesting them, some of these predators seem to have established a symbiotic relationship with the single-celled creatures that they ingested, and so the first internal organelles came into existence, later to develop into the mitochondria, chloroplasts, and Golgi apparatus of eukaryotic cells. Each of these, and the nucleus of these cells itself, came to be membrane-bound separately within the parent cell. This is the key distinction between prokaryotes and eukaryotes. Both names come from the Greek, πρό (pro), meaning 'before', and καρυόν (kayron), meaning nut or kernel. The Greek εὖ (eu) means 'true' or 'well', implying that eukaryotes have true, internal, membrane-bound organelles like the kernels of nuts, while the simpler prokaryotes, earlier life forms, do not. It is assumed that all subsequent plant and animal life on our planet evolved from these larger, more complex eukaryotic single-celled entities, while the bacteria and archaea continued to go their own way as prokaryotes, surviving in a vast variety of forms until the present day. As noted above, they remain the most successful life forms on the planet, with a total biomass thought to be at least equal to that of the eukaryotes, while individual species have evolved a capability of survival in almost any environment, including boiling springs, arctic glaciers, and even solid rock. Some can flourish without oxygen and without organic nutrients, making it likely that some could survive almost any earthly catastrophe. By comparison, we mesophilic, placental mammals are pathetically vulnerable.

In 1735 the great Swedish naturalist Carl Linnaeus (1707-78) published his *Systema Naturae*, the most comprehensive attempt made up to that date at categorising all living things. It was he who, in the year 1758, coined the title *homo sapiens* for our species. Linnaeus recognised only two basic 'kingdoms' of living things, namely animals and plants. Over the following century, however, as microscopes improved, the number of kingdoms was increased to five, animals, plants, fungi, protozoa (single-celled eukaryotes), and bacteria. These five kingdoms reigned until the age of DNA analysis, when it became clear that not all 'bacteria' were the same. The tiny archaea, long thought to be bacteria, were in fact as different from bacteria as bacteria are from the most primitive protozoans. While the physical structure of archaeans as viewed through microscopes is very similar to that of bacteria, their genetic structure was found to be entirely different, resembling that of eukaryotes far more than that of bacteria. Their cell walls are also different and unique, based on lipids, giving them immunity to those viruses that attack bacteria. Interestingly, no archaean has yet been discovered that is pathogenic to humans: only bacteria and parasitic eukaryotes cause human diseases. But we should not be too hard on bacteria either: out of some 151,000 identified species, only 585 are pathogenic to humans. This sounds like a lot, but is only 0.36% of the whole, and not even all of those give rise to serious ailments: 99.64% of all known bacteria are completely harmless to humans. Archaea also differ from bacteria in that they are the most successful extremophiles,and only they are capable of producing methane as a by-product of their metabolism. Together with billions of bacteria, the human body also plays host to billions of archaea. Both live in happy symbiosis with their hosts, aiding our digestive processes. The archaea find the human bowel to be a particularly congenial environment, where their methogenic properties may occasionally cause you some embarrassment, but they will never do you any harm!

It is, however, the genetic differences between archaca and bacteria that are the most significant. In 1977 this discovery led University of Illinois biologist Carl Woese (1928-2012) to propose an entirely new category of life, the 'domain', which he placed above kingdoms. This new term became generally accepted in 1990. His three 'domains' were Archaea, Bacteria, and Eukarya, a new term, with this last domain embracing all other life forms apart from the first two. Because a whole new taxonomic classification had been established, and because Woese had developed new techniques of gene sequencing, these developments have become known as the Woeseian Revolution, and Woese himself has been hailed by some as 'the Einstein of biology'! There is still some dispute among taxonomists over just how many kingdoms should be distinguished below Woese's 'domains', but the British system recognises four, all under the domain Eukarya: Animalia, Plantae, Fungi, and Protista, with this last a catch-all grouping designed to include all life forms that do not fall clearly into any of the first three categories. The Archaea are thus given an entire domain to themselves. Most archaeans are anaerobic, and can live only in the absence of oxygen, which is a poisonous element for them. This makes them prime candidates for the first life on earth, or at least as one of its earliest forms, for the early earth had no free oxygen, and of course the hydrothermal vents were regions of high pressure and temperatures, exactly the environments preferred by some of the archaean extremophiles of today.

The evolution of life on earth at first proceeded very slowly. For at least two billion years the prokaryotic bacteria and archaea had the world to themselves. It was only about 1,850 million years ago that the first clear evidence of the more complex eukaryotic cells appears in the fossil record. By about 1,200 million years ago these single eukaryotic cells had evolved a form of sexual reproduction through the more efficient exchange and repair of genetic material, which may have accelerated the evolutionary process. Nevertheless, another 400 million years passed before the first multicellular life forms emerged, such as fungi, algae, and slime molds. From 800 million years ago life forms such as these slowly diversified into protozoa, later to develop into animals, and protophyta, later to develop into plants. Truly multicellular organisms, with variegated cells which performed different functions within their metabolisms, had appeared by 580 million years ago, and their emergence heralded the beginning of the so-called Cambrian Explosion of sea life some 580 to 500 million years ago, when the first recognisable animals began to appear as sea creatures, jellies, sponges, corals, worms, and sea anemonies. The Burgess Shale fossil beds, laid down 508 million years ago in the Rocky Mountains of British Columbia in Canada, show that a great variety of hard- and soft-bodied sea creatures were flourishing in those times. The Burgess Shale deposits have been celebrated by the distinguished palaeontologist Stephen Jay Gould (1941-2002) in his 1990 book, *Wonderful Life*.

Plant life first invaded the land about 435 million years ago, probably having evolved from green algae, and by the beginning of the Carboniferous Period, 363 million years ago, plant and insect life was firmly established on dry land. More developed animal life followed soon afterwards in the form of crustaceans, arachnids, and amphibians. Small reptiles had evolved by 250 million years ago, and the first small mammals, shrew-like creatures, some 160 million years ago. From that time onwards, a great variety of advanced life forms on land and in the seas has continued to flourish on our planet, which might therefore be assumed to be extremely life-friendly. Comparatively speaking this is true, when our Earth is compared with other planets in the solar system: it has certainly made life *possible* for highly evolved and vulnerable creatures like ourselves. But has it made life *easy* for them? That is quite another question. In reality, every life form ever to have emerged on our planet has faced severe challenges to its survival.

For example, the earliest stages of Earth's formation are known as the Hadean Era after 'hades', because for the first half billion years of its existence conditions on our planet were truly hellish. It accreted from the impact of numerous planetessimals and meteors to become a molten mass, and was then impacted by Theia, thought to have been a Mars-sized object, some four and a half billion years ago. This impact gave rise first to rings, and then to our moon, which was originally in very close orbit around the Earth, causing huge land and sea tides to sweep our planet after its crust had formed and its oceans had condensed out of the primordial steam. Earth was then subjected to the so-called 'late heavy bombardment' between 4.1 and 3.8 billion years ago, as the remaining comets and meteors left over from the formation of the planets orbited inwards towards the sun. It is termed 'late' to distinguish it from the initial heavy bombardment which Earth underwent during its formation. The craters that may still be seen on the moon today are a legacy of that period. On Earth billions of years of erosion and plate tectonics have erased all evidence of this late bombardment, but on the lifeless and airless moon with no plate tectonics, its effects can still be seen.

For the next billion years Earth settled down as a mainly water world with very little dry land on its surface, and an atmosphere that had been provided essentially by volcanic emissions. The lighter gasses, hydrogen and helium, had long been driven off by solar radiation, and it is thought that Earth's early atmosphere was made up of carbon dioxide, methane, ammonia, and water vapour. These are all powerful greenhouse gasses, but Earth seems to have needed them to keep its oceans liquid in those times of a weaker sun. Later, nitrogen, carbon dioxide, and some methane came to predominate. There was of course more volcanism in this period, but safe in their womb of the hydrothermal vents, the first primitive life forms were already beginning to take shape. It might have been assumed that these prokaryotes, the archaea and bacteria, would have been secure enough in the ocean depths, independent of the sun, unaffected by the tides, and with their own source of volcanic chemical energy, but their own kind betrayed them.

As explained above, the cyanobacteria, clumping together into colonies, floated to the surface of the seas and, by exploiting their unique ability to photosynthesize, began the long process of the oxygenation of Earth's atmosphere and oceans. Dissolved oxygen penetrated to the ocean depths, where it proved to be lethal to organisms that had evolved in anaerobic environments with no free oxygen. This so-called 'Oxygen Catastrophe' could therefore be regarded as Earth's first great extinction event, which came to threaten even the cyanobacteria themselves. This is because, as explained above, their oxygenation of Earth's atmosphere is believed to have given rise to the first great Ice Age, the Huronian Glaciation of just over two billion years ago, during which time ice covered the surface of the oceans, which had been the habitat of the cyanobacteria themselves! However, some open water may have remained near the equator, and the cyanobacteria quickly evolved and adapted, with some species learning how to live within the solid ice itself, where they may still be found to this day. Some bacteria and archaea also clearly managed to survive this 'Oxygen Holocaust', for these are the most adaptable and enduring of organisms, capable of surviving even the most severe of catastrophes.

'Snowball Earth' conditions returned between 750 and 580 million years ago when it is thought that there were four periods of severe glaciations, each one lasting about ten million years. There is still debate over whether ice sheets straddled the equator, but these Ice Ages cannot be regarded as extinction events at that time, although they certainly would be in our own time. This is because all life 580 million years ago was still sea life, and water possesses a unique property. Most elements and compounds are denser in their solid state than in their liquid state. This is to be expected, because heated elements expand and become progressively less dense, eventually vaporizing as a gas. Water, however, is different. In its solid state water forms a crystalline structure that is actually less dense than water in its liquid form. A bar of iron thrown into a cauldron of molten iron will sink to the bottom of the cauldron, but a block of ice thrown into a pond of water will float on its surface. This unique property of H2O was all that saved sea life from an extinction event during the Ice Ages. It meant that water froze from the top down, and not from the bottom up. Cold water is indeed denser than warm water and tends to sink, but as soon as ice is formed this ice floats to the surface, so that water freezes from the top down, forming an insulating layer that can reach down to only a limited depth. But imagine what would have happened if water had instead frozen from the bottom up! The oceans could have become solid blocks of ice, making life impossible for many organisms. Again, extinction would not have been total. The many hydrothermal vents would have kept the water liquid in their vicinities, continuing to harbour primitive life forms, just as they still do today. As it was, however, life forms had to adapt to colder seas, but there is no evidence of mass extinctions. Indeed, since the final ending of these total Ice Ages some 580 million years ago heralded the Cambrian Explosion of new forms of sea life, they might actually have served as a spur to evolution. The fossils of the Burgess Shales testify to the existence of a huge variety of primitive animal life in our seas some 508 million years ago.

No sooner had the Cambrian Explosion begun, however, than the extinction rate of marine organisms also began to rise, or so the palaeontologists tell us, with high extinction rates between 540 and 440 million years ago. This may be put down to nature experimenting with new animal life forms, which proved to be ill adapted for long-term survival. In addition, however, five major separate and well defined mass extinction events have been recognised in the last 500 million years as the complexity, and so the vulnerability of Earth's life forms steadily increased. It is important to realise, however, that these extinction events did not occur because the Earth was becoming a more dangerous place. On the contrary, it was probably more life-friendly than ever before, with fewer extreme climate swings, no total glaciations and, from 600 million years ago, a well-developed ozone layer in the upper atmosphere which, although it varied in thickness over time, usually shielded the surface of the planet from some 97 to 99 per cent of the sun's ultraviolet radiation, just as it still does today. Without this ozone layer land-dwelling life forms would need to have developed their own shielding from these harmful rays, and their eyes too would need to have been specially adapted to cope with reflected ultraviolet light.

In addition to a long period of moderate temperatures, both carbon dioxide and oxygen levels in the atmosphere varied only between tolerable levels, perhaps regulated by plate tectonics as explained above. In fact, the mass extinction events were due not to a more hostile Earth, but rather to the increasing vulnerability of the more complex life forms which were now coming to occupy it. Earth had always been a rather dangerous place for life forms, but rapidly reproducing and evolving single-celled sea-dwelling organisms had possessed many advantages in the survival stakes, enabling them to survive events that would have been fatal to terrestrial animals. There would have been many, many more extinction events in pre-Cambrian times had the life forms of those eras been vulnerable to them.

Although Earth's climatic variations over the last 500,000 years have been moderate and tolerable compared to those of earlier eons, and certainly by comparison with the climate changes suffered by Venus and Mars, we would regard them as being extreme if we were to experience them today. Palaeoclimatologists now speak with some confidence about climatic conditions of the distant past, because they can draw on a wide range of evidence on the extent of climate change. This includes core samples taken from deep lakes and the seabed, pollen analysis, oxygen isotope levels in the shells of marine creatures, and deep ice core samples taken from both Arctic and Antarctic ice sheets. These last are the most valuable, since Earth's poles have been ice covered for the last two million years. Some core samples have yielded evidence on the climatic conditions of 800,000 years ago. They contain not only trapped air bubbles from ages long gone, but also pollen grains, yielding evidence on past vegetation, and volcanic ash, testifying to previous levels of volcanism. The main points from their findings are summarized in the table below, showing the percentages of oxygen in Earth's atmosphere, and the concentrations of carbon dioxide in parts per million. These concentrations of up to 4,500 parts per million should be compared with our recent pre-industrial levels of 280 ppm, and today's level of 400 ppm. It should also be noted that the natural carbon dioxide levels of the last two-and-a-half million years have been very low (on average) by comparison with those of the distant past, and that these levels on their own do not appear to have been the decisive factor influencing temperature changes.In the table below dates are given in millions of years before the present , with the figures taken from Wikipedia entries for each Period.

Table A (Dates in millions of years before the present)

Period	Dates	O2 % Vol.	CO2 ppm	Av. Temp.
Cambrian	541- 485	12.5	4500	21 c
Ordovician	485 - 444	13.5	4200	16 c
Silurian	444 - 419	14.0	4500	17c
Devonian	419 - 359	15.0	2200	20c
Carboniferous	359 - 299	32.5	800	14c
Permian	299 - 252	23.0	900	16c
Triassic	251 - 201	16.0	1750	17c
Jurassic	201 - 145	26.0	1950	16.5 c
Cretaceous	145 - 66	30.0	1700	18 c
Paleogene	66 - 23	26.0	500	18 c
Neogene	23 - 2.59	21.5	280	14 c
Quaternary	2.59 - Present	20.8	250	14 c

The Quaternary Period, characterized by the recent glaciations, is subdivided into the Pleistocene, from 2.59 million to 11,700 years ago, and the Holocene from 11,700 BC to the present. This division refers to the beginning of the last Ice Age, 2.59 million years ago, which our Earth is still experiencing, since there is still ice cover over both poles, and the beginning of the last interglacial period, when the ice sheets last began their retreat from northern Europe. Within the last 200 years, of course, carbon dioxide levels in our atmosphere have increased sharply, from 250 to some 400 parts per million, but over the entire Quaternary Period, the average level was quite low. Now I am not a climate change denier: obviously, the Earth's climate is changing all the time. But the above figures call into question the influence of CO2 levels in the atmosphere as playing a crucial role, and also question the importance of man's contribution to this level. The table above shows a rather poor correlation between movements in average temperatures and CO2 concentrations in the atmosphere over Earth's long history. Note the Silurian/Devonian period, and the Jurassic/Cretaceous periods, when falls in atmospheric CO2 levels were associated with *rising* temperatures. Even more questionable is the importance of humankind's contribution to this level, since

CO2 concentrations have clearly fluctuated widely on Earth long before man's arrival on the scene. In addition, 97% of the annual CO2 production in our present atmosphere comes from natural sources, mainly the ocean-atmosphere exchange as dissolved CO2 is released at sea level, but also from plant and animal respiration, together with soil respiration and decomposition, plus a small amount from volcanoes. Only 3% comes from man's contribution, that is 3% of the .04% concentration of this gas in our atmosphere. In a recent book by William Soon (ed.), *Global Warming, a Guide to the Science* (2002), several contributors point out that over the last 150 years average global temperatures have fluctuated very closely in line with sunspot activity, while the match with atmospheric CO2 levels has been a poor one. Specifically, global temperatures spiked between 1920 and 1960 while CO2 levels in the atmosphere barely moved. But this spike did correlate very closely with sunspot activity over those years, and sunspot activity has again been on the increase since 1980. Two graphs illustrating those movements are reproduced from Soon on p. 37 of the book *Global Warming* (2009) edited by Professor Stanley Feldman (1930-2016). A further iconoclastic blast against the present consensus may be found in Patrick J. Michaels (ed.), *Shattered Consensus: The True State of Global Warming* (2005).

From Cambrian to Neogene times, that is the last 540 million years or so, the average temperature of the Earth has been 17 degrees centigrade, as against today's average (Ice Age) temperature of 14 degrees centigrade, and this despite a steadily warming sun over that period. In terms of its last half billion years of history, our Earth has in fact been unusually *cold* for the last 2.9 million years. It would be ironic indeed if, having made Herculean efforts to move to a 'net zero carbon' economy we were then to find to our dismay that the Earth continued to warm in any case, owing to natural factors that were completely beyond our control.

However, it must be admitted that climatology is an extremely difficult science, because of the large number of unpredictable variables that must be taken into account. As noted above, atmospheric CO2 passes through a carbon cycle, with most of this gas being produced from natural sources, and then reabsorbed again by plants, the oceans, and 'silicon sinks'. In 2020 some 750 billion tons of CO2 passed through this cycle, with human activity contributing roughly 25 billion tons to the process, that is 3.1% of the .04% of our atmosphere that is made up of CO2. This sounds like a very small contribution, but the carbon cycle is in delicate balance. Only 40% of our increased contribution is absorbed by the Earth's 'sinks' each year, so that the surplus steadily builds up, raising the concentration of CO2 in our atmosphere from 280 to 400 parts per million since 1880, as noted above. This higher concentration can have only a warming effect on our climate, and so, despite the controversy that still rages over this issue, it would seem wiser to do what we can to reduce our CO2 emissions. Clearly, very small increases of atmospheric CO_2 can have a significant warming effect in our times. However, my fear is that Boris Johnson's 'green agenda' will be carried through to the great advantage of Boris's wealthy friends, but at very great cost to the rest of us.

On a geological time scale, despite an overall tendency towards a cooling Earth over the last half billion years, climate swings have been moderate. Variable as our climate has been, we should remember that the climates of Venus and Mars have varied much more than our own. It is believed that both Venus and Mars once hosted oceans in their early years, but radical climate change over billions of years wiped them out. Only Earth has retained its surface water, and remained relatively life friendly. Nevertheless, the last 500 million years have been characterised by five major extinction events. The first distinct crisis to affect post-Cambrian life is known as the Ordovician-Silurian Extinction Event, so called because it straddled the two geological periods which followed the Cambrian, some 455 to 439 million years ago, although a peak in extinctions occurred 444 million years ago. In this global disaster it is believed that some 50 to 60 percent of all marine genera and nearly 85 per cent of all marine species were wiped out. Although this was the second most severe of the five events, it is also the most mysterious, defying any conclusive explanation, partly because of its great distance in time. Increased volcanism, falling temperatures, glaciations, and metal poisoning of the seas have all been suggested, but never conclusively proven. Even a gamma ray burst from a nearby magnetar has been proposed, a sure sign of desperation on the part of the palaeontologists!

Next came the Late Devonian Extinction of 375 to 360 million years ago, which seems to have been a prolonged event with no distinct crisis. It affected only sea life, but there was still little vulnerable life on land at this time, apart from plants and insects. Some 19 per cent of all sea creature families disappeared, and about 50 per cent of all genera. Brachiopods, trilobites, and corals were particularly hard hit, but convincing explanations for this event have again eluded the scientists, although various suggestions have been put forward.

The third crisis, the Permian-Triassic Extinction Event, was the most severe of the five, with a clear crisis striking 252 million years ago. The fossil record suggests that up to 96 per cent of all marine species and 70 per cent of all terrestrial vertebrate species became extinct. It also marks the only known mass extinction of insects, which had flourished in the oxygen-rich atmosphere of Carboniferous and Permian times. Those were the days of giant dragonflies with four-foot wingspans. It seems that some 50 per cent of all families and 83 per cent of all genera were lost. Once again a variety of explanations has been put forward to account for this catastrophe, including a possible large meteor strike, but the prime suspect in the frame is a series of extensive volcanic eruptions from the Siberian Traps. These eruptions were not sudden, violent, and explosive, thereby injecting great clouds of dust and ash into the stratosphere, but rather steady and sustained, releasing instead large amounts of greenhouse gasses. They occurred in the region that is today central Siberia, but 252 million years ago all of the Earth's land mass was concentrated together in the one single supercontinent of Pangaea, and much of the area that experienced these eruptions was actually beneath the sea. The large basaltic lave flows that were emitted may still be traced today, covering an area of about two million square kilometres, roughly that of Western Europe, in what is now Siberia. It is believed, however, that at their full extent these flows could have covered up to seven million square kilometres. Up to four million cubic kilometres of lava could have been extruded in this, the largest known eruption episode in the history of the Earth. This long period of eruptions would of course have sharply raised carbon dioxide levels in the atmosphere, but in addition lava flows may have caused methane hydrates on the seabed to dissociate into free methane and water, causing an increase in atmospheric methane as well. These two powerful greenhouse gasses would have caused a temperature rise of six to eight degrees centigrade across the planet, but it is thought that sea temperatures may have risen by more than this. In addition, released hydrogen sulphide and carbon dioxide caused acidification and anoxic conditions to develop in the oceans, since carbon dioxide dissolves in water 28 times more readily than oxygen, forming carbonic acid ($CO2 + H2O = H2CO3$). Dying sea creatures caused deoxygenation of the oceans as they decayed, for aerobic bacteria flourished on their bodies, draining the depths of oxygen. Acid rain probably killed most land plants, as indicated by a lack of coal beds and other carboniferous deposits dating from this time. The fossil record suggests that it took between ten and thirty million years for land and sea life to recover fully from this disaster.

Only twenty million years after this recovery, however, Earth was struck by a fourth extinction episode, known as the Triassic-Jurassic Extinction Event. This occurred within the fairly short period of only 10,000 years some 201.3 million years ago, just before Pangaea began to break apart to create the present configuration of continents. At least half of all the species known to have been living on the Earth at that time became extinct over this fairly short period. Once again large-scale volcanic eruptions are the prime suspect as the cause of this disaster, centring this time on the Central Atlantic Magmatic Province, an area located in the middle of what is now the Atlantic Ocean. A huge basaltic lava plain was created, comparable in size with that of the Siberian Traps, but the spreading of tectonic plates from both directions along the Mid-Atlantic Ridge has now pushed the remains of this basaltic plateau to both sides of the Atlantic Ocean. The effects of these eruptions would have been similar to those of the great Permian-Triassic extinction Event.

Following this disaster Earth enjoyed a fairly stable period for 135 million years before being struck by its most recent great extinction episode, the Cretaceous-Palaeogene Extinction Event of 66 million years ago which, confusingly enough, is often referred to in abbreviated form as the 'K-T Extinction'. This is because the Cretaceous Period was named for the many layers of chalk strata which characterise it, and the Latin term for chalk is *creta*. However, this era was first intensively studied by German palaeontologists, and their word for chalk is *Kreide*. They used the single letter 'K' as an abbreviation for the Cretaceous, and their usage has stuck. The 'T' of the K-T comes from the Tertiary, which was an alternative sub-division falling within the Paleogene. For good measure of confusion, reference is also often made to the 'K-PG boundary'.

By any name, however, this was a disastrous event, wiping out some three-quarters of all the plant and animal species on Earth, both land and sea creatures, in a period of just 10,000 years. Among those lost were the giant dinosaurs that had ruled the Earth in Jurassic and Cretaceous times. Some have argued that the dinosaurs were already in decline before the K-T event, which was merely the last straw for them, but there can be no doubting the magnitude of the disaster. On this occasion, the prime suspect as a cause of the K-T event was the collision of a large asteroid, some 10 to 15 kilometres in diameter, with the Earth. A crater consistent with this scale of impact has been identified just off the northeast corner of the Yucatan Peninsula in the Gulf of Mexico, with its formation dated to 66 million years ago. The crater itself is 180 kilometres wide, and has been dubbed the Chicxulub crater after a nearby Mexican town of that name. However, it is also possible that Earth suffered multiple impact strikes at this time as the large asteroid broke up on its approach to Earth, much as the Shoemaker-Levy comet broke up on its approach to Jupiter in 1994. A second suspected crater has been identified in the Arabian Sea just off Mumbai on the west coast of India, dubbed the Shiva Crater. Its origins are still disputed, although it is also believed to be about 66 million years old. What is more certain, however, is that another large scale and long term volcanic eruption was going on in this area at the same time, producing the Deccan Traps flood basalts. This volcanism may have been stimulated by impactor strikes, particularly that of the Chicxulub asteroid. The latest thinking on the combined effects of asteroid impacts and the Deccan eruptions is well explained by John Reilly in his fascinating book, *The Ascent of Birds* (2018) pp. 13-19. Other craters dating from this time have also been detected in the Ukraine and the North Sea. But the Chicxulub asteroid, the largest fragment, struck a region of sulphur-rich carbonate rock (gypsum), much of which was vaporised, injecting sulphuric acid aerosols into the stratosphere. These alone could have reflected back into space some 50 per cent of the sun's radiation in addition to causing acid rain and ocean acidification. Giant dust clouds also circled the Earth, conditions that gave rise to a 'nuclear winter' effect. Sea and air temperatures plunged by ten degrees centigrade, and there is strong evidence to indicate that plant life was devastated over a ten-year period, with disastrous consequences all the way up the food chain.

The K-T extinction event was certainly a disaster for most life forms of the times, especially the more cold-blooded species like most of the dinosaurs, but perhaps we humans should feel grateful for it, since it ended dinosaur domination of the world, although some warmer-blooded species survived to evolve into today's birds. Without this event our mammalian ancestors might have remained as small, nocturnal, burrowing creatures, feeding on roots, seeds, insects, and earthworms, while hiding in fear from reptilian raptors further up the food chain. Mammalian and marsupial species, which were warm-blooded and so could generate their own internal heat, definitely survived the KT event more successfully than the more cold-blooded species that relied partially on external heating, and although the spread and diversification of the mammals was certainly slow after the event, clearly they flourished in the millions of years that followed it. But had the main asteroid struck just a few miles further east, out in the deep ocean instead of on shallow coastal waters, or had it vaporized harder, igneous rocks, its consequences would have been far less severe, and the dinosaurs might have survived, to our cost. On such threads hang our existence.

But why all this science? It is hoped that the above review has proved to be interesting in itself, but its purpose has been to present a large body of evidence to prove that, *pace* Paul Davies, the universe is *not* 'just right for life' at all. Only a physicist could have made a statement like that. The ecologist, the palaeontologist, and the astrobiologist would hold very different views. Our universe does indeed make life *possible*, which is miraculous enough, especially bacterial life on the few planets that are possessed of those special conditions that will permit it. But when it comes to the emergence and survival of advanced life forms like ourselves, the universe is a decidedly hostile place. Even here on Earth, that most life-friendly of all conceivable planets, life has had a very difficult time of it over the last half billion years, enduring one major extinction event every 100 million years on average, and numerous minor ones. It seems that life was frequently endangered by Earth's unpredictable volcanism. Sometimes rising columns of very hot magma from the asthenosphere break through the lithosphere to erupt as volcanoes. These are dangerous enough, but sometimes this hot magma pools as a large deposit just below the surface, where it continues to build up, perhaps lurking for thousands of years before erupting explosively as a supervolcano. Even just 75,000 years ago there was a major eruption from the Mount Toba supervolcano on the island of Sumatra, which is believed to have caused a decade-long 'nuclear winter' effect. The resulting caldera, 100 kilometres long and 30 kilometres wide, is now the site of Lake Toba. Some have argued that the Earth's human population was reduced to just a few tens of thousands by this event, but these claims remain controversial. Nevertheless the fact that another supervolcano, comparable in scale to Mount Toba, is currently bubbling away beneath Yellowstone National Park in Wyoming, is rather unsettling. Indeed, some 20 potential supervolcanoes have been detected around the globe! If any one of them were to erupt, they would produce another Mount Toba disaster: we live eternally just one supereruptionfrom catastrophe. Every textbook you can find assures us that at least 99 per cent of all the species that have ever existed on the Earth are now extinct: indeed, some put the figure at 99.999 per cent! A life-friendly planet? Well, to a degree. But when it comes to calculating extinction rates, I have often wondered who has done the counting, and just who the lucky survivors of today are. On these points the books are strangely silent, but one must assume that the ubiquitous bacteria and archaea are among their numbers.

Moreover, how many Earth-like planets can there be? As pointed out above, our sun is an unusually large star occupying an unusually remote position in the galaxy. Our solar system is almost certainly atypical to say the least, and even within this our planet is certainly the weirdest of the bunch. Mercury is typical, the moon is typical, Mars is typical, Jupiter and Saturn are typical of the gas giant planets that you might expect to find around other stars, but life forms like ourselves could not survive on any of them. Our Earth is in fact freakishly *atypical* of any planet that you might expect to find. To briefly recap, it is the only planet in our system that has liquid water on its surface, but also at the same time large areas of dry land, which are absolutely essential to allow for the emergence of very advanced life forms. How many other planets can be so gifted? If Earth had remained the water world that it was in its earliest days, evolution could never have progressed beyond the fishes. Indeed, we are all descended from fish, as Neil Shubin so eloquently explains in his 2007 book, *Your Inner Fish.* As the human embryo 'climbs up its own evolutionary tree' from single cell to fully developed baby, it displays, in its very early stages, eight distinct gill arches just below the head. At this stage, the human embryo is almost indistinguishable from that of the shark. (p. 91)

But this land-water mix is not Earth's only unique feature. Only our planet displays ongoing plate tectonics, a crucial factor for the evolution of advanced life, for it was these tectonics that threw up our dry land. Only Earth has a large, single moon which stabilizes the tilt of its axis. Among the rocky inner planets only Earth generates a strong magnetic field which deflects charged particles from the sun and outer space away from its surface, and protects our atmosphere from 'sputtering'. Only Earth has an ozone layer which protects it from ultraviolet radiation, and an oxygen-rich atmosphere which at the same time contains just enough greenhouse gasses to keep its oceans liquid, and its average temperature (of the last half billion years) 35 degrees centigrade higher than that of its airless moon. In short, it is a freakishly improbable planet which, by the laws of chance, ought scarcely to exist at all! Moreover, it is only within that thin surface film known as the biosphere that advanced life forms can live, even on this world: just ten kilometres above or below this layer no unprotected advanced life form could survive. But even within this highly improbable world, the most improbable development of all was ourselves. SETI programmes (The Search for extraterrestrial Intelligence) have been running since the 1960s using radio telescopes to search for intelligent radio signals, but so far without success, suggesting that we are very lucky to be here. The evidence to date implies that we are alone, at least in this galaxy and at this point in time. One might call this evidence 'the ominous silence'.

(e) How Secure is Our Future?

I have always believed that, 'The ingenious man is never defeated', and ingenuity is certainly a quality in no short supply within our species. We are also capable of superhuman levels of collective achievement, as in times of war. On those grounds I would tend to be optimistic, but the challenges that lie ahead for us in the next century are certainly formidable. Will our intelligence be up to the task?

But why do we possess this preternaturally high level of intelligence? What possible evolutionary advantage could our ancient ancestors have derived from an ability to compose symphonies, paint masterpieces, write novels, and perform calculations in higher mathematics? Every other animal on the planet today has managed to survive very happily with levels of intelligence far lower than our own. Our closest living animal relatives are now the bonobos and chimpanzees, whose DNA is almost 99% identical to ours, yet we are incomparably more intelligent than they are. This wide disparity is difficult to account for in purely evolutionary terms, making us humans a uniquely freakish development indeed, even on this uniquely freakish planet. In his 2015 book *Homo Deus, a Brief History of Tomorrow*, Yuval Noah Harari suggests that we may have crossed a crucial evolutionary threshold, in that we are now so intelligent that we are capable of manufacturing artificial forms of intelligence that are more intelligent that we are! This claim, of course, is highly dependent on a precise definition of 'intelligence': is it the same thing as consciousness or creativity? It is true that in 1997 IBM's Deep Blue computer beat the world chess champion Gary Kasparov at his own game, something that I never expected to see in my lifetime. Deep Blue won only on aggregate, suffering some defeats by Kasparov, but in 2015 Google's AlphaGo programme beat world Go champion Fan Hui by five games to nil! This Chinese game of Go is even more complex than chess, played on a board with 361 squares as against a chess board's 64. In 2016 a programme known as MogAI developed by American Professor Allan Lictman successfully predicted a Trump victory in the 2016 presidential election race, confounding all the human pundits! Artificial intelligence would appear to be already greater than our own in some fields. In December 2017 newspapers reported the development of a new computer programme called Alpha Zero, a product of the American company Deep Mind, that was able to teach itself chess in just four hours, and is now able to beat convincingly all other chess computers, and every human player as well, every time. Some might describe the speed of developments in this field as frightening. The definition of 'intelligence' remains a moot point, but the fact is that the score so far stands at computers three, humans nil! Moreover, the development of quantum computers, which will be much more powerful, is now expected in the near future. Harari predicts that the rise of machine intelligence and genetic engineering will give us god-like powers, greatly extending human life spans and our technological abilities. But intelligent machines may also begin to steal human jobs, threatening large-scale unemployment, and worsening our present problems of social inequality. In fact Harari predicts something of a dystopian future as machines come to know us better than we know ourselves, so that we will be forced to continually turn to them for advice on how we should live our lives, right down to which marriage partners we should choose: not so much *homo deus* as *homo servus*! The possible advantages, and possible dangers of strong AI are enlarged upon by Max Tegmark in his recent book, *Life 3.0: Being Human in the Age of Artificial Intelligence* (2017). It may be that we are just a little too clever for our own good.

But all this evidence has been presented mainly to make the point that within this impossibly improbable universe, we live in an atypical solar system on the most improbable of all improbable planets. Yet even this most life-friendly of all conceivable planets is not *that* life-friendly, as its many extinction episodes have shown. We are exceedingly lucky to be here. We should all be down on our knees every day thanking whatever gods we believe in for our extreme good fortune. Even so, we may yet be in the position of the optimist who fell off the roof of a skyscraper and shouted in the window of every floor that he passed on the way down, 'I'm all right so far!' We should not take our extreme good fortune for granted. At the present time, however, we have even more than this to be grateful for, as the sections below will make clear.

The science of classification on the tree of life is known as taxonomy. There are many grades and sub-grades within it, and some variations of terminology from country to country, but basically below the three Domains mentioned above fall four Kingdoms, all within the domain Eukarya, those of Animalia, Plantae, Fungi, and Protista. The Kingdoms are divided into Phyla, and the Phyla into Classes. The Classes are divided into Orders, the orders into Families, and the Families into Genera. Finally, the Genera are divided into Species and Subspecies, the distinction between the last two and the rest being that while members of the same species may successfully interbreed, members of different species cannot.

For example, we humans can be taxonomically categorised very precisely. We belong to the Domain *Eukarya*, and the Kingdom *Animalia*. We are of the Phylum *Chordata*, which is to say that we have a spinal cord. Within this we are of the Subphylum *Vertabrata*, which means that our spinal cord is encased in a backbone. We belong to the Class *Mammalia*, giving birth to live young which are then breast fed. We are of the Order *Primates*, which includes the chimpanzees, our closest relatives, gorillas, bonobos, and orang-utans. Within this we are of the Family *Hominidae*, which included *homo habilis* and *homo erectus*, species now extinct. We are then of the Genus *Homo*, and the Species *Sapiens*, which included Neanderthal Man and Cro-Magnon man, species now also extinct. Finally we are of the Subspecies *Homo Sapiens Sapiens*, the only surviving members of the species *Homo Sapiens*.

This taxonomy casts us in a rather sinister light. The final extinction of *homo erectus* dates to about 50,000 years ago in Asia, around the time that our own species, *homo sapiens sapiens* was beginning to spread to that region. Where now is Peking man, and Java man? The disappearance of other subspecies of *homo sapiens*, such as the Denisovans of eastern Asia and the pygmy *homo floresiensis* of Indonesia also seem to have coincided with the arrival of our own subspecies in these regions. Further, what became of the Neanderthals and the Cro-Magnons? Both subspecies are now extinct. The Neanderthals were a sturdy and muscular race, well adapted for survival in the conditions of Ice Age Europe, while the Cro-Magnons were a tall, artistic and creative people, as may be seen from their surviving body ornaments, figurines, and cave paintings. Some of these paintings were discovered in the caves of Lascaux in the Dordogne in 1940. It is reported that when Picasso saw them he gasped with astonishment and declared, 'We have learned nothing in 30,000 years!' The story may be apocryphal, but the paintings are certainly impressive. Surviving skeletal remains show that both the Neanderthals and the Cro-Magnons had larger cranial capacities than our own – in other words, they had bigger brains. But what became of them? The archaeological record is clearest for the Neanderthals, and it shows that they retreated steadily across Europe from east to west between 50,000 and 30,000 years ago, just as our own subspecies was occupying the continent. The remains of the last Neanderthals, found in caves at Gibraltar, have been dated to c28,000 BC. But why the retreat? This is what Nick Barton, Professor of Paleolithic Archaeology at the University of Oxford, has to say about the Neanderthals in his book, *Ice Age Britain* (2005):

Ever since the first Neanderthal fossils were discovered in the 19th century in Europe, the popular picture of these prehistoric humans has been one of brutish cave dwellers, relegated to the margins of humanity as an evolutionary sideshow. But in recent years this image has been transformed by new excavations and analyses which show Neanderthals as fellow human beings with sophisticated tool-making skills and a complex social organization…Far from being 'dumb brutes', the Neanderthals were in fact highly intelligent and resourceful creatures, who had overcome most natural obstacles and become the human survival experts *par excellence* of the Ice Age world…in the end, we are left with the impression of a highly gifted people who survived in Europe for a much longer time than we have so far imagined. Perhaps, rather than considering them as failed models of ourselves, it is high time they were treated as equals in their own right. (pp. 79, 96)

Since the Neanderthals had survived successfully in Europe for tens of thousands of years, there are no obvious natural reasons for their fairly sudden demise. Perhaps they were not simply migrating across Europe from east to west but rather fleeing – from us. At last they reached Gibraltar, and then there was nowhere left to run to. But why was it not *homo sapiens sapiens* that retreated before the Neanderthals? It may be that we were not the biggest, nor the strongest, nor the fastest, nor even the most intelligent – we were simply the most murderous members of our species, which succeeded in wiping out all of its closest relatives. Even our closest surviving relatives, the bonobos and chimpanzees, are now officially listed as an endangered species. This of course is mere speculation, but the thesis is supported by the very evident fact that, having wiped out everyone else, we then set about trying to wipe out each other, in a series of ever-fiercer wars and genocides. Perhaps we should heed this warning from prehistory.

Our own subspecies is believed to have originated in east-central Africa some 250,000 years ago, and to have spread out from there to occupy the rest of the world in a series of migrations between 100,000 and 50,000 years ago. This proved to be bad news for other members of the Family *hominidae*, but they were not the only species which suffered. Palaeontologists of the future will find in the fossil record evidence of a sixth great extinction event, which began about 10,000 years ago, but which has gathered pace with frightening speed in just the last 300 years, affecting in particular the megafauna of the world. But the palaeontologists will not have to rely on fossil evidence alone for an explanation of this latest disaster, for its causes have already been well documented in written records. We are in fact living through the first great extinction with a purely biological cause since the Oxygen Catastrophe of two billion years ago. That cause is, of course, ourselves.

This latest extinction is variously referred to as the Holocene Extinction, or the Sixth Extinction, or sometimes the Anthropocene Extinction. Many scientific disciplines are now coming to recognise a new era, which has been named 'The Anthropocene' (from the Greek άνθωπος, *anthropos*, man) and dated, by general agreement, from 1950, because the so-called 'Great Acceleration' in humankind's influence on the planet has been dated from the middle years of the twentieth century.But this term has been so recently coined that it has not yet found its way into most dictionaries. As the name implies, it suggests that mankind itself has now become the principle agency of change, the key factor in shaping the development of our world, and the current 'Sixth Extinction' has been only one example of the impact of our species. In his splendidly detailed book,*Extinction: A Radical History* (2016) Ashley Dawson has suggested that the present pace of extinctions may be running at the rate of 100 species a day, if plants, fish, birds, insects, and all land animals are to be considered. This would make it the worst ecological disaster since the K-T event of 66 million years ago. Dawson links these developments to the capitalist ethos which pervades our society, and in particular to the 'let 'er rip' capitalism of the last few decades, politely named 'neoliberalism', although other terms have been used to describe it. It is certainly true that neoliberals tend to take a somewhat dismissive approach towards one of the most prominent concerns of our time, the issue of climate change. The cavalier attitude adopted by Friedrich Hayek towards the preservation of Earth's natural resources will be noted in the Economics section below. Nigel Lawson (b.1932), who served as Chancellor of the Exchequer under Margaret Thatcher from 1983 to 1989, is another example of the neoliberal genre. Global warming? Sure, but why worry? With a background in journalism, Lawson published a short book in 2008 with the title, *An Appeal to Reason: a Cool Look at Global Warming.* Nigel had done his homework on this one, bringing out clearly all the uncertainties of the science on climate change. He then took us into a detailed cost/benefit analysis on the problem of what to do about it. Here, although the science was so uncertain, there was no doubt about Nigel's conclusions: battling global warming simply wasn't worth the cost: warming was even good for you. 'Warmer but richer is in fact healthier than colder but poorer.' (p. 33) He concludes his book with the lines,

> We appear to have entered a new age of unreason, which threatens to be as economically harmful as it is profoundly disquieting. It is from this, above all, that we really do need to save the planet. (p. 106)

So that's clear enough then: we simply cannot afford to do anything about global warming. It seems that very serious political, social, economic, and ecological challenges lie ahead for us. On November 4, 2016, the Paris Agreement on Climate Change came into force. Nearly all of the world's countries were signatories to the Agreement, but it amounted to little more than pious declarations of intent to cut greenhouse gas emissions on their part. President Trump announced that he would pull the USA out of the Agreement in 2017. Since then China and India have been dragging their feet, pointing out that the West grew rich by burning fossil fuels, but is now lecturing them for doing the same. Russia too has been dragging its feet, since global warming could actually benefit its vast northern territories, and it has vast reserves of oil and natural gas, which form its main exports. while Australia has massive coal reserves that it is eager to mine and sell to China and India, both of which still rely heavily on coal-fired power stations. The prospects for concerted and effective global action in the near future to reduce greenhouse gas emissions look poor. The COP 26 meeting of November 2021 was far from a resounding success.

When it comes to ecology, the problems facing us are most clearly spelled out by Tony Juniper of the Cambridge Institute for Sustainability Leadership in his book, *What's Really Happening to Our Planet?* (2016). The figures, on the face of things, look alarming. World population has recently quadrupled in just a single lifetime; my lifetime as a matter of fact, rising from roughly two billion in 1940 to almost eight billion today. Clearly, this rate of growth cannot be sustained: another quadrupling over the next 80 years would be a disaster. Not only would we have more people, but the populace would also expect something like the present European standard of living on a global scale: it has been estimated that we would need another two planets just to provide enough raw materials for us all! However, there is hope for the future. People are living longer, but a rapidly falling birth rate in the world as a whole means that the pace of population growth is slowing. According to current United Nations Reports, the populations of China, India, Europe, Russia, and Indonesia should actually be in decline by 2100. Only the populations of Nigeria and the USA will still be increasing. Plummeting birth rates mean that the sustainability goal of only two births per woman on average may have been reached by 2050. Only in Africa is the birth rate expected to be higher, and even there it should have fallen to under three births per woman. This offers some hope that world population will level off at somewhere between nine and eleven billion by 2100 or shortly after, and will cease to grow after that.

Of course, these projections depend on the assumption that living standards will rise in the Third World, and that infant mortality rates will therefore decline. Rising living standards and the emancipation of women always bring with them lower birth rates. It is therefore in the interests of the richer countries to help the underdeveloped world to achieve economic growth, something that was at least their intention between about 1947 and 1977. With the rise of neoliberal economic philosophies, however, the role of the developed countries changed to become one of exploiters rather than assisters. Drawing heavily on economic history to prove his points, the Cambridge economist Ha-Joon Chang brilliantly chronicles this sad transition in his 2007 book, *Bad Samaritans*. Neoliberal economic policies such as free trade, 'sound' money, deregulation, and no state support for their infant industries were imposed on underdeveloped nations, actually slowing their rate of economic development in many instances, most notably in Latin America. But assuming that the IMF (International Monetary Fund), the World Bank, and the WTO (World Trade Organization) can see the error of their ways in time, we may yet achieve the fall in birth rates that our planet so desperately needs. In addition we will need a massive move away from fossil fuels to sustainable energy sources, and a whole new technology directed at the production of goods that are almost 100% recyclable. Perhaps we can devise vegetable-based meat substitutes that taste just like the real thing, and turn to 'vertical farming' in warehouses under controlled conditions. But these are tall orders indeed, and of course we may fail: greed, selfishness, and short-termism may take their toll. Nor has the threat of nuclear annihilation vanished simply because it is less talked about these days. This is more likely to occur by accident or miscalculation than by deliberate intent, but today we see a dangerous war in Ukraine, while China is threatening Taiwan, which the USA has promised to defend. For a species like ours, warfare is not an unusual occurrence. That would be a fine joke indeed: *soi-disant homo sapiens sapiens*, *stupor mundi*, the wonder of the world, so bloody intelligent that he managed to wreck his only planet and wipe himself out. You could die laughing at that one. But David Attenborough in his recent book *A Life on Our Planet* (2020) suggests that we are already well down the road to doing precisely that, unless we can very quickly change our ways. Further worst possible scenarios have been sketched out for us by Mike Berners-Lee in *There is no Planet B* (2019) and David Wallace-Wells in *The Uninhabitable Earth* (2019). Even if our fears over climate change have been exaggerated, many other problems lie ahead: pollution, soil degradation, species loss, overpopulation, etc. We had better keep our fingers crossed. So far we have been very lucky indeed, but we should not take our good fortune for granted: time is desperately short. If we have not achieved sustainability by 2100, we will be in very serious trouble indeed, and 2100 is now only one human lifespan away. There is no doubt that we *can* do it: but will we? The steps we will need to take to achieve 'net zero' carbon economies are clear enough, and recycling technologies that can bring us to zero waste economies already exist: both of these measures simply need to be scaled up. I believe we will succeed, but the path ahead will be a hard one. The present world economy has such a momentum behind it that it will be difficult to change its course.

In the meantime, just how lucky have we been? Next time you walk down the street, do not take the people that you pass for granted: they are not 'normal' and everyday creations. Within the context of the universe, they are freakishly abnormal entities indeed. You are looking at the product of four billion years of fortuitous evolution. Just a few million years ago the ancestors of those people were primitive, shambling, ape-like creatures little removed from the beasts, but now, members of that species are unravelling the secrets of the universe. When you pass a motor car, do not assume it is 'usual': in the context of the universe it is not, so pause to wonder. The carbon and iron that make up the steel of its body were forged in the raging heart of a long-dead star billions of years ago. On the violent death of that star, the constituent elements that it had created were driven into space to become stardust. That dust found its way into the accretion disc surrounding our own infant sun, and later coalesced to form part of the crust of our planet. From there they were extracted, and worked by the hands of the most improbable beings in the galaxy into the machine that you see before you. In the context of the universe, a car is not just a car: it is a miracle of improbability.

The appreciation of facts like these should, in my view, contribute to the happiness of the philosopher. This chapter has been dedicated largely to showing just how unusual our planet is, and how lucky we are to be here at all. But in addition we should remember that our remarkable planet has played host to a huge variety of life forms, of which our species is only one. The odds against you being born as a member of *our* species were also enormous, but you were improbably lucky again. In addition, you were fortunate enough to be born in the right place at the right time if you happen to live in the developed world.

We who live here in the early twenty-first century have many reasons to be grateful. You are a member of what Warren Buffett called, 'the lucky sperm club'. You are enjoying a higher standard of living now than has any generation of the past, and higher too than that of many other people on the planet today. How lucky can you get? Do not take for granted the advantages that Science has bestowed upon you. If you were to be transported back in time to the year 1750 and forced to live then, you would feel that you had been delivered into hell. Can you imagine the standards of dentistry, of medicine, of sanitation, of housing, that prevailed in those times? No electricity or central heating for the people of those days: no clean, running water in every home: there was only a stream, a well, or the parish pump, all sources liable to pollution. There was no knowledge of how bacteria and viruses caused diseases, and so no awareness of the importance of cleanliness. Could you live with no bathrooms, no toilet paper, no sanitary protection, no toothpaste, and with permanent infestation by fleas and lice? I could go on (trust me, I'm a social and economic historian) but you get the general picture. Worst of all was the ignorance of the times, that stifling, blanketing cloud of unknowing that drove eighteenth-century intellectuals to despair. Of all the benefits that life in the twenty-first century has conferred upon me, it is the precious gift of knowledge that I value most of all. For the first time we have at last a credible explanation for our existence. So give thanks – ingratitude would be most inappropriate.

The philosopher with a knowledge of science has many 'reasons to be cheerful'. However, the personal circumstances of some individuals may make it difficult for them to feel happy nevertheless. Is there a scientific formula for happiness? Perhaps not for, as noted above, happiness is subjective. But the question of happiness will be examined in the Conclusion to this volume, with the help of what might be described as a 'scientific' approach.

I should at this point perhaps acknowledge the existence of a great rival to my thesis on the importance of ideas in the person of Jared Mason Diamond (b. 1937), an American scientist born in Boston Massachusetts. Having studied at both Harvard and Trinity College Cambridge, he became a professor of physiology at UCLA Medical School in Los Angeles in 1968. However, over the years his interests moved to environmental history, and he became a professor of geography at UCLA in 2002. In 1991 he brought out his first well-known book entitled, *The Third Chimpanzee: The Evolution and Future of the Human Animal.* A later edition was entitled, The *Rise and Fall of the Third Chimpanzee: How Our Animal Heritage Affects the Way We Live.* Then in 2004 he produced what might be described as the definitive edition with the title, *The Rise and Fall of the Third Chimpanzee: Evolution and Human Life.* Finally, in 2014 Diamond brought out a fourth, abridged version with the title, *The Third Chimpanzee for Young People.* Each edition included amendments to its predecessor.

Diamond's best-known book, *Guns, Germs, and Steel: A Short History of Everybody for the Last 13,000 Years* came out in 1997, but a later edition of 2016, with amendments, was entitled, *Guns, Germs, and Steel: The Fates of Human Societies.* Both of these two latter books make the same case. Diamond argues that it was not ideas that shaped the destinies of nations, but rather physical factors, geographic, technological, and biological. Taking these as his yardstick, Diamond compares Western Europe with other parts of the world, and concludes that it was these factors which gave the Europeans technological and biological advantages in the eighteenth and nineteenth centuries, enabling them to conquer and colonize other parts of the world. He rules out racial superiority as a factor in the success of the Europeans. Well, we can all agree with that. The Europeans of the nineteenth century certainly *thought* that they were racially superior to everyone else, but today we know better. As shown above, all humans in the world today are not only members of the same species, *homo sapiens*, but also all members of the same subspecies, *homo sapiens sapiens*, the only surviving hominid on the face of the planet today. Racism is therefore simply unscientific, as well as being socially unacceptable.

In his book *Guns, Germs, and Steel* Diamond argues that European firearms in the eighteenth and nineteenth centuries were superior to all those to be found in other parts of the world, which is a reasonable proposition. His reference to steel applies mainly to the ships built by Europeans in the nineteenth century, which again were superior to those then being built in other parts of the world. These two factors certainly gave Europeans the edge, once they had made the philosophical decision to go out conquering and colonizing other parts of the world. But when it comes to germs, Diamond is on less firm ground. His thesis applies best here to Australia and to the Americas, whose populations had been isolated from other parts of the world for thousands of years before the arrival of the Spanish and Portuguese to the Americas in the sixteenth century. Neither had they been great keepers of livestock: the majority in those continents had been hunter-gatherers. This meant that their populations had not acquired resistance to European diseases, in particular those zoonotic infections acquired from domesticated livestock, such as flu, tuberculosis, and anthrax. These diseases, together with smallpox, pneumonia, measles, and plague (the Black Death) which were still endemic in Europe at that time, devastated native populations once they had been introduced by

European invaders. Diamond argues that those diseases helped the Europeans to subjugate, and in some cases almost wipe out, the native populations, making conquest and colonization that much easier for them. This thesis applies well in Australia and the Americas, but less well in Africa, India, tropical Indo-China, and Indonesia. When it came to diseases, those regions gave better than they got: indeed, Africa was known as 'the white man's grave' in the nineteenth century. Waiting for the Europeans when they arrived in central Africa were malaria, yellow fever, sleeping sickness, typhus, dengue fever, hepatitis, and numerous other tropical diseases. These infections in fact acted as a *defence* against European penetration of the continent. By contrast, the only disease that the Americas had been able to give to Europeans was syphilis. India, Indo-China, and Indonesia too had their fair share of native tropical diseases, including malaria, hepatitis, typhoid, dysentery, jaundice, cholera, hookworm infestation, and numerous intestinal infections. During the Burma campaign of World War II the British 14th Army suffered a disease to battle casualty ratio of 121 to one in 1943, 19 to one in 1944, and 3.4 to one in 1945 as the army slowly learned how to deal with tropical diseases. (Philip, B. 'Scrub Typhus in World War II' *The Journal of Parasitology* Vol. 34 No. 3 (June 1948) p. 169) As in Kenya, the British in India preferred to withdraw to the 'White Highlands' as much as possible so as to escape from pestilence. The populations of Africa, India, Indo-China, and Indonesia were *not* of course driven to near extinction by European diseases. Rather, it was the Europeans themselves who were decimated by native diseases when they entered those regions.

China and Japan were of course never fully conquered by Europeans as part of their colonial adventures, but both were bullied by them in the mid-nineteenth century with the aid of superior European ships and guns. The Western powers wanted to buy Chinese goods, especially their silks, cottons, porcelain, and tea, but also pepper and ginger. On the other hand, there was very little that the Chinese wanted to buy from the West, so foreigners were forced to pay for Chinese goods with silver, draining them of specie. As trade expanded the Westerners became increasingly desperate to find a product that they could sell to China, to improve their trade balances. It was the British who first hit upon the idea of opium, made from the opium poppies which grew in abundance in British India. But the Chinese resisted the import of opium into their country because of its detrimental effects on their population. This resulted in the First Opium War of 1839-42 in which China was defeated, forced to accept free trade in opium, and to cede the port of Hong Kong to Britain. But China still tried to restrict opium imports, and this resulted in the second opium war of 1856-60, in which Britain was joined by France, Russia, and the USA. China was again defeated, and again forced to pay heavy reparations in silver. More trading concessions were demanded from China, together with the opening of a number of Chinese ports to Western trade. The treaties which ended these wars were referred to by the Chinese as 'The Unequal Treaties'. They certainly were.

Japan too was bullied by Western powers in the nineteenth century. It had been alarmed as early as 1808 by the threatening attitude of the British frigate Phaeton in Nagasaki harbour, the only Japanese port then open to foreigners, and began to make some efforts to update its antiquated cannons, but made little progress. They were therefore still unprepared when Commodore Matthew Perry (1794-1858) of the US navy arrived at Tokyo Bay in July, 1853 with a small American fleet of steam-powered vessels. This area had been banned to foreign shipping, but Perry sailed boldly in, ignoring Japanese requests to withdraw. In negotiations Perry demanded that Japan should open its ports to trade with the USA. His ships were armed with the new Paixhans cannons, invented by the Frenchman Henri-Joseph Paixhans (1783-1854). These were still muzzle loaders, but weighed 2.5 tonnes each, had a calibre of 220 mm, and could fire explosive shells on a straight trajectory over a range of two miles. Invited aboard Perry's ships, the Japanese quickly realized that they were completely outgunned. A thinly veiled threat by Perry to bombard Tokyo was enough to bring the Japanese to terms. When Perry returned in February 1854, with eight vessels, steam powered and well armed, the Japanese were ready to negotiate, and signed the Convention of Kanagawa in March, 1854. In 1858 a number of other treaties were forced on Japan by Western powers, notably the Treaty of Amity and Commerce with the USA. But those were to be the last 'unequal treaties' imposed on Japan by 'gunboat diplomacy'. The country began to modernize immediately, quickly acquiring Western technologies at a much faster pace than did China. In consequence Japan was able to defeat Russia in a war of 1904-5, a ground-breaking achievement for a non-white power at that time: the Europeans should have taken note. Later, Japan was able to seize Taiwan and Korea, and in the 1930s to occupy large swathes of China itself. In 1941, just 87 years after Perry's bullying visits, Japan felt powerful enough to challenge the USA for control of the Pacific. This remarkable development had nothing to do with a change in the natural conditions of Japan, rather everything to do with a change in Japanese philosophy over the intervening 87 years. But Japan had in fact moved only from one wrong philosophy to another, from a firm belief in smug isolationism to a firm belief in overseas conquest and colonisation. In this, of course, they were simply following the rather bad example that had been set for them by the Europeans. But their new philosophy was to have serious consequences for Japan. Their notorious attack on Pearl Harbour Pearl Harbour took place on December 7, 1941, and was a superficial success, but the admiral in charge, Isoroku Yamamoto (1884-1943) had his misgivings. He is said to have declared, 'We have simply roused a sleeping giant, and have filled him with a terrible resolve'. Ironically, it could be argued that America itself had done much the same thing when it had forced Japan out of isolationism in the previous century. But Japan was to change its philosophy again after 1945, this time for the better.

The question now arises of why China and Japan had fallen so far behind the West in military technology that they could be so easily bullied by Western powers in the mid-nineteenth century. The answer to this question has nothing to do with geography, biology, or natural resources, but everything to do with philosophy; political philosophy in this case. Some centuries earlier, both countries had made the political decision to adopt isolationist policies, and to minimize as far as possible all trade and contact with the West. Their decisions had arisen from arrogance and complacency. Both countries believed that they already had everything that they needed, and regarded Westerners as 'barbarians', who could have nothing but a corrupting influence upon their sophisticated cultures. It had been their isolationist philosophies that had allowed them to fall so far behind the Europeans in technological terms.

In an interview given to the journal *Edge* for June 6, 1999 entitled, bizarrely enough, 'How to Get Rich' (available on line) Diamond had this to say about the disadvantages of isolationism and, he could have added, the disadvantages of having a powerful, centralized, conservative, and dictatorial government, another product of political philosophy. Diamond wrote,

> To understand these losses in extreme isolation, the easiest case to understand is Japan, because the loss of firearms in Japan was witnessed and described. It took place in a literate society. Guns arrived in Japan around 1543 with two Portuguese adventurers who stepped ashore, pulled out a gun, and shot a duck on the wing. A Japanese nobleman happened to be there, was very impressed, bought those two guns for $10,000, and had his sword maker imitate them. Within a decade Japan had more guns per capita than any other country in the world, and by the year 1600 Japan had the best guns of any country in the world. And then, over the course of the next century, Japan gradually abandoned guns.
>
> What happened was that the samurai, the warrior class in Japan, had been used to fighting by standing up in front of their armies and making a graceful speech, the other opposing Samurai made an answering graceful speech, and then they had one-on-one combat. The Samurai discovered that the peasants with their guns would shoot the Samurai while the Samurai were making their graceful speeches. So the Samurai realized that guns were a danger because they were such an equalizer. The Samurai first restricted the licensing of gun factories to a hundred factories, and then they licensed fewer factories, and then they said that only three factories could repair guns, and then they said that those three factories could make only a hundred guns a year, then ten guns a year, then three guns a year, until by the 1840s when Commodore Perry came to Japan, Japan no longer had any guns. That represents the loss of a very powerful technology. (pp. 8-9)

There is much to arouse our suspicions in this account. Sixteenth-century firearms were notoriously inaccurate, and to bring down a bird on the wing with one would have been a prodigious feat. The instantaneous transformation of swordsmith into gunsmith seems unlikely, and how can Diamond be sure that in 1553 Japan had 'more guns per capita than any other country in the world'? Why did the Samurai put up with peasants shooting them for so long before they finally banned guns? The $10,000 figure is suspiciously round, and of course Perry visited Japan in the 1850s, not the 1840s. However, assuming that the gist of the story is true, it would account for the lack of personal firearms in nineteenth-century Japan. But both the forms of government adopted in China and Japan and their isolationist policies had been the fruits of political philosophy, and nothing to do with physical factors. Diamond undermines his own case by taking them as examples. Now the Europeans too could have decided to trade only with themselves. Europe too had everything that it needed – all the timber, all the coal, all the mineral ores, and all the food-producing capacity. But the Europeans adopted a very different philosophy. They were outward-looking and adventurous, eager to explore the rest of the world, to trade widely, and to colonize underdeveloped areas. The advanced technologies developed by the Europeans in the nineteenth century would have had little impact on the rest of the world but for the adventurous and outward-looking spirits of the Europeans who, from 1500 onwards took a strong interest in overseas exploration, trade, conquest, and colonization.

But had the philosophies of East and West been reversed, the world could be a very different place today. In the fifteenth century, it was China that enjoyed a technological lead over the rest of the world. The number of inventions that China had to its credit by 1400 is far too long to list here, but they are conveniently catalogued for us by Wikipedia, under the simple heading, 'List of Chinese Inventions'. Chief among them were paper making, printing using movable type, paper money, the compass, and gunpowder. From this last came cannons, rockets, and mortar bombs. The Chinese had also invented the crossbow and trebuchet centuries before the Europeans, and had both the cupola furnace and the blast furnace, with bellows powered by water wheels. The Chinese had mastered the puddling process and the finery forge for the production of steel by 300 AD. Long-distance canals with multiple locks were in existence long before the Europeans had thought of the idea. Chinese clocks were also far in advance of any that could be found in Europe. A host of everyday things such as oven-baked bricks, the wheelbarrow, and the saw had first been devised in China. The Wikipedia list is culled mainly from Joseph Needham's monumental seven-volume *Science and Civilisation in China* (1954-2008), and runs to 173 items up to 1400. Diamond argues that rivalry between the independent European powers acted as a spur to invention among them, but China proved that large, monolithic empires could also be extremely inventive.

Moreover, perhaps most significantly of all, Chinese shipbuilding technology was the most advanced in the world by 1400. Not only were Chinese junks of the time far larger than any ships to be found in Europe, but they also incorporated multiple watertight bulkheads, unlike European ships, and had heavy, iron-bound keels to provide stability together with cleverly designed rudders to aid with steering, mounted on large sternposts. S.K. Church, writing in the journal *Monumenta Serica* (Vol. 53(2005) pp. 1-43) describes the discovery by Chinese archaeologists in 1962 of the rudder remains of one of the largest junks. The rudder post was 36 feet long and 1.25 feet in diameter. Such a rudder would have been appropriate for steering a vessel of up to 500 feet in length. This would have been one of the legendary 'treasure ships', the largest of the junks, said to have been built with up to nine masts and many-sectioned hulls. However, Church confined herself to a more detailed investigation of smaller craft in her article, 'Zeng He: An Investigation into the Plausibility of 450-Foot Treasure Ships'. By comparison, Nelson's HMS *Victory*, one of the largest wooden ships ever built in the West, had measured only 227.5 feet from stem to stern. Controversy still rages over whether such large wooden ships could have been seagoing, but even China's smaller junks must have been among the largest wooden ships ever built.

Between 1405 and 1433 the Ming government sponsored seven naval expeditions under the command of admiral Zeng He (1371-1433). His fleets consisted of a number of specialized craft, depending on the destinations of each voyage. Some carried horses, some troops, and some were warships armed with cannons. There were also fresh water transports and supply ships carrying, among other things, citrus fruit to prevent scurvy, and brown rice to ward off beriberi. There is good documentary evidence to suggest that Zeng's first fleet consisted of the staggering number of 317 ships with 28,000 crewmen. (Tamura, E.H. et al., *China: Understanding its Past* (1997) p. 70) Other sources suggest 250 ships, still a remarkable number. Such fleets could easily have circumnavigated the globe, stopping off for fresh supplies. In fact one writer, Gavin Menzies (1937-2020) argues that they did do just that in his book, *1421: The Year China Discovered the World* (2002), discovering most of the world en route. But his views have been rejected not only by British sinologists, but also by the Chinese themselves. In any event, whatever the Chinese may have achieved with their voyages was of no consequence, for the Chinese made nothing of their discoveries on that alleged circumnavigation. In the event, this feat was left to the Europeans with the Magellan-Elcano expedition of 1519 to 1522, nearly a century later. It had been a desperate venture: of the five ships and 270 men who had set out, only one ship with 18 survivors limped back to Seville. All of the other crewmen, including Magellan himself, had been lost en route. The voyage was completed by Magellan's second-in-command, Juan Elcano. But those 19 Europeans had done it: the very first undisputed circumnavigation of the globe.

Zeng He confined himself to the Indian Ocean, visiting Brunei, Java, Thailand, Southeast Asia, India, the Horn of Africa, Arabia, and the east coast of Africa. From this last destination Zeng brought back exotic animals, zebras, ostriches, and even a giraffe for the amusement of the Chinese court. On Zeng's fourth voyage he brought back envoys from thirty states around the Indian Ocean to pay their respects at the Ming court. These were essentially prestige voyages, designed to impress the region with the overwhelming might of China, although tribute was demanded from only a few states. The point here is, however, that Zeng's fleets could easily have gone much further. They could have sailed to the east, crossed the Pacific, and reached the west coasts of North and South America. They could have sailed further south, and reached the north coast of Australia. Had the Chinese been bent on colonization, they could easily have achieved it. At that time China, the most technologically advanced country on the globe, had the world at its feet. The great age of European exploration and colonization had not yet begun: the world lay open for the taking. China had the guns, the steel, the ships, the population, and at least as many endemic diseases as the Europeans. Indeed, the bubonic plague had originated in China. They could easily have colonized the Indonesian Islands, the north and east coasts coast of Australia, the East coast of Africa, and the west coasts of the Americas. Large parts of Africa, Australia, Indonesia, and the Americas could have been Chinese-speaking today. As it happened of course, the whole of North and South America, Australia, and many parts of Africa speak European languages today, while English is the second language of India and Pakistan. With the languages came European cultures, European mores, and of course Christianity, spreading across the globe, making it the world's most widely followed religion today. But there was also a dark side to all that European expansion. In North and South America, in Africa, and in Australia millions of native inhabitants were slaughtered or enslaved to make way for the Europeans. Their expansion had entailed genocide on a scale far greater than that of the Holocaust. But while the Holocaust is vividly remembered, that genocide is conveniently forgotten. Only the Holocaust stirs in us a particular horror. Could this be because its victims were white?

Meanwhile, China had remained confined to its traditional territories. But in the fifteenth century it was the Ming dynasty that had available to it all the material resources necessary to achieve global colonisation. The fact that the Chinese did not do so was entirely down to their philosophy. The Xuande Emperor, who ruled from 1426 to 1435, concluded that such overseas expeditions were simply not worth the effort. He declared,

> 'Some far-off countries pay their tribute to me at much expense and through great difficulties, all of which are by no means my own wish. Messages should be forwarded to them to reduce their tribute so as to avoid high and unnecessary expenses on both sides'. (Chang, K., 'The Maritime Scene in China at the Dawn of Great European Discoveries' *Journal of the American Oriental Society* Vol. 94 No. 3 (1974) p. 347)

This had seemed like a sensible philosophy at the time, since the seven prestige voyages had been very expensive to launch. China was complete in itself, and obviously superior to any other country, so why bother to have anything to do with them? China was unrivalled at sea, but ever threatened by northern 'barbarians', pressing on their northern frontier. The great fleets were mothballed, left to rot in their harbours, and China built no more. Her policy of minimizing contact with the rest of the world dated from this time, with momentous consequences for the futures of Africa, Australia, Indonesia, the Americas, and indeed China itself. Like Islam at roughly the same time, China sank into a kind of self-satisfied torpor, allowing the Europeans to draw far ahead of both of them in terms of technological developments, and also in terms of political and scientific thought. In the last analysis, for good or ill, it is their philosophies, in particular their political and economic philosophies, that decide the destinies of nations.

V On Politics

(a) Introduction

When it comes to the vexed question of how we should be governed, our species is still far from reaching a consensus view. Immediately following the fall of the Berlin wall in 1989 the American political scientist Francis Fukuyama (b. 1952) published a short article in the journal *The National Interest* (Summer 1989) with the intriguing title, 'The End of History?' which he later expanded into a book following the collapse of the Soviet Union in 1991,*The End of History and the Last Man* (1992).The gist of his thesis was that, with the collapse of Communism, the world-wide triumph of Western-style liberal democracy, accompanied by free enterprise private capitalism, was inevitable. It would now be only a matter of time before this system was adopted everywhere around the globe. This would mark the final end point of humanity's political and economic evolution and would be, in this sense, the end of history. Well, all that was thirty years ago now, and we are still waiting to see the fulfilment of Fukuyama's prophecy. Many nasty little dictatorships are still in existence around the world, and even some major powers, such as Russia and China, are still far from being Western-style liberal democracies. But when it came to his forecast on the spread of free enterprise private capitalism, Fukuyama was much more on the money. Today, even the world's nominally Communist countries, such as Cuba and China, tolerate large private enterprise sectors in their economies. In Cuba these deliver some 25% of annual GDP, while in China, according to Chinese government figures released in November 2019, private enterprises accounted for 60% of GDP, 80% of urban employment, and 90% of all new jobs created in that year.

Fukuyama himself began his career as a neoconservative politically, and a neoliberal economically but, like Karl Popper, he later distanced himself from both movements as they became more extreme. Writing in the *New York Times Magazine* for February 19, 2006 Fukuyama declared, 'Neoconservatism, as both a political symbol and a body of thought, has evolved into something I can no longer support.' In an interview with the *New Statesman* for October 17, 2018 Fukuyama was asked about his views on 'socialism'. He replied,

> If you mean redistributive programmes that try to address this big imbalance in both incomes and wealth that has emerged then yes, I think not only that it can come back, it ought to come back. This extended period, which started with Reagan and Thatcher, in which a certain set of ideas about the benefits of unregulated markets took hold, in many ways it's had a disastrous effect. At this juncture it seems to me that certain things Karl Marx said are turning out to be true. He talked about the crisis of overproduction...that workers would be impoverished and there would be insufficient demand.

In the Economics chapter below, we will see how politics and economics are very closely interrelated. In the Conclusion it will be shown how our so-called 'democracies' in the West remain very vulnerable to plutocratic subversion, and what we should do to change that situation.

But the best way to understand how we have arrived at the forms of government that we know today is to view their development from a historical perspective. In paragraph six of Book IX of his *Confessions*, an autobiographical work published posthumously in 1782 (understandably in view of its contents) Jean-Jacques Rousseau (1712-1778) declared, 'J'avais vu que tout tenait radicalement à la politique et que, de quelque façon qu'on s'y prit, aucun people ne serait que ce que la nature de son gouvernement le ferait etre'. (I had come to see that everything depends entirely upon politics, and that whichever way you look at it, no nation will ever be anything other than what the nature of its government may make it). This was a very sweeping, Rousseauesque sort of statement, but it can scarcely be denied that he had something of a point there, underlining the importance of political thought in the history of our social and economic development. His casual statement about the importance of government was later to be heartily endorsed by Daron Acemoglu and James A. Robinson in their 2012 book, *Why Nations Fail: the Origins of Power, Prosperity, and Poverty*. Here, they stress the importance of institutional factors in determining the wealth of nations, adducing a great deal more evidence in support of their proposition than was ever supplied by Rousseau. The question of how we should live as individuals is challenging enough, but the question of how we should live as communities is even more challenging, and more important. From the historical perspective, however, it is appropriate that we should have considered both philosophy and religion before turning to politics, because over the course of human history our political structures have been underpinned first by force, later by religion, and finally by philosophy, specifically political thought. In more recent times, economic thought too has come to play an increasingly important role in political decision making.

After two thousand years of thought on the subject of political philosophy, by 1770 Edmund Burke (1720-97) could write towards the end of his *Thoughts on the Causes of the Present Discontents*,

> It is the business of the speculative philosopher to mark the proper ends of government. It is the business of the politician, who is but the philosopher in action, to find out the proper means towards these ends, and to employ them with effect. (2009 ed.) p. 49

This theme was later taken up by the German philosopher Heinrich Heine (1797-1856), who wrote *The History of Religion and Philosophy in Germany,* first published in 1834. In Vol. III he declares,

Mark this well, you proud men of action! You are, after all, nothing but the unwitting agents of the men of thought who, often in quiet self-effacement, mark out most exactly all your doings in advance. (p. 19)

Much the same kind of observation had also been made by Friedrich Hegel (1770-1831), and his fellow idealist, the Italian philosopher Benedetto Croce (1866-1952), who claimed that politics was but 'philosophy in action'. Even making allowance for the inbred arrogance of philosophers, there is certainly more than a grain of truth here. Napoleon Bonaparte, despite his dictatorial tendencies, was clearly a man of Enlightenment thought, as was illustrated by his Code Napoleon, while Lenin, Stalin, and Mao Zedong had certainly been influenced by the writings of Karl Marx. It usually takes quite some time for the thought of philosophers to filter through to the politicians, but if we accept Rousseau's point about the supreme importance of political regimes, then we must also accept that the philosophical principles on which those regimes were based are also of supreme importance.

Politics is basically about power, and its distribution within a society. Men seem to have a natural tendency to divide themselves into the leaders and the led, an inclination that probably pre-dates our humanity. Troops of monkeys and packs of wolves also adopt hierarchical social structures with dominant males, while herds of African elephants prefer a matriarchy, with a dominant female taking the lead. Leadership, however, has always been associated with power. In our early human societies, it was the strongest and the bravest male who tended to take a leading role. When the Plains Indians of North America were first discovered by early European settlers, they were still a Stone Age people, living in migrating hunter-gatherer bands, ignorant of all forms of metal working, and even of the wheel. But they had their tribal chieftains, and sometimes also a council of elders. The son of a chieftain might have a better chance of becoming a chief himself, but only if he was up to the job: there was no strict hereditary principle. The tribes of course fought with each other, and so prowess in battle was highly prized.

Palaeontologists are an argumentative group, but the balance of opinion today is that our particular sub-species, *homo sapiens sapiens* (truly smartarsed man) emerged in east-central Africa some 200,000 to 250,000 years ago. But for at least the first 190,000 years of our existence on the planet, we lived as hunter-gatherers. During this time, the archaeologists and anthropologists tell us, a great variety of hunter-gatherer societies came into existence. Some had head men or councils of elders, but others were highly egalitarian, with a rotating leadership, or no fixed pattern of leadership at all. This makes generalisations about hunter-gatherer societies rather difficult, and it remains a controversial area. However, some form of tribal leadership system was probably the norm. The rich grave goods found with some individuals at hunter-gatherer burial sites suggest that these men had taken a leadership role. Tribal warfare would have meant that hunter-gatherer societies would have needed good leaders. Some tribes may of course have lived peacefully in isolation, but the only two major nomadic groups that Europeans were able to observe in the nineteenth century, The Plains Indians of North America and the Aborigines of Australia, both engaged in intermittent tribal warfare. It may indeed have been tribal warfare, in conjunction with a rising population, that spurred the first migrations of our particular species out of their homeland in east-central Africa some 100,000 years ago, led by our more enterprising cousins, the Neanderthals.

It seems that leadership roles, with an associated concentration of power, have long been endemic in human societies, certainly pre-dating the Neolithic Agricultural Revolution. But equally ancient must have been tribal spiritual beliefs, and here again leadership figures would have emerged in the form of shamans and witch doctors. To be human is to wonder, to speculate about the nature of the world, and to imagine the existence of gods and spirits. At Göbekli Tepe, an archaeological site in southern Turkey, a number of nomadic tribes appear to have co-operated in the raising of a stone circle temple, similar to Stonehenge, that has been dated to c. 9600 BC, before settled agriculture had appeared in this region. Göbekli Tepe is claimed to be the oldest religious site ever discovered, and it suggests that at least some of our hunter-gatherer ancestors pursued active spiritual lives. On the other hand, nomadic peoples did not normally go in for carved stone architecture, and Göbekli Tepe must be highly unusual, perhaps even unique for its time. The site is discussed in *National Geographic* magazine for June, 2011.

Although the Neolithic Agricultural Revolution marked a most significant milestone in human history, setting us on the path to the modern world, its immediate effects were not entirely beneficial. For the first 190,000 years of our existence as a sub-species, 'politics' as we would understand the term today, with the cut and thrust of organised confrontational groupings, scarcely figured in our history. Archaeologists and anthropologists base this conclusion on archaeological evidence and on their studies of the few hunter-gather groups that had survived into the nineteenth century, like the Hadza and the Han of southern Africa, the Kalahari Bushmen, the Haida of British Columbia, and the Aborigines of Australia. In some tribal societies there had indeed been chieftains and councils of elders, but because every man was a warrior as well as a hunter, and because tribal groups were quite small, everyone could have a say including, it seems, women too, and a form of democracy could be practised. The tribe gave people a great sense of identity, camaraderie, and common interest. There was little envy or jealousy among tribal members, because everyone was equally poor. Instead there was mutual support, with the tribe almost a kind of extended family, sharing childcare. There was very little private property to be had, and what there was could be shared in times of need. It was a kind of communistic society, approaching the French Revolutionary ideal of, 'liberty, equality, and fraternity'. If the river ran dry, or the trees were not bearing well, or the game herds moved on, the nomadic hunter-gatherers could simply abandon their rough huts or pack up their tepees, and find a more congenial environment for themselves elsewhere. The human population density was low, and there was plenty of land for all. When the first American settlers told the Plains Indians that they now 'owned' part of their lands, the Indians were astonished. 'How can anyone "own" the land?' they asked. 'Can you own the wind, or the sky?' In addition, hunter-gathering was a healthy lifestyle. There was no alcohol, little tobacco, and a diet of fresh fruits, nuts, and roots supplemented by fresh meat and fish was low in salt, sugar, and fat. Gathering, foraging, and chasing game were good forms of exercise, and hunter-gatherers seem to have enjoyed reasonable life spans, though shorter than today's averages. There must have been infectious diseases of some kinds among the tribes, but of course evidence for these is hard to find. What is certain is that many of our modern diseases, known collectively as zoonotic infections, were acquired from our domesticated animals after farming had been adopted. Common vectors were flu viruses, salmonella, campylobacter, and E. coli. Epidemiologists believe that measles, tuberculosis, and smallpox all reached humans through forms of these diseases in cattle.

Controversy rages over the extent to which tribal warfare was a blight on hunter-gatherer societies, but the examination of nomadic skeletons for evidence of war wounds suggests that it was not a major problem, although warfare certainly did occur. There is less controversy, however, over the question of how hard hunter-gatherers had to work for a living. The precise length of their 'working week' is disputed, but there is general agreement that it was a good deal shorter than that of the first farmers! Hunter-gatherers did not try to create a surplus: they ate their fill, and then went out to find some more. This left plenty of time for cooking, talking, telling stories around the campfire, dancing to primitive instruments, or just lazing around. It was not a bad lifestyle at all. A lost Eden, perhaps? No wonder we stayed with it for 190,000 years! But now that we have eaten of the fruit from the tree of knowledge, there is no going back.

The first farmers tended to overspecialise in one crop, such as wheat or rice, which made for a less healthy diet. It has been argued that our early farming ancestors enjoyed less freedom, were overworked, undernourished, and more prone to diseases than their hunter-gatherer forebears. In addition, because they farmed in settled areas, the first agriculturalists had in effect nailed their flag to the mast. The new farmland had to be tended, usually by labour-intensive irrigated or 'hydraulic' methods in those early riparian societies, and it had to be defended. The first farmers were also hostages to climate change. It was no longer so easy to simply up sticks and leave, a valuable survival strategy that had been enjoyed by the hunter-gatherers. In addition of course, the social structures of the farming communities rapidly became very different from those of their hunter-gatherer predecessors.

(b) Might Makes Right: Rule by Force

In our hunter-gatherer days, every adult male had been a warrior as well as a hunter, which had guaranteed a kind of basic equality amongst them. The womenfolk had done the gathering, and it had required the efforts of the whole tribe just to produce enough food for all. But with the Neolithic Agricultural Revolution, which began around 8000 BC, some farming communities, especially those in the fertile river valleys of the Nile, Tigris, Euphrates, and Yellow River, found that they could now produce a food surplus over and above the needs of their farming population. This was a development of the greatest significance in human history, because it meant that, for the first time, not everybody had to be concerned with food production. Some people could be released from the agricultural labour force to specialise in other forms of production including metal working, which emerged soon after the establishment of the first agricultural societies. The very first cities arose in Mesopotamia, 'The Land Between the Rivers', the rivers Tigris and Euphrates in present-day Iraq. As the Agricultural Revolution gathered pace, more and more specialised craftsmen began to emerge, exchanging their wares with the farmers for food, in what might be described as an early Industrial Revolution. It was not long, of course, before money replaced the barter system as a much more convenient medium of exchange, first as silver shekels of a fixed weight, or other items deemed 'valuable', and later as stamped coins. But it was not only craftsmen who emerged at this time. As the farmers formed settled communities they became more aware of the climate in their areas, and the significance of the changing seasons. Would the rivers flood on time? Perhaps this was all controlled by the gods, who would need to be propitiated to ensure that the annual rains came, and so priestly classes began to emerge from the witch doctors and shamans of earlier times.

Nor were they the only new classes to emerge. As the first agricultural societies became more productive and more specialised, increasingly those who farmed only farmed, and those who crafted only crafted, while those who prayed only prayed. But the new communities still needed to be defended, and so another new specialisation emerged – those who fought. The soldiers and the craftsmen and the priests were all supported basically by the agricultural surplus now being produced by the farmers. But societies of such diversity and sophistication needed to be organised, and from the former chieftains and the priestly classes emerged another new group: those who ruled. As the Agricultural Revolution spread across Europe and Asia, this kind of diversified and hierarchical society, dominated by a small ruling class, became the normal pattern in classical and medieval times. The rulers emerged as either the soldiers themselves, as in the cases of the highly trained and well equipped armoured knights of medieval Europe and the Samurai of feudal Japan, or they were those who raised and controlled the armed forces, like the emperors of China and Rome.

The warrior class, or those who controlled them, ruled in those early societies by the same right as the biggest and fiercest monkey had ruled the troop. Our early political structures were therefore not so different from the law of the jungle – God's law. This point is well illustrated by the famous Melian dialogue, as related by Thucydides in his *History of the Peloponnesian War*, fought between Athens and Sparta from 431 to 404 BC, although the *History* runs only to 411 BC. Thucydides was himself an Athenian general who fought in the war, but he tried hard to be objective in his *History*, writing it after he had been exiled from Athens in 423 BC for an alleged military failure. Indeed, the Melian story hardly shows his own side in a good light. Melos was an island in the Cyclades which had sympathised with Sparta during the war. In 416 BC the Athenians sent envoys to Melos, supported by a strong military force which encamped on the island. The envoys demanded its surrender and submission to the Athenian empire. But the Melians claimed that they were neutral, and asked the Athenians, already well known as philosophers, how they could morally justify the invasion of a small and peaceful island. A debate ensued, but the envoys brought it brutally to an end by declaring that in this world, 'The strong do what they can, and the weak suffer what they must'. Foolishly, the Melians decided to resist. On land, the Spartan infantry was invincible, but Athens ruled the waves with her mighty fleet. Melos lay at her mercy. The Athenians attacked. All the men of Melos were slaughtered, and the women and children sold into slavery, a bitter lesson in *realpolitik*, the notion that might makes right. It is believed by some that Niccolò Machiavelli (1469-1527) was influenced by Thucydides in the writing of his notorious little book *The Prince*, published in 1513. In this handbook of *realpolitik* it is argued that winning and maintaining power are the only things that matter to a prince, and so any means may be used to secure these ends. The prince may legitimately employ lying, treachery, murder, slaughter, and terror as instruments of policy: might made right. This point is again well illustrated in the poem, *Tubal Cain*, written by the Scottish poet Charles Mackay (1812-1889) in the year 1851. Tubal Cain was a biblical character, mentioned in Genesis 4:22 as the son of Lamech and Zillah, and so a direct descendent of Cain, the first murderer. He is described as, 'an instructor of every artificer in brass and iron', or in other words, the first craftsman. Inspired by this image Mackay wrote his poem, the first verse of which is quoted here.

Old Tubal Cain was a man of might
In the days when the earth was young:
By the fierce red light of his furnace bright
The strokes of his hammer rung.
And he lifted high his brawny hand
On the iron glowing clear,
Till the sparks rushed out in scarlet showers

As he fashioned the sword and spear.
And he sang, 'Hurrah for my handiwork!
Hurrah for the spear and the sword!
Hurrah for the hand that shall wield them well,
For he shall be king and lord!'

In more recent times this brutal reality was given new expression by Mao Zedong (1893-1976), the leader of the Chinese Communist Party. On November 6, 1938, in his concluding speech to the Sixth Plenary Session of the Party, Mao made famous a phrase that he had first coined in 1927: it was, 'Political power grows out of the barrel of a gun'. Sadly, in the last resort, this remains true. Even in Europe, during the Second World War we saw that regimes could be overthrown and replaced by the power of the gun alone. But just because it *can* be done does not mean that it *should* be done. There is usually a better way. As a young man, firearms held a certain fascination for me. I learned how to shoot in Canada, with the ubiquitous, standard issue BB gun, and later became a very good shot with air weapons, .22, and .303. Although I can hardly believe it now, the record will show that I was once a keen member of my school's Combined Cadet Force, and a crack shot on the school's rifle team. Later, I was a member of Cambridge University's Officer Training Corps. But I now believe that a man with a gun is a potential tragedy, whether he wears a uniform or not. If he doesn't, it's a tragedy for society, and if he does, it's a tragedy for himself. History is littered with examples of such tragedies. Unfortunately, warfare is sometimes necessary, because there have always been fools in history who have believed that they can gain by war. It is becoming increasingly clear, however, that nobody ever 'wins' a war. The winners may come out marginally ahead of the losers, but both sides only ever suffer terrible losses: a tragedy indeed.

The diversity, the hierarchical structure, and the authoritarianism of the new agricultural societies were well reflected in the utopian state imagined by Plato in his great work, *The Republic,* written around 380 BC. Here, Plato envisaged a city-state (πολις) ruled by 'Guardians'. This elite group had been educated and trained from early youth for their leadership role. The Guardians were divided into two classes, the Guardians proper, and the Auxiliaries, whom Plato described as 'the men of gold' and the 'men of silver'. The men of gold did the actual ruling, while the men of silver enforced their rule as the army and police force. Below them were the men of bronze, or of iron, and finally, we must assume, the men of dross! Although Plato does not actually mention this last group, we must assume its existence as the numerous slave class which was then typical of Greek society. It has been estimated that in first-century Rome roughly one third of the population were slaves, and the position in Athens must have been similar. So much for the egalitarian structure of the hunter-gather communities! The men of bronze and of iron were to be the merchants, craftsmen, and farmers who were expected to keep their places, have nothing to do with government, and get on with the jobs they were trained for, namely providing resources for themselves and the ruling classes. Since they were allowed no power at all, they were permitted to own property in the form of goods, lands, and slaves. However, Plato did allow for a degree of social mobility, accepting that a man of bronze might have a child of gold. This should be recognised, and the child of gold trained up as a Guardian, although just how this child was to be recognised at a very early age was not made clear.

But surely the most interesting aspect of Plato's imaginary state was the lifestyle that he would impose on his Guardians. They were to be allowed no private property, and no family life, so that nothing would distract them from their task of ruling wisely and justly. Within the Guardian community, all property was to be held in common, and also all wives! Children were to be raised by the community as a whole, ignorant of whom their fathers were. This meant that women too would have to be carefully selected, and trained up in exactly the same way as the male Guardians, with the same education, and also the same rigorous physical training. Plato declared that female Guardians should exercise naked with the men in the gymnasiums. This did in fact happen in Sparta, but in Athens this idea ran so entirely counter to the accepted role of women in those times that it was considered to be a scandalous suggestion. Indeed, even the radical Plato accepted that a man of gold was superior to a woman of gold, but he did suggest that a woman of gold might be superior to a man of bronze. This reflected Plato's obsession with eugenics, and his firm belief that some were 'natural' leaders, and some 'natural' slaves, so that the Guardian class, the master race, had to be kept 'pure'. Downward social mobility for the Guardians was also allowed. Just how far female Guardians were supposed to actually rule as distinct from merely supporting the men was never made clear, but the female Auxiliaries were definitely imagined by Plato as a race of Amazonian warriors! This again was an outrageous suggestion, since even the Spartans did not send their women to war (they left that to us!). The Auxiliaries would of course have been very important in an age when might made right. Later, in the Roman Empire, emperors were often made and unmade by the army, or murdered by their own praetorian guards.

Plato's fantasy republic of course never came into being, but his idea that the Guardians should be allowed no private property or family lives was an interesting one. The power of the Guardians was absolute, and this was all very well, '*Sed quis custodiet ipsos custodes?*' as the Roman poet Juvenal enquired in his *Satires,* written around 100 A.D. (Who will guard the guardians?) Plato seems here to have anticipated by more than 2,000 years the famous observation made by the Victorian historian John Edward Acton, later Lord Acton (1834-1902) who noted, 'Power corrupts, and absolute power corrupts absolutely'. By denying the Guardians private property and family lives Plato was hoping to make it impossible for them to feather their own nests, or promote their own families rather than the best interests of the state that they were meant to serve.

Quite how fully justified Plato's concern over this point was has been amply borne out by history. Over the centuries very few ruling cliques have been able to resist the temptation of enriching themselves and promoting their families at the expense of the states they were ruling. Even today, we see this sort of thing still going on in Africa, the Middle East, and North Korea. Of course, this is always a question of degree: even here in Britain we have had the scandal of MPs' expenses, the private funding of political parties, and the link between powerful corporations and those politicians (or their spouses) who take highly paid jobs with them after 'retirement'. However, things were a good deal worse in the Middle Ages! The attitude of rulers in those days was well reflected in a statement made by Giovanni di Lorenzo de' Medici (1475-1521) who was elected Pope in 1513 as Leo X. On his election he is reputed to have said, 'God has given us the papacy: now let us enjoy it!' He had been made a cardinal at the age of 14 through the influence of his father, Lorenzo the Magnificent (1449-1492), although he had never trained as a priest. He had still not taken holy orders when elected Pope in 1513. Thereafter he borrowed heavily, spent lavishly, and sold indulgencies. Martin Luther certainly had a lot to complain about!

But the kings of the time were no better. Their principal objective was clinging on to power, and founding a dynasty to succeed them. This was their main reason for keeping law and order in their kingdoms, and if they were able to do that, then they felt that their duty to their subjects had been discharged. Any notion that they might have been there to improve the lives of those they ruled over never entered their heads. To paraphrase Leo X, 'God has given us the monarchy, now let us enjoy it!' Their subjects were there to provide them with rents and taxes, so that they could live lavish lifestyles and fight wars for their greater personal glory. If the subjects did not like it, they could argue with the soldiers, but this never got them very far! The strong did what they could, and the weak suffered what they must. In reality, the law of the jungle applied. Kings ruled their realms by the same right that the biggest and fiercest monkey had ruled the troop: might made right. If the Kings were the Guardians, then their feudal host, which owed them military service in return for the lands that they held of the king, were the Auxiliaries who enforced the king's power. These men were the barons, knights, and armed retainers under their command. Unfortunately for the ruled, however, these men were *not* denied private property or family lives, with predictable consequences! These consequences were most clearly illustrated during the anarchy of King Stephen's reign between 1135 and 1154.

In theory the power of a medieval king was absolute, but in practice it rested on the support of his armed auxiliaries. So long as the king could keep their support, his position was secure. However, if he lost the support of enough of his baronial feudal host, wherein the real military power of the kingdom lay, then he could find himself in trouble. Stephen was the nephew of his predecessor Henry I, but the throne was also claimed by Henry's daughter Matilda, usually referred to as the Empress Matilda because she was the widow of the Holy Roman Emperor Henry V. By 1135 she was the wife of the powerful Geoffrey of Anjou, and enjoyed the support of her uncle David I of Scotland and her half-brother Robert of Gloucester, a powerful baron. In 1139 Matilda invaded to claim the crown, and some of Stephen's barons rallied to her support. The ensuing civil war lasted until 1153, with neither side able to control the entire country. As the tide of war flowed back and forth, soldiers looted, raped, and pillaged at will, torturing the peasantry to force them to reveal where their food stores were hidden, and then leaving them to starve. Men said of those times that, 'Christ and all his angels slept'. Never was the rule of the 'robber baron' more clearly illustrated: the populace stood no chance against the soldiers. What is not widely understood, however, is the fact that the age of the robber baron continued for longer than most people realise. It was only in the nineteenth century that governments in Europe at last began to feel that perhaps they owed some kind of duty of care to those over whom they ruled. Prior to that date, the ruling classes of Europe had been little better than kleptocracies, robbing their hapless subjects to support their own lavish lifestyles. With the ruling classes in mind, Pierre-Joseph Proudhon (1809-1865) in his *Inquiry into the Principle of Right and Government* written in 1840 had famously asserted that, 'property is theft'. Up until that time, this had very largely been true, and to a degree it remains true even in our own day, as we shall see.

Prior to the nineteenth century, 'constitutional evolution' had represented nothing more than an ongoing struggle for power between the Guardians and the Auxiliaries, that is between the crown and the ruling class that supported it. The Magna Carta of 1215, for example, far from being the product of carefully considered political thought, represented little more than a temporary peace treaty in the power struggle between king John and his barons. Both sides approached the document in bad faith, and it had to be reissued with amendments in 1216, 1217, 1225, and 1297. As an attempt to place an absolute king under the restraint of law it was a partial success, but it brought very little benefit to the mass of the population. It achieved only a small shift of power within the ruling class. If the baronial class, or a large majority of it, were to unite against the king then they could indeed force concessions from him, as in the case of the Second Barons' War of 1263-4. A revolt against King Henry III was led on this occasion by Simon de Montfort, Earl of Leicester (1208-1265). In May, 1264, de Montfort defeated and captured the king at the Battle of Lewes, and became *de facto* ruler of England for just over a year. In 1265 he called De Montfort's Parliament, which included representatives from the towns for the first time. His 'reign' was short lived, however. Henry III's son Edward rallied baronial support and defeated de Montfort at the Battle of Evesham in August 1265, making sure that de Montfort himself was killed in the conflict. But de Montfort's parliamentary reforms survived as a permanent constitutional change: the towns never lost their representation.

In reality, kings were always dependent for their power upon the ruling classes that supported them. This was once again demonstrated during the Wars of the Roses between 1455 and 1487, and during the English Civil War of 1642-1651. This latter was certainly *not* a class war, as Marxist historians like E.P. Thompson, Eric Hobsbawm, and Christopher Hill would have us believe. Rather, the ruling class on this occasion split along religious and political lines, fighting on both sides. Of course, by the seventeenth century the feudal system was dead, and the new ruling class consisted of the king, the aristocracy, and the gentry who between them owned most of the land of England. However, they were still robber barons of a sort, extracting rents and other dues from their tenants who actually did the work of farming the land, while the great lived high on the hog at their expense.

(c) The Mandate of Heaven: Rule by Divine Right

The English Civil Wars of 1642 to 1651 are more properly called the British Civil Wars, since Scotland and Ireland were also involved: indeed, sporadic fighting in Ireland dragged on until 1653. Religion played a very important part in these wars, and this brings us to a consideration of the role of religion in politics. Let us look first at 'the divine right of kings'. In the Ancient World, some rulers got straight to the point by declaring that they actually *were* divine themselves, like the pharaohs of ancient Egypt or the emperors of Rome. One of the first Mesopotamian god-kings was Shulgi of Ur, who proclaimed himself divine in 2006 BC, according to records carved onto baked clay in Sumerian cuneiform. The emperors of Japan also enjoyed divine status by right of their descent from the sun goddess Amaterasu, while the various rajas and sultans of Southeast Asia also claimed divine sanction for their rule in one form or another. In China, successful emperors could claim the 'mandate of heaven' as justification for their position. This mandate, however, did not grant the Chinese emperors unconditional tenure of their office. In theory, heaven could be displeased by an unjust ruler and therefore withdraw its mandate, bestowing it instead on a rival claimant to the throne. This theory therefore allowed a right of rebellion, at least from the time of the Zhou dynasty (1046-256 BC), which had devised this philosophy to justify their overthrow of the previous Shang dynasty (1600-1046 BC). In ancient Persia the Zoroastrian religion taught that rulers were indeed the representatives of God on earth, but they deserved allegiance only as long as they possessed *farr*, that is a kind of divine blessing or 'mandate of heaven' which they had to earn by ruling wisely and well. This religion too, therefore, allowed a right of rebellion. These are the earliest known examples of 'resistance theory', which could overrule divine right under certain circumstances. This idea was to come to prominence in seventeenth-century England, costing Algernon Sidney (1623-83) and several others their heads!

Although the claiming of some form of divine sanction for their rule was almost ubiquitous amongst rulers in the Ancient World, it came to assume a special significance in Christian Europe. The Old Testament had seemed to make it clear that monarchy was a form of government ordained by God, as witnessed by the many kings of Israel. King David, the second king of the united kingdom of Israel, was shown special favour by Yahweh. In Psalm 89:19-23 God says,

> I have laid help upon one that is mighty: I have exalted one chosen out of the people. I have found David my servant: with my holy oil have I anointed him; with whom my hand shall be established: mine arm also shall strengthen him. The enemy shall not exact upon him, nor the sons of wickedness afflict him. And I will beat down his foes before his face, and plague them that hate him.

Verse 36 adds, 'His seed shall endure forever, and his throne as the sun before me'. In ancient Hebrew the term 'messiah' means 'the anointed one'.

The New Testament too seemed to recommend unquestioning submission to 'the powers that be'. Jesus himself had said, 'Render unto Caesar the things which are Caesar's' (Matthew 22:21), and had told Pilate that his authority came from God (John 19:11). St. Paul took up this theme, writing in Romans 13:1-2, 'Let every soul be subject unto the higher powers, for there is no power but of God: the powers that be are ordained of God. Whosoever therefore resisteth that power resisteth the ordinance of God, and they that resist shall receive to themselves damnation'. St. Peter too urged obedience to the secular powers. 'Submit yourselves to every ordinance of man for the Lord's sake, whether it be to the king as supreme, or unto governors, as unto them that are sent by him for the punishment of evildoers, and for the praise of them that do well, for so is the will of God' (I Peter 2:13-15).

The subject's duty of obedience was made clear enough by such injunctions, but the Bible was far less clear on how the 'divine right' of rulers was to be acquired. Was it a hereditary thing, or was it to be decided by 'the God of Battles'? Victory in war was often taken as a sign of divine favour. It was this question indeed that had divided Moslems at the great Battle of Karbala in 680. The Shiites, who believed that the Caliphs should be the hereditary successors of Muhammad, were heavily defeated by the Sunnis, who believed that the Caliph should win his authority by the sword in *jihad*, or by the popular support of the faithful. It seemed that God had spoken in the outcome of this battle, and the Sunnis remain by far the largest sect in Islam to this day. A similar ambiguity may be traced in medieval England. Hereditary right was greatly respected, but it did not prevent Richard II from being overthrown by Henry IV in 1399, or Henry VI being overthrown by Edward IV in 1461, or Richard III being overthrown by Henry VII in 1485, all by appeal to 'the God of Battles'. With the coming of the Tudor dynasty of 1485 to 1603, however, we see the beginnings of a whole new ball game. In Europe, the Achilles' heel of divine right monarchy had lain in the fact that the king's divine sanction had been bestowed upon him *through the Catholic Church* which of course had a leader of its own in the Pope, who claimed a spiritual jurisdiction over secular rulers. In England, each new king was anointed with holy oil at his coronation ceremony by the Archbishop of Canterbury, who thereby ordained him to monarchy. This archaic ceremony is still practised in Britain to this day, although it is now a great rarity. In most other monarchies it has been replaced by a simple inauguration ceremony. Of course, everywhere else it is also extremely unusual to find an heir to the throne who insists on having his clothes hand-washed by lackeys, his shoelaces ironed, and toothpaste put onto the brush for him by his valet!

According to Shakespeare, Richard II had placed great faith in his anointing, and in his divine right. As Henry Bolingbroke closed in on him, Richard remained optimistic, declaring,

Not all the water in the rough, rude sea
Can wash the balm from an anointed king.
The breath of worldly men cannot depose
The deputy elected by the Lord.
For every man that Bolingbroke hath pressed
To lift shrewd steel against our golden crown,
God for his Richard hath in heavenly pay
A glorious angel. Therefore, if angels fight,
Weak men must fall, for heaven still guards the right.
(Act Three, Scene II, lines 54-62)

Shakespeare was, however, being somewhat anachronistic here, speaking much more for his own time than for the fourteenth century. The issue of divine right had assumed a far greater significance by Shakespeare's day than it had enjoyed in the days of Richard II. This was in large measure due to the actions of King Henry VIII, who had ruled from 1509 to 1547, and had famously broken with Rome over the issue of the annulment of his marriage to Catherine of Aragon, setting up the independent Church of England, with himself as supreme head thereof. Clement VII, who was Pope from 1523 to 1534 had, for reasons that remain obscure, but may have been based on an ill-founded fear of Charles V, the Holy Roman Emperor, refused to grant Henry this annulment, although it had not been an unusual request for the times. Desperate to be rid of Catherine so that he could marry Anne Boleyn, Henry had Parliament pass the Act in Restraint of Appeals in 1532, cutting off Catherine's right of an appeal to Rome, so that the case could be tried only in Henry's courts. For this act of blatant defiance of papal authority, Henry and his archbishop, Thomas Cranmer were excommunicated. It seems that Clement grossly overestimated the strength of his position relative to that of the king, who was desperate for a male heir. Previously a loyal son of the Church, Henry was virtually forced out of the Catholic fold. Henry married Anne in January 1533, and in September their only long-surviving child, Elizabeth, was born. In 1534, with the Acts of Supremacy, parliament recognised Henry as supreme head of the new Church of England. As far as this Church was concerned, Henry had become Pope as well as King: he was now untrammelled by any form of external spiritual jurisdiction.

This fact in itself greatly increased the king's power, but in addition Henry's tame parliament passed another series of Acts between 1536 and 1539 which dissolved all the monasteries and priories of England, transferring their lands and wealth to the Crown. It has been estimated that about one fifth of all England's landed wealth changed hands, and brought the king an additional annual revenue of some £120,000 in rents alone, a vast sum for those days. At this point in time, Henry VIII had a better chance of establishing an absolute monarchy in England than had ever been available to his recent predecessors, or was to be for his successors. Parliament, as we know from history, clearly had the potential to develop itself into a formidable political force, but by 1540 Henry VIII also had the potential to vastly increase the powers of the crown. Such an opportunity was not to occur again: Henry's position was unique. His father, Henry VII had famously 'muzzled the bloody-minded barons', fining them heavily for keeping private armies of 'retainers', and effectively removing their military threat to the crown. Meanwhile, parliament in 1540 was still cowed and compliant, with all its members in fear of the wrath of the king. Henry was known to be very ready with the axe! Such an opportunity was never to recur again. Only during Henry's reign were the barons at last down, and parliament not yet up.

Although parliament had the potential to greatly increase its power, so too had the crown. After violent and disruptive civil wars, succeeding monarchs tended to be allowed much more power by the political nation than would otherwise have been the case. Henry II (reigned 1154-69) benefited from this effect after the anarchy of Stephen's reign, just as Henry VII and VIII were to do after the Wars of the Roses, and as Charles II and James II did after the civil wars of the seventeenth century. Henry VIII, however, found himself in a particularly strong position owing to the vagueness of English law at that time. The king enjoyed a shadowy independent legislative authority known as the power of proclamation. Royal proclamations at that time were in theory not able to create new law, but only to draw attention to or reinforce existing law. However, just how much fell within the scope of proclamations remained a murky area. Only the judicial arm, the courts, could decide this, and of course Henry himself had the appointing and dismissing of judges, just as he then had the appointing of bishops. Indeed, it was not impossible at that time for even parliament itself to agree to a great extension of the power of proclamation. This did in fact happen in 1539 with the Statute of Proclamations, which declared that proclamations made by the king with the assent of his Privy Council should have the force of statute law, provided they were not prejudicial to 'any person's inheritance, offices, liberties, goods, chattels, or life'. This statute was indeed repealed in 1547, but only after Henry's death. He certainly had the potential to build up an independent legislative power for himself, converting his power of proclamation into something very like the edicts issued by the kings of France in the seventeenth century.

The position of parliament in Henry's England was also uncertain. It was called only by royal prerogative: Henry was under no legal obligation to call it at all. He needed it for only two things: legislation and money. But Henry could have expanded his independent legislative power, and controlled the judiciary through his appointment of judges. Had he also kept for himself all the lands and wealth of the monasteries which he had looted, he need never have felt obliged to call parliament for money again, and could have set England well on the road to the kind of royal absolutism that was shortly to emerge in France, and which would have required a French-style revolution to overthrow it. Had Henry VIII possessed anything like the astuteness of his father Henry VII or his daughter Elizabeth I, this could easily have happened.

Fortunately for England's constitutional development, however, Henry VIII was a greedy, petulant, vainglorious idiot. He threw away the great advantages that he might have enjoyed in return for immediate ready cash, selling off his monastic lands at knock-down prices to any gentleman or merchant who could afford them. Given the importance of land in those days, these sales represented a very significant transfer of political potential. The sales made Henry rich, but not for long. He squandered the money on a series of futile wars against Scotland and France, which won him nothing, and left him bankrupt again by the time of his death in 1547.

Henry had destroyed the wealth of the crown, but not its prestige. His daughter Elizabeth (1533-1603) ruled wisely, well, and frugally, avoiding war as far as was possible, and greatly enhancing the standing of the monarchy. Moreover, the tide of history was flowing in her favour. Wearying of religious conflicts and civil strife, the ruling classes of the day were beginning to reconcile themselves to the idea of a strong monarchy. The political thinkers of the time reflected this trend. In 1576 Jean Bodin (1530-96), the French jurist and philosopher, published *Les Six Livres de la République*, shortly after the St. Bartholomew's Day massacre of 1572. An expanded Latin version of the text appeared in 1586, and Richard Knolles produced an English translation in 1606 as *The Six Books of a Commonweale*. 'Commonwealth' was indeed a better translation than 'republic' as we would understand it today, because Bodin in fact argued for an absolute monarchy, justified by divine right, in this treatise.

The divine right theme was taken up by an Englishman, Robert Filmer (1588-1653), a country gentleman, lawyer, and magistrate. His most famous work, *Patriarcha*, was written in the 1620s or 1630s, but not published until 1680, when it provoked a vigorous response from Locke and Sydney, which is its main claim to fame. However, Filmer wrote a second book in 1648 which *was* published in his lifetime, *The Necessity of the Absolute Power of all Kings*, a title that more clearly expressed his views. Filmer's arguments were based entirely on biblical texts, with an emphasis on the Old Testament idea of kingship. The Bible was also cited as his authority by Jacques-Bénigne Bossuet (1627-1704) Bishop of Metz, court preacher, and tutor to the French Dauphin from 1670 to 1681. As part of his instruction to the young prince, Bossuet wrote his best known discourse, *Politics Drawn from the Very Words of Holy Scripture* in 1679, although the work was not published until 1709. Here he argues for absolute monarchy on the grounds of divine right.

Divine right theory was to be firmly and finally rejected in England with the 'Glorious Revolution' of 1688-9, but in France it went from strength to strength. Louis XIV (1638-1715) king of France from 1643, is often seen as a paradigm of absolute monarchy, able to legislate independently by the issuing of royal edicts, and in sole control of a large standing army, which allowed him to tax his subjects in an arbitrary fashion. This model was soon to be emulated by other European rulers. Indeed, the eighteenth century is often referred to as 'The Age of Absolutism', as other rulers sought to cast themselves in the mould of Louis XIV, notably in the Spanish and Russian empires. However, this growing stress on divine right theory was at least a step away from the 'might makes right' ideology of the Melian Dialogue and the Middle Ages. It was to be debate over this concept that was to place Britain and France at the forefront of political thought on a global scale in the seventeenth and eighteenth centuries.

Another self-styled political thinker of the day was James Stuart (1566-1625). James' father Lord Darnley was murdered in February 1567, probably at the instigation of his mother, Mary Queen of Scots, who was in consequence forced to abdicate in July of that year. Her son was crowned King of Scotland as James VI on July 29, 1567 at the age of thirteen months by rebel nobles who acted as regents during James' minority, and it was 1583 before he gained a measure of control in his kingdom. Married to Anne of Denmark in 1589, James produced two sons, Henry (1594-1612), and Charles (1599-1649). Very significantly for later British history, the marriage also produced Elizabeth (1596-1662), whose grandson was later to reign as George I of Great Britain.

James had been well educated, and fancied himself as a scholar, producing two books of political advice, written for his son and heir, Henry. The first of these, *The True Law of Free Monarchies*, was written in 1598, and the second, the *Basilikon Doran* (Royal Gift) in 1599. There was much wisdom, good advice, and common sense to be found in both books, but James also made it clear that he believed a king's rule should be absolute, on the basis of the divine right of kings. In his 'free monarchy' it was not the people who were to be free, but rather the king himself – free to do whatever he liked! Monarchy had preceded all other forms of government, 'and so it follows of necessity that kings were the authors and makers of the laws, and not the laws of the kings'. This was a fine theory, but in reality the monarchs of both Scotland and England were still dependent upon the support of their ruling classes, as James' mother had found to her cost. However, in a speech made to Parliament in 1610 James had declared,

> The state of monarchy is the supremest thing upon earth, for kings are not only God's lieutenants upon earth and sit upon God's throne, but even by God himself they are called gods. (G.W. Prothero, *Select Statutes* (1906) p. 400)

This statement, 'Even God calls me god' must surely be one of the most arrogant ever made, unsupported by any biblical text. James had simply misread several Old Testament passages, especially Psalms 82:6. The Jews were strict monotheists, and would never have dreamed of calling any of their kings God. Despite his grandiose claims, however, James was basically a sensible and kindly man, a lover of peace, and not one to provoke a conflict. On the death of Elizabeth I in 1603, he was recognised as King James I of England, by virtue of his descent from Henry VII. As King of England he managed his parliaments well in difficult times, kept taxes low, and was genuinely mourned at his death. His two books of advice had been written for his son Henry, but he had died of typhoid in 1612, so this advice passed to his second son Charles, later Charles I from 1625. Unfortunately Charles overlooked all his father's recommendations for wise and responsible kingship, and took up only his grandiose ideas about absolutism. He pursued the wrong political and religious policies, engaged in foolish wars, antagonised parliament, and brought the country to a ruinous civil war, which culminated in his own execution in 1649. The 'divine right' in which he so passionately believed had served him no better than it had Shakespeare's Richard II.

The execution of Charles I of course severely dented the notion of divine right, but the idea had come under fire even in the sixteenth century mainly, ironically enough, for religious reasons. Catholic writers like Juan de Mariana (1536-1624) had opposed it because he disapproved of Protestant sovereigns like Elizabeth I, and Protestants like John Knox (1514-1572) and Christopher Goodman (1520-1603) had written against it because they disapproved of the Catholic rule of Mary Queen of Scots and Mary I of England. But the most trenchant piece of criticism of the theory, and one of the earliest, was surely penned by John Ponet (1514-56), the Protestant Bishop of Winchester and Marian exile. His major work was *A Short Treatise of Politike Power*, published in 1556. He had of course been inspired to write it by the Catholic rule of Mary Tudor. Here he flatly rejected the idea of divine right, argued for tyrannicide, championed the rule of law, and advocated a limited and responsible form of monarchy. In his classic work on *The English Reformation* (1978) A.G. Dickens wrote,

> Ponet's treatise comes first in a new wave of anti-monarchical writings...it has never been assessed at its true importance, for it antedates by several years those more brilliantly expressed but less radical Huguenot writings which have usually been taken to represent the tyrannicide theories of the Reformation. (p. 391)

Ponet's pamphlet was republished on the eve of Charles I's execution, and Ponet has even been credited with introducing the idea of clearly separating the executive, legislative, and judicial branches of government. This, however, is incorrect. The legend seems to have arisen from a misconception on the part of John Adams (1735-1826), the second President of the USA. In a multi-volume biography and collection of the President's papers produced by Charles Francis Adams (1807-86), a grandson, he quotes John Adams as saying that Ponet's work contained, 'all the essential principles of liberty, which were afterwards dilated on by Sidney and Locke, including the idea of a three-branched government.'(Vol. VI, p. 4) However, on reading Ponet's works for myself I find no evidence of any such suggestion at any point. It would have been remarkable, indeed incredible, for any sixteenth-century writer to have put forward such an advanced proposition, for in those days the three branches of government were inextricably linked together, and for contemporaries it would have been inconceivable to imagine any other arrangement.

The executive branch in those days was essentially the king, although by custom he was supposed to act with the advice of his Privy Council, a body of the great and good of unspecified size and membership. This was fine for day-to-day matters, but for major issues the king was expected to consult with his Great Council, that is the Lords and Commons assembled in Parliament. This gave Parliament a small degree of executive power, although it was fundamentally the legislative branch of government, giving it a foot in both camps. The king, however, was not obliged to accept any advice, and could in theory act as the executive branch entirely on his own. In addition, the king intruded into the legislative sphere with his power of proclamations, which carried a quasi-legislative authority. The king also claimed 'dispensing and suspending powers' over the laws of the land. The first was the power of dispensing with a law as it applied to a particular case, which was simply an extension of the royal prerogative of granting pardons, a power that remains with heads of state to this day. The suspending power, however, was much more threatening. Here, English kings claimed the right to suspend any law of the land, including statute law, for as long a period as they chose. This meant that no man could break that law, because for the time of its suspension it did not apply. The last king to exercise this power was James II, who reigned from 1685-8. In addition, of course, the king retained a veto over all new statute law, because until it received the royal assent no Act of Parliament could pass into law. This gave the monarch another measure of legislative power. In Britain, this is still the case. Indeed, in the sixteenth century the king was allowed all this independent legislative power on the assumption that all laws were the king's laws. The three branches of government were inextricably linked.

In a well constituted government, the legislative branch has the sole right to create or amend laws, the executive executes the laws and runs the country, while an independent judiciary interprets the laws, making their meaning clear in difficult cases. However, in sixteenth-century England the king not only enjoyed legislative powers, but also independent judicial powers through his prerogative courts. Here, the discretionary powers, privileges, and legal immunities of the crown were exercised. In the sixteenth century these were the Court of the Exchequer, the Court of Chancery, and the Court of Star Chamber. Star Chamber was essentially the king's Privy Council sitting as a court, assisted by some judges. The king himself did not sit on this court, but since it was composed of the king's hand-picked Privy Councillors and hand-picked judges, it could always be relied upon to bring in verdicts of which the Crown approved. It was in effect the king sitting as Chief Magistrate of the Realm by proxy, for kings had traditionally been judges as well as rulers. But Star Chamber became an instrument of oppression, used against perceived opponents of the crown, and it was abolished in 1641.

The two leading law courts of the land were the Court of King's Bench, which dealt with statute law cases, and the Court of Common Pleas, which was intended to deal with common law matters, although the jurisdictions of the two courts became interchangeable with time. It was the king, however, who had the appointing and dismissing of all judges, and this too gave him *de facto* judicial power. To add to the confusion Parliament too possessed a judicial power of sorts with the process of impeachment, whereby the Commons might accuse a man of a crime and the Lords try him, and the Act of Attainder, whereby any man might be voted guilty, even on the flimsiest of evidence, by a simple majority of those present to vote in both Houses, with the royal assent.

In short, the three branches of government were so inextricably intertwined in 1556 that John Ponet would need to have been impossibly precocious to have imagined a radically different system. But Ponet is a man of special interest for me because he was a graduate, fellow, and bursar of my old college, Queens'. He designed the elaborate and colourful sundial which may still be seen high on the north wall of Old Court. Remarkably, it is also a moondial, enabling you to tell the time at night as well if the moon is bright enough! (Image available online)

With his tyrannicide theory, Ponet had hinted at the idea of contract, suggesting that the tenure of kings was not unconditional. This contractual concept was to figure prominently in the seventeenth and eighteenth centuries, particularly in England, but it was not an entirely new idea. Plato had floated the proposition in Book II of his *Republic*, where Glaucon is in argument with Socrates about the nature of justice. In the rather racy translation by Lee in my Penguin Classics edition Glaucon declares,

> What they say is that our natural instinct is to inflict wrong or injury, and to avoid suffering it, but that the disadvantages of suffering it exceed the advantages of inflicting it. After a taste of both, therefore, men decide that, as they can't have the ha'pence without the kicks, they had better make a compact with each other and avoid both. They accordingly proceed to make laws and mutual agreements, and what the law lays down they call lawful and right. This is the origin and nature of justice. It lies between what is most desirable, to do wrong and avoid punishment, and what is most undesirable, to suffer wrong without redress. Justice and right lie between these two and are accepted, not as being good in themselves, but as having a relative value due to our inability to do wrong. (pp. 89-90)

Later in the text however, Socrates, who speaks for Plato, rejects this definition of justice as a mere convenience agreed upon by the hoi polloi amongst themselves, arguing that it is an altogether higher concept than this, a virtue in itself, and something that can be administered only by the all-knowing, all-powerful Guardians, with everyone else keeping to the place assigned for them by the Guardians. Epicurus of Samos also looked at this theme, stating as No. 31 of his *Principal Doctrines* that, 'Natural justice is a pledge of reciprocal benefit, to prevent one man from harming or being harmed by another'.

Some early thoughts on the 'social contract' therefore saw it not as a compact made between the ruler and the ruled, but rather an agreement made amongst the ruled themselves. This theme was taken up by one of the earliest and also one of the most famous advocates of contract theory in modern times, Thomas Hobbes (1588-1679) a Wiltshire man who was rather unkindly referred to by his opponents as 'the pig of Malmsbury'. An able scholar and an Oxford graduate, Hobbes was at first supported by the mercantile wealth of his uncle, Francis Hobbes, after his father had deserted the family. In 1609, however, he was appointed as personal tutor to William Cavendish, son of the Baron of Hardwick, who later became the Earl of Devonshire. The two young men embarked on a 'grand tour of Europe' together in 1610, something that was then considered an obligatory part of a young gentleman's education. Here Hobbes was exposed to contemporary European thought, which inspired him with an interest in philosophy that lasted for the remainder of his life.

Hobbes was a prodigious writer, publishing many books in his lifetime, but his most famous work by far appeared in 1651. This was, *Leviathan, or the Matter, Form, and Power of a Commonwealth, Ecclesiastical and Civil*. Here, Hobbes argued that the ruler of a 'commonwealth', who need not necessarily be a king, should be invested with absolute power in every branch of government, executive, legislative, judicial, and ecclesiastical. The ruler must also have a power of censorship, and be able to suppress free speech at will. In *Leviathan* Hobbes considered aristocracy and democracy as alternative forms of government, but concluded that a monarchy, absolute rule by just a single person, was the surest path to political stability.

To our modern eyes, Hobbes' ideal government looks very like a tyranny. What could possibly induce people to place themselves under such a regime? Hobbes did in fact admit that such a government might include tyrannical elements, but like Machiavelli he suggested that the end justified the means. That end was internal peace and stability, a priceless asset which Hobbes believed could be achieved in no other way. An aristocracy could divide against itself, as Hobbes had witnessed with his own eyes during the English Civil War, while in a democracy disagreements were even more likely, increasing the chances of a descent into anarchy. It was this anarchy that Hobbes feared most of all, understandably in view of the trauma that his country had just experienced during a violent civil war. He did not try to claim that tyranny was an ideal form of government – only that it was preferable to the alternative of anarchy, and indeed the best guarantee against anarchy.

This is an interesting idea, and would be valid if the state in question had a marked tendency to descend into anarchy when strong government was removed from it. Sadly, we can see this scenario being acted out in our own day with the tragic consequences of the so-called 'Arab Spring' that has recently swept the Middle East. For many decades past, Israel has been the only democracy in the region. All of the other governments have been monarchies, theocracies, or secular dictatorships. The West had always disapproved of those regimes, and at first welcomed uprisings against them in Tunisia, Libya, Egypt, Iraq, and Syria. However, with the removal of the strong hand of their governments, all of those nations then descended into at best instability, and at worst anarchy to a greater or lesser degree. Their former dictators were certainly evil men, exploiting their countries, ruthlessly arresting , torturing and murdering their political opponents, and even employing poison gas against dissident groups, as we have seen in Iraq and Syria. Many died at their hands, but not as many as later died in the anarchies that followed their overthrow. It would seem that, under certain circumstances, Hobbes' arguments do apply: tyranny is preferable to anarchy. However, in the Middle East rather special circumstances existed. The area was a seething cauldron of ancient resentments, aggravated by religious factors. In addition, the region had no 'political' traditions, in the fullest sense of that word. It was these factors that made civil wars very likely once the strong hand of a dictator had been removed.

Hobbes himself was a timid man, always taking flight at the first threat to his security, which perhaps explains how he managed to live so long! 91 was a very exceptional age to reach in those times. He had an excessive fear of anarchy, which he called 'the state of nature' and 'the war of all against all', a situation in which everyone was in 'continual fear, and danger of violent death; and the life of man solitary, poor, nasty, brutish, and short'. (*Leviathan, XIII*) But where does contract theory come into this? Hobbes argued that to avoid the terrible consequences of 'the state of nature' men mutually agreed to place themselves under an absolute ruler in whom all power was vested and whom all had agreed to obey. This 'Leviathan' could then maintain order in the state, and allow civil society to flourish. This might occasionally require some tyrannical actions, but that was a price well worth paying. Most significantly, *there had been no contract made between the ruler and the ruled*, but only between the ruled themselves. The ruler therefore could not be held to account or overthrown for 'breaking' the contract, because he himself had not been a party to the contract. He had been placed in office by common consent, a form of democracy, and he was required to do nothing more than keep order in the kingdom. Whatever he did to achieve that, therefore, nobody had any right to complain of since, 'He that complaineth of injury from his sovereign complaineth of that whereof he himself is the author, and therefore ought not to accuse any man but himself, no nor himself of injury, because to do injury to oneself is impossible'.

This last argument sounds rather dubious. Men obviously *can* do injury to themselves, and what if the ruler failed in his prime duty, that of keeping order? Also dubious is Hobbes' concept of the 'state of nature, wherein men live without government'. Is this always as bad as Hobbes believed? We know a great deal more about 'the state of nature' today than ever was known in Hobbes' time, thanks to the work of our anthropologists and archaeologists. In hunter-gatherer societies, we find no evidence of one supreme ruler dictating in a tyrannical fashion to everyone else. Within the tribes every man was a warrior as well as a hunter, but these men did not spend all their time attacking and killing one another. Rather, the norm within these communities was co-operation and mutual support. This was only common sense. Hobbes could have observed the same kind of behaviour in packs of wolves. What, are we lower than the beasts? Yes, there was inter-tribal warfare on occasions, but equally there could have been war between two Hobbesian states. Indeed, history has proved that dictatorships are actually more inclined to go to war, simply provoking thereby a different form of anarchy.

Although Hobbes was such a powerful advocate of absolutism, his treatise in fact represented a move away from the idea of the divine right of kings, and instead took thought in the direction of contract theory, putting forward a secular and rational justification for absolutism rather than a divine one. Hobbes himself was an outright materialist, denying the existence of 'incorporeal substance' as a contradiction in terms. By saying this he was denying the existence of the soul, and exposing himself to the charge of atheism, which his enemies were quick to take up. Hobbes' religious views were certainly unorthodox, but he always strenuously denied the charge of atheism, surviving the attacks of his opponents to live to a ripe old age, while the idea of 'contract' which he had introduced into political discourse rapidly took on a life of its own. It was mainly as a result of the development of this idea of contract that England was shortly to emerge as a world leader in terms of innovative political thought.

However, the Hobbesian theory of contract was not the only piece of radical political thought to be thrown up by the convulsions of the British Civil Wars of 1642-51. During this period, Englishmen in particular showed themselves to be capable of great originality and independence of thought in the political field. The very idea that a king could be tried as a 'traitor' to his country by a quasi-judicial process, and then formally sentenced to death by his own subjects flew directly in the face of divine right theory, which had been in the ascendant up to that time. On January 6, 1649, the purged House of Commons, which by then was little more than the cat's paw of the New Model Army, abolished the monarchy and the House of Lords and passed what was, for the time, this astonishing resolution:

> That the people are, under God, the original of all just power; that the Commons of England in Parliament assembled, being chosen by and representing the people, have the supreme power in this nation; that whatsoever is enacted or declared for law by the Commons in Parliament assembled hath the force of law, and all the people of this nation are concluded thereby, although the consent and concurrence of King or House of Peers be not had thereunto. (*Commons Journals Vol. VI, pp. 107-8*)

Today, we might accept these points as being fair enough, but in 1649 they were about 300 years ahead of their time. They meant that the king was tried as plain Mr. Charles Stuart, 'that man of blood', as Cromwell described him. (He was a fine one to talk!) After the execution of Charles, the 'Commonwealth of England' embarked upon an experiment in republicanism that was to last until the Restoration of 1660.

Radical ideas on social change also emerged in this period, from egalitarians like John Lilburne (1614-57) the 'Leveller', who argued for a democratic government and society, and Gerald Winstanley (1609-76) the 'Digger', who would have abolished private property in land. Both men became Quakers in later life. In 1649 Winstanley produced a short tract with the title, *A Declaration from the Poor Oppressed People of England* in which he addressed England's great landowners, declaring,

> The power of enclosing land and owning property was brought into creation by your ancestors by the sword; which first did murder their fellow creatures, and after plunder or steal away their land, and left this land successively to you, their children. And therefore, though you did not kill or thieve, yet you hold that cursed thing in your

hand by the power of the sword; and so you justify the wicked deeds of your fathers, and that sin of your fathers shall be visited upon the heads of you and your children to the third and fourth generation, and longer too, till your bloody and thieving power be rooted out of this land. (p. 1)

Historically, Winstanley was quite correct here. Following the Battle of Hastings in 1066, William I was held to be the 'owner' of all the land in England by right of conquest. He held it by the sword, but then let out the right to occupy it to his feudal supporters, the barons and knights, in return for military service from them. These men over time acquired a title of full ownership of the lands they occupied, forcing the peasants who worked the lands to pay them rents. Nevertheless, they were frequently obliged to fight for their titles in bloody conflicts. It also remains true that the hereditary ownership of land, sometimes huge amounts of land, is still with us even today. That 'bloody and thieving power' is with us yet.

Religious thought too moved in highly radical directions during this turbulent period. The Quakers and the Baptists may both trace their origins back to these times, and a host of other sects emerged as well, such as the Fifth Monarchists, Seekers, Arians, Socinians, and Antinomians. Collectively they were known as the Sects or the Independents, for they did indeed show great independence of thought in religious matters. From 1649 to 1660, however, all were tolerated, for the regime at this time was supported entirely by the bayonets of the New Model Army, which itself was made up almost entirely of Independents, since these men had been the most radical and ardent anti-royalists. Cromwell himself was an Independent, with religious ideas that were entirely his own. One soldier is reported as saying, 'If I should worship the sun or moon like the Persians, or that pewter pot upon the table there, no one has anything to do with it'. (D. Masson, *The Life of Milton* (1880) Vol. III p. 525) Again, this degree of religious freedom is taken for granted in the present day, but in the intolerant atmosphere of the 1640s such an attitude was centuries ahead of its time. The other religious groups of the day, the Catholics, Anglicans, and Presbyterians were much more typical of their age. They hated the Independents, referring to them as 'that hydra-headed monster of accumulated heresies'. (*Ibid*, p. 135) As soon as the power of the army collapsed under the leadership of Oliver's son Richard Cromwell, the regime fell, and the monarchy and intolerant Anglican religion were restored.

Following the Restoration of 1660, two names emerge as most prominent in a new wave of radical political thought that swept England in the second half of the seventeenth century, those of Algernon Sidney (1609-83) and John Locke (1632-1704). Sidney was an ardent republican, which was rather surprising, in view of both his background and his experiences with the British Commonwealth and Protectorate. His pedigree could scarcely have been more aristocratic. His father was Robert Sidney, second Earl of Leicester, and his mother Dorothy Percy, daughter of the ninth Earl of Northumberland. Despite this, however, he was one of the minority of his class who fought against the King, bravely leading a charge at the Battle of Marston Moor in 1644, and later serving as a colonel in Cromwell's New Model Army. Because Sidney was a younger son and not in line for his father's title, he was technically a commoner, and therefore able to sit in the House of Commons, serving as a member of the Long Parliament from 1645 to 1649. He even acted as a commissioner at the trial of Charles I in 1649, after the king had lost the civil war. He was dismayed, however, when a majority of the 150 commissioners appointed to try the king voted for the death penalty. Sidney believed that this was going too far, and he squared up to Cromwell, pointing out that a king could not be tried in his own courts, and that in fact no man could be tried by that particular court, since it lacked all legality and credibility. But Cromwell had no time for legal niceties, and a 'short way' with opponents. 'I tell you', Cromwell thundered back, 'we will cut off the king's head with the crown upon it!' (C.H. Firth, *Oliver Cromwell* (1900) p. 218)

This was of course done, and later, in 1659, Sidney came around to thinking that it had been the right thing to do after all. His relationship with Cromwell did not improve, however. After the establishment of the Protectorate in 1653, he came to regard Cromwell as a tyrant, a reasonable enough point of view. The New Model Army, on which Cromwell's power rested, consisted almost entirely of Independents, religious radicals who believed in toleration for all religious beliefs, so long as these did not include 'popery or prelacy'. This latter meant any church governed by bishops, which included the Church of England. All Anglicans and Catholics, therefore, who between them made up the great majority of the population, were excluded from Cromwell's 'toleration'. The Presbyterians, the next largest religious group, *were* tolerated by the Independents, who recognised them as another bishop-free sect like themselves, but the Presbyterians were certainly *not* ready to return the favour and tolerate the Independents, whom they regarded as unconscionable heretics! Indeed, the Independents could not possibly have represented more than ten per cent of the whole nation. Sidney put this point to Cromwell, asking him how he could hope to rule when nine men in every ten were against him. Cromwell did not disagree with the figures. 'Aye', replied Cromwell, 'but how if I should disarm the nine and put a sword in the tenth man's hand? Would not that do the business?'(J.H. Jesse, *Memoirs of the Court of England* (1840) Vol. III p. 67) Indeed it could. With a standing army of little more than 57,000 men, Cromwell was able to hold down three kingdoms and levy the taxes necessary for the support of his troops. In Cromwell's mind, nothing was more important than securing freedom of worship for his co-religionists, the Independents, and the army was their only guarantee of this freedom. A constitutionalist Cromwell was not: his only concern was with doing 'God's work' on earth. In Cromwell's mind, this was his 'divine right' to rule.

Algernon Sidney, on the other hand, was a profound constitutional thinker, despite his almost fanatical dedication to republicanism. He was in Rome in 1660 when the Restoration took place, and because of his republican reputation he thought it wiser to remain abroad for a few years. While in France in 1666 he wrote *Court Maxims*, a short treatise in which he argued that the Restoration had been a mistake, declaring, 'as death is the greatest evil that can befall a person, monarchy is the worst evil that can befall a nation'. With remarkable prescience, Charles II had sent agents abroad in the 1660s to hunt Sidney down and kill him: two attempts on his life failed narrowly, and Sidney was forced to keep on the move. In the calmer atmosphere of the 1670s, however, Sidney at last returned to England hoping to live quietly, but soon found the lure of political involvement to be too strong for him. In 1679 England was overtaken by the Exclusion Crisis, with a majority in the House of Commons attempting to exclude James, Duke of York from succession to the throne on the grounds of his Catholicism and absolutist beliefs. Charles II had no legitimate children, and his younger brother James was next in line for the throne. He was not without support, and in 1680 his faction printed and distributed Robert Filmer's *Patriarcha*, which had not previously been published. This strenuous defence of divine right theory provoked a vigorous response from the exclusionists, with three counter-arguments being penned almost immediately. James Tyrrell's *Patriarcha non Monarcha* was published in 1681, while Algernon Sidney began work on his *Discourses Concerning Government*, not published until 1698. At the same time John Locke (1632-1704) began work on his celebrated *Two Treatises of Government*, finally published in 1689, but completed well before this date. These latter two works, both inspired by the Exclusion Crisis, are now recognised as milestones in the history of political thought, exerting a profound influence upon the Founding Fathers of the American Revolution, and subsequently upon political theory around the world. Much of what they had to say was basically anticipated in the *Tractatus Politico Religio* of Baruch Spinoza that had been published in 1670, but Spinoza's work was ignored at the time outside a small academic circle, and he exercised no influence upon contemporary events. It was the later nineteenth century before his work became widely appreciated.

Sidney's *Discourses* were essentially a chapter by chapter refutation of the views of Filmer in his *Patriarcha*. Both books consisted of three chapters divided into numerous sections, with Sidney flatly contradicting all the points which Filmer had put forward. He argued that people had a basic right to choose their own leaders, and a basic right to depose them as well if they proved to be unsatisfactory. Furthermore, kings and other leaders should be subject to the law, and this law could be created only by the representatives of the people, meeting in a parliament. Partly because neither Sidney nor Locke was able to get their works published immediately, however, the exclusionists lost their argument, and succeeded only in provoking a royalist backlash.

Charles II completely outmanoeuvred them, and in 1681 was able to dissolve Parliament, declaring that he would rule without it for the rest of his reign.

Driven to despair, the exclusionists hatched a wild plan known as the Rye House Plot. The aim here was to assassinate both Charles and James as they returned to London from the races at Newmarket, and to establish a republic in Britain. Never likely to succeed in any case, the plot was betrayed, and Sidney identified as one of the conspirators. After a trial of dubious legality, Sidney was executed in December 1683, together with a dozen others.

John Locke (1632-1704) was too young for involvement in the civil wars, but he came from a middle-class Puritan family. His father, a Somerset man, was a country lawyer who had fought on the parliamentary side as a captain of cavalry in the wars, and the family's sympathies were clearly with the parliamentarians and dissenters from the established Church of England. Educated at Oxford, Locke stayed on there to take a master's degree in 1658, and returned there later to take a medical degree in 1674. For several years before this, however, Locke had been studying medicine in London and elsewhere, and in 1667 he joined the household of Antony Ashley Cooper (1631-83) who was from 1672 the First Earl of Shaftsbury, acting as the Earl's personal physician. Shaftsbury proved to be a dangerous patron, however. A strong parliamentarian and anti-Catholic, he fell from royal favour in 1675, and in 1677-8 was even imprisoned in the Tower of London for his radical views. Locke himself left the Earl's household in 1675 to travel in France for a few years, returning in 1679 at the Earl's request. Shaftsbury wanted Locke by his side as a propagandist, because he had by then emerged as the leader of the exclusionists during the Exclusion Crisis. He may have encouraged Locke to begin work on his *Two Treatises of Government* as early as 1679. The policy of Exclusion was, however a failure, and in July, 1681, Shaftsbury was arrested on a charge of high treason, and again found himself imprisoned in the Tower of London. At his trial he was on that occasion acquitted, but fearing that further charges would be brought against him later, Shaftsbury fled to the Netherlands, where he died of natural causes in January, 1683.

Shaftsbury's political career seemed at that point to have been a complete failure, but his views were to be triumphantly vindicated just a few short years after his death by the events of the Glorious Revolution of 1688-9. Among other things, he is also remembered as the founder of the Whig party, another development to emerge from the Exclusion Crisis. The exclusionists were at first known as the Petitioners, because they were continually petitioning Charles II to recall Parliament, so that they could get their Exclusion Bill passed. Those who opposed them were known at first as Abhorrers, because they abhorred the idea of excluding James, Duke of York from the throne. It was not long, however, before both sides invented pejorative nicknames to apply to each other. The Petitioners dubbed their opponents 'Tories'. The original Tories were the half-barbarous bands of Irish brigands who infested the more desolate parts of the country after the Irish rebellion of 1641. They were of course Catholics. The original 'Whigs' on the other hand were the lawless Calvinist Covenanters who held out in the Lowlands of Scotland after the failure of an insurrection there in 1679. They too were not Anglicans, having sworn a 'Covenant' to resist the authority of the Church of England, which remained the faith of the great majority south of the border. These two terms were, therefore, the most insulting available to Englishmen at the time, since neither group was English, neither was Anglican, and both were wild, lawless, and rebellious. However, once coined, the two terms 'Whig' and 'Tory' stuck, and were to dominate political discourse for the next 200 years, with the Tories generally in favour of the monarchy and Church of England, while the Whigs championed ever-greater powers for Parliament and religious toleration for Protestant dissenters. Both sides, however, hated the Catholics.

Because of his close association with Shaftsbury, Locke himself became an object of suspicion, and following the failure of the Rye House Plot in 1683, he too fled to the Netherlands. He did not think it safe to return to England until after the Glorious Revolution, accompanying William of Orange's wife Mary back to England in December, 1688. Because of the radical nature of his writings, Locke had felt it unsafe to publish them until after the Glorious Revolution of 1688-9. During his time abroad, however, Locke had been able to concentrate on his writing, and his published works reveal him to have been a man of very wide interests, and a true philosopher in the fullest sense of the word. For example, in his *An Essay Concerning Human Understanding* (1690) Locke made a major contribution to epistemology with his definition of subjectivity and the conception of the self, while his *Letters Concerning Toleration* of 1689-92 show him to have been far ahead of his time in this regard, advocating full toleration for even non-Christians, and the separation of church and state. His thoughts on toleration were taken up by the Founding Fathers of the American Constitution. He was also an economic thinker. His *Some Considerations on the Consequences of the Lowering of Interest and the Raising of the value of Money* (1691) revealed him to be a monetarist and a mercantilist, declaring that England should always strive to achieve a favourable balance of trade, and an accumulation of bullion, while in his second *Treatise* he put forward a labour theory of value. He was also a strong advocate of education, believing that men were shaped by what they learned. In his *Some Thoughts Concerning Education* (1693) Locke wrote, 'I think I may say that of all the men we meet with, nine parts of ten are what they are, good or evil, useful or not, by their education'.(p. 1) There are echoes here of the ancient Greek idea that only the sage could be virtuous.

The most famous of all Locke's writings, however, were undoubtedly his *Two Treatises of Government* published (at first anonymously) in 1689, although written long before, probably during the Exclusion Crisis of 1679-81.

The two treatises were always published together as a single book, although they are very different in character. The first is devoted entirely to an attack upon Robert Filmer's *Patriacha* and its theory of the divine right of kings. Here, Locke followed closely in the footsteps of Algernon Sidney's *Discourses Concerning Government*. It was only in the second *Treatise* that Locke put forward his own views on how government should be organised. Unlike Sidney, Locke was not a fervent anti-monarchist, but he was a strong parliamentarian, believing that in the last analysis Parliament should be the supreme power in the state, able to override royal authority, and even able to depose an unsatisfactory king. Here he followed Sidney as an advocate of resistance theory, which was still a very dangerous thing to do at the time of the Exclusion Crisis. He further argued that all just power derived from the people, and that government should be only by the consent of the governed, or at least the consent of the majority. The will of the people was to be expressed through their elected representatives in Parliament. But even this legislative body could itself be overthrown by the people if it failed to govern justly, since it was there to rule for the benefit of the people, and this was its prime duty. In his second *Treatise* Locke wrote,

> Though...there can be but one supreme power, which is the legislative, to which all the rest must be subordinate, yet the legislative, being only a fiduciary power to act for certain ends, there remains still in the people a supreme power to remove or alter the legislative when they find the legislative act contrary to the trust reposed in them. For all power given with trust for the attaining an end being limited by that end, whenever that end is manifestly neglected or opposed, the trust must necessarily be forfeited, and the power devolve to the hands of those that gave it, who may place it anew where they shall think best for their safety and security. (Chapter XIII, Section 149)

This idea, that all just power derives from the will of the people or the consent of the governed, was still a radical and revolutionary one in 1689, and helps to explain why Locke at first published his *Treatises* anonymously. On a superficial reading these make Locke sound like the ultimate democrat, but on closer inspection his credentials here become suspect. For just who were 'the people' who had the right to depose kings and dismiss legislators? Who should be allowed to vote? Only a small minority of the populace enjoyed this right in 1689: indeed, after the Glorious Revolution the franchise emerged as even more restricted than it had been before. When Locke talks about 'the people' it seems clear that he has in his mind not *all* the people, but only 'the political nation', or essentially the landowners and the wealthy in the towns who had the vote. A key question, therefore, was that of how many people could vote. The first firm figures that we have on this date from 1780, when Parliament ordered a survey to be carried out. This revealed that in England and Wales only 214,000 people out of a total population of some eight million had the vote: rather less than three per cent. This proportion could not have been very different in 1690. In Scotland the figures were even worse, with only 4,500 voters in a population of 2.6 million. Ireland, which had its own Parliament, was not included in the survey, but the franchise there was also very restricted.

In his second *Treatise* Locke again follows Sidney when he clearly implies a right of violent resistance to unjust rulers, although he does not specifically spell this out. Once again, however, such resistance could be led and organised only by members of the ruling class, who might well divide against themselves once more as they had done during the civil wars of the seventeenth century. Locke was, therefore, no rabble-rousing democrat. He was writing for an audience of middle-class property owners like himself. Although his second *Treatise* makes much of the 'natural equality' of all men and their 'natural rights', he himself became an investor in the English slave trade when he bought shares in the Royal African Company in 1671. Again, while Shaftsbury's secretary at this time he had a hand in drafting the Fundamental Constitutions of Carolina, which was then just a single colony. This constitution established a virtual feudal aristocracy, and allowed for slavery and 'indentured servitude', which was little better than slavery. Again, this causes us to wonder just who 'the people' were who should enjoy these 'natural rights' and liberties. However, Locke made a lasting and profound contribution to political thought with his concept of 'natural rights', a legacy that is assuming an ever-greater importance in our own day with, for example, the rather controversial European Court of Human Rights. Locke argued that in the 'state of nature' every man had a 'natural right' to defend his own life, liberty, and property, but that this responsibility devolved onto the civil authorities once a government had been established by consent. Even then, however, men retained a 'natural right' to overthrow that government by any means necessary if they found it to be unsatisfactory. In reality, of course, there is no such thing as 'natural' rights at all. In God's world, the real world that existed before humans arrived on the scene, no creatures had any 'natural rights', but only *powers* to do what they could. This idea of 'natural rights' is as much a purely human and artificial invention as our concepts of 'morality' and 'justice'. In reality, we have precisely no more 'natural rights' than those that we choose to invent and extend to one another: there is nothing 'natural' about them. But again, this invention is no bad thing. As I have noted before, God's world is just not good enough for us.

Locke particularly stressed the duty of government to provide safety and security for property, which was fine for those who owned substantial amounts of property, like himself. In particular, property owners were to be protected from 'unjust' taxation! In short, his second *Treatise* was far from being a charter of democracy. Rather, like Magna Carta, it was just another episode in the long-running rivalry between the Guardians and the Auxiliaries, between the Crown and the ruling class that supported it. Locke was arguing for a massive and decisive shift in the balance of power in favour of the ruling classes, but as usual the bulk of the population were to have nothing to do with it. Locke made no suggestions for the extending of the franchise or for improving the material conditions of the labouring poor in any way. On the contrary Locke supported 'the unlimited accumulation of wealth', something that could be done, of course, only by those who had some wealth to begin with. He acknowledged that this might lead to great inequality, a potential cause of conflict, but suggested only that government should be ready to deal with that problem, without saying how this should be done. Moreover, although Locke put forward a labour theory of value, saying that he who combined his labour with raw materials thereby acquired a right to ownership of the finished product, he saw nothing wrong with the idea of one man owning the land that was worked by another man, and taking a rent from it, without any input of his own labour at all! Locke was not a consistent economist. Beside his labour theory of value, he also stressed the law of supply and demand which of course gives rise to an entirely different way of establishing 'value'.

Like Sidney, Locke never specifically mentioned Thomas Hobbes by name, but he must have read his works, and he certainly introduced two of Hobbes' basic ideas into his own political theory. These were the concept of the 'state of nature' and the idea of a 'social contract'. However, Locke disagreed with Hobbes in his definition of these two concepts. Firstly, he took a more optimistic view of the 'state of nature' than had Hobbes, arguing that it was more a state of peace than a condition of eternal warfare of all against all. From what we now know of hunter-gather societies, it would seem that Locke's definition of the state of nature was closer to the truth than Hobbes'. Clearly, the members of individual tribes did not spend all their time fighting and killing one another, although there was some warfare between tribes, just as there has always been warfare between states, no matter what their forms of government. Therefore, a temporary collapse of government, leaving a reversion to the 'state of nature' for a while, was nothing to be feared, and should serve as no deterrent to the overthrowing of a tyrannical regime. However, while in the state of nature every man had a 'natural right' to defend himself and his property, yet some form of social organisation was always to be preferred, because the setting up of a form of government that all had agreed to obey guaranteed greater security for the lives, liberties, and property of all. Towards this end, therefore, men entered into a social contract with some form of governing power. But here Locke differed fundamentally from Hobbes by declaring that this was not a contract made simply amongst the governed themselves, but was rather a contract made *between the governed and the government*. This meant that *both* sides were bound by obligations, one to the other. Hobbes had argued that the ruler was not a party to the social contract made among the ruled and was therefore under no specific obligations to them beyond the keeping of order, and once in power he could not be deposed. But Locke's governments most certainly *were* under specific obligations, and *could* be removed. Their tenure of office was conditional upon their keeping the terms of the social contract that they had made with the ruled, and if they broke those terms, then that government could be dismissed by the people. However, in Locke's mind 'the people' were in fact the 'political nation', a very small proportion of the total population.

The whole thrust of Locke's *Two Treatises* was directed towards the avoidance of 'tyrannical' government. To this end Locke advocated a clear separation of the powers of government into executive, legislative, and 'federative' branches so that each branch could balance and moderate the others, although in the last resort the legislature, elected by the people, should have supreme power. Commentators have long been puzzled by Locke's failure to use the term 'judicial' in his advocacy of the separation of powers. The strange term 'federative' that he introduces does carry legal overtones, but seems to refer to unspecific, non-statute law. Some have also argued that Locke was suggesting that the judicial power was somehow subsumed within the executive power, an acceptable enough concept to him since the executive power was itself to be under the control of the legislature. The truth seems to be, however, that Locke was simply no jurist, leaving it to later writers like Montesquieu and Blackstone to stress the crucial importance of the judicial branch in its role of *interpreting* the law in difficult cases. Because judges and magistrates exercised a kind of executive power in enforcing the laws, Locke seems to have conjoined the two branches of government, executive and judiciary, into one in his own mind. A similar error was made later by Thomas Paine in his celebrated *Rights of Man.* Both men also failed to stress the importance of a fully independent judiciary within a constitutional framework. But Locke was at least a firm champion of the rule of law, to which all should be subject, even the highest in the land. He also advocated the separation of church and state, with full religious freedom for all, even non-Christians. At this time of course, the rather intolerant established Church of England was the official church of the nation, as it remains even to this day, so here Locke was making another very radical suggestion as far as England was concerned. However, in America the Founding Fathers took up his suggestion. The First Amendment to the American Constitution, drawn up in 1791, declares, 'Congress shall make no law respecting an establishment of religion.'

Because for printing reasons the earliest texts of Locke's *Two Treatises* are all dated 1690, it was for long assumed that the Glorious Revolution had inspired the philosophy, rather than the philosophy inspiring the Revolution. However, more recent scholarship has established that Locke in fact wrote his *Treatises* well before 1688. But they were not widely read before 1690, and it is purely fortuitous that political events of the time took a turn that seemed to be very largely in accordance with what Locke had advocated. The truth is that the *Treatises* neither inspired the Glorious Revolution, nor were they written subsequent to the Revolution as a justification for it. Their chronological coincidence was purely fortuitous, although Locke's views did perhaps reflect something of the changing temper of the times.

But just what was the 'Glorious Revolution' and how did it come about? It was given the title 'Glorious' because it was in its early stages largely bloodless, although there was later to be bitter warfare in Ireland and Scotland. But the Glorious Revolution is worth considering in some detail because of its profound influence upon England's constitutional development, and subsequently upon political structures around the world. As with the Exclusion Crisis, the person of James, Duke of York, later James II of England and VII of Scotland, was central to developments. James II was therefore to exercise a most profound influence upon the history of English constitutional development, although ironically his influence turned out to be exactly the opposite of the one he would have wished for! James Stuart (1633-1701) came to be known while Duke of York as a staunch Catholic and fervent admirer of Louis XIV of France, whose style of government he would, ideally, like to have emulated. These features of his character did nothing to endear him to the great majority of Englishmen. The Catholics were for him because he would have granted them full toleration and civil rights, but the Catholics were only a very small proportion of the population by 1680. Across the country James' views were so unpopular that a majority in the House of Commons was ready to pass a Bill excluding him from succession to the throne during the Exclusion Crisis of 1679-81. But the country at large was divided on the issue. Englishmen had already rid themselves of one king in 1649, and the result had been the tyrannical and highly unpopular dictatorship of Oliver Cromwell and the Independents of the New Model Army. Moreover, James still had considerable support as the legitimate heir to the throne. Did the country want to risk a second descent into a ruinous civil war? These considerations, and the personal astuteness of Charles II, saved the throne for his brother. He so successfully outmanoeuvred the exclusionists that by 1681 the country at large had swung around to the idea that the legitimate heir to the throne must be accepted as king however unpopular his views, because the alternative of rejecting him was just too difficult and too dangerous.

In February 1685 Charles II died without any legitimate children, and the crown passed to his younger brother James with very little trouble. Charles' eldest illegitimate son, the Duke of Monmouth, did try to raise a rebellion in the West Country to claim the throne for himself as a good Protestant, but he met with no support, and was executed for his trouble in July, 1685. By that time Englishmen had decided that they must knuckle down and accept James as king rather than risk any alternative. James' first wife Anne Hyde (1637-71) had borne him eight children, but only two daughters, Mary (1662-1694) and Anne (1665-1714), had survived childhood. Both daughters had been raised as Protestants on the orders of Charles II, and so in 1685 the Protestant Mary was heir to the throne. Englishmen believed that they could put up with James for a few years until Mary succeeded him. James had married a second wife, Mary of Modena in 1673, but her health had been poor. They had produced no children, and by 1685 it was assumed that they never would. Much to the consternation of England's Protestant Establishment, however, Mary unexpectedly gave birth to a healthy male child, James Francis Edward Stuart, on June 10, 1688. As a son the boy took precedence in the line of succession over his two half-sisters Mary and Anne. Moreover, he would certainly be raised as a Catholic, since his mother was, like James II, also a devout member of that faith. This birth completely changed the situation by opening up the prospect of an unending Catholic dynasty holding the throne of England.

During his three-and-a-half years on the throne James had pressed recklessly ahead with a policy of Catholic toleration, using his dispensing and suspending powers to abrogate the Test Acts of 1673 and 1678, which had been designed to exclude all non-Anglicans from public offices. James had then shamelessly appointed Catholic supporters, and some Dissenters, to numerous key posts, including the officer ranks of his new standing army. By 1688 he had managed to build this up to a force of 34,000 men spread across his three kingdoms. All this had confirmed the worst fears of his opponents: now the birth of a healthy son to his wife was the last straw. James would have to go, whatever the dangers involved. But James would, of course, have to be replaced. Englishmen had had enough of republicanism under Oliver Cromwell! Fortunately, a suitable alternative was not far away. James' daughter Mary was married to William of Orange (1650-1702) the Protestant Stadtholder of the Dutch Republic. William had a good claim to the British throne in his own right as a grandson of Charles I: his wife Mary was also his first cousin. There could be no more obvious choice.

Usually at odds, both Whigs and Tories, Lords and Commons, were now united in their determination that something must be done. The desperate lie was invented that James Francis' birth had been a fraud, with James himself a changeling smuggled into the birth chamber. In fact there had been some 200 witnesses to the reality of the birth, as was the custom of the time. This lie was readily believed, however, which gave the political nation an excuse to invite William of Orange to invade England to defend his wife's right to the succession. This excuse was also a lie – their real hope was that James II would be overthrown. Fortune favoured the enterprise. An amphibious invasion would be a very risky venture, as William knew well. Exactly 100 years earlier, the Spanish Armada had failed spectacularly. But William feared that the alternative would be another Anglo-French alliance and an attack on the Netherlands, as had happened before in 1672. Therefore, with great difficulty William persuaded the Dutch estates to back him, and launched an invasion fleet in November, 1688. Contrary winds, tides, and fog almost scuppered the enterprise, but at the last moment the wind changed, the fog lifted, and William was able to land safely at Torbay in Devon with his army. Once it became known that he was ashore, more and more towns declared for William, and leading officers from James' army deserted to him, including John Churchill, later the Duke of Marlborough. William's march to London was almost unopposed. Fearing for his life, James lost his nerve, and finally fled to France on December 23rd. This enabled Parliament to claim that James had abdicated, and that the throne was now 'vacant', a totally unprecedented situation, but a very satisfactory one from the point of view of the political nation.

In January, 1689, a parliamentary election was held, with both houses convening on January 22. This new assembly went under the name of the Convention Parliament, because of the unusual circumstances of its convening. The horse trading with William could now begin. Parliament wanted Mary to be Queen with William as regent, but William insisted that he must have the title of king, ruling as a joint sovereign with Mary. If this was refused, he declared that he would return to the Netherlands taking his wife with him, and leave the English to sort out their own affairs. Mary supported her husband in his demand, leaving Parliament with no choice but to accept William's terms. William and Mary were recognised as joint monarchs in February, 1689, and were crowned on April 11th. Scotland, as a separate kingdom, made its own settlement with William, and William and Mary were crowned there on May 11th, 1689. Catholic Ireland, however, resisted the new monarch, and William had to conquer Ireland by force, securing a decisive victory at the Battle of the Boyne over forces led by James himself, on July 11, 1690.

The occupancy of the throne was now settled, but Parliament was in no mood to leave the constitutional status quo in place, for this might allow for the rise of another James II in the future. There must now be radical constitutional change. On January 29, 1689 the Commons recorded in their Journal that William, 'cannot take it ill if we make conditions to secure ourselves for the future, in order to do justice to those who sent us hither'. These 'conditions' were to amount to a full-scale constitutional revolution. The changes were implemented by three monumental pieces of legislation, all passed by Parliament and approved by the Crown. The first of these was the Coronation Oath Act of February, 1689. This substantially reformed the oath that had been taken by monarchs hitherto, making it shorter but at the same time more explicit. Instead of undertaking to, 'protect and defend the bishops and churches under my government' the king was now to promise to, 'maintain the true profession of the gospel and the Protestant Reformed Religion Established by Law'. Further, future kings were to, 'solemnly promise and swear to govern the people of this kingdom of England, and the dominions thereunto belonging, according to the statutes in Parliament agreed on, and the laws and customs of the same'. This was another important change from the previous oath, which had defined laws as being the grant of the king, rather than the creation of Parliament. The relationship between king and Parliament was being fundamentally redefined in this new oath.

The second highly significant piece of legislation to be passed was the so-called Bill of Rights, which received the royal assent on December 16, 1689. It thereby became, of course, an Act and a Bill no longer, but for most of 1689 it had been worked on by Parliament as a Bill, and the name stuck. It was based on the Declaration of Right that had been presented to William and Mary in February 1689, prior to their accepting the crown, and William had agreed to its terms. As an Act, the Bill of Rights began with a long list of complaints about the behaviour of James II, making it clear that such behaviour would not be tolerated from any monarch in future. The positive terms of the Act were then stated, and they are worth enumerating, for they were to have great significance for the future of Britain, and indeed of the world.

The use of the dispensing and suspending powers without the consent of Parliament was banned. No taxation should be levied without the authority of Parliament. The right to petition the monarch should be without prejudice. No standing army was to be kept in peacetime without the consent of Parliament. Protestant subjects (but not Catholics) had the right to keep and bear arms. Parliamentary elections should be free and according to law. Freedom of speech in Parliament should not be infringed, nor challenged in any court outside of Parliament. Excessive bail should not be required, nor excessive fines imposed, nor cruel and unusual punishments inflicted. Jurors should be empanelled according to law and without interference from the crown. Parliaments should be held frequently. Finally, Catholics were to be permanently banned from the throne of England since, 'it hath been found by experience that it is inconsistent with the safety and welfare of this Protestant kingdom to be governed by a papist prince'.

Echoes of this Act, and sometimes its very wording, were later to be heard in the Bill of Rights appended to the American Constitution, in the French Revolution's Declaration of the Rights of Man, in the United Nations Universal Declaration of Human Rights, and in the European Convention on Human Rights. It radically altered the English constitution of the time, massively shifting the balance of political power in Parliament's favour. Charles II and James II had both ruled for years without consulting Parliament at all, but from 1689 Parliament has remained in annual session every year from that day to this. But the revolutionary changes of the time were not yet complete.

The third major piece of legislation that was to transform the political scene in England was the Act of Settlement of 1701, which altered the line of succession to the English throne, ultimately vesting it in George Ludwig, Elector of Hanover (1660-1727) in 1714. The 1689 Bill of Rights had declared that the throne would pass first to Mary's children, but in the absence of these then to her sister, the Princess Anne, second daughter of James II, and to her heirs, or failing these to any heirs of William by a later marriage. These provisions had seemed adequate enough, but fate took a hand. By 1701 Mary

(1662-94) was dead, leaving no surviving heirs. William (1650-1702) had not remarried, and it seemed unlikely that he would produce surviving heirs either. This proved to be the case. Queen Anne, who succeeded him in 1702 was married to Prince George of Denmark, but her health was poor, and despite seventeen pregnancies, she too died with no surviving heirs in 1714. Foreseeing that this might well be the case after Anne's only surviving child, Prince William, died in 1700, the English Parliament decided that further steps needed to be taken to secure the succession in Protestant hands. This was the main reason for passing the Act of Settlement in 1701. However, that was not its only provision.

As a replacement for James II, William of Orange had been the almost perfect alternative, but not quite. Although he had not been a Catholic, he had not been an Anglican either. William was a Calvinist, of that sect known in England as the Presbyterians, and he had pressed for the toleration of his co-religionists, and other dissenting sects, securing for them the Toleration Act of 1689, which allowed them freedom of worship, but left them, like the Catholics, excluded from political offices. These were to be reserved exclusively for members of the Anglican Establishment. William, however, had been allowed to serve as Supreme Governor of the Anglican Church whilst not being an Anglican himself. He had not been required to change his religion, but this privilege was not to be extended to future monarchs. The first provision of the 1701 Act of Settlement declared that all future sovereigns, 'shall join in communion with the Church of England' or forego the crown.' This was, however, something of a cosmetic requirement. George I and George II were allowed to remain in practice Lutherans, 'conforming' only occasionally and as ceremonial required. The supreme importance of religion in the Settlement was, however, further underlined in the new order of succession to the throne which it laid down. James II, who was still alive when the 1701 Act was passed, was excluded from the throne, together with his surviving children by Mary of Modena, James Edward and Louisa Maria, and their heirs. The reason for their exclusion was primarily their Catholicism. Also excluded were all the descendents of James' sister Henrietta, also a Catholic, from whom later Jacobite pretenders were descended. Altogether more than 50 Catholic heirs, all with a better hereditary claim to the crown than George of Hanover, were passed over. The Act also declared that any future sovereign who became a Catholic, or married a Catholic, would thereby forfeit the crown. This clause was repealed only in 2013. So fiercely anti-Catholic was parliament at this time that one could almost believe that they would have had a Moslem or a Hindu as king had that been the only way to keep a Catholic off the throne!

In future, no person who held a paid office under the monarch or who received a pension from the Crown could become a Member of Parliament. The aim here was to prevent the Crown from filling Parliament with 'placemen', who would be the king's creatures, not a difficult thing to do in those days of 'pocket boroughs' and a very limited franchise. This still allowed for Privy Councillors to be appointed by the Crown, but in practice it permitted the emergence of a whole new form of executive government. In 1701 the office of 'Prime Minister' was unknown, as was the idea of 'cabinet government'. However, both were later to emerge as an unforeseen consequence of the Act of Settlement. The idea of this 'Place Clause' was to further diminish the Crown's ability to exert an influence over Parliament, thus taking a further step towards a clearer separation of the executive and legislative branches of government. In Britain, however, this separation was never to be made as clearly and decisively as it is under the constitution of the United States of America. In this country, all members of the executive branch of government must also be members of the legislature, while in the U.S. no member of the legislature may also be a member of the executive branch. This came about in Britain because, although in theory the executive branch in 1701 consisted of the king and his Privy Council which advised him, after 1714 it became customary for a smaller, select group known as the Executive Committee of the Privy Council to take all the important decisions regarding advice to be given to the monarch. This group came to be called the Privy Cabinet, and later just 'The Cabinet', whose leader, as a minister of the Crown, came to be called the 'Prime Minister'. George I's ignorance of the ways of British government, and his readiness to rely on his ministers and accept their advice, meant that this 'Cabinet', headed by the 'Prime Minister', rapidly became the *de facto* administrative branch of government during the reigns of George I and George II from 1714 to 1760. The first clearly recognised 'Prime Minister' was of course Robert Walpole (1676-1745) who held this office from 1721 to 1742. The Cabinet which he led consisted entirely of members of the House of Commons and the House of Lords and this tradition, although never laid down as law, persists to this day.

But how does this tradition square with the Place Clause in the Act of Settlement? Surely the Prime Minister and Cabinet members are the king's ministers? Yes, indeed they are, and to this day the UK government is referred to as 'Her Majesty's Government'. However, in Walpole's day neither the Prime Minister nor Cabinet members, nor members of Parliament were paid anything by the Crown, and only *paid* ministers had been excluded by the Act. Cabinet members, like MPs, were supposed to be men of independent means. Moreover the executive, in the form of the Cabinet, was in practice 'appointed' by Parliament rather than the Crown, and they could be dismissed by Parliament. Even today, the Prime Minister must retain the confidence and approval of a majority of the House of Commons. If a vote of confidence in the Prime Minister is called in the Lower House, and the Prime Minister loses that vote of confidence, then he must resign, and all his Cabinet with him. In this way, Cabinet government was able to co-exist happily with the Place Clause. The Clause still retains some relevance today, however, because MPs who wish to resign from their seats must do so by applying for an archaic paid office under the Crown, usually the Stewardship of the Chiltern Hundreds or of the Manor of Northstead. Today of course MPs are paid, but via a legal technicality they are not paid by the Crown.

A third important provision of the Act of Settlement laid down that in future all judges once appointed could hold their offices *quamdiu se bene gesserint* (during good behaviour) which meant in effect for life, or until they decided to resign. This clause of course diminished the judicial power of the Crown by making it impossible for the king to dismiss judges who brought in rulings of which he disapproved. In practice moreover, George I and George II appointed judges on Cabinet advice, and this tradition has been retained to this day.

Fourthly, although a power of pardon was left to the Crown, and is still allowed to heads of state today, this power was not to extend to anyone who was impeached by the House of Commons and found guilty by the House of Lords after a proper trial, on the basis of a simple majority vote. This meant that Parliament retained a measure of judicial power over those who had offended it, further blurring the separation of powers in Britain.

The remaining clauses in the Act of Settlement related to George I as a foreigner and a ruler of foreign lands, since he was also the Duke of Brunswick-Luneburg within the Holy Roman Empire, better known as the Elector of Hanover, its capital. These clauses were designed to protect British interests, but they became increasingly irrelevant as time went on.

The Act of Settlement completed the revolutionary legislation of 1689-1701 which had transformed the English constitution. But it had applied only to England, Ireland, and Wales. Scotland remained a separate kingdom, with a deeper attachment to the Stuart line than existed in England, since the Stuarts had originally been a Scottish dynasty. Most of the Scots were Protestants of the Calvinist school, sharing with the English a hatred of Catholicism, but in the sparsely populated Highlands the old Catholic faith still found favour. As late as 1745 the Young Pretender Bonnie Prince Charlie, grandson of James II, could still raise an army of wild Gaelic swordsmen in the Highlands who were ready to fight a last forlorn battle for the Stuart cause. In order to secure the Revolution Settlement, Scotland had to be brought on board. This was achieved by an unsavoury combination of threats, bribery, and cajoling which eventually persuaded the Scottish ruling class to agree to the Treaty of Union in 1706. This treaty was then enshrined in legislation under the Union with Scotland Act passed in England in 1706, and the Act of Union with England Act passed in Scotland in 1707. Under the terms of these Acts the independent Scottish Parliament was abolished, and Scotland instead sent 45 MPs to the now united Parliament at Westminster, where they joined 513 English and Welsh members. 16 Scottish peers joined the now British House of Lords.

Presbyterianism was accepted as the established Church of Scotland, and the Scots were allowed to keep their own existing laws, courts, and legal system. The Scots accepted all the terms of the Revolution Settlement including the new line of succession, and the two nations then became officially the United Kingdom of Great Britain.

George I had been a desperate choice as monarch. He had almost nothing to recommend him except the fact that he was not a Catholic, and was prepared to conform, at least nominally, to Anglicanism as a condition of accepting the Crown. In his German lands he had ruled as an absolute monarch, and he never fully understood the British constitution, which was indeed a rather complicated instrument by 1714. He spoke almost no English, and made little attempt to learn the language, conversing with his ministers in French. He made numerous return visits to his native Hanover, where he died and was buried in 1727. He tried to claim that he ruled England by hereditary right, since he was indeed the Protestant with the best title to the Crown as the great-grandson of James I. However, this ignored the fact that more than 50 Catholic heirs with a better hereditary claim than his own had been passed over. In reality, nothing less than elective monarchy had been established in Britain by his accession to the throne. Every subsequent monarch had to remember that in Britain, one king had been executed by his people and another driven into exile. It was clear to all that in Britain the monarch too served only *quamdiu se bene gesserint* (only during good behaviour). What had happened before could happen again. Contempt for authority is the beginning of wisdom. In the sixteenth century the English and the Scots had shown contempt for the authority of the Pope by abandoning Catholicism. Now they were showing contempt for monarchical authority by deposing one king and installing another who was entirely one of their own choice. On this rebellious island not only had the theory of divine right been jettisoned beyond recall by these developments, but even the principle of strict hereditary succession to the Crown had been thrown out of the window after it! The new united nation of Great Britain was in 1707 leading the way with constitutional changes that were later to be emulated across the world.

The Revolution Settlement of 1689-1701 and the Acts of Union had constituted a massive victory of the Auxiliaries over the Guardians, of the British ruling classes over the Crown, of the legislature over the executive. Under its terms the new British Parliament became the most powerful legislative body in Europe, and indeed of the world. But this raises an interesting question. How far were these changes inspired by the political thought of the times, and how far by purely fortuitous factors? In 1963 Harold Macmillan was asked by a young reporter what he found to be the most difficult aspect of his job as Prime Minister. With a weary sigh the old PM replied, ‘Events, dear boy, events!’ To do justice to the role of ‘events’ and chance factors in this case, it seems that a brief foray into counterfactual history is called for. What if the wind had not changed and the fog had not lifted on that fateful November day in 1688? What if William's invasion fleet had been driven onto the rocks and wrecked like the Spanish armada? What if James II had not been the king that he was, but instead had embraced Anglicanism? Almost certainly, given the temper of the times, he would never have been deposed, and the whole Revolution Settlement would not have occurred at that time. James produced healthy male heirs, and indeed the Stuart line persists to this day, as does an enormous respect for the monarchy here in Britain. Indeed, what if George I had not been the man that he was? Would the Revolution Settlement have had the same impact? Consideration of such factors might lead us to believe that the writings of Algernon Sidney and John Locke had little influence on the course of events. Perhaps the crucial player in the Revolution Settlement should be seen as being Henry VIII, who had set England on the road to becoming a sincerely Protestant nation. But again, what if the Pope had simply granted him the longed-for annulment of his marriage to Catherine of Aragon? Would England ever have turned Protestant? Probably not. Prior to his divorce issue, Henry had been a very sincere Catholic. We certainly cannot ignore the role of chance factors in History.

On the other hand, however, the political thought of the time did have a part to play. John Locke's *Two Treatises* had been published in 1689, and Algernon Sidney's *Discourses Concerning Government* in 1698. It has been argued that this latter work was in fact more influential at the time than the former because of its more straightforwardly anti-monarchical tone, although both had ridiculed the notion of divine right. These works certainly reflected the new temper of the time, and were probably influential when it came to drawing up the Act of Settlement, but there can be little doubt that the prime motivation for the Glorious Revolution of 1688-9 was the pressing and immediate necessity of getting rid of James II. In retrospect of course, Sidney and Locke came to be seen as the intellectual heroes of the Glorious Revolution, and were credited with a greater influence upon events than perhaps was merited.

(d) The Age of Ideology: Rule by Philosophy

In general, history would seem to suggest that radical new works on political thought do not have an immediate impact at the time of their publication, but philosophy will out. In the longer term, their influence can be very considerable indeed. This point is quite well illustrated by the trajectory of French political thought in the eighteenth century. After 1714 the British settled down to digest the great political changes of the previous 25 years, and to adapt to their radically new constitution. The torch of innovative political thought then passed to the French-speaking world. Collectively, those innovative thinkers of eighteenth-century France in this age of the so-called 'Enlightenment' were known as the *philosophes,* and their thinking ranged well beyond the political sphere alone. In particular the *encyclopédistes* took the whole range of human knowledge as their field, publishing the famous *Encyclopédie* in 28 volumes between 1751 and 1772. This was the world's first true encyclopaedia, although it had in fact been inspired by the work of an Englishman, Ephraim Chambers (1680-1740), who had published his two-volume *Universal Dictionary of Arts and Sciences* in London in 1728. The editors of the *Encyclopédie* were Denis Diderot (1713-84) and Jean d'Alembert (1717-83) but its most prolific contributor was Louis de Jaucourt (1707-79), who wrote no less than a quarter of all the entries himself! Many of these entries were challenging in tone, highly critical of the political and social structures then current in France, and critical too of the Catholic Church, advocating toleration and religious freedom for all. In 1759 the work was officially banned, but because it had highly placed admirers the ban was never enforced. Diderot declared that his aim was 'to change the way people think', which was quite a dangerous venture under the absolute monarchy of eighteenth-century France. Indeed, Diderot suffered a spell of imprisonment in 1749 for his materialist views. The volumes promoted the advancement of science and secular thought, supporting tolerance, rationality, and open-mindedness. The contributors were, however, in no way agitators or revolutionaries. It was not their intention to sow the seeds of a full-scale revolution, but in the event they in fact contributed substantially to this outcome.

Another group of *philosophes* who ranged beyond the political sphere were the so-called 'Physiocrats' who were later given this title, although at the time they called themselves *économistes*. Their concern was mainly with economic affairs, but this inevitably led them on to fiscal issues, and so to a consideration of the political structure of France. The leading names in this field were those of François Quesnay (1694-1774), Jacques Turgot (1727-81) who briefly held the office of France's Controller–general of Finance from 1774-6, and Vincent de Gournay (1712-59) who served as France's *intendant du commerce* from 1751. They built on the work of earlier thinkers such as Pierre Le Pesant (1646-1714) and Richard Cantillon (1681-1734) who had been essentially anti-mercantilists, critical of government controls over trade and manufacturing. The Physiocrats were certainly indicative of the bold and orginal thinking that was to be found in France at this time, and were indeed to be the inspiration for Adam Smith's *Wealth of Nations* after Smith had visited France in the 1760s and had met several of them, but this group will be considered more fully in the Economics chapter below.

Others among the *philosophes* were brilliant satirists like François-Marie Arout (1694-1778), better known to history by his pen name of Voltaire. His first satire, *Micromégas,* appeared in 1752, and his better known satire, *Candide*, in 1759. In both works he denounced the hypocrisies, injustices, and absurdities of the *AncienRégime*, and argued staunchly for political reform and religious toleration. These were dangerous opinions to hold in eighteenth-century France. Voltaire suffered imprisonment, exile, and was twice beaten up by thugs on the orders of offended members of the French nobility. Another brilliant satirist was Charles-Louis de Secondat, Baron de Montesquieu (1689-1755). The best known of his satirical writings was his *Lettres Persanes,* in which an imaginary Persian visitor to France is alternatively astonished and appalled by the absurdities and unfairness of French society. But Montesquieu was much more than a satirist: like Voltaire, he was also a great philosopher and profound political thinker. Both men were admirers of the new British constitution which had come into full effect in 1714. In his most famous work, *De l'Esprit des Lois*, published anonymously in 1748, Montesquieu ranged over every aspect of government and society, bringing in climatic and other physical factors in his attempt to classify the various different forms of government and constitutions. His work has earned him from some the title of 'father of anthropology', while in his preface to the French edition of his *General Theory of Employment, Interest, and Money* first published in 1936, John Maynard Keynes (1883-1946) described Montesquieu as, 'the real French equivalent of Adam Smith, the greatest of your economists, head and shoulders above the Physiocrats in penetration, clear-headedness and good sense (which are the qualities an economist should have)'.

Multi-talented as he was, however, Montesquieu is best known for his doctrine of the strict separation of powers within a constitutional framework. Although he was a noble and a landlord, Montesquieu had also been trained as a lawyer, and fully understood the importance of the rule of law and therefore of the key role that a fully independent judiciary should play under a limited, constitutional monarchy. A fine classicist, he had published in 1734 *Considérations sur les Causes de la Grandeur des Romains et de leur Decadence*, exploring the history of the Ancient World, where we may trace the seeds of his later thoughts on constitutional frameworks. Seeing what had happened to the Romans, Montesquieu was very concerned to avoid a descent into *le despotisme* in his native France. Indeed, he was instrumental in introducing the term 'despotism' into the political lexicon, a term later taken up by Quesnay in 1767. In Montesquieu's view, the best guarantee against 'despotism' was a sharing out of power between the executive, legislative, and judicial branches of government, with each branch being separate from, and independent of, the other two. This was the main thrust of his 1748 master work, *De l'Esprit des Lois*, which was very well received in Britain, North America, and some parts of Europe, but not in France itself. Indeed, in 1751 the Vatican placed it on the Index of Prohibited Books. This was something of an overreaction since Montesquieu had not been a bitter critic of the Church, and like the Encyclopaedists and the Physiocrats, he was no revolutionary, no great champion of the common man, and no supporter of colonial independence. Despite this, however, Donald S. Lutz writing in *The American Political Science Review* for March, 1984, was able to show that in 916 political writings penned by prominent Americans between 1760 and 1805, Montesquieu was cited more often than any other authority except the Bible, and his influence may be clearly seen in the structure of the American Constitution to this day.

As an accomplished jurist, Montesquieu was able to fill the gap in the separation of powers theory that Locke had left incomplete, by clearly stressing the judicial dimension, and its role of interpretation. But England too had produced its great jurists, and some of these also deserve a mention at this point, for the principle of the rule of law had long been respected in England, although not always observed by either rulers or people. The first great English jurist was Henry de Bracton (1210-68) who attempted an early codification of such English law as existed at the time with his four-volume *De Legibus et Consuetudinibus Angliae*, left uncompleted at the time of his death. Even at this early date, Bracton was able to argue here that in England the king was far from being an absolute potentate, declaring,

> The king has a superior, namely God. Also the law, by which he was made king. Also his curia, namely the earls and barons, because if he is without a bridle, that is without law, they ought to put the bridle on him...The king must be under no man, but under God and the law, because the law makes the king...there is no rex where will rules rather than lex. (Vol. 2, pp. 33, 110)

These were grand words indeed, but at the time they were rather wishful thinking. It had been no law that had made William the Conqueror king in 1066, but simply the force of his arms, and even 200 years after the Conquest Bracton still had to admit that the king could be curbed in the last analysis only by the power of his barons. But English jurists maintained their touching belief in the majesty of the law.

We might look next at Sir John Fortescue, a Devon man educated in law at Exeter College Oxford, who enjoyed a long and eventful life between 1394 and 1480. He rose to become the Chief Justice of King's Bench, an office that he held between 1442 and 1460, and wrote several treatises on English law, although none of them was published in his lifetime. The best known of these was *De Laudibus Legum Angliae* (In Praise of English Laws) written around 1470, but not published until 1543. In this work he famously described England as a *dominum politicum et regale*, that is to say not an absolute monarchy, but a kingdom in which the king ruled under the law. Ever since the granting of Magna Carta in 1215 this had been true in theory, but it had not prevented English kings from playing fast and loose with the law whenever they thought they could get away with it. Henry VIII, for example, came as close to being an absolute monarch as made no difference, able to change the law virtually at will by resorting to the simple expedient of terrorising his parliaments. Oliver Cromwell had ridden roughshod over all English laws and precedents, and even in the late 1680s James II was still able to make a mockery of the laws of England by the free use of his suspending powers. Nevertheless, a framework of basic laws was in existence, growing in complexity and efficiency as the centuries passed. Following the revolutionary legislative programme of 1689-1701 it could at last be said that Fortescue's *dominum politicum et regale* had finally come into existence. The Glorious Revolution had represented not only a victory of the political nation over the king, but also a victory for the rule of law, which had at last been removed, *de facto,* from any further royal manipulation. However, the battle to reach this point had been a long and hard one, with the common and statute laws of England often requiring their doughty defenders against royal encroachments.

One of England's greatest defenders of its legal framework was Sir Edward Coke (1552-1634) a Norfolk man of good family who moved from Trinity College Cambridge to the Inns of Court, where he qualified as a barrister. Thanks to his family connections, he was made Attorney General for England and Wales in 1594, in which post he acquitted himself well, being promoted on merit to the office of Chief Justice of the Court of Common Pleas in 1606. James I soon came to regret this appointment, however, for Coke proved to be a great champion of the rule of law, in opposition to the pretensions of the Crown. His proclivity in this regard was never better illustrated than in the *Case of Prohibitions* of November, 1608. Here, James I argued that as head of both church and state he might 'prohibit' the trying of any case in any court, lay or ecclesiastical, withdrawing it to judge the issue himself in person, declaring, 'In cases where there is not express authority, the king may himself decide in his royal person, for the judges are but delegates of the king...the king protecteth the law, and not the law the king'. James was very well educated, and had earlier noted in his *Basilikon Doran* that there had been kings before there were laws, and that therefore the kings had created the laws, and not the laws the kings. All laws were therefore the gift of the king, since even statute law could not be created without the royal assent. This implied that what the king had given the king could take back, which indeed he legally could at that time with his suspending power. All laws were the king's laws, and all courts the king's courts. Who then was better qualified to act as a judge? In these claims James was historically and legally entirely correct, as he was in his belief that kings had always acted as judges. He argued too that the law was based upon reason and common sense, and that he had reason as well as the judges. But these were not the sort of arguments that Coke wanted to hear. He recorded the king's words and his own counter case in the twelfth of his famous *Reports*.

To which it was answered by me that true it was that God had endowed his majesty with excellent science and great endowments of nature, but his majesty was not learned in the laws of his realm of England, and causes which concern the life, or inheritance, or goods, or fortunes of his subjects are not to be decided by natural reason but by the artificial reason and judgment of the law, which law is an act that requires long study and experience before that a man can attain to a cognisance of it, and that the law was the golden met-wand and measure to try the causes of the subjects, and which protected his majesty in safety and in peace. With which the king was greatly offended, and said that then he should be under the law, which was treason to affirm, as he said. To which I replied that Bracton saith *quod rex non debet esse sub homine, sed sub Deo – et lege.* (G. Wilson (ed.), *The Reports of Sir Edward Coke, Knt.* (1777) Report 12, pp.63-4)

James was infuriated by this reply, and Coke was saved from imprisonment only by the special pleading of his powerful friends, who interceded with the king on his behalf. The lawyers could twitter on as much as they liked about their *dominum politicum et regale*, where the king was under the law, but James 'God calls me god' Stuart wanted nothing to do with the concept. The battle to establish the unchallenged rule of law in England was to be a long and hard one. .By making a stand, however, Coke did win a victory of sorts. No future kings of England ever again proposed to try cases in person, instead using their powers to appoint and dismiss judges to secure verdicts favourable to the Crown. Because of his 'perpetual turbulent carriage' Coke himself was dismissed by James from the Court of Common Pleas in 1613, and made Chief Justice of King's Bench instead, where it was felt he would be less of a nuisance. However, James had underestimated Coke, and had to dismiss him from King's Bench as well in 1616! Coke then became a Member of Parliament, where he continued to make trouble for the Crown.

Returning to the contribution of eighteenth-century francophone thinkers to political theory, however, just one more name remains for serious consideration at this point, that of Jean-Jacques Rousseau (1712-1778). Rousseau was in fact born as a citizen of Geneva, which was then a Calvinist city-state within the Swiss Confederacy. However, French was his native tongue, and he spent most of his adult life in France. Rousseau's father had been a watchmaker, but he had married well to a woman of good family. Unfortunately Rousseau's mother died soon after his birth, and Rousseau never knew her, but he was later to receive a small legacy from her family. Because he had been trained as a watchmaker by his father before taking up his career as a writer, it could be said that Rousseau belonged to that small group of craftsmen-philosophers which included Spinoza the lens grinder, and Tom Paine the stay maker. The class background of these thinkers was considerably lower than that of most writers on philosophy, and this fact coloured the views of all three, making them outsiders who stood somewhat apart from the philosophical mainstreams of their day. Rousseau's formal education had been sparse and patchy, but he was an avid reader, and he became essentially, like Spinoza and Paine, a self-educated man. He spent much of his life in poverty, however, drifting from one expedient to another, and often dependent on the favour of patrons. His private life was turbulent, and his mental stability often in question, but Rousseau was multi-talented, and could show flashes of genius. Best known as a political philosopher, he was also a very good novelist, and the composer of several impressive musical pieces. A prodigious writer on various subjects his publications were very numerous, but he was not a consistent thinker. Rousseau was in fact a mass of contradictions, which makes him one of the most difficult to grasp of all the political philosophers. Because of the breadth of his scope, and the large number of his works, almost anyone of any political persuasion at all can find support for their views in Rousseau's writings. These included contributions to Diderot's Encyclopaedia which he was making from 1749, mainly on musical subjects. He first came to prominence, however, by winning an essay competition sponsored by the *Académie de Dijon* in 1750. The theme set was the question of whether the development of the arts and sciences had been morally beneficial for mankind. Rousseau won the prize with his *Discours sur les Sciences et les Arts* by arguing strongly against the proposition, declaring that the rise of civilization had brought the mass of mankind nothing but poverty, misery, oppression, and moral decay. He elaborated on this theme in his second major philosophical work, *A Discourse on the Origin and Basis of Inequality Among Men*, completed in 1754. At the same time he continued to write for Diderot's Encyclopaedia, and in 1755 he made his most important contribution with his entry on *Economie Politique*. It was this entry that was later to be expanded into Rousseau's most important work, *Du Contrat Social, Principes du Droit Politique*, usually referred to as simply *The Social Contract*, published in 1762. All of the Rousseau quotes which follow below are taken from this work. Important as it was, however, *The Social Contract* was itself only a fragment of a larger work which Rousseau had envisioned and which he mentions in his autobiographical *Confessions*, referring to it as his *Institutions Politiques*. This work, however, was never competed.

Because of his tendency towards self-contradiction, it is rather difficult to isolate those concepts in which Rousseau firmly believed, but his class background certainly made him more painfully and directly aware of the consequences of the grotesque social inequalities of his day, and his credentials as a democrat can scarcely be doubted. He firmly believed that sovereignty resided in the people, echoing here the seventeenth-century views of thinkers like Lilburn, Spinoza, Sidney, and Locke. He went beyond them, however, with his belief in direct democracy, rejecting the idea of indirect democracy through elected representatives. He was clearly influenced here by his notions of classical republicanism, the example of the Greek city-states, and the peasant communes of his native Switzerland which he had witnessed in operation. In *The Social Contract* Rousseau wrote,

> When one sees groups of peasants deciding their affairs under an oak tree and how sensibly they always conduct themselves, it is difficult not to distrust the refinements of other nations, who have made themselves illustrious and miserable with so much artifice and mystery. (Book IV, chap. i)

Direct democracy is of course impossible in a large nation-state, but Rousseau envisaged a solution to this problem in federalism. In the closing passages of his *Social Contract* Rousseau looked ahead to his *Institutions*

Politiques, a work which was either never written or subsequently lost. Speaking of the international anarchy of his day, he declares,

> We shall examine the kind of remedy men have sought against these evils in Leagues and Federations which, leaving each state master in its own house, arm it against all unjust aggression…we shall enquire what are the means of establishing a good form of federal association and what can give it permanence, and how far we can extend the rights of federation without touching on those of sovereignty.

Would Rousseau have sounded 200 years ahead of his time on those issues? One immediately thinks of NATO and the European Union of our own day. Rousseau had in fact already written two short essays on those themes at some time during the 1750s, which were discovered only after his death. One was entitled *A Lasting Peace* and the other *The State of War*, which is only a fragment. In the former he proposes a federal structure for European states, with all disputes being settled by 'the Tribunal of Europe'.(Both available online)

Rousseau was a harsh critic of the kind of 'civilisation' that had followed from the Neolithic Agricultural Revolution, sharing with Hobbes and Locke a conception of the 'state of nature' that had obtained before elaborate government structures had been created. We would think of our hunter-gatherer days here, which indeed compared very favourably with the lot of the early agriculturalists. Like Locke, Rousseau believed that the state of nature was fundamentally one of peace, because man was fundamentally good, although he had been corrupted by 'civilisation'. The agricultural societies of the Ancient and Medieval Worlds had developed strictly hierarchical social structures, with power highly concentrated at the apex of the pyramid. The distribution of material wealth within those societies had closely paralleled the distribution of political power, leading to the impoverishment of the great bulk of the population, and bitter competition for scarce resources. Rivalries and jealousy had thus corrupted public morals.

But although Rousseau had been such a scathing critic of 'civilisation', the first of his seeming contradictions emerges here, for at the same time we find him agreeing with Plato and Hegel in arguing that mankind can find its true and highest fulfilment only within the context of civil society, provided that this society is properly governed. Needless to say, this meant government along the lines suggested by himself. Rousseau was obsessed by notions of liberty and equality. Both his entry on *Economie Politique* and his *Social Contract* had included the memorable line, 'Man is born free, and everywhere he is in chains', impoverished and enslaved by the social and political structures under which he laboured. But there was a remedy. Instead of being highly concentrated, political power should be distributed as widely as possible. A more equitable distribution of wealth would inevitably follow. In his imagined federation of democratic communes, 'everyone hastens to the assemblies…as soon as anyone says of the affairs of a state, "Of what importance are they to me?" we must consider the state as lost…the better constituted a state is, the more do public affairs outweigh private ones in the minds of the citizens.' (Bk. III, xi) In his new, imagined Commonwealth, 'No citizen should be rich enough to be able to buy another, and none poor enough to be forced to sell himself…tolerate neither rich people nor beggars.' (Bk. II, xi)

This sounds like something of a fantasy state indeed, no more likely to become a practical reality than Plato's *Republic*, but Rousseau was making a very important point here when he stressed the parallel between the distribution of political power and the distribution of wealth within a state. Here is a lesson for our own times, as I shall try to show in the Conclusion below.

The sovereign people were of course meant to be the supreme legislative body, with local magistrates enforcing the law, but what kind of law? It is here that Rousseau introduces the concept for which he is most famous, his idea of 'the general will'. This was not an entirely new idea. Spinoza had spoken of the *mens una* within a state, and Montesquieu had mentioned the *volonte general*, but it was Rousseau who explored this concept in the greatest depth. His 'general will' was not the will of the majority nor even the sum of each individual will divided by the population, but in an almost mystical way it was in fact the will of all, whether everyone realised this or not, in the same way that an electron mysteriously takes the 'sum over paths' from point A to point B so that it somehow takes every possible path simultaneously. Moreover, while individual wills could err, the 'general will' was somehow always right. Mysterious as this concept may seem, it is important to try to understand it, because Rousseau was insistent that this 'general will' should be enforced, by quite draconian means if necessary upon all, including those in charge of government.

Because the 'general will' was in essence the will of all whether they realised it or not, those who dissented from it must be subjected to compulsion, since the 'general will' in fact guaranteed the freedom of all. Therefore, in a memorable phrase, those who dissented should be 'forced to be free'. This sounds rather like an oxymoron, or at best a charter for dictatorship, and it has indeed been employed as such in fascist and communist states. This enforced sociability was elevated to something like a religious dogma in Rousseau's mind. He himself was accused of religious indifference, and even atheism, since he had moved from Calvinism to Catholicism and then back to Calvinism again during his lifetime. But Rousseau was no atheist, and deeply resented that charge against him. He is perhaps best seen as a deist of sorts. However, although he had argued for religious freedom, he was quite prepared to impose a kind of secular religion upon the citizens of his imagined state. In the following quotation, Rousseau sees 'the sovereign' as being the people themselves. Having argued earlier for religious freedom, he then later adds,

> There is, however, a purely civil profession of faith, the articles of which it is the duty of the sovereign to determine, not exactly as dogmas of religion, but as *sentiments of sociability*, without which it is impossible to be a good citizen or a faithful subject. While it can compel no one to believe them, it can banish from the state anyone who does not believe them...it can banish him not for impiety, but as an anti-social being, incapable of truly loving the laws and justice, and of sacrificing, at need, his life to his duty. (Bk. IV, 8)

This sounds quite harsh, but Rousseau then goes even further, declaring that if anyone *pretends* to believe in this 'sociability' but then acts against it, he should be put to death for, 'he has committed the greatest of crimes: he has lied before the laws'. This is a strange kind of 'freedom' indeed, but typical of the contradictions to be found in Rousseau's writings.

Can anything therefore remain to be said in favour of Rousseau's concept of 'the general will'? Perhaps the idea is not quite so threatening as it sounds. Perhaps it is simply what people *ought* to believe. First we must remember that it rests, as the title of his greatest work suggests, upon a social contract. This was essentially the same kind of arrangement as was envisaged by Hobbes and Locke, under which men agree to surrender a measure of their individual freedom for the common good, the idea being to elevate themselves from the 'state of nature' onto an entirely higher plane of existence which can be achieved only within the context of a well constituted civil society. Rousseau set out to,

> ...find a form of association which may defend and protect with the whole force of the community the person and property of every associate, and by means of which each, while uniting himself with all, may nevertheless obey only himself, and remain free as before. (Bk. I, 6)

Under this contract men, who are naturally unequal, are made equal by convention and legal right, and so are protected from oppression and exploitation by one another and by the state. Now this concept of the 'general will' which all must be forced to obey can be made to seem less threatening if we choose to regard it as simply the law of the land, which we are indeed all forced to obey, including those in government, and harsh penalties exist for those who refuse to obey it. For example, we all want to be protected from assault, robbery, murder, and rape by the law. There is a consensus of agreement that such deeds should be banned, and those who do not agree with the consensus and act accordingly must be dealt with by society. These are extreme examples of course, but the law of the land in fact lays down a myriad of rules and regulations which we are all expected to obey on pain of punishment, and we seem to find all this quite acceptable on the whole. We are indeed 'forced to be free' of undesirable behaviour by the law. So, is this concept of 'the general will' really so threatening after all? Is it simply the consensus view?

Of course, this 'general will' is something that cannot be established overnight: there is a historical dimension here. Our laws are in fact the product of many centuries of experience, undergoing constant change and evolution. Rousseau seemed to acknowledge this point when he referred to, 'particular regulations that are merely the arching of the vault of which manners, slower to develop, form at length the immovable keystone'. (Bk. II, xii) It is the general *acceptance* of these laws which becomes 'the keystone which closeth up the arch of government', to borrow a phrase from Charles I, although he was talking about the monarchy there.

(e) A Perfect Constitution? The USA. in 1791

It might be interesting to pause at this point for an examination of the first fruits of all that political thought which had been in circulation prior to the 1770s. The most striking example of thought being transformed into action with the creation of an entirely new structure of government is surely to be seen in the constitution of the United States of America, which emerged in its final form with the addition of the first ten amendments to the constitution in 1791. There are several remarkable aspects to this document. First of all, it stands as the oldest basically unchanged constitution in the world. No other country on earth is still governed under essentially the same constitution as it had in 1791. 'Aha', you may say, 'but has not that constitution been amended 27 times?' This is true, but the first ten amendments should be seen as part of the original constitution itself, and are known as 'The Bill of Rights'. Moreover, some of the later amendments cancelled each other out, like the 12th. Amendment of 1803, superseded by the 20th.of 1933, or the 18th. Amendment of 1919 which banned the sale of alcohol across the entire USA, and the 21st. Amendment of 1933 which repealed it. In sum, only nine ratified amendments have explicitly superseded or modified the text of the original constitution, viz. numbers 11, 12, 13, 14, 16, 17, 20, 22, and 25. This is a very remarkable record for a constitution that is now 229 years old, surviving virtually intact through centuries of profound social and economic change. Moreover, the American Constitution is not only the oldest in the world, it is also the shortest, the original document of 1791 with its first ten amendments taking up just five parchment pages. In addition, this was not a constitution for a city state, a Swiss canton, or a small country, but one designed for the government of a land mass on a continental scale. The fact that this constitution has stood the test of time for so long would suggest that it must have instituted a near-perfect form of government. But did it? This suggestion merits closer examination.

We might begin by looking at America's famous Declaration of Independence, drawn up by Thomas Jefferson (1743-1826) and issued on July

4, 1776. Its second paragraph opens with the ringing phrase, 'We hold these truths to be self-evident: that all men are created equal, that they are endowed by their Creator with certain unalienable rights, that among these are the rights to life, liberty, and the pursuit of happiness.' That last phrase, 'the pursuit of happiness', was an entirely new proposition, and a deviation from the writings of Locke and the English Bill of Rights of 1689, both of which had spoken of the protection of life, liberty, and *property.* It was a reflection of the idealism of Jefferson, and the fact that he was a self-professed Epicurean. These were fine words indeed, but the proof of the pudding lay in the eating, as later history was to prove. But even at the time, that opening line was open to criticism.

First of all, it was inaccurate. All men are *not* created equal in God's world, the real world. Some are born with exceptional talents and abilities, and others with mental or physical handicaps, while the rest of us are on a scale somewhere in-between. Nor is it true that anyone possesses 'natural' or 'inalienable' rights. The concept of natural rights will be discussed more fully later, but basically in the pre-human world, the natural world, no creature had any 'rights' at all, natural or otherwise. They had only their own power to rely on, and had the 'natural right' to nothing more than they could win for themselves. Our modern idea of 'rights', like our conceptions of justice and morality, are entirely human inventions. We have precisely those 'rights' which we choose to invent and accord to one another, no more and no less: there are no 'natural rights'. Moreover, in making that statement, Thomas Jefferson himself could be accused of hypocrisy. He was at that time a slave owner, and in fact had a child by one of his female slaves. Did he believe that his slaves possessed 'unalienable rights'? The truth was that no white man at that time believed a black man to be his equal, and nor, for that matter, a red man or a yellow man or a brown man either. These attitudes were a long time a-dying. Rudyard Kipling (1865-1936) expressed them well in his 1899 poem, *The White Man's Burden*, in which he urged America to follow in the imperialist footsteps of Britain.

> Take up the White Man's burden,
> Send forth the best ye breed:
> Go send your sons to exile
> To serve your captives' need:
> To wait in heavy harness
> On fluttered folk and wild –
> Your new-caught, sullen peoples
> Half devil and half child.

When he wrote in his *Barrack Room Ballads,*

> Though I've belted you and flayed you,
> By the Living Gawd wot made you,
> Yer a better man than I am, Gunga Din!

Kipling was being entirely ironic.

But in the America of 1791 not even all white men were considered fully equal! If all men really were equal, then all should be entitled to vote in a representative democracy, which is what the new country professed to be. However, the Constitution of 1791 did not guarantee a universal franchise at all. Instead, it left the question of who could vote to the individual state legislatures, and after independence had been won, not one of them opted for universal manhood suffrage. Instead, the privilege of voting was restricted to adult, white, male property owners, just as it had been under the mother country from which independence had just been won. Gradually, each individual state did extend the vote to all males over 21, but this was a long, slow process, stretching into the twentieth century. Nor was it accepted that a black man was the equal of a white man: indeed, it took some Americans a very long time indeed to accept this idea. The 1791 constitution did nothing to prohibit slavery, which was practised in all 13 of the original colonies in 1791, and seventy years later Abraham Lincoln was still a racist himself, openly declaring that a black man was of course not the equal of a white. Even the issue of slavery was not his prime concern. In a letter to the *New York Tribune* of August 22, 1862, Lincoln wrote,

> My paramount object in this struggle is to save the Union, and is not either to save or destroy slavery. If I could save the Union without freeing any slave, I would do it; and if I could save it by freeing all the slaves, I would do it; and if I could do it by freeing some and leaving others alone, I would also do that.

Following the victory of the northern states in the bloody and bitter civil war of 1861-5, in which the USA lost more men than in the two World Wars combined, slavery was indeed abolished by the 13th Amendment in 1865, and an effort was made to accord full civil rights to coloured persons with the 14th and 15th Amendments of 1868 and 1870. However, it was to be another hundred years before the southern states fully accepted the spirit of these Amendments. For example, the 24th Amendment of 1964 prevented the southern states from disenfranchising coloured voters on the grounds of non-payment of taxes. Women too were of course denied the vote until the 20th century, as was also the norm in Europe, but the 19th Amendment of 1920 compelled the states to extend the franchise to all women over 21. In 1971, under the 26th Amendment, the voting age for all was lowered to 18.

The remarkable fact remains, however, that this eighteenth-century constitution needed so few amendments to modernise it for the twenty-first century. The secret of its success lay perhaps in its minimalism, and the way in which it accorded such wide powers of self-government to the individual states themselves. Each state was allowed to make its own laws, tailored to their individual circumstances, so long as these laws did not contradict the basic principles of the federal constitution. 'That government rules best which governs least' has always been a watchword of American political thought. However, this arrangement has caused many tensions between the central and the state governments, tensions seen at their worst in the American Civil War.

The Americans could also draw upon certain invaluable political traditions which they had inherited from their mother country, including parliamentary government and the invaluable concept of the rule of law, to which all were meant to be subject, including the highest in the land. The Americans were able to build here upon a great body of statute and common law derived from their British heritage, in addition to a long record of jurisprudence, neatly and conveniently summarised for them in Sir Edward Coke's *Reports,* which had been published in complete form in 1777, and the *Commentaries upon the Laws of England*, by Sir William Blackstone (1723-80), a four-volume work that was finally completed in 1769. This latter work in particular profoundly influenced America's Founding Fathers, and was frequently cited in later Supreme Court decisions. The principle of the rule of law was accepted from the earliest days of the new republic.

However, the 1791 Constitution can be criticised for instituting a one-man executive in the form of the President. The Founding Fathers had little excuse for this decision, for the model of British cabinet government was there for them to see. Here, a collective body took joint decisions after due discussion, and each member of the cabinet took individual responsibility for all decisions made. Although the Prime minister was *primus inter pares*, he could be overruled by a cabinet revolt or the threat of mass resignations. This was a very desirable arrangement. History provides us with many examples of the superiority of collective decision making over individual leadership, for the latter is far too subject to irrational whims and human error. Indeed, in many instances a wise collective decision was later reversed on the word of one man who held supreme power, with disastrous consequences. As an illustration of this we could look as far back as to the Crusades, and the Battle of Hattin, fought on July 3-4 in 1187. Leading the crusaders was Guy of Lusignan (1150-94) who had become King of Jerusalem just a year earlier. This was a dangerous time for the Christian kingdom, for Saladin the Kurd (1137-93) had recently united numerous Arab tribes, and had conquered much of the Middle East. His next move was clearly going to be against Jerusalem. In May 1187 word reached Guy that Saladin had gathered an army of 30,000 men at Tell-Ashtara near the Sea of Galilee. Guy was able to raise a Crusader army of 20,000, and marched north to meet Saladin, taking up a strong defensive position at the Spring of La Saphorie, an easy march from Saladin's army. There the Crusaders waited for the Muslims to attack, but Saladin knew well that in an attack on this fortified position with its own water supply, the odds would be against him. He therefore moved first to attack the Crusader fortress of Tiberius on the Sea of Galilee. This was held by Raymond III, Count of

Tripoli and Prince of Galilee (1140-87). Raymond himself had left to join the Crusader army, leaving his wife Eschiva in charge at Tiberius. In itself the fortress was a small prize, but Saladin hoped that by besieging it the Crusaders, with their knightly code of chivalry, would feel obliged to rescue a damsel in distress, and would try to raise the siege. This would draw the Crusader army out of their fortified position and onto a waterless desert plain on the road to Tiberius. The ploy was an obvious trap, but Guy called a council of war with his barons on the evening of July 2 to discuss their next move. The near-unanimous decision was that Tiberius should be sacrificed to save the Crusader army, for if the army was lost, Jerusalem itself would fall to the Muslims. Even Raymond III urged this council, saying that should Tiberius fall, his wife would be safe in Saladin's hands, and could be ransomed later. The army must remain at La Saphorie to save Jerusalem. Having made that wise decision, the council dispersed. Later that evening, however, Raynald de Chatillon (1125-87), a newcomer to the Holy Land, approached the king in private. He argued that Raymond was a despicable coward to be prepared to leave his wife in danger, and that Guy himself would be seen as a coward for evermore if he did not move to relieve Tiberius. This fatuous argument was enough to persuade the king. The Crusaders were dismayed to find when they awoke the next morning that they were to march immediately for Tiberius. It was clear to all that they would be placing themselves in great danger, but Guy was the king, and his word was law. Saladin must have been delighted at the success of his ploy: he could scarcely have dared to hope that the Crusaders would be so foolish. After a few hours of marching under the desert sun on July 3rd the straggling Crusader column, exhausted by heat and thirst, made an easy target for harassing Muslim raids. By the end of the day they found themselves forced to camp on an open plain, cut off from a water supply and surrounded by Saladin's forces. On the following morning Saladin threw his entire army into an attack. The Crusaders were cut to pieces, their army destroyed with no more than 3,000 escaping the carnage. King Guy was captured, and Raynald de Chatillon, who had persuaded Guy to his monumental act of folly, was beheaded by Saladin himself, who held a personal grudge against him. With its garrison now fatally weakened, Jerusalem itself fell to Saladin's forces on October 2nd. All these disasters had come about because a wise collective decision had been overruled by the whims of one all-powerful individual.

Moving to more recent times, another illustration of the dangers of one-man rule was provided by the fate of Arctic Convoy PQ 17 in July, 1942. The convoy consisted of 34 British and American merchant ships bound for the Russian arctic port of Archangel with supplies for their Russian ally. A powerful naval task force had been deployed with the merchantmen on convoy protection duty, consisting of 15 surface warships and two submarines, for the waters north of Norway were known to be very dangerous. Germany had conquered Norway, and had deployed a strong naval force on its western coast. The admiralty in London received dubious intelligence which suggested that this force might be on its way northwards to intercept PQ 17. In actual fact this fleet had not deployed at all, and most of the Admiralty's strategic advisors, making a collective decision, believed that the convoy and its escort should proceed on its way. The final decision, however, rested with the First Sea Lord, Admiral of the Fleet Sir Alfred Dudley Pound (1877-1943). Sir Alfred was in poor health, and in fact died in the following year, but he made the unilateral decision to withdraw the convoy's protecting escort, ordering it to turn back to meet the imagined German naval threat. The merchant ships, now defenceless, were ordered to disperse. Before they could properly do so, however, they were spotted by German air reconnaissance, and attacked by German submarines and torpedo bombers based in northern Norway. Of the 34 ships that had set out, only 11 eventually limped in to Archangel, many of them damaged. This was not only a military and human catastrophe, but also a diplomatic disaster. The Russians were furious, refusing to believe that so many ships could have been lost, and accusing their allies of being half-hearted about supplying them. The Americans were also enraged, because the convoy had been a joint Anglo-American exercise, but the Americans had allowed the British to take command of the operation, which was now seen as having been a terrible mistake. They resolved to take part in no more joint convoys under British command. The whole anti-Nazi alliance was severely strained by the episode.

Convoy PQ17 had been a great German victory, but the German nation itself was also under the unilateral command of just a single individual, Adolph Hitler. It is difficult to believe that some of Hitler's decisions, such as his Jewish policy or his plan to conquer Russia, could ever have emerged as the result of collective decision making, following from reasoned discussion and debate. Policies like that could have emerged only from the mind of one demented individual, illustrating once again the perils of trusting to a one-man executive. The policies were clearly insane, but Hitler was in supreme command, and no one could say him nay. In our own day it might be noted that the government of China, although hardly democratic, at least provides a collective leadership that has served China well in the economic sphere, greatly raising the material standard of living of her people. With regard to the American Constitution, it seems ironic that after their Declaration of Independence had presented such a long list of the grievances that Americans held against George III, they should then have set up an executive that was so much like a monarchy. Even the American method of *electing* their president was flawed. Under the Electoral College system, it was possible for the College to elect a president who had not won a majority of the popular vote. This did in fact happen in 1824, 1876, 1880, and 2000. Recently, it has happened again with the election of Donald Trump in 2016. Trump won a narrow majority of Electoral College votes with 290 out of 570, but lost the popular vote by roughly 61 million to 62 million, causing great consternation across America. Moreover, once elected the Constitution made it very difficult to remove a president who was incompetent, or became ill, while the electoral process meant a delay of two months between the election of a new president and his actually taking office.

Turning to the Bill of Rights, which was allegedly added to the Constitution to protect the rights of citizens, we may again detect some flaws. For example, the notorious Second Amendment read, ‘A well-regulated militia being necessary to a free state, the right of the people to keep and bear arms shall not be infringed’. Of course, in 1791 ‘the people’ meant white, adult, male property owners, and militias had served America well in its fight for independence. In addition, an armed populace was seen as a further guarantee of democracy, the ultimate safeguard against state tyranny. However, it is hardly necessary to spell out here the consequences of that amendment. Designed for the protection of the citizens, it has in fact resulted in the deaths of many thousands of them, and the wounding of many thousands more. Nor did the Eighth Amendment provide much protection. It read, ‘Excessive bail shall not be required, nor excessive fines imposed, nor cruel and unusual punishments inflicted’. This last phrase, like the militia clause, was taken word for word from the English Bill of Rights of 1689. However, it did not prevent the introduction of the electric chair as a new method of execution in 1890. This punishment was certainly ‘unusual’, since it had never been used before, and it was also very cruel. Had America decided to dip a man repeatedly into a large vat of boiling water until he died there would have been outrage around the world at such a barbarous method of execution, but slowly boiling him alive in his own blood was evidently acceptable. Death was not instantaneous, since the electricity was administered in a series of bursts, each one raising his temperature higher as the victim’s body acted as a resistance to the electric current. The condemned are forced to wear a heavy nappy for their execution, since boiling urine and faeces are excreted during the process. The expanding brain forces eyes from their sockets, while an extractor fan in the ceiling of the execution chamber removes the smoke and steam that rises from the victim. The first condemned in 1890 took eight minutes to die, but later victims have taken as long as twenty. Where was the protection of the Eighth Amendment against this entirely unusual and very cruel form of punishment?

It seems clear that even this venerable and enduring constitution, which has served as a template for so many others, was riddled with flaws. In our own day, it has proved only too vulnerable to manipulation by the rich and big business interests. For example, American workers have not enjoyed a real-terms pay rise since the 1970s, while wealthy Americans have grown enormously richer. Can a perfect constitution, one that truly works in the best interests of *all* a county’s citizens, ever be devised? Perhaps not, but this question will be addressed in our Conclusion below.

(f) Imperfect Constitutions: France, 1791-1958

Drawing up an enduring constitution is certainly no easy task. An exactly contemporary constitution with that of the American document of 1791 proved to be far less successful and far less enduring. This was the constitution of the French First Republic, adopted on September 30, 1791, following from the outbreak of the French Revolution of 1789. Under its terms the French monarchy was retained, but supreme power in the state passed to a unicameral legislative body, the newly established National Assembly. However, this constitution lasted intact only until August 10, 1792, rather less than one year. It had included in its preamble the famous *Declaration of the Rights of Man and the Citizen,* which had been promulgated on August 26, 1789. It had also accepted the sovereignty of the people, abolished feudal customs in France, and instituted a clear separation of powers between the executive, legislative, and judicial branches of government. On the face of things, it appeared to be a very reasonable document. However, it foundered upon Louis XVI's refusal to co-operate with the National Assembly. Moreover, he treacherously conspired with foreign powers, encouraging them to invade France and crush the Revolution. This led to the 'August Insurrection' of 1792 and the calling of a National Convention to replace the National Assembly. This new body was the first in France, and indeed in the world, to be elected by universal male suffrage, since even the individual states in America still retained a property qualification for voters at this time. The Convention abolished the monarchy, and declared France to be a republic on September 22, 1792. In June, 1793, another new constitution was drawn up, the so called 'Constitution of Year One', which again allowed for universal manhood suffrage.

The violent and bloody course followed by the French Revolution from 1792 onwards is too well known to require repetition here. After the September massacres of that year, Louis XVI was executed on January 21, 1793, and his queen Marie Antoinette followed him to the guillotine on October 16. The Committee of Public Safety headed by Maximilien Robespierre (1758-94) then instituted the notorious 'Reign of Terror' from September, 1793 until Robespierre was himself guillotined on July 28, 1794. After the fall of Robespierre a new constitution was promulgated on August 22, 1795, the 'Constitution of Year III' according to the new French Revolutionary calendar. It closely resembled the original constitution of 1791, but with a five-man 'Directory' replacing the king as the executive. Manhood suffrage was abolished, with only payers of direct taxes being allowed to vote. In its turn this was replaced by the Constitution of Year VIII on December 24, 1799 following Napoleon's coup of November 9. This established a Consulate of Three as the executive branch, but in practice all power lay with Napoleon as First Consul. The new regime was so close to being a dictatorship that 1799 is usually taken as marking the official end of the French Revolution. Its dictatorial nature was confirmed in the new Constitution of Year X which made Napoleon First Consul for life in 1802, and the later Constitution of Year XII, which declared Napoleon to be Emperor of the French on May 18, 1804. This title was to be hereditary in Napoleon's line. Napoleon's rise had been another example of political power growing out of the barrel of a gun, for he owed his success to his skill as a general. But all of these constitutions were of course swept away with the final military failure of Napoleon at Waterloo in 1815, with the Bourbon Restoration calling for yet another new constitution. This meant that France had experimented with no fewer than seven different constitutions in the 24 years between 1791 and 1815, and even that of 1815 was not to endure for long.

This was a sorry end to the high hopes that the French Revolution had engendered in its early stages, when William Wordsworth (1770-1850) could write of those times in *The Prelude*, 'Bliss was it in that dawn to be alive, but to be young was very heaven!', and William Blake could celebrate its coming in his fragment, *The French Revolution*, written in 1791. After the dust had settled on all the turmoil that had convulsed France from 1789 to 1815, the only tangible legacies that endured from all the upheavals were the *Declaration of the Rights of Man and the Citizen* of August, 1789 and the Code Napoleon, a legal system devised by Napoleon himself, and based upon Enlightenment principles. This Code was retained in France and was later to form the basis of the legal structures of several European states. In a broader sense, however, the Revolution had demonstrated once again that monarchs could be deposed and executed by their subjects, and that radical and drastic change could be implemented within a very short space of time. In France this had included the sweeping away of all feudal customs overnight, a redistribution of land, the framing of an entirely new constitution, the setting up of a republic, and even at one point the introduction of universal manhood suffrage as an element in representative democracy. In these respects the French Revolution was a milestone in European, and indeed in world history. Thanks to the conquests of Napoleon, Enlightenment ideas were spread across the whole of Europe: the world was never to be the same again.

After the final defeat of Napoleon in 1815 the Bourbon monarchy was restored, brought back in the baggage train of the conquering armies of the Alliance, and imposed on a defeated France. However, the restoration of the monarchy did not bring lasting political stability. France was to suffer revolution once again in 1830, in 1848, and in 1870. The restored monarchy was replaced by the Second Republic of 1848-51, which was in turn replaced by the Second Empire under Napoleon III. This fell as a result of the Franco-Prussian War in 1870, and the Third Republic was instituted, lasting until France's defeat by Germany in 1940. The Fourth Republic followed from 1946 to 1958, until collapsing under the strain of the Algerian crisis. The constitution of the Fifth Republic, instituted in 1958, is the one under which France is still governed today. By comparison with the efforts of the French to establish a lasting constitution in 1791, the American Constitution of the same year, for all its flaws, appears to have been a resounding success! Before we laugh too hard at the French, however, we should remember that our own unwritten British constitution of today is also enormously different from our constitution of 1791, and the same applies also to every other state in Europe and the world. The American achievement in establishing a lasting constitution at so early a date was not only exceptional, it was unique. Even this constitution, however, has its flaws as we have seen. This underlines the difficulty faced by all states in drawing up a constitution that will truly operate for the greatest good of the whole population. Despite centuries of political thought and endless experimentation, this problem remains a highly challenging one, but it will be addressed in our Conclusion below.

(g) The Age of Responsible Government

It was only in the nineteenth and twentieth centuries, with the spread of representative democracy, that the governments of European countries at last began to show some concern for the well-being of the great majority of their citizens. Prior to that time, and indeed well into the nineteenth century, the governments of Europe had been essentially kleptocracies, whose primary aim had been to divert as much of their countries' wealth as possible into their own hands, at the expense of the rest of the populace. The whole focus of the law had been towards the protection of private property. Their concern to keep order and promote political stability in their states had been entirely self-interested: the status quo had suited them extremely well. For the same reason they had looked to national defence, lest foreign invasion should threaten their existing positions. This situation was to change only slowly, as a movement towards greater representative democracy was led by the middle classes in both Britain and France. Indeed, in France it had been this class that had initiated the French Revolution, only later drawing on support from the classes below them. In Britain the Parliamentary Reform Acts of 1832, 1867, and 1884 had also been designed primarily to accommodate the property-owning middle classes: the 1884 Act still left 40 per cent of adult males and all women without a vote. It was only in 1918 that the franchise was finally extended to all men over 21, regardless of property qualifications, and to women over 30. It was 1928 before the vote was extended to all women over 21 as well.

Running parallel with the extension of this kind of 'democracy' in Britain and Europe was the growth of what might be described as 'conscience' amongst the ruling classes, although the cynical might rather describe it as vote chasing. In so far as it was informed by any philosophy at all, however, I would identify this philosophy as being essentially Utilitarianism. This creed is based upon the simple proposition that the government which governs best does all it can to provide for the greatest happiness of the greatest number of its population. The implication of course was for the greatest happiness of *all* the people, not just the greatest happiness of the wealthiest ten per cent, far less the happiness of the wealthiest one per cent. But a proposition such as the above immediately calls for a definition of the term 'happiness', without which the statement has no specific meaning. This definition will be supplied in the Conclusion below, together with a definition of morality, but since this chapter is already overlong, I would rather not attempt these definitions here. Suffice to say at this point that the achievement of happiness, like the achievement of health, must always be a joint venture between the individual and the state. Both must take responsibility and work together here towards the reaching of this goal, with the role of the state being more that of removing the obstacles to the reaching of happiness by the individual. Obviously the state cannot *impose* happiness upon anybody. Nevertheless, what we have with Utilitarianism is a fundamentally very good idea that was later so refined, analysed, and dissected that it floated upwards into abstruse realms where it threatened to become of no practical use to anyone. Philosophers are often guilty of this sort of thing. Let's just keep it simple. For example, it was later suggested that perhaps 'the greatest *good* of the greatest number' might be a better definition of Utilitarianism. But this simply raises more problems than it solves. Should the government give people what is 'good' for them rather than open the way to happiness? I see this as being a dangerous course, for while no government can impose happiness upon people, it might very well try to impose upon them what it believes to be 'good' for them. This opens the way to an Orwellian state, with things like compulsory PE for all, a ban on alcohol as in the USA from 1917 to 1933, or China's one child policy. Even if these things are 'good' for you (which is debatable) this is too high a price to pay. I would much prefer that we stuck with the term 'happiness', even although I myself have in fact gone in for regular exercise, a virtual alcohol ban, and a two-child policy.

Today Utilitarianism is a familiar creed in the history of political thought, but it has been subjected to numerous definitions over the years, and even the origin of the concept itself remains controversial. Its principles can be traced back at least as far as the writings of Francis Hutcheson (1694-1746), a Scottish academic who was tutor to Adam Smith at the University of Glasgow, and whose writing influenced David Hume. His book entitled, *An Inquiry into the Original of our ideas of Beauty and Virtue* appeared in 1725. In the second section of this book subtitled, *An Inquiry Concerning Moral Good and Evil*, Hutcheson adopts a clearly utilitarian approach to the question of the morality of actions, arguing that they should always tend to the general good of mankind. In chapter III of this work, he actually declares that they should make for, 'the greatest happiness of the greatest number'. Hutcheson was of Scottish Presbyterian stock, educated at the University of Glasgow, where he later held the chair of Moral Philosophy, although he was actually born in County Down, Northern Ireland. In his 1725 book he argued that the morality of any action was directly proportional to the number of people to whom that action brought happiness, while moral evil, or vice, was proportionate to the number of people made to suffer from it. The best actions were therefore those that procured the greatest happiness for the greatest numbers, and the worst the ones that caused the most misery. He did not actually set up his precept as a criterion to be followed by governments, but in all other respects he anticipated Jeremy Bentham (1748-1832) by half a century, even to the extent of devising a spurious set of mathematical algorithms to compute the 'morality' of all actions. How easily can philosophers lose their way. Bentham too devised a fatuous 'hedonic or felicific calculus' to measure the precise morality of individual actions.

Two of Hutcheson's protégés later became more famous than their master. One was Adam Smith, but the other was the great Scottish empiricist philosopher David Hume (1711-76) who, in 1751, published what he himself believed to be his greatest work, *An Enquiry Concerning the Principles of Morals*. Here, he judges each individual action according to how useful or beneficial it is to society as a whole. His chapters are liberally sprinkled with the terms, 'useful', 'beneficial', and 'practical', but the terms 'utility' and 'utilities' also make frequent appearances throughout, especially in chapter IV, 'Of Political Society'. Indeed, chapter V is actually titled, 'Why Utility Pleases'. In the first sentence of Part I of this chapter, Hume declares,

> It seems so natural a thought to ascribe to their *utility* the praise that we bestow on the social virtues, that one would expect to meet with this principle everywhere in moral writers as the chief foundation of their reasoning and enquiry. In common life, we may observe that the circumstance of *utility* is always appealed to, nor is it supposed that a greater eulogy can be given to any man than to display his usefulness to the public, and to enumerate the services which he has performed to mankind and society. (My italics)

A third figure who is generally regarded as a precursor of nineteenth-century Utilitarianism was William Paley (1743-1805), a Peterborough man and graduate of Christ's College Cambridge. He became an Anglican clergyman, and was essentially a theologian, but in 1785 he published *The Principles of Moral and Political Philosophy*, which took him slightly outside his usual theological sphere, but not very far out. He argued that a benevolent God obviously wanted everyone in His creation to be happy, and that therefore all actions that contributed to the happiness of others were moral actions. His views were not only simplistic, but highly derivative, drawing on the writings of Leibniz (1646-1714), Hume (1711-46), John Gay (1699-1745), and William Derham (1657-1735). Partly because it provided a useful summary of the views of others, however, Paley's book was widely read in academic circles of the time. Today he is remembered chiefly for his 'watchmaker' analogy, arguing that just as a watch showed evidence of intelligent design, so too did the human body, which should serve as powerful evidence for the existence of God. This point was later to be answered in Richard Dawkins' book, *The Blind*

Watchmaker (1986). It has also been suggested that it was the publication of Paley's *Principles* in 1785 that spurred Bentham on to publish his own great work, *An Introduction to the Principles of Morals and Legislation*. This had been basically completed in 1780, but Bentham did not get around to publishing it until 1789.

There is also debate about just when the term 'Utilitarianism' was originally coined. The philosophy was first firmly labelled as *Utilitarianism* by John Stuart Mill (1806-73) in his book of that title, which appeared in 1863. In his first footnote of the book, however, Mill declared that although believing himself to be the first person who brought the term 'Utilitarian' into use, 'he did not invent it, but adopted it from a passing expression in Mr. Galt's *Annals of the Parish*'. This latter was a rather obscure 1821 novel about Scottish country life by the Scotsman John Galt (1779-1839), quite a prolific novelist, who was concerned about the increasingly obvious effects that the nascent Industrial Revolution were having on the society around him. In chapter 35 of his *Annals*, one of his characters, a Presbyterian minister, declares to his congregation that he 'thought they had more sense than to secede from Christianity to become Utilitarians, for that would be a confession of ignorance of the faith, seeing that it was the main duty inculcated by our religion to do all in morals and manners to which the newfangled doctrine of utility pretended.' The fact that Galt used a capital letter to describe the 'Utilitarians' suggests that he already regarded them as members of a recognisable creed, although whether this was quite the same creed as Mill espoused remains a moot point.

The man who is today regarded as the founder of Utilitarianism in its classic form is of course Jeremy Bentham, but even he modestly disclaimed the coining of its title. In his 1821 work, *On the Liberty of the Press and Public Discussion*, Bentham claimed on p. 4 that he had picked up the name from a 1768 tract by Joseph Priestly (1733-1804), *An Essay on the First Principles of Government*. Here Priestly had written, 'The good and happiness of the members, that is the majority of the members of any state, is the great standard by which everything relating to that state must finally be determined.' (p. 17)

At this point Joseph Priestly deserves a mention in his own right, because during his lifetime he was regarded as one of the three arch-radicals of the late eighteenth century, together with Tomas Paine and Richard Price, and he was duly demonised as such. All three advocated republicanism, democracy, religious toleration, and egalitarianism, ideas that were to receive general acceptance only long after their deaths. As a result, all three were ruthlessly lampooned by cartoonists of the day such as James Gillray, Thomas Rowlandson, and William Dent. Born into a dissenting family in the West Riding of Yorkshire, Priestly became, like Richard Price, a dissenting minister, a Unitarian, and a polymath. In addition he was also a polyglot, a student of no fewer than nine ancient and modern languages. Like Bentham he had been a child prodigy, and like Price he had been educated at one of the many excellent dissenting academies which had sprung up all over England in the eighteenth century to provide higher education for dissenters, since only Anglicans were admitted to Oxford and Cambridge at that time. Although his range of interests was very wide, he is best known for his scientific work in the fields of chemistry and electricity. In 1766 Priestly was elected as a Fellow of the Royal Society, and was awarded the coveted Copley Medal by the Society in 1773. The University of Edinburgh granted him the degree of Doctor of Law in 1764. He published more than 150 works in his lifetime, some of them influential books on education and theology, but Priestly was also a political radical. He was a vehement critic of the government of the day, welcomed the French Revolution, and was basically a republican. His religious and political views made him unpopular, however, as the general mood in England began to swing against the French Revolution. In July 1791 a 'church and king' mob, probably incited by local magistrates, attacked his home and meeting house in Birmingham, burning both to the ground, although Priestly himself escaped. In 1794, as the government stepped up its persecution of radicals with the notorious Treason Trials of that year, Priestly was forced to flee to America with his family. He died in Pennsylvania in 1804.

Although 'utilitarian' thought had clearly been abroad for much of the eighteenth century, the doctrine is, of course, most closely associated with the name of Jeremy Bentham (1748-1832). Bentham was born at Houndsditch in London to a wealthy legal family with a Tory and Anglican background. He was an exceptionally bright child. After attending Westminster School he secured a BA degree from Queen's College Oxford at the age of 15, and a Masters at the age of 18. He then studied law at Lincoln's Inn and was called to the bar in 1769 while still only 21, although he never practised as a lawyer. Thanks to his family's wealth, Bentham was instead able to make a name for himself as a writer, philosopher, jurist, and social reformer. He never became known as a dangerous radical in the mould of Price or Paine, however. In 1776 he wrote a tract opposing the American Declaration of Independence, and became an outspoken critic of the violence of the French Revolution after 1792. Although in his youth he had been a member of the Bowood House group that had included radicals like Richard Price and Joseph Priestly among its membership, he never became tarred with the radical brush. However, his writings contributed greatly to later Poor Law reform, penal reform, and health and sanitation legislation, although he himself did not live long enough to see his ideas on those measures come to fruition. Bentham appears to be an entirely commendable figure, sincerely dedicated to the wellbeing of mankind.

His best known work is of course, *An Introduction to the Principles of Morals and Legislation* which he completed in 1780, although it was not published until 1789. On the first page of this famous work he declares,

By the principle of utility is meant that principle which approves or disapproves of every action whatsoever according to the tendency which it appears to have to augment or diminish the happiness of the party whose interest is in question: or, what is the same thing in other words, to promote or to oppose that happiness. I say this of every action whatsoever, and therefore not only of every action of a private individual, but of every measure of government.

It was Bentham's great achievement to transform a system of moral philosophy into a tenet of political thought, but stated as baldly as it is above, his proposition seems simplistic, and open to challenge, apparently lacking a moral dimension. First, his definition of 'happiness' as 'a predominance of pleasure over pain' is jejune, and meaningless without a definition of 'pleasure'. Not only does he fail to adequately define 'happiness' anywhere in his text, but his creed would appear to justify the Roman Games, because only a few people were tortured to death to keep a large number 'happy'. Therefore the aggregate total happiness of all those present was increased, and so the Games should be seen as a good thing. However, P.J. Kelly in his 1990 book, *Utilitarianism and Distributive Justice: Jeremy Bentham and the Civil Law* successfully clears Bentham of the immorality charge by pointing out that his principle was intended to operate within the framework of civil law, which would preclude inflicting suffering on some to increase the happiness of others. Indeed, such a proposition would have run entirely counter to Bentham's humanitarian proclivities.

These proclivities emerge clearly enough in Bentham's central work of 1789. Here, Bentham put forward suggestions that were 200 years ahead of their time, advocating prison reform, the decriminalisation of homosexuality, a full equality of rights for women, and the abolition of corporal punishment for children. This last was an astonishing suggestion in an age when the public flogging of both adult men and women was still a legal penalty. He was of course a leading opponent of slavery, and was also the earliest exponent of humane treatment for animals, famously stating that, 'The question is not can they reason nor can they talk, but can they suffer?' (Chpt. 17, n. 122) Bentham's concern was in fact for the greatest happiness not just of humanity, but of all sentient creatures. He was surely one of history's great humanitarians.

It was in one of his earliest works, *A Fragment on Government*, published in 1776, that Bentham first provided a utilitarian definition of morality. Just a few lines into his Preface he declares, 'It is the greatest happiness of the greatest number: that is the measure of right and wrong'. Although this was Bentham's first statement of that fundamental principle, however, its propagation was not the primary purpose of *A Fragment on Government*. The main thrust of this work was an attack upon Sir William Blackstone's *Commentaries upon the Laws of England*, finally completed in 1769. It was one of Bentham's dearest wishes to secure a simplification and codification of English law, which he dubbed, 'the Demon of Chicane'. There were echoes here of Oliver Cromwell's views on 'the tortuous, ungodly jungle of the law', which partly explained his disdain for legal niceties. Both men were entirely correct. By 1769 England's laws had indeed become highly complex, convoluted, and very unfair, heavily favouring the propertied classes. Despite a lifetime of campaigning and good intentions, however, Bentham completely failed to secure any significant structural law reform at all.

The history of Utilitarian thought after Bentham provides us with a classic example of a fundamentally very good idea later worked to death by subsequent commentaries upon it. John Stuart Mill, often seen as almost a co-founder of Utilitarianism together with Bentham, was the first to muddy the waters in his 1863 book, *Utilitarianism*. He struck at one of the weak points in Bentham's theory, namely his failure to adequately define 'happiness'. He argued that intellectual pleasures provided 'higher' and therefore more desirable forms of happiness than mere physical ones. But this was only the beginning of the slippery downward slope into controversy. The dissection of Utilitarianism continued until the end of the nineteenth century, and right through to the end of the twentieth. Related concepts such as Ideal Utilitarianism, Act Utilitarianism, Rule Utilitarianism, Two-Level Utilitarianism, Preference Utilitarianism, Negative Utilitarianism, and Motive Utilitarianism had all emerged by the end of the twentieth century. One of the sharpest critics of Utilitarianism in the last century was the British philosopher Professor Sir Bernard Williams (1929-2003), erstwhile husband of Shirley Williams, the Labour politician. In his book *Utilitarianism: For and Against* (1973), co-authored with J.J. Smart, Williams comes down very firmly against Utilitarianism, arguing that all moral decisions are essentially personal decisions, so that no objective definition of 'morality' is possible. But this is the worst kind of relativism and defeatism, completely selling the pass and opening the door to moral anarchy. Utilitarianism in fact provides us with an excellent basis for a discussion of morality, as will be seen in the Conclusion below, where a definition of 'morality' will be offered.

Some of these twentieth-century refinements and debates on Utilitarianism were interesting enough, and it says a lot for the concept that it was able to inspire continuing interest and debate for over two hundred years. But we need to keep our eye on the ball here. One of the central reasons for the enduring interest in and importance of Utilitarianism lies in the fact that it established a link between happiness and morality, and went on to impose a duty of morality upon governments and the state. This represented an entirely new dimension of political thought, the novel idea that perhaps governments owed a duty of care to *all* those over whom they ruled. Perhaps legislation should be so directed as to promote the economic and social welfare of the citizenry, a startlingly new concept that had scarcely been considered before. It is important to stress at this point just how truly radical eighteenth-century 'utilitarianism' was in terms of political thought, running as it did entirely contrary to the assumptions of the ruling classes of the day. In those times the poor were expected to look after themselves, with no assistance at all from national government. Even the poor laws of the time were entirely a local, parish matter, often amounting in effect to the poor supporting the poor. The Speenhamland System, which was common in England between 1795 and 1834, had been quite effective as a means of poor relief, but it was abolished by the Poor Law Amendment Act of 1834, which aimed at punishing the poor for their poverty. We will see in a later section just how hard Margaret Thatcher tried to revive this nineteenth-century concept, using words from her own lips.

To understand the full significance of Utilitarianism, however, clear definitions of both 'happiness' and 'morality' are required. These will be offered in the Conclusion below. We must also address there the question of to what extent the governments of Britain and Europe really did work to provide for 'the greatest happiness of the greatest number' in the nineteenth and twentieth centuries. Of particular interest to us here in Britain, we must also ask to what extent the governments of the UK and the USA are truly catering for 'the greatest good/happiness of the greatest number' in the twenty-first century. We will see how, over the last one hundred years, it is economic thought that has come to occupy centre stage, although the political dimension, as ever, retains its importance. Is it possible to devise a system of government that is not susceptible to corruption by wealthy individuals? It remains true that the distribution of wealth in a nation closely parallels the distribution of political power within that nation, as true today as in the eighteenth century or the Middle Ages. Can any system be devised that will not enormously favour the rich? Have we in the UK really succeeded in moving on from the situation that prevailed in the eighteenth century, namely rule by kleptocracy? What should be the role of the state in the national economy? How much 'Socialism' is good for a country? These questions will be addressed in the Economics chapter, and in the Conclusion below.

Finally, since I write in 2020, the great political issue of our own day deserves a mention. This is of course Brexit, which has at last been decided upon, although many details remain to be settled, even after our 'no tariffs, no quotas' deal with the EU. Our nation was very evenly divided between 'Leavers' and 'Remainers' on this issue, and it is extremely difficult to determine which side had the stronger case to make, or to predict what sort of future awaits Britain outside the EU. Views were strongly held on both sides, and all that I can do here is to explain my own experience in the debate. Basically, I was disgusted with the EU. There is so much wrong with that organisation that I could write a book about it, but I don't have to, because that book has already been written. It is, *The Euro: How a Common Currency Threatens the Future of Europe* (2018 ed.) by the Nobel laureate Joseph Stiglitz. In fact it is about much more than just the euro, exposing clearly the 'democratic deficit' of the EU and the results of its insane neoliberal economic policies. The imposition of the misery of austerity upon debtor nations actually made it *less* likely that they would ever be able to repay their creditors. Also worth a read is, *The Left Case Against the EU* (2019) by Costas Lapivitsas.

I was disgusted with the EU because it was big enough and strong enough to have stood up to the bankers and to plutocratic domination, but it chose not to do so. Multinational companies and banks could not have deployed their usual threat of pulling out and setting up business elsewhere unless the bloc kow-towed to their demands, because the EU was immune to that form of blackmail. As the world's third-largest economy it was simply too big and too prosperous to ignore: no one could have afforded *not* to do business in Europe. This gave the EU the potential to impose a uniform rate of corporation tax across the entire bloc of 28 countries, and a uniform top rate of income tax. It could have brought in wealth taxes, inheritance taxes, a financial transactions tax, and a number of other measures, such as cleaning up at least its own tax havens. Several prominent economists have made the point that high tax rates have never stopped any company from investing in an area where they were sure that profits could be made. Of course they would prefer low taxes as well, but tax levels have never been the key consideration in their decision making.

It might be argued that imposing common tax rates across the union would have been too ambitious a target. I would disagree there. In fact, instead of imposing those very sensible, highly beneficial, and entirely feasible measures, the EU embarked on an even more ambitious programme, the introduction of a common currency, the euro, and of the common interest rates that went with it, in 19 of the 28 member states. One is reminded here of those, 'blind guides, who strain out a gnat and swallow a camel'. (Matthew 23:24) The policy was a disaster. The states of Europe had initially begun to draw together with the European Coal and Steel Community, set up in 1952. Its six member states were intended to form the core of a wider and closer union of European countries in years to come. The main purpose of this union was to draw France and Germany closer together, in the hope of avoiding another European war between them. This small core progressively grew into today's EU, and indeed we have had no major war in Europe now for 75 years. But this has been no thanks to the EU. Rather, it has been NATO and the *pax atomica* which have kept this peace, and we would have enjoyed it even if the EU and its predecessors had never existed. The EU was therefore conceived in error. It was never needed in the first place for the purpose that inspired its creation, and having been conceived in error, it was then driven forward by mindless fanaticism. Mere geographical location was considered to be enough to qualify European countries for membership, regardless of the condition of their economies. This error was then compounded by the imposition upon 19 of them of a common currency and common interest rates, which came into full operation in January, 2002, without regard to the great differences in the economies of member states. The world financial crisis of 2007-9 and the euro crisis of 2012 threw these errors into sharp relief. In its determination to maintain the value of the euro the EU, working with the European Commission, the European Central Bank, and the International Monetary Fund, imposed austerity measures across the eurozone. These hit the southern countries of Greece, Italy, Portugal, and Spain particularly hard, stunting their rates of economic growth and causing high levels of unemployment, especially youth unemployment, in all four. This was done of course to defend the value of their precious euro, mainly for prestige reasons, but once again, the poor were made to pay for the folly and greed of the bankers. As we shall see in the Economics chapter below, it is only the poor who suffer from 'austerity'. After 2012, as John Rapley commented sadly on this austerity programme, 'Whatever path the EU had once charted, it showed that its future would now be thoroughly neoliberal.' (*Twilight of the Money Gods: Economics as a Religion, and How it all Went Wrong* (2017) p. 384) Neoliberals, as will be shown in the Economics chapter below, always consider money to be more important than people, and are ever ready to kow-tow to bankers and plutocrats as part of their religion. Whatever happened to the idea of promoting the greatest happiness of the greatest number? Whatever had happened to democracy? Yanis Varoufakis, academic economist and former Finance Minister of Greece answers this question in his two books, *And the Weak Suffer What they Must?* (2017) and, *Adults in the Room: My Battle with Europe's Deep Establishment* (2018). It has of course been Greece that has suffered most severely from EU economic policies, as Stiglitz explains clearly in *The Euro* (2018), pp. 191-202.

For years I had cherished high hopes for the EU, because I believed that only a multinational union of countries would be powerful enough to counter the economic power of multinational corporations, internet giants who gather our personal information for commercial purposes, money managers, very rich individuals, and the threat of plutocracy replacing democracy. I was to be bitterly disappointed. In 2016 I voted to leave the EU, but not because I wanted to leave. I retained my hope that one day the EU might see sense, and use its great economic power to curb the neoliberal plutocrats in the way that only a large, multinational coalition could do: it was still our last, best hope for countering the power of multinational corporations. My aim was only to put a shot across their bow. Like all the politicians and all the pundits I believed that the British people could never possibly vote to leave, because of all the difficulties and upheaval that this would entail. But I also thought that the minority of leave voters would be large, and I sought to increase it in the hope of terrorising the EU into changing its ways. 'My God, we nearly lost the UK! What a disaster *that* would have been! Perhaps it's time that we stood up to the plutocrats after all: perhaps it's time we started governing in the interests of our people instead of our bankers.' But it was not to be. I miscalculated the surprise result. Instead of a shot across the bow, my shell missed its mark, struck squarely amidships, and blew the EU apart. In so doing, I simultaneously shot myself in the foot. My fear now is that, freed from all restraints, our neoliberal plutocrats here in Britain will forge ahead with policies that are entirely in their own interests, but highly detrimental to the rest of us. I fear the further removal of regulations, especially environmental regulations, and further moves by this Tory government to favour the rich at the expense of the poor. We are left, therefore, with the abiding question of how to defend our democracies from plutocratic subversion. This issue will be further addressed in the chapters which follow.

VI On Economics

Taking a very broad view, we might say that different categories of philosophical thought have successively come to the fore in the course of recorded history. In classical times, and in the Dark Ages, despite all the teachings of the Buddha, Confucius, Jesus, and the Stoics, the predominant philosophy remained one of 'might makes right'. This applied even to the philosophy-loving Greeks, as the Melian dialogue showed. But with the rise of Islam and Christianity in the Middle Ages and the sixteenth century, it was religious thought that took centre stage in Europe and the Middle East. In seventeenth-, eighteenth-, and early nineteenth-century Europe, it was political thought that came to the fore. In the second half of the nineteenth century, and on into the twentieth, it was scientific thought that assumed the greatest importance in the intellectual field. This brief survey is of course an over-simplification. In reality, the terrible doctrine of 'might makes right' lurked always in the background, to receive its worst expression in the First and Second World Wars. Religious thought too remained, and still remains eternally with us, and political thought also stays as a continual preoccupation. The outline suggested above applies to the emphasis only, but may be helpful as a guide. So now, in the later twentieth and early twenty-first centuries, what form of thought has come to the fore? Why, it must surely be economic thought, that poor relation in the eyes of academic philosophers, a school of thought not considered worthy of even a nominal Nobel Prize until 1968 but now, it could be argued, the most immediately relevant field of all. The stone which the professional philosophers hath rejected, is now become the head of the corner. Or, in the memorable phrase that Bill Clinton kept on display in the Oval Office, 'It's the economy, stupid!'

In considering economic thought, it is important to distinguish between microeconomics and macroeconomics. The former, as its name suggests, concerns the workings of economic principles on a small scale, that of the individual consumer or firm, while macroeconomics considers the handling of national economies. It is generally assumed that this places microeconomics on a sounder rational footing than macroeconomics, since it deals with simpler, basic concepts such as the effects of supply and demand, the relative marginal utility of different products, wage levels, opportunity costs, and the effects of monopoly supply. However, even microeconomics assumes the existence of totally rational consumers with a firm grasp of the concept of marginal utility and a complete knowledge of the market. In practice of course, none of these provisos usually applies, so that even microeconomics remains far from being an exact science. Ultimately it depends upon the behaviour and emotions of individual human beings, and as noted above, few things are as unpredictable as human behaviour, or as irrational as human emotions. Since Economics has a great deal to do with both, it can never be regarded as a science, despite the aspirations of the economists. As Immanuel Kant put it in 1784, 'Out of the crooked timber of humanity, no straight thing was ever made.' (*Idea for a General History with a Cosmopolitan Purpose:* Proposition 6) En masse and on average certain general principles might apply, but when it comes to the marketing of an individual product, it remains very difficult to predict its success. Macroeconomics, which deals with the handling of national economies, is decidedly more complicated than microeconomics, and operates on rather different principles, but it is this latter that will be our main field of interest here, since it is macroeconomics which relates much more closely to politics and ecology, and so is a subject of general concern for our times.

It is at this point perhaps worth quoting once more the Cambridge economist Ha-Joon Chang, who declared in his book, *23 Things They Don't Tell You about Capitalism* (2011),

> Ninety-five percent of economics is common sense made complicated, and even for the remaining five per cent the essential reasoning, if not all the technical details, can be explained in plain terms. (p. xviii)

Now this may be true in the case of microeconomics: indeed, we all become microeconomists ourselves when we run our household budgets. But I cannot entirely agree with the implications of that statement when it comes to the field of macroeconomics, which involves the managing of national economies. Its theoretical aspects may indeed be explained in simple terms, but applying them in practice to ensure the successful management of the wealth and wellbeing of nation states has proved to be extremely difficult, certainly too difficult for all of our academic economists so far. If it is all so simple then why, as examples, do we still have eternal swings between boom and bust, why are national debts spiralling upwards to alarming proportions, why are inequalities of income and wealth grotesque and increasing, why is youth unemployment such a problem in Europe, why the continuing debate over how much state regulation of the economy is desirable, and why is the issue of free trade still proving to be so problematical? Above all, why did we experience a disastrous financial crash in 2008, which the poorer people of Britain, Europe and America are still paying for, even although they had nothing to do with causing it? John Maynard Keynes once defined his discipline as, 'the science of thinking in terms of economic models combined with the art of choosing models which are relevant to particular situations'. It is the artistic side of the formula which has proved to be by far the more difficult. The macroeconomic management of national economies is, unfortunately, not a simple matter at all: rather it is a subject of infinite complexity, and we in the Western World have been getting things badly wrong recently, as we shall see. Writing an obituary of Alfred Marshall in 1924, Maynard Keynes declared,

> The master economist must possess a rare combination of gifts. He must be mathematician, historian, statesman, philosopher...he must study the present in the light

of the past for the purposes of the future. No part of man's nature or his institutions must be entirely outside his regard. (*The Economic Journal* Vol.34, Issue 135, p. 322)

In short, the good economist must concern himself with far more than just 'Economics', as defined in the narrow academic sense. In particular it is ecological issues, the movements of financial markets, and the problems of rising material inequalities which have been sadly neglected in recent times by 'mainstream' economists. In view of its complexity, it is therefore a brave man who presumes to pronounce on macroeconomic matters at all, but if we approach the subject from a historical point of view, that should help us at least to understand how we have arrived at our present situation.

Much depends here upon the school of economic thought that is currently holding sway, for fashions in this field have changed over the years. The economists, like the philosophers, have tried desperately hard to jump aboard the science bandwagon, attempting to employ 'scientific' methods in their analyses and claiming scientific status for their discipline. However, because macroeconomics too has a great deal to do with human behaviour and human emotions, they have met with no more success in their efforts than have the philosophers. Their beliefs have indeed been described as more akin to a religious faith than a scientific discipline by such writers as Robert Nelson in his, *Economics as Religion* (2001), and John Rapley in his, *Twilight of the Money Gods: Economics as a Religion and How it All Went Wrong* (2017). His title was of course intended to echo Nietzsche's famous work, once translated as *Twilight of the Gods* (1888), but more accurately rendered as *Twilight of the Idols*. Nietzsche in turn had the Wagner opera in mind. Unfortunately, as his title suggests, our economic thought has taken a seriously wrong turning since the 1970s, as we shall see.

There are numerous brief histories of economic thought currently available which will bring the reader right up to date in this field, such as Agnar Sandmo's *Economics Evolving* (2011), Niall Kishtainy's *A Little History of Economics* (2016), and Alessandro Roncaglia's *A Brief History of Economic Thought* (2017). There is no need, therefore, to explore the historical dimension too deeply here. Broadly speaking, however, it might be said that, around the globe, a central question has always been that of just how much government intervention in the workings of national economies has been either necessary or desirable. In the Middle Ages and on into the eighteenth century, European governments granted monopoly rights to manufacturing guilds and to overseas trading companies while excise, that is consumption taxes on popular items such as beer, were levied on the common people, as shown in the Paine section above. In addition import tariffs were levied on some goods, and export bounties granted to others, raising their price at home. It could be said that all this represented excessive and undesirable state interference in the national economy, but in the seventeenth century, these measures were justified under the economic philosophy known as mercantilism. Mercantilists attached great importance to the accumulation of gold and silver bullion in the homeland, seeing this as a measure of the country's 'real' wealth. There was some justification for this outlook in the days before paper money, when even pennies were made of silver, with no copper coinage being officially struck in Britain until 1797. Today of course, silver pennies are found only in the Maundy money bags handed out by the Queen each year. With the founding of the Bank of England in 1694 the first 'bank notes' were issued, promising to pay the bearer bullion on demand, a great convenience for large transactions. However, the lowest denomination of these notes was fifty pounds, more than twice the annual median wage at the time. In 1745 this minimum dropped to twenty pounds, and in 1793 to five pounds. Until these changes, a shortage of bullion could have had serious effects on the money supply, potentially disrupting the entire economy. Mercantilists therefore argued that it was essential to maintain a favourable balance of trade, exporting more in goods or services than your country imported, thus forcing the foreigner to pay for the difference in bullion. This accumulation of bullion would increase the 'real' wealth of the country. However, this could be overdone, with a surplus of money leading to inflation. Between 1500 and 1650 prices in England rose some six fold, due in part to larger bullion imports, sourced from new ore discoveries in South and Central America.

Until the end of the eighteenth century, therefore, it could be argued that the state had been interfering excessively, and unfairly, in the workings of national economies. This interference bore particularly heavily upon the poor in the form of numerous taxes, and tariffs imposed upon imported goods. The English Corn Laws of 1689, for example, had paid grain dealers bounties for the export of rye, malt, and wheat, while at the same time imposing import duties on those basic commodities, raising their prices in the home market. Thomas Paine was able to show that in 1788 for England alone a state revenue of some 15.5 million pounds was raised. Less than two million of this came from the land tax, which fell upon all landowners, great and small. The rest was raised by consumption taxes on essential items needed by the less well off, such as malt, sugar, beer, salt, leather, soap, and candles, together with such impositions as stamp duties, and import levies. In addition, tenant farmers were obliged to pay rent to their landlords, and tithes to the church. All this was onerous enough, but in France the position was even worse. Here, the land-owning aristocracy paid no tax at all, while a land tax known as the *taille* was imposed on the peasantry. In addition France was burdened with internal customs barriers, and numerous consumption taxes such as the *gabelle*, a tax on salt. Suggestions for the reform of this very unfair system had emerged as early as the 1690s in the writings of Pierre le Pesant (1646-1714), a minor noble, born at Rouen in Normandy. His principle work was, *Le Détail de la France; la Cause de la Diminution de ses Biens et la Facilité du Remède* (1694) Here, he attacked the mercantilist system established in France by Jean-Baptiste

Colbert, Louis XIV's Finance Minister, advocated a reform of the *taille*, the suppression of internal customs duties, and greater freedom of trade.

However, it was only during the second half of the eighteenth century that a new and coherent economic philosophy began to emerge in France, giving that nation the leadership in economic thought for those times. It originated with a body of men who called themselves '*Les Economistes*', but who are better known to history as the Physiocrats. Physiocracy meant 'rule by nature' and this school advocated less government interference in the national economy so that 'natural' economic laws could apply. One of them, Pierre Samuel du Pont (1739-1817) wrote a book with the revealing title, *Physiocratie, Ou Constitution Naturelle du Government le Plus Advantageux au Genre Humain* in 1768. The leaders of the movement, however, are generally recognised as being François Quesnay (1694-1774) and Anne-Robert-Jacques Turgot (1727-81). They were patronised by Vincent de Gournay (1712-1759) who was the *Intendant du Commerce* from 1751 until his death. He was one of the first to recognise a law of diminishing returns from productive resources, the first to coin the term '*laissez faire'* and the first to use the term *bureaucratie*, meaning literally 'government by desks' which reflected his contempt for overregulation by government officials. Others who contributed to the movement were Francois Forbonnais (1722-1800) and Louis Paul Abeille (1719-1807).

The Physiocrats instituted numerous periodicals in eighteenth-century France which dealt with economic questions, but their most famous publication was Quesnay's *Tableau économique* which appeared in 1758. Quesnay was a medical doctor, and in his *Tableau* he likened the workings of a national economy to the functioning of a human body, with each separate part related to the functioning of the others. This work essentially summarised the views of the Physiocrats, and showed them to be wrong-headed in many respects. They exaggerated the importance of land and agricultural production, dismissing craftsmen and merchants as 'sterile' classes within their economic framework. However, they did argue strongly for free trade, being highly critical of government-imposed tariffs and the monopolistic effects of the French guild system.

As noted above, the term 'physiocracy' means 'rule by nature', free from 'unnatural' restrictions. This idea of living in accordance with nature was a very old one, going back to the ancient Greeks, who had believed that only the sage could achieve true 'virtue', because only the wise could understand how to truly live in accordance with nature. This idea had also appeared in Confucian thought, which taught that there could be good government only when a perfect harmony existed between the ways of man and the way of nature. François Quesnay in particular was a great admirer of Confucianism. It was indeed the stress laid by Confucius upon agrarian policies that had influenced Quesnay's own thinking in this regard. The Chinese conception of the 'way of nature' may be rendered as 'wu wei' in Western script, and in French this was translated as 'laissez faire'. Although de Gournay was the first to actually coin the term, based on his reading of Quesnay's writings on China, in particular his *Le Despotisme de la Chine* published in 1767, it was Quesnay who later popularised its use, expanding it into the phrase, '*Laissez faire et laissez passer, le monde va de lui même!*' The Physiocrats, like the Encyclopaedists, were not revolutionaries. Indeed their leader Quesnay was such an admirer of Chinese government that he favoured a system of enlightened despotism for France. However, the Physiocrats made it clear from their writings on economic matters that they believed the government of France at that time to be far from enlightened enough! Adam Smith (1713-90) met both Quesnay and Turgot during a visit to France in 1765-6, and was clearly influenced by their thought.

This influence can be seen in the way that Smith too stressed the existence of 'natural' laws of economics in his *Wealth of Nations* (1776), laws that the state should recognise, and should interfere with only to a minimal extent. If men were left to themselves, with each one pursuing his own self-interest, the economy would regulate itself, guided by the 'invisible hand' of natural economic laws, achieving fair prices and optimum output levels. Smith accepted that, under such a system some people, notably those with capital, would rapidly become richer than others in the 'natural' course of events, but he argued that greater inequality was a price worth paying in order to achieve a higher overall level of production. As noted in the Philosophy chapter, however, Smith was not an advocate of complete *laissez faire*, recognising a role for the state in the building of public works like roads, bridges, harbours, and prisons. He also believed that schools and a police force should be paid for by national taxation. While in general he favoured free trade, he was also prepared to accept some protective tariffs to encourage infant industries, and because he favoured competition among producers in a free market, he also saw a role for the state in the curbing of monopolies, decrying the selfishness of monopoly-seeking manufacturers.

Because Adam Smith (1723-90) is regarded as being such a pivotal figure in the history of economic thought, he deserves some more detailed consideration here. In 1886 the socialist Beatrice Webb (1858-1943) described the writings of Adam Smith as being 'the employers' gospel', but a close reading of Smith reveals this to be far from true: indeed, he was an ardent champion of the working man, as we shall see. Smith does indeed recognise a fundamental selfishness in humankind, but at the same time Smith had a keen sense of morality and fair play, believing that this selfishness should never be allowed to degenerate into immoral behaviour, but rather should be harnessed for the general good of all. He was a close friend of fellow Scot David Hume (1711-76) who had also been deeply concerned with moral issues. Both men had in turn been influenced by the thought of Francis Hutcheson (1694-1746), the celebrated Glasgow University teacher. Cited below are two of Smith's most famous passages from *The Wealth of Nations.*

It is not from the benevolence of the butcher, the brewer, or the baker that we expect our dinner, but from their regard to their own interest. We address ourselves not to their humanity, but to their self-love, and never talk to them of our own necessities, but of their advantages. (Book I, Chpt. 2, 2012 ed., p.19)

As every individual, therefore, endeavours as much as he can, both to employ his capital in the support of domestic industry, and so to direct that industry that its produce may be of the greatest value, every individual necessarily labours to render the annual revenue of the society as great as he can. He generally, indeed, neither intends to promote the public interest, nor knows how much he is promoting it. By preferring the support of domestic to that of foreign industry, he intends only his own security; and by directing that industry in such a manner as its produce may be of the greatest value, he intends only his own gain; and he is in this, as in many other cases, led by an invisible hand to promote an end which was no part of his intention. (Book IV, Chpt.. 2, 2012 ed., p. 445)

Smith is here laying stress upon 'natural' laws and individual freedom, but this does not mean that he is favouring employers over workers. In fact, he often speaks disparagingly of masters and great landowners, while he is unfailingly in support of the labourers. Indeed, he occasionally hints at the fundamental equality of all men. Early in *The Wealth of Nations* he declares,

The difference between the most dissimilar characters, between a philosopher and a common street porter, for example, seems to arise not so much from nature as from habit, custom, and education. When they came into the world, and for the first six or eight years of their existence, they were, perhaps, very much alike, and neither their parents nor playfellows could perceive any remarkable difference. (Book I, Chpt. 2, 2012 ed., p. 20)

Far from being the employers' champion, Smith in fact reserved some of his sharpest criticism for 'the great merchants and master manufacturers', writing of them on the last pages of Book I, Chapter II, Part 3,

Merchants and master manufacturers are, in this order, the two classes of people who commonly employ the largest capitals, and who by their wealth draw to themselves the greatest share of the public consideration...As their thoughts, however, are commonly exercised rather about the interest of their own particular branch of business than about that of society, their judgment, even when given with the greatest candour (which it has not been upon every occasion) is much more to be depended upon with regard to the former of those two objects, than with regard to the latter. Their superiority over the country gentleman lies not so much in their knowledge of the public interest as in their having a better knowledge of their own interest than he has of his. It is by this superior knowledge of their own interest that they have frequently imposed upon his generosity, and persuaded him to give up both his own interest and that of the public, from a very simple but honest conviction that their interest, and not his, was the interest of the public. The interest of the dealers, however, in any particular branch of trade or manufactures, is always in some respects different from, and even opposite to, that of the public. (p. 257 of 2012 ed.)

Now the country gentry were, of course, the main political class of the day, completely dominating the House of Commons, and frequently promoted up to the House of Lords as well. For 'country gentry' we may safely read, 'the politicians' here. We are powerfully reminded in this passage of how the plutocrats of our own day have sold the doctrine of neoliberalism to our own political classes with dazzling success, to the great benefit of themselves but to the detriment of the rest of us. Later in this same passage Smith goes on to criticise the naivety of the politicians of his own day for being too ready to pass legislation in the interests of this greedy and selfish class, declaring,

The proposal of any new law or regulation of commerce which comes from this order, ought always to be listened to with great precaution, and ought never to be adopted till after having been long and carefully examined, not only with the most scrupulous, but with the most suspicious attention. It comes from an order of men whose interest is never exactly the same with that of the public, who have generally an interest to deceive and even to oppress the public, and who accordingly have, upon many occasions, both deceived and oppressed it. (pp. 257-8 of 2012 ed.)

Later on, employers are again criticised, while the interests of workers are championed.

We rarely hear, it has been said, of the combinations of masters, though frequently of those of workmen. But whoever imagines upon this account that masters rarely combine, is as ignorant of the world as of the subject. Masters are always and everywhere in a sort of tacit, but constant and uniform combination, not to raise the wages of labour above their existing rate. (Book I Chpt. 8, 2012 ed., p. 71)

Servants, labourers, and workmen of different kinds make up the far greater part of every great political society. But what improves the circumstances of the greater part can never be regarded as any inconveniency to the whole. No society can surely be flourishing and happy in which the far greater part of the members are poor and miserable. It is but equity, besides, that they who feed, clothe, and lodge the whole body of the people should have such a share in the produce of their own labour as to be themselves tolerably well fed, clothed, and lodged. (Book I Chpt. 8, 2012 ed., p. 83)

In raising the price of commodities, the rise of wages operates in the same manner as simple interest does in the accumulation of debt. The rise of profit operates like compound interest. Our merchants and master manufacturers complain much of the bad effects of high wages in raising the price, and thereby lessening the sale of their goods, both at home and abroad. They say nothing concerning the bad effects of high profits; they are silent with regard to the pernicious effects of their own gains; they complain only of those of other people. (Book I Chpt. 9, 2012 ed., p. 103)

Whenever the legislature attempts to regulate the differences between masters and their workmen, its counsellors are always the masters. When the regulation, therefore, is in favour of the workmen, it is always just and equitable; but it is sometimes otherwise when in favour of the masters. (Book I Chpt. 10 Pt. 2, 2012 ed., p. 148)

The great landowners too come in for criticism, with Smith declaring that they should be paying much more in taxation. Having condemned the 'violence, rapine, and disorder' of the age of the robber barons, Smith goes on to say,

> But what all the violence of the feudal institutions could never have effected, the silent and insensible operation of foreign commerce and manufactures gradually brought about. These gradually furnished the great proprietors with something for which they could exchange the whole surplus produce of their lands, and which they could consume themselves, without sharing it with either tenants or retainers. All for ourselves, and nothing for other people, seems in every age of the world to have been the vile maxim of the masters of mankind. As soon, therefore, as they could find a method of consuming the whole value of their rents themselves, they had no disposition to share them with any other persons. (Book III, Chpt. 4, 2012 ed., pp. 405-6)

Smith was here complaining about the tendency of great landowners to purchase imported foreign luxuries, which gave no employment to workers at home. Smith again showed his concern for the workers when it came to the elementary education of the labourers. Smith believed that the state should step in, establishing a school in every parish that should be subsidised with public money, rather like the system already obtaining in his native Scotland.

> For a very small expense the public can facilitate, can encourage, and can even impose upon the whole body of the people the necessity of acquiring those most essential parts of education. The public can facilitate this acquisition by establishing in every parish or district a little school, where children may be taught for a reward so moderate that even a common labourer may afford it, the master being partly, but not wholly, paid by the public. (Book V, Chpt. 1, Part 3, Article 2, 2012 ed., pp. 780-1)

Smith also believed that the rich should pay more tax as a proportion of all state revenues, declaring,

> The luxuries and vanities of life occasion the principle expense of the rich, and a magnificent house embellishes and sets off to the best advantage all the other luxuries and vanities that they possess. A tax upon house rents therefore, would in general fall heaviest upon the rich and in this sort of inequality there would not, perhaps, be anything very unreasonable. It is not very unreasonable that the rich should contribute to the public expense not only in proportion to their revenue, but something more than in that proportion...ground rents are a still more proper subject of taxation than the rent of houses. A tax upon ground rents would not raise the rent of houses; it would fall altogether upon the owner of the ground-rent, who acts always as a monopolist, and exacts the greatest rent that can be got for the use of his ground. (Book V, Chpt. 2, Part 2, Article 1, 2012 ed. pp. 842-3)

There are echoes here of Spinoza, Paine, and Henry George. A few pages later, (p. 859), Smith recommends the imposition of inheritance taxes.

In short, the whole of *The Wealth of Nations* is suffused with a keen moral sense, and a sympathy for the underdog. In this regard it may be seen as an extension of Smith's earlier work, *The Theory of Moral Sentiments* (1759). This book is available online in PDF, and the quotes below are from that version. Here once again, Smith hints at the basic equality of all mankind, and disparages the rich and powerful.

This disposition to admire – and almost to *worship* – the rich and the powerful, and to despise, or at least neglect, persons of poor or mean condition is, (on the one hand) necessary to establish and maintain the distinction of ranks and the order of society and, (on the other), the great and most universal cause of the corruption of our moral sentiments. Moralists all down the centuries have complained that wealth and greatness are often given the respect and admiration that only wisdom and virtue should receive, and that poverty and weakness are quite wrongly treated with the contempt that should be reserved for vice and folly. (Part I, Section 3, Chpt.3, PDF p. 33)

The proud and unfeeling landlord views his extensive fields and – without a thought for the wants of anyone else – imaginatively consumes himself the whole harvest that grows on them; but what of it? The homely and common proverb *The eye is larger than the belly* is exactly true of this landlord. The capacity of his stomach bears no proportion to the vastness of his desires, and won't receive any more food than does the stomach of the lowest peasant...They consume little more than the poor; and despite their natural selfishness and greed, and despite the fact that they are guided only by their own convenience, and all they want to get from the labours of their thousands of employees is the gratification of their own empty and insatiable desires, they do share with the poor the produce of all their improvements. They are led by an invisible hand to share out life's necessities in just about the same way that they would have been shared out if the earth had been divided into equal portions among all its inhabitants. And so, without intending it, without knowing it, they advance the interests of society as a whole, and provide means for the survival of the species. When Providence divided the earth among a few lordly masters, it didn't forget or abandon those who seemed to have been left out in the distribution – these too enjoy their share of all that the earth produces. In terms of the *real* happiness of human life, they are in no respect inferior to those who seem to be so far above them. In ease of body and peace of mind, all the different ranks of life are nearly on a level; the beggar sitting in the sun beside the highway has the security that kings fight for. (Part IV, Chpt. 1 PDF pp. 98-9)

As for all the rich man's possessions,

They may keep off the summer shower, but not the winter storm. They always leave the rich man as much – sometimes even *more* – exposed to anxiety, fear, and sorrow; to diseases, danger, and death. (loc. cit.)

Smith's sympathies extended even to Negro slaves, whom he admires for their courage and fortitude in their captivity.

> There's not a Negro from the coast of Africa who does not in this respect have a degree of magnanimity that the soul of his sordid master is too often hardly able to conceive of. Fortune never used her dominance of mankind more cruelly than when she subjected those nations of heroes to the sweepings of the jails of Europe, to wretches who don't have the virtues of the countries they come from, or of the ones they go to – wretches whose levity, brutality, and baseness so deservedly expose them to the contempt of the vanquished. (Part V, Chpt. 2, PDF p. 109)

It would appear, therefore, that far from being the author of an 'employers' gospel', Adam Smith's sympathies lay wholly with the labouring poor. His attitude in *The Wealth of Nations* is entirely in line with that expressed in his *Theory of Moral Sentiments* (1759) where he stresses empathy with our fellow men. Neoliberals and their institutions such as the Adam Smith Institute credit Smith with creating for us a vision of the totally selfish individual, *homo economicus*, who shows no concern for the wellbeing of others. But Smith himself rejected this picture, writing in his *Theory of Moral Sentiments,*

> How selfish soever man may be supposed, there are evidently some principles in his nature which interest him in the fortune of others, and render their happiness necessary to him, though he derives nothing from it except the pleasure of seeing it. (Part I, Section 1, Chapter I, p. 1)

This is the very first point that Smith makes in the book, but in this as in so much else the neoliberals have completely failed to grasp his underlying philosophy. Had Smith lived long enough to read Part II of Thomas Paine's *Rights of Man* (1792),and his *Agrarian Justice* (1795) where Paine suggests the setting up of an embryonic welfare state, he would surely have sympathised with those views. It is true that Smith advocated less state intervention for his times, but we must remember that in his day state intervention had operated in the main *against* the interests of the working poor, with its support of monopolies, import duties, and unfair taxation. Even poor relief was not organised by the national government, but rather was a parish affair, with each parish being responsible for the relief of its own poor. But the local poor rate in fact usually amounted to the poor supporting the poor, since the great landowners and merchants were generally able to avoid paying their fair share, although some of them did set up private charities, such as schools and hospitals. Had the interventions of national government at the time been actually *beneficial* for the poor, it seems likely that Smith would have taken a much more favourable view of state intervention, while nevertheless retaining his fundamental belief in the power of free market forces, and of a basically private enterprise economy. While he believed in economic freedom, he clearly felt that this freedom should not extend to a licence for the economically strong to exploit and despise the economically weak. If only today's members of the

Adam Smith Institute had taken the trouble to read Smith properly instead of contenting themselves with a half-baked understanding of his views. Smith himself would have been disconcerted to see the policies which they are now promoting in his name.

The first British economist to take up Adam Smith's views on 'natural laws' and the workings of an 'invisible hand' was Thomas Robert Malthus (1766-1834), an Anglican clergyman and scholar. In 1798 he published his most influential work, *An Essay on the Principle of Population*. Here he argued that population would increase by a geometric progression (2, 4, 8, 16, etc), while the food supply of a nation could increase only much more slowly, by an arithmetic progression (1, 2, 3, 4, etc). Therefore, the rate of population growth would always outstrip the growth of food supply, leading inevitably to what became known as a 'Malthusian Catastrophe', when famine and disease would intervene, drastically reducing the population, and bringing it back to its 'natural' level once more, i.e. that which could be supported by existing food supplies. Here was a harsh 'natural' law indeed. After 1798 Malthus became a prodigious writer on economic matters, with his *Principles of Political Economy* (1820) being the best known of his later works. In general he followed Adam Smith in arguing for less government interference in the economy, even attacking the Poor Laws.

Other economists of the day, greatly impressed by *The Wealth of Nations*, also followed Smith, arguing that, left to their own devices, markets would be self-regulating and would operate at optimum levels. One of them was the French economist Jean Baptiste Say (1767-1832) who, in his *Traité d'economie politique* of 1803 introduced his famous Say's Law. This declared that any increase in aggregate supply within a society would automatically increase the aggregate demand for goods within that society, thus making the whole society richer. This implied that a general glut (a widespread excess of supply over demand) could not occur within a free market. Another supporter of classical theory was David Ricardo (1772-1823), a Jewish banker and stock broker of independent means. He too followed Adam Smith in his best known work, *Principles of Political Economy and Taxation* (1817), supporting a labour theory of value and arguing strongly for free trade, suggesting that free trade would always be beneficial to both parties, whatever their comparative economic circumstances, taking trade between England and Portugal as his example. He also enlarged upon the definition of 'rent', declaring it to be an unearned surplus of any kind, not just that arising from the rent of land.

A close friend of David Ricardo was James Mill (1773-1836), the father of John Stuart Mill (1806-1873). Like his son, James too was an economist and philosopher, who wrote on a wide variety of topics. His best known work on economics, however, was his *Elements of Political Economy* (1821), in which he very largely supported the views of Ricardo. Together, these men are generally regarded as being the founders of that school of economic thought known as 'classical economics', which was to hold sway until the later years of the nineteenth century, when it was superseded by a generally more sophisticated school which came to be known as 'neoclassical'. Both schools, however, advocated minimal government interference in the working of national economies believing that, left to their own devices, free markets would be self-regulating and would, despite some ups and downs, operate at optimum levels overall. This belief persisted until the onset of the Great Depression in 1929.

As noted by Keynes and Hayek in the Introduction above, it took some decades for the ideas of economic thinkers to be acted upon by the political classes, but by the 1840's the adoption of what came to be known as the 'classical' school of economic thought by Britain's ruling classes was complete. Its final triumph came with the repeal of the Corn Laws in 1846. These were the Corn Laws of 1815, amended in 1822, 1828, and 1842, but all imposing import duties on foreign cereals until domestic prices reached very high levels, with the aim of keeping the price of cereals high at home for the benefit of British landowners and their tenant farmers. However, well organised opposition to the Corn Laws from non-agricultural interests had been growing since 1815, and the final blow against them came with the onset of the Irish potato famine in 1845. The rising classes of industrial manufacturers and townspeople had long opposed the Corn Laws, and now the onset of famine in Ireland and scarcity in England made their repeal seem imperative. Prior to the arrival of potato blight, potatoes had provided some 60 per cent of Ireland's food needs, at prices that were affordable for the poor.

The onset of famine in Ireland had been the tipping point in turning political opinion against the Corn Laws. But in fact, their repeal did little to help the Irish, most of whom could still not afford to buy wheat at its new domestic price. Indeed, a great deal of the more expensive foodstuffs such as beef and pork, butter, oysters, peas and beans, and also some wheat, continued to be exported from Ireland even at the height of the famine. In the 1780s, when wheat prices in England had been high, the export of wheat was banned for a time, but in the 1840s this was seen as being contrary to free trade principles. Of course, people are more important than principles, but the British ruling classes of the day did not seem to be capable of grasping that point. There was in fact enough food on their island throughout the famine to feed everyone, but most of the Irish could not afford to buy it. The worst conditions were found in the west and south of Ireland, while in the north-east, which was mostly Protestant, and in Dublin, people were better off. There was always plenty of food available in Ireland for those who could afford it. About four times as much wheat was imported into Ireland during the famine as was exported from it. For the rest, a great deal of maize was imported from the USA, and sold cheaply to the masses. In addition the British government set up soup kitchens from March to September in 1847, bringing relief to some three million people. However, the idea of giving free food to Irish Catholics was not popular on the other side of the Irish Sea. The British quickly experienced compassion fatigue, and the scheme was abandoned, never to be revived.

Although 'classical' economic theory, with its insistence on free trade, had at last brought down the Corn Laws, on balance the doctrine did the Irish more harm than good. It laid stress on minimal government interference in the economy, so that 'natural' laws could operate. But these 'natural' laws taught that periodic famines were only to be expected, as population growth outran food supplies, leading to the kind of 'Malthusian Catastrophe' that had recently been predicted by Malthus himself. The famine was therefore seen by the English as a kind of Act of God, a righteous punishment inflicted upon the Irish for being Catholics, lazy, stupid, and frankly sub-human. Such an attitude is difficult for us today to understand, but we must remember that racism was the creed of the times, shared by all Europeans. No one doubted for a moment that a white man was 'better' than a black man, or a brown man, or a yellow man. While it had to be admitted that Irish Catholics were in fact white, if you could see beneath the grime that usually covered their faces, in English minds they were classed with the coloured races. Indeed, Negroes were later to be referred to as 'smoked Irishmen'. The racism of the times is difficult for us to understand.

The Irish Famine of 1845-52 was therefore not a 'Malthusian' catastrophe at all. Rather it was a political catastrophe, an economic catastrophe, and most of all a human catastrophe. It was the result of the racial, religious, and doctrinaire attitudes of the British ruling classes of the day, and the doctrine to which they were adhering was that of classical economic theory. The truth is that the Irish were allowed to starve on the doorstep of what was then the richest country in the world. The British could easily have afforded to send to Ireland the minimal free relief supplies that would have prevented starvation on the island, but they chose not to do so. Census figures for the time are somewhat inaccurate, but they suggest that the population of Ireland was just over eight million in 1841. The 1851 census returned a count of some six and a half million, but the census commissioners themselves estimated that the population would have grown to nine million by that time without the famine, a shortfall of some two and a half million. It seems likely that about two million Irish emigrated in that decade, with deaths from starvation and diseases exacerbated by malnutrition accounting for the rest of the shortfall.

It might be thought that in retrospect the British would have felt ashamed of themselves for the way they had treated Ireland, but they seem to have learned nothing from the experience. During British rule in India, a great famine of 1876-9 killed some six to ten million people, and from 1896 to 1902 an even worse famine killed even more people. Estimates range somewhere between 6 and 19 million. The Bengal famine of 1943 killed some two to three million more: once again the dead were never counted. What did it matter? Famines were 'natural' in India: a righteous judgement of God upon a pagan and backward people. In reality, however, the British themselves had contributed towards causing famine in India by insisting that Indian peasants should switch from food production to the growing of cash crops that were more profitable to export, such as cotton, jute, indigo, or poppies, used to produce opium for sale to China. Food supplies were also exported from India, even during the famines. Once more racial, religious, and doctrinaire thinking meant that the British authorities again even in 1943 made only minimal and completely inadequate gestures towards famine relief. Local British administrators, including the Viceroy, could see how serious the situation was becoming, and appealed to London for help. Churchill was not unsympathetic, and made some efforts to divert grain shipments to India, but was continually frustrated in his efforts to get more wheat to India by the attitude of his war cabinet and by shipping shortages: supplies were desperately needed in other theatres. At last, in a fit of temper, he uttered words that he was later to come to regret, blaming the Indians themselves for the famine because they 'bred like rabbits'. This was classic Malthusian thinking. In September 1943 Churchill lost patience with appeals for help, declaring to Leopold Amery, Secretary of State for India, 'I hate the Indians. They are a beastly people with a beastly religion.' When informed that the situation was worsening, he growled, 'Then why hasn't Ghandi died yet?' (Madhusree Mukerjee, *Churchill's Secret War: the British Empire and the Ravaging of India* (2010) p. 274) Racism died hard – a long, slow death that took most of the second half of the twentieth century. Is it completely dead even now? I am old enough to remember seeing notices in landladies' windows which read, 'No blacks or Irish', something that would never be allowed today. We need to remember that racism was still the predominant form of thinking in 1943, so that no one of those times should be condemned simply for being of their time. But classical economic thinking and religious prejudice also played their parts in the Bengali famine, which could certainly have been relieved to a far greater extent than it was. Churchill was not devoid of humanitarian feeling, but his top priority was always the winning of the war.

Despite the rise of classical economic theory in the early nineteenth century, however, at the same time we can detect the first glimmerings of a realisation by the state that perhaps it owed some kind of duty of care to its citizens. This was illustrated by the Health and Morals of Apprentices Act of 1802, sometimes known as the first Factory Act. It was introduced by Sir Robert Peel (1750-1830), the father of the later Prime Minister, who was to repeal the Corn Laws. The elder Peel was a cotton magnate, as well as an MP, and he became upset by seeing the working conditions in his own and other cotton mills of the time. The Act required that the mills were to be kept clean and well aired, while the apprentices themselves were to be given clothing, and a basic education, that was to include religious instruction. Their hours of work were to be limited to twelve a day, for six days a week. Some of the children covered by the Act were as young as eight. Peel meant well, but the Act was ineffective, because the cotton masters simply stopped calling their child workers 'apprentices', and called them 'free labourers' instead.

A second Act of 1819 banned the employment of children under nine years of age in cotton mills, but it too was ineffective for lack of an adequate enforcement mechanism. Further Acts were passed in 1825, 1829, and 1831 seeking to improve working conditions for children in cotton mills, but again little was achieved. The first effective Factory Act was therefore that of 1833, known as Althorp's Act after Lord Althorp, who had sponsored it. This Act applied to *all* textile factories, i.e. woollen, silk, and jute mills as well as cotton mills, but again it sought only to limit the working hours of children, and to ensure that they received at least *some* education while working. This time, however, factory inspectors were appointed to ensure that the terms of the Act were enforced. Subsequent Acts of 1836, 1838, 1843 and 1844 extended protective legislation to mines and collieries, improved enforcement measures,

and limited working hours for women. During the second half of the nineteenth century progressively more and more legislation was introduced aimed at improving working conditions in mines and factories, restricting the freedoms of employers, particularly when it came to the employment of women and children.

A further blow against child labour in mines and factories was struck by William Forster's Education Act of 1870. It was a poor enough measure at the time, relating to elementary education only. Census data suggested that in England and Wales in 1870, while some one million children had access to church schools and a further 1.3 million to state aided voluntary schools, two million children still had access to no schools at all in their parishes. This contrasted sharply with the position in Scotland, where Education Acts of 1633 and 1646 had required the setting up of schools in every parish, to be financed by local landowners, who were to pay for school buildings and a salary for the schoolmaster. Under the 1870 Act, School Boards were set up to provide schools funded by local rates in local authority areas where provision was lacking, for children aged five to thirteen. Optional by-laws could make attendance compulsory, and by 1873 40 per cent of the population lived in compulsory attendance districts. This was the first step towards making school attendance compulsory for all children, and subsequent Education Acts further extended this principle. By 1918 schooling was compulsory for all, and in that year the Fisher Education Act raised the school leaving age to 14, abolished all fees in state elementary schools, and widened the provision of medical inspection, nursery schools, and special needs education.

Nineteenth-century legislation on working conditions and educational provision represented the return of state interference in the economy to a degree, but the underlying preference for *laissez faire* remained the keystone of government policy in most branches of the economy. Caring legislation for women and children was one thing, but the assumption still was that the state should interfere as little as possible with the workings of the national economy.

During the later years of the nineteenth century however, a recognisably new school of economic thought arose in Europe which came to be called 'neoclassical economics'. The term was coined only in 1900 by Thorstein Veblen (1857-1929), the witty Norwegian-American critic of capitalism, but the development of the school had been in train well before then. Its early exponents were William Stanley Jevons (1835-82) with his, *A General Mathematical Theory of Political Economy* (1862) and his *Theory of Political Economy* (1871), Carl Menger (1840-1921), the founder of the 'Austrian School' of Economics, with his *Principles of Economics* (1871), and Léon Walras (1834-1910), the French mathematical economist and Georgist, with his multi-volume *Elements of Pure Economics* (1874-7). Here, Walras was the first to introduce general equilibrium theory, suggesting that all markets would naturally adjust to a general equilibrium. His 'equilibrium', however, related only to supply and demand considerations, and did not exclude the possibility of an 'equilibrium' that settled at low levels of demand with high unemployment resulting. One of the greatest later exponents of the neoclassical school in all its aspects was the Englishman Alfred Marshall (1842-1924). His *Principles of Economics* (1890) became the standard Economics textbook in Britain for decades. It was Marshall who succeeded in introducing the first Economics degree course to Britain in 1903, while he was Professor of Political Economy at Cambridge. Prior to that time, Economics had been taught only as part of the Historical and Moral Sciences Tripos – a 'poor relation' indeed!

Essentially, neoclassical economic theory was more statistical, more mathematical, and therefore, as the economists hoped, more scientific than mere classical economic theory. The concepts of demand and supply curves were introduced, making it possible to represent graphically the effects of monopoly supply on prices. While the classical school had argued that price levels were determined entirely by production costs, the neoclassical school stressed rather demand in relation to supply as the decisive factor. It was Alfred Marshall who settled the debate by pointing out that arguing over whether production costs or demand levels determined prices was like asking which blade of a pair of scissors did the cutting!

Neoclassical economic theory certainly represented an advance over classical economics, which seemed simplistic by comparison. For example, while classical economic thought had been reluctant to accept the idea of trade or business cycles, periods of 'boom and bust', these were accepted by the neoclassicals as an inevitable concomitant of an advanced capitalist system. However, the neoclassicists still relied heavily on rational behaviour theory, and their neat little econometric equations therefore often did not accurately predict what actually happened in the real world of markets. They laid great stress on the marginal utility of goods to the consumer, so much so that the advent of neoclassical economics is sometimes referred to as 'the marginal revolution'. This was later refined into the concept of 'ordinal utility', stressing that some goods could be seen as being of greater marginal utility than others. Despite the greater sophistication of their analyses, however, the neoclassical school retained the basic assumption of classical economics, namely that the state should interfere as little as possible in the workings of the national economy. They believed that, despite some ups and downs, free markets would always be self-regulating, and that the 'invisible hand' of 'natural' economic laws would always ensure optimal levels of output and employment in the long run.

This cosy assumption held sway until the onset of the Great Depression in 1929, a world-wide phenomenon that lasted in one form or another until the outbreak of the Second World War in 1939. It was this tragedy that destroyed forever the myth that, left to their own devices, markets would be self-correcting and would operate at optimum levels of output and employment, with no interference from government agencies. The neoclassicists had casually accepted the idea that natural swings in the trade cycle would lead to periods of 'boom and bust' at intervals, but they had failed to notice something about those swings that was not lost on Karl Marx (1818-83). In his famous work, *Das Kapital*, Marx had noted that each swing of the trade cycle was becoming lengthier, and its extremes more pronounced. He therefore predicted that eventually a long period of prosperity would be followed by the greatest crash of all, so severe that it would bring down the entire capitalist system, leaving socialism as the only alternative. With the onset of the Great Depression of the 1930s, it began to look as though Marx might have been right. The nineteenth century had also suffered from stock market crashes, bank runs, and business failures. Indeed, the term 'Great Depression' had originally been applied to the years between 1873 and 1896, when Europe and North America had suffered from a long period of price deflation, slower growth, and higher unemployment, but these problems had never reached crisis proportions. Today this period is usually referred to as the 'Long Depression', or sometimes the 'Long Recession', to distinguish it from the Great Depression of the 1930s, which was of a completely different order.

The Great Depression began in the United States, with a collapse of the New York stock market. After the great boom of 'the roaring twenties' the economy had begun to slow by the end of the decade. There had been a serious fall in stocks from September 4, 1929, but a major stock market crash occurred between October 24 (Black Thursday), continuing on October 28 (Black Monday), and concluding on October 29 (Black Tuesday) when precipitous falls ended. In just four days of trading the New York Stock Exchange lost 29% of its value. Stock markets in other American cities also fell. In just a few days the Dow Jones Industrial Average of all stocks had plunged from 350 to 200. To an extent, this had been simply a common enough market correction. During the 'roaring twenties' the Dow Jones Industrial Index had soared from 70 to a peak of 381.2 on September 3, 1929. It was not to reach this level again until November 23, 1954. The Index had reached 200 by the end of 1927, and then accelerated sharply in the following two years until September, 1929. The 'Great Crash' therefore had merely restored the stock values of two years earlier, with the Dow Jones index hitting a nadir of 198.6 on November 13. In fact, the market had simply overheated badly in the two years before the crash, fuelled by what Robert Schiller was later to call *Irrational Exuberance* in his 2000 book of that title. The stock market had been rising so strongly for so long that people had come to believe that buying shares was a certain way to make money. Many had actually borrowed money to buy shares, certain that they would make a profit on them, and even banks had bought shares, using their depositors' money. These people were hit hard when the value of their shares suddenly dropped to considerably less than they had paid for them, leaving them in debt with no means of recouping their losses. But how did what was after all just a very reasonable stock market correction in America lead to a world-wide Great Depression?

The answer lay partly in a failure by the governments of the day to realise just how serious and threatening the slump of 1929 to 1931 really was, together with their enduring faith in neoclassical economic doctrines. Herbert Hoover (1874-1964), who served as President from March 1929 to March 1933, was convinced that the downturn of those years was just a normal part of the trade cycle, and that the situation would soon correct itself. The economy had already been slowing in the run up to 1929. In November 1929 he declared, 'Any lack of confidence in the economic future or the basic strength of business in the United States is foolish'. By March 1930 3.2 million Americans were unemployed, but Hoover declared that the worst was over, and that the situation would right itself within two months. Captains of industry supported his view. John D. Rockefeller (1839-1937) declared, 'These are days when many are discouraged. In the 93 years of my life depressions have come and gone. Prosperity has always returned, and will again.'

It was certainly true that America had already experienced a number of booms, slumps, and panics, which the neoclassical economists had explained as just the inevitable swings of the trade cycle. The first of these had struck in 1819, and the last as recently as 1920-1. But the downturn of 1929-33 was of a new order. Never before had Americans borrowed so much or so recklessly to buy themselves some of the new wonders of the 1920s – motor cars, refrigerators, radios, vacuum cleaners, and a host of other items. Never before had the banks lent so much on such poor security. Never before had people speculated so rashly on the stock exchange, many using borrowed money to do so, pushing stock prices far beyond their true value. For their part, U.S. banks kept, on average, only ten per cent of their depositors' money in cash. The rest they lent out at interest, hoping to make a profit. Moreover, some banks had also been using their depositors' money to buy shares. All this had left the American economy in a vulnerable position, ill-equipped to weather a major financial storm.

This storm struck in the early 1930's with a general collapse of confidence in America – confidence in investment, confidence in the banks, and confidence in the stock market. Economic systems are rather like a religion – they will work for only so long as people believe in them, for only so long as people have faith. If this faith is lost then that system is at best in serious trouble, and at worst may collapse completely. After a brief rally in 1930 the stock market continued to fall. On July 8, 1932 the Dow Jones Index bottomed at 41.22, only 10.8% of its peak level of 381.2 in the September of 1929. Millions of shareholders lost a great deal of money, and began to default on their bank loans. This weakened the position of banks, and depositors began to withdraw their money, fearing a collapse of their bank. Their fears were well founded. Banks desperately tried to call in their loans to pay depositors, foreclosing on unpaid mortgages, but many banks failed, beginning with the smaller ones. Then, in December 1931, the New York Bank of the United States failed, with a loss to depositors of some 200 million dollars. It was the biggest single bank failure in U.S. history. This further undermined confidence in all banks, and 'bank runs' accelerated. During the 1930s nearly 9,000 U.S. banks failed, some one third of the total. Much of the money withdrawn from banks simply disappeared from circulation as people hoarded it, hiding cash at home. This is what economists call a 'liquidity preference', although usually readily available cash is held in banks, where it can be lent out for investment. But under the new circumstances people no longer trusted banks, preferring to hide cash under the mattress, so the money supply in America contracted sharply, by some 35%. This caused a deflationary spiral, with average prices falling by 33% in the 1930s.

People hoarded money because they had come to distrust the banks, and because they feared for their jobs in an uncertain future. The unemployment rate in 1929 had been 3.2%, but in 1930 it rose to 8.9%, in 1931 to 16.3%, in 1932 to 24%, peaking in early 1933 at 25%. Another reason for saving money was that, in deflationary times, its value was steadily increasing as prices fell. Why buy today when prices would be lower tomorrow? This meant that those in debt were further disadvantaged by what the economists call 'debt deflation' but which in practical terms, is really debt *inflation* for its victims. Prices and wages both fell during the Great Depression. This increased the value of money relative to goods and services. But those in debt had to make their repayments in cash, making their debts relatively more costly for them in real terms. All this led to a drastic falling off of demand in the U.S. economy, proving the falsity of Say's Law of Markets. Jean Say had argued in 1803 that any increase in production within a society would always lead to an overall increase in demand as well, so that market gluts would be impossible. But in 1930s America production outstripped demand, with too many goods and too little money to buy them, leading to just the kind of gluts that Say had claimed could never occur. Factories began to close, raising the unemployment rate, which further reduced demand. The United States found itself trapped in a deadly downward spiral.

A leading American economist, Milton Friedman (1912-2006), a monetarist and neoliberal, has argued that America's central bank, the Federal Reserve, could have done much to prevent that situation from developing. He claimed that if the Federal Reserve had provided emergency lending to key, large banks like the Bank of the United States and the Bank of Tennessee, they could have been kept afloat, restoring confidence in the whole banking system. The Federal Reserve should have lowered interest rates, printed money, or simply bought government bonds on the open market to increase the money supply in circulation. More banks would have survived, and they could have lent more to industries: the vicious spiral could have been nipped in the bud. But the Federal Reserve, America's Central Bank, stood back and did nothing, waiting for the system to self-correct.

There is something to be said for Friedman's arguments, but another problem with the U.S. economy at that time was its adherence to the gold standard. The belief in those days was in 'sound money' to prevent inflation, so every U.S. dollar carried the promise that it could be exchanged for a fixed amount of gold. However, the Federal Reserve kept enough gold in its vaults to redeem only 40% of the dollars issued. To a large extent, this tied the hands of the Federal Reserve, limiting the amount of money that it could put into circulation. Further, the deflationary spiral which had set in was largely beyond the bank's power to control in any case. Friedman blamed the banks for a shortage of money in the American economy, but in reality it was the American people themselves who had caused a shortage. All the money was out there – all that the 'Fed' could legally issue, but people were hoarding it rather than spending it. Moreover, they were not even hoarding it in banks, which people no longer trusted. Rather, it was being hidden under mattresses, or in private safes at home. Even if the Fed had been able to issue more money, it would have met with the same fate, disappearing into the hands of hoarders. The real value of private hoards was increasing all the time in real terms. Why buy today, when everything would be cheaper tomorrow?

The 'gold standard' itself was, moreover, just another act of faith, faith in the expectation that there would be no attempt at the mass conversion of dollars into gold. However, in the early 1930s this is exactly what was threatened, not only by Americans seeking the security of gold, but also by foreign governments trying to maintain their own gold standards. In 1929 other advanced countries such as the UK, Belgium, France, Poland, Switzerland, Germany, Italy, Hungary, Japan, Brazil, Argentina, and the Scandinavian countries had also adhered to a gold standard, but all were forced to abandon it in the 1930s. They found that higher interest rates in countries trying to maintain their own gold standard, like the USA, led to a gold outflow from countries with lower interest rates, forcing them to raise their own interest rates. This resulted in an increase of the value of money relative to goods, forcing them to pursue deflationary policies if they wished to maintain their own gold standards. While wholesale prices fell by 32% in the USA from 1929 to 1932, in Britain they fell by 33%, in France by 34%, and in Germany by 29%. It was recognised in retrospect that the gold standard had been a major factor in transmitting depression from one country to another. Those countries which left the gold standard earlier recovered from depression more quickly, while countries like China, which worked on a silver standard, scarcely experienced depression at all, although this was partly because their economies were less well developed, and they were less dependent on foreign trade.

When Franklin Roosevelt became President in March, 1933, he immediately grasped the seriousness of the situation, and took America off the gold standard on April 5, 1933. On the same day Roosevelt issued an executive order making the private ownership of gold certificates, bullion, and coins illegal. These two measures curbed the run on gold, although some continued to be held illegally. They also took pressure off the Federal Reserve, allowing it to print more money. However, the Central Bank did not take full advantage of this change immediately, partly because of another shibboleth of laisser-faire economic thought. This was known as the liquidation hypothesis, which basically said that depressions were a good thing, because they weeded out the weaker industries and banks, leaving only the soundest free to flourish and grow. This was entirely the wrong philosophy for the time. If there had been too much government interference of the wrong sort in Britain's national economy up to 1790, it had become clear by 1933 that there had been too little government intervention of the right sort in America's economy under the prevailing neoclassical doctrine of laissez-faire: it was time for a change.

The monetarist argument, blaming a shortage of liquidity for America's Great Depression, is persuasive, but does not account for all the facts of the time. First, the initial downturn in the stock market and of industrial activity in 1930 and 1931 took place before there was any noticeable shortage of liquidity. Indeed, the supply of money seems to have exceeded the demand for it. The main run of bank failures and fall of the money supply seems to have occurred only after 1931. Secondly, Roosevelt's assumption of office in March, 1933 was enough on its own to stimulate an immediate rise in economic activity as expectations for the future improved, even although the money supply was then at its nadir.

No doubt a shortage of money, a loss of confidence, and a downward deflationary spiral all contributed to the length and depth of the Great Depression. But an additional explanation was put forward by John Maynard Keynes (1883-1946) in his classic work, *The General Theory of Employment, Interest, and Money* (1936). Here Keynes argued that a sustained falling off of *demand* had been the main cause of the Great Depression. Left to its own devices, a free enterprise capitalist economy could suffer a downward spiral of falling demand and rising unemployment, which led to a further falling of demand and more unemployment. This downward spiral could be checked only by vigorous government intervention in the form of stimuli aimed at increasing demand once more. These stimuli should take the form of government work-creation schemes, financed by government borrowing, to reduce unemployment levels, together with tax reductions. Both of these measures would put more money into people's pockets, increasing their demand levels with the aim of 'kick starting' the economy and putting it on the road to recovery.

Herbert Hoover, despite his basic belief in laissez faire, was not entirely unaware that something needed to be done. In 1929 he slightly reduced income tax, and on June 17, 1930, he signed the Smoot-Hawley Tariff Act, which initially raised import duties on some 900 items, but later on many more as well. The aim was to create more employment at home, but foreign countries retaliated with anti-American tariffs of their own, so there was little net benefit to the U.S. The only result was a trade war, in which all countries suffered, as the volume and value of world trade plunged by over 50%. But in January and February of 1932 Hoover did persuade Congress to lend three billion dollars to struggling banks, which saved many from collapse.

The road to recovery really began, however, on March 4, 1933 when Franklin Delano Roosevelt (1882-1945) assumed the office of President. Unlike Hoover, he had no faith in laissez faire at all, believing that only heavy and sustained government intervention in the American economy could save the country from its existing plight. On March 9, 1933 he announced his plans for a 'New Deal' in America which he proposed to implement in three stages. This New Deal involved heavy government expenditure on work creation projects, aimed at reducing unemployment and so raising demand in the economy. In effect, Roosevelt was a Keynesian even before Keynes had fully expounded his views in 1936. The measures taken by Roosevelt to deal with the depression are too numerous to mention here, but they may be seen on line under several 'Timelines of the Great Depression' and numerous entries on the subject. To finance his projects Roosevelt borrowed heavily, increasing the national debt from 23 billion dollars in 1933 to 49 billion in1941, even before the outbreak of war with Japan. He raised the top rate of income tax from its 1929 level of 24% to 79% in 1936, and 81% in 1940. He also repealed Prohibition, so that he could tax alcohol sales for extra revenue. From January 17, 1920 to December 5, 1933, America had been 'dry', with a ban on all sales of strong drink under the Eighteenth Amendment to the Constitution. Repeal took place under the Twenty-First Amendment, passed in 1933.

Roosevelt's projects, such as the Civilian Conservation Corps, the Civil Works Administration, the Works Project Administration, and the Tennessee Valley Authority employed some 15 million Americans during the 1930s, and the unemployment rate began to fall, to 21.7% in 1934, 20.1% in 1935, 16.9% in 1936, and 14.3% in 1937. But in 1938 FDR cut back on his investing, hoping to balance the federal budget, and unemployment immediately rose again to 19%, showing how crucial his intervention measures had been. He then resumed his heavy investing, and unemployment fell to 17.2% in 1939. There was a further fall to 14.6% in 1940 as America increased its defence expenditure, and to 9.9% in 1941. However, this was still a depression level of unemployment. What really changed the situation was America's entry into World War II in December, 1941 and the beginning of truly massive government expenditure. By 1942 unemployment was down to 4.7%, a reasonable peacetime norm, and in 1944 it stood at 1.2%.

Between 1933 and 1937 FDR had increased America's national debt by 17 billion dollars in his efforts to pull the USA. out of depression. But in 1943 and 1944 alone he increased the debt by 128.5 billions in order to win the war. Had Roosevelt been allowed to borrow on that scale in the 1930s, he could have stopped the depression in its tracks by 1935. But of course, political factors prevented him from doing this. In 1935 the Supreme Court ruled that one of the new agencies set up by Roosevelt, the National Recovery Administration, was unconstitutional, and Roosevelt was forced to abandon it. The same fate befell his National Labour Relations Board in 1937. The Tennessee Valley Authority, a government project designed to bring hydroelectric power and employment to one of the poorest parts of America, did survive, but was described as 'stark Communism' by right-wing Republicans. Roosevelt went as far as was politically possible for him with government initiatives, but all his measures were still not enough, given the depth and severity of the depression. He was forced to backtrack in 1938, trying instead to balance the budget, and no major New Deal legislation was passed after this date. Only the vast amounts of government money spent on rearmament from 1942 to 1945 were enough to finally remedy the situation.

Americans suffered terribly during the Depression because of their firm belief that free enterprise capitalism on its own was enough. The American tradition of 'rugged individualism' had meant that every American male was expected to provide for himself and his family without any form of welfare assistance whatsoever. Americans had always been suspicious of government, preferring freedom over security. 'That government governs best which governs least' had been their watchword. These assumptions had been more feasible in the days of the 'Wild West', when land was cheap and plentiful, while labour had been scarce and expensive, with high wages. However, as the economy developed and became more sophisticated, people's expectations changed. A log cabin on a farmstead with no piped water, electricity, or sanitation was no longer enough, and medical costs also rose as medicine too became more sophisticated. While America had been only five per cent urbanised in 1790, by 1930 56.1% of the population lived in cities. (81% by 2010) Most Americans had already become urban wage earners, entirely dependent on salaries, rather than self-sufficient rural food producers. Under these new conditions, 'rugged individualism' was no longer enough.

Remarkably, in 1935 America was still the only advanced country in the world to have no form of national social security in place. As a result, there were no unemployment benefits available for the millions of Americans who became unemployed in the early 1930s. Many could not keep up their mortgage payments, and lost their homes. Some two million Americans became homeless, and were forced to build rough shacks for themselves on city outskirts, where they scratched a living as best they could. Collections of these shacks were dubbed 'Hoovervilles', a bitter reproach to Herbert Hoover who, it was thought, had not done enough to ease the Depression. Millions more were housed only in the work camps set up by Roosevelt as accommodation for workers on his state-financed employment projects.

Even sturdy, independent, landowning farmers were hard hit as nature combined with economic folly to deepen the misery of Americans. The 1930s were the hottest and driest years ever recorded in the mid-western United States. Temperatures of over 100 degrees Fahrenheit were commonplace for long periods and in 1936, the hottest summer on record, five states experienced temperatures of 120 degrees. Rainfall was far below average. In 1934 80% of American states recorded extremely dry conditions, and drought was reported by 27 states. Hardest hit were New Mexico, Colorado, Oklahoma, Kansas, Nebraska, and northern Texas. These states were the main focus of the 'dust bowl', as their parched and overworked topsoil crumbled into dust, and began to blow away in great dust storms, whipped up by searing desert winds. In May, 1934, a three-day dust storm blew an estimated 350 million tons of soil as far east as New York and Boston, reducing visibility in those cities. In the Midwest, entire farmsteads were buried beneath drifting dunes. The misery of Midwestern farmers and of many others was poignantly recorded by the American photojournalist Dorothea Lange (1895-1965) in many moving images, and also in John Steinbeck's novel, *The Grapes of Wrath* (1939). FDR did something to help American farmers with his Emergency Farm Mortgage

Act of May 1933 designed to save farms from foreclosure, and in February, 1935 he passed the Soil Conservation and Domestic Allotment Act, which paid farmers to plant soil-binding crops, but these moves were not enough to save American farmers from the consequences of drought and falling prices for their produce.

A more significant measure, however, came on August 14, 1935, when America's first Social Security Act was signed into law by FDR. It provided only the basis of a comprehensive social security system, but again FDR went as far as was politically possible for him at the time. The Act provided first for old age pensions for all workers over 65, to be paid for by a payroll tax, levied on workers and employers. It also provided the first federal unemployment benefits for the many unemployed. Child benefits were also introduced, together with measures for maternal and child welfare. Provisions were also made for the blind. Much more was required in later years to build a comprehensive welfare system, but at least a start had been made, most notably in the crucial field of unemployment benefits.

The bitter lesson of the Great Depression induced a sea change in the attitude of most Americans towards state intervention in the running of the national economy. The central lesson of Keynesianism, that unrestrained capitalism was not enough, and that some degree of government regulation of the economy was essential, had been well learned. It came to be felt by many that it should be the duty of the state to keep unemployment down to tolerable levels, and to act vigorously if a future depression should be threatened again. This new attitude was adopted not only in the USA, but also in other economically advanced countries around the world. They too had experienced boom conditions in the 1920s, followed by severe depression in the 1930s, for much the same reasons that had obtained in America. The USA had been hardest hit, followed by Germany, where unemployment levels increased by 232% between 1929 and 1932. But in America they rose by 607% over the same time span. Germany's foreign trade declined by 61% over the same period, but America's fell by 70%, and while industrial production in Germany went down by 41%, in America the decline was 46%. Other advanced economies suffered similar declines.

The misery of the 1930s was of course followed by the even greater misery generated by the Second World War, fought between 1939 and 1945, with America, Russia, and Japan joining the fray in 1941. Following the victory of the Allies in 1945 there was a strong feeling that an opportunity presented itself for the building of a new world order, where peace would be preserved through the agency of the newly formed United Nations, and in which depressions, mass unemployment, and even the usual trade cycles of boom and bust, would become things of the past, with welfare states established in every developed country. It became accepted that all this would require a great deal more government intervention in the working of national economies than had been the case in the past, together with higher taxation.

On the economic front, this meant a turning to the thought of John Maynard Keynes, as expounded in his classic work. *The General Theory of Employment, Interest, and Money* (1936), written in response to the depression conditions of the times. It is best described as an emergency plan, designed primarily as a means of pulling economies out of depression. Essentially, Keynes argued that only strenuous government intervention could do this. He recommended that in times of depression, governments should borrow heavily, increasing the national debt, and use the cash to invest in sensible, productive schemes such as the Tennessee Valley hydroelectric development, or other plans similar to those which FDR had already put into place. These would revive the economy by reducing unemployment and increasing demand, which would lead to increased investment in new factories, further reducing unemployment. This theory is known as the multiplier-accelerator model, a Keynesian concept, but one spelled out in detail by Paul Samuelson (1915-2009) and Alvin Hanson (1887-1975) in 1939. The idea of 'the multiplier' was that every dollar put into the economy by government projects would be spent more than once. The previously unemployed worker would spend the money with a grocer, who would spend it with his wholesaler, who would spend it with a farmer or food processor. The farmer or processor, seeing that demand was picking up, would then invest in more machinery or plant to increase his output. This capital investment was referred to as the 'accelerator stage', since more plant increased both employment and output, leading to a larger GDP, and faster economic growth. But the initial demand stage could also be initiated by the government simply cutting taxes, thereby putting more money into the pockets of those who were already employed, although both methods would increase the national debt.

Keynes stressed the importance of government intervention to increase demand under conditions of depression, essentially mass demand, which would stimulate mass production and more employment, thus creating a beneficial cycle in place of the vicious spiral which had taken America and other countries down into depression. However, Keynes added a caveat which too many of our modern politicians seem to have conveniently overlooked. Once full employment and prosperity had been restored, the economy would grow and tax revenues would increase. Keynes stressed that these higher revenues should then be used to pay down the national debt through higher taxation, increasing tax rates if necessary. However, our politicians have found that while it is very easy to borrow money, it is very difficult to pay it back so that, by and large, they have generally not bothered to do so, resulting in massive and increasing national debts in countries around the world. But running national economies on the basis of massive, permanent, and increasing public debt had never been any part of Keynes' proposals. This development will be re-examined below.

What followed the Second World War was a new economic consensus, broadly accepted by academic economists and politicians in advanced nations, known as the neoclassical synthesis. This combined the macroeconomic thought of Keynes with neoclassical economics into a synthesis generally described as neo-Keynesian economics, with Keynesian thought applied in the macroeconomic field and neoclassical thought in microeconomics. The theoretical framework which explained and justified this synthesis was provided by the British Economist Sir John Hicks (1904-1989) and the French economist Maurice Allais (1911-2010), with their work summarised and popularised by the American Economist Paul Samuelson (1915-2009). Samuelson's key book was his very popular, *Economics: An Introductory Analysis*, first published in 1948, but reprinted many times. To date it has sold nearly four million copies in 40 languages. All three of those economists were awarded the Nobel Memorial Prize in Economics between 1970 and 1988. The basic Keynesian principle of heavy government involvement in the management of national economies had been accepted by all three.

For 30 years after the ending of World War II this economic synthesis, sometimes called 'the Samuelson Consensus', worked extremely well in promoting economic growth in the developed First World. Those thirty years are best known by the title coined for them by the French economist Jean Fourastié (1907-1990) as *les trente glorieuses*, although in Germany they were known as the *das Wirtschaftswunder*, and in Italy as the *il miracolo economico*. Recovery began immediately after 1945, but growth was most rapid between 1950 and 1970, when it averaged four per cent a year in Europe, falling back to 1.5-2% from 1970 onwards. The wider world also benefited, with global trade increasing at an annual average rate of 7.3%, and global industrial output at an average annual rate of 5.6%. Western Europe was helped on its way in the immediate post-war years by America's Marshall Plan, an economic aid programme for Europe. This had been implemented by General George C. Marshall (1880-1959), who had served as Army Chief of Staff between 1939 and 1945, later taking the civilian post of U.S. Secretary of State between 1947 and 1949, but he was working under the orders of President Harry S. Truman (1884-1972), who was President from 1945 to 1953. It was indeed the so-called 'Truman Doctrine' which did more for Europe than the Marshall Plan. Truman chose not to exploit America's very favourable trade position after 1945 but instead to import freely from European nations, stimulating their economic growth. The idea was to 'restore the fabric of Europe', and to prevent the spread of Communism. Mindful of how depression conditions in Germany had facilitated the rise of Hitler, America was anxious to prevent anything similar from happening in post-war Europe, specifically the rise of Communism. However, the Marshall plan was in operation for only four years, from 1948 to

1952, during which time America contributed only 13 billion dollars worth of aid to Western Europe, with most of this going to France, the UK, and Western Germany. This had been a very small sum in relation to America's war expenditure, and economists believe that it added only 0.3% to Europe's growth rate over those years. The main cause of growth had been the adherence of Europe's political leaders to allegedly neo-Keynesian economic policies, but there was rather more to it than this.

Ironically, while the economic philosophy that had inspired *les trente glorieuses* did indeed include Keynesian elements, the system as a whole could hardly be described as Keynesianism, which had after all been devised as an emergency measure, designed to rescue economies from severe depressions. While governments in Europe accepted the Keynesian principle of much heavier involvement by the state in the running of national economies, his demand-side theories, and his views on the relationship between unemployment and inflation, they also went much further down the road of state intervention than Keynes had ever envisaged. In particular they laid great stress on the development of comprehensive welfare states, an aspect which Keynes had relegated to a footnote. In addition trade union rights were recognised, progressive taxation was introduced, and every effort was made to see that all classes benefitted equally from the striking economic growth of those 30 years, through what amounted to a state-sponsored redistribution of wealth downwards towards the poorer classes. In fact, the post-war systems that were established in Western Europe were better described as examples of the 'social market economy'. This term was first coined by the German economist, anthropologist and politician Alfred Müller-Armack (1901-1978) in 1946. He envisaged a mixed economy, based on free enterprise capitalism, but subjected to heavy state regulation, with government ownership of public utilities and some key heavy industries. Economies, Müller-Armack stressed, should be designed to serve all humanity. Following Müller-Armack's lead, one of the chief architects of this new system was the West German Chancellor Konrad Adenauer (1876-1967), who was in office from 1949 to 1963. He began by reforming the institutional framework of the state, a policy known as ordoliberalism, from the German *Ordonnanz,* meaning 'orderly' in a military sense, a policy devised in Germany between the Wars. Later, he took more positive steps to introduce a social market economy. In the UK Clement Attlee (1883-1967), prime minister from 1945-51, worked with his Minister of Health Aneurin Bevan (1897-1960) to build a welfare state, the National Health Service, and a social market economy. In addition to the utilities, key industries like coal, steel, and the railways, the 'commanding heights of the economy', were nationalised, and strongly progressive taxation was imposed. In France similar policies were introduced under President Charles de Gaulle (1890-1970) and his prime minister Georges Pompidou (1911-74). Indeed France went even further down the road of extensive state regulation of the economy and widespread nationalisation of industries than had either Germany or the

UK. This extreme interventionism came to be termed *dirigisme*, from the French *diriger*, 'to manage, steer, or direct'. Later, neoliberals were to decry this social market economy as one of high taxation and 'big government', which was anathema to them.

For some 30 years after 1945 social market principles such as these were accepted by all political parties in the UK, France, Germany, and Italy. Indeed, in the UK the prominent Conservative politician Sir Keith Joseph (1918-94) was one of the strongest advocates of social market principles, working with Margaret Thatcher in setting up the Centre for Policy Studies to promote them in 1974, and authoring its first publication, *Why Britain Needs a Social Market Economy* (1975). However, both Joseph and his Centre were shortly to swing sharply over to neoliberal beliefs. In the USA, with its stronger traditions of free market capitalism, nothing like a social market economy was introduced, but further steps towards the building of a welfare state were taken, and Keynesian principles were broadly accepted, especially on the key point of the duty of the government to intervene in the running of the national economy whenever necessary. In 1971 Richard Nixon (1913-94), who was President from 1969 to 1974, made his famous confession, 'I am now a Keynesian in economics', although he never spelled out exactly what he meant by that remark. He made it immediately after taking America off the gold standard on August 15, 1971, and so he may have had only monetary policy in mind, since Keynes had always opposed the idea of a gold standard for international currencies.

No sooner had Nixon made this confession, however, than the Keynesian idyll began to unravel. During the *trente glorieuses*, while governments had accepted that it was their duty to regulate national economies, they had assumed that their main concern should be to maintain a balance between the level of unemployment and the rate of inflation, with a little touch on the tiller now and then, using fiscal or monetary measures. The neo-Keynesian assumption had been that an inverse relationship existed between these two factors, with higher unemployment leading to lower inflation as demand fell off, while full employment would increase demand, threatening higher inflation. This relationship could be plotted graphically, with inflation levels on the vertical axis, and unemployment rates on the horizontal. The resulting graph displayed what was known as a Phillips curve, named after the New Zealand economist, adventurer, and polymath William Phillips (1914-1975). However, in 1968 the American neoliberal economist Milton Friedman (1912-2006) argued that the Phillips curve would be applicable only in the short run. Over the longer term, while high unemployment might indeed decrease the inflation rate, inflation on its own would not necessarily decrease unemployment levels. Under certain circumstances, it would be entirely possible for both inflation and unemployment to increase together. His words were soon seen to have been prophetic when, during the recession of the 1970s inflation and unemployment rates in Europe and America did indeed increase together, coupled with a falling off in growth rates, giving rise to a new phenomenon, which was quickly dubbed 'stagflation'.

This new development called into question the neo-Keynesian economic consensus which had delivered low inflation, steady growth, and virtually full employment to Western Europe and North America for some 30 years after the Second World War. What had gone wrong? The truth was that neo-Keynesianism, operated within the framework of a social market economy, was more fragile than anyone had realised. It was far from immune to both exogenous and endogenous economic shocks, as the 1970s were to prove. Its weaknesses could be traced back to the Bretton Woods Conference of 1944. This had been an international gathering, held on the outskirts of Carroll, a small New Hampshire town, with the intention of hammering out a new economic order for the world. The only significance of the site was that it served the Bretton Woods ski resort, where accommodation for skiers was provided by the large and opulent Mount Washington Hotel, conveniently underused in the summer months. In July 1944, following the success of the D-Day landings, Allied armies were advancing through France, while Russian armies encroached on Germany from the east. It had become clear that Nazi Germany would be crushed like a nut in a vice, and that the war in Europe would be over within a year. There was a determination amongst the delegates at Bretton Woods during their July meeting that the new world order would be better than the old.

Three key institutions emerged from the conference: the International Monetary Fund (IMF), the International Bank for Reconstruction and Development (the World Bank), and the General Agreement on Tariffs and Trade (GATT). This last bound all the attending countries to reduce their import duties and tariffs over time, so that world trade would flow as freely as possible. There was to be no return to the dark days of the 1930s, when countries had tried to beggar each other in trade wars which had served only to deepen the depression. The World Bank would provide loans from richer countries to poorer ones, to help them on the road to economic growth, so that they could then repay the loans. The IMF was a more complicated instrument, designed to balance world trade. The idea was that all participating countries would make a deposit with the IMF as a kind of rainy-day fund. If they then imported more than they exported, they could draw on the fund to cover their trade gap until they got their trade back into balance again. The plan was to incentivise countries to do this. On the other hand, some countries would habitually export more than they imported. What was to be done with them? Here, there was some disagreement.

The Bretton Woods Conference had been attended by two key figures. One was John Maynard Keynes, representing Britain, and the other was Harry

Dexter White (1892-1948) the American representative. Both men were in poor health. Keynes was to die just two years after the Conference, and White just two years later, in 1948. But White was a fascinating figure. Although born in Boston, he was of entirely Jewish descent, and although educated as an economist, he had spent most of his working life at the U.S. Treasury Department as a civil servant. His reputation had been tainted by charges of spying for Russia during the war, when the two countries had been allies, but he seems to have been much more of a Keynesian than a Communist. Nevertheless, McCarthy witch hunters had been hot on his trail when he died in 1948. His sincere hope had been that the Russian-American alliance might be continued after the war, as a guarantee of world peace. Intellectually he was no match for Keynes, but as the American representative, he held the ultimate power to make the major decisions. This was because, with Europe in ruins, Japan devastated by bombing, Russia exhausted after a hard war, and the rest of the world in a state of economic underdevelopment, the USA. bestrode the planet like a colossus. In 1945 America accounted for one third of the world economy, and more than half of its industrial output. Moreover, America was then the world's chief creditor nation. Everyone owed, or was to owe her money, including, in no small measure, the U.K.

Although he agreed with Keynesian theory, White saw his first duty at the Conference as being the promotion of American interests. He therefore clashed with Keynes on two key issues. One was which currency would be used in future to conduct world trade. Keynes favoured the introduction of a new international unit of currency, the 'bancor', issued by the 'International Clearing Union', in effect a world bank, with foreign exchange reserves held in bancors by countries' central banks, in addition to their national currencies. The bancor would be exchangeable at fixed but flexible exchange rates with those national currencies, allowing them in effect to devalue or revalue their currencies within fixed limits allowed by the ICU. In theory, this was a clever plan. Countries that imported too much would see their stock of bancors diminishing, and realise that they had to import less or export more to improve their balance of trade if they wanted to continue trading on world markets. Those who exported too much and built up a big stock of bancors would find their surplus simply confiscated by the ICU beyond a certain limit. This would encourage them to spend more on buying in imports, rather than lose their bancors for nothing, thus helping those countries with balance of trade deficits, and so overall world trade could be kept roughly in balance, or so Keynes hoped.

Dexter White, however, insisted that the US dollar should be the currency of world trade, backed by American gold reserves held at Fort Knox in Kentucky. These amounted to some three-quarters of the world's official gold stocks. Against the advice of Keynes, White set the price of this gold at $35 per ounce. This was tantamount to restoring the gold standard for world trade, despite the experiences of the 1930s, since other countries agreed to keep their currencies pegged to the dollar, with adjustments allowed only under exceptional circumstances. But America was to discover, in 1971, that a gold standard was no more sustainable then than it had been in the 1930s. It is important to stress at this point that Keynes was *not* in favour of rigidly fixed exchange rates for international currencies, based on a gold standard. In the absence of his bancors, he argued at Breton Woods that nations with persistent trade deficits, importing more than they exported, should be allowed to devalue their currencies to some extent against others so as to make their imports dearer and their exports cheaper and so more desirable on world markets. Conversely, those countries with a persistent trade surplus should be obliged by the IMF to revalue their currencies, making their exports more expensive on world markets, thus bringing world trade more into balance.

But this is not what was done. The Conference decision, or rather diktat by White, gave the USA. for a time what President de Gaulle was later to call 'an exorbitant privilege'. If international trade was to be carried out in dollars, then other countries would have to store their dollar reserves in the American banking system instead of each country storing its bancors in their own central banks, as would have happened under Keynes' plan. That in turn meant that the USA, in control of dollar production, would be able to pay for its imports simply by printing dollars, or by lodging an IOU in its trading partners' American accounts. The use of dollars for world trade also meant that New York would now take precedence over London as the world's financial capital. This, indeed, had been White's intention. Keynes of course had opposed this move, but was forced to look impotently on.

The other point on which White clashed with Keynes was over the question of how world trade could be kept in balance. Under the IMF proposals countries which habitually imported more than they exported could draw on their reserves with the Fund to cover their trade gap, and if their reserve became exhausted, the IMF could then lend them more, but only under strict conditions. The errant country would be forced to reduce its imports and cut back on its spending at home so as to restock its reserves, a penalty that was later to be described as 'austerity'. This penalty would not have been necessary under Keynes' bancor system, since deficit countries could still have used their own currencies for internal trade. But what was to be done with countries that habitually exported more than they imported? Surely they too should be subjected to disciplinary measures, forcing them to reduce their exports, revalue their currencies, increase their imports, or all three. For Keynes, the picture was quite clear. Over the world as a whole, the trade deficits of those countries that imported heavily must be exactly matched by the trade surpluses of those countries that exported far more than they imported. To avoid great imbalances in world trade, the excessive exporters should be just as strictly disciplined as the excessive importers, in particular, said Keynes, persuaded to loosen their purse strings and buy in more from their trading partners. This idea of spending your way out of trouble was very Keynesian, and somewhat epicurean. But White was more of a stoic and would have none of it, perhaps because he expected that, after the war, the USA. would be a surplus exporter herself. He insisted that only those countries in trade deficit should be disciplined. But perhaps the ideal of a perfectly balanced world trading system had always been a pipe dream in any case. Things certainly did not work out that way in practice.

In retrospect it appeared that Keynes had been right and White wrong on both of those two major issues that had divided them. The so-called 'Bretton Woods System' would have functioned more fairly and more efficiently if Keynes' advice had been taken, but in addition it had other weaknesses. Russia was present at the Conference, but Stalin refused to sign up to its recommendations, while Germany, Japan, and their satellites, as enemy aliens, were not represented at all. Neither, of course, were all the new nations that came into existence in the 1950s and 1960s as the old European colonial empires collapsed. In all, only 44 countries were represented at Bretton Woods, while by 2018 no fewer than 195 sovereign nations had come into existence. Moreover, the 'free' trade that GATT was supposed to institute turned out to be not so free after all in its operation, especially with regard to those states which had not been represented at Bretton Woods. For example, GATT, which had laid down only vague guidelines, did not in practice prevent the industrial nations from imposing import tariffs on textiles and foodstuffs, the very commodities in which underdeveloped countries were most likely to be able to compete with the more advanced powers. In both Western Europe and North America governments displayed a great concern for the protection of their farming communities, in part because they were important political constituencies.

Third World countries were allowed to export only tropical produce, and raw materials like rubber, timber, oil, jute, mineral ores, and raw cotton to the developed nations tariff-free. But during the *trente glorieuses* these products were in abundant supply, keeping their prices down, while the price of manufactured goods rose, in part because the Third World had to import manufacturing machinery from the First World in their efforts to industrialise their own economies, and so the terms of trade turned against the underdeveloped world. In addition, newly independent countries had to conduct their world trade in dollars, always having to set aside a portion of what they earned in trade and deposit it with America's central bank under IMF rules. As a result, regardless of their political independence, poor countries would always struggle to reverse the flow of economic surpluses to the rich countries. Many came to feel that they had merely exchanged one form of servitude for another. Instead of being subject to political imperialism, they were now being subjected to economic imperialism. It was certainly true that, until the 1970s, the First World had prospered at their expense. While the wealth of the developing nations did increase slowly, the wealth of the First World rose much more rapidly, increasing rather than diminishing the wealth gap between them. There had been a dark side to the *trente glorieuses* which Keynesians have been reluctant to acknowledge. To some extent, this element of exploitation is still present in the early twenty-first century, as the Cambridge economist Ha-Joon Chang explains in his book, *Bad Samaritans* (2008). But the Western World was to experience a setback in the 1970s.

In that decade it was discovered that the Western economies, for all their apparent success during the *trente glorieuses*, had an Achilles heel. Their prosperity had been very heavily dependent upon cheap oil imports from Third World oil producers. All had gone well until 1973, but in that year fate took a hand. How often can fortuitous events change the course of history. In 1948 the state of Israel had been successfully established on former Arab lands in Palestine, against strenuous Arab opposition. Thereafter, the new country frequently had to fight to maintain its existence. In 1967, in response to an attempted Egyptian sea blockade, Israel launched a surprise attack on Egypt and its allies Jordan and Syria. The result was the 'Six Day War', of June 5 to 10 1967, during which Israel was able to capture the Gaza Strip and Sinai Desert from Egypt, the west bank of the Jordan from Jordan, and the Golan Heights in northern Israel from Syria. The Arabs had been humiliated, and were left smarting for revenge. In 1973 they in their turn launched a surprise attack on Israel, the so-called 'Yom Kippur War' of October 6 to 26. The war was so called because Saturday, October 6 was, in that year, the day of Yom Kippur, the holiest day of the Judaic year, the 'Sabbath of Sabbaths', the annual Day of Atonement for all Jews. It is marked by 25 hours of fasting and prayer in the synagogues while forgiveness is asked of God. It is preceded by a day of heavy feasting. There was no day of the year on which Israel was less prepared for a surprise attack, although it should be added that October was also the month of Ramadan for Moslems in that year. Both the Israeli and the American intelligence agencies, usually very alert, had failed to notice preparations for the strike.

In the first few days of the war the Arab armies made heavy incursions into Israeli-held territory, and the Israelis lost a lot of military hardware. The Israeli Prime Minister, Golda Meir, made a desperate appeal to America for a resupply, but at that point the Arabs launched their secret weapon. The king of Saudi Arabia informed President Nixon that if the USA resupplied Israel it would face an oil embargo not just from Saudi Arabia but from all the then members of OPEC (The Organisation of Petroleum Exporting Countries). In 1973 these were the Persian Gulf oil producers plus Indonesia, Libya, Algeria, Nigeria, Ecuador, and Gabon, 13 nations in all. They agreed to cut back significantly on their oil sales to the world market, while the USA plus all countries supporting Israel, including the UK, would face total embargos. But

President Nixon felt that he could not be seen to give way to blackmail, and so Israel was resupplied, and the embargo began. The USA produced some of its own oil, and non-OPEC states kept up their supplies, but Saudi Arabia alone was the world's largest oil producer, capable of influencing world oil prices on its own. Within weeks the world price of oil shot up, because demand for this product was what the economists call 'inelastic'. As the price went up, demand barely fell at all. The West depended on oil to power its motor cars, while its ships, aircraft, and many of its trains burned varieties of diesel. Western machinery also needed to be lubricated. Many power stations of the day burned oil, and in the countryside, far from gas pipelines, many homes depended on oil-fired central heating. The oil still had to be bought, whatever its price. Within weeks, the world price of oil had quadrupled, from two dollars a barrel to eight dollars a barrel.

Not only were Westerners forced to pay more for their oil, but also their transport costs went up, affecting the prices of all other commodities. The value of money relative to goods therefore declined, and people could buy less with their wages. Demand fell off, and therefore so did production. Workers were laid off, and the GDP growth rate of the oil-importing countries slowed. This was the so-called, 'First Oil Shock'. But although serious, it was of fairly short duration. The Israelis rallied their forces, and within three weeks had beaten all the Arab armies back to their original lines and beyond. The Arabs were forced to sue for peace, and the total embargos against America and the Western powers which had supported Israel were lifted. But the oil price remained high, since the oil producers had realised that just a small cutback in their production levels could cause a disproportionately large rise in oil prices, thanks to the inelasticity of demand for their product. From 1974 to 1978 they averaged twelve dollars a barrel. The vulnerability of First World countries was laid bare.

During the 'stagflation' years of the 1970s and early 1980s not only did economic growth rates slow in both Western Europe and America, but unemployment levels and inflation rates surprisingly rose together, in contradiction of the predictions of the Phillips curve. In 1972-3 the growth rate of America's GDP (Gross Domestic Product) had averaged 5.5% annually, but between 1974 and 1982 this rate fell to an average of only 2.04% a year. At the same time the USA's unemployment rate, which had averaged only four per cent between 1965 and 1970, averaged 7.1% between 1971 and 1983, peaking at 10.4% in 1983 before beginning to decline once more. Simultaneously America's inflation rate, which had also averaged only four per cent in 1971-2, rose to average 8.76% between 1973 and 1982, peaking in 1981 at 10.35%. At the same time the UK, being more reliant on imports, was even harder hit by rampant inflation. The inflation rate as measured by the consumer price index (CPI) had stood at 4.7% p.a. in 1968, but it rose dramatically in the early 1970's to peak at 26% p.a. in 1975, following the 'First Oil Shock'. Thereafter there was a sharp decline to only 7% in 1978, but then the 'Second Oil Shock' sent it soaring again to 21% in 1979. There was some decline thereafter, but in 1980 the inflation rate was still a frightening 16.4% p.a. At the same time the unemployment rate rose steadily, from 3.4% in 1973 to 11.9% in 1984. The Phillips Curve, one of those neat little calculations produced by the neoclassical school, was utterly discredited. Output in the UK also fell in the 1970s. In 1973-4 the annual growth rate of UK GDP had been five per cent, but in the remainder of the 1970s this declined to average only 1.6% p.a., dropping to a nadir of minus four per cent in 1980 before slowly recovering in the following decade.

To prevent this stagflation from developing into a full-scale depression, First World governments had applied the balm of Keynesian economic theory, pumping money into their economies by increasing both government expenditure and their national debts. In the mid-1970s this seemed to be having the desired effect of at least preventing stagflation from developing into anything worse, though at the cost of more debt and high inflation. But then, in 1978, the 'Second Oil Shock' struck. This time, the culprit behind the oil price rise was Iran. Iran too had been a major oil producer, and a friend of the West, but in 1978 an Islamic revolution overthrew its then ruler and would-be moderniser Shah Mohammad Reza Pahlavi (1919-80), installing the Moslem cleric ayatollah Ruhollah Khomeini (1902-89) in his place. The fall of the Shah had been preceded by widespread demonstrations and strikes which had paralysed Iranian oil production. The 1978 world oil price of $12.79 a barrel rose to $26.19 in 1979 and $35.52 in 1980, a near tripling in just two years. Again oil prices remained high until 1985, and again First World oil importers reeled under the blow. Would Keynesian stimulus be enough to save them this time? Many now believed not, as the thought of the American economist Milton Friedman (1912-2006), a monetarist and a neoliberal, was coming to the fore. But there was one country in Europe which kept the Keynesian faith, and that country was France.

In 1981 the Socialist François Mitterrand (1916-96) and his party won a national election in France. From 1960 to 1974 the unemployment rate in France had averaged only 2% but by 1981 it was nearing 6%, while the inflation rate stood at 13%, with production stagnating. Mitterrand's answer was a dose of Keynsian stimulus. He set the unemployed to work on government projects, provided pay rises for government employees, and strengthened the bargaining power of unions. The world watched with interest to see what the outcome of this last throw of the Keynesian dice would be. Mitterrand's policies certainly increased demand levels from French workers, and was very successful at increasing economic output, but it was German economic output. Mitterand had reckoned without the impact of the EEC (European Economic Community), the forerunner of today's EU, which had established free trade between its members. In the 1930s, when Keynesianism had been devised, countries could set their own trade tariffs and control the flow of their foreign exchange, but the situation in Europe was now very different from that of Britain or America in the 1930s. While France had been increasing the wages of its workers, German firms could keep their labour costs lower and so sell their goods more cheaply into the avaricious French market. Mitterrand soon realised that his policy had been a disaster. The national debt had soared, while French GDP had barely increased at all. In 1983 he sharply reversed course, selling off nationalised industries to reduce the national debt, weakening the unions, cutting back on state spending, and putting an end to extravagant pay rises. By 1985 he had wrestled the inflation rate down to 3% a year, although the stagnation of output continued. The world adjudged this last Keynesian experiment to have been a resounding failure. Keynesianism had been utterly discredited by two fortuitous 'oil shocks' and the structure of the EEC. But it was not only Keynesian economic theology that died in 1983: with it died also the whole concept of the social market economy, a mixed economy with strongly progressive taxation, designed for the benefit of all and not just for a privileged few. The fatal blows had been struck in the 1970s. Until that point inequality in the UK and USA had been on the decline, and the way had seemed to be open for the building of even fairer, happier, healthier, and more equal societies on both sides of the Atlantic. How often can the destinies of nations be swayed by fortuitous happenings. As a result of events in the 1970s, the way was instead opened for the advent of a different economic creed. Unfortunately for humanity, a much more sinister economic philosophy had long been lurking in the wings, waiting for its chance.

This creed goes by many names: neoliberalism, free market capitalism, 'let 'er rip' capitalism, free market fundamentalism, the new normal, loss of moral compass, and many others. Writing in *The Guardian* for August 18, 2017, Stephen Metcalf called it, 'Neoliberalism: the Idea That Swallowed the World', which is only too sadly true. Anyone who wishes to understand the philosophy which informs our modern economic policies should read that article. It is available online under the entry, 'Neoliberalism'. So whatever we would like to call it, let us stick with neoliberalism, because that is its official name, and the term has a long and interesting history. It was first coined as 'neo-liberalism' in 1938 by the German economist Alexander Rustow (1885-1963) at the Paris Colloque Walter Lippmann, a meeting of economists and sociologists called to discuss Walter Lippmann's 1937 book, *An Enquiry into the Principles of the Good Society*. Walter Lippmann (1889-1974) was an American writer, journalist, and political commentator who was highly regarded in his time, although today his views appear to be somewhat elitist. In his 1937 book he had discussed economic and social issues.

'Liberal' economists in those days were essentially *laissez-faire* free marketeers, but those policies had just caused the Great Depression of the 1930s. The aim of the conference therefore was to seek out a middle way between USA-style *laissez-faire* and Stalinist state planning, which might offer greater economic stability for the future. For that reason Colloquy members did not like to call themselves just 'liberals', but rather 'neo-liberals'. The tone of the gathering was certainly against socialism and collectivism, but it was also opposed to that form of free-wheeling capitalism that had caused the kind of disaster from which the world was still suffering in 1938. The framework which emerged suggested that a basically capitalist, free enterprise market economy was desirable, but under the guidance and rules of a strong state, a model that came to be known as the *social market economy*, a mixed economy with key services such as the utilities and transport nationalised and under direct government control. This was certainly *not* intended to equate with the older concept of *laissez-faire*. Although the system was to be basically on of free enterprise capitalism, there was to be heavy government intervention and regulation of this capitalism to ensure that it worked for all, especially in the maintaining of full employment and an effective welfare state. This was essentially the system that was applied, and operated with great success in Western Europe for three decades after the Second World War. We should never forget that *this* was the original meaning of neo-liberalism. It became so much the new normal after 1945 that the term neo-liberalism dropped out of use, and its original meaning was forgotten.

When the term re-emerged in the 1970s in its new guise as 'neoliberalism' it was first of all applied by Spanish-speaking economists to the extremely free market economic policies then being pursued in Chile by the military dictatorship of General Augusto Pinochet (1915-2006). In September 1973 Pinochet had seized power in a USA-backed military coup, and remained in control of the country until 1990. As a result, from 1973, the term was then more widely adopted in the West to apply to extremely free market forms of private capitalism, with a minimum of state intervention or regulation. How easily can words change their meaning. This, the 'new' neoliberalism is, therefore, only the remote descendent, and indeed almost the very antithesis, of the creed that emerged from the Colloque Walter Lippmann in the 1930s. It had become not so much the New Liberalism as the Old Conservatism – that is to say, Disraelian Toryism!

The 1938 colloquium was attended by 26 intellectuals, including its convener, the French philosopher Louis Rougier (1889-1982), Friedrich Hayek (1899-1992), and the free market Viennese economist Ludwig von Mises (1881-1973), who had heavily influenced Hayek. The advent of the Second World War interrupted their proceedings, but in April, 1947, many of the same figures reconvened at a conference called by Friedrich Hayek to take up the themes discussed in 1938. The venue was the Swiss ski resort of Mont Pèlerin, a village near the city of Vevey, and so those attending chose to call themselves, in English, the Mont Pelerin Society (MPS). That first meeting in 1947 was attended by 39 scholars, mostly economists, with some historians and philosophers. While many of the old faces from 1938 were there, significantly there were some new faces too, notably those of Karl Popper, Milton Friedman, George Joseph Stigler (1911-91) and Antony Fisher (1915-88) who went on to establish many think tanks around the world to promote MPS ideas. The aims of the MPS were at first quite moderate and reasonable. Their *Statement of Aims* drawn up on April 8, 1947 included intended investigations into,

> Methods of re-establishing the rule of law and of assuring its development in such a manner that individuals and groups are not in a position to encroach upon the freedom of others, and private rights are not allowed to become a basis of predatory power.
>
> The possibility of establishing minimum standards by means not inimical to initiative and the functioning of the market.
>
> Ways to facilitate an exchange of ideas between like-minded scholars in the hope of strengthening the principles and practice of a free society, and to study the workings, virtues, *and defects* of market-oriented economic systems. (My italics) (Available online)

However, these moderate aims of neo-liberalism were later to be entirely superseded by the much more radical policies of neoliberalism, as we shall see. Perhaps the best way into an understanding of neoliberalism is indeed through a study of two of its leading philosophers, and of three of its most famous practitioners. Let us look therefore at Friedrich Hayek and Milton Friedman as philosophical founders, with Ronald Regan (1911-2004), Margaret Thatcher (1925-2013), and of course dear old General Augusto Pinochet (1915-2006) as leading practitioners of this creed. The first four were all well meaning individuals, with Hayek and Friedman genuinely seeking for what they believed to be the most efficient and productive of economic systems, while Thatcher and Regan were great patriots, striving to deliver what they genuinely believed to be in the best interests of their countries. All four, however, allowed themselves to be made the unwitting dupes of the plutocrats, as we shall see.

Friedrich Hayek (1899-1992) and Neoliberal Theory

Despite their moderation, the philosophy which underlay the 1947 aims of the Mont Pelerin Society was based in large measure upon the views expounded in a celebrated book written by the convener of that first meeting, Friedrich Hayek in his famous, *The Road to Serfdom* (1944). This book was written between 1940 and 1944, at the height of the Second World War, which largely explains the tone of its contents. Hayek displayed a profound distrust of the state, forecasting that the relentless growth of state power would undermine personal liberties, including freedom of speech and thought. For me the book, rather like its title, displays overtones of paranoia and hysteria in its antigovernment stance, but perhaps this was understandable in view of the times in which it was written. Fascist governments had recently come to power in Spain, Italy, and Japan, while Hitler's Nazism and the Communism of Joseph Stalin (1878-1953) and Mao Zedong (1893-1976) were creeds with identical characteristics as far as the suppression of their subjects' individual liberties were concerned. But even in democracies like the UK and the USA the state had taken greater powers under wartime conditions, and again personal liberties had been curtailed as wartime emergency measures. However, although it had been Fascism and Nazism that had taken over most of Europe in the 1940s, it was against the threat of Socialism that Hayek directed his fire in *The Road to Serfdom*, fearing that after the ending of World War II the trend in the Western World would be towards Socialism. With Fascism defeated and discredited, Hayek's fear was that it would next be Socialism, which Hayek seemed to confuse with Communism, that would pose the greatest threat to his much-vaunted 'freedom'. By always using the term 'Socialism' when he clearly meant 'Communism', Hayek did the Left a great disservice, by implying that all socialist policies would eventually and inevitably lead to Communism. He defined both equally as 'statism'. But this, of course, is nonsense. I would say, for example, that the British Labour Party was socialist, but certainly not Communist, nor ever likely to be so. To my mind the social market economy that worked so well in Europe for thirty years after 1945 was also socialist, but again certainly not Communist.

Hayek was born in Vienna in 1899, making him a close contemporary of Popper, who had also been born in Vienna, in 1902. The two were later to become good friends, although their views did not entirely coincide. While both had been founder members of the Mont Pelerin Society, Popper carefully distanced himself from it in later years as its economic theories moved more to the Right. In addition, Popper had been totally unambiguous when it came to his views on unelected dictatorships, declaring, 'I personally prefer to call the type of government which can be removed without violence as 'democracy' and the other 'tyranny'. (*Conjectures and Refutations* (2002 ed.) p. 464). But while Popper would have no truck with dictatorships, Hayek took an ambiguous view on the subject, finding some merit in the regime of General Augusto Pinochet, who ruled Chile from 1973 to 1990, because of the neoliberal economic policies which Pinochet adopted. However, there could scarcely have been a worse advertisement for what was then a new creed. Even by the standards of Latin America at the time, the Pinochet regime had an appalling human rights record: there could scarcely have been a clearer example of a tyranny. Having won power through a USA-backed military coup, Pinochet then enforced his rule by instituting a reign of terror. His political opponents were subjected to arbitrary arrest, imprisonment, torture, and murder. Statistics on such a regime are always questionable, but the best estimates would suggest that some 3,200 persons were murdered, 30,000 tortured, and 80,000 subjected to arbitrary imprisonment. A further 200,000 were forced to flee the country. Many Chileans chose to oppose the military regime with arms, and it was captured members of these groups who were subjected to torture in an attempt to force them to reveal the names of accomplices or the whereabouts of guerrilla groups. Being a mountainous country with many swift rivers, Chile enjoyed ample supplies of hydroelectricity, and this was the chosen instrument of the torturers. High voltage electric shocks were applied to the genitalia of both men and women. Twenty women reported suffering miscarriages as a result of torture, and 316 reported being raped *and* tortured by the military, but the unreported instances were probably much more numerous in both cases.

There was precious little 'freedom' to be had under such a regime. But for Hayek, freedom of choice in the supermarket was preferable to freedom of choice at the ballot box. He seems to have forgotten that supermarket freedom was available only to those with the wherewithal to enjoy it. Hayek drew a careful distinction between 'authoritarianism' and 'totalitarianism'. For him, the rule of Pinochet was only 'authoritarian', while that of his predecessor, the socialist President Salvador Allende (1908-73), had been 'totalitarian', because Allende had attempted to reform both the economy and the society of Chile in the interests of the poor. In an interview with the right-wing Chilean Newspaper *El Mercurio* given on April 12, 1981, Hayek said,

> Well, I would say that, as long-term institutions, I am totally against dictatorships. But a dictatorship may be a necessary system for a transitional period. At times it is necessary for a country to have, for a time, some form or other of dictatorial power.

That could have been Vladimir Lenin speaking, as he advocated his temporary 'dictatorship of the proletariat'. But Hayek went on,

> As you will understand, it is possible for a dictator to govern in a liberal way, and it is also possible for a democracy to govern with a total lack of liberalism. Personally, I prefer a liberal dictator to democratic government lacking liberalism.

By 'liberal' here Hayek meant a free enterprise capitalist economy subject to a minimum of state control. One is left with the strong impression that Hayek would have been perfectly happy to see his 'temporary' dictatorship become permanent, so long as it enforced free market, private capitalist principles. Neither did Hayek have much time for what he scornfully dismissed as *The Mirage of Social Justice* in Vol. 2 of his trilogy, *Law, Legislation, and Liberty* (1978). However, unlike many neoliberals, Hayek was not entirely devoid of humanitarian principles. Even in his 1944 *The Road to Serfdom* Hayek had written,

> There is no reason why, in a society that has reached the general level of wealth which ours has attained, that security against severe physical privation, the certainty of a given minimum of sustenance for all; or more briefly the security of a minimum income, should not be guaranteed to all without endangering general freedom...there can be no doubt that some minimum of food, shelter, and clothing, sufficient to preserve health and the capacity to work, can be assured to everybody. Indeed, for a considerable part of the population of England, this sort of security has long been achieved.

Nor is there any reason why the state should not assist...individuals in providing for those common hazards of life against which, because of their uncertainty, few individuals can make adequate provision. Where, as in the cases of sickness and accident, neither the desire to avoid such calamities nor the efforts to overcome their consequences are as a rule weakened by the provision of assistance – where, in short, we deal with genuinely insurable risks – the case for the state's helping to organise a comprehensive system of social insurance is very strong...there is no incompatibility in principle between the state's providing greater security in this way and the preservation of individual freedom. Whenever communal action can mitigate disasters against which the individual can neither attempt to guard himself nor make the provision for the consequences, such communal action should undoubtedly be taken. (2007 ed., pp. 147-8)

Some three decades later Hayek had not changed his mind on those points, writing in his *Law, Legislation, and Liberty*,

There is no reason why, in a free society, government should not assure to all protection against severe deprivation in the form of an assured minimum income, or a floor below which nobody needs to descend...So long as such a uniform minimum income is provided outside the market to all those who, for any reason, are unable to earn in the market an adequate maintenance, this need not lead to a restriction of freedom, or conflict with the rule of law. (Vol. II, 1976 ed., p.87)

But one can almost hear the tone of reluctance in Hayek's voice here as he grudgingly admits that there might be some merit in a provision which he could not help suspecting smacked of socialism. His top priority remained the preservation of 'individual liberty' within the context of a free market, capitalist economy.

Hayek attached supreme importance to prices within this free market economy, as an infallible guide to the most efficient allocation of productive resources. One is reminded here of Oscar Wilde's famous definition of a cynic as 'someone who knows the price of everything, and the value of nothing'. This point is best illustrated by Hayek's cavalier attitude towards soil degradation. In his book, *Out of the Wreckage: A New Politics for an Age of Crisis* (2018 ed.) George Monbiot cites an article on 'Soil Degradation' which appeared in the journal *Food Security* Vol. 7 No. 2 (April 2015), a collective work by no fewer than six ecologists and economists. This article pointed out that, according to UN estimates, six million hectares (14.8 million acres) of new farmland will be needed every year to keep up with global food demand as world population increases. But currently, 12 million hectares a year are being *lost* through soil degradation. Monbiot writes, 'This is not an unanticipated side effect of the system; it *is* the system.' He then quotes from Hayek's *The Constitution of Liberty* (1960) where Hayek argues,

> 'Soil mining' may in certain circumstances be as much in the long-range interest of the community as the using up of any stock resource....Such resources share with most of the capital of society the property of being exhaustible, and if we want to maintain or increase our income, we must be able to replace each resource that is being used up with a new one that will make at least an equal contribution to future income. This does not mean, however, that it should be preserved in kind or replaced by another of the same kind, or even that the total stock of natural resources should be kept intact...There is nothing in the preservation of natural resources as such which makes them a more desirable object of investment than man-made equipment or human capacities.

In other words, as Monbiot continued,

> Soil should be treated like any other form of capital: disposable, and exchangeable for money. Our sole duty to each other is to maximise income. As long as we replace the soil we mine for profit with something else – a new factory for example – its exhaustion is of no account. What happens when we exhaust the soil everywhere appears, strangely, to be beyond the scope of his analysis. (pp. 117-8)

Hayek bought in completely to Adam Smith's idea of the 'invisible hand', which would ensure that an unplanned, free market economy would always function with greater efficiency than any state planned economy ever could. His views on those points had been reinforced by the writings of Carl Menger (1840-1921) and Ludwig von Mises (1881-1973). He dismissed 'socialist' state planning as *The Fatal Conceit* in his 1988 book of that title, since the complexities of national economies were beyond human understanding, and best left to the 'invisible hand' to sort out. Hayek believed that this 'invisible hand' was in fact a kind of highly rational collective mind, capable of marshalling more information, and making more efficient decisions, than any single human mind ever could. But Hayek then went on to argue that a free economy would inevitably give rise to a free society, where individualism and human rights would be respected, and individual initiative would be given room to flourish. These ideas were initially put forward in his collection of essays, *Individualism and the Economic Order* published in 1948, and later in his book, *The Constitution of Liberty*, first published in 1960, with a definitive edition appearing in 2011. However, this was a rather odd conclusion to draw. Had their free enterprise, capitalist economies prevented the rise of Mussolini in Italy, or of Franco in Spain, or of Hitler in Germany? These men were dictators all, with very little time for individualism or human rights. Their populations had not been saved from the grossest violations of their rights and freedoms by their capitalist, free enterprise economic systems. It would seem that it was perfectly possible for tyrannies to exist in tandem with free enterprise economies. Later, Chile was to provide another case in point.

Throughout his writings, Hayek made clear his somewhat maniacal obsession with the concept of 'freedom', which he certainly rated above equality, placing even security as a poor second on his wish list. However, Hayek never defined exactly what he meant by his term, 'freedom'. Perhaps, therefore, we should remember here the somewhat more refined definition of freedom put forward by Sir Isaiah Berlin (1909-97) in his inaugural lecture as Chichele Professor of Social and Political Theory at the University of Oxford, delivered in 1958. In this Berlin distinguished carefully between 'negative freedom', which he defined as freedom from external direction or restraint, and 'positive freedom', which he defined as what we are actually *able* to do, as distinct from only what we are left free to do. This second form of freedom, by far the more desirable of the two, of course requires both health and money before it can be enjoyed. Few things constrain this more valuable form of freedom more effectively than poverty, which of course can have a bearing on health as well. As David Harvey put it in his *A Brief History of Neoliberalism* (2007 ed.), 'Neoliberalism confers rights and freedoms on those whose incomes, leisure, and security need no enhancing, leaving a pittance for the rest of us'. (p. 38) It will be noticed that all those who value freedom above security already have security, which they seem to take for granted. For people who lack security of employment, housing, or income, the concept of 'freedom' has very little significance.

The rich of Chile certainly did very well under the Pinochet regime. It is alleged in Naomi Klein's book, *The Shock Doctrine: The Rise of Disaster Capitalism* (2008) that the wealthiest ten per cent of Chile's population saw their real incomes rise by 83% under Pinochet. (p. 105) The exact figure may be questionable, but the trend was clear enough. Meanwhile, what about the poor? In this context it is perhaps worth noting that according to World Bank figures, the proportion of Chile's population living below an internationally defined poverty line rose from 17% in 1970 to 45% in 1985, and 48% in 1988 under General Pinochet's neoliberal policies. This proportion still stood at 40% in 1990, but after the fall of Pinochet in that year it declined rapidly to only 20% in 2000, according to the 2004 World Bank publication, *Chile: Successes and Failures in Poverty Eradication.* At the same time levels of unemployment, which had averaged 4.7% under Allende in 1973, averaged 18.1% under Pinochet from 1974 to 1989. Despite these World Bank figures, however, in a letter to *The Times* of London dated July 26, 1978 Hayek declared, 'I have not been able to find a single person even in much maligned Chile who did not agree that personal freedom was much greater under Pinochet than it had been under Allende'. Did Hayek never meet any members of the deprived 45% during his visits to Chile, or did he simply never understand the true meaning of the word 'freedom'? This was a serious failing in a philosopher, since many of Hayek's economist supporters and opponents saw him as being primarily a philosopher rather than an economist. Maynard Keynes, J.K. Galbraith, Paul Krugman, and Milton Friedman were among them. Friedman is quoted as declaring himself, 'an enormous admirer of Hayek, but not for his economics. I think his *Prices and Production* is a very flawed book, and his *Pure Theory of Capital* is unreadable.' (Quoted in the LSE's *Hayek Society Journal* Vol. 5 No. 2 (2003) p. 1) In 1950, when Hayek sought an Economics appointment at the University of Chicago Friedman, who was already well established there, vetoed his application to the Economics Department, insisting that he should be appointed as Professor of Moral and Social Sciences instead. Maynard Keynes too had a low opinion of Hayek as an economist. Writing of his *Prices and Production* (1931), Keynes said,

> The book, as it stands, seems to me to be one of the most frightful muddles I have ever read, with scarcely a sound proposition in it...It is an extraordinary example of how, starting with a mistake, a remorseless logician can end up in bedlam. *Collected works*, Vol. XII, p.252

In view of his rather less than complete understanding of his favourite word, 'freedom', however, Hayek's credentials as a philosopher might also be called into question. Nevertheless, in 1974 Hayek shared the Nobel Memorial Prize in Economics with the Swedish economist, sociologist, and philosopher Gunnar Myrdal (1898-1987). Their citation announced that they had won the prize 'for their pioneering work in the theory of money and economic fluctuations and for their penetrating analysis of the interdependence of economic, social, and institutional phenomena'. But as noted in the Popper and Einstein sections, the award of Nobel Prizes has often proved to be rather a curious business, and once again there was a certain irony here. Although they had worked in related fields, Myrdal's conclusions had essentially contradicted Hayek's, and Myrdal himself resented being bracketed with Hayek, whom he regarded as being a reactionary. Perhaps we should, at this point, take a closer look at the 'Nobel Prize in Economics'.

Alfred Bernhard Nobel (1833-96) was a Swedish businessman, chemist, engineer, inventor, and philanthropist. By the time of his death in 1896 he held 355 different patents, the most famous of which was for dynamite. He was also a manufacturer of cannon and other armaments. After reading a premature obituary on himself in 1888, which condemned him as 'a dealer in death', he decided to bequeath his fortune to the setting up of the Nobel Prizes for achievements in five fields which Nobel believed could be of real benefit to humanity. The five fields were Physics, Chemistry, Physiology or Medicine, Literature, and Peace. As noted above, there were no prizes instituted for Philosophy or Economics, because Nobel considered these disciplines to be theoretical in nature. Indeed, in the fields of Chemistry, Physics, and Medicine Nobel stressed in his will that mere *theories* in these fields too were not to be rewarded either. Only actual inventions or discoveries that could be of obvious practical use to humanity were to qualify. After some dispute over Nobel's will, the first prizes were awarded in 1901. It was only in 1968 that a 'Nobel Prize in Economics' was instituted by the Sveriges Riksbank (Sweden's central bank) to celebrate the 300th anniversary of the bank's foundation. The bank put up a large sum of money to fund the prize, which was officially named, 'The Sveriges Riksbank Prize in Economic Sciences in Memory of Alfred Nobel', although the name is usually shortened to 'The Nobel Memorial Prize in

Economics', or just, 'The Nobel Prize for Economics'. Interestingly though, it was set up by big business interests, and there was some suspicion at the time that the prize had been instituted primarily to give 'the oxygen of publicity' to right-wing economists like Hayek and Friedman, both of whom were early recipients of the Prize. It was noted that some early members of the selection committee were associates of the Mont Pelerin Society.

Members of the Nobel family themselves were unhappy with the decision to institute the Prize and to associate it with Nobel's name. Among them was the Swedish human rights lawyer Peter Nobel (1931-2016) who declared that no member of the Nobel family had ever had the intention of establishing a prize in Economics. He explained that, 'Nobel despised people who cared more about profits than society's well-being' and that, 'There is nothing to indicate that he would have wanted such a prize.' Peter saw the Prize as, 'a PR coup by economists to improve their reputation'. One suspects that he must have been speaking here about the post-1888 Alfred Nobel, after he had experienced his Scrooge-like conversion. It is difficult to believe that Nobel had cared nothing about profits before that date. Returning to Friedrich Hayek, however, it is interesting to note that Hayek himself launched a trenchant piece of criticism against the Prize, even while he was in the process of accepting it. In his acceptance speech at the 1974 award ceremony Hayek declared, 'If I had been consulted on whether to establish a Nobel Prize in Economics, I should have decidedly advised against it.' After having expressed some doubts about the impartiality of the selection committee, Hayek went on to, 'my second cause of apprehension'.

> It is that the Nobel Prize confers on an individual an authority which in Economics no man ought to possess. This does not matter in the natural sciences. Here, the influence exercised by an individual is chiefly an influence on his fellow experts; and they will soon cut him down to size if he exceeds his competence. But the influence of the economist that mainly matters is an influence over laymen: politicians, journalists, civil servants, and the public generally. But there is no reason why a man who has made a distinctive contribution to economic science should be omnicompetent on all the problems of society – as the press tends to treat him, till in the end he may himself be persuaded to believe it. One is even made to feel it a public duty to pronounce on problems to which one may not have devoted special attention...I am therefore almost inclined to suggest that you require from your laureates an oath of humility, a sort of Hippocratic oath, never to exceed in public pronouncements the limits of their competence. (Friedrich von Hayek, Banquet Speech, available online)

These were probably the wisest words that Hayek ever spoke. He was indeed more of a philosopher than an economist.

Milton Friedman (1912-2006) and Neoliberal Theory

Milton Friedman has been hailed as 'the greatest economist of the second half of the twentieth century', ranking in stature with John Maynard Keynes over the century as a whole. .But this, of course, is nonsense. History will recognise Friedman as being the extremely bad economist that he was, and will hold him culpable for the misery that the implementation of his policies has inflicted upon many millions of people. However, he certainly stands with Friedrich Hayek as one of the greatest promoters of neoliberalism. As a monetarist and a neoliberal he was delighted to see Chile becoming the world's first neoliberal state, and like Hayek he was prepared to forgive Pinochet for his atrocities because of the 'greater good' that Pinochet had delivered for Chile. He visited Chile in March 1975 just as Pinochet's repression was at its bloodiest, to deliver a series of lectures on the glories of neoliberalism at the Pontifical Catholic University of Chile and elsewhere. During the visit he met with Augusto Pinochet, and in the following month he wrote a long letter to the dictator, advising him in some detail on how to set up a neoliberal economy in Chile. Because of this rather cosy relationship, the award of the Nobel Memorial Prize in Economics to Friedman in 1976 caused an international outcry. Giving a lecture at the Adam Smith Institute on November 1, 1991 Friedman declared,

> I have nothing good to say about the political regime that Pinochet imposed. It was a terrible political regime. The real miracle of Chile is not how well it has done economically; the real miracle of Chile is that a military junta was willing to go against its principles and support a free market regime designed by principled believers in a free market...In Chile, the drive for political freedom, that was generated by economic freedom and the resulting economic success, ultimately resulted in a referendum that introduced political democracy. Now, at long last, Chile has all three things: political freedom, human freedom, and economic freedom. Chile will continue to be an interesting experiment to watch to see whether it can keep all three or whether, now that it has political freedom, that political freedom will tend to be used to destroy or reduce economic freedom. (Wikipedia entry, Friedman)

In Friedman's eyes, democracy was suspect, and not necessarily desirable at all. However, as shown above, the neoliberals' contention that a free enterprise capitalist economy will always be the mainstay of political freedom simply does not stand up to historical examination, as in the cases of Germany, Italy, and Spain. In the case of Chile, there is a consensus of agreement that it was political rather than economic factors that worked to bring Pinochet down. Moreover, in the light of his quotation above it seems that Friedman, like Hayek, was a little suspicious of democracy, fearing that democratic regimes might be rather too inclined to redistribute wealth in favour of the poorer majority to the prejudice, they believed, of rapid economic growth. They were entirely mistaken on that point, as history was to prove.

Neoliberals are unduly concerned with the annual rate of growth of Gross Domestic Product, but GDP is a rather unsatisfactory and incomplete way of measuring the wellbeing of nations: it can even be misleading. As we have seen from the case of Chile, it is perfectly possible for GDP to be growing, while a large section of the population is actually becoming poorer. It was Robert Kennedy (1925-68) who once observed, 'GDP measures everything except the things that matter'. This point is substantially supported in the 2010 book by Richard Wilkinson and Kate Pickett, *The Spirit Level: Why Equality is Better for Everyone*.

But even if we accept their contention that GDP growth rates are of primary importance, by that measure the neoliberals are hoisted on their own petard by the evidence on growth rates in Western Europe during the second half of the twentieth century. All of the available figures from the World Bank and the OECD tell the same story: annual GDP growth rates in Western Europe were actually higher under the social market economies that prevailed in Europe during the third quarter of the twentieth century than they were in the last quarter, as neoliberalism tightened its ideological grip upon the continent. There may be some argument over details, but the trend is unmistakable. Delivering the Tawney Memorial Lecture to the Economic History Society's conference in April 1994, N.F.R. Crafts was able to show that between 1950 and 1973 GDP growth rates in Western Europe had averaged 4.6% annually, while between 1973 and 1993 the rate fell to average only 2%. (Available online, p. 8). Crafts later developed this lecture into a book, *Economic Growth in Europe since 1945* (1996). The same point was made by the leading American economist and Nobel laureate, Joseph Stiglitz (b. 1943) in his 2012 book, *The Price of Inequality*, adducing ample evidence to support his case. (pp. 104-147) These figures are hardly surprising. From 1950 to 1973 all classes in Western Europe were growing richer together, thereby stimulating demand, especially mass demand. But after 1973, and particularly from the 1980's, real wage levels stagnated as a larger and larger proportion of the nation's growing wealth was siphoned off into the pockets of the rich. This group had a higher propensity to save and invest rather than to spend, and more of what they did spend went on imported luxuries. Even the home-produced goods they did buy tended not to be of the mass produced variety. This was not the best way to stimulate mass demand, employment, and economic growth at home.

Milton Friedman was born in Brooklyn, New York, on July 31, 1912, but he was of entirely Jewish descent. His parents had been nineteenth-century immigrants from Hungary. A very gifted student, he was able to graduate from Rutgers University in New Jersey in July, 1932 while he was still only 20, taking a joint degree in Mathematics and Economics, gaining a Master of Arts degree in the following year. However, in those hard times Friedman was unable to find a permanent academic post, and was obliged to work as a jobbing economist and civil servant for many years, eventually taking his Ph.D. from Columbia University in New York in 1946. In September of that year he finally got a tenured academic post at the University of Chicago, which was to remain his *alma mater* for the rest of his life. Friedman quickly rose to prominence within the university's Economics department, and made that university the world centre of the creed that later came to be called 'neoliberalism', with his famous 'Chicago School'. As noted above, he worked with Friedrich Hayek and Karl Popper to found the Mont Pelerin Society, which held its first meeting on April 8, 1947.

Intellectually speaking, Friedman's thought revolved around two big ideas. Even more than Hayek, he was obsessed with the concept of 'freedom', especially in the area of free market capitalism, becoming a libertarian in the extreme. Secondly, he attached great importance to control of the money supply as a means of regulating national economies. These beliefs became two of the main pillars of the neoliberal creed, which advocated almost complete state disengagement from the management of national economies. As Friedman and the neoliberals saw it, state intervention could be nothing but a drag on the pace of economic growth, and therefore the less state intervention the better. They had complete confidence in the power of unrestrained free market forces to be stable and self-regulating, despite the warning lesson of the Great Depression in the 1930s.

Their creed is often contrasted with Keynesianism, but as noted above, this is something of an oversimplification. Keynesianism was designed to be an emergency measure only, to rescue economies from the kind of desperate straits in which they found themselves in the 1930s. Yes, it advocated temporary heavy government borrowing to provide the means of implementing a variety of measures designed to create employment and revive demand in national economies, but once these economies had been revived, Keynes then believed that taxes should be raised and the heavy government debts incurred paid off. He certainly did not advocate permanent deficit financing of the kind we have seen since 1975.

Initially, after 1945, governments in Western Europe and America bought into the idea of state intervention to regulate and direct their economies, building on and expanding Keynes' ideas into the construction of those 'social market economies' described above. It was these social market economies and 'big government' rather than just Keynesianism that became the target of the neoliberals. One of the aims of Keynesianism, or perhaps we should call it neo-Keynesianism after 1945, one aspect of the 'Samuelson Consensus' mentioned above, had been the maintenance of 'full' employment. But 'full' in this context was a rather elastic term, because of course it never meant absolutely zero rates of unemployment: this was an unobtainable ideal. Rather it meant 'tolerable' levels of unemployment, with rates ideally at somewhere under five per cent. Friedman, however, introduced the opposing concept of 'natural' rates of unemployment, below which inflationary pressures would be generated.

These rates might well exceed five per cent on some occasions. For Friedman, it was inflation rather than unemployment which was the great enemy that needed to be conquered, through higher unemployment levels if necessary, but above all via control of the money supply. He first declared that 'Inflation is always and everywhere a monetary phenomenon' in his 1963 book, *Inflation: Causes and Consequences*, and later expanded on that statement in the annual Harold Wincott Memorial Lecture, delivered at Chatham House on November 1, 1970 entitled, *The Counter-Revolution in Monetary Theory*. Here he declared,

> Inflation is always and everywhere a monetary phenomenon in the sense that it is and can be produced only by a more rapid increase in the quantity of money than in output...A steady rate of monetary growth at a moderate level can provide a framework under which a country can have little inflation and much growth. It will not produce perfect stability; it will not produce heaven on Earth; but it can make an important contribution to a stable economic society. (Wikiquote, Friedman on inflation)

This was a more nuanced statement than his bald declaration of 1963, and Friedman's doubts about this central tenet of his economic philosophy continued to grow over the years. Was control of the money supply really the best way to keep inflation down and to regulate the economy in general? Towards the end of his life, in an interview with Simon London of the *Financial Times*, Friedman admitted, 'The use of quantity of money as a target has not been a success...I'm not sure I would as of today push it as hard as I once did.' (*Financial Times*, June 7, 2003) This was a timely admission. To try to claim, for example, that the 'cost push' effects of the two 'oil shocks' of the 1970s had nothing to do with the inflation experienced in that decade was simply unrealistic. Nor is it correct to say that a mere increase in the money supply will always cause inflation. Inflation is caused not just by an increase in the money supply, but rather by an imbalance between supply and demand: by *too much money chasing too few goods*. If you can increase the money supply in such a way as to stimulate an increased production of goods and services that are in demand to match the increase in the money supply, then there will be no inflation. However, this rather basic point was one that the somewhat intellectually challenged Friedman seemed to be incapable of grasping.

Unfortunately, by that time Friedman was ready to ease up on his 'hard pushing' his propaganda had already done its damage, convincing many influential people that inflation was the supreme threat. I began to suspect that things were going seriously wrong on the morning of May 17, 1991 while listening to *Yesterday in Parliament* on Radio Four. There I heard Norman Lamont, who was then Chancellor of the Exchequer, delivering his economic credo to the House. He said, 'Rising unemployment is a price well worth paying in order to keep inflation in check'. Now by this he did not of course mean that *he* was nobly volunteering to become unemployed himself and live on the dole, in order to maintain the value of the pound. Oh dear me no. What he meant was, '*Somebody else's* unemployment is a price the *I* am more than ready to pay in order to maintain the value of *my* money!' At that point I began to fear that our world was moving into dark times indeed.

But in addition, as the second mainstay of his economic philosophy, Milton Friedman was desperate to prove that unrestrained free markets would always be stable and self-regulating, despite the lesson of the 1930s. Rather than admit that unregulated capitalism was unstable and ultimately self-destructive, Friedman tried to blame the U.S. government for the Great Depression! In his autobiographical volume which related largely to his marriage to Rose Director (1910-2009), *Two Lucky People* (1998), Friedman declared,

> The Fed was largely responsible for converting what might have been a garden-variety recession, although perhaps a fairly severe one, into a major catastrophe. Instead of using its powers to offset the depression, it presided over a decline in the quantity of money by one-third from 1929 to 1933...Far from the depression being a failure of the free-enterprise system, it was a tragic failure of government. (p. 233)

In reality of course, the Fed's hands had been very largely tied by the gold standard then being adhered to by the USA., which limited the quantity of money that it could issue, by the rise of private hoarding, and by the political constraints of the time, as explained above. Far from government causing the Great Depression, it was government, and only government under the direction of Roosevelt, that saved Americans from the worst consequences of the inbred self-destructive nature of unregulated capitalism, as outlined above. However, by constantly harping away on his theme from 1963 when it was argued in his book, *A Monetary History of the United States, 1867-1960*, produced jointly with Anna Schwartz, Friedman succeeded in convincing many influential people that unregulated capitalism was just fine, and that government was to blame for the Great Depression! Speaking at a conference held at the University of Chicago on November 8, 2002, in honour of Milton Friedman, Ben Bernanke (b. 1953) who served two terms (2006-14) as Chairman of the Federal Reserve, the central bank of the United States, was ready to say,

> Let me end my talk by abusing slightly my status as an official representative of the Federal Reserve. I would like to say to Milton and Anna: regarding the Great Depression, you're right. We did it. We're very sorry. But thanks to you, we won't do it again. (Reprinted in M. Friedman and A. Schwartz, *The Great Contraction* (2008 ed.) p.247)

That declaration was made only six years before unrestrained capitalism once again caused a major world financial crisis, the second occasion within the span of just one human lifetime, and while Bernanke was still Chairman of the Federal Reserve. Despite his brave promise of 2002, Bernanke found that there was nothing that he could do to head off the deepening crisis of 2008. Once again it was only massive government intervention *after* the event that saved the Western World from the truly catastrophic economic consequences that were always the potential of unregulated capitalism, but only at the cost of soaring national debts followed by subsequent austerity, the burden of which fell mainly on the poor. Conveniently, Friedman had died in 2006, in time to miss witnessing the awful consequences of his misplaced faith in market rationality, but many of his most loyal acolytes did live to see it. Prominent among them was Alan Greenspan (b. 1926) who had served as Chairman of the Federal Reserve from 1987 to 2006. He had been completely taken in by Friedman's preaching on 'freedom', and in the wake of the Great Crash of 2007-9 an ashen-faced Alan Greenspan was forced to confess, 'I still don't understand why it happened'. (John Rapley, *Twilight of the Money Gods* (2017) p. 341)

But Greenspan and the other acolytes had little excuse for their surprise. Many warning voices on the dangers of unregulated capitalism had been raised for decades. One of the earliest had been that of Hyman Minsky (1919-96), an economist at Washington University in St. Louis. Referring to the Great Depression of the 1930s, Minsky had published a book in 1982 with the title, *Can 'It' Happen Again?* warning against the 'let 'er rip' ethos of neoliberalism. He followed this up in 1986 with a second volume, *Stabilizing an Unstable Economy*, providing some timely advice on much-needed government regulation. Another early Casandra was Charles Kindleberger (1910-2003), a leading architect of the Marshall Plan, and later a Professor of International Economics at the Massachusetts Institute of Technology. His book, *Manias, Panics, and Crashes: A History of Financial Crises* (1978) explained just how easily these disasters could happen in unregulated markets. It was reprinted in 2000, on the eve of the dot-com crash, which brought down many companies that had chosen to trade exclusively via the internet. Their shares became absurdly overpriced, but then crashed. In the same year, 2000, Robert Schiller (b. 1946) a Professor of Economics at Yale University since 1982, published his celebrated *Irrational Exuberance*, a carefully researched piece of work which once again demonstrated how booms and busts of ever-greater proportions could develop in unregulated economies as a result of irrational expectations. His work directly contradicted Milton Friedman's assumptions of market rationality, something that economists referred to as 'the efficient markets hypothesis'. Finally, Raghuram Rajan (b. 1963), an Indian economist who in 2005 was serving as Chief Economist of the International Monetary Fund, attempted to warn America's central bank, the Federal Reserve, of the dangers of the new and highly complicated financial instruments that had recently been developed. In that year he presented a paper to the Federal Reserve's annual conference with the title, 'Has Financial Development made the World Riskier?' He concluded that it had, but only two years before the onset of the great financial crisis of 2007-9, his work was ignored. The good times were rolling, and everything seemed to be going well.

After the event, interest in all these writers revived, and their books were dusted off to be read again with greater appreciation. In 2016, Adair Turner, who had been Chairman of Britain's Financial Services Authority in 2008, conceded that the work of Hyman Minsky in particular had been, 'largely and dangerously ignored in his lifetime'. Rapley helps to explain this by pointing out that all of these critics were regarded as economic heretics, beyond the pale because they had defied the economic theology of their day. Further, he writes, 'Eschewing the applied mathematics that had become the *sine qua non* of economic scholarship, Minsky's and Kindleberger's more traditional narrative approaches precluded them from serious consideration. You can't work at the Vatican if you don't speak Latin'. (op. cit., pp. 378-9) All of these writers had warned against the folly of unregulated capitalism, of the kind advocated by Friedman. As events were to prove therefore, both of the central tenets of Friedman's economic philosophy, his emphasis on the money supply and his faith in market rationality, were shown to have been entirely mistaken.

In addition, when it came to how businesses should behave, Friedman preached greed and irresponsibility. During a recorded interview with Phil Donahue on SiP TV held in 1979, Friedman is on record as saying,

> Is there some society that you know that doesn't run on greed? You think Russia doesn't run on greed? You think China doesn't run on greed? What is greed? Of course, none of us are greedy, it's only the other fellow who's greedy. The world runs on individuals pursuing their separate interests. (Available online)

So greed is good, risk is good, but do large corporations owe some kind of duty of responsibility towards society as a whole? In the article, 'Milton Friedman Responds' which appeared in the journal *Chemtec* for February,1974, Friedman gave his own emphatic answer to that question. He said,

> So the question is, do *corporate executives,* provided they stay within the law, have responsibilities in their business activities other than to make as much money for their stockholders as possible? And my answer to that is, no they do not. (p. 72)

So that is clear enough then: in Friedman's book it is just fine for large corporations to exploit their workforce, pollute the environment, and avoid or evade the taxes that they ought to pay, just so long as they are delivering nice, fat dividends to their shareholders.

But what else did Friedman advocate to win for himself such a high reputation as an economist? He shared with Hayek an almost fanatical obsession with the concept of freedom, coupled with a paranoid suspicion of the state, but this did not preclude him from having some good ideas. Friedman was against business monopolies, which in the USA are called 'trusts', on the grounds that these reduced competition. This was fine in theory, but in practice we have seen that neoliberalism in fact leads to the building of monopolies as banks and corporations swallow each other and become ever larger. Under neoliberalism, the building of a monopoly has come to be seen as a reward for 'efficiency'. In *The Wall Street Journal* for September 12, 2014, Peter Thiel (b. 1967), a co-founder of PayPal, wrote the Saturday Essay. It was entitled, 'Competition is for Losers', and extolled the virtues of building a monopoly. The American economist Joseph Stiglitz (b. 1943), a Nobel laureate, noticed that this was becoming a general trend among U.S. corporations. In the journal *Project Syndicate* for March 11 2019, he wrote an article entitled, 'Market Concentration is Threatening the U.S. Economy'. Here he said of American corporations,

> Why bother to produce anything of value when you can use your political power to extract more rents through market exploitation [monopolies]? Political investments in getting lower taxes and fewer regulations yield far higher returns than real investments in plant and equipment...Add to that the globalisation of corporate power and the orgy of deregulation and crony capitalism under Trump, and it is clear that Europe will have to take the lead if reforms are to be made. (Available on line)

Unfortunately, however, Europe too has recently been succumbing to the neoliberal creed. Stiglitz himself had already linked falling productivity rates and lower rates of growth in GDP in both Europe and America to the rise of neoliberalism in the first edition of his book, *The Price of Inequality* (2012).

Like Keynes, Friedman favoured flexible exchange rates for international currencies, an eminently sensible idea, adhered to by all countries after 1971, until the introduction of the Euro in 1999, which fixed exchange rates for member states. Another good idea that Friedman had was the abolition of conscription for young men, known in America as 'the draft'. This was finally abolished after a long debate in Congress in March, 1973. Friedman had been one of 15 members of the Gates Commission, set up by Richard Nixon in 1969, and reporting in 1970 on the conscription issue. All 15 members recommended the abolition of the draft. It met under the chairmanship of Thomas S. Gates (1906-83) a former Secretary of Defence, and not of Friedman, as wrongly reported in Wikipedia. However, in 1995 Friedman described his role in helping to secure this abolition as his proudest accomplishment.

Also in 1995 Friedman declared himself to be an anti-interventionist in foreign policy, having opposed both the Gulf War and the Iraq War. Friedman also claimed that he stood for fiscal probity, that is to say that governments should not spend money that they did not have by borrowing to cover the gap between their incomes and their expenditure, but instead should balance their budgets from year to year. One of his favourite quotations was, 'There is no such thing as a free lunch'! Friedman did not originate the phrase, but he certainly popularised it. Here again his views were in agreement with those of Keynes, who advocated deficit financing as a means of pulling countries out of depression, but only as a temporary measure. Once prosperity had been restored, Keynes advocated higher taxes, the paying off of the government debt, and a return to fiscal probity thereafter. One can only agree with such common sense views.

However, neoliberal policies have led to precisely the opposite result. In Europe and North America the level of national debts has never been higher since the Second World War and its aftermath and, alarmingly, these debts are still growing in many cases, and coming down only slowly in others. It is our present governments which now seem to be demanding the 'free lunch', by living permanently on borrowed money! This was true even before the Covid pandemic, and has been the direct result of their having adopted neoliberal policies, trusting in unrestrained capitalism, for it was this that led to the great financial crisis of 2007-9. This in turn forced governments everywhere to borrow large sums of money to bail out the banks and financial institutions that had speculated so rashly and greedily as to threaten the stability of the world's financial system. But what is the scale of the present debt problem? Under the terms of the Maastricht Treaty of 1992 no EU country was supposed to acquire a national debt larger than 60% of its GDP, but the crisis shattered this ideal. According to figures from America's Central Intelligence Agency and the IMF, the UK's figure for 2017 was 90.4%. In Europe, even frugal Germany's 2017 figure was 64.1%, with France and Spain's figures nearing 100%, while Greece, Italy, Portugal, Cyprus, and Belgium all had public debts of over 100% of their GDP. Canadian public debt in 2017 stood at 89.7% of GDP, while in the United States for the same year the figure was 103.8%. Would you be happy if your personal debts came to some 100% of your annual income? China, on the other hand, which practices a highly attenuated form of the neoliberal creed, had a debt to GDP ratio of only 18.6%.

Another of Friedman's better ideas appeared early in his career in a collection published in 1953, *Essays in Positive Economics*. The first essay in the book was entitled, 'The Methodology of Positive Economics'. Here, Friedman explored the difference between positive and normative economics, that is the distinction between what actually *is* and what *ought to be* in economic affairs. Just as the logical positivists had tried to put philosophy onto a 'scientific' basis, here Friedman was trying to do the same thing with economics by adopting an empirical approach. He argued that a worthwhile economic theory should be judged not by the superficial plausibility of its arguments, but firstly by its simplicity in its ability to predict at least as much as an alternative theory, but needing less information to do so. Secondly, it should be fruitful in the precision and scope of its predictions, i.e. it should be judged by its predictions of events which later actually happened. These criteria formed the epistemological basis of Friedman's later approach to economic thought. Of course, as noted above, when it comes to philosophy, it is extremely difficult to produce a completely original idea. Here, Jesus had scooped Friedman by almost 2,000 years with his much more succinct observation, 'By their fruits ye shall know them'. (Matthew 7:20) All this sounds sensible enough, but by this criterion the neoliberals are once again hoisted by their own petard, for the consequence of following Friedman's economic doctrines was of course the disastrous world financial crash of 2007-9, while Friedman had predicted that unregulated financial markets would always be rational, and could safely be left to their own devices. Writing in the *New York Review of Books* for April 10, 2008, Paul Krugman (b.1953), Distinguished Professor of Economics at the City University of New York and a Nobel Laureate in Economics, said of Friedman that he, 'slipped all too easily into claiming both that markets always work and that only markets work. It is extremely hard to find cases in which Friedman acknowledged the possibility that markets could go wrong, or that government intervention could serve a useful purpose.'

Friedman was so strongly anti-government that he could quite understand the anarchist point of view. But he was prepared to concede that after all government was necessary, so long as it confined itself to protecting the interests of big business and did not try to meddle with the economy. In a celebrated interview with *Playboy Magazine* for February, 1973 Friedman declared,

> I wish the anarchists luck, since that's the way we ought to be moving now. But I believe we need government to enforce the rules of the game. By prosecuting anti-trust violations, for instance. We need a government to maintain a system of courts that will uphold contracts and rule on compensation for damages. We need a government to ensure the safety of its citizens – to provide police protection. But government is failing at a lot of these things that it ought to be doing because it's involved in so many things that it shouldn't be doing...What kind of society isn't structured on greed? (Available online)

A few years later, as reported in *The Times Herald* of Norristown, Pennsylvania on December 1, 1978, Friedman said,

> There's a sense in which all taxes are antagonistic to free enterprise...and yet we need taxes...I would like to see a great deal less government activity than we have now, but I do not believe that we can have a situation in which we don't need government at all. We do need to provide for certain essential government functions – the national defence function, the police function, preserving law and order, maintaining a judiciary. So the question is, which are the least bad taxes? In my opinion the least bad tax is the property tax on the unimproved value of land, the Henry George argument of many, many years ago. (Available online)

This conception of the 'least bad' form of taxation is an important one, which will be revisited in the Conclusion below. Although not mentioned above, Friedman also believed that the state should provide free primary and secondary education for its citizens, although he thought that this should be done by the issuing of school vouchers to parents, which could be redeemed at schools of their choice, rather than expecting all children to attend their local high schools. However, like Hayek, Friedman was very suspicious of social security, arguing that it could lead to a culture of welfare dependency in his 1962 book, *Capitalism and Freedom* (pp. 182-9). But again like Hayek he acknowledged that, at the end of the day, the handicapped and the destitute were entitled to some form of state support. He advocated a negative income tax as the best means of establishing at least a minimum standard of living for all. But he was against any minimum wage laws, and Friedman was also in favour of unlimited immigration, both legal and illegal, into the United States, believing that by increasing the labour supply, the immigrants would keep wage costs down. Also like Hayek, he had complete faith in the price mechanism as an infallible guide for markets, writing in his 1980 book *Free to Choose*,

> The price system works so well, so efficiently, that we are not aware of it most of the time. We never realise how well it functions until it is prevented from functioning, and even then we seldom recognise the source of the trouble...the price system transmits only the important information and only to the people who need to know. (p.13)

So great was Friedman's confidence in the price mechanism that he tended towards the belief that things with no price had no value. This would mean that all voluntary service, both within the home and outside the home, was worthless because nothing was paid for it. The same would apply to donations to food banks. On the other hand, the possibility that some shares and other financial products could become absurdly *overpriced*, far beyond their true value, never seems to have occurred to him, and nor did the potentially disastrous consequences of this overpricing, as seen in the great world financial crash of 2007-9. One is tempted to suggest that such grotesque misconceptions could have emerged only from a seriously unbalanced mind.

On the wilder shores of Friedman's libertarian thought we find him advocating the legalisation of prostitution, an arguable proposition, but also the legalisation of all drugs for private use, which is rather more questionable. In addition, he devoted his PhD thesis to an attack on the AMA, the American Medical Association, for insisting that all doctors should be qualified and licensed to practice by the state! Friedman believed that medical licensing was a form of state imposed monopoly and that unlicensed doctors should also be allowed to practise, in accordance with free market principles! What might be described as the collateral damage which could well result from such a policy was evidently, in Friedman's view, a price well worth paying for the sake of medical 'freedom'. In his 1962 book *Capitalism and Freedom* he wrote,

> I am myself persuaded that medical licensure has reduced both the quantity and quality of medical practice; that it has reduced the opportunities available to people

who would like to be physicians, forcing them to pursue occupations they regard as less attractive; that it has forced the public to pay more for less satisfactory medical service, and that it has retarded technological development both in medicine itself and in the organisation of medical practice. I conclude that licensure should be eliminated as a requirement for the practice of medicine. (p. 148)

It would appear that it is not only cynics, but also economists too who sometimes know the price of everything, but the value of nothing. In short, what are we to make of Friedman as an economist? Despite his great reputation, I do not regard Friedman very highly. If any modern economist is to be compared with Maynard Keynes, I believe that man to be Joseph Eugene Stiglitz (b. 1943). I would say that if Einstein was the most overrated physicist of the twentieth century, then Friedman was the most overrated economist. Unlike Einstein, however, Friedman's ideas have done a great deal of harm to a great many people, as we shall see. Friedman has done more than anyone else to legitimise greed, selfishness, and irresponsibility in the minds of far too many, to the great detriment of the rest of us.

Augusto Pinochet (1915-2006) and Neoliberalism in Chile

Because Chile was indeed the first test bed of what was then the new and untried economic creed of neoliberalism, the case of Chile is worthy of further examination, since it was Chile that first introduced neoliberalism to the world. Ironically, it could be argued that it was Salvador Allende (1908-73), a lifelong dedicated socialist, who was responsible for the instigation of this first neoliberal experiment. Elected as President of Chile in 1970, Allende at once embarked on a recklessly extravagant left-wing programme of social and economic reforms. He nationalised several of Chile's large-scale industries, including the copper mining industry, which accounted for most of Chile's export earnings. Also nationalised were the largest banks, the health care system, and the education system, organisations that had long been under state control in some of the more advanced countries. But Allende went further, breaking up the large estates of the great landowners, the *latifundia*, by outright government confiscation. The land was redistributed to smaller farmers, on the understanding that no holding was to exceed 80 hectares, about 200 acres, in size. This programme was an extension of one begun by Allende's predecessor as President, Eduardo Frie (1911-82), who was in office from 1964 to 1970. The new, smaller holdings became *asentamientos*, a form of tenure under which the new farms were run as joint enterprises between the state and the peasants who had lived on the land as tenant farmers. The state provided loans, land, and technical guidance, while the peasants provided their labour and took any profits that the land might yield, minus interest on their loans. 1,408 large estates were expropriated in this way under Frie, and a further 3,479 under Allende, together making up some 40% of Chile's agricultural land. By the end of 1972, no *latifundia* remained.

During 1970 and 1971 Allende raised all wages and pensions by fiat, and introduced price controls. In addition he embarked on an extensive state supported housing programme, building an average of 52,000 houses a year during his time in office. He also greatly expanded educational and cultural provisions at all levels, and provided free milk and free school meals for all children aged seven to fourteen. Health services too were greatly expanded. In addition, Allende also instigated many more policies of a very socialist nature, too numerous to mention here. His policies were all very worthy and well meaning, but completely unrealistic given the strength of the Chilean economy. The national debt soared, and Chile was obliged to default on its foreign loans. By 1972 the Chilean escudo was suffering from an annual inflation rate of 140%, while average real GDP (Gross Domestic Product) contracted at an annual rate of 5.6% between 1971 and 1973. From an index of 100 at the beginning of Allende's rule real wage levels rose to 119 in the first few months, but then fell rapidly to only 31 at the time of Allende's fall, thanks to rampant inflation. Allende's price controls resulted in the disappearance of basic provisions from the shops, and black markets arose for the supply of rice, beans, sugar, and flour, all essential, basic commodities. In short, Allende's idealistic socialist programme had been devised in Cloud Cuckoo Land, and was quite unsustainable even on its own.

In addition, however, Allende faced both internal and external headwinds. The world price of copper fell by nearly one-third during Allende's presidency, and the nationalisation of the copper mines was not a success. He was constantly challenged by the Chilean Congress, which accused him of acting unconstitutionally, and of seeking dictatorial powers. Allende's predecessor, Eduardo Frei, who had been President from 1964 to 1970, turned against him, supporting opposition to Allende's policies. He too had been a socialist, raising taxes and redistributing wealth in Chile, but he believed that Allende was moving too far too fast, an accurate enough assessment. In addition the USA had long feared an Allende presidency, seeing his policies as being at least Marxist, if not outright Communism. This was unfair, since a large private sector still remained in Chile under Allende's reforms, and the new *asentamienos* were hardly collective farms on the Soviet model, but the USA was desperate to suppress any move that might lead to the rise of Communism in Latin America. The USA did all it could to damage the Chilean economy under Allende, placing embargoes on the export of vital machine parts to Chile, disabling one-third of Chilean motor vehicles. This was a serious handicap in a long, thin country like Chile, which measured almost 3,000 miles from end to end. Meanwhile the CIA supported, though it did not instigate, the final military coup against the Allende regime. But in truth, Allende had brought his troubles upon himself through the damage his policies had done to the Chilean economy, with even his predecessor, the socialist Frei, supporting the coup. Besieged in his presidential palace by the military, Allende fought to the last, and finally committed suicide when he saw that all was lost.

When Augusto Pinochet took power as a military dictator on September 11, 1973, he immediately set about building the world's first neoliberal state. In this he was closely advised and supported by America's Central Intelligence Agency, and by the 'Chicago Boys', a team of Chilean economists who had trained at Friedman's Economics Department at the University of Chicago, or at its affiliated institution, the Pontifical Catholic University of Chile. The results of Pinochet's policies were mixed to say the least, as he resorted to shock therapy as a cure for Chile's economic ills. He threw all of Allende's policies sharply into reverse, cutting government expenditure, including family allowances and unemployment benefits, returning nationalised industries and land to private ownership, suppressing the trade unions, and keeping a tight control over the money supply to curb inflation. These were classic neoliberal policies. According to figures from the United Nations Statistics Division, the annual growth rate of Chilean GDP fell to -5% in 1973, and -13% in 1975, but thereafter it rose rapidly to average 7% p.a between 1976 and 1981. In 1975 Pinochet renamed the Chilean escudo as 'the peso', reverting to its pre-1960 appellation in an attempt to give the currency more credibility.

Unfortunately, however, on the advice of the 'Chicago Boys', Pinochet also removed all government regulation from the banking and financial sectors, aiming for a completely *laissez faire* economic system. This opened the way to that same 'irrational exuberance' that always follows from deregulation, and was later to cause the worldwide financial crash of 2008. In 1982 Chile faced a similar economic crisis, with a surge in unemployment and a meltdown of the financial sector. 16 out of 50 Chilean financial institutions faced bankruptcy, and Pinochet was forced to nationalise five of the largest banks, and place more under government supervision, returning some financial controls. As in the 1930s, government was forced to come to the rescue of the excesses of unregulated capitalism. The annual growth rate of Chile's GDP plunged to -14% in 1982, and the unemployment rate rose to 33%. Pinochet then sacked the 'Chicago Boys', and turned to less radical and more pragmatic economic advisors, although privatisations continued, and the emphasis remained on a *laissez faire* approach. Thereafter there was steady economic recovery, with annual GDP growth rates averaging 5.9% between 1984 and 1990, the highest in Latin America. In 2010 Chile was deemed 'rich' enough to gain membership of the exclusive OECD club of what was then 31 members, the first country in South America to do so.

While all this was happening, however, we should remember those World Bank figures cited above, which indicated that under Pinochet unemployment rates remained high at an average of 18.1%, while the proportion of Chile's population living below an internationally defined poverty line rose from 17% in 1970 to 48% in 1988. Under neoliberalism, a large proportion of the Chilean population had actually become poorer, while overall national wealth had been increasing. The greatest beneficiaries of Pinochet's policies had been the richest 10% of the Chilean population. But in 1988, thanks to dwindling internal support, Pinochet was forced to agree to a plebiscite on the question of whether he should enjoy another eight years as President. Pinochet lost this popular vote, and under its terms he had no alternative but to step down in 1990, although he remained as Commander-in-Chief of the army until 1998. A democratic regime was re-introduced in 1990, and it was only under Pinochet's two successors as President, Patrico Aylwin (1918-2016), and Eduardo Frei, the son of the former President, (b. 1942) that at last something was done to help the poor of Chile.

Under Aylwin, in office from 1990 to 1994, taxes imposed on the richer half of Chile's population were increased by some 15%, and the additional government income was spent on helping the poor. During the Aylwin presidency spending on education rose by 40%, and on health provision by 54%. The minimum wage was increased by 36% in real terms between 1990 and 1993, while a new Solidarity and Social Investment Fund was set up to direct aid towards the poorest communities. Family allowances, pensions, and benefits for the unemployed and disabled were also raised. A new labour law, introduced in 1990, fully legalised trade unions and collective bargaining, while also increasing severance pay for dismissed workers. The poorest workers, those on the minimum wage, benefited most from these changes, but for all workers real wages increased at an average annual rate of 4.6% under Aylwin, while the unemployment rate fell from 7.8% to 6.5%. A slum clearance programme was also initiated, aiming to build 100,000 new houses a year. These policies were continued under Eduardo Frei, President from 1994 to 2000, and according to United Nations figures the proportion of the population living below an internationally defined poverty line fell steadily, from some 40% in 1990 to 33% in 1993, 20% in 2000, and 14.4% in 2010. According to World Bank figures, the GINI index for Chile fell from 57.2 in 1990 to 47.2 in 2013. This compared with an index of 34 for the UK in 2014. The GINI index is a measure of income inequality in a country, with an index of zero indicating absolute equality of all incomes, while an index of 100 would indicate that one man enjoyed all the income while everyone else had nothing. Of course, the extremes of this scale are never reached in practice. But these figures are very difficult to measure, and different authorities will give different estimates. Perhaps only broad trends should be recognised. There is, however, a broad consensus of agreement that, despite recent improvements, income inequality in Chile remains very high, certainly the highest of the OECD (Organisation for Economic Co-operation and Development) countries. This is reflected in the structure of Chilean cities, which have affluent centres surrounded by shanty towns that have only communal supplies of clean water and sanitation facilities. The distribution of wealth in Chile is even more unequal. Writing in the Latin American journal *Alborada* for December 16, 2017, Orr Yeoli-Rimmer in his article 'Redressing the Balance? Inequality in

Chile' claimed that the richest five percent of the population owned 42% of all the wealth in 2017. (Available online).

What then are the lessons to be learned from the experience of the world's first neoliberal economy? From the Chilean example we may conclude that, while neoliberal policies might increase the overall rate of economic growth, they also tend to make the poor poorer and the rich richer, increasing wealth inequality within nations. It also suggests that once deregulation of financial markets has been introduced the state will, sooner or later, be obliged to step in to save free enterprise capitalism from its own self-destructive tendencies. One is reminded here of the old adage, 'An ounce of prevention is worth a pound of cure.' It would surely be more sensible, and cheaper, to keep free enterprise capitalism closely regulated in the first place.

Margaret Thatcher (1925-2013) and British Neoliberalism

It is now time to consider in more detail just how neoliberal thought has impacted in practice upon some other countries. Let us begin by looking at one of its most famous practitioners. Margaret Thatcher was born as Margaret Roberts on October 13th 1925 in the town of Grantham, in Lincolnshire. Her father Alfred was a man of some standing in the town, a Methodist lay preacher, the owner of two grocery shops, an alderman, and mayor of Grantham from 1945-6. Thanks to her father's influence, Margaret remained an avowed Christian in adult life, although she converted to Anglicanism in 1951. Significantly, her father was a self-made man, an independent tradesman, an employer of labour, and not a wage earner himself. Perhaps also significantly, Margaret was educated at the local grammar school, the Kesteven and Grantham Girls' School, where she served as head girl in 1942-3. Despite this distinction, however, Margaret was fortunate to win a place at Somerville College Oxford in 1943. Oxbridge in those days was very much a male preserve, with most colleges admitting men only: Cambridge at that time had only two women's colleges, Girton and Newnham. But Oxford had five, which improved Margaret's chances. Even so, she was initially rejected by Somerville, and offered a place only after a preferred candidate had dropped out. She chose to do a four-year Bachelor of Science degree, which was actually a higher qualification than the standard Oxford MA. She took a second class in Chemistry, which at Oxford in those days equated to a 2-1 degree elsewhere. In another sense, however, Margaret was later to score a double first, becoming not only Britain's first female Prime Minister, but also its first Prime Minister to hold a Science degree, a fact of which she was very proud.

The choice of a Science degree might seem odd for one who was later to devote most of her life to politics, but Margaret had always been an all-rounder, with a wide range of interests. In 1946 she became President of the undergraduates' Oxford University Conservative Association, and was already avidly reading the works of Friedrich Hayek and other *laissez faire* economists, with an eye towards law and later politics. After graduating in 1947 she worked as a research chemist for a year, and then applied for a job with Imperial Chemical Industries. However, her interviewers turned her down, reporting that, 'This woman is headstrong, obstinate, and dangerously self-opinionated.' (Wikipedia entry on Thatcher) Who can doubt the accuracy of that assessment? Undeterred, Margaret continued to work as a chemist for the next few years, while associating herself as closely as possible with the Conservative Party. She joined local Conservative Associations, and attended the annual Party Conference. She also joined the famous Vermin Club, an association of enthusiastic grassroots Conservatives who were proud to adopt that name after Aneurin Bevan had described the Tories as being 'lower than vermin' in a speech of July, 1948. Thanks to her enthusiasm, Margaret rose rapidly through the ranks of this organisation to become a 'Chief Rat' in 1949. At its peak the Club had some 120,000 members, but it was wrapped up in 1951.

Through her political interests Margaret came to the notice of the Dartford Conservative Association which happened to be looking for a candidate to stand for this safe Labour seat at the general election of 1950. Margaret was then only 24, but despite her youth and sex she applied for and was selected as the Conservative candidate for Dartford in January 1950. She was defeated in the general election of February 1950, and again in the general election of October 1951. However, at a dinner following her formal adoption as candidate for Dartford in February 1950 she met her future husband Dennis Thatcher (1915-2003), a wealthy divorcé, successful businessman, and of course member of the Tory party. They married in December, 1951, and Margaret became the Margaret Thatcher known to history. With financial help from Denis and her parents, Margaret then studied Law, and qualified as a barrister in 1953, specialising in taxation. In that same year her twins, Carol and Mark, were born. It was not until October 1959 that she finally succeeded in being elected to Parliament as the Conservative member for Finchley, which was at that time a constituency in north London.

Once in Parliament, as with the Vermin Club, Thatcher rose swiftly through the ranks. Harold Macmillan promoted her to Parliamentary Undersecretary at the Ministry of Pensions and National Insurance in October 1961. Following the Conservatives' election defeat in 1964 she became a spokesman on Housing and Land, advocating the sale of council houses to existing tenants, and in 1966 was promoted to the shadow Treasury team, where she opposed Labour's prices and incomes controls as undue state interference in the workings of the economy. At the 1966 Conservative Party conference she denounced the high tax policies of the Labour government as being a step, 'not only towards Socialism, but towards Communism'. We may detect here the same notes of paranoia and hysteria that characterised the writings of Hayek himself. Also in 1966 she voted in favour of a Bill to decriminalise male homosexuality, and in favour of a Bill to legalise abortion. These moves were in the libertarian traditions of Hayek and Friedman, but in 1968 she voted against the relaxation of the divorce laws, and in 1970, according to John Campbell's extensive study *Margaret Thatcher,* she declared to the *Finchley Press* that she would like to see a 'reversal of the permissive society'. (Vol. I, *The Grocer's Daughter* (2000) p. 191) Always something of a disciplinarian, she also voted during the 1960s for the retention of hanging and birching: it is noticeable that neoliberalism approves of Victorian values.

Following the Conservative election victory of 1970, Thatcher was promoted to the Cabinet as Secretary of State for Education and Science by Edward Heath. Here, she did all she could to delay the introduction of comprehensive schooling, managing to save 94 grammar schools during her time in that office. However, Heath coped badly with the effects of the first oil shock and rising inflation, and his leadership fell under a cloud. The Tories lost the general election of 1974, and a leadership election was held in 1975 with Thatcher as one of the candidates. She came from behind to win the election, becoming leader of the Conservative Party on February 11, 1975. It was only then that Thatcher began to emerge as a passionate ideologue. Always a great admirer of the Institute of Economic Research, Thatcher began attending lunches there on a regular basis. The Institute was a think-tank founded in 1955 by Antony Fisher (1915-88), a successful British business man. As mentioned above, he was in 1947 a founder member of the Mont Pelerin Society, together with Milton Friedman and Fredrick Hayek, whom he knew personally and greatly admired. Fisher was someone who well understood both the power of ideas, and how the dissemination of neoliberal principles could contribute mightily to the filling of his pockets, if only he could sell them to governments at home and around the world. To this end, he later founded the International Institute for Economic Research in 1971, and the Atlas Network in 1981. Through this last, by 1984 Fisher had been able to establish a score of neoliberal think-tanks in eleven countries, and after Fisher's death in 1988 the network that he had founded went on to establish nearly 500 neoliberal think tanks in over 90 different countries.

Fisher had not hesitated to spend his own money liberally in support of these think-tanks, regarding it as a sound investment for the future, and so it was to become for members of his class, but ironically, not for Fisher himself. One is reminded here of the parable of the rich fool, that we read in Luke 12:15-20. The rich man became obsessed with laying up for himself treasures upon Earth, and was planning to build bigger barns to store his ample produce. But the Lord God said unto him, 'Thou fool, this night shalt thy soul be required of thee: whose then shall those things be which thou hast provided?' By dying in 1988, Fisher never reaped the full fruits of all his efforts: indeed, he was knighted only four weeks before his death, barely living long enough to enjoy that honour either. However, the evil that men do lives after them. Inspired by Fisher's example, many other rich individuals and powerful corporations also poured money into numerous similar think-tanks and 'right-thinking' university Economics departments everywhere, and were only too successful at selling their creed in Britain, in Europe, in North America, and in many other parts of the world.

Margaret Thatcher provides us with a classic example of someone who had been completely brainwashed by the ideas of Friedrich Hayek and Milton Friedman. John Ranelagh in his book *Thatcher's People* (1992) relates an incident at a meeting of the Conservative Research Department, attended by Thatcher, which took place in July, 1975. The guest speaker had been declaiming on the merits of moderation in Conservatism, but Thatcher rudely interrupted him. Pulling a copy of Hayek's *The Constitution of Liberty* from her briefcase, she 'held the book aloft for all of us to see. "This", she said sternly, "is what we believe!", and banged Hayek down on the table.' (p. ix) After the Conservatives won the general election of May 3, 1979 under their new leader Margaret Thatcher, she proved to be as good as her word. For example, she bought in entirely to Friedman's paranoid fear of the state. Invited to speak to European Commission members at Bruges in September, 1988 Thatcher declared, 'We have not successfully rolled back the frontiers of the state in Britain, only to see them re-imposed at a European level by a European super-state exercising a new dominance from Brussels.' (Senden, L. *Soft Law in European Law* (2004) p. 9)Winning three successive elections, she remained in power until 1990, and during that time she imposed a full neoliberal agenda upon Britain.

Thatcher's first move was on taxation rates. Now national taxation is a very complicated field, a matter of infinite detail. However, at least the broad outline of taxation changes between 1979 and 2019 may be discerned with the help of figures provided by the Office for National Statistics, the Institute for Fiscal Studies, the Office for Budget Responsibility, the United Kingdom Statistics Authority, and HMRC, all available on line. Although a plethora of information is provided by all these sources, some figures are estimates, and some sources contradict each other. Once again therefore, only broad trends should be considered as reliable. These show that the main thrust of Thatcher's changes was in the direction of reducing direct taxes on incomes, while increasing indirect taxes, such as purchase taxes. Economists would describe this as a move towards 'regressive' taxation. The term sounds pejorative, but for economists it is simply the antonym of 'progressive' taxation. This latter is so called because it progressively increases in line with rises in the level of a tax payer's income, or the amount of wealth that he holds. A 'regressive' tax is any levy imposed on persons whose income has not increased, obliging them to pay the new tax from existing income. A change of emphasis to this form of taxation bears more heavily on those with low incomes, who do not pay much income tax in any case, but who have to spend nearly all that they do earn on everyday items, now made more expensive by purchase taxes. This move hit in particular young couples trying to get a home together, because they had to buy so much for their homes at that stage. But it favoured the more elderly, who had already been able to accumulate most of what they needed. In addition the elderly enjoyed state pensions, no prescription charges, free bus passes, and free TV licences, all this financed by taxes paid by the young.

A central tenet of neoliberal doctrine has always been the aim of shrinking the state, and thereby achieving lower taxation. But we should remember that a shrinking of the state also means a shrinking of democracy, since the power lost by the state passes into the hands of private capitalists. We should also ask, 'Lower taxation for whom?' It is interesting to trace the history of the top rate of income tax levied in Britain since 1945, the rate paid only by those with the very largest incomes. Between 1945 and 1971 this rate was very high, at 19/6 in the pound, or 97.5%. In 1971 this top rate was cut to 75%, but a new surcharge of 15% was imposed on investment income, keeping the overall rate of income tax still very high for the wealthiest, at some 90% on average. In 1974 the top rate on earned income was again raised, to 83%, with the investment income surcharge kept at 15%, raising the overall rate for the very wealthiest to around 98%. This applied only to earnings over the £20,000 threshold in 1974, equivalent to about £205,000 p.a. in 2018 terms. Only some 750,000 people in the country were liable to pay that rate, roughly 1.3% of a population of 56 millions, but it acted as a deterrent to board members paying themselves enormous salaries and bonuses, since most of their extra money would go in tax. But money earned under the £20,000 threshold was taxed at lower rates, leaving the wealthy still much richer than the average wage earner.

This remained the state of play until Margaret Thatcher's first budget in 1979. Here, the top tax rate was reduced from 83% to 60%. Later, the investment income surcharge was completely abolished in 1985, and the top rate of income tax was further cut to 40% in 1988. This left the very wealthy substantially richer than before, especially since board members then found it much more worthwhile to pay themselves enormous salaries and bonuses, since they could now keep most of the money for themselves. The result was a sharply rising disparity between the pay of the average worker and that of the CEOs (Chief Executive Officers) of Britain's large companies. In 1970 when those earning over £20,000 p.a. would have had to pay tax at the rate of 97.5% on any additional income over that sum, the CEO to average worker's pay ratio was between 20:1 and 30:1. But according to research carried out by Bloomberg Surveillance and published in January 2019 (available on line) this ratio had risen to 40:1 by 1978, 120:1 by 2000, and 133:1 by 2017. They support this claim by citing the actual pay levels of the CEOs of Britain's top ten companies in 2017. These ranged from £10.5 million p.a. for Bob Dudley of BP up to £47 million p.a. for Jeff Fairburn of Persimmon. The average CEO's pay among the top ten was £20.8 million p.a. In the USA the disparity was even greater. Bloomberg cites figures gathered from America's 350 largest companies by the Economic Policy Institute in 2017. These show the average CEO's pay in that country to be 312 times that of the average worker. In his book , *23 Things They Don't Tell You About Capitalism* (2010), Ha Joon-Chang agrees with those figures, and spends a few pages (148-53) comparing the pay rises of US executives with rises in the productivity of both themselves and their companies. He concludes,

US managers have increased their relative pay by at least ten times between the 1950s and today. The average CEO used to get paid 35 times the average worker's salary then, while today he is paid 300-400 times that, but this is not because their productivity has risen ten times faster than that of their workers. (p. 257)

The real reason is, of course, that thanks to tax cuts it is now much more worthwhile for board members, who are in the happy position of being able to set their own remuneration, to pay themselves as much as they can get away with. Moreover, it is important to remember that in no way do those board members actually *earn* the enormous salaries that they pay themselves. They simply *get* the money because of the positions that they occupy. Board members used to be happy to work for far less, but the greed of the greedy knows no bounds. This indeed is a point that was noted long ago: 'He that loveth silver shall not be satisfied with silver, nor he that loveth abundance with increase: this also is vanity.' (Ecclesiastes 5:10) The great gainers from Thatcher's tax reforms have been the wealthy and the fabulously wealthy. The average tax payer is left no better off, and young couples trying to get a home together are actually worse off, thanks to the 20% VAT tax on all goods and services.

In the UK the 40% top tax rate lasted until 2010, when the newly-elected Conservative-Liberal Democrat coalition government tried to raise the top rate of tax from 40% to 50% on incomes of over £150,000 p.a. To their dismay, however, they found that top rate tax receipts actually fell under this new regime, although the number of very wealthy people in the country remained the same. But they had become reluctant to surrender the great tax gains that they had made over the previous 30 years. The very wealthy had simply found ways to avoid or evade the new tax rate, forcing the government to retreat on this issue. In 2012 the top rate was cut from 50% to 45% for 2013-14. This resulted in an *increase* in the yield from top rate tax payers of eight billion pounds, from £38 billion to £46 billion. The then Tory Chancellor of the Exchequer, George Osborne (b. 1971) congratulated himself on having been very clever indeed, choosing to ignore the ominous implication of this development, namely that taxpaying by the very rich was a voluntary activity, subject to their own control. Nothing was done to remedy the situation. In part this was because the development was seen as simply a vindication of the so-called 'Laffer curve', a theoretical economic concept associated with the name of Arthur Laffer (b. 1940), an American economist who began his career at the University of Chicago. However, Laffer himself declared that his 'curve' was simply a very old idea relating to optimum levels of taxation, originally outlined by the Moslem philosopher Ibn Khaldun (1332-1406), and mentioned by Adam Smith and Maynard Keynes. Laffer had simply expressed it as a graph, which showed tax receipts rising to a certain point as tax rates were increased, but then beginning to decline after that point if tax rates were raised any higher. In consequence, for the tax year 2019-20 the top rate remained at 45% for incomes of over £150,000 p.a.

Meanwhile, what had been happening to tax rates for the poorer members of the community? With fewer indirect or regressive taxes, the basic or lowest income tax rate in 1979 was quite high at 33%. However, this was paid only on taxable income, what was left after personal tax allowances had been deducted. These were quite generous in 1979 at £1,165 for a single person and £1,815 for a married man, with child allowances at £365 for each child. This meant that a married man with two children could earn £2,545 p.a. before paying tax. The average wage at that time for a low-paid adult male manual worker in full-time employment was about £6,000 p.a., so assuming he earned this low wage our married man with two children would pay tax at 33% only on his taxable income of £3,455, or £1,140 on his £6,000 income, a tax rate of only 19%.

How have things changed? According to the Annual Survey of Hours and Earnings published by the Office for National Statistics, the median annual income for someone in full time employment in 2018 was some £28,500 p.a. The personal allowance in 2018 was £11,500, so the median wage earner would pay tax on £17,000. At a tax rate of 20% this would come to £3,400, some 12% of his gross pay for a single man. But the married man with two or three children would now find himself paying at the same rate with no allowances for his wife and children, unless he earned less than £16,105 p.a., in which case he could apply for child tax credits. If his wife was a non-taxpayer, she could transfer £1,250 of her unused allowance to her husband, which would increase his after tax income by just £250 p.a. But both would be paying considerably more in purchase taxes, and the wage earner's increased national insurance contributions. Moreover, many in full-time employment earned less than the median wage, and not everyone was in full-time employment. According to the Office for National Statistics, out of a total UK labour force of 32,597,000, only 24,035,000 were in full-time work. The remaining 8,562,000, rather more than one quarter of the whole, were part-timers. Some of these were very part-time indeed, working on 'zero hours' contracts, a condition unknown in 1979. This meant that they were on call for work, but only at the employers' discretion. No weekly hours were guaranteed. In 2017, 901,000 workers were 'employed' in this way. In 2018 this number fell to 844,000, but largely because employers, responding to the bad reputation of 'zero hours', had begun to change the name of this kind of work to 'short hours' contracts instead. This could mean as few as four hours a week, not a great improvement on the previous year's situation. We are reminded here of how the early factory owners circumvented the 1802 Health and Morals of Apprentices Act by simply calling their child workers 'free labourers' instead.

As for income tax rates in 2019-20, after a personal allowance of £12,500 each, tax was levied at 20% on the first £37,500 of taxable income (the 'basic rate'), a range that covered the average earner. At £37, 501 to £150,000 the rate was 40% (the 'higher rate'), and over £150,000 it was 45% (the 'additional rate'). The basic rate of 20% in 2019 was indeed lower than the 33% rate of 1979, but there were no longer the same marriage or child allowances in 2019. This meant that in 1979 lower earners who were family men had in fact not been paying a 33% rate on earnings over their personal allowances, nor even a 20% rate in most cases, but no one earning over £12,500 p.a. in 2019 could avoid paying the 20% rate on earnings over this amount. Moreover, we have to consider here National Insurance contributions as a deduction from incomes, for these were not negligible, and they rose appreciably between 1979 and 2019. In 1979 workers paid 6.5% of their gross incomes above £900 p.a., but this rate had risen to 12% on earnings over £8,424 p.a. by 2019. The corresponding employers' contribution went up from 11% to only 13.8% over the same time period, a much smaller proportionate increase than had been levied on employees. Of course, many people in the UK do not pay any income tax at all, and their numbers are increasing. According to the Institute for Fiscal Studies, 34.3% of the adult population fell into this category in the tax year 2007-8, and 43.8% in the tax year 2015-16. This was only partly due to increasing poverty, however. Many non-taxpayers were married women supported by their husbands, and many more were pensioners, whose numbers are increasing with a rising proportion of the aged in our population

We need also to consider here the question of indirect taxes. Value Added Tax or VAT was instituted in the UK on January 1, 1973 when the UK joined the European Economic Community. Previously, since the Second World War there had been purchase taxes in the UK, but these had been 'progressive' in that basic necessities had been low rated, and luxury items high rated. From 1973 to 1979 VAT had been levied at a standard rate of 8% with a 12.5% rate on petrol and some luxury goods. But in 1979 Margaret Thatcher 'harmonised' both rates at 15% to help pay for tax cuts for the rich, although some items such as most foods and children's clothing remained zero rated. In 1992 John Major's government raised the standard rate to 17.5%, and in January 2011 David Cameron raised the rate again to 20%. With a few exceptions, this rate applied to all goods *and services* purchased in the UK, whether they were 'luxuries' or not, and whether the purchasers could afford to pay income tax or not. This kind of tax would clearly be described by economists as 'regressive', because it had to be paid by everyone at the same rate regardless of their incomes. This tax bore more heavily on the low paid, who had to spend a higher proportion of their incomes, indeed often all of it, on purchases each month, while the rich would not. Moreover, there were no longer 'luxury taxes' on items that the rich were more likely to buy. Of course, the more the rich spent the more they paid, which has enabled some economists to argue that a flat rate VAT is in fact a 'progressive' tax after all! According to the Institute for Fiscal Studies, in 2016 indirect taxes, including VAT, national insurance contributions, duties of various sorts, import levies, etc. made up 44.5% of total UK government revenue. Additional duties above the VAT threshold were levied on beer, wine, spirits, cigarettes, and motor fuel. Again, these duties hit the poor harder than the rich. Meanwhile, income tax returned only 25.4% of all government revenue, and inheritance tax only 0.7%. These latter two would be described as 'progressive' taxes in that they were paid in proportion to the wealth of the taxpayer, while the consumption taxes would be described as 'regressive' in that they were 'flat' taxes, paid at the same rate by all, regardless of their incomes. It is easy to see where the emphasis lies here.

In addition, of course, house owners or those buying their homes with a mortgage had to pay council taxes to their local authorities. In 2016 council tax amounted to 4.2% of national taxation. Taken together, all government taxes meant that the total tax take amounted to some 37% of GDP in 2019, as opposed to the 34% level of 1979. The Institute for Fiscal Studies forecasts that government receipts will be 37.4% of national income in 2020-21. With the increase of VAT from 8% to 20%, a higher proportion of this will be in the form of indirect taxation, which is more of a burden on the lower paid and the young.

Corporation tax is a complicated business, with lower rates for smaller companies and some exemptions, but the trend here is clear. With the introduction of Advance Corporation Tax in 1973 it could be said that the 'headline' rate of tax on the profits of large companies peaked at 52%, but this rate was steadily reduced, to 35% in 1983, 28% in 2010, and 20% in 2015. The Institute for Fiscal Studies forecasts that this rate will be further reduced to 17% for the tax year 2020-21, the lowest rate amongst the G20 group of economically advanced nations. Despite this rate reduction, however, HMRC figures show that corporation tax receipts have risen from £28.5 billion in 2003 to £54.6 billion in 2017, owing to the increasing profitability of UK companies.

All those reductions in the top rates of income tax and corporation tax, the latter leaving more money available for large salaries and bonuses for board members and dividend pay outs to shareholders, while VAT rates have been raised, might make it appear that the tax system has become heavily biased against the poorer members of the community. But taxation is a complicated business. Because, under neoliberalism, the very rich have become so much richer than the rest of us so rapidly, it is still they who pay most of our income taxes. Remembering that in 2015-16 only 56.2% of the adult population of the

UK paid any income tax at all, within that percentage the top 1.2% of income tax payers (less than 1% of the whole population) accounted for 30.5% of total income tax liabilities in the tax year 2015-16. This is the figure provided by HMRC on their website *UK Income Tax Liabilities Statistics*,posted on May 25, 2018. The threshold of payment for the top tax rate of 45% (the 'additional rate') has remained fixed at incomes of £150,000 p.a. from 2012 to 2020 meaning that, with inflation and other factors, more are now paying at the 45% rate. In addition, personal allowances are gradually tapered off to zero on incomes over £100,000 p.a. HMRC estimates that this percentage, some 30% of all income taxes being paid by 1.2% of taxpayers, will be little changed by 2020, assuming that very rich people remain in this country. But this is not a foregone conclusion. The headline on *TheTimes* of London for March 7, 2019 read, 'British billionaires rush to world's top tax havens'. The story below explained that one third of British billionaires had moved abroad to tax havens over the previous ten years. What is the matter with these people? They are prepared to leave their homes, their country, and their wider families and move off to some remote jurisdiction, all in pursuit of something that they already possess in abundance, namely money. By so doing they erode the nation's tax base, and so rob us all, but especially the poor who depend upon state support. This immoral behaviour suggests that they have been crazed by greed. We need a new word in the English language to describe this condition. I would suggest 'pleonechosis', from the ancient Greek πλεουέκτης, which means 'greedy', 'selfish', or 'grasping'. Those who suffer from it should be described as 'pleonechotics'. These very rich people could easily afford to pay the taxes that they owe and still remain very rich. That story would seem to illustrate the futility of a 'race to the bottom' on corporation tax and the top rate of income tax. No matter how low you go, there will always be some small jurisdictions with lower expenses that will be able to undercut you.

More likely to stay in the UK are the next percentile down of income tax payers, those paying at the higher rate of 40%. These made up 14.5% of all taxpayers in 2016, and accounted for 37.1% of total tax liabilities. The remaining 84.3% of taxpayers, paying at the 20% rate over personal allowances, paid only 32.4% of all income tax receipts. This meant that the richest 15.7 % of taxpayers paid 67.6% of all income taxes in 2015-16. This makes the picture look rather fairer, but the 20% VAT rate still bears much more heavily on the poor than on the rich, as do the rises in National Insurance contributions for employees. The Conservatives have proved to be 'the low tax party' rather more for some then for others. It will be noted, however, that while Margaret Thatcher started the ball rolling on tax cuts for the better off paid for by purchase tax increases, her successors have out-Thatchered Thatcher, not hesitating to go further than Mrs. T. on both VAT rate rises and corporation tax cuts.

Next on Margaret Thatcher's list of priorities was the privatisation of state-owned industries, in the best neoliberal traditions. The Conservative manifesto of 1979 had not listed this as a major issue, promising only to 'sell back into private ownership the recently nationalised aerospace and shipbuilding concerns', but when in office the Tories also privatised the nuclear research company Amersham International, British Petroleum, and half of Cable and Wireless as well. After the Conservative election victories of 1983 and 1987 the programme was accelerated, with the privatisation of Associated British Ports in 1983, Jaguar in 1984, the Trustee Savings Bank in 1985 and British Gas in 1986, with Rolls-Royce, the British Airports Authority, and British Airways following in 1987. British Leyland was privatised between 1982 and 1988, and British Telecom between 1984 and 1993, with British Steel also privatised in 1988. The water companies of England and Wales were privatised in 1989, followed by all the electricity companies of England and Wales in 1990.

All this was radical enough, since the above list is far from complete, illustrating highlights only. By the time Margaret Thatcher left office in 1990 more than 40 UK state-owned businesses employing some 600,000 workers had been privatised. Over 60 billion pounds worth of state assets had been sold, and the share of the labour force working in nationalised industries had fallen from just under 10% to just under 2%. But the number of private shareholders in the UK had risen from about three million in 1979 to about twelve million by 1990, remaining at much the same level in 2015.

These were impressive achievements, but again Margaret Thatcher's successors did not hesitate to out-Thatcher Thatcher in this field as well. Scottish Power was privatised in 1991 and Northern Ireland Electricity in 1993, both against strenuous local opposition, with British Coal following in 1994. There then began the most ambitious privatisation scheme of all, with the whole of British Rail passing into private hands between 1994 and 1997. Even Thatcher herself had baulked at this prospect, calling it 'a step too far' and predicting that it would be 'our Waterloo' if the Tories were to attempt it, but the rail scheme was carried through, and between 2013 and 2015 even the Royal Mail was privatised, although it retained that name while in private hands. Piecemeal, several prisons too were contracted out, to be run by private companies. Between 1992 and 2017 fourteen prisons were contracted out to be managed in this way. Even an attempt to part-privatise the probation service was made, but in 2019 it was recognised that this had been a disastrous failure. By 2015 the great bulk of state assets had been sold off via 195 separate transactions.

The above institutions had been owned nationally by central government, but local government assets too passed into private hands during Margaret Thatcher's time in office, mainly in the form of the sale of council houses to sitting tenants. Thatcher had supported this idea from as early as 1964 when she had served as Conservative Spokesman on Housing and Land, and the Labour Party too had floated the idea in their manifesto for the 1959 general election, which they subsequently lost. Local councils had always been allowed to sell council houses to sitting tenants at their discretion, and some were already being sold in the 1970s: some 7,000 were sold to their tenants in 1970, and more than 45,000 in 1972. However, after Margaret Thatcher became Prime Minister in May, 1979, the Right to Buy was enshrined in statute under the Housing Act of October 1980. This Act opened the flood gates, with more than one million council houses being sold to their tenants by 1987. By 2017 some 1.5 million council homes had been sold to tenants, with home ownership rising from 55% of households in 1979 to 70.9% in 2003. However, there has since been a decline to only 62.6% in 2017. The homes sold in this way were a great bargain at an average discount of 44% off the going market price, with up to 70% off for council flats. However, the concomitant of this rise in private ownership was an even greater proportionate decline in the availability of social housing in the UK, which fell from nearly 6.5 million units in 1979 to roughly two million units in 2017. This had not been entirely due to the sale of council properties, but rather to the fact that local councils had ceased to be builders of council housing, and could no longer afford to rent private housing on any scale for needy people in their areas owing to increasingly severe cuts to their central government funding.

Those tenants who had bought their council homes at great discounts were the gainers from this policy, especially if they were able to hold on to their homes for a number of years. But as with share ownership, many sold out quickly to make a profit, and many of their homes were bought by buy-to-let landlords. A survey conducted by *The Guardian* (June 28, 2013) showed that one third of Right to Buy houses were then owned by private landlords. For London alone, the proportion was 36%, and here 52,000 homes were being rented by councils from Right to Buy landlords. A report published by the London Assembly in 2013 described the council house sales as ' incredibly poor value for money to taxpayers', noting that it had, 'helped to fuel the increase in the housing benefit bill, heaped more pressure on local authority waiting lists, and led to more Londoners being forced into the under-regulated private rented sector'. Some councils had bought back houses they had been forced to sell, at many times their original selling price.

The selling off of public assets was a shrewd political move from Thatcher's point of view. She reasoned that people who were home owners and share owners would be more likely to vote Conservative. In addition the government revenue from the sales enabled her to keep taxes down, and the newly privatised industries were a profitable source of investment for her wealthy supporters, who could afford to buy shares in them. However, industries like the utilities were natural monopolies, and after privatisation they had to find additional cash to pay for the very high salaries of board members, and dividends to shareholders. This meant that prices for consumers went up. Moreover, national assets could not be sold twice. Once they were gone they were gone, leaving the state with no assets to set against its rising national debt in future years.

A point that is often overlooked about all these privatisations is that a great deal of public land also passed into private ownership with the privatisation of industries like British Coal, the British Airports Authority, and the water companies. More followed as cash-strapped local authorities were forced to sell off council houses with their land, school playing fields, and public spaces in towns as their grants from central government were steadily reduced. The Swedish historian Brett Christophers (b. 1971), Professor of Social and Economic Geography at the University of Uppsala, has documented this transition in his recent book, '*The New Enclosure: The Appropriation of Public Land in Neoliberal Britain* (2018). He estimates that since 1979 10% of the land area of Britain, one half of all publicly held land, has been sold off into private hands. In financial terms, the value of all that land has been estimated by Christophers to be approximately £400 billion. If wisely spent, a sum of that magnitude could have paid for a lot of doctors, nurses, and hospitals. It might even have enabled the state to look after dementia patients properly, instead of forcing them to sell their homes to pay for their own care. We should remember, however, that the acquisition of public land had been very largely a twentieth-century phenomenon, resulting primarily from the requisitioning of private land by the state during the First and Second World Wars, for airfields, army camps, firing ranges, naval dockyards and the like. This was not, however, confiscation, since private owners received financial compensation for their loss. More land followed into public ownership with the nationalisation of many industries by the Labour government in the years following the Second World War. As with so much else, it seems that today's neoliberals would like to see a return to Victorian days as far as the public ownership of land is concerned.

Thatcher next turned her attention to the problems of the inflation rate and the trade unions, which in her mind were closely linked. For neoliberals, inflation was the great enemy that needed to be defeated, certainly a greater threat than rising unemployment. The 1970s with their two 'oil shocks' had seen the highest inflation rates since the First World War, with rises in the Retail Price Index peaking at 26% in 1975 and 21% in 1979, as prices and wages had chased each other upwards. Thatcher decided that the point at which this spiral should be broken was at the wages link, by curbing wages. This was not a new idea. The Labour Party too had been concerned about the problem of over-powerful unions and the question of how to keep inflation in check. In 1969 Barbara Castle (1910-2002), who was then Secretary of State for Employment and Productivity, had introduced a white paper entitled *In Place of Strife* which would have made ballots before strikes compulsory, and set up arbitration panels with legally binding powers. This plan was not adopted, but the Labour Prime Minister James Callaghan (1912-2005), who was in office from 1976 to 1979, had also tried to impose pay restraint, working with the Britain's trade unions to agree pay rises of 5% or less from 1976 to 1979. This policy had worked well, but following the 'Second Oil Shock' of 1978-9 and the surge in inflation rates, the unions refused to accept any further pay restraint, and resorted to widespread strike action in support of much higher wage claims. The result was the notorious 'Winter of Discontent' (1978-9) with numerous services disrupted, the dead left unburied, and rubbish piling up uncollected in the streets. In all 29,474,000 working days were lost, the highest number since the General Strike of 1926. The public was greatly inconvenienced, and the popularity of both the Labour Party and the trade unions plunged. Opinion polls had suggested that Callaghan could have won an election held in the Autumn of 1978, but in the Spring general election of 1979 he lost heavily to Margaret Thatcher and the Conservatives, leaving the Labour Party out of office until 1997.

Margaret Thatcher decided on a two-pronged strategy to curb the power of trade unions, using both legislation and confrontation to steadily whittle away union power. Her legislative programme was essentially embodied in seven Acts, the 1980 Employment Act, the 1982 Employment Act, the 1984 Trade Union Act, the 1986 Public Order Act, the 1988 Employment Act, the 1989 Employment Act, and the 1990 Employment Act. Thatcher wisely decided upon gradualism, taking a piece-by-piece approach towards breaking the power of the unions.

The first Act became law on August 1, 1980, relating mainly to picketing and the 'closed shop'. This latter applied to industries where membership of its trade union was compulsory for all who wished to work there. This law declared the closed shop to be illegal, unless 80% of its members voted for it. The government offered funds to pay for union ballots. 'Flying pickets' were also declared to be illegal. These were workers not in dispute with their own employer who gave picketing support to the striking workers of another employer. The number of pickets legally allowed to act was specified as six per dispute, but this law was widely ignored.

The 1982 Act came to be known as 'the Tebbitt Act' or 'Tebbitt's Law' because it was introduced by Norman Tebbitt (b. 1931) who was then Secretary of State for Employment. Tebbitt made it clear that its purpose was, 'to redress the imbalance of bargaining power to which the legislation of the last Government had contributed so significantly.' (Hansard, Feb. 8 1982, Col. 738) The legislation defined more closely what was to be regarded as a legal dispute, and made the unions liable to be sued for damages resulting from illegal action for the first time since the Trades Disputes Act of 1906. Many forms of industrial action, such as sit-ins, were now deemed to be illegal. Compensation of up to £250,000 could now be claimed from union funds. With the definition of a 'legal' strike being further tightened, employers were empowered to fire striking workers without facing unfair dismissal claims. Tebbitt boasted in his memoirs, 'I have no doubt that Act was my greatest achievement in government, and I believe it has been one of the principal pillars on which the Thatcher economic reforms have been built.' (*Upwardly Mobile* (1991) p. 233).

The 1984 Act made the re-election of union leaders by secret ballot every five years compulsory, with ballots on political funding to be held every ten years. Secret ballots were also made compulsory before any legal strike action could be taken, but a 55% majority for a strike remained sufficient. The 1986 Public Order Act imposed further restrictions on legal picketing, and the Acts of 1988, 1989, and 1990 simply reinforced and extended all the measures that had already been passed.

Armed with new legislative weapons, Margaret Thatcher then moved on to the second prong of her attack upon what she saw as excessive union power, which was confrontation. She chose as her first opponent the NUM, the National Union of Mineworkers, one of the largest and most powerful of Britain's trade unions. They owed their strength to the fact that most of Britain's electricity generating stations were coal-fired at that time, so that a coal strike could cut off electricity supplies, and paralyse the whole country. In 1972 and 1974 the NUM had organised strikes for higher wages, and on both occasions electricity supplies had been hit. In 1972 a state of emergency was declared from February 9 to 19, and voltage was reduced across the entire national grid. In 1974 it had proved necessary to introduce a three-day working week for most industries from January 1 to March 7 in order to conserve coal supplies and prevent total blackouts. Most of the coal industry was at that time nationalised, and so the miners were in negotiation with the government as their employer. On both occasions the government was defeated, and the miners got their pay rises. Again, in February 1981 the government announced plans to close 23 pits across the country, but was forced to back down by the threat of a national coal strike. From that moment, Margret Thatcher was determined that next time a strike was threatened, the government would be ready to deal with it. Following the successful conclusion of the Falklands war against Argentina in June, 1982, Thatcher was riding high on a wave of nationalistic popularity, and she felt sure that the country would be behind her.

The next major coalminers' strike began on March 6, 1984, and continued until March 3, 1985, but contrary to general belief it was not specifically provoked by Margaret Thatcher, and nor was it initially called by Arthur Scargill (b. 1938), the leader of the NUM. Rather, it began spontaneously with a walkout at Cortonwood Colliery in South Yorkshire as a protest against the proposed closure of the pit. Other pits in Yorkshire and Scotland then followed

Cortonwood's example, and it was only on March 12 that Scargill declared his support for the strikers in Yorkshire and Scotland, and called for supporting action from all NUM members, arguing that *all* pits would face closure sooner or later. He did not, however, hold a national ballot on strike action, which was a bad mistake. As a result, a High Court judgement of September 1984 ruled the strike to be illegal, encouraging some miners to return to work. The timing of the strike was also unfortunate for the NUM, beginning as it did in Spring when demand for electricity was falling off.

The closure of uneconomic pits had been going on since the 1960s, but it was predictable that this programme would sooner or later lead to a major strike by the miners. Most pits were uneconomic to run by 1984, and although specific figures on this point must always be questionable, one estimate has claimed that British coal was being produced at an average loss of £3.05 per tonne in 1984, with coal some 25% cheaper on the world market than the home produced product. The uneconomic nature of the pits would seem to be clear enough from figures like these, but the argument of Scargill and the miners was, 'Coal, not dole'. By this they meant that coal mines in many areas were the biggest employer by far, so that if the pits were closed there would be high levels of regional unemployment, throwing workers onto social security payments. The cost of these payments could amount to more than the coal subsidies.

Even if this had been true, however, the miners were on a hiding to nothing. Coal was a fuel whose time had passed, with a move increasingly towards gas, oil, and nuclear power stations as the means of electricity generation. From its peak in 1920 when coal mining had employed 1.2 million workers, by 1984 only 160,000 were still working in the industry. Moreover, in contrast to the somewhat reckless behaviour of Arthur Scargill, Margaret Thatcher had prepared her ground carefully, assiduously laying in reserve stocks of coal since February 1981, moving some power stations over to oil firing for their steam dynamos, preparing 'flying squads' of police to protect strike breakers from picketers, and fleets of lorries to transport coal around the country. As a result, there were no power cuts during the strike. The NUM was supposed to provide strike pay for its members, but its funds soon ran low, and many miners were forced back to work by poverty. The NUM had a federal structure, and in some areas, such as North Wales, South Derbyshire, and Leicester only about ten per cent of miners were striking by 1985. The result of all this was a total defeat for the NUM. On March 3, 1985 the strike was officially called off, and the miners were forced to return to work with virtually no guarantees against further pit closures. The exhausted NUM was never able to mount a national strike again, and pit closures proceeded apace both under Margaret Thatcher and her successors. By 2018 all the deep pits had been closed, and the industry employed only 2,000 workers on opencast mines. Such additional coal as was needed was imported from abroad. As Scargill had forecast, many mining communities were devastated by the loss of their pits, suffering high unemployment levels for years afterwards. But gradually, adjustments were made.

This monumental defeat proved to be a landmark not only for the coal mining industry, but for the whole UK trade union movement. It was followed in 1986 by the much-publicised Wapping dispute, a strike by print workers in London against Rupert Murdoch's News International group. This strike lasted for 54 weeks, making it longer than the miners' strike, but it too ended in total defeat for the strikers. In the wake of these two disputes, the UK trade union movement became totally demoralised, and trade union membership fell away. In 1979 there had been some 13 million trade unionists, but by 2012 numbers were down to 5.8 million, with only about one quarter of full-time workers belonging to a union. According to Gregor Gall writing in *The Guardian* for August 4, 2016, in 1979 29.5 million man-days had been lost to strikes in the UK, but in 2015 only 170,000 were lost in that way, a negligible number on a national scale. He went on to cite a TUC report which claimed that since 2007 UK workers' real wages had fallen by 10.4%, a worse fall than in any other of the 36 OECD countries except Greece. Figures from the Centre for Economic Performance, based at the LSE, showed that the UK, Greece, and Portugal were the only three OECD countries that had seen real wages fall over this 2007-2015 period. (Both available online).

Now it could be argued that in 1979 UK trade unions had been hair-triggered, Luddite, and too inclined to ignore the law of the land, so that they needed to be 'cleaned up' and put into better order. But it could also be argued that the ideal of the neoliberal Tories would have been a return to the Combination Acts of 1799 and 1800 which had bluntly declared all forms of trade union activity to be illegal, or at least a return to the Combinations of Workmen Act of 1825, which allowed trade unions, but severely restricted their activity. In effect, after the plethora of anti-union legislation passed by Thatcher and her successors, this was indeed the situation that had been returned to by 2015. This proves once again that 'neoliberalism' is in fact nothing more than old-fashioned nineteenth-century Toryism. For neoliberals, trade unions represented simply a 'distortion' of the labour market. Their ideal was the extreme of 'labour flexibility' with the 'gig economy' of zero hours contracts and short hours contracts. The 'self-employed' ruse was also very popular with some neoliberal employers such as Uber, the international taxi company. They insisted that their employees should declare themselves to be self-employed contract workers. This arrangement provided many advantages to Uber, since it meant that their drivers would be entirely responsible for making their own national insurance contributions and pension provisions. The drivers could not appeal to employment tribunals, since they were self-employed. They had no entitlement to holiday pay, sick pay, or even the national minimum wage, and of course they had no guarantee of working hours, and no security of employment. However, in a series of court cases around the world, this ruse was progressively ruled to be illegal.

The British government itself had done nothing to prevent this kind of exploitation of employees. The creed of neoliberalism was, 'every man for himself'. While the state had felt a duty to protect the physically weak from the physically strong, passing laws against robbery, assault, rape, etc., under neoliberalism it felt no duty to protect the economically weak from the economically strong. Individuals should look out for themselves. In an interview with Douglas Keay of *Woman's Own* magazine for September 23, 1987 Thatcher declared,

> I think we have gone through a period when too many children and people have been given to understand, 'I have a problem. It is the government's job to cope with it!' 'I am homeless: the government must house me!' and so they are casting their problems on society, and who is society? There is no such thing! There are individual men and women, and there are families and no government can do anything except through people, and people look to themselves first. (pp. 8-10)

There was little compassion to be detected in such a statement, but in addition to say, 'there is no such thing as society' was one of the most frankly stupid statements ever made by anybody. On the contrary, we humans have nothing *but* society: without it, we are utterly lost. Did you build your own house? Do you raise your own food? Did you manufacture your own car? Did you make your own clothes? Could you cure your own cancer? Of course not. All these things are provided for you by society, in return for the contribution that you made to society. We humans can achieve enormously more as a collective than any one of us ever could as an individual. More than the ants, more than the bees, more than the termites, more than a community of naked mole rats, we humans are the most social species on the planet! We are utterly dependent upon one another, and it is mutual co-operation, not mutual rivalry, that has made us what we are. But this is a point which the neoliberals appear to be incapable of understanding. True, there are some among us who, through age, handicap, or illness are more dependent than others, but these people are entitled to help from those of us who have been more fortunate.

However, there was little sympathy for the poor to be found in the Thatcher regime. Richard Dowden, writing in the *CatholicHerald* for December 22, 1978, quotes Thatcher as declaring that the poor are simply suffering from a 'personality defect'. Nor was there much sympathy for the unemployed. The regime's approach here was well represented by the person of Norman Tebbit (b. 1931) Mrs. Thatcher's faithful rottweiler, aka 'The Chingford skinhead'. In a speech to the Conservative Party Conference, delivered on October 15, 1981 just after his appointment as Secretary of State for Employment, Tebbit had this to say about the July riots in Handsworth and Brixton, areas of very high unemployment.

I grew up in the 1930s with an unemployed father. He didn't riot. He got on his bike and went out to look for work, and he kept looking until he found it. (Wikipedia entry on Tebbit)

Tebbit's father was lucky. Even if all the unemployed of the 1930s had 'got on their bikes' and spent all their time looking for work very few would have found any, because there were simply not enough jobs available for all those seeking them at the time. Economists call this 'structural unemployment', a very real phenomenon which the neoliberals would like to believe does not exist, because it is usually caused by corporate mismanagement, insufficient government regulation, and 'irrational exuberance' in the stock markets, leading to a general economic collapse. But neoliberals always prefer to blame the unemployed themselves for their unemployment.

Remarkably, although Thatcher had cautiously declined to go ahead with rail privatisation, she then plunged ahead with an even more daring policy that proved to be her downfall by instituting the so-called 'poll tax', although its official title was the Community Charge. This might be described as the ultimate in regressive taxation, since it was to be paid by all regardless of their income. It could also be described as a 'flat tax', although reductions were to be available for those living on benefits. The idea was to replace the existing rating system as a means of providing funding for local government services. Thatcher argued that since everyone received equal benefits from local services, everyone should pay an equal amount for them. The rates had always been heavily subsidised by grants from central government to pay for local services like education, the police, and highway maintenance, but domestic rates too had formed an important part of local government income. Based on property values, higher rates had been paid by the owners of larger properties, less by the owners of smaller ones, and usually none by tenants, especially tenants of cheaper properties. But under the poll tax everyone, including tenants, would pay the same tax for their local areas. This would mean great savings for large property owners, but a very considerable burden for most of the population.

The tax was rolled out in Scotland in 1989, and in England in 1990. The Duke of Westminster, who paid £10,000 p.a. in rates, would now pay only £400 p.a. in poll tax. However, Nicholas Ridley (1929-1993), who had inherited the title of Baron Ridley of Liddesdale and was serving as Secretary of State for the Environment in 1989, could see nothing wrong with that. In July 1989 he declared, 'The Duke of Westminster and his gardener will now pay the same in Community Charge. What could be fairer than that?' This was the authentic voice of neoliberalism. There had certainly been problems with the old rating system, but the Poll Tax was seen as yet another blatant attempt to 'make the poor pay', and to transfer wealth from the poor to the rich. There were mass refusals to pay, many were taken to court, and Tory ratings in the opinion polls plunged. Since the idea had been driven forward by Thatcher herself, her popularity too plunged within the Tory party. In November 1990 she narrowly survived a leadership challenge from Michael Heseltine, but completely lost the support of her cabinet. It was they who forced her resignation later in that month. The Poll Tax was abolished, and replaced by our present Community Charge, which very closely resembles the old rating system.

We see then that the policies of Thatcher and the neoliberals included tax reforms, with income tax cuts for the rich and corporation tax cuts for big business, coupled with higher purchase taxes and national insurance contributions, especially for employees, the selling off of state assets into private hands to the great advantage of the new owners, and the crushing of trade union power. There was, however, a fourth platform of neoliberalism which proved to be the most damaging of all. This involved the deregulation of financial markets. Under Margaret Thatcher, the biggest single step in this direction was the Financial Services Act of 1986. This took effect on October 27 of that year, a day dubbed by the London Stock Exchange as the 'Big Bang' because of the radical changes that it introduced into the London stock market.

Previously, there had been a requirement that stock jobbers and stock brokers should act independently, both of each other and of any wider financial group. Stock brokers acted as agents for their clients, while stock jobbers made the markets by buying and selling, theoretically providing liquidity by holding their own lines of stocks and shares on their books. In addition, foreigners were excluded from stock exchange membership. All this changed in 1986. Individuals were allowed to act as both brokers and jobbers, and banks themselves were allowed to trade in shares. Foreigners were admitted to the Exchange, and many old stock broking firms were taken over by large banks, both foreign and domestic. There had never been formal legislation in the UK to separate retail banking from merchant banking, unlike the situation in the USA, where the Glass-Steagall Act of 1933 had specifically banned retail banks from stock trading or merchant adventuring, but in the UK there had been simply a kind of gentlemen's understanding that retail banking was one thing, and merchant banking another. After the 'Big Bang' of 1986, however, the two functions began seamlessly to merge, placing retail bank deposits at risk. These changes were justified by the Thatcher government on the grounds that London banking had been in decline thanks to over-regulation and the dominance of elitist old boy networks. The solution lay in the introduction of 'light touch' regulation, and more competition to allow the rise of a meritocracy in the banking industry. This policy was accepted, and actually expanded upon, by the 'New Labour' government of Tony Blair and Gordon Brown, which was in office from 1997 to 2010.

That policy was to prove both reckless and foolish, opening the way to greedy and improvident speculation by the banks. Speaking on the Radio 4 programme *Analysis* ('A price worth paying?') on February 1, 2010, Nigel Lawson (b. 1932), who had been Tory Chancellor of the Exchequer from 1983 to 1989 and who had presided over the 'Big Bang', admitted that one of its unintended consequences had been the great global financial crash of 2007-9. He explained that UK merchant banks had previously been very cautious, since they were operating with their own money, but after merging with major retail banks, they were able to gamble with their depositors' savings as well as their own money. This not only greatly widened their scope, making them more 'competitive' on world markets, but also carried the added advantage of making them 'too big to fail' since now, if they went down, the whole retail banking system could be brought down with them, paralysing the country. The government would be forced to step in to save them, bailing them out with billions of pounds of public money. This is indeed what happened between 2007 and 2012, with the UK government putting many billions into a rescue package, mostly in the form of guarantees. In effect bankers' profits remained their own, but their losses were covered from the public purse.

Knowing that this would happen had made some banks more reckless and greedy with their speculative investments than others. Worst hit by the crisis was Northern Rock, formerly a building society, but from 1997 a bank with its headquarters at Newcastle upon Tyne. It had recently grown to be the fourth biggest bank in the UK by share of lending, but its 'assets' included financial instruments that were heavily dependent upon the American sub-prime mortgage market, and on high risk, unsecured credit card debts. In addition, the bank had borrowed on the international money markets to extend its lending. When these markets lost confidence in sub-prime mortgages, Northern Rock faced a severe liquidity crisis, and seemed in danger of collapse. This led to the first run on a British bank for 150 years, as depositors queued outside branches to take their money out of Northern Rock, in such numbers that the bank collapsed, again the first failure of a British bank due to a bank run for 150 years. The government was forced to nationalise the bank in 2008 to keep it in existence, but its branches and other retail operations were sold to the Virgin Group in 2012, and rebranded as Virgin Money. The merchant banking side, with its higher risk assets, was sold to Cerberus Capital Management in 2016, but the government lost billions of pounds by these transactions. Such was the inglorious end of Northern Rock, which had been in existence since 1850.

The only other major recipients of government money were Lloyds Bank and the Royal Bank of Scotland, which would certainly have failed without it, probably bringing other major banks down with them, but government intervention prevented this from happening. Other large banks, such as Barclays, HSBC, the Nationwide, and Standard Chartered were shaken, but managed to get by in various ways without further government support. The government was forced to buy shares in RBS and Lloyds which were later sold off at a loss. The net loss to taxpayers is disputed, but believed to be between one and two billion pounds on those transactions.

In part the crisis was caused by the fact that the banks had lent money to each other. Speaking at the annual conference of the Institute for New Economic Thinking, held at Bretton Woods on April 11, 2011, Gordon Brown (b. 1951) who was Chancellor of the Exchequer from 1997 to 2007, admitted,

> We know in retrospect what we missed. We set up the Financial Services Authority believing that the problem would come from the failure of an individual institution. So we created a monitoring system that was looking at individual institutions. That was the big mistake. We didn't understand how risk was spread across the system, we didn't understand the entanglements of different institutions with each other and we didn't understand, even although we talked about it, just how global things were, including a shadow banking system as well as a banking system. That was our mistake, but I'm afraid it was a mistake made by just about everybody who was in the regulatory business. (Minutes 44-6 of videoed speech by Gordon Brown under 'Crisis and Renewal – Bretton Woods 2011', available online)

The financial crisis, in conjunction with neoliberal economic policies which insisted on tax cutting, had a disastrous impact on UK national debt levels. In 2006 this debt had stood at £500 billion, but by 2011 it had reached one trillion pounds, and £1.5 trillion by 2016. In March 2019 the debt stood at £1.8 trillion, or 84.6 % of GDP, more than tripling since 2006. As noted above, other European countries, which had also suffered badly from the financial crisis of 2007-9, had also been left with very high levels of public debt. What was to be done? Clearly, there are different solutions to the problem. The French economist Thomas Piketty, in his celebrated book *Capital in the Twenty-First Century* (2013) declared,

> How can a public debt as large as today's European debt be significantly reduced? There are three main methods, which can be combined in various proportions: taxes on capital, inflation, and austerity. An exceptional tax on private capital is the most just and efficient solution. Failing that, inflation can play a useful role: historically, that is how most large public debts have been dealt with. The worst solution in terms of both justice and efficiency is a prolonged dose of austerity – yet that is the course Europe is currently following. (p. 541 of 2014 English translation)

His book is a massive tome, running to 655 pages with footnotes, but it is entirely devoted to adducing a great mass of evidence in support of one simple proposition, namely that the rate of return on capital will always exceed a country's rate of economic growth. This means that the capital-owning classes will steadily become richer and richer by comparison to the rest of the population. Left unchecked, this process will lead to inequalities of wealth so grotesque as to threaten the stability of society. It is up to the governments of individual countries to step up to the plate and fulfil their obvious duty to redistribute wealth among their citizens in one way or another. For let us be quite clear about what is meant by this term 'austerity'. It means austerity *for the poor only*. The rich remain totally unaffected by 'austerity'. They can afford to buy private education and private health for themselves, and they never become dependent on social services. Moreover, it is not only the rich who are unaffected: the comfortably-off middle classes also feel no pain, people like myself and all those who live around me on this estate (sorry, 'development of executive homes'). Nearly everyone here is retired, and we have our gold-plated pensions, our mortgage-free homes, our big cars and our private health insurance. It is especially the working poor and the young who suffer from cuts to public libraries, state schools, bus transport, the National Health Service, the police, and all the social support services needed by the poorer elderly and disabled. It is they and they alone who pay the price of 'austerity', although they played no part in bringing about the need for it.

Indeed, 'make the poor pay' would seem to be an unspoken mantra of the neoliberals. There are too many examples of this to be listed here, but let me mention just two of them. The first relates to solar panels on the roofs of private homes. Wealthier people could afford to have them installed, and so enjoyed a 'feed-in tariff' from the electricity companies, who paid them for the power that they produced, whether they themselves used that power or not. I have such panels myself. But of course, payments to panel owners put up the general price of electricity for everybody else, because the tariffs paid per unit produced by panels were well above the retail costs of units sold to the public, and they were index linked. Or let us consider the National Lottery. Who buys lottery tickets? Richard Branson? Phillip Green? Me? Of course not. It is primarily the poor, desperate to escape from their poverty, who spend money that they can ill afford each week in the hope of fabulous riches that almost none of them will ever see. However, their lottery money allows the government to play Lady Bountiful, handing out cash for the support of sports centres and village halls. But make no mistake, the money spent there is the money of the poor. They have been left to the mercy of pay day loan sharks like Wonga, who have found that 'there's money in poverty'. Make the poor pay.

'Austerity' clearly represents an attempt by governments to reduce their outgoings at the expense of the poor and needy as a means of reducing their massive debts. God help the poor when they become a minority in a plutocracy. But there is another way to decrease national debts, and that is through raising government income by increased taxation, especially taxation of the rich. However, it is not only the rich who could afford to pay more in taxes, but also us, the comfortably off middle classes. Personally, I would prefer to live in a country that is poorer, but fairer, even if this meant that I myself became poorer. I can afford to be, while many others cannot. However, we need to be careful here. It is of no use trying to tax the *money* of the rich, for they have access to a plethora of tax havens all around the world where they can secrete their surplus wealth away, safe from the tax man. [See N. Shaxson, *Treasure Islands* (2012) and G. Zucman, *The Hidden Wealth of Nations* (2015)]. Even their financial wealth which cannot be hidden is protected by a small army of clever lawyers and accountants who can drive a coach and horses through the tax laws, ensuring that their tax payable is minimised. At the moment, the richer you become, the lower a rate of tax you pay. The only solution is to tax *property*, in the form of land and buildings which cannot be hidden away. This is the old argument of Baruch Spinoza, Adam Smith, David Ricardo, Henry George, and even Milton Friedman. Such a tax should apply in particular to buildings and land in London, much of which is foreign owned. But in addition there is another unavoidable tax which the rich could be forced to pay, and this is a financial transactions tax. So many financial transactions are carried out by the City of London, before Brexit the world's greatest financial centre, that just a very small tax, say 0.1% on each transaction imposed upon institutions that are very rich indeed, could return very large revenues. It is only fair that the banks and other financial institutions that caused the great crisis of 2007-9, and who were then bailed out with public money, should be forced to pay for its consequences, instead of throwing this burden onto the poor. Our public services are in desperate need of additional funding.

Another means by which the rich and the very rich might be forced to make a more adequate contribution towards the maintenance of the state is by means of a revision to the UK inheritance laws. There can be few better examples of the need for such reforms than the case of Hugh Grosvenor, the seventh Duke of Westminster (b. 1991). On the death of his father Gerald, the sixth duke, on August 9, 2016, Hugh inherited an estate worth £9.3 billion, consisting mainly of property in London. He was just 25 years of age. By 2019 his fortune had grown to an estimated worth of £10.1 billion. Under our present inheritance laws, he should have paid inheritance tax on such a vast sum at a rate of 40%, which is of course far too high, encouraging the rich to make every effort to avoid paying any inheritance tax at all. At the moment this tax applies, with allowances to married couples, to all inheritances worth more than the tax-free threshold of £325,000, which today is too low. But how much did the young duke in fact pay? Not one penny. The family lands had been placed into a trust, which enabled the young duke to claim that he was not their 'owner' at all, but was simply holding them in trust for future generations. Of course, he could still enjoy the revenues from these lands for his lifetime, but could not sell them. Well, if you think about it, you will see that the enjoyment of our property for our lifetimes is all that any of us can hope for. The duke's London rents were so high that he had no need to sell any land to make ends meet. I would suggest that this obvious tax dodge should be made illegal, and that inheritance tax should be paid whether the property is in trust or not. However, it should be levied at a rate of only 10% on inheritances worth over one million pounds, and at only five per cent on inheritances worth between half a million and one million. I invoke the theory of the Laffer curve here. While the wealthy will move heaven and Earth to avoid an inheritance tax rate of 40%, I hope they would see 10% as being very fair, and not worth avoiding. There should be no inheritance tax on estates worth less than half a million pounds. All of these figures should be regularly revised to keep pace with inflation. But all these very fair, obvious, and necessary measures will not be implemented by the form of government that we have at the moment. Of course we must have free enterprise capitalism, and of course we must have inequality, but our present system needs to be attenuated. This problem will be addressed in the Conclusion below but for now, let us examine a one last case of neoliberalism in action.

Ronald Reagan (1911-2004) and American Neoliberalism

Ronald Reagan was born on February 6 in Tampico, a small town in northern Illinois, as the younger son of Nelle and Jack Reagan. Jack was a travelling salesman, and the family was quite poor, living in rented accommodation that was usually a small flat. After several moves the family eventually settled in nearby Dixon, a town on the Rock River, capital of Lee County Illinois. This was in 1920, when Ronald was just nine years old, and it was here that the family bought their first house, now carefully preserved as a memorial site. Reagan attended Dixon High School where he discovered his talents for acting, sports and, like his father who was of Irish descent, storytelling. In 1928 he moved on to nearby Eureka College, a liberal arts school, where he studied Economics and Sociology. He was no great scholar, graduating in June 1932 with a 'C' grade overall, but it was here that he developed his talents for acting, oratory, sport, and student politics, being elected Student Body President in 1931.He was a keen member of the college football team, and captain of the swimming team, with a part-time job working as a lifeguard at Lowell Park on the Rock River from 1927 to 1933.

Graduating in the depths of the Great Depression in 1932, Reagan was fortunate to find a job as a radio announcer, specialising in baseball commentaries for the Chicago Cubs. While travelling with the team in California in 1937, Reagan took a screen test that led to a seven-year contract with Warner Brothers studios, and his career as a movie actor was launched. He won successively larger parts, and by 1942 was earning $3,000 a week, a great sum for those times. However, Reagan had been a member of the Army Enlisted Reserve since 1937, and in 1942 he was called up for active duty. His poor eyesight excluded him from serving overseas, but Reagan applied for a transfer to the Army Air Forces, where he was able to play a useful role in making training films for aircraft pilots, rising to the rank of army captain.

After the war Reagan was released from service in December, 1945, and returned to film acting. Thanks to his oratorical skills and penchant for politics, he was elected as President of the Screen Actors Guild in 1947, and re-elected to that position each year until 1952. Reagan was a fervent anti-communist, but he disliked the witch hunting of the McCarthy era. Forced to testify to the Un-American Activities Committee in October, 1947 on Communist sympathisers in the film industry, he reminded his interrogators that, 'we should never compromise any of our democratic principles through fear or resentment'. This was a bold statement for Reagan to make in 1947, when America was in the grip of its 'Second Red Scare'. The 'First Red Scare' had followed the ending of the First World War and the emergence of Communism in Russia. Now, in 1947, the USA was entering its Cold War phase, with the Soviet Union seen as being the new enemy after the defeat of Fascism. 'Reds under beds' were sought everywhere, with the witch hunt led by the fanatically Right-wing senator Joseph McCarthy (1908-57), ably assisted by J. Edgar Hoover as head of the FBI from 1935 to 1972.

In 1954 Reagan moved to television when he was hired by the General Electric Company to host *General Electric Theatre*, a weekly TV drama series. This show ran until 1962, raising Reagan's national profile. In his final year with the show Reagan was paid $125,000, equivalent to roughly one million dollars in 2019 currency. In 1964-5 Reagan appeared as host and performer in the television series *Death Valley Days*, another highly paid role. It was the large sums that Reagan earned in those years that enabled him to retire from acting in 1965, and turn his attention entirely to politics.

In 1938 Reagan had co-starred in the film *Brother Rat* with actress Jane Wyman (1917-2007). He courted her, and they were married in January, 1940. They had one daughter, Maureen, and adopted a son, Michael but the marriage came under strain owing to the demands of Reagan's position as President of the Screen Actors Guild. In addition, Wyman was an ardent and registered Republican, while Reagan was still a Democrat at that time, and effectively a trade union leader for screen actors. Eventually they decided upon a divorce in 1949, although they remained as friends. Ironically, Reagan was to become an ardent Republican himself in later years, joining the Republican party in 1962. Just after his divorce in 1949 Reagan met actress Nancy Davis (1921-2016) whose name had appeared on Hollywood's Communist blacklist by mistake. She appealed to Reagan as President of the Screen Actors Guild, and he was able to establish that the Communist sympathiser had been another minor actress with the same name. The two became close, and married in March, 1952. They had two children, Patti (b. 1952) and Ronald Jr. (b. 1958). Their marriage was very successful, and lasted until Reagan's death in 2004.

During the 1950s Reagan found himself moving steadily to the Right in politics, supporting Eisenhower for President in 1952 and 1956, and Nixon in 1960. It should be noted, however, that by the standards of US politics today, Eisenhower and Nixon, nominally Republicans, would be seen as liberal Democrats. It was under Nixon that America's Medicare scheme was first mooted, a modest enough proposal that was to provide national health insurance, funded by a payroll tax, only for those over 65, and a few others with chronic illnesses. Even then it covered only half of their costs, so that they still needed to take out private health insurance in addition to obtain full cover. But even this was too much for Reagan. In 1961 in an address to the American Medical Association, he declared that the plan would, 'mean the end of freedom in America'. If the AMA did not oppose it, 'we will awake to find that we have *socialism*. And if you don't do this, and if I don't do it, one of these days you and I are going to spend our sunset years telling our children, and our children's children, what it was once like in America when men were free'. This sounded irrational and hysterical enough, but Reagan went further in 1964 with his support for the extreme Republican candidate in that year's presidential election campaign, Barry Goldwater. In his famous campaign speech, 'A Time for Choosing', Reagan declared,

> The Founding Fathers knew a government can't control the economy without controlling people. And they knew, when a government sets out to do that, it must use force and coercion to achieve its purpose. So we have come to a time for choosing...You and I are told we must choose between a left or right, but I suggest that there is no such thing as a left or right. There is only an up or down. Up to man's age-old dream – the maximum of individual freedom consistent with order – or down to the ant heap of totalitarianism...those who would trade our freedom for security have embarked on this downward course. (Available online)

What had happened to the old, Democratic Reagan, the trade union leader, the opposer of McCarthyism? It seems all too clear that he had fallen under the malign influence of the ideas of Friedrich Hayek. We see here the same confusion of socialism with communism, the same paranoid fear of the state, the same maniacal emphasis upon 'freedom'. In addition, Reagan's comments above could have been made only by a man who had recently accumulated a great deal of money for himself, and who knew that he personally would be financially secure for life. It is always easy enough for such a man to rate 'freedom' above security. In the 1960s he went on to oppose the Democrats' Food Stamp Programme, the raising of the minimum wage, and the establishment of the Peace Corps. He became a climate change sceptic, on the grounds that nature produced more greenhouse gases than humanity. He also joined the National Rifle Association, becoming a lifetime member. In later years he went on to make many scathing remarks about the federal government, even after he had become the head of it, such as, 'Government is not the answer to our problems: government *is* the problem!' and 'Government is like a baby: an alimentary canal with a big appetite at one end and no sense of responsibility at the other'. He was also fond of quoting Milton Friedman's quip, 'If you put the federal government in charge of the Sahara desert, in five years' time there would be a shortage of sand.' Ludicrous as these observations are, they represent a good reflection of the neoliberal mentality.

Playing on his celebrity as a national TV star, Reagan next decided upon forging a political career for himself, announcing in 1965 that he would run for election as Governor of California. He won the election in 1966, and served as Governor of California from 1967 to 1975. Extremely ambitious, he also campaigned for nomination in the 1968 presidential campaign as the Republican candidate, but lost the nomination to Richard Nixon, who subsequently served as President from 1969 to 1974. As Governor of California Reagan promised to 'send the welfare bums back to work' and 'clear up the mess at Berkeley'. This latter referred to student demonstrations at the Berkeley campus of the University of California. The 1960s were a time of student protest in America, both against the Vietnam War and, after 1967, against the Israeli treatment of the Palestinians following their victory in the Six Day War of that year. On May 15, 1969 during a demonstration on the People's Park at Berkley, Reagan sent in the California Highway Patrol and other officers to quell the protest. This resulted in a riot situation which came to be known as 'Bloody Thursday'. One student was killed, and a carpenter who had joined the demonstration was blinded. 111 police officers were injured, one seriously. Reagan then called out 2,200 National Guard state troopers who occupied the city of Berkley for 17 days, preventing any further demonstrations. Questioned about campus protest one year after 'Bloody Thursday' Reagan declared, 'If it takes a bloodbath, let's get it over with. No more appeasement'. (L. Cannon, *Governor Reagan: His Rise to Power* (2003) p. 295) Dear me – could this be the state using, 'force and coercion to achieve its purpose'? Surely that was something only nasty 'socialist' states did? Whatever had happened to good old, all-American freedom? Behind the genial smile and the folksy quips lurked the mind of a ruthless neoliberal.

Two other issues on which Reagan also displayed a confusion of principles were those of abortion and divorce. When Reagan had been governor for only four months, the California state legislature sent up a bill for his signature, the 'Therapeutic Abortion Act'. This liberalised the state abortion law by allowing for the well-being of the mother, including her mental well-being, to be taken into account. Reagan was instinctively against abortion, but he reluctantly signed the bill into law on June 14. As a result some two million abortions were carried out in California during Reagan's lifetime, and he came to bitterly regret his decision to sign the bill, campaigning strenuously against abortion for the rest of his political career. Neoliberalism had always laid great stress on freedom of choice for the individual, but evidently not in this case, proving once again that neoliberalism is simply Victorian Conservatism writ large. Reagan's tender concern for human life did not extend to the death penalty, for example, which he strongly supported throughout his career, another example of a Victorian mindset.

On divorce, Reagan signed into Californian law the Family Law Act in 1969. This was to become the first 'no fault' divorce legislation in the United

States, making divorce easier in the state of California. This was another decision which Reagan later came to bitterly regret, campaigning against divorce later in his career, even although he was divorced himself. On issues such as these, Reagan's religious faith played a major part. His father had been a Roman Catholic of Irish descent, but his mother had been an enthusiastic evangelical, a member of The Disciples of Christ church, and a supporter of the Social Gospel Movement, which advocated social reforms in 1930s America. His mother was the stronger influence upon him, and Reagan came down on the evangelical side, joining The Disciples of Christ in 1922, and declaring himself to be a 'born again' Christian. He was at first sympathetic to the idea of social reforms, joining the Democratic Party, but later changed his mind on those issues as well.

Reagan was re-elected as Governor of California in 1970, but did not seek a third term in 1974, concentrating instead upon his presidential ambitions. In 1976 he again campaigned for the Republican presidential nomination, but lost out on that occasion to the sitting President, Gerald Ford (1913-2006). However, Ford lost the election of 1977 to the Democrat Jimmy Carter (b. 1924). This gave Reagan his chance, and in 1980 he at last won the Republican nomination to run for President against Jimmy Carter. Reagan won that election, running on a platform of lower taxes to stimulate the economy, smaller government, states' rights, and a strong national defence.

Ronald Reagan was in office from January 20 1981 to January 20 1989, overlapping with Margaret Thatcher's term as Britain's Prime Minister, and their policies too were quite similar. The parallel to Thatcher's handling of the coal miners' strike of 1984-5 was Reagan's handling of the strike by PATCO, the Professional Air Traffic Controllers Organisation, which was attempted in August, 1981. As with the coal miners, the demands of the strikers here were somewhat unrealistic. 12,645 controllers sought a total pay rise of $600 million over three years, coupled with a cut in their working week to only 32 hours over four days. Again, like the coal miners, they overestimated the strength of their position. While the UK had moved to the Left after World War II, electing a Labour government, in the USA the opposite had happened. Following the 'socialism' of the New Deal and heavy state control of the economy during that war, America had lurched back to the Right as soon as peace had been restored, seeking a return to 'traditional' American values. After the war wages fell and unemployment increased, leading to the most widespread wave of strikes in American labour history during 1945 and 1946. The response of a Republican-controlled Congress was to pass the Labour Management Relations Act on June 23, 1947, mustering a two-thirds majority in both houses to override an attempted veto by President Truman. This amended the National Labour Relations Act of 1935, which had guaranteed the rights of workers to form unions and to take strike action. The 1947 legislation is better known as the Taft-Hartley Act, after the two congressmen who had sponsored it. At one fell swoop this Act had introduced all of the anti-union legislation that it had taken Margaret Thatcher years to build up, effectively emasculating US trade unions. In addition union leaders were required to file sworn affidavits declaring that they were not supporters of the Communist Party, and federal employees were prohibited from striking altogether.

Thanks to the Taft-Hartley Act, Reagan had no need for additional legislation to deal with PATCO – his weapons lay ready to hand. The traffic controllers were acting in clear breach of the law, gambling on the fact that they would be very difficult to replace, and that the Taft-Hartley Act was a kind of nuclear option, that no President would dare to use. But they had underestimated Reagan. Within hours of the union declaring its strike on August 3, 1981 the President appeared on national television to condemn their action as illegal, quoting the 'solemn oath' sworn by all the controllers as federal employees, not to go on strike. He then declared that they had 48 hours to return to work, or they would all be sacked. Only 1,300 controllers did so, and on August 5 Reagan fired the 11, 345 controllers who had remained on strike, and banned them from federal service for life. Using the non-strikers, air traffic supervisors who had a separate union, military personnel, and partly trained operators, the government was initially able to keep 50% of national flights available, and stepped up the training of new controllers. As more trainees qualified the situation steadily improved, but it took almost ten years for complete normality to be restored. America paid a price for Reagan's victory, but as with the UK miners' strike, his success was pivotal. If PATCO could be defeated, there was no union that could not be defeated. David Schultz in his *Encyclopedia of Public Administration and Public Policy* (2004) declared that the firing of the PATCO strikers had 'sent a clear message to the private sector that unions no longer needed to be feared.' (p. 359) America had been made safe for employers.

Another favourite policy of neoliberals like Thatcher and Reagan was of course tax cuts for the rich. Reagan wasted no time here, passing the Economic Recovery Tax Act in August, 1981, which cut the top rate of income tax from 70% to 50% over three years. By the same Act Reagan also cut the maximum capital gains tax to 20%. The lowest income tax rate of 14% was also cut to 11%. Later, the Tax Reform Act of 1986 cut the top rate further to only 28%, and raised the lowest bracket from 11% to 15%, but with the expansion of tax reliefs. The top rate of income tax in the U.S. had peaked at 92% in 1952, but this had been only on incomes of over $3.77 million p.a. in terms of 2018 dollars. Thereafter the top rate had declined steadily to reach 70% in 1971, but starting at the lower threshold of $1.24 million in 2018 terms. Reagan's 1981 cut lowered the threshold to $222,000, and by 1988 his 28% rate was being paid by all those earning over $63,000 p.a. This meant that his top rate of tax was now being paid by people who could be described as middle class, since some 25% of the population earned more than this. However, this threshold was steadily raised again to $430,000 in 2013 in terms of 2018 dollars, which confined the top rate to only one per cent of individual income earners in 2017. Moreover, by 2013 the top rate had been raised again to 40%.

Reagan trumpeted his credentials as a tax-cutting President, but for the great majority of the U.S. population this ploy was all smoke and mirrors. What Reagan gave with one hand, he took away with the other. In fact he imposed tax increases of one kind or another in every year from 1981 to 1987 to make up for his giveaways to the rich. Just one of these new impositions, the Tax Equity and Fiscal Responsibility Act of September 1982, has been described by official sources as, 'the largest peacetime tax increase in American history'. Average federal income tax revenues over Reagan's two terms amounted to 18.2% of GDP as compared to a national average rate of 18.1% over the period 1970-2010. By comparison with other OECD countries this seems like a low percentage, but U.S. citizens had also to pay state and local taxes. The important point is that the only permanent gainers from Reagan's tax cuts were the rich and the very rich. Reagan also cut the top rate of inheritance tax from 75% to 55%. After World War II the top rate of federal taxation had never fallen below 70%: from 1950 to 1964 it had averaged 90%. After Reagan's reforms, it never rose above 40%. (Piketty (2014) pp. 499, 503) Despite this, U.S. governments took an ever-larger share of GDP in tax. By 2015 this proportion had reached 27.1%, with the poorer classes now bearing a larger share of the burden, mainly through increased consumption taxes and insurance contributions, according to OECD figures. This was still a low national rate, but Americans also had to pay state and municipal taxes. The comparable national figures for the UK and Denmark were 34.4% and 50.8% respectively in 2015. However, we must remember that figures like these are very difficult to compile, and are more reliable in relative rather than absolute terms.

Like most neoliberals, Reagan was much more worried about inflation than about unemployment, because inflation reduced the value of all that money held by his very rich supporters. To that end, Reagan ordered an investigation into the establishing of some kind of gold standard in the US to defend the value of the dollar, although this came to nothing. By the end of his term Reagan had brought the inflation rate down to 4.4%, but the unemployment rate had averaged 7.5% during his time in office. Also in the best neoliberal traditions, Reagan cut the budgets of programs designed to help the poor, such as Medicaid, food stamps, federal education programmes, and the Environmental Protection Agency. He froze the minimum wage at $3.35 an hour, slashed federal assistance to local governments by 60%, cut the budget for public housing and rent subsidies in half, and cancelled the antipoverty Community Development Block Grant programme. All of these welfare cuts helped to finance his tax cuts for the rich at the expense of the poor. But there was one area of public expenditure that Reagan did expand, and this was the defence budget, which was increased by 40% during his presidency. Owing to this heavy expenditure and his tax cuts, the US national debt under Reagan rose from $997 billion to $2.85 trillion, almost tripling. So what? That was posterity's problem, and how many votes did posterity have? Neoliberalism preached fiscal probity, but it has in fact delivered frighteningly high levels of public debt across Europe and North America. It also at first trumpeted the values of free and fair competition, but is now changing its tune to argue that there is something to be said for monopolies after all, as explained above. One is reminded here of how the slogans parroted in *Animal Farm* changed from, 'Four legs good, two legs bad' to 'Four legs good, two legs better'.

Enough has been said by now to convey the flavour of 'Reaganomics' a cult all too typical of neoliberalism. At its heart lay the theory of 'supply-side' or 'top-down' economics, which held that tax cuts for the rich and big corporations would promote investment, and so increase production and employment, providing benefits for all. This was 'trickle down' theory, which argued that benefits for the rich would 'trickle down' to provide wealth for the poor as well. The idea harked back to Say's law of 1803, mentioned above, which held that increased production would create its own demand. This 'law' had been debunked clearly enough by the Great Depression of the 1930's, which had shown that supply could easily exceed demand, leading to deflation and unemployment. But this was a lesson that neoliberals chose to ignore. They needed some excuse to make tax cuts for the rich and benefit cuts for the poor, and 'supply-side' economic theory provided it. In reality of course, 'supply-side' economics is simply an absurd idea. No manufacturer is going to invest in production before he can be sure that there will be a demand for the goods that he will produce. Both economic growth and economic recovery must begin with assured demand. Supply will not increase its own demand, but demand will increase its own supply. That is why the policies of John Maynard Keynes and FDR were so successful at pulling America out of the Great Depression, and would have been more successful still if political factors had allowed FDR to take them further.

The converse of 'supply-side' economics is of course 'demand-side' economics, the finding of ways to increase the prosperity of the masses by ensuring full employment, through government investment if necessary, preferably on schemes to develop a more productive infrastructure. Generous benefits for the poor can also contribute to this end. Such were the conditions during the *trente glorieuses* in Europe and America, when all classes of society grew wealthier together, as explained above. But progressively, under neoliberalism, nearly all the fruits of economic growth become channelled into the pockets of the wealthiest ten per cent of society, with most of that going to the wealthiest one per cent. The policies that Reagan set in train led the French economist Thomas Piketty to fear for the future of the US, as he foresaw the rise of a plutocratic oligarchy in that nation. He wrote,

The history of progressive taxation over the course of the twentieth century suggests that the risk of a drift towards oligarchy is real, and gives little reason for optimism about where the United States is headed. It was war that gave rise to progressive taxation, not the natural consequences of universal suffrage. The experience of France during la Belle Epoque [1871-1914] proves, if proof were needed, that no hypocrisy is too great when economic and financial elites are obliged to defend their interests – and that includes economists, who currently occupy an enviable place in the US income hierarchy. Some economists have an unfortunate tendency to defend their own private interests while implausibly claiming to champion the general interest...it also seems that US politicians of both parties are much wealthier than their European counterparts and in a totally different category from the average American, which might explain why they too tend to confuse their own private interest with the general interest. Without a radical shock, it seems very likely that the current situation will persist for quite some time. The egalitarian, pioneering ideal has faded into oblivion, and the New World may be on the verge of becoming the Old Europe of the twenty-first century's globalised economy. (op. cit. p. 514)

Ronald Reagan must bear a heavy burden of responsibility for the introduction of neoliberal policies into the US economy, but once he had opened the way, as was the case with Thatcher, his successors did not hesitate to out-Reagan Reagan after seeing what he had been able to get away with. The evil that men do lives after them. One of the pillars of neoliberal belief is the idea that all forms of state control and regulation serve only to stifle economic growth, and are best disposed of. One of the most disastrous aspects of this creed proved to be banking deregulation. This trend had already begun in 1980 with the Depository Institutions Deregulation and Monetary Control Act, which served to deregulate commercial banking. Further deregulation came in 1987 when banks were allowed to underwrite corporate debt and equity. Next came the Riegle-Neal Interstate Banking and Branch Efficiency Act of 1994, and finally, following the lead given by Thatcher's 'Big Bang' of October, 1986, the Gramm-Leach-Bliley Act of 1999 was passed by Congress, which repealed most of the Glass-Steagall Act of 1933 and the Bank Holding Act of 1956, both of which had served to sever investment or merchant banking from commercial, deposit banking. From 1999 onwards, a bank could now offer commercial banking, securities, and insurance services under one roof. Ominously, this therefore enabled them to use the current accounts of their depositors for speculative investment purposes.

It did not take long for the new, multipurpose banks to begin to invent extremely complicated financial instruments to take advantage of their new status. These included the introduction of hedge funds, and the use of derivatives such as credit default swaps and collateralised debt obligations. Without trying to explain the complexity of these instruments, suffice to say that they served to confuse everyone in the finance industry, even those who had invented them. They enabled banks to 'slice and dice' a number of different investment products up into separate packages for sale to investors, packages that were of such complexity that nobody really understood the implications of their contents. Too late, it was discovered that many included a range of 'toxic assets', to such an extent as to undermine the integrity of the entire package. Chief among these toxic assets were stakes in the US sub-prime mortgage market. Desperate to exploit their new freedoms, US banks began to make ever-riskier loans in attempts to expand their portfolios for what they hoped would be larger profits. But sub-prime mortgages were a step too far. These were loans granted to persons not previously considered to be credit worthy, on the assumption that if they defaulted on repayments, their homes could be seized and sold. This new policy expanded the demand for houses, pushing up their nominal value, and making such loans look to be advantageous. However, it gradually became clear that most of those sub-prime borrowers were in fact incapable of keeping up their mortgage repayments, and they began to abandon their homes, often simply pushing their keys into banks' night deposit boxes and walking away, leaving the banks with their homes to sell. The banks came to dread the sound of 'jingle mail'. Suddenly, there was a surplus of houses for sale, and house prices plummeted to levels below the value of the mortgages that had been granted. Cheap homes in America were timber-framed and planking-clad, with tar shingle roofing, and if abandoned, they quickly fell into disrepair, reducing their value further. They became 'toxic assets', on which the banks could only lose money.

The sub-prime mortgage fiasco was the worst example of reckless lending by US banks in their greedy quest for ever-larger profits, but they were not the only 'toxic assets' to be found in the new investment packages, again the fruits of reckless lending by the banks. Moreover, having created these new securities, the next profit-making opportunity spotted by US investment banks was the idea of selling their packages abroad, mainly to banks in Europe and Asia, where they were eagerly snapped up. The assumption was that the US government and its regulators were keeping a close eye on their banks, curbing any reckless behaviour. Unfortunately, the very opposite was true: US regulators had been asleep at the wheel. Not only had the US government and the Federal Reserve been lifting regulations for years, but they had also been pressing their regulators to go easy even on those few controls that remained. In effect, they had been allowing the banks to do more or less what they liked, and what the banks liked was taking higher risks in the hope of making larger profits.

With the regulators virtually nullified, it fell to private ratings agencies like Moody's or Standard & Poor's to assess the risks inherent in the new investment packages. But the agencies tended towards a Pavlovian reaction whenever they saw the term 'mortgages', associating it with high security. In addition, the banks that were asking the agencies to rate their products were the very people paying for the ratings! If their products were rated too harshly, the banks threatened to take their business elsewhere. The result of all this was that the agencies rated nearly all of the 'mortgage-backed' new packages as AAA, indicating that they were as close to risk free as possible. This of course helped with their sale abroad. In this way the world's banks invested in each other, lent to each other, and borrowed from each other, becoming highly interdependent. If just a few of the larger banks were to fail, they could bring down their closest partners, setting off a chain reaction which could destroy the entire world's financial system. This is what very nearly happened in the great financial crisis of 2007-9, when major banks like Lehman Brothers and Bear Stearns in America, together with UK banks like Northern Rock, the Royal Bank of Scotland, and even Lloyds, found that they were facing collapse. Lehman Brothers, the fourth-largest investment bank in the US, was in fact allowed to fail, but the others were saved by massive bailouts from public funds, lest the contagion should spread around the world. This was done, however, only at the expense of heavy government borrowing in Europe and North America, leading to the very high levels of national debt mentioned above. In the UK national debt as a percentage of GDP rose from 41.2% to 76.3% between 2007 and 2010, while in the US federal debt as a percentage of GDP rose from 62% to 90% over the same period. Meanwhile, the bankers who had caused the crisis kept their jobs, their salaries, and their bonuses. The price of their folly and greed was to be paid by others.

Most worrying of all, insufficient measures were taken after the crisis to ensure that it could never happen again. The banks were ordered to lay in larger reserves, but to date, this does not seem to have happened. Incredibly, the Glass-Steagall Act of 1933, repealed in 1999, was not reinstated in the US, and no measures were taken in the UK either to separate commercial from investment banking. This meant that in both countries the banks could continue to use the current accounts of their depositors for speculative purposes. In addition, they remained 'too big to fail', lest the failure of just a few large banks brought the whole world's financial system crashing down with them, leaving depositors to discover that even their current accounts had evaporated. Moreover, the same high levels of public and private debt remain, now even larger than before the 2007-9 crisis. We are today entirely dependent upon the discretion of the banks, who are being trusted not to engage in the same kind of reckless speculations as those which caused the last crisis. Even America's Dodd-Frank Act of 2010, designed to restore some safeguards, was largely repealed by Donald Trump in 2018.

So far we have been lucky, but I have noted that in this life a phenomenon applies which I call 'the declension of morality'. The cheat or the thief begins in a small way, and finds that he has got away with it. This encourages him to greater crimes, and so on by small degrees, until at last he is taking such inordinate risks that he is caught, still failing to realise just how far down the road to depravity he has travelled. I fear that this same principle may apply to bankers and their investments over time. So far, they have behaved themselves, but for how much longer? After every crisis, governments and bankers assume that they have learned their lesson, and that a crisis like the last will never occur again because, 'this time is different'. However, in a very detailed study published in 2009 Reinhart and Rogoff argue powerfully that 'this time is never different' because the same fundamentals always apply, and that the next crisis is always waiting in the wings. Today, instead of their dependence upon sub-prime mortgages, our banks are highly dependent upon promises to pay made to each other. They therefore resemble a number of dominoes stood on end and arranged in a circle. I would say that the wobbling domino today is the Banca d'Italia, but I could be wrong.

On line, the Wikipedia entry on 'Financial Regulation' includes a very revealing graph drawn up by its authors which shows the number of banking crises experienced by 70 countries between the years 1800 to 2000. Although this is the authors' own version, they point out its similarity to the graph which appears as Figure 10.1 in the 2009 book by Carmen Reinhart and Kenneth Rogoff, *This Time is Different: Eight Centuries of Financial Folly*, which draws upon the experiences of 66 countries over these years. In my 2011 edition of that book, this graph appears on p. 156. Both graphs show a significant absence of any banking crises anywhere in the world between 1945 and 1971, the years during which the Bretton Woods system was in operation, in marked contrast to the periods both before and after that time. Reinhart and Rogoff put this down to the reduced mobility of international capital during this period, which is certainly a valid point, but in my view there were other explanations as well. These included the facts that,

(a) The banks were properly regulated.
(b) Investment banking was separated from commercial banking.
(c) The rich were properly taxed.
(d) Large corporations felt a sense of responsibility to society as a whole, including their duty to pay taxes.
(e) The greed genie was still firmly in the bottle.

Unfortunately, none of these provisos any longer applies. The last point is the most worrying of all, because once the greed genie is out of the bottle, it will prove to be extremely difficult to push it back in again. Even Alex Proud, Economics Correspondent of the *Daily Telegraph,* which is hardly a left-wing publication, wrote in that paper on May 4, 2015 with reference to *The Sunday Times Rich List*,

> Rather than a cheeky gawp into the hidden world of the wealthy, it now feels like an uncritical celebration of how bloody brilliant it is to have tons of money...Every day is an uncritical celebration of wealth. In modern Britain being rich is everything. It's the only thing. And it's becoming almost impossible to opt out of this ghastly money-go-round. The Rich Listers are over 100 per cent better off than they were ten years ago, this despite most of the decade being taken up by the worst recession since the 1930s. By contrast, the average Briton is only as well off as they were before the

financial crisis: by some measures **they may be worse off.** (Original bold type) 'Inequality is Ruining Britain – So Why Aren't We Talking About It More?'(Available online)

Moreover, the greed of the greedy knows no bounds: the greedy man never has enough. Let us once again call to mind that now highly relevant observation from the past, 'He that loveth silver shall not be satisfied with silver, nor he that loveth abundance with increase: this also is vanity.' (Ecclesiastes 5:10) This is reflected in the ever-rising levels of pay and bonuses voted to themselves by board members, and in the size (and number) of super yachts owned by very wealthy individuals like Sir Phillip Green.

Neoliberalism: the Tally

The first thing to be noted about neoliberalism is the scale of its failures on a number of fronts. Neoliberalism promised us faster economic growth, which was only to be expected from their more 'efficient' system. But in fact, as has been clearly shown by N.F.R. Crafts and Joseph Stiglitz mentioned above, rates of economic growth in Europe and the USA have actually slowed as neoliberal economic policies have been brought in. Growth rates were distinctly higher within the social market economies of the *trente glorieuses*.

In the same way, neoliberals at first trumpeted the merits of free and fair competition in open markets as the best road to efficiency. Even Milton Friedman acknowledged that one of the few duties of governments was to step in to prevent the rise of monopolies. But under today's neoliberalism, we see nothing being done to prevent more and more corporate and banking mergers, while monopoly-seeking retail giants like Amazon and Sports Direct threaten the survival of our high streets. Once a monopoly has been established, however, the simplest demand/supply curve graph will show how the monopolist can squeeze out higher profits by restricting supply levels, much as OPEC did during the 1970's. But today's neoliberals now applaud the rise of monopolies as a reward for 'efficiency': another broken promise of neoliberalism.

We should also remember the spurious neoliberal slogan, 'A rising tide raises all boats'. The argument was that by allowing the rich to get richer faster we would stimulate economic growth, and so there would be a 'trickle-down effect' to the poorer members of society, thus benefitting all. But as we have seen, their doctrine has in fact raised some boats much higher than others, while 'trickle down' has proved to be more of a 'Niagara up'. Median real wages in North America have virtually stagnated since the 1970s, showing little if any rise, while both the incomes and the wealth of the richest ten per cent, and especially of the richest one per cent, have greatly increased. The scale of this development has been best illustrated in Thomas Piketty's monumental work, *Capital in the Twenty-First Century* (2013), where he shows clearly that the rate of return on capital will always exceed the overall rate of national economic growth. Therefore, those with capital to invest will rapidly become richer than those who have no such surplus. If governments refuse to step in to redistribute wealth down the social scale, then these disparities will continue to increase until they reach grotesque proportions. But governments wedded to neoliberal thought will be very reluctant to do this: another failure of neoliberalism.

The Pew Research centre published a very revealing study on the movement of real wage levels in the USA in 2018 (available online). They found that average (not median) hourly wage rates in the US had risen steadily from 1949 to 1972, when they stood at $4.80 per hour. By 2018 this figure had risen to $22.65 per hour. But after allowing for inflation in the meanwhile and in terms of constant 2018 dollars, the real wage level had peaked at $24.04 in 1972, fallen to $19.95 in 1995, and risen again to only $22.65 in 2018. What they found was a virtual stagnation of real wage levels in the USA from the late 1960s to the present day. Phillip Larkin would ask, 'Why aren't they screaming?' In real terms, American wage earners were no better off in 2018 than they had been 50 years ago, over the very period during which neoliberal thought was rising to prominence. Meanwhile, in constant dollar terms, the GDP of the USA had risen from $1.9 trillion in 1970 to $19.39 trillion in 2015, according to World Bank figures, a ten-fold increase, while the population had risen from 203 millions in 1970 to 325 millions in 2017, less than doubling. Clearly, average wealth per head should have risen by more than five-fold, so why did wage earners become no better off over this period? Why had the 'rising tide' not raised their boats? The answer is, of course, that US neoliberalism has channelled all the fruits of economic growth into the pockets of the rich and the better off. The Congressional Budget Office of the USA published a report in 2013 which showed that, since 1989 the share of national wealth held by the richest 10% had increased from 30% to an incredible 73%, while the share of wealth held by the poorer 50% of the population had remained the same at one per cent or less (available online). Even allowing, as always, for substantial margins of error in statistics such as these, again the trend is clear. Here in the UK we have not suffered so badly, with real wages roughly doubling from 1980 to 2020, although median wage levels have seen a sharp decline since 2008. Meanwhile, our GNP over the last 40 years has grown by approximately 140%, according to figures from our Office for National Statistics. (Available online)

While neoliberals were prepared to admit that their policies might lead to growing material inequalities and increasing environmental pollution in the short term, the 'faster' rate of GDP growth that neoliberalism would provide would eventually level out these inequalities by making everybody richer. By the same token, rising environmental pollution would also solve itself because richer societies would be better able to deal with the problem. They illustrated their case by introducing us to the so-called 'Kuznets curve'. This was the brain child of Simon Kuznets (1901-1985) who was born into a Lithuanian-Jewish family, but who emigrated to the USA in 1922, where he made a career for himself as an economist. From 1927 to 1961 he worked at the National Bureau of Economic Research, and from 1961 until his retirement in 1970 Kuznets taught Economics at Harvard university. He specialised in analysing long-term swings in economic history, and in the above two cases his Kuznets curve resembled the Laffer curve, taking the form of an inverted 'U' with an extended base. This represented levels of inequality and pollution first of all increasing, but then slowing and diminishing again over time. These were fine ideas, but history has proved his curves to be just another neoliberal misconception. The evidence to date shows that the 'Niagara up' to the rich is simply gathering pace, leaving most of us little better off. In fact the poor have become worse off, as neoliberal theology has dismantled and diminished the welfare state, displaying no feelings for the poor other than contempt. In the same way pollution levels, on a world scale, have shown no signs of diminishing, nor even of levelling off. The truth is that unless governments step in to do something about it, there will be no curve at the top of these Kuznets curves: they will simply continue to rise indefinitely. The envisaged 'Kuznets curves' have proved to be just another error of neoliberal economic thought.

Then we should also remember the insistence of early neoliberals upon fiscal probity, an eminently sensible idea. 'There is no such thing as a free lunch' was one of Milton Friedman's favourite quotations. Ronald Reagan quipped, 'The trouble with governments is that they always run out of other people's money', while Margaret Thatcher, speaking to the annual conference of Conservative Trade Unionists in November, 1980, declared, 'It is neither moral nor responsible for a government to spend beyond the nation's means, even for services which may be desirable. So we must curb public spending to amounts that can be financed by taxation at tolerable levels and borrowing at reasonable rates of interest'. But today we see national debts at record levels in North America and Europe, partly because of the financial crisis caused by neoliberalism, but also because neoliberal governments everywhere always decide to borrow more rather than impose higher taxes on their very rich supporters. This represents a disgraceful display of irresponsibility towards future generations, and another failure of neoliberalism. Governments should spend no more each year than they can raise in taxation: the desirability of living within your means is too obvious a point to need emphasis. Today in fact we should institute a sinking fund, dedicated solely to the steady reduction of the national debt. Harking back to Burke's idea of an intergenerational social contract, this should be seen as a moral duty that we owe to posterity. But this would mean higher taxes for the rich.

Neoliberalism also invited us to trust in market rationality, better known as 'the efficient markets hypothesis'. Guided entirely by price levels, we were told that markets could never get things wrong, and should just be trusted to get on with the job, hampered by as few government regulations as possible. The high priest of this doctrine was Eugene Fama (b. 1939) as argued in his two books *The Theory of Finance* (1972) and *Foundations of Finance* (1976). He was supported by Robert Lucas (b. 1937) in such works as *Studies in Business-Cycle Theory* (1981) where he put forward his conception of 'rational expectations'. Both men were 'Chicago boys', needless to say. The counterattack against their views was led by Robert Shiller (b. 1946), Sterling Professor of Economics at Yale University, in such books as *Irrational Exuberance* (2000), updated in 2005, *The New Financial Order* (2003) and, with George Akerlof, *Phishing for Phools: The Economics of Manipulation and Deception* (2015). Fama and Shiller were jointly awarded the Nobel Memorial Prize in Economic 'Science' in 2013. Now the vagaries of Nobel Prize committees have already been commented on in relation to the cases of Einstein and Millikan, Hayek and Myrdel, Karl Popper, and Bertrand Russell, but here they surely hit a new low. Those two economists had flatly contradicted one another, with Fama arguing that unregulated markets were rational and trustworthy, and Schiller arguing the exact opposite. Quite clearly, only one of them could be right, in which case the other must have been talking absolute nonsense. In no way could *both* men deserve the prize for their 'genius'. However, such were the abilities of the Nobel Economics Committee that they found the arguments of both men to be entirely convincing, and so they could see only one way out of their dilemma. But surely, they could at least have decided to honour each man in a separate year, rather than admit to their crass incapability. Unlike the committee, I have no difficulty in drawing a distinction here. The man who was right was obviously Shiller. I am astonished to see that anyone could retain their faith in unregulated markets after the fiasco of 2007-9. 'Irrational exuberance' sums up the case very well.

Finally, the globalisation of world trade and finance has of course played straight into the hands of neoliberal multinational corporations and international financiers, at the expense of large sections of society in both the developed and the developing world. How this has come about is fully explained by Joseph Stiglitz in his two books *Globalisation and Its Discontents* (2002) and *Globalisation and Its Discontents Revisited* (2017). Here he points out that globalisation could have been managed in such a way as to bring benefits to all, but that, sadly, it has not been. He writes,

> Even with the rules of globalisation that were far from ideal, globalisation could have been managed better, especially by the advanced countries. It could have been managed in ways that would have prevented large segments of the population from suffering from the effects of globalisation – ways which simultaneously could have led to more growth, stability, and equality. Most of the advanced countries (including the United States) did not do so – and for much the same reasons that the rules of globalisation had been originally 'distorted'. Corporate interests that had shaped globalisation in a way which led to lower wages were not interested in 'correcting' this

problem: they liked the lower wages, and they disliked the taxes that would have to be imposed to prevent workers from suffering significant income losses...the corporate forces that have created a globalisation that works for them, but not for the rest, are not going to easily and willingly give up their power. (Globalisation Revisited, p. xxii)

We see therefore than neoliberalism stands condemned as a failure on all counts, morally bankrupt, utterly discredited, shot to pieces by its critics, and yet still the zombie walks, like some hideous, lurching monster out of a horror film. While they remain in control of our governments, our plutocratic masters will never allow neoliberalism to die, because it is so hugely advantageous to themselves to keep it alive. Despite all of its manifest failures, yet still governments in North America and Europe in particular cling to neoliberal economic policies. 'There is no alternative', said Margaret Thatcher. Neoliberal globalisation is 'a force of nature' said Bill Clinton.

But of course, there *is* an alternative. It is the re-introduction of the social market system that worked so well for everyone between 1945 and 1975, a time when the prosperity of all was increasing at equal rates. Capitalism can in fact adopt many different forms, as has been well illustrated by Charles Hampden-Turner and Fons Trompenaars in their book, *The Seven Cultures of Capitalism* (1994). Today, the pendulum has simply swung too far to the Right, and a corrective is badly needed. Yes, of course we must have free enterprise capitalism, and of course we must therefore accept a measure of inequality, but at the moment we also need more state intervention, more regulations, more sense of our social responsibilities to one another, and higher taxes for the more affluent elements in our societies. Every successful economy must have a free enterprise capitalist system at its core, but capitalism alone is not enough: the state must also play its part. Completely unregulated capitalism is only too likely to lead to disaster, as we have recently seen.

But of course, neoliberal governments will never introduce the measures suggested above, and we have to ask ourselves why not. Perhaps we could begin by asking, 'Well, who benefits from neoliberalism?' The answer to this question is clear – it is the rich and the very rich. Could it be that they are dictating economic policies to our governments? It would certainly appear that we live today in a kind of bandit state, where the rich are robbing the poor, the old are robbing the young, and this generation is robbing the next, by piling up huge levels of public debt for it to repay. Politicians of every stripe always find it easier to borrow more rather than tax, pushing the bill on to posterity, so that they can look good for the moment. Why not? They will be out of office in a few years time, and the debt will be somebody else's problem. But now that we have heard what Hayek and Friedman, the high priests of neoliberalism, have had to say, and have seen what Pinochet, Thatcher, and Reagan have actually done, we are in a position to draw up,

The Credo of the Neoliberals/Plutocrats

1.) Down with the state, and down with the EU. States tax and regulate. Only 'little people' and 'losers' pay taxes (Leona Helmsley, 1989) and regulations stifle business enterprise. Deregulate the financial markets. Give us FREEDOM. 'I wish the anarchists luck'. (Milton Friedman, 1973) 'We have not successfully rolled back the frontiers of the state in Britain only to see them re-imposed at a European level'. (Margaret Thatcher, 1988)

2.) Down with democracy. 'I prefer a liberal dictator to a democratic government lacking liberalism.' (Friedrich Hayak, 1981) Genuinely democratic states would never allow us to get away with all the tax dodging that we do, and might even expect us to contribute towards helping the poor and supporting the nation's infrastructure. We certainly don't want that: the present arrangement suits us fine.

3.) Public enterprise bad, private enterprise good – so privatise everything, even natural monopolies like the public utilities, even the Post Office, even the prisons – and the railways, of course. This will push up prices for consumers, but guarantee nice fat payouts to shareholders and board members. Make the poor pay.

4.) The duty of private companies is only to make profits. They have no other responsibilities whatsoever. Never mind the environment, the workers, or the national tax base, and never mind the future. We want profits *now!* (Milton Friedman, 1974)

5.) Smash the trade unions: they interfere with 'labour flexibility'. Zero hours contracts and the 'self-employed' wheeze suit us just fine. Keep wages down for fatter profits. Make the poor pay. Down with security of employment and company pensions – there's no profit in pensions!

6.) Everyone knows that rich people need to be paid more to make them work harder, but poor people need to be paid less to make them work harder. So tax cuts and pay rises for board members, but social security cuts for the poor. Let them eat from food banks. Force the 'disabled' into work. Make the poor pay: they don't deserve anything better: they are just 'welfare bums'. (Ronald Reagan, 1968)

7.) 'There is no such thing as "society": there are only individuals'. (M. Thatcher, 1987) We owe no duty of care to one another whatsoever. It's every man for himself, and devil take the hindmost. We are all in competition with each other, and if you are not a winner then you are a 'loser'. It's the war of all against all. If you are poor or unemployed then that is *your* fault, and you must be made to *feel* that it is entirely your fault, you sad loser. 'Collectivism' is always evil.

8.) Greed is good: risk is good: inequality is good, and ought to be guaranteed, to provide everyone with an incentive to work. Back to the nineteenth century!

9.) Globalisation is just great. It gives us a plethora of secretive tax havens all around the world for us to hide our money in, no questions asked. It also forces governments into a race to the bottom to win our favours, with ever-larger cuts to corporation tax and top rates of income tax. It enables us to blackmail them all with threats to leave their countries unless they play ball with us.

10.) Closely assess all employees at regular intervals to keep them up to the mark. Give them quotas to fulfil, and targets to reach. Those who fall short must be ruthlessly sacked. Efficiency is more important than humanity. We don't care about people: we worship money. The price mechanism is the only measure that matters: if something has no price, it has no value. (Milton Friedman, 1980)

11.) The government's annual spending deficit and the national debt should *never* be reduced by imposing higher taxes on those who can best afford to pay them, i.e. us. Instead of increasing government *revenue* to reduce the deficit, we will see to it that government *expenditure* must always be reduced on things like the social security budget. Vital public services like the health service, the police, and education should also have their funding cut, together with municipal facilities like libraries and museums. Make the poor pay.

12.) The poor deserve nothing but contempt. 'Poverty is indicative of a personality defect'. (M. Thatcher, 1978) Any relief afforded to them should be kept down to a minimum, and they should be forced to grovel even for this subsistence. People who work for low wages to help others, like nurses, teachers, and social workers, are just mugs and fools. They don't realise that money is the only thing that matters. They're not smart like us. When the country runs into financial trouble, the first recourse should be to freeze their wages. We will ensure that our fettered governments always follow this course.

13.) Climate change? Ha! We'll be all right Jack for our lifetimes. We want to make money *now*!

All this, of course, has done the mental health of most of us no good at all, as shown by Matt Haig in his *Notes on a Nervous Planet* (2018). There is no kindness to be detected in neoliberalism, no sympathy, and no mercy. It is hard to imagine a creed better designed to ensure the greatest happiness of the smallest number, and the greatest misery of the largest number. It is a very brutal and self-interested creed indeed. The picture it paints of humankind as mere *homo economicus* is an oversimplification, a caricature, indeed a travesty of the complicated truth. The above 13 points read like a satire, but unfortunately they are simply true. By citing what Hayek and Friedman have said, and what Pinochet, Thatcher, and Reagan have actually done as shown above, the true nature of this creed has been proved beyond any reasonable doubt. It has become abundantly clear that the future of our planet is *not* safe in neoliberal hands, because neoliberals will always put profits ahead of environmental concerns. Moreover, by driving the poor to despair, it has increased the incidences of crime, alcoholism, drug addiction, homelessness, mental illness, and even dementia on both sides of the Atlantic, while at the same time denying society the adequate resources needed to deal with those social problems that neoliberalism has created. I would therefore like to propose here,

A Counter-Creed to Neoliberalism

(a) Humanitarianism should always trump ideology. People are more important than principles. They should not be sacrificed on the altar of adherence to a rigid economic creed, especially when that creed becomes clearly discredited because it is obviously not working, having broken all of its promises and failed on every count.

(b) People are more important than money. Governments should pursue policies that are genuinely in the public interest, not those most likely to attract party funding from rich donors. Rather than a GDP index, we need a GHI (General Happiness Index) or perhaps, more realistically, an LMI (Least Misery Index), as Karl Popper suggested.

(c) Those who have lent money can afford to lose it far better than those who have borrowed it can afford to pay it back. For every reckless, imprudent borrower, there has been a greedy, imprudent lender. Why should the borrower alone be expected to bear all of the resulting suffering arising from this mutual folly? The Greek debt, for example, can never be repaid, and should be forgiven.

(d) Mass unemployment is NOT a price well worth paying to keep inflation in check. The maintenance of full employment should be the prime aim of every government's policy.

(e) Humanity is more important than efficiency. We need more state intervention, higher taxes, more economic regulations, and more controls towards the achieving of that principle.

(f) It is very important to have an efficiently run economy, but it is even more important to have an efficiently run society that provides adequately for all of its members. To achieve this it will be necessary to prise just a small proportion of their vast wealth out of the greedy paws of the rich by imposing higher taxation upon them. A land tax, a property tax, and a very small financial transactions tax, together with an inescapable inheritance tax at 10% for all inheritances of over £1 million could achieve this end. Make the plutocrats pay. But these desirable measures can be brought in only after some political reforms have been made.

(g) Economic sustainability is more important than economic growth, and should be the target to be aimed for. Endless compound economic growth clearly cannot be sustained. Economic growth in the developed world should no more than keep pace with population growth, and ideally population growth itself should be curbed, aiming for population stability. I have been acutely aware of this from an early age. After my wife and I had produced two healthy children, I had myself sterilised. It is time that our obsession with GDP growth, which fails to measure any of the things that really matter, was replaced by a determination to build a fairer and happier society for us all through a measure of redistribution, together with a renewed concern for the environment.

Neoliberalism is a clear enough case of a wealth grab by the rich, thinly disguised under the tattered cloak of a failed and utterly discredited economic philosophy. However, I am a historian and not a polemicist, so my first and only allegiance must be to the quest for truth, the whole truth, and nothing but the truth. What I have said above seems to me to be undeniable, just the plain, unvarnished truth about neoliberalism, proven beyond a reasonable doubt. This creed has made a substantial net contribution to human misery. But on the other hand, is there anything good to be said about it? This side of things should also be considered.

Economics is a very complicated business, so much so that even the darkest of its creeds may have some merits. The attitude of the neoliberal plutocrats towards the poor is inexcusable, as is their determination to pay little or nothing in taxation to support the society that has done so well by them. But in other respects it could be argued that rule by plutocrats is not so bad – there have been many worse regimes. The plutocrats say, 'Just give us all the money and all the political power so that we can be sure of keeping all the money, and that will be fine with us. In return we will give you FREEDOM to manage as best you can on whatever resources you can muster after we have helped ourselves to our grotesquely disproportionate share. There will be no midnight arrests, no military crackdowns, no torture, no arbitrary imprisonment: we can rule without any of those. You can vote for whatever party you like, and it won't make any difference to us: we will simply buy your existing governments with our large-scale private funding, or blackmail them with threats to leave their countries to get what we want. We believe in crony capitalism, always holding open the revolving door to a well paid, low effort post-retirement job for those politicians who will play ball with us. Money is the only thing that matters to us, so what we want of course is fat government contracts, lower taxes for ourselves, and the ready availability of secretive tax havens all around the world, so that we can avoid paying even the lower taxes that are asked of us. At the moment we are doing very nicely for all three, thank you very much.

Freedom of speech and of the press will be guaranteed. You can say what you like. It won't do you any good, because our money will always talk louder than your words, but you will be free to say them: and we own most of the press and other media anyway. As a cosmetic exercise, we will even pretend to speak up for fair play ourselves sometimes. And you can continue to enjoy the illusion of living in a democracy: we will be very careful not to undermine *that* myth! Ignorance is our friend: so long as you 'little people' don't realise how badly we are ripping you off, you can live on in delusional happiness, or at least accept that your poverty is entirely your own fault. Freedom of religion too will be guaranteed – anything that distracts people from thinking about economics and politics, or believing that other things are more important, is really great for us. Take a healthy dose of the 'opium of the people', and imagine that everything is just fine – it sure is for us! This means that we don't want to rock the boat: the status quo suits us admirably. That means that we want to avoid physical warfare. Class warfare is OK, since we're winning that one hands down, but physical warfare disrupts international trade, brings insecurities, and forces governments to tax us under emergency measures. So you can always count on us to steer our fettered governments away from at least major wars, although there is sometimes a profit to be made out of minor ones, especially if oil is involved. Neoliberals are the party of peace and (usually) non-intervention!'

It could be further argued that by keeping the masses poorer, neoliberalism has choked back demand, slowed the rate of economic growth, kept inflation in check, and also contributed to birth rate decline in the developed world. This much seems obvious from all the available statistics. But is that such a bad thing? Do we really need faster economic growth, or endless economic growth? Surely, for the good of the planet, economic sustainability is of far greater importance than economic growth. As far as the Developed World is concerned, we are already more than rich enough to provide adequately for all of our people, even if we were to move to zero growth tomorrow. Our failure to provide for them has been a political failure and an ideological failure arising from neoliberalism, not an economic failure: almost the Irish Famine case revisited. *Prosperity Without Growth* is a book first published in 2009 by Tim Jackson, Professor of Sustainable Development at the University of Surrey, although my own copy is the second, enlarged edition of 2017. In this edition Jackson declares,

> This narrow pursuit of growth represents a horrible distortion of the common good and a misrepresentation of our underlying human values. It also undermines the legitimate role of government. A state framed narrowly as the protector of market freedom in the unbounded pursuit of consumerism bears no relation to any meaningful vision of social contract. At the end of the day the state is society's commitment device par excellence, and the principle agent in protecting our shared prosperity. A new vision of governance that embraces this role is crucial. (p. 199)

This theme of aiming for economic sustainability and a more equitable distribution of income has recently been taken up by the Oxford economist Kate Raworth in her book, *Doughnut Economics: Seven Ways to Think Like a 21st-Century Economist* (2018). Ideally, we should put a stop to economic growth in the Developed World and leave all future growth to the Emerging Economies, which are in much more desperate need of it than we are.

But for the moment, there can be no doubt that the remedy for our present social and economic ills can lie only in the political sphere. Something must be done to break the stranglehold which plutocrats currently exercise over our governments, and to restore genuine democracies once more. Only when we have achieved political reforms will it be possible to proceed to the necessary economic reforms of our present system. These should consist of imposing higher taxes on the rich, who can very easily afford to pay them, by the means suggested above, which include a tightening up of inheritance laws. In addition, a sinking fund should be set up, dedicated entirely to a steady reduction of the national debt. The immorality of continually pushing debt on to future generations should end. Well-meaning economists and investigative journalists everywhere have already done all that they can to expose the evils of neoliberalism, but our fettered governments refuse to listen to them. It must therefore now be the turn of political thinkers to step in with some suggested solutions to our current ills. That will be the main thrust of the Conclusion to this volume.

Finally of course, 2020 will go down in the annals of history as a second *Journal of the Plague Year.* In that year, with its desperate 'lockdowns', the pandemic corona virus Covid-19 has had us on the ropes. In 2021 we struck back with an effective vaccination programme, but Covid 19, with its many variants, remains far from conquered, and it may become an endemic seasonal infection like flu, that we will simply have to live with. But the prolonged 'lockdowns' which it has necessitated will have a devastating effect on our economy, massively increasing the national debt and the budget deficit, and calling the survival of many enterprises into question. Our new relationship with the EU will add to our economic problems. How will our Tory government deal with this? It is to be hoped that they will not 'double down' on 'austerity', once again throwing the whole burden onto the backs of the poor. As noted above, it is high time that the rich were obliged to pay their fair share of taxation, via the means suggested above. Perhaps our government's hand will at last be forced on this issue. But there are some who argue that massive public borrowing or quantitative easing is nothing to worry about, even at the levels that will be required by the Covid 19 crisis. They crusade under the banner of 'modern monetary theory', (MMT) which is fully explained in the works by Mosler (2013) and Kelton (2020) listed in the bibliography of this book. I cannot entirely agree with their arguments, but the American economist Stephanie Kelton in her book *The Deficit Myth* (2020) does make some good points. For example, she notes,

> Whenever the topic of Social Security comes up, or when someone in Congress wants to put more money into education or health care, there's a lot of talk about how everything must be 'paid for' to avoid adding to the federal deficit. But have you noticed that this never seems to be a problem when it comes to expanding the defence budget, bailing out banks, or giving huge tax breaks to the wealthiest Americans, even when these measures significantly raise the deficit? As long as the votes are there, the federal government can always fund its priorities. That's how it works. Deficits didn't stop Franklin Delano Roosevelt from implementing the New Deal in the 1930s. They didn't dissuade John F. Kennedy from landing a man on the moon. And they never once stopped Congress from going to war. (p. 4)

Kelton might have added at this point, 'Neither did it deter the UK from establishing the National Health Service and a welfare state in 1948, despite being deeply in debt after World War II'. Further on, making light of deficits and the national debt she declares,

> The real crises that we're facing have nothing to do with the federal deficit or entitlements. The fact that 21 per cent of children in the United States live in poverty – that's a crisis. The fact that our infrastructure is graded at a D+ is a crisis. The fact that inequality today stands at levels last seen during America's Gilded Age [1870-1900] is a crisis. The fact that 44 million Americans are saddled with $1.7 trillion in student loan debt is a crisis. And the fact that we ultimately won't be able to 'afford' anything at all if we end up exacerbating climate change and destroying the life on this planet is perhaps the biggest crisis of them all. These are real crises. The national deficit is not a crisis. (pp. 11-12)

Theresa May famously said, 'There is no magic money tree', and Kelton quotes Margaret Thatcher as saying, 'We know that there is no such thing as public money: there is only taxpayer money'. But Kelton challenges the veracity of both of those statements, writing of Thatcher's declaration,

> Was it an innocent mistake or a carefully crafted statement designed to discourage the British people from demanding more from their government? I'm not sure. Regardless of her motives, Thatcher's remarks concealed the currency-issuing power of the state. (p. 20)

In fact there *is* a 'magic money tree'. It is the Bank of England in the UK, and the Federal Reserve in the USA, both of which can print and distribute as much money as they like. The only constraints on this process are inflationary pressures, which in turn are dependent upon the strength, or rather the potential strength, of the real economy. If this can be stimulated to produce more goods and services by quantitative easing to match the increased money supply, there will be no inflation. During the Great Depression of the 1930s and again after 2008 there was massive quantitative easing on both sides of the Atlantic, but no disastrous inflation resulted. No sovereign nation with the ability to print its own money as a fiat currency can ever go bankrupt, and that created money well spent can produce good returns in times of depression, without pushing up inflation rates. Indeed, during severe depressions, such as that of the 1930s, there is a danger of *deflation* setting in. It is *the real economy* that matters, and the real economy that must be sustained. This was the argument of John Maynard Keynes, and as a good Keynesian myself I can only applaud our Prime Minister's announced intention to 'build, build, build' our way out of the depression that will almost certainly follow in the wake of Covid 19. We desperately need improvements to our infrastructure, and his announced plans will provide jobs for the unemployed. But history has taught us that depression recovery programmes are usually underfunded. They help, but not enough. We saw that in the 1930s, and again after the collapse of 2007-9, when the banks and the bankers were saved with public money, but not the many millions on both sides of the Atlantic who lost their jobs and homes. Following his announcement of a $787 billion relief programme, President Obama proposed a further $75 billion package to help struggling mortgage payers to keep their homes, but ran into fierce Right-wing opposition. On February 19, 2009 CNBC reporter Rick Santelli, interviewed at the Chicago Mercantile Exchange, demanded a referendum 'to see if we really want to subsidise the losers' mortgages', rather than, 'rewarding people that can actually carry the water instead of drink the water... do you want to pay for some loser who had an extra bathroom put into his house, and now can't pay his mortgage? We're thinking of having a Chicago Tea Party in July'. His interview 'went viral', and the Tea Party Movement was born. (Rapley, op. cit. pp. 381-2) The danger we face today is that once again government relief measures will help, but will be insufficient to deal with the full aftermath of the Covid 19 crisis. History so often repeats itself. Governments seem to lack the courage needed to make full use of their monetary powers in times of crisis. If the political will is there, then the money is always there too. Carefully managed, especially in periods of depression, quantitative easing can be entirely beneficial, and will not lead to inflation, provided that it produces more goods and services to balance the increased money supply. All that is required is the courage to make full use of the 'magic money tree' to save those businesses that were viable before Covid 19, and to institute new, sensible projects providing goods and services that are in demand, to counter high unemployment. The very worst response to depression is to raise taxes for the masses, since they are the mass consumers. This will merely choke back demand and slow the recovery. Higher taxes should be imposed only *after* the recovery has taken place, as Keynes recommended.

In her book *The Deficit Myth* (2020) Stephanie Kelton devotes chapter 7, 'The Deficits That Matter' (pp. 191- 228) to a detailed and heart-rending exposé of the devastation wrought upon the majority of Americans by their government's adherence to neoliberal policies. Among other points she writes about pension arrangements in the USA,

> In 1975 nine out of ten workers in private companies had a defined benefit pension plan. These pensions were often the result of labour negotiations, before unions lost bargaining power. By 2005, that number had dropped to one in three (p. 170). 77 percent of Americans do not have adequate retirement savings for their age and income level. In June, 2019, one in five people over the age of 65 were still working, if not actively searching for a job. Another 2019 poll from the Associated Press-NORC Centre for Public Affairs Research found that nearly one quarter of Americans expect to never retire at all. (pp. 200-201)

The really frightening possibility is that the USA of today could be the UK of tomorrow, if present trends continue. If you read only two economics books in your life, make one of them Kelton's book, and the other John Rapley's *Twilight of the Money Gods* (2017). Both are written in good, plain English. If they whet your appetite for more information, as they certainly should, then read the books by Joseph Stiglitz listed on the Bibliography below. These volumes speak more eloquently of our present dilemma that I have been able to do here with the limited space available to me.

Conclusion

What then, can we conclude from the above reviews of philosophy, politics, and economics? Whilst economic and ecological questions would appear to be our major preoccupations at the moment, it seems that the answers to both questions can be found only in the political sphere. Ecology is dependent upon economic structures, and economies are controlled by politicians. We might do well to remember here once again that highly relevant observation made by Jean-Jacques Rousseau early in Book IX of his *Confessions*, published posthumously in 1782: 'I had come to see that everything depends entirely upon politics, and that whichever way you look at it, no nation will ever be anything other than what the nature of its government may make it'. How true. Closer to our own times, Kwame Nkrumah (1909-72) noted in his autobiography, 'Seek ye first the political kingdom, and all things shall be added unto you'. By this he meant that until a nation gets its government right, it has very little chance of getting anything else right. Unfortunately, here in the UK our government is in rather desperate need of long-overdue reform at the moment.

On Constitutional Reform:

But what has our UK government managed to do for us so far? We might begin here by displaying some humility, and an appropriate sense of gratitude. Government is an extremely difficult business, and by world standards we have not come out of it all too badly. Our governments have done quite well at keeping us out of major wars since 1945 despite some backsliding into minor ones, and we have a reasonably sound set of political and judicial institutions, with most people in this country managing well enough economically. By world standards, we are a rich country. Of course, nobody's perfect. Anyone harbouring the delusion that our institutions are paragons of integrity should read *The Establishment and How They Get Away With It* (2014) by Owen Jones, and *How Corrupt Is Britain?* (2015) by David Whyte (ed.) as correctives. For the latest exposés of greed, corruption, and self-serving that estimable journal *Private Eye* is essential reading. As for our courts, we should remember the cases of Jeremy Thorpe and Stephen Ward.

Moreover, our population does include a large minority of poor people who are only just managing to make ends meet, and some who live permanently in misery and real poverty, while a small minority have aggregated a disproportionately large share of the nation's wealth to themselves. The UK's Office for National Statistics reported that in 2016 the richest 10% of UK households enjoyed 44% of all the nation's wealth, with the richest one per cent holding nine per cent of the wealth on their own. Meanwhile, the poorer half of the population had to share just nine per cent of all the wealth between them. More than a fifth of the population lived on incomes below the government-defined 'poverty line', even although most of those households were in work. Nearly one in three children lived in poverty by the government's own definition, and the use of food banks was increasing. On April 19, 2016 the Institute for Fiscal Studies reported that the poorest nine per cent of households possessed no net wealth at all, because their debts exceeded their assets. In the same report they estimated that the richest 10% of households then enjoyed 50% of all privately held wealth in the UK. (Both available online). A further plethora of depressing figures is provided in Stephen Armstrong's book, *The New Poverty* (2017), and in Danny Dorling's, *Inequality and the 1%* (2019 ed.). As ever, we must remember that figures like these are very difficult to compile, and their absolute accuracy should not be relied upon. But the general picture emerges clearly enough.

These facts represent our country's 'dirty neck', which needs to be scrubbed clean. There is no need for this state of affairs. We are a wealthy country with more than enough resources to provide adequately for all. What is needed is just a comparatively small redistribution of resources to put more money into the hands of those who desperately need it, and also into the hands of those public services on which they rely. I am thinking here primarily of our National Health Service and social services, but also of our police, schools, and library services. This will still leave the rich very rich. It does mean an increase in taxation, but I for one would gladly pay more, and the imposition of property taxes and a very small financial transactions tax together with changes to the inheritance laws as suggested above, would be enough to greatly ease the current situation, if imposed on top of existing tax structures. Running a civilised society is an expensive business, but a country like ours ought to be prepared to pay for one. It should be seen as a national disgrace if we fail to discharge our obligations in this regard.

What we need in the UK today is a political reformation, a moral reformation, and a reformation in the happiness index of that large poorer section of our society. As noted above, it was Karl Popper who so wisely observed that the aim of governments should not be to achieve the greatest happiness of the greatest number, but rather the least misery of the greatest number. This is because happiness is a very abstract, intangible, and subjective concept, the idea of which will vary from individual to individual, while misery is very real, evident, and unmistakable. If I might rephrase Leo Tolstoy, all happy people are happy in different ways, while all who suffer misery are miserable in the same ways. Drug addiction, alcoholism, and criminality are usually the results of poverty. The rich can look after themselves, and even we, the middle classes, can look after ourselves. Governments need to step in only to aid those at the bottom of the social pyramid, a duty that they should consider to be their prime responsibility.

As regards present government policies, the manifest failures of neoliberalism have by now been laid bare for all to see. Allowing the rich to become very much richer than the rest of us has not resulted in faster economic growth, but in slower economic growth and a slower increase of real wage levels, accompanied by a sharp rise in inequality and growing social unrest. This unrest has resulted in the Brexit vote in Britain, the election of Trump in the US, and the selection of Jeremy Corbyn as leader of the Labour Party. It has benefitted nobody except the rich themselves, and yet governments in North America and Europe continue to pursue neoliberal policies. The only possible explanation for this must be the power that big money, now bigger than ever before, is exerting over our governments around the globe. For the latest expositions of this trend see Peter Geoghegan's *Democracy for Sale: Dark Money and Dirty Politics* (2020) and Tom Burgis' *Kleptopia: How Dirty Money is Conquering the World* (2020). For who is it that is handing over very large sums of money to finance political parties? The poor? I think not, and that is why they are being treated so badly. God help the poor when they become a minority in a plutocracy. Suggestions for putting the world to rights lie beyond the remit of this volume: there are far too many corrupt little dictatorships around the world to be dealt with here. But we could perhaps make a start by doing what we can here in the UK. Given the importance of government, we should begin by looking to the political scene, where a considerable reformation is needed to bring our institutions up to date, and to restore a measure of real democracy. A good idea would be the introduction of a written constitution, which would dispense with the vagaries, ambiguities, and anachronisms of our present unwritten constitution, one which relies very heavily upon traditional practices. This constitution should be one which makes it more difficult for plutocrats to seize control of our government. But what should our written constitution lay down?

Winston Churchill is famously reported as saying, 'Democracy is the very worst form of government – except for all the rest'. Well, one can see what he meant: democracy is difficult, cumbersome, and fallible, as we have seen with the American Constitution: simply the 'least worst' option perhaps, a point also made by Spinoza in Chapter 16 of his *Tractatus Theologico-Politicus* in 1670. (*Complete Works*, 2002 ed., p. 531) It has been said that, 'democracy speaks only through its anus', and one can see the point there. Nevertheless, we must have representative democracy, and we must have private capitalism, and we must have inequality. But it should be truly representative democracy, and regulated, controlled, and responsible capitalism, together with a tolerable degree of inequality in material terms, rather than the grotesque inequalities that we see at the moment. History teaches us that the distribution of wealth within a society has always very closely paralleled the distribution of political power within that society, and so here in the UK, if we want to see a happier, more stable and more equitable country, I would begin by advocating more power to the people. The first step to be taken in this direction is obvious enough – we must deal with the elephant in the room, which is the private funding of political parties, in both North America and Europe. There is no public service that more desperately needs to be nationalised than government, even more in the USA than in the UK. The private funding of political parties should be made a serious criminal offence, carrying a custodial sentence. This funding should be seen for what it is – bribery. Where much is given, much is expected. Political parties will always dance to the tune of their paymasters, whether they are parties of the Right or of the Left, because both need private funding to help them win elections. If we want to have governments that will truly govern in the interests of *all* the people in an even-handed way, then *all* the people must provide the funding for them, and not just small, sectional interest groups as at the moment. The public funding of political parties need not cost very much at all – certainly far less than the cost of *not* funding them! Allowing the private funding of political parties must be the worst example of a false economy in history. The private funding of political parties must cease. As George Monbiot put it in his book, *Out of the Wreckage: a New Politics for an Age of Crisis* (2017),

> If this dam breaks, the political system goes with it. It is a revolutionary transformation from which many others will follow, in America and around the world. The US government, elected by means more plutocratic than democratic, wielding extraordinary power, has impeded progress towards a more generous, inclusive politics in global forums and in many other nations. If the current political funding system is swept away, this is the point at which everything changes. (p.180)

Just listen to the desperate squawking that will emanate from the plutocrats once the idea of state funding for political parties has been floated, and begins to gain traction. In addition, of course, it should also be made illegal for any retired cabinet minister to subsequently take a highly paid, low effort job with a major corporation. This prospect is just another means by which, at the moment, plutocrats exercise control over our governments.

To be fair, the above points are so blatantly obvious that even our present UK governments have been very gradually groping their way towards addressing them in recent years. Indeed, we could look as far back as the Corruption and Illegal Practices Act of 1883, although this concerned only constituency candidates, their campaign expenses, and their agents. The next milestone came with the Honours (Prevention of Abuses) Act of 1925, passed in response to Lloyd George's blatant sale of honours and titles to finance his then Liberal Party. Much later, in August 1976, the Committee on Financial Aid to Political Parties, chaired by Lord Houghton of Sowerby, proposed that state financial aid to political parties should be given in two forms, firstly block grants to the central organisations for their general purposes, and secondly a limited reimbursement of election expenses to parliamentary and local government candidates. These were eminently sensible suggestions as far as they went, but they did not go on to say that *only* those forms of funding should be allowed to political parties. Had they done so they could, if implemented, have gone a long way towards solving the problem at a stroke. But Margaret Thatcher was shortly to come to power, and these suggestions were very largely ignored.

Speaking of Margaret Thatcher brings us to another scandalous aspect of private funding, which is the sale of honours and titles to raise money for party funds. In his book *The Honours System* (1992 ed.), Michael De-la-Noy had this to say on the subject:

> The difference between Mrs. Thatcher's methods of raising party funds and rewarding contributors and Lloyd George's seems only to have been one of refinement; in Mrs. Thatcher's case, she dispensed with the middleman. In principle, the objectives were identical. Rumbled by the Labour Research Department, she immediately agreed to a request from the Political Honours Scrutiny Committee for a tightening up of vetting procedure. The matter was raised in the House of Commons under the ten-minute rule on 6 December 1983 by a Labour MP, Mr. Austin Mitchell, but little fuss seems to have been made, and compared to the uproar engendered by Harold Wilson's resignation honours list, or any of the other honours scandals of the past, Mrs. Thatcher's apparent sale of honours for party purposes, on the face of it a blatant prostitution of the honours system, caused scarcely a ripple on the surface of a society by now grown cynical in such matters to the point of inertia. Not a voice was raised in surprise when, in the 1991 New Year Honours List Mrs. Thatcher rewarded the chief executive of Trafalgar House, Mr. Eric Parker, with a knighthood. Trafalgar House was a leading corporate donor to the Tory party.
>
> Even before Mr. Parker's knighthood had been announced, Mrs. Thatcher's Resignations Honours List, published on 21 December 1990, had prompted Adam Raphael to comment in the *Observer* that 'no prime minister this century, with the exception of Lloyd George, has been more ruthless or calculating in the use of patronage than Mrs. Thatcher'. (pp. 134-5)

The 'middleman' referred to above was in fact Maundy Gregory (1877-1941), Lloyd George's notorious honours broker, a character so colourful that he deserves a whole book to himself. But things are not so different in our own day. When the reason given for the bestowal of honours is 'for political services', this is usually a euphemism for 'big donations'. A blatant example of this was the knighthood awarded in 2017 to Sir David Ord, the Bristol port owner. He was a beneficiary of Tory privatisations when the Port of Bristol Authority, part of Bristol City Council, was obliged to grant a 150-year lease to the Bristol Port Company, of which Ord became the Managing Director and co-owner. In 2014 the council sold the freehold of the port to the company for £10 million. Just how profitable this deal proved to be for Ord was reflected in the fact that between 2013 and 2017 he was able to donate £930,000 to the Conservative Party. His knighthood was awarded for 'political service and service to the community in the South West'. But his 'community service' amounted to no more than being South West regional treasurer of the Conservative Party. We must assume, therefore, that his 'political service' amounted to precisely his very large cash donations. A storm of criticism ensued, and Downing Street tried to justify his knighthood by issuing a statement declaring, 'Being involved in political parties is generally considered to be an important part of civic society, and the alternative is having state funding for political parties, which is not where the consensus lies'.(*The Guardian,* December 30, 2016) Yes, the Tories would like to think that, wouldn't they? Those were weasel words indeed, but the behaviour of New Labour under Tony Blair was hardly any more creditable.

De-La-Noy's second edition came out in 1992, but had it been published just a few years later he would surely have also mentioned the great Life Peerages Scandal of 2006-7, which seems to have played a part in the resignation of Tony Blair on June 27, 2007. Too many life peerages had apparently been doled out to those who had made large 'loans' to the Labour Party. On March 20, 2006, New Labour admitted that just 12 individuals had recently loaned £13,950,000 to the party. Some connection between loans and peerages was sought, with a police investigation being carried out to see whether offences had been committed under the Public Bodies Corrupt Practices Act of 1889 or the Honours (Prevention of Abuses) Act of 1925. Tony Blair became the first serving Prime Minister to be interviewed by police, although not under oath, and in the end no charges were brought. Of course, under the banner of 'New Labour' Tony Blair and Gordon Brown had made every effort to toe the neoliberal line and to cosy up to big business. They were duly rewarded for it, but are still referred to as 'traitor Blair' and 'traitor Brown' within the Labour movement today. When asked at a dinner in 2002 what she believed to be her greatest achievement, Margaret Thatcher replied without hesitation, 'New Labour'. (*The Independent,* April 8, 2013). Neoliberalism has a claim for being the most successful confidence trick in the history of the world.

After Lord Sowerby's Report of 1976, the next important step taken towards the cleaning up of party financing was the Political Parties, Elections, and Referendums Act of 2000. This established the Electoral Commission, and required all political parties to register with it. The Commission was to oversee all future elections and referendums in the UK, and registered parties were allowed to accept donations of over £500 only from 'permissible donors'. These were not to include foreign donors or anonymous donors, but could include any individual on a UK electoral register, or any companies, trade unions, 'or similar organisations' registered in this country. This was a remarkably broad remit, and of course it did nothing to limit the amounts that these 'permissible donors' could give to political parties. However, the Act did place strict limits on how much each party could spend on electioneering before a General Election. In 2019 this stood at £30,000 per constituency contested within 365 days of the election, up to a maximum of £18.84 million overall. This, of course, allowed the maximum outlay of £30,000 to be concentrated on marginal seats.

Next came Sir Hayden Phillips' Inquiry of March, 2006 into the funding of political parties. He reported a year later, recommending that individual donations should be limited to £50,000 each, with a further capping of expenditure on political campaigns. He also recommended increasing state funding for the parties by £25 million, and expanding the uses to which this money could be put. Then in 2008 the Ministry of Justice released a White Paper which analysed party finance and expenditure. It recommended the tightening of controls on spending by parties and candidates, a substantial strengthening of the powers of the Electoral Commission, and more transparency on the sources of donations. Finally, in November 2011 the Committee on Standards in Public Life, chaired by Sir Christopher Kelly, published a report entitled, 'Political Finance: Ending the Big Donor Culture'. This recommended a contribution limit of £10,000 per donor per year, although this limit should not apply to trade union affiliation fees, provided such fees were raised under an 'opt in' system, so that they could be regarded as party membership fees. The existing limits for campaign spending should be cut by a further 15%, and in addition to the existing 'policy development grant' eligible parties should be granted public funding at the rate of £3.00 per vote in Westminster elections, and £1.50 per vote in devolved and European elections. Income tax relief should be available only on donations of up to £1,000, together with membership fees for political parties. (Online information)

All this did at least show a degree of public and government concern over the issue of private funding for political parties, but most of the recommendations put forward since 2000 have never been implemented and essentially, still in 2022, nothing substantial has been done to curb this abuse. All of the legislation passed since 2000 is so full of loopholes as to be virtually useless. For example, although contributions from foreign donors are supposed to be banned, any wealthy oligarchs who buy property here and become ratepayers then appear on local electoral rolls, and are therefore 'on a UK electoral register', and so qualified to donate. In effect, any wealthy foreigner can thereby purchase the right to fund a political party. Had our governments been serious about a ban on foreign funders they could simply have limited acceptable funders to British citizens. *Private Eye,* Issue No. 1504 for September 2019 reported in relation to the Brexit negotiations of the time,

> The list of Tory donors who suddenly became very generous as Theresa May's deal sank below the waterline and the good ship Boris loomed on the horizon gives a good idea of those in whose direction the tide is turning...Those with most to gain from Johnson's likely lassitude towards the loaded proved especially forthcoming. Lubov Chernukhin, the wife of Russian oligarch Vladimir who famously wrote a large cheque to play tennis with Johnson in 2014, suddenly upped what had been regular donations in the low tens of thousands to a £200,000 handout. (p. 7)

In addition 'loans' made at commercial rates of interest did not need to be declared as funding, and it remained possible for donors to give large sums to parliamentary candidates at elections while remaining anonymous, by channelling those donations through a members' association such as the United and Cecil Club. Clearly, these abuses must also be ended. Without going into details, it should be noted that other countries both in Europe and further afield are already far ahead of the UK in their moves towards restricting private donations and introducing full public funding for their national parties. In Europe these include Germany, France, Austria, Sweden, the Netherlands, and Poland. Further afield Canada, Australia, Israel, Mexico and Japan have also made moves in this direction, although no country has yet introduced complete public funding.

As noted above, in 2019 each party was allowed to spend up to a maximum of £18.84 million on each general election campaign. I would suggest that the parties should be given a taste of their own austerity here, for it is neither necessary nor appropriate to spend such large sums on electioneering. This obviously gives an advantage to the best funded party, which in our case is always the Tories, with their big money backers. I would suggest that an electoral commission should be set up, composed of civil servants, not politicians, to decide on how much money should be spent, and in what ways, on electioneering. All of this money should then be provided by the state, and I would expect it to amount to a good deal less than £18 million per party per election! The details can be left to the commission, but obvious things would be, for example, funding for all parties to enable them to send a party manifesto to every household in every constituency where they chose to field a candidate. Some might say that this in itself would be enough 'campaigning'! Their policies would also be discussed in the media, with interviews, analyses, etc. Local supporters could also knock on doors canvassing for support, so long as they were not paid. All parties could also be allowed equal amounts of free air time for party political broadcasts. But the details of any further campaigning expenses allowable could be left to the commission, together with how much should be allowed for the running of party headquarters, etc.

There should, however, be some exceptions allowed for non-state funding. Parties should be allowed to keep the membership fees of their party members, provided that the state imposes a uniform fee for every member of all parties, adjusted for inflation each year. There should also be exceptions made for new parties trying to get off the ground. Private funding should be allowed here until that party wins five per cent of the national vote, at which point public funding, in line with that made available to the other parties, should be the only form of funding allowable to them apart from their membership fees. The whole point of all this should be to end the pernicious effects of private funding once and for all. Public funding for political parties would put an end to all the scandals and sleaze that have been reported in our newspapers for many years past – cash for honours, cash for titles, cash for questions, cash for political influence, etc.

The public funding of political parties would in itself be a giant step back towards real democracy, and away from our present plutocracy. But in addition, better use could be made of our existing bicarmal legislature as a further step towards democracy. The lower House should be elected by a system of proportional representation as happens, wholly or partially, in 40 out of the 43 countries generally considered to lie within the continent of Europe. The absurdity of a two-party system was noted as early as 1882 by W.S. Gilbert in the libretto of his comic opera Iolanthe. In Act II he has his character Private Willis sing,

> I often think it's comical how nature always does contrive
> That every boy and every gal that's born into the world alive
> Is either a little Liberal or else a little Conservative.

In reality of course there are shades of political opinion in every country, and more than two parties to vote for, even here in the UK. A PR system would allow the minority parties some say, and therefore far better reflect the real feelings of the nation as a whole. The absurdity of our present system was pointed up by the fate of UKIP, the only party campaigning on a platform of getting the UK out of the EU. At the 2015 general election UKIP secured over 3.8 million votes (12.6% of the total), replacing the Liberal Democrats as the third most popular party, but it secured only one seat at Westminster. On the other hand, in the 2014 elections for the European Parliament, held under a PR system, UKIP won the greatest number of votes (27.5%) of any British party, and so was able to return 24 MEPs. The irony of the situation was further underlined by the notorious Brexit referendum of June, 2016, when a majority of the electorate (51.89%) voted to leave the EU, although their views on this major issue had gone virtually unrepresented for years in the House of Commons under our 'first past the post' system. The absurdity of our present arrangements was once again illustrated by the general election of December, 2019. Boris Johnson called the outcome of that election, 'a decisive vote for Brexit' when in fact it was nothing of the kind. The Tories won 43.6% of the popular vote as against only 32.2% of that vote for Labour, so it was indeed a decisive Conservative victory over Labour, but not a vote for Brexit. The Liberal Democrats won a further 11.5% of the popular vote, the SNP 3.9%, and the Green Party 2.7%. Sinn Fein won 0.6%, and Plaid Cymru 0.5%, while the Alliance Party and the SDLP won 0.4% each. All of those parties mentioned favoured either a second referendum, or to remain in the EU. Together they won 52.2%, a majority of the popular vote that was more decisive than the 2016 majority vote (51.89%) that took us out of the EU. Had a second referendum been held, this majority might well have voted to remain. I would certainly have done so. Many of those who voted 'leave' in the 2016 referendum might well have changed their minds by 2020, having seen all the difficulties and dangers involved in leaving the EU. It is surely time for a change to our present electoral system.

A PR system with each voter casting just one vote for the party of his choice would keep things simple. However, under a PR system MPs returned would be chosen from party lists and would represent only the policies of their parties, and not any specific regional area of the country. The leader of the party with the largest number of seats under PR would become the head of government, or Prime Minister if you will. It would then be his or her job to form a coalition government with a majority in the Lower House, and a cabinet composed of members from parties to the coalition, in rough proportion to the size of the parties forming that coalition. Voters for the Lower House would therefore be choosing the executive branch of government as well as membership of the more important legislative body. This cabinet, reaching decisions by debate, chaired by the Prime Minister or perhaps a Deputy Prime Minister in the PM's absence or illness, and taking collective cabinet responsibility for all decisions as today, would constitute the executive branch of government. It is most important to retain this form of collective leadership by debate, for this is one of the great strengths of our present system. It is always a very bad idea to have a one-man executive under any form of constitution, including that of the USA. Individual cabinet members could be responsible for the running of the various government departments just as they are at the moment. The Lower House would then represent much more accurately the true will of the people at an ideological level. To make this doubly sure, voting should be made compulsory as in Australia, Belgium, and Luxembourg, with fines for those who failed to do their civic duty without a good excuse. Turning out once every three years to vote for the Lower House is not, I would suggest, an intolerable burden, and elections to this Lower House should be triennial. The voting age should be lowered to 16, as in the recent Scottish independence referendum. Since this Lower House would be the one truly representative of the political wishes of the people, it should be called 'The House of Representatives'. This would do away with the invidious and typically English obsession with class distinctions, as in the present titles of 'Commons' and 'Lords'.

But the existence of a bicameral legislature in our land provides us with the opportunity to retain the best features of our existing system, while at the same time introducing the above changes, thereby enabling us to enjoy the best of both worlds. The problem of regional representation could be solved by making better use of our second chamber. The House of Lords should be abolished and replaced by an elected chamber, the Senate. Officially, this is already the policy of all parties except the Conservatives, but nothing is being done about it. Since there is seating for only 400 in the Lords' chamber, this should be the membership of the new Senate, to save the expense of building a new chamber!

Each senator should be elected by a majority vote, arrived at by the use of a single transferable vote system. However, no more than four candidates for each Senate seat should be allowed, selected on the grounds of individual merit by local authorities. The single transferable vote should be used here to help ensure that each winning candidate really did have majority support from those who chose to vote, since voting for a representative in the Senate should not be compulsory. A points system could be used, with four points for a first place vote, three for a second, and so on. The candidate with the largest number of points would win.

Senate constituencies would be larger than those at present, with boundary changes allowed according to population movements, so that each senator represented a roughly equal number of people. We could afford to have larger constituencies for the Senate than for our present Commons, since it would be the prime duty of each senator to represent the interests of his constituents in the Upper House, just as MPs do today in the Commons, but with the important difference that all senators could then concentrate mainly on their duties as representatives and helpers of their constituents, without being distracted by cabinet responsibilities or party loyalties, although they would also be called upon to vote on national issues. The senators should not previously have served in the lower house to make them as non-partisan as possible, and should be 40 years of age or more on taking office, so that they could bring experience from outside politics to this upper chamber. The senators should be allowed full freedom of information, in case the present Freedom of Information Act, already under attack, is scrapped altogether. They should also be able to name suspects free from the fear of slander charges, a privilege enjoyed by Commons MPs today. The senators could then concentrate mainly on representing and serving their constituencies while conversely, those in the Lower House could concentrate exclusively on the business of government, without being distracted by representational duties.

Those running for the Senate would also be allowed public funding, but now from local government sources. This would include a salary for their senator, and election expenses for the four candidates once every five years, not a great financial burden. The candidates should be allowed one mail shot each to every household in their constituency, consisting of a booklet explaining their background, their views, and their priorities, with their expenses on much the same lines as for those in the Lower House, as decided by the civil service commission. The four candidates should be chosen by elected local authority bodies on the basis of interviews with all those who put themselves forward, and examination of their CVs. Elections to the Senate should be held every five years, so as not to coincide with elections to the Lower House. As a further safeguard, the one should be elected in April, and the other in September, to ensure that people are asked to concentrate on only one issue at a time. Voting for Senate membership should not be compulsory. The two chambers could still be called Parliament, as at present. A membership of 501 for the lower House would seem to be about right, to allow for one Speaker, who should remain as neutral as possible. This Speaker, and two Deputy Speakers, should be elected by members of the Lower House as today. Again as today, the Speaker would lose his vote in the Chamber, but the Deputy Speakers could retain theirs unless they were in the chair when a division was called. In that case, they would have only the casting vote, if one was required.

The senators should vote, by a process of elimination, to choose from one of their number who volunteered for the job, a President, who would be head of state, and two Vice Presidents, all of whom could chair Senate debates, although normally the President would be in the chair. Those men or women should have served for at least five years in the Senate before being eligible for these offices, and so would be at least 45 years of age. The election of the President by Senate members rather than by the populace as a whole should be a safeguard against a populist coming to power, as has happened recently in the USA. On being elected, the President would be obliged to give up his Senate constituency, where a by-election would be called to replace him or her, but the Vice Presidents could retain their constituencies, under the same rules as Deputy Speakers in the Lower House. This would bring Senate membership up to 401. It is important that there should be an even number of senators, because in the event of a tied vote, the President would have the casting vote, although normally he would not vote in divisions at all. The President should remain, like the Queen today, as far as possible above party politics. The Vice Presidents, who could retain their constituencies, could also retain their Senate votes, unless one of them was chairing a debate in the Upper House, in which case he or she would have the casting vote, if one was required. They could speak in Senate debates, but their primary duty would remain the representation of their constituents, since normally the President would be in the chair, acting in much the same way as the Speaker in our present House of Commons, in addition to performing ceremonial and diplomatic duties. In the unlikely eventuality of the President and Vice Presidents all being incapacitated at the same time, senators could elect one of their number to act as chairman in a temporary capacity. Presidents and Vice Presidents would normally serve for only five years each, although they could make themselves available for re-election. All members of the Senate would be deprived of their right to a vote in national elections, as is the case for members of the House of Lords today, as a further step towards ensuring their at least nominal political impartiality, although they could vote in local elections, and in Senate divisions.

The senators should remain, as far as possible, above party politics, making it clear that their main task is to consider the overall best interests of their constituents and of the country as a whole. To this end, if the Lower House should become deadlocked in some way, the President should have the power to order a mid-term election in the hope of resolving the problem.

Alternatively, he could order a referendum to be held on a specific issue. But it should be only for the President, and not for the Prime Minister, to decide whether and when a mid-term election or a referendum should be held. It should not lie within the powers of the President or the Prime Minister to order a mid-term prorogation (as distinct from referendum or election) of Parliament for any reason whatsoever, but both Houses could decide by majority votes on adjournments of not more than three weeks outside normal periods of recess to fight elections, prepare for referenda, or hold party conferences, if they wished.

Normally, legislation would be initiated by the Lower Chamber, as it is today, and then sent up to the Senate for ratification by a simple majority vote. However, by a majority vote of those present, the Senate could also, after debate, vote to amend the legislation, and then send it back to the Representatives, who may or may not accept the amendments. If they do not, then the Senate may accept their decision. However, if they feel strongly on the issue the Senate may, by a two-thirds majority of the whole House, veto the legislation in the hope of forcing their amendments through. The Senate could also initiate legislation, but this would have to be first sent down to the Lower House for their approval by a simple majority before it could go any further. Both Houses could of course form parliamentary committees to look at specific issues, as today. Just as the Law Lords left the Upper House in 2009 to form our new Supreme Court, so the bishops should also leave the Upper House, abandoning politics to concentrate entirely on their spiritual duties.

These provisions would give the Senate a real measure of political power, which it would deserve as an elected chamber. It would be the senators who were more in touch with the grass roots feelings of their specific constituencies, since they would be the recipients of correspondence from their constituents, and so become aware of their concerns and needs at practical levels. The Representatives would concern themselves more with ideological issues, and broad trends of policy. It would therefore be entirely appropriate that our elected Senate should enjoy a greater measure of political power under our new constitution then the House of Lords does under our present one. A division of powers between the different branches of government is something that should always be seen as desirable, just as a concentration of powers into too few hands should always be seen as dangerous.

If these reforms could be implemented, then the UK would at last have earned the right to call itself a genuinely representative parliamentary democracy, having finally broken the yoke of plutocracy. On the face of things, these might appear to be radical suggestions, but I would call them evolutionary rather than revolutionary. Notice how much would remain unchanged. Our system of local government, our judicial systems, and our civil service could all remain exactly as they are now. Our bicameral legislature would still be in place, and crucially our compound executive, reaching decisions by debate and taking collective cabinet responsibility for all decisions made, would also still be in place. Ministers in the Lower House could still be responsible for individual departments, as today, but no senators would be allowed to serve as ministers. Apart from voting on Bills sent up to them, the only other duty of senators would be to represent the interests of their constituents, without fear or favour. Senators should be given immunity from libel and slander laws, a privilege which, I am sure, would be used responsibly, just as is the 'naming' privilege allowed to Commons MPs today.

Senators would have no party leadership to court in the hope of obtaining a ministerial office. Under this system there would be more voting for the people to do since the Senate too would now have to be elected, but this is merely an extension of voting procedures already in operation, a normal part of parliamentary democracy. In fact, since unexpected mid-term elections would be much rarer under this system than they have been in the past, there would at least be less voting to do in that respect.

Under these changes, the best aspects of our existing system would be retained, while its more archaic and ludicrous elements would be eliminated. I therefore see nothing radical or revolutionary about the above suggestions. Here I bow the knee to Edmund Burke and to Karl Popper, both of whom warned against the dangers of radical political change over short periods of time. We might also take a lesson from evolutionary biology here: slow and steady change can give rise to superior life forms, but sudden genetic mutations are more likely to produce monsters. We saw this happening in political terms with the French Revolution, the rise of the Nazis in Germany, and the rise of the Bolsheviks in Russia. But the reforms that I have suggested here are entirely in keeping with our evolutionary traditions. It is in fact the plutocrats rather than myself who have been the radicals, who have undermined and suborned our present pseudo democracy, and who have been the real 'enemies of the people'. My suggestions will simply put us back onto a democratic path, and provide us with a form of government of which we can be truly proud. Of course, our present politicians are so hopelessly set in their ways that they will be very reluctant to implement the above suggestions. No matter. We writers need concern ourselves only with the quality of our pearls, and not with the nature of the swine before whom they are cast. All that we can do is to point the way: we should not be upset if the world hurries by, preoccupied and unheeding. 'The old Masters: how well they understood'. You can lead a horse to water, but you cannot make it drink. As numerous philosophers have noticed, it usually takes decades for new ideas to penetrate into the dim awareness of politicians. But I have no doubt that one day the reforms which I have suggested here, or something very like them, will be implemented, although certainly not in my lifetime.

I must now make a very personal confession. When I consider today's monarchy and House of Lords, I feel ashamed of my country, ashamed to be an Englishman. Both represent the tattered remnants of an entirely wrong-headed age. Again, I have not changed my views in this regard since the 1960s. Both institutions are ludicrous anachronisms in the twenty-first century. Both are unelected but, even more reprehensibly, both retain a remnant of political power, inherited from the days of the Dark Ages! Ideally, they should both be abolished with all speed, and replaced by an elected Senate and President. Let us first consider the House of Lords. In 2019 its membership stood at 779, consisting of 92 hereditary peers, 26 Lords Spiritual, bishops and archbishops, and 661 life peers, appointed by the Queen but on the advice of governments of the day. This gives those governments a power of patronage, and a means of rewarding large donors to their parties. At 779 members the House of Lords is down in size considerably from the 1144 members of 1990, but it still remains the second largest second chamber in the world, surpassed only by that of Communist China. Other nations manage perfectly well with much smaller numbers in their upper houses. France has 348, Spain 257, Italy 321, and Germany only 69, while the entire EU parliament in 2019 had an upper chamber of only 28 members! The Indian upper house has only 254 members, while the USA's Senate of course has only 100. But a membership of 401 for our Senate could be justified by the constituency work that our senators would have to do. In 2019 the peers could all claim expenses of £305 a day simply for turning up and signing in. They could then immediately go home again without ever voting, speaking, or doing any committee work. Most of the business of the Upper Chamber is in fact carried out by a small, hard core of 'working peers'. Having an elected Senate would be no cheaper than the existing system, but we could at least be sure that all senators were working equally for their money!

When it comes to the monarchy, it is high time that we recognised that institution for what it is, namely a branch of the entertainment industry, just one endless photo-opportunity. How else would our newspapers and numerous magazines be illustrated? However, as entertainers this troupe is utterly talentless. All that is required of them is the ability to walk, smile, wave, and engage in a few lines of banal conversation. They also occasionally read out speeches, usually written for them by speech writers. Yet we are supposed to be moved to ecstasies of delight by their mere presence! The puppy-like devotion which the English in particular still display towards this anachronistic institution in the 21st century might be regarded as a harmless foible, faintly amusing to other nations, who must regard us as at least soft in the head if not actually demented, but nothing more than that. Unfortunately, however, the matter *is* rather more serious than that. In fact, Queen worship is an abomination in the eyes of God and man. The notion that any human being should be regarded as, if not quite divine, then certainly at least so much 'better' than the rest of us that we are actually supposed to bow and scrape before her every time she is graciously pleased to favour us with her presence is both obnoxious and toxic, taking us back to the days of the divine right of kings. It reinforces the notion that some people should be simply entitled to privilege, adoration, and vast wealth for achieving nothing more than being born in the right bed. Moreover, this privilege extends not only to the monarch herself, but to the whole tribe of her rather extensive family! This notion of undeserved entitlement then diffuses downwards to pollute other bodies of society, reaching beyond the House of Lords, whose members are also entitled to respectful forms of address, to managing directors and members of company boards. In no way could these latter ever be said to 'earn' the enormous salaries and bonuses that they pay themselves, even if their companies are successful. They simply *get* the money out of a sense of self-awarded 'entitlement'! This 'entitlement' of course continues to apply even if their companies are unsuccessful. Enormous salaries and bonuses continue to be paid right up to the eve of liquidation. Our limited liability laws then ensure that they are allowed to keep all the money that they have taken out of the company before it collapsed and paid to themselves. Our athletes who win gold medals for us at the Olympics after years of arduous training, doing what nobody else in the world has been capable of, are worthy of admiration. So too are our nurses, teachers, and headmasters who put in a lifetime of hard, vital work for modest material rewards. The royals perform only the lightest and most undemanding of duties, with plenty of time off, and are massively over-rewarded for those slight tasks, spoiled, pampered, and waited upon all their lives. What is there to admire there?

The royal family provides, moreover, a rather expensive source of entertainment for the nation. According to official figures released in June 2019, the annual net cost of the monarchy to the British Taxpayer had been £67 million, a rise of 41% over the previous year. But this seemed to be a suspiciously small sum, considering all their homes which need to be kept up, and the very numerous staff that man them. In 2019 £30.4 million was set aside from the Sovereign Grant (which replaced the Civil List in 2011) for the refurbishment of Buckingham Palace alone. Moreover, the cost of royal protection was excluded from this £67 million figure. Why? According to an exposé by Susie Boniface first published in the *Daily Mirror* on July 11 2010, with figures later updated to January 27, 2012, the costs of royal protection were about £100 million p.a. even then. For this sum 21 members of the royal family were being protected for 24 hours a day by highly trained and armed police officers. Because they worked in shifts and needed time off for holidays, sick leave etc. this involved some 1,000 handsomely paid officers. The Royalty Protection Squad of London's Metropolitan Police, known as SO14, consisted of some 120 persons ranging in rank from a sergeant earning £50,000 p.a. to a chief superintendent on £80,000-plus. One third of these, the 'front line' staff, could also earn a 'special allowance' bonus of up to £15,000 p.a. after passing the rigorous selection process. The remaining two-thirds were support officers and civilian staff, who could also claim large allowances and overtime. The Met also devoted a further 400 more uniformed officers to guard duties at royal residences in London, including Buckingham Palace, St. James's Palace, Kensington Palace, and Clarence House. A further 120 uniformed officers guarded Windsor Castle and Prince Andrew's home, Royal Lodge. Sandringham, was permanently guarded by some 20 officers and dedicated armed response teams. Prince Charles's Gloucester home at Highgrove had 30 to 40 local officers guarding it, as did Prince Edward's Bagshot Park home in Surrey. Balmoral Castle was also closely guarded by Met officers for two months every summer during the Queen's visit there. To those ten royal residences should also be added Frogmore Cottage at Windsor, the former residence of Prince Harry and his family, Gatcombe Park in Gloucestershire the home of Princess Anne, and the Palace of Holyrood in Edinburgh, used occasionally by the Queen for official duties in Scotland. No figures are available for protection costs at those residences. A programme aired on Chanel Five on the evening of February 16, 2019 entitled, 'Spending Secrets of the Royals' put the true cost of the extensive royal family to the British taxpayer at £345 million per annum at that time.

All of those police officers had been allocated to royal protection duties at a time when the national police budget had just been cut by 25%. If we had no monarchy, they could all have been devoted to protecting the rest of us instead. Our particular form of monarchy is a ludicrously anachronistic anomaly in the twenty-first century. The puppy-like devotion displayed towards this archaic institution by the English in particular must make our national judgment suspect. Personally, I see the monarchy as being a great embarrassment, ranking with *The Archers* as a national disgrace. All of its members could be pensioned off to live very comfortably on their private wealth. This would not only be a further step towards turning our country into a true representative democracy, but also a giant stride towards dragging our reluctant nation into the twenty-first century. Buckingham Palace and Windsor Castle, already maintained by the public, should be made permanently open to the public once they have been cleared of the royals.

Having said all that, however, I know my countrymen. Although the abolition of the monarchy would be the least consequential of all the changes suggested above, the idea would be greeted with howls of outrage on a scale that could be exceeded only by a proposal to cancel *The Archers.* The English love a soap opera and the monarchy, of course, has proved to be the longest-running soap opera of them all. Assuming, therefore, that the last remnants of political power would be removed from the monarchy under our new, written constitution, this bauble of the entertainment industry could be retained with no damage to our parliamentary democracy, provided that it was managed more on the lines of the other constitutional monarchies still extant in Europe today. I am thinking here of the constitutional monarchies of Norway, Sweden,

Denmark, and Holland. We could even continue to call ourselves a monarchy, with the monarch and the President as joint Heads of State. The monarch's title would be an honorary one, however. The de facto powers of our Head of State would remain with the President as outlined above, but the monarch could ease the presidential burden by sharing ceremonial duties with him or her. As for the honours system, the granting of life peerages would clearly have to end, and no more hereditary titles would be awarded either, but the awarding of other honours could remain much the same as today, their distribution decided upon by an Honours Committee, and not by politicians. Existing hereditary peers and baronets could continue to use their titles just as the European old aristocracy does, even in republican countries. Hopefully, the retention of those baubles would lessen the shock of change for the credulous, and make it likelier that the more necessary and important reforms suggested above would prove to be acceptable. But what should be the goals of this new government under our new constitution?

On Happiness:

Prior to writing his masterwork *Das Kapital*, a young Karl Marx (1818-83) had produced eleven short *Theses on Feuerbach*, written in 1845, but not published as a complete collection until 1888. Ludwig Feuerbach (1804-72) was a contemporary materialist philosopher, and a bitter opponent of Christianity, and so he was of great interest to Marx, although Marx was critical of him. The eleventh and last thesis of the series ends with the famous line, 'Philosophers have so far only interpreted the world in various ways: the point is to change it'. I would not agree with this statement: in my view, political thinkers had already changed the world with the American and French Revolutions, and were even then continuing to change it with the emergence of new creeds like Utilitarianism and classical economics. However, in the sixth of these short theses, as at various points in *Das Kapital*, Marx argued that human nature was not immutable, but could change according to the changing material circumstances under which people lived. It is certainly to be hoped that human nature can change – for the better. Indeed, in his book *The Better Angels of our Nature* (2011) Steven Pinker suggests that this process may be already in train. However, even making allowance for this point, it is surely true that certain basic requirements for happiness will remain essential and eternal even if human nature can change, which is perhaps a pious hope.

But before looking to human nature, let us look at the role of governments in the promotion of happiness. Assuming that the above constitutional changes could be introduced, what should our new government be doing to promote the happiness of us all? Well, what is the first essential requirement for happiness or, as Karl Popper would prefer to say, the avoidance of misery? Surely it is good health, always your most precious asset: chronic ill health, or even temporary ill health, is enough to dampen anyone's spirits. For this reason, every state that can afford it ought to institute a national health service for all, free at the point of use. No one in our country should be denied essential medical treatment because of their inability to pay for it. Yes, this will be expensive, and poorer countries will not be able to afford it at all, but countries like ours certainly can, and ought to do so. Having set up this service it will then need to be properly maintained, and it is rather questionable whether our own National Health Service is being properly funded at the moment. This of course is the result of 'austerity', the need for which was not the responsibility of the ill. The remedies for this should therefore be provided primarily from the resources of those who caused the need for this 'austerity' in the first place, namely bankers, stock brokers, and hedge fund managers. But even if the state is fulfilling its bounden duty in this regard, there is more to the maintenance of good health than the existence of an efficient health service: the individual too must take a share of responsibility in this regard. Obviously, we should avoid the ingestion of toxic substances such as recreational drugs, alcohol, and tobacco smoke. Surprisingly, it is perfectly possible to live very happily without ingesting any of the above: I do so myself. We should also be very careful about what we eat: we have something of an obesity crisis in this country at the moment. My private mantra has always been, 'Drink is the devil's brew, food is very bad for you, and smoking is for mental defectives'. Of course, nobody's perfect. I will take a drink sometimes for social reasons (people are more important than principles) and I am something of a chocoholic, but it's a good mantra to bear in mind. We also need to take exercise. I have a simple workout regime that I can follow at home, but the most enjoyable way to exercise is through sport. This can be any sport at all so long as it is vigorous tennis, squash, rowing, or cycling would be fine, or a team sport perhaps. Even in old age you can still play short tennis and table tennis, or at least take regular walks. After that it's up to God. You can do all the right things and then die from cancer at 30 if you have the wrong genes. On the other hand, you can have the genes of a Winston Churchill, who was a heavy smoker and drinker all his life, never bothered to exercise, and lived to be 90. Man proposes, but God disposes, and God knows nothing of justice.

The next requirement for the avoidance of misery is physical security, that is security from criminals at home and foreign enemies abroad. Some would say that the provision of these securities is the primary duty of the state, and of the state alone. Certainly, if you lived in a high crime area or in a war zone, the importance of this factor in the avoidance of misery would be forcibly brought home to you. We can see some of this on our own TV screens in the lamentable case of Ukraine today. In the absence of physical security, it is very difficult to find happiness. More important than your health is your physical survival, but since that is not seriously threatened by war or crime in our land, I would say that health provisions are of the greater importance for us at the moment, despite the cuts to our police force imposed by neoliberal austerity.

The next essential requirement for the avoidance of misery is the possession of a material sufficiency or, in the vernacular, an ability to 'make ends meet'. An insufficient income is not only a source of stress and anxiety but also, as noted above, a serious limitation upon your degree of 'positive freedom', as defined above by Isaiah Berlin. The state has taken some steps towards helping the poor in this regard by instituting minimum wage legislation and a social security 'safety net' for the unemployed and chronically ill, but more still needs to be done in this area for the poorest 30% of our population and for those public services upon which they rely. The war in Ukraine, following hard on the heels of Brexit and the Covid lockdowns, have combined to do us great economic damage, forcing a disastrous rise in the cost of living. The government is now implementing temporary relief measures for the poorest, but a more permanent solution should be sought for the long run. The guarantee of a basic minimum income for all regardless of whether they are in work or not is an idea that deserves to be taken seriously. Indeed, it has been taken seriously in the past, both in Europe and, surprisingly, also in the USA. In his very interesting book *Utopia for Realists* (2018 ed.) Rutger Bregman includes a chapter entitled, 'The Bizarre Tale of President Nixon and his Basic Income Bill' (pp. 77-100) which tells of just how close America came to rolling out just such a scheme on a national scale. This episode will be looked at in more detail below.

'Security' is indeed a key word in this context. The achieving of physical security, health security, and financial security are of course of primary importance, but within these contexts housing security should be recognised as a distinct issue, with an importance of its own. Too many young couples, especially those with children, are today caught in the 'renting trap'. Since Margaret Thatcher opened the flood gates to the sale of council housing, more and more young couples have been forced to rent from the private sector, and private sector landlords always seek to extract the maximum rent that the market will bear. With rents taking a third or more of their net incomes, it is almost impossible for average wage earners to save enough money for the deposit that would enable them to take out a mortgage to buy a house of their own. Their chances of saving would have been better in council-owned property. However, on principle it is always undesirable for one man or institution to own the roof over another man's head: ultimate security of tenure comes only with ownership. Surely the state could step in here to help those with only a small deposit, or no deposit, by providing publicly funded mortgages, or mortgage deposits. The applicants would have to be carefully screened for credit worthiness of course, and an appropriate rate of interest for the times would have to be charged. There must be no reckless lending on the lines of the 'sub-prime' fiasco that recently afflicted the USA, and later the world. Moreover, even with a state mortgage, borrowers with the state scheme would not be entirely secure, since a long spell of unemployment could lead to the state repossessing their home. This is another reason why the state should always aim for policies that will maintain full employment. But most mortgage holders today do in fact manage to repay their entire loan over a period of decades, until at last the blessed day dawns on which they find themselves the sole owners of a mortgage-free home. All that most people need is help with that crucial first step onto the 'housing ladder'. From that moment on, they will strain every sinew to make sure that their mortgage debt continues to be paid. Pride of 'ownership', and the ability to improve their properties will act as powerful incentives.

Then of course, in the majority of cases, people prefer to choose a partner with whom to share their lives: they need a love interest. Even today commitment to such a relationship, be it gay or straight, usually takes the form of marriage, and of course choosing the right marriage partner can have a great bearing on your level of personal happiness. So too can your ability to keep your partner happy! 'Happy wife, happy life', as the saying goes, with the converse applying to the distaff side. The maintenance of a successful personal relationship must be a key factor in the happiness of nearly all of us.

Once these basic essentials of happiness have been achieved, it might be said that we have achieved 'contentment', a kind of fundamental happiness. But to be truly 'happy', we need in addition a love interest, or an interest that we love. This can be anything at all: a sport, a hobby, a religion, some form of communal activity, anything that you find to be personally enjoyable. Why, some people might even derive enjoyment out of writing a book about philosophy! Clearly, any form of eccentricity will do. Speaking of philosophy however, I might add here that this too can be a vital factor in the quest for happiness. This is because everyone has a philosophy, whether they realise it or not. Even the practical man who says, 'Philosophy? Huh! I don't want anything to do with *that*! I just deal with situations as they arise in a sensible and practical way. I'm a pragmatist'. But alas, there is no escape! Pragmatism too is a recognised school of philosophy, as expounded by such luminaries as the Americans Charles Sanders Peirce (1839-1914), William James (1842-1910), and John Dewey (1859-1952). When it comes to philosophy, there really is nothing new under the sun, although this is partly because, as Cicero noted long ago, 'There is nothing so ridiculous that it has not been said by some philosopher or another!' But if we can cultivate a philosophy that incorporates a deep sense of gratitude for our miraculous good fortune, as explained above, this too should surely contribute to the happiness of us all.

Of course, nearly all of us must work for a living, and the nature of the work that we have to do can exercise a profound influence on our level of happiness, or misery. This is where the element of job satisfaction comes in, a factor not always related to pay levels, as we see in the cases of so many of those who work in the NHS. Security of employment might also figure highly in the minds of some. It behoves all of us to choose our line of work carefully, not always with an eye to obtaining the highest of pay levels, although of course this factor will usually figure prominently in the minds of most. Another important aspect of this choice is making sure that your job will provide you with a good pension after retirement, so that eventually you are actually paid for doing nothing at all! Like the very few who inherit so much money that they are not required to work, we pensioners are often envied for our 'freedom'. But freedom on its own is of little value in the absence of those factors mentioned above: freedom can be 'just another word for nothing left to lose'. We all surrender our freedom when we choose to live in civil society, when we start a job, when we take out a mortgage, when we choose a partner to share our lives, or decide to raise a family. But the freedoms that we lose can add greatly to our happiness. In short, we achieve happiness not by acquiring freedoms, but rather by surrendering them. In my opinion, freedom has been seriously oversold as a desideratum.

Those of us who can manage to get all seven of the above factors right (the Seven Pillars of Happiness?) are very unlikely to be miserable. Some may detect echoes here of Maslow's Hierarchy of desiderata for happiness, the brainchild of Abraham Maslow (1908-70), but my views differ substantially from his. In his book *Sapiens: A Brief History of Humankind* (2014) Yuval Noah Harari too devotes Chapter 19 (pp. 376-396) to a long discussion of happiness which, to a degree, parallels my own discussion here, but again our views on this subject are substantially different.

Notice, however, that the achievement of individual happiness must be a joint venture between the state and the individual. It is the duty of the state to keep us out of wars abroad, and to keep our streets safe at home. By subjecting our capitalist economy to proper regulation it must deflect the system from its inherent tendency towards self-destruction, and prevent the occurrence of financial crises, stock market crashes, and periods of mass unemployment. Left to its own devices, unregulated capitalism will also generate increasing degrees of material inequality within our populations, as Thomas Piketty has shown so clearly. The state must recognise its responsibility not only to regulate capitalism, but also to redistribute wealth downwards towards the poorest 30% of our population, in order to prevent levels of inequality arising which are simply grotesque and unsustainable, giving rise to serious social unrest. In other words, the state must see to it that the rich pay their fair share in taxes. In addition of course every state that can afford it should institute a national health service for all of its citizens, free at the point of use, together with those other social services that are needed by the poorest members of our society. The state should also be prepared to help those members of society who are credit worthy to make that crucial first step onto the housing ladder. Once it has done all that, responsibility for the achievement of happiness moves from the state to the individual, as indicated above.

On the keeping of peace, however, in the sense of not participating in war, a separate word needs to be said here. Just as capitalism is not enough without state regulation, so too well intentioned pacifism is not enough without the means to ensure that going to war will never be necessary. 'If you seek for peace, prepare for war'. Would-be aggressors will always calculate carefully as to whether they are likely to gain more than they will lose by an act of aggression. In order to deter them, we are obliged to maintain strong military forces of our own, and preferably also to be a member of a military alliance of nations. Unfortunately, the cost of maintaining armed forces is always going to be high. This might be seen as an unavoidable expense, but surely defence expenditure should be for just that: defence, and nothing more. In this context our four Trident-armed nuclear submarines may be seen as defensive, because they serve as a deterrent to any potential aggressor. However, the defence budget should not be spent on weapons that are designed primarily for aggression. I am thinking here of the two new 'Elizabeth class' aircraft carriers currently being built for the Royal Navy. These can hardly be seen as defensive weapons. Land based air, properly dispersed, is always more effective than carrier-based air. You do not 'defend' your country with aircraft carriers. The only point of those weapons is the projection of military power far from home or, to be more blunt, to beat the hell out of somebody else's country. These ships are not defensive weapons: they are aggressive weapons. Moreover, in these days of satellite surveillance and precision-guided hypersonic missiles, those craft are very vulnerable. All this would be bad enough, but now we come to the costs involved. These two carriers, the Queen Elizabeth (named after Elizabeth I, not Elizabeth II) and the Prince of Wales are expected to cost £6.2 billion. But this is only for the basic craft before a plethora of optional extras are added. The planes for them will be F35Bs, bought from the USA. On January 19, 2018 the Public Accounts Committee reported to Parliament that the cost of the first 48 of these aircraft would be £13 billion, assuming an exchange rate of $1.55 to the pound. But of course the exchange rate has fallen since then to average $1.30 to the pound in 2019 and is still going down, making the final cost to us by 2023 more like £15 billion. Each ship can carry 48 planes, so their final total cost will be nearer to £30 billion. Since building costs for the two ships are also escalating, a realistic estimate of the total cost once both are fully operational in 2023 will be around £40 billion. That money could have done a lot for our Health Service, schools, and police force. Our two carriers, like the monarchy itself, should be seen as a national disgrace.

On Morality:

If we look at the etymology of words like 'morality' and 'ethics' we find that they come from similar roots. 'Morality' derives from the Latin *mores*, the plural of *mos,* a custom. 'Ethics' has a similar root from the Greek ἔθος, ethos, which again means a custom. This would suggest that 'ethical' behaviour or 'morality' involves simply acting in accordance with the customs of the times, doing what society considers to be 'moral' or 'ethical' at any particular point in its history. But this definition is not good enough, for these are shifting sands.

Slavery was once considered to be entirely acceptable, but is so no longer. The Roman 'games' were once considered 'ethical' – having people torn to pieces or otherwise tortured to death for the amusement of watching crowds. Public floggings and public executions were also seen as forms of entertainment even in our own country until the early nineteenth century. These were established customs of the times, and so seen to be entirely 'ethical'. Nearer our own day, bull baiting, bear baiting, dog fighting, hare coursing, and fox hunting were once considered to be quite legitimate, but these activities are now frowned upon. Conversely, living together before marriage, having children out of wedlock, and homosexuality were once considered to be terribly wrong: indeed, the last was actually illegal. Today, of course, all of these activities are entirely acceptable to our society. Therefore, simply behaving in accordance with the customs of the times is not, in reality, an adequate definition of 'morality', for these mores are always changing. But where can we find firmer ground?

If we are to ask simply, 'What is morality?' the question would seem to be unanswerable, in much the same way that the question, 'What is time?' asked in the Einstein section, appeared to be unanswerable. The only way forward was to turn the question around a little, and to come at it from a different angle. In the case of time, we had to ask, 'Well, what *creates* 'time', or rather, our impression of time passing?' Put that way, we were able to move forward on the issue. In this case, we should again turn the question around a little and ask instead, 'Well then, what is *immorality?*' Just as misery is much easier to define than happiness, so immorality is much easier to define than morality and (let's be honest here) also much more interesting as a study. If I might once again rephrase Tolstoy, 'All moral people are moral in the same way, but all immoral people are immoral in different ways.' In essence, all forms of immorality might be defined as simply unenlightened selfishness, a determination to increase your own happiness at the expense of the happiness of others. But this selfishness can take different forms. Therefore a plurality, and indeed a gradation, of immoralities may be identified. Some of them are,

(a) The immorality of intent:

This is the most culpable form of immorality, as practised by the sadist, the bully, the burglar, and the fraudster. Into this last category would fall the large-scale financial swindler, a very broad category indeed. This kind of person can increase his own happiness *only* by deliberately diminishing the happiness of others, and even revelling in the sense of his domination over them. These people are the worst kind of reprobates imaginable, the lowest possible forms of humanity. Quite rightly they are condemned for cruelty to animals as well, for as Bentham has reminded us, 'We should not ask, "Can they reason?" or "Can they speak?" but only, "Can they feel?"'

(b) The immorality of indifference:

This was the kind of immorality practised by the Victorian factory owner who allowed his employees to work with dangerous machinery for starvation wages: he was motivated entirely by selfishness and greed. His intention was not to deliberately decrease their happiness, but only to increase his own profits: he was simply utterly indifferent to any consequential suffering that might have resulted from his behaviour. Another example might be that of a couple who meet, fall in love, and decide that they want to get married. The only problem is that they are both already married to someone else! So they decide to divorce their existing spouses so that they can marry each other, utterly indifferent to the suffering that this might cause to their former partners, or to any existing children. Their intention is not to decrease the happiness of their ex-partners, but only to increase their own: that is all that they think about. They remain indifferent to any collateral suffering that might be inflicted upon others. Of course, if the divorced spouses happen to heartily agree with the new arrangement, so that all the adults come out of it happier, then only a lesser immorality has been perpetrated, although any children involved might still suffer

(c) The immorality of ignorance:

Then there is also the immorality of ignorance, whereby one person diminishes the happiness of another not by intent, nor solely in order to increase their own happiness, but just through thoughtlessness or carelessness. This can involve just careless talk, like complaining about the national obesity crisis when there is an overweight person in the room. It could be a case of the rambler who fails to secure farm gates properly, allowing livestock to escape. There might be no *intention* on the part of these people to diminish anyone's happiness, but the *consequences* of people's actions are always much more important than the *motivations* for them (*pace* Kant). Mere thoughtlessness perhaps, but as John Milton declared in *Samson Agonistes*,

> All wickedness is weakness: that plea therefore
> With God or Man will gain thee no remission. (Lines 833-4)

I have always thought that judgement to be rather harsh, for as humans we all suffer from weaknesses. But then, in this poem at least, Milton played the rather stern Puritan.

(d) The immorality of contingency:

Speaking of weakness though, what about a couple who embark on an affair together even although they are both married to someone else, and have every intention of staying married to them? They are extremely careful in their behaviour, so as not to cause their spouses any offence. Their intention is simply to increase their own happiness, without diminishing the happiness of anyone else. Nothing wrong with that, surely? They are simply increasing the total amount of happiness in the world, so does that let them off the hook in moral terms? Not entirely, since they are nevertheless gambling with the happiness of others. They might take every possible precaution and be guilty of no kind of folly, but some totally fortuitous factor which they could not possibly have foreseen might still intervene and blow the gaff on them, causing great unhappiness all round.

This might be termed the immorality of accident, or of contingency. The odds were highly in their favour, but they still gambled and lost. However, this raises another interesting question. What if they had gambled and won? Suppose that they did get away with it? Suppose that it was a well calculated risk? Suppose that eventually the affair fizzled out, and the guilty parties simply went their own separate ways, leaving nobody any the wiser about what they had done. Would there then have been anything immoral about their behaviour at all? Indeed, what if their brief affair had simply made both realise how precious their existing partners were to them, and so had improved both of their marriages? In that case their affair, although an immorality, would have turned out to be the right thing to have done. This is an important point to grasp: we have to recognise that behaviour that is immoral can occasionally also be at one and the same time either beneficial, necessary, or expedient, or correct, as is explained further below. But immorality remains immorality in absolute terms. Is it still immoral to gamble with other people's happiness even if you gamble and win? I would say that the answer is 'yes'. Gambling with the happiness of others in order to increase your own is certainly a lesser sin than deliberately decreasing their happiness for that end: a less reprehensible form of immorality, perhaps: but it is still an immorality. Now here I am beginning to sound a little like John Milton in Puritan mode myself, and I would hasten to add that, despite my very best intentions, I have of course not always been a paragon of virtue myself. But I have at least thought deeply about the concept of morality, and my conclusion is that morality is absolute, not relative.

(e) The immorality of necessity:

We have looked now at the immorality of intent, the immorality of indifference, the immorality of ignorance or incompetence, and the immorality of contingency. But we should, perhaps, also recognise a final category, namely the immorality of inevitability, or the immorality of necessity, if you will. This involves immoral behaviour which is also, in context, the correct behaviour. The ultimate immorality is war, which is also the ultimate obscenity and the ultimate absurdity. And yet, what choice do you have when a regime like that of Nazi Germany's is trying to invade your country? Do you just let them march in and murder all your Jews while you stand by wringing your hands, in order to avoid war? Sometimes you are forced to fight, because the alternative is unacceptable, however immoral war may be. That is the reality of the situation, and reality must always trump morality, for morality is of man, while reality is of God. Thus, we are rendered immoral by necessity, we are made fools by compulsion: we must become immoral in order to prevent an even greater immorality. It is important to understand that moral behaviour, or even morally neutral behaviour, can on occasions be not only boring and unhealthy, but actually shameful and wrong. Deliberate immorality can sometimes be necessary, as in the punishment of criminals, for example. Vegetarians and vegans would also argue that the raising of animals for food is an immorality, since we aim to benefit at their expense. However, this is a moot point – the animals so raised are at least given a life thereby that they might not otherwise have had, and a well fed and comfortable one too for the most part. But when all is said and done, immorality remains immorality in absolute terms, and folly remains folly. As your grandmother would have said, 'Two wrongs do not make a right!'

Well, we have dealt with immorality, but who then is the moral individual? He who avoids doing any of the above, lives quietly, observes the mores of his time and does nothing to increase his own happiness at the expense of someone else's happiness might be regarded as a moral and upright citizen. But this is something of a neutral state. He has not been immoral or anti-social, but he hasn't done anything particularly commendable either. I think we need one or two new words in our vocabulary here, terms like 'pro-social' and 'metamoral', for example. These could be applied to people who do not just passively go along with the mores of the times and keep a low profile, but who are actually pro-active in doing good work for their community, even at the expense of their own comfort or convenience. The fact that we do not have such terms in our vocabulary says something about our society. These people ought to be recognised and celebrated. Sometimes, indeed, they are, but I still say that our vocabulary needs to change: terms like 'pro-social' and 'metamoral' should be applied to those people, replacing such epithets as 'do-gooder' and 'holy Joe'.

Speaking of 'necessary and acceptable immorality', however, leads us on to consider competitive situations. If ten people go for one job and only one person gets it by deliberately proving himself better than the other candidates, then he has increased his own happiness, but only at the cost of diminishing the happiness of the other nine applicants. Has he therefore committed an immoral action? One could ask the same question about all forms of competitive sport. By winning, one side always increases its own happiness and that of its supporters, but only at the cost of diminishing the happiness of the other side and their supporters. This conundrum of course casts moral doubt over our whole capitalist system, which is very heavily based upon competition. But perhaps we can introduce another refinement here. There exists in English law a doctrine known as the *volenti non fit injuria* rubric, which translates roughly as, 'He who has volunteered to be injured has not been injured at all as far as the law is concerned, even if he is injured'. (The law is like that.) So we might say that all the competitors who enter into competitive situations do so voluntarily, knowing that their happiness might be diminished if they lose the competition. This lets those who have deliberately diminished their happiness by winning the competition off the hook in moral terms. 'If you can't take the heat, don't go into the kitchen', as Harry S. Truman once observed. Of course the injured party remains just as injured as if he hadn't volunteered, but we have to remember that our human laws, in terms of jurisprudence, are just as much our own invention as our whole concept of morality in the first place, so it is perhaps logical enough that the one might cancel out the other in some cases. However, when it comes to job applications the candidates often do not have any choice about whether they enter into a competition or not – they desperately need to get a job! It could well be argued therefore, as Marx in fact did, that our whole capitalist system is immoral because it is based upon competition and exploitation. Companies compete with each other in an attempt to establish themselves as monopoly suppliers, landlords collect rents for very little effort, and labourers are exploited. The employer makes a profit only by creaming off the surplus value of the labour of his employees and keeping it for himself. The value of the worker's product must always be greater than the cost of his wage plus the raw materials on which he works.

Now under Communism, these elements in theory disappear. There is no competition for jobs, because work is created for everyone. No one is exploited by a private capitalist because there are no private capitalists: instead everyone works simply for the greater prosperity of the community as a whole. There are no great inequalities of wealth, while health, education, social services, and pensions are provided freely to all, and so in theory we have here the perfectly moral state. There is just one problem: history has taught us that in practice, Communism doesn't work. An example from agricultural history provides an illustration of why this might be so. In early eighteenth-century England most village communities enjoyed access to an area of 'common' land in their vicinity. This land belonged to the community as a whole, and could be used for rough grazing, fuel gathering, turf cutting, etc. But the problem was that everyone wanted to take something out of the common, and nobody wanted to put anything back in. Despite local by-laws that made some attempt to husband the common resource, anyone who drained the common, or irrigated the common, or planted the common, or fertilised the common, would be regarded as a fool, because all his efforts would go to the benefit of others. This meant that, in those days of scarce resources, nobody in fact ever tried to improve the common land at all, and so it was denuded of timber, and its soil quality deteriorated. Only when the common was enclosed and parcelled out into private ownership did people begin to think that it might be worthwhile to improve their particular portion of it for their own benefit, and so the productivity of the once-common land was increased. Sadly, when you have a common resource, everyone strives to take more out of it than they put into it, and where you have an entirely communist system, you find this problem writ large: everyone strives to take more out of it than they put in. I remember one worker from an ex-communist land reflecting wearily, 'We pretended to work, and they pretended to pay us!' Unfortunately, the profit motive is hard-wired into out psyches, and Communism throws the profit motive into reverse: since there is nothing to be gained by working harder, since everyone still gets the same however hard they work, the only way to make a 'profit' out of the arrangement is to put less in, by working less hard. In the end, the entire system collapsed.

With regard to the eighteenth-century enclosure movement in England, however, there was of course another side to this development. When it came to enclosure by Act of Parliament and the parcelling out of the common land, the lion's share of the enclosure always went to the lord of the manor, the parson, and the local gentry. The small proprietor was often left with so little land of his own that the extra size of his holding was not an adequate compensation for his loss of common rights. Many found that they were left without enough grazing to keep a cow, and that their smallholding was no longer economically viable. They were forced to sell up, and become tenant farmers on the estates of the great landowners. Sometimes entire villages were cleared after enclosure to make way for the private landscaped parks that surrounded stately homes, as in the case of Nuneham Courtenay in Oxfordshire. Essentially, the parliamentary enclosure movement had been another act of theft by the kleptocracy that ruled in eighteenth-century England. The commons, although badly managed, had at least been the people's land, but now most of it was taken from them and handed over to the rich. In 1770 the poet Oliver Goldsmith (1728-74) bewailed these developments in his long poem *The Deserted Village*, some lines from which are quoted below. I cannot help feeling that they are surprisingly apposite for our own day, for Goldsmith could have been writing here about our very own city traders and overpaid CEOs, especially those based in London. He wrote,

Ill fares the land, to hastening ills a prey,

Where wealth accumulates and men decay...
Ye friends to truth, ye statesmen who survey
The rich man's joys increase, the poor's decay:
'Tis yours to judge, how wide the limits stand
Between a splendid and a happy land...
Hoards even beyond the miser's wish abound,
And rich men flock from all the world around.
Yet count our gains: this wealth is but a name
That leaves our useful products still the same.
Not so the loss. The man of wealth and pride
Takes up a space that many poor supplied...
Where then, ah where, shall poverty reside
To scape the pressure of contiguous pride?...
If to the city sped, what waits him there?
To see profusion that he must not share;
To see ten thousand baneful arts combined
To pamper luxury, and thin mankind:
To see those joys the sons of pleasure know
Extorted from his fellow-creatures' woe...
Oh luxury! Thou, curst by Heaven's decree,
How ill exchanged are things of worth for thee!
How do thy potions, with insidious joy,
Diffuse their pleasures only to destroy!
Kingdoms by thee to sickly greatness grown
Boast of a florid vigour not their own.
At every draught more large and large they grow,
A bloated mass of rank, unwieldy woe;
Till sapped of strength, and every part unsound,
Down, down they sink and spread a ruin round!

Yes, our bankers certainly 'spread a ruin round' in 2008 and have gone unpunished for it, continuing to enjoy enormous salaries and bonuses at our expense. It is rather depressing to think that, after 250 years, we have simply moved from one kleptocracy to another. Ill fares the land indeed. Some very enlightening reading on this point is to be found in Andrew Sayer's book, *Why We Can't Afford the Rich* (2016) and Nicholas Shaxson's, *The Finance Curse: How Global Finance is Making Us All Poorer* (2018).

Nor has the system been reformed: we have every reason to fear that the great crash of 2007-9 could happen again. I should say once more at this point that I remain a friend of capitalism, a friend of democracy, and I accept that we must always have a degree of inequality. But I am not the friend of the kind of capitalism that we have at the moment, nor of our present pseudo-democracy, nor of the grotesque levels of inequality that are currently tolerated in our society. There is much work to be done here, but the answers lie in reform rather than revolution. I continue to have no faith in Communism, but an injection of some much-needed socialism into our present unbalanced system is an entirely different proposition. As Karl Popper so wisely observed, we should aim for moderation in all things, and today the pendulum has simply swung too far to the Right. When Popper wrote about *The Open Society* he had in mind primarily a society that was open to change, and open to the reception of new ideas in ways that the communist and fascist societies of his own day certainly were not. It is to be hoped that our own societies of the present time in Europe and in North America are still 'open' enough to be capable of change, despite their current obsession with neoliberal thought. In the UK in particular, change is badly needed both in the constitutional sphere and in terms of the economic philosophy currently being adhered to by our government.

Do We Live in a Neoliberal Plutocracy?

The above suggestion sounds rather extreme and depressing, but unfortunately all of the available evidence points in that direction. Robert Peston's book, *Who Runs Britain?* (2008) does nothing to allay our suspicions. (See in particular chpt. 8, 'Democracy for Sale', pp. 256-303). Thanks to the rise of neoliberalism the plutocrats, now richer than ever before, have been able to tighten their grip on governments not only in the UK, but throughout the Western World. A responsible government that was not under plutocratic control would never have countenanced the insane policy of financial deregulation. This was an open invitation to precisely the kind of financial disaster that overtook the Western World in 2007-9. This forced governments on both sides of the Atlantic to greatly increase their borrowing to bail out the banks, leading to much higher levels of public debt. Annual budget deficits too increased to service the higher debts. What was to be done? A responsible government would have taken the obvious course of forcing the offenders to pay, raising state income by imposing wealth taxes, inescapable inheritance taxes, and a small financial transactions tax. But for governments under plutocratic control such measures would of course be unthinkable. Instead, to reduce national budget deficits and debt, their only available solution was to cut public *expenditure* in the hope of balancing the books in that way. This meant the imposition of austerity, with severe cuts to public services, pay in the public sector, and welfare benefits. But here I must stress once again that 'austerity' means austerity *for the poor only*. It lets the rich off scot free. They can afford to buy private health care, private education, private transport, and even private security for themselves. They never become dependent upon those social services that are such a vital lifeline for the poor. As a public policy therefore, the imposition of 'austerity' was clearly immoral, disgraceful, and utterly contemptible. It forces the poor to pay for the folly and greed of bankers and hedge fund managers. It looks very much like the kind of policy that would be forced upon a government by its plutocratic masters. During the AIDS epidemic of the 1980s the slogan emerged, 'Don't die of ignorance'. This meant, 'Be aware of the dangers posed by this disease, and take appropriate countermeasures'. Today we are having the financial lifeblood drained out of us by a class of greedy and selfish plutocrats, who are getting away with it because so few people are aware of what is really going on. Become aware. Don't die of ignorance.

Another clue to the rule of plutocrats lies in the laxity of our taxation systems for the rich, not only here in the UK but throughout the Developed World. We have already seen how top rates of income tax have been slashed in recent decades, together with rates of corporation tax in many wealthy countries. Inland revenue staff have also been cut back, and those remaining advised not to be too 'officious' with their 'customers'. There is no need to ask who has benefitted from these changes. Moreover, by employing armies of clever lawyers and accountants to work for them, wealthy interests are not even paying all the tax that they owe at these reduced rates. *The Financial Times* for August 28, 2007 reported that in the previous boom year of 2006 one-third of the UK's 700 largest businesses had paid no corporation tax at all.

Warren Buffet (b. 1930) is one of the world's richest men, and a noted philanthropist who pays a good deal of tax to the US government. He has himself criticised the absurdity of our taxation systems. On surveying the pay of his own office staff in 2006 he discovered that he was paying the lowest *rate* of tax of any of them, including his receptionist. He paid only 19% of his income in federal and state taxes, while his employees paid 33% of theirs, despite making much less money. 'How can this be fair?' he asked, 'How can this be right? There's class warfare all right, but it's my class, the rich class, that's making war and we're winning'. (Quoted in *The New York Times* for November 26, 2006) This is the situation that prevails on both sides of the Atlantic: the richer you become, the less income tax you pay as a proportion of your income. But Buffett does at least have a social conscience, having given billions of dollars away to various charities on a regular basis. The same cannot be said for most of his plutocratic class. More typical is Leona Helmsley (1920-2007), an American property speculator and convicted tax evader who died worth eight billion dollars. She was better known as 'The Queen of Mean', and during her trial for tax evasion in 1989 she was famously quoted in *Newsweek* magazine for July 24, 1989 as saying,

> *We* don't pay taxes. Only the *little people* pay taxes. (p. 11)

Leona never attempted to deny this quote, which is indeed too true to be funny. Leona was speaking here not only for herself, but for the whole class to which she belonged. Originally sentenced to 16 years for blatant tax evasion, she eventually served only 19 months thanks to the work of her very clever lawyers.

The situation in France is no better. Thomas Piketty, the celebrated French economist, explains why this is so.

Take Lilliane Bettencourt, the L'Oréal heiress and the wealthiest person in France. According to information published in the press and revealed by Bettencourt herself, her declared income was never more than five million a year, or little more than one ten-thousandth of her wealth (which is currently more than 30 billion euros). Uncertainties about individual cases aside (they are of little importance), the income declared for tax purposes in a case like this is less than a hundredth of the tax payer's economic income. The crucial point here is that no tax evasion or undeclared Swiss bank account is involved (as far as we know). Even a person of the most refined taste cannot easily spend 500 million euros a year on current expenses. It is generally enough to take a few million a year in dividends (or some other type of payout) while leaving the remainder of the return on one's capital to accumulate in a family trust or other ad hoc legal entity created for the sole purpose of managing a fortune of this magnitude, just as university endowments are managed. (*Capital in the 21st. Century* (2014 ed.) p. 525

These measures, of course, are designed to avoid taxation. This is precisely why, as Piketty points out, the rich will continue to become progressively richer and richer than the rest of us, unless governments have the will and the courage to step in to redress the situation. But it also means that there is no point in raising the income tax rates of the rich, because it is so easy for them to avoid paying income taxes, perfectly legally. Piketty's proposed solution is the imposition of wealth taxes instead, particularly on wealth held as land and buildings. I would agree here, but add that we also need 'trust-proof' inheritance taxes, and a small financial transactions tax.

But for those who are hell-bent on paying no tax at all, either legally or illegally on certain sums of money, a plethora of tax havens exists all around the world, ready and eager to service them, be they drug dealers, gun runners, human traffickers, or corrupt dictators, feathering their own nests at the expense of their countries. These havens are too numerous to list here, but they are named, shamed, and explained in four excellent publications, James Henry's *The Blood Bankers: Tales from the Global Underground* (2005), Nicholas Shaxson's *Treasure Islands: Tax Havens and the Men Who Stole the World* (2012), Gabriel Zucman's *The Hidden Wealth of Nations: The Scourge of Tax Havens* (2015), and Bastian Obermayer's, *The Panama Papers: How the World's Rich and Powerful Hide Their Money* (2017). Interestingly, Zucman's book was published by the University of Chicago Press: the first glimmerings of repentance by sinners? These books expose the whole sordid business: the secrecy jurisdictions, the zero-tax islands, the bogus trusts, the transfer pricing and the 'laddering' used by multinational corporations such as Apple, Google, and the American International Group, the shell companies, the money laundering, and the bogus foundations. Thomas Piketty points out the obvious when he declares,

The most plausible reason why tax havens defend bank secrecy is that it allows their clients to evade their fiscal obligations, thereby allowing the tax havens to share in the gains. Obviously, this has nothing whatsoever to do with the principles of the market economy. No one has the right to set his own tax rates...that is outright theft. (op. cit. p. 521-2)

Now the point about all of these tax havens is that they could all be shut down, or their banking systems cleaned up, if the political will to do so existed. Two of the most notorious, for example, Jersey and the Cayman Islands are still, in the last analysis, under the direct rule of London. The American Virgin Islands and American Samoa lie in the same relationship with the USA. Others are independent states like Luxembourg and Switzerland which are very vulnerable to economic sanctions imposed upon them by surrounding countries. The Wikipedia entry on Tax Havens includes all the latest information available on this topic, and makes the following statements on the scale of tax loses for those countries that are not tax havens:

Estimates of the financial scale of taxes avoided vary, but the most credible have a range of US$100-250 billion per annum. In addition, capital held in tax havens can permanently leave the tax base (base erosion). Estimates of capital held in tax havens also vary: the most credible estimates are between US$7-10 trillion (up to 10% of global assets). The harm of traditional and corporate tax havens has been particularly noted in developing nations, where the tax revenues are needed to build infrastructure. (Available online)

Since the harm being done by tax havens is well known, it might be expected that the honest countries of the world would unite to do something about them. However, both Shaxson and Zucman complain bitterly about the lack of progress being made on dealing with these tax havens. Such measures as have been taken so far they describe as, 'inadequate', 'a whitewash', a 'fig leaf', and 'toothless'. They suggest that this might be because the world's largest tax havens are never named on any blacklists because they are in fact the USA and its satellites, and the UK and its overseas territories! Could this in turn be because the USA and the UK are also the two most ardently neoliberal countries in the world? Richard Brooks explains how the UK became a tax haven in his book, *The Great Tax Robbery: How Britain Became a Tax Haven for Fat Cats and Big Business* (2014), while Oliver Bullough in his book, *Moneyland: Why Thieves and Crooks Now Rule the World, and How we can take it Back* (2019) devotes a chapter to 'Tax Haven USA' (pp.256-70) Taking a global view, Shaxson in his *Treasure Islands* notes, 'Overall, taxes have not generally declined. What has happened is that the rich have been paying less, and everyone else has had to take up the slack'. (p.24) This would be entirely in the best neoliberal traditions. In addition, of course, this explains why interest rates are currently so low around the world. Even tax havens must find someone to borrow their money in order to make a profit out of holding it, and there is now a plethora of this money to be lent. This in turn is the result of an increasing amount of national incomes going into the pockets of the rich, who have a much higher propensity to save than the poor. They enjoy gloating over their bank balances, and are obsessed with adding to them, even at very low rates of interest. They think rather of the tax that they are not paying on those sums, which more than makes up for low interest rates. As a result there is a great deal of 'cheap money' sloshing around the world, but it is not causing inflation because to do this the money must be *spent*, increasing the demand for goods and services, the prices of which will rise if supply cannot match the increased demand. If most of an increased money supply is simply salted away in secret bank accounts it will *not* cause inflation: this is the situation we are in today. Friedman, with his jejune understanding of monetarism, completely failed to recognise this. But low interest rates are very hard on ordinary savers, trying to save modest sums for rainy days, and for small investors trying to live on income from their capital. It makes them easy prey for bogus schemes offering higher interest rates.

However, as time goes on we are at least learning more and more about who is using these tax havens, thanks to the work of public-spirited individuals who have leaked information from them. The first of these leaks was only a small one and, uniquely, the information was sold for cash on this occasion. It emerged from a Liechtenstein bank in 2008, naming 1,250 of its customers, many of whom were subsequently prosecuted for tax evasion. The next leak emerged in 2013 from a much larger haven, the British Virgin Islands, this time naming 2.5 million haven clients. The third leak came from Luxembourg in 2014, revealing the affairs of more than 340 multinational companies based in Luxembourg. A fourth leak came from Switzerland in 2015 and concerned the British multinational bank HSBC. Its Swiss subsidiary, HSBC Private Bank (Suisse) had, allegedly with the knowledge of head office, been advising clients on tax avoidance and evasion schemes in tax havens around the world. Data was provided on over 100,000 private clients and 20,000 companies which were using offshore banking facilities. But the biggest leak so far emerged in the form of the notorious 'Panama Papers', anonymously leaked to the German journalist Bastian Obermayer in 2015. These were the records of the Panamanian law firm Mossack Fonseca, so extensive that Obermayer had to recruit the help of journalists from 107 media organisations in 80 countries to help him to analyse the data, which was eventually published in 2016. Again clients of the firm had been directed to tax havens around the world, and among the prominent names revealed was that of David Cameron, who was then Prime Minister of the UK.

The most recent leak emerged in 2017 and took the form of the so-called 'Paradise Papers'. They were so named because they provided a wealth of information on numerous tax havens which were a 'paradise' for tax dodgers. They consisted mainly of the records of the law firm Appleby, which had offices in tax havens around the world, including Bermuda, the British Virgin Islands, the Cayman Islands, the Isle of Man, Jersey, Guernsey, and Hong Kong, but also revealed were the records of the corporate service providers Estera and Asiaciti Trust, together with the business registries of 19 other tax jurisdictions. In all, seven legal and financial firms were named, most of them under investigation by tax authorities at the time. Collectively, they are often referred to as the 'Offshore Magic Circle', because they can make your tax bills magically disappear. Individuals using these havens included U.S. Secretary of Commerce Wilbur Ross, and James Sassoon, better known as Baron Sassoon of the UK House of Lords who, from 2007-8 was President of the international Financial Action Task Force on Money Laundering. Also named as users of these havens were Queen Elizabeth II and her son Prince Charles. (Wikipedia entry on Tax Havens).

But perhaps the most alarming aspect of these tax havens is the fact that most of their users are not criminals. They are unethical perhaps, immoral possibly, unpatriotic certainly, but what they are doing is often not actually illegal, thanks to the help of their very clever lawyers. Why pay tax when it is so easy to move your money into a tax-free jurisdiction like Jersey? Anyone can do it – well, anyone with the money to hire expensive lawyers and accountants anyway. Moreover, there are so many of these havens, several of them sovereign states, and they are patronised by so many powerful politicians and billionaires. What hope is there of ever closing them down, or persuading them to mend their ways? At present, the greatest attraction of tax havens is the secrecy that they afford to their clients. Some people might be holding money there quite legitimately, while others might be determined tax evaders, and at the moment tax authorities have no means of distinguishing between them. Many havens now claim to be 'transparent' because they will release 'on demand' information on individual clients on request. But there are strings: the enquirers must first show 'good cause' as to why they need the information. As Shaxson put it,

> No fishing expeditions –or general trawls to find tax cheats – are allowed. You can't prove criminality until you get the information, and you can't get the information until you can show criminality. *Catch 22's* Captain Yossarian would have appreciated the double bind. On request information is a fig leaf. It lets tax havens claim they are transparent, while continuing business as usual...Geoff Cook, chief executive of Jersey Finance, confessed in March 2009 that in the seven years since Jersey signed a tax agreement with the US, it had exchanged information with American investigators on just 'five or six' cases. (*Treasure Islands* pp. 212-213)

In reality, even the most 'transparent' of tax havens are absolutely furious when genuinely full information about their clients is leaked, as has been happening on an increasing scale. With every leak they thrash about desperately, looking for someone to sue. Many tax havens have now signed 'on demand' treaties with specific countries, but Zucman informs us,

> Yet through these treaties countries like the United Kingdom gather only a few dozen pieces of information each year, whereas hundreds of thousands of UK residents have foreign bank accounts. In spite of the resounding declarations of progress, defrauders go about their business with almost complete impunity. (op. cit., p. 60)

Also very worrying is the fact that the amount of money being moved into these havens is rapidly increasing. This means, of course, that the tax base of countries around the world is being steadily eroded. Gabriel Zucman, who has done pioneering work on quantification of the scale of offshore tax evasion, points out that by charging for their 'services', the tax havens are in fact robbing the more honest nations:

> No matter what one does, fraud originating in French or US banks is impossible, because they fully and truthfully exchange their information with tax authorities. It is only thanks to the lack of effective cooperation of a number of offshore private bankers that ultra-rich individuals are able to illegally evade taxes by not declaring income on their wealth. And although it is not alone, Switzerland is still to this day the number-one place for offshore private banking...According to the latest available information, in the spring of 2015 foreign wealth held in Switzerland reached $2.3 trillion. Since April 2009 – the date of the London summit during which the countries of the G20 decreed the 'end of banking secrecy' – it has increased by 18%...The growth is stronger in the emerging Asian centres, Singapore and Hong Kong, so that globally, according to my estimate, offshore wealth has increased by about 25% from the end of 2008 to the beginning of 2014. (op.cit. pp. 29, 46)

All this is very depressing. It suggests that, thanks to the triumph of neoliberalism, the fox is in charge of the chicken coop, the robbers are running the banks, and the lunatics have taken over the asylum. By 'the lunatics' I mean those who have been unhinged by greed, the 'pleonechotics', crazed with a manic desire to accumulate more and more and more of that which they already possess in abundance, namely money. I believe that the technical description for such a form of government is 'kakistocracy', government by the worst, from the Greek κάκιστος, 'worst'. The rich want to enjoy all the advantages supplied to them by the state's infrastructure, but do not want to make a fair contribution towards maintaining it. We see here the very same 'take-more-out-than-you-put-in' syndrome that brought down Communism.

I would like to stress again at this point, however, that I do not advocate making the rich poor. Both Thomas Piketty in his latest publication, *Capital and Ideology* (2020) and Albert Einstein, are a little too 'lefty' for me. The rich need to be persuaded to give over just a fair proportion of their wealth towards the relief of the poor. If they simply paid the taxes that they owed, this would help a lot. But can they be persuaded to do so? The outlook is bleak, but there are some glimmerings of hope on the horizon. Both Zucman in his *Hidden Wealth of Nations* (pp. 110-116) and Shaxson in his *Treasure Islands* (pp. 280-292) make some very practical suggestions for dealing with the problem of tax havens. Shaxson indeed suggests ten specific measures that could be taken. Although Shaxon is entirely right – all of his suggestions should be implemented - one is tempted to think on each point, 'Easier said than done' For example, as his tenth proposal he declares,

The final and most important element on my list is to **change the culture.** When pundits, journalists, and politicians fawn over people who get rich by abusing the system – getting around tax and regulations and forcing everyone else to shoulder the associated risks and taxes – then we have lost our way. (p. 290)

This echoes my own point about our need for a moral reformation, and reminds me poignantly that this very same point was made by Adam Smith in his *Theory of Moral Sentiments* (1759). He wrote,

Moralists all down the centuries have complained that wealth and greatness are often given the respect and admiration that only wisdom and virtue should receive, and that poverty and weakness are quite wrongly treated with the contempt that should be reserved for vice and folly. (Part I, Section 3, Chapter 3)

Again we have to ask ourselves, 'How much has changed in 250 years?' But I see two further grounds for hope in two points that were not made by either Zucman or Shaxson. One is that as more and more of the wealth of developed nations disappears into tax havens, the tax base of those countries will become more and more eroded, putting their governments under increasing pressure to take collective action against tax evaders. There is a limit to how far the burden of taxation can be moved down the social scale onto the shoulders of the less prosperous members of society. The second point lies in the hope that more whistle-blowers, insiders who are outraged by what they see, will take the risk of anonymously releasing large tranches of information on the users of tax havens, such as the Panama Papers and the Paradise Papers. Clients of these havens hate to have the spotlight of publicity focussed upon them, exposing them to at least a loss of reputation, and at worst a prison sentence. More leaks, please. It is further encouraging to note that the Panama Papers were not leaked to governments or to police forces, but to the German investigative journalist Bastian Obermayer of the Munich-based newspaper *Suddeutsche Zeitung* who could be trusted to give them maximum publicity. He was able to call to his aid the International Consortium of Investigative Journalists (ICIJ), rallying scores of journalists from around the world to help him in processing the vast amount of information that was released (11.5 million separate documents in all). This serves as a refreshing reminder that not *all* of the press is owned by plutocrats, and not all publishing houses allow themselves to be intimidated by them.

'Freely have ye received, freely give', said Jesus. (Matthew 10:8) That sounds entirely reasonable to me. What we really need to see, of course, is a moral reformation on the part of the rich, as they come to a full understanding of the term, 'immorality', which I have tried so hard to define above. This is what I meant when I spoke of the need for a moral reformation: it is the rich who need to reform. They should be capable of realising for themselves the importance of paying their taxes, so as to maintain the fabric of society in their own interests, as much as in everybody else's. This is not an entirely pious hope. Jean Paul Getty (1892-1976), known to be a notorious miser, discovered something of the joy of giving towards the end of his life, and was generous with endowments in his will. The life of Alfred Nobel (1833-96) followed a similar pattern. Moreover, some of the rich have been great philanthropists in the past, such as Andrew Carnegie (1835-1919) and John D, Rockefeller (1839-1937) in the USA, and Joseph Rowntree (1836-1925) and Antony Ashley Cooper (1801-85) in Britain. In 2020 Warren Buffett and Bill Gates, who vie for the title of world's richest man, are also today's greatest philanthropists, each one having given away tens of billions of dollars. Both men have demonstrated a lively social conscience, and a deep understanding of the world's ills. In fact, let us remember that Warren Buffett quotation once again.

There's class warfare all right, but it's my class, the rich class, that's making war, and we're winning. (*New York Times*, November 26, 2006)

In 2020 four out of the world's five richest billionaires signed the Giving Pledge, instituted by Gates and Buffet. This commits them to giving half of their private fortunes to charitable causes, either during their lifetimes or in their wills. Only the richest of them all, Jeff Bezos, CEO of Amazon, has declined to join in, but even he has been steadily increasing his philanthropic activities. In February 2020 he announced that he would contribute $10 billion over a period of years towards the battle against climate change. Unfortunately, however these men are exceptions to the rule. Most of the rich are obsessed with prestige, using conspicuous consumption as a means of demonstrating their status. Moreover they think it is clever, rather than disgraceful, to avoid paying the taxes that they owe, even although they could easily afford to pay them. Together they form a plutocracy that wields enormous political influence, and they will be extremely difficult to dislodge. Those rich plutocrats, crazed with greed, compare very unfavourably to the ordinary, decent people that you meet all around you every day. I find that these people are always ready to help one another, to contribute to charities, and to give some of their time for voluntary work. What a contrast they present to our greed-crazed, plutocratic masters.

I can well understand the despair felt by Thomas Paine as he reviewed the prospects for political reform in Britain. Despite his instinctive revulsion for violent methods, (his moderation had got him into trouble in revolutionary France) he came to believe that Britain's ruling kleptocracy of the 1790s was so firmly entrenched that it could be removed only by violent revolution. Well, I am not advocating bloodshed in the streets (although it may come to that if present trends continue) but I would like to see substantial political reform in our country, based on our existing institutions.

The multinationals and their extremely rich CEOs can hardly be blamed for caring nothing about the National Health Service, the Welfare State, decent pensions for all, full employment, good wages, and a more equal society. They have no need to do so. Neither is it their job to do so; these things do not fall within their remit. It is their job simply to maximise the profits of their companies, the dividends to their shareholders, and the incomes of themselves, regardless of any collateral environmental or social damage they may cause (in accordance with the sacred teachings of St. Friedman). They will not even pay their taxes if governments allow them to get away with it. 'Let 'er rip capitalism' will never build a fair and responsible society and a sustainable world for us all to live in. If this is what we want, then it is governments that must step up to the plate and enforce the stringent measures that will be necessary to bring this better world about. *In the last analysis the state is stronger than the plutocrats.* We can use the state to bring the plutocrats to heel once we have wrested control of our own governments back out of plutocratic hands via the constitutional reforms suggested above. If things are simply left as they are then the rich of the world will continue to get richer at an ever-increasing rate, their political power will increase in proportion, inequality will reach intolerable levels, environmental damage will continue, and our Welfare State provisions and National Health Service will continue to deteriorate. Moreover, if the rich are allowed to continue with tax avoidance at the present rate, then national debts will continue to increase until they reach unsustainable levels. Covid 19 has already forced our government into unprecedented levels of borrowing in peacetime.

In terms of wealth and income distribution, the UK has already become a very unequal country indeed. As Piketty and Dorling have shown so clearly, it was only the impact of two world wars during the twentieth century that forced governments to set about a redistribution of wealth in their countries, mainly by imposing higher taxes on the rich and by making better welfare provisions for the poor. After World War II the idea of higher taxes for the wealthy lingered on for some 30 years, providing the basis of the *trente glorieuses* and the remarkable rates of economic growth seen in that era. Things then took a turn for the worse in the 1970s. But hope for change is held out in several recent publications. One is the remarkable best seller by the Dutch historian and author Rutger Bregman, *Utopia for Realists and How We Can Get There* (2018 ed.). *Pace* Margaret Thatcher, Bregman made the resounding observation, 'Poverty is not due to a lack of character: it's due to a lack of cash'. This was not an entirely original point – others had made it before him – but Bregman certainly gave it maximum publicity, since his book has been translated into 23 languages. He also noted, 'You can't pull yourself up by your own bootstraps if you have no boots'. Bregman proposed the creation of Utopias through the elimination of poverty. He suggested that this could be done by the provision of one-off cash grants to the poor, or by the institution of a universal basic income, payable by the state to everyone. These too were not original ideas. In 2010 Joseph Hanlon, Barientos Armando, and David Hulme had published their remarkable book, *Just Give Money to the Poor: the Development*

Revolution from the Global South in which they detailed the results of experiments in giving cash grants to the poor of the Developing World. In 2017 Guy Standing, professor of Development Studies at SOAS, University of London, had published, *Basic Income: And How We Can Make It Happen*. In Chpt. I of this publication Standing traces the history of this idea back through Bertrand Russell, William Morris, Henry George, Thomas Paine, Charles Louis Montesquieu, and Thomas More with his original *Utopia*, right back to Pericles and Ephialtes in the days of ancient Athens. As noted in the Philosophy chapter above, it is extremely difficult to come up with a new idea these days. Well, it is certainly true that in our own time the obscenely large amounts of money being allowed to the rich, with their self-awarded pay rises, their tax cuts, and their tolerated tax havens, would seem less obnoxious if we could at least be sure that the poor were being properly looked after: but how should this best be done? They are certainly not being well looked after at the moment.

Because of the rise of automation and strong AI, plans for the introduction of a universal basic income may indeed represent an idea whose time has come. In his book *Utopia for Realists*, Bregman includes a chapter on, 'The Bizarre Tale of President Nixon and his Basic Income Bill' (pp. 77-100). The full details of the scheme are related in Brian Steensland's book, *The Failed Welfare Revolution: America's struggle Over Guaranteed Income Policy*. Nixon was in office from 1969 to 1974, and having presided over America's first manned moon landing, he then aimed to cement his place in history by also abolishing poverty in the USA! He planned to do this by establishing a basic income for all. These would have been two memorable achievements indeed, and had he succeeded he would have set a precedent for other countries to follow. Steensland's book shows just how close Nixon came to achieving his aim, but his plans foundered in Congress, he was himself overtaken by scandal, and then the *trente gloriouses* drew to a close as neoliberalism reared its ugly head. The idea of handing out free money to 'welfare bums' became unthinkable. But its time may be coming around again.

Ironically, Nixon had been dissuaded from his basic income bill partly by stories about a similar scheme that had been tried in England 150 years earlier. It was known as the Speenhamland System after the village of Speen in Berkshire, where local magistrates, meeting at the Pelican Inn on May 6, 1795, had first instituted the system. This scheme was quickly taken up by other counties in the agricultural south of England, and similar schemes were introduced further north. Scotland had its own system of poor relief. The Speenhamland system was never enforced by national legislation, but simply spread on its own merits. Britain was, at that time, at war with revolutionary France, and there were fears among the ruling classes that revolutionary ideas might spread in England if the poor were not properly provided for. Each parish in the scheme agreed to provide a basic income for its poor based on a sliding scale that rose with the price of bread and in accordance with how many children were in each family. For example, when a gallon loaf (which weighed 8½ lb.) cost one shilling, a married man with two children was guaranteed a basic income of seven shillings and six pence a week, *whether he was in work or not*. If the price of a loaf rose to one shilling and sixpence, this guaranteed income rose to ten shillings and three pence, with higher rates for more children. If a man was in work, but being paid less than these figures, the parish rates made up the difference, so that this level of basic income was always guaranteed. No distinction was made between the 'deserving' and the 'undeserving' poor. The assumption was simply that *all* who were poor deserved this money in order to subsist, as a basic human right.If this could be understood in 1795, then why not now? The scheme worked very well in relieving poverty wherever it was practised, and by keeping up demand for food benefitted farmers as well, and stimulated the entire economy. But in the early years of the twentieth century the scheme came under attack from historians of both the Left and the Right. Leftists described it as an 'employers' charter' because it enabled them to pay less than living wages to their workers, telling them to, 'get the rest from the parish'. Rightists attacked it as a disincentive to labour, since it was paid to the unemployed, and as an encouragement to have large families. But the truth was that it succeeded very well in its primary objective, which was the relief of poverty: there was no French Revolution in England. Indeed, by 1830 France herself had a monarchy again in the person of Louis Philippe I, who adopted a friendly attitude towards England. The danger from France had passed, and concern for the poor waned, to become rather a concern about the cost of the poor rates. Moreover, in that same year the Swing riots broke out across the south-eastern, agricultural counties of England. The rioters were agricultural labourers protesting about high cottage rents and tithes, but the main object of their wrath was the new, horse-powered threshing machines which were depriving them of seasonal work, namely winter threshing. Many machines were smashed during the riots. Notice, however, that the Speenhamland system had not made those labourers lazy and welfare dependent – on the contrary, they were demanding *work*.

However, the riots provided a further incentive for looking into the poor laws. In 1832 a Royal Commission was set up to investigate the Speenhamland System, and in 1834 it produced a lengthy report, complete with statistical appendix, which was utterly damning of the old poor law. For years historians accepted it as an accurate piece of research, but in fact it was a complete fraud, a piece of black propaganda designed to discredit the old poor law, which had come to be seen as too expensive. The true nature of the Royal Commission Report was first exposed by Mark Blaug in his article, 'The Poor Law Report Reexamined' (*Journal of Economic History (June 1964)* pp. 229-45). Other historians took up the theme, and it is now recognised for what it was. But in 1968 Nixon was not yet aufait with the latest historical research. The Speenhamland system was held up to him by right-wing advisors as an example of the failure of a basic income scheme. The Poor Law Amendment

Act of 1834 swept away the old system, and brought in a harsh new regime. Henceforth, all who needed relief would have to enter a workhouse, where families were separated, with separate houses for men, women, and children, and the regime made deliberately as gruelling as possible, under the principle of 'less eligibility'. But the 1834 Act succeeded in its primary goal: once the new system was fully operational, the proportion of national income being spent on poor relief fell from 2% to 1%. (Hanlon et al., pp. 16-17) In fact, the Speenhamland system had been incomparably better for the poor than its successor after 1834. This episode underlines the importance of acquiring a proper understanding of history. Nixon would never have allowed himself to be swayed by tales of the 1834 Poor Law Report if he had known at the time that it was an utterly bogus piece of propaganda, and might well have pushed ahead with his plans. Had he done so he could have relieved the poverty of millions in the USA, and set an example for the rest of the world. Instead of occupying just a footnote in history, this episode deserves to be headline news. Nixon's plan had been modest enough, proposing a universal basic income of $1,600 p.a., while the median US family income in 1969 was $9,400, although the median income of Negro families was only $6,000 p.a., according to figures from the US Census Bureau. However, Bregman declares that, 'his plan would have distributed cash assistance to some 13 million more Americans, 90% of them working poor'. (op. cit. p. 81). More significantly, however, the scheme would have established the principle, in the best traditions of Speenhamland, that those people were *entitled* to that money, *entitled* to have their poverty relieved, simply by dint of being human beings, and citizens of the richest country in the world. The entitlement of the poor to relief from their poverty is certainly more justifiable than the assumed 'entitlement' awarded to themselves by certain other groups.

In March 2020 Guy Standing published another book with the title, *Battling Eight Giants*. This title was intended to reflect the aims of the Beveridge Report of November 1942. Its official title had been, *Social Insurance and Allied Services* (Cmd. 6404) and it was the work of the Liberal economist William Beveridge (1879-1963). In this he named five 'giants' that needed to be defeated in order to build a better future for all after World War II. He named these as, 'want, disease, ignorance, squalor and idleness'. By this last he really meant, 'unemployment'. His report formed the basis of our National Health Service and welfare state, which came into full operation from 1948. But by 2020 Standing was arguing that the welfare state had failed, since the 'giants' which now needed to be defeated had multiplied to eight, and were somewhat changed in character. He identified them as, inequality, insecurity, debt, stress, precarity, automation, populism, and the threat of extinction. He once again advocated a universal basic income as part of the solution to all of those problems.

The arguments in favour of a universal basic income put forward in their books by Bregman and Standing are certainly interesting, but I cannot help feeling that the majority of people in this country are in no need of an additional income at the moment. Therefore, 'universal basic income' should not be truly 'universal'. There should be a cut-off point once earned income has reached a certain level. In the USA of 1969 this might have been $40,000 p.a., or in the UK of today perhaps £40,000? In the America of 1969, poor families on $6,000 p.a. would have been greatly helped by an additional $1,600 p.a., but as incomes rose $1,600 would have become of progressively less relative value to the wage earner in any case.

On the other hand, our large minority of poor are in desperate need of additional funding right now. Surely any additional resources should be focussed on them? It might therefore be wiser to begin by taking the less ambitious (and less expensive) route of simply guaranteeing a basic income to all of them according to family size whether they are in work or not. If this could be done under the Speenhamland System 200 years ago, then why not now? Alternatively, the handing out one-off lump sums to the poor could be trialled. This may seem to be an idealistic proposal, but schemes of this kind have already been extensively trialled, notably in Africa, but also in Mexico, India, and Brazil. An assumption has always been made that poor people must be 'bad with money' – that is why they were poor in the first place. But those trials proved this to be entirely untrue. In fact, poor people are extremely *good* with money. This discovery was hardly surprising: the poor *have* to be good with money, because they are used to having so little of it. The block grants handed out were put to very good and responsible use, often turning people's lives around on a permanent basis. On pp. 25-73 of his book Bregman outlines several examples of the success of similar trials in the developed world too, in Holland, in Canada, and even in the USA, and goes into detail about one such trial carried out in London.

The subjects of the trial were 13 homeless men who had been sleeping rough on the streets of London's Square Mile for some time. Each man was given a lump sum of £3,000 in May, 2009. There were no strings attached: every man could spend the money however he wished. Surprisingly, the money was very carefully, wisely, and slowly spent on a variety of items which the men themselves felt they most needed. After one year they had spent an average of only £800 each. Later,

> A year and a half after the experiment began, seven of the thirteen rough sleepers had a roof over their heads. Two more were about to move into their own apartments. All thirteen had taken critical steps towards solvency and personal growth. They were enrolled in classes, learning to cook, going through rehab, visiting their families, and making plans for the future. (p. 26)

Previously, many had resorted to petty crime, and 'Between police expenses, court costs, and social services, these thirteen troublemakers had racked up a bill estimated at £400,000 or more per year.' (p.25) On the other hand, the lump sum scheme had cost only, 'Some £50,000 a year, including the social workers' wages.' (p. 27). Providing the men with money had, at a stroke, relieved financial pressure upon them and given them a foothold in life, and hope for the future. It seems that the people who best know what is needed by the poor are the poor themselves. Perhaps a one-off block grant scheme, if rolled out nationwide could result in a win-win situation. It might actually be cheaper than our present Universal Credit system. It would be simpler to administer, and certainly more humane. Universal Credit is proving very costly to administer, and seems to be causing a great deal of hardship and stress to benefit seekers. 'Just Give Money to the Poor', as Joseph Hanlon et al. have recommended in their 2010 book. Perhaps block grants could at least be trialled on test groups as supplements to Universal Credit to see whether lump sums might indeed enable some to get back onto their feet and off welfare altogether. No doubt some would abuse the system, but trials run to date show this to be a great rarity.

I see the most urgent and immediate necessity in our country today as being that of making better provision for our poor, whether by introducing a basic income for them, by lump sum grants, or by simply making the provisions of Universal Credit more generous and less oppressive. The poor do not need contempt, or lectures, or sanctions, or humiliating interviews, or impossibly difficult forms to fill in: they just need cash. The present system seems to be deliberately designed to oppress, humiliate, and punish the poor for their poverty, very much like the Poor Law Reform Act of 1834, and should be seen as a national disgrace. It is once again an attempt to return to nineteenth-century conditions, which seems to be a cherished aim of neoliberals. It is the very antithesis of Karl Popper's recommendation to strive for 'the least misery of the greatest number'. An organisation already exists for promoting the reform of our benefits system, in particular for the reform of benefits for the disabled, who are among the most humiliated by universal credit. It is called the Centre for Welfare Reform. It is based in Sheffield and is headed up by Dr. Simon Duffy. Look them up on the web, subscribe to their newsletter, and lend them your support.

But of course, desirable as changes to our welfare system may be, only prior political reforms will make these changes possible. Here, I believe we should begin our attack against the present system's weakest point, which is the private funding of political parties. The Establishment already has a guilty conscience about this one, as has been clearly demonstrated by the many attempts to modify the present funding system that I have outlined above. What we need is the founding of a pressure group dedicated specifically to bringing in state funding, and *only* state funding, for all of our political parties.

Alternatively, perhaps one of our existing parties could be persuaded to adopt public funding as a plank in their campaigning platform. Obviously this could not be the Conservative Party, which benefits greatly from our existing system, and in which our ruling plutocrats are heavily concentrated, but one or all of the opposition parties might be persuaded to do so. In this respect, the UK has the opportunity to set a lead for the world.

The possibility of persuading one of our present parties to this idea, or even of starting up an entirely new party to support it, is more than just a pipe dream. In his book *Out of the Wreckage: a New Politics for an Age of Crisis* (2017) George Monbiot goes into some detail about the campaign of Bernie Sanders (b. 1941) who ran for nomination as the Democratic Party's presidential candidate in the US election of 2016. Initially, as the 'socialist' candidate, he appeared to be a complete no-hoper. Monbiot wrote,

> When Sanders officially launched his campaign in May 2015, everything seemed to be against him. Just 3 per cent of the electorate recognised his name. He was treated by much of the media as a marginal and superannuated figure (he was 74) whose policies were so far removed from the consensus that he could be safely ignored. His programme – the redistribution of income and wealth from the rich to the poor and middle; the break-up of the big banks; radical action on climate change; universal healthcare provided by the state; major restrictions on campaign finance – was considered either laughable or diabolical by the political mainstream. He refused to court major funders, relying instead on small donations from his supporters...By the time the contest was over, he had captured 22 states and 46% of the pledged delegates. In other words, he almost won, without compromising his political position. Had he succeeded – well, who knows what would have happened?...Perhaps only Sanders could have beaten Trump.
>
> So how did this man, dismissed from the outset as a no-hoper, come so close to securing the nomination? Part of the answer is provided in the most encouraging book I have read in years. *Rules for Revolutionaries: How Big Organising Can Change Everything* (2016), written by two of Sanders's campaigners, Becky Bond and Zack Exley, explains how, with hardly any staff and a tiny initial budget, they built the biggest voter-contact operation ever unleashed in a presidential primary. Had they known at the beginning of the campaign what they knew by the end, Sanders would have been irresistible. But by the time they stumbled across the strategy that almost won the nomination, it was too late. They see this not as a cause of frustration, but as a source of hope: if the methods they developed are used from the beginning, they could transform the prospects of any campaign for a better world. (pp. 166-7)

Monbiot then goes on to explain in some detail just how the Sanders campaign was run. (pp. 167-181) *Rules for Revolutionaries* is currently available in paperback from Amazon at £9.79. It is worth reading by anyone who hopes to achieve change from the grass roots upwards: by anyone who hopes to make the impossible possible. It is even conceivable that one day we might be able to bring in state funding, and *only* state funding, for our own political parties here in the UK. We already have our own campaign group that is pressing for the reform of our voting system in Britain. It is called the

Electoral Reform Society, based in London and sadly, it is the world's oldest operating organisation concerned with political and electoral reform. I say 'sadly' because it was founded in 1884 as the Proportional Representation Society. Although it has achieved some success in Ireland, it has clearly not made much progress in Britain in 136 years! This is a reflection of the innate conservatism of the British people, a godsend to the neoliberal plutocrats who are currently controlling our political parties, and proving so successful at robbing us all to satisfy their own greed.

The Electoral Reform Society favours the introduction of the single transferable vote. Under this system, each voter has only one vote, but on his ballot paper he can list some or all of the candidates standing for the different parties in order of preference. In this way, no vote is wasted, since if the voter's first choice of candidate is eliminated through not getting enough votes, the voter's choice moves to his second preference, and so on down his list. This strikes me as being quite a reasonable arrangement as a basis for proportional representation in the absence of the more radical reforms proposed above. The ERS also favours a smaller, and elected House of Lords. They declare on their website that from February 2014 to January 2015, £21 million was paid out in fees and expenses to members of the Lords, with the average peer receiving £25,826. Those monies came to them tax free, and from April 2020 peers will be able to claim £323 per day just for signing in and going home again. You may agree with the aims of the ERS or you may agree with my own suggestions for constitutional reform outlined above, but please become involved. Sign their online petition for Lords reform: subscribe to their newsletter: lend them your support. Contact them to suggest that their main aim should be the securing of public funding for political parties: I have already done so. Let me say again that in the last analysis the state is stronger than the plutocrats, and if we can use our democracy to wrest control of the state out of their hands, then the state can be used to bring them to heel. But let me also say again that I do not advocate making the rich poor. Let them stay extremely rich if that is so important to them. We simply need a fair proportion of their wealth to help our poor, to invest in our infrastructure, to adequately fund our public services, and to protect our environment.

I hope that I have said enough in this book to convince any reasonable person that both our electoral system and our economic policies are in desperate need of reform, with ecological reform of course dependent upon economic reform. Unfortunately, however, the present system suits our ruling plutocrats far too well. As Bernie Sanders has noted, 'Reform never comes from above: it always comes from below'. If we want to see change for the better for all of us, then all of us must work for those changes. Write to your MP: campaign for electoral reform: but above all, become aware and become involved. We can use our democracy to change the game, and to build a better world for ourselves and our children. I have played a small part here by writing this book, but what is really needed is collective, large-scale action, arising from an awareness of the undesirability of our present situation. The neoliberal plutocrats are getting away with it because not enough people are aware of what is going on. 'Don't die of ignorance'. Now that we have seen what kind of position we are in with our current political system and economic policies, and where present trends are leading, we are faced with a clear choice. Either we can sit back and do nothing, and simply watch the greed-crazed (pleonechotic) plutocrats diverting a larger and larger share of the national wealth into their own pockets while paying less and less in taxes, ensuring that their political power steadily grows. Or we can get off our backsides and start trying to do something about it: the choice is ours. Our planet is not safe in the hands of neoliberal plutocrats. Something must be done.

Select Bibliography

Introduction

Eliot, T. S. *Four Quartets* (1943)

Hemingway, E. *For Whom the Bell Tolls* (1940)

Guirand, F. (ed.) *The Larousse Encyclopaedia of Mythology* (1959)

Jones, D. S. *Masters of the Universe: Hayek, Friedman, and the Birth of Neoliberal Politics* (2012)

Keynes, J. M. *The General Theory of Employment, Interest, and Money* (1936)

Khayyam, O. *The Rubaiyt* (1859 translation by E. Fitzgerald)

Pascal B. *Pensées* (1670)

Pope, A. *An Essay on Man* (1734)

Popper, K. *Unended Quest* (1977 ed.)

Shakespeare, W. *Hamlet* (1600)

Russell, B. *A History of Western Philosophy* (1946)

Tegmark, M. *Our Mathematical Universe* (2014)

Tolstoy, L. *War and Peace* (1869)

On Religion

Armstrong, K. *Islam, a Short History* (2000)

Beaver, R.P. et al. (eds.) *The World's Religions* (1982)

The Bible (1611 ed.)

Ciapalo, R.T. (ed.) *Postmodernism and Christian Philosophy* (1997)

Cross, F.L. (ed.) *The Oxford Dictionary of the Christian Church* (1958)

Eaton, C.L. *The Book of Hadith* (2008)

Fowler, J.D. *Hinduism: Beliefs and Practices* (1997)

Hutton, R. *The Stations of the Sun: A History of the Ritual Year in Britain* (1996)

Jacobs, A. (ed.) *The Essential Gnostic Gospels* (2006)

James, W. *The Varieties of Religious Experience* (1902)

Jung, C.G. *Psychology and Religion: West and East* (1938, 1970 ed.)

Kant, I. *Critique of Pure Reason* (1781, 1996 ed.)

Mack, B. L. *The Lost Gospel: The Book of 'Q' and Christian Origins* (1993)

Metzger, B.M. *The Oxford Companion to the Bible* (1993)

Pelikan, J. (ed.) *The World Treasury of Modern Religious Thought* (1990)

Pelikan, J. (ed.) *The Koran* (1992)

Popper, K. *The Open Society and its Enemies* (1945, 2002 ed.)

Rahman, A. *Muhammad: Encyclopedia of Seerah* (2017)

Romer, J. *Testament: the Bible and History* (1989)

Rahula, W. *What the Buddha Taught* (1974)

Smart, N. *The World's Religions* (1992)

Wray, W. *The Sayings of the Buddah* (1993)

On Philosophy

Barnes, J. (ed.) *Aristotle: The Nicomachean Ethics* (2004)

Basore, J.W. (ed.) *Seneca: De Beneficiis* (1989)

Byrom, T. *Dhammapada: The Sayings of the Buddah* (1993)

Campbell, R. (ed.) *Seneca: Letters from a Stoic* (2004)

Chang, H. *23 Things They Don't Tell You About Capitalism* (2010)

Douglas, C.L. (ed.) *Boethius: The Consolation of Philosophy*(2009)

Dylan, B. *Mr. Tambourine* Man (1965)

Falconer, W.A. (ed.) *Cicero: De Divinatione* (2008)

Fukuyama, F. *The End of History and the Last Man* (1992)

Harris, J. (ed.) *Epictetus: Complete Discourses* (2018)

Hegel, G.W. *The Philosophy of Law* (1833 ed.)

Hegel, G.W. *History of Philosophy* (1837)

Heidegger, M. *Being and Time* (1927)

Heidegger, M. *What is Philosophy?* (1956)

Hobbes, T. *Leviathan* (1651)

Jowett, B. (ed.) *Plato: Complete Works* (2020)

Kalupahana, D.J. *A History of Buddhist Philosophy (1994)*

Kant, I. *Prolegomena* (1787)

Kresge, S. (ed.) *Hayek on Hayek: An Autobiographical Dialogue* (1994)

Legge, J. (ed.) *Confucius:The Great Learning* (2016 ed.)

Leibniz, G. *Théodicée* (1710)

Magee, B. *The Story of Philosophy* (1998)

Murray, G. *The Stoic Philosophy* (1915)

Nietzsche, F. *The Gay Science* (1882)

Nietzsche, F. *Twilight of the Idols* (1889)

Nietzsche, F. *Thus Spake Zarathustra* (1891)

Pelikan, J. (ed.) *The Analects of Confucius* (1992)

Pascal, B. *Pensée* (1670)

Robertson, D. (ed.) *Meditations by Marcus Aurelius* (2019)

Rousseau, J.J. *The Social Contract* (1762)

Russell, B. *My Philosophical Development* (1959)

Sartre, J.P. *A Critique of Dialectical Reason* (1960)

Sartre, J.P. *La Nausée* (1938)

Schlipp, P.A. *The Philosophy of Karl Popper* (1974)

Spinoza, B. *Tractatus Theologico-Politicus* (1670)

Spinoza, B. *Tractatus Politicus* (1677)

Saint-Andre, P. (ed.) *The Vatican Sayings of Epicurus* (2010)

Stalley, R.F. (ed.) *Aristotle: The Politics* (2002)

Wittgenstein, L. *Tractatus Logico-Philosophicus* (1921)

Wittgenstein, L. *Philosophical Investigations* (1953)

Youge, C.D. *Epicurus: Principal Doctrines* (2019)

Four Great Philosophers

Baruch Spinoza

Deleuze, G. *Spinoza: Practical Philosophy* (1988)

Dockstader, N. 'Benedict de Spinoza: Epistemology' *The Internet Encyclopaedia of Philosophy* (September, 2009 edition, available online)

Gatens, M. *Spinoza's Hard Path to Freedom* (2011)

George, H. *Progress and Poverty* (1879)

Kaufmann, W. *The Portable Nietzsche* (1954)

Nadler, S. *Spinoza: A Life* (2018)

Newlands, S. 'Spinoza's Modal Metaphysics' *The Stanford Encyclopaedia of Philosophy* (Winter 2013 edition, available online)

Newton, I. *Principia* (1687)

Newton, I. *Opticks* (1704)

Nietzsche, F. *Beyond Good and Evil* (1886)

Scuton, R. *Spinoza* (2002)

Spinoza, B. *A Short Treatise on God, Man, and His Wellbeing* (1660)

Spinoza, B. *On the Improvement of the Understanding* (1662)

Spinoza, B. *The Principles of Cartesian Philosophy* (1663)

Spinoza, B. *The Ethics* (1674)

Spinoza, B. *A Compendium of Hebrew Grammar* (Unfinished in 1677)

Wolf, A. (ed.) *The Correspondence of Spinoza* (1928)

Yalom, D. *The Spinoza Problem* (2013)

Thomas Paine

Ayer, A.J. *Thomas Paine* (1988)

Burke, E. *Speech to the Electors of Bristol* (1774)

Burke, E. *Reflections on the Revolution in France* (1790)

Burke, E. *An Appeal from the New to the Old Whigs* (1791)

Fructman, J. *The Political Philosophy of Thomas Paine* (2009)

Hawke, D. E. *Paine* (1974)

Kaye, H.J. *Thomas Paine and the Promise of America* (2006)

Keane, H.J. *Tom Paine: A Political Life* (1995)

Middleton, C. *A Free Enquiry into the Miraculous Powers Which are Supposed to have Subsisted in the Christian Church* (1749)

Nelson, C. *Thomas Paine: His Life, His Time, and the Birth of Modern Nations* (2007)

Paine, T. *Common Sense* (1776)

Paine, T. *Rights of Man* (1792)

Paine, T. *Agrarian Justice* (1795)

Paine, T. *Open Letter to George Washington* (1796)

Paine, T. *The Decline and Fall of the English System of Finance* (1796)

Paine, T. *Observations on the Construction and Operation of Navies* (1797)

Paine, T. *The Age of Reason* (1794-1807)

Paine, T. *An Essay on the Origin of Freemasonry* (1810)

Roosevelt, T. *Life of Governor Morris* (1888)

Pearsall, M. *The Land Tax, 1692-1963* (1966)

Price, R. *A Discourse on the Love of our Country* (1789)

Price, R. *Observations on the Nature of Civil Liberty* (1776)

Price, R. *Observations on the Importance of the American Revolution* (1784)

Prior, J. *Life of Burke* (1854)

Rubel, D. (ed.) *Days of Destiny* (2001)

Sinclair, J. *A History of the Public Revenue of the British Empire* (1785)

Tone, T.W. *Memoirs of Theobald Wolfe Tone* (1827)

Watson, R. *An Apology for the Bible in a Series of Letters to Thomas Paine* (1796)

Albert Einstein

Atkins, P. *Four Laws That Drive the Universe* (2007)

Bjerknes, C.J. *Albert Einstein: The Incorrigible Plagiarist* (2002)

Bjerknes, C. J. *Albert Einstein: The Incorrigible Racist* (2016)

Calaprice, A. *Dear Professor Einstein: Albert Einstein's Letters to and from Children* (2002)

Calaprice, A. *TheUltimate Quotable Einstein* (2011 ed.)

Carus, T.L. *De Rerum Natura* (c. 60 BC)

Courant, R. & Hilbert, D. *Methods of Mathematical Physics* (1924)

Cox, B. & Forshaw, J. *Why Does* E=Mc^2? (2010)

De Pretto, O. 'Hypothesis of the Aether in the Life of the Universe' *Proceedings of the Royal Venetian Institute of Science, Letters, and Arts* Vol. LXIII Part II (Nov. 1903) pp.439-500

Einstein, A. 'On a Heuristic Point of View Concerning the Production and Transformation of Light' *Annalen der Physik* Series 4 Vol. 17 (1905) pp. 132-48

Einstein, A. 'On the Movement of Small Particles Suspended in Stationary Liquids Required by the Molecular-Kinetic Theory of Heat' *Annalen der Physik* Series 4 Vol. 17 (1905) pp. 549-60

Einstein, A. 'On the Electrodynamics of Moving Bodies' *Annalen der Physik* Series 4 Vol. 17 (1905) pp. 891-921

Einstein, A. 'Does the Inertia of a Body Depend on its Energy Content?' *Annalen der Physik* Series 4 Vol. 18 (1905) pp.639-41

Einstein, A. *Relativity: The Special and the General Theory* (1916)

Einstein, A., Thomson, J.J., & Planck, M. (eds.) *James Clerk Maxwell: A Commemorative Volume* (1931)

Einstein, A., Podolsky, B., & Rosen, N. 'Can the Quantum-mechanical Description of Physical Reality be Considered Complete?' *The Physical Review* Series 2 Vol. 47 (1935) pp. 777-80

Einstein, A. & Russell, B. *The Russell-Einstein Manifesto* (1955)

Einstein, A. *The World as I See It* (1956)

Einstein, A. *Essays in Humanism* (1978)

Einstein, A. *Ideas and Opinions* (2005 ed.)

Green, B.R, *The Fabric of the Cosmos* (2004)

Hasenohrl, F. 'On the Theory of Radiation of Moving Bodies' *Annalen der Physik* Series 4 Vol. 15 (1904) pp. 344-70

Isaacson, W. *Einstein: His Life and Universe* (2007)

Jammer, M. *Einstein and Religion* (1999)

Lorentz, H. 'Considerations on Gravitation' *Proceedings of the Academy of Science of Amsterdam* Vol. 2 (1900) pp.559-74

Lorentz, H. 'Electromagnetic Phenomena in a System Moving with Any Velocity Smaller Than That of Light' *Proceedings of the Royal Netherlands Society of Arts and Sciences* Vol. 6 (1904) pp. 809-31

McLaren, S. *Saving Einstein* (2021)

Ohanian, H.C. *Einstein's Mistakes: The Human Failings of Genius* (2009)

Perrin, J.B. *Les Atomes* (1813)

Planck, M. 'On Irreversible Radiation Processes' *Annalen der Physik* Series 1 (1900) pp. 69-122

Poincaré, H. 'The Theory of Lorentz and the Principle of Reaction' *Archives nèerlandaises des Sciences exactes et naturelles* Series 2 Vol. 5 (1900) pp. 252-278

Rodgers, N. & Thompson, M. *Philosophers Behaving Badly* (2005)

Rosenthal-Schneider, I. *Reality and Scientific Truth* (1980)

Seelig, C. (ed.) *Ideas and Opinions by Albert Einstein* (2005)

Wheaton, B.R. 'Philipp Lenard and the Photoelectric Effect, 1889-1911' *Historical Studies in the Physical Sciences* Vol. 9 (1978) pp. 299-322

Karl Popper

Cohen, R.S. & Parusniková, Z. *Rethinking Popper* (2009)

Comte, A. *Cours de Philosophie Positive* (1835)

Crews, F. *Freud: The Making of an Illusion* (2017)

Edwards, P. (ed.) *The Encyclopedia of Philosophy* (1967)

Feyerabend, P. *Against Method* (1975)

Feyerabend, P. *Farewell to Reason* (1987)

Hume, D. *Treatise of Human Nature* (1739)

Intellectus Vol. 23 (July-September 1992)

Kant, I. *Critique of Pure Reason* (1781)

Ladyman, J. & Ross, D. (eds.) *Scientific Metaphysics* (2013)

Nola, R. *After Popper, Kuhn, and Feyerabend* (2001)

Popper, K. *All Life is Problem Solving* (1994, 2001 ed.)

Popper, K. *Unended Quest* (1974, 1977 ed.)

Popper, K. *The Two Fundamental Problems in the Theory of knowledge* (1933, 2008 ed.)

Popper, K. *The Logic of Scientific Discovery* (1934, 1959 ed.)

Popper, K. *Realism and the Aim of Science* (1956, 1982 ed.)

Popper, K. *The Poverty of Historicism* (1957)

Popper, K. *The Open Society and its Enemies* (1945, 2011 ed.)

Popper, K. *The Open Universe: An Argument for Indeterminism* (1982)

Popper, K. *The Future is Open* (1985)

Popper, K. *Conjectures and Refutations: The Growth of Scientific Knowledge* (1963)
Schlipp, P.A. (ed.) *The Philosophy of Karl Popper* Vol. 2(1976)

Schopenhauer, A. *TheWorld as Will and Idea* (1819)

Shearmur, J. & Turner, P.N. (eds.) *Karl Popper:After the Open Society: Selected Social and Political Writings* (2011)

Zerin, E. (ed.), 'Karl Popper on God: The lost interview' *Skeptic* Vol. 6 No. 2(1998) pp. 29-35

On Science

Attenborough, D. *A Life on Our Planet* (2020)

Barnes, L.A. 'The Fine–Tuning of the Universe for Intelligent Life' *Publications of the Astronomical Society of Australia* Vol. 29 (June 2012) pp. 529-564

Barnes, L.A. 'The Fine Tuning of Nature's Laws' *The New Atlantis* Issue 47 (Fall, 2015) pp.87-97

Barton, N. *Ice Age Britain* (2005)

Batygin, K., Laughlin, G. & Morbidelli, A. 'Born of Chaos' *Scientific American*Vol. 314 Issue 5 (May 2016) pp. 1-24

Berners-Lee, M. *There is no Planet B* (2019)

Broom, N. *How Blind is the Watchmaker?* (1998)

Brown, B. & Morgan, L. *Miracle Planet* (1990)

Chang, H. *Bad Samaritans* (2007)

Chang, K. 'The Maritime Scene in China at the Dawn of Great European Discoveries' *Journal of the American Oriental Society* Vol. 94 No. 3 (1974) pp. 347-359

Chown, M. *We Need to Talk About Kelvin* (2009)

Church, S.K. 'Zeng He: An Investigation into the Plausibility of 450-Foot Treasure Ships' *Monumenta Serica Vol. 53* (2005) pp. 1-43

Coveney, P. & Highfield, R. *The Arrow of Time* (1990)

Cox, B. & Forshaw, J. *Why Does E=Mc²?* (2009)

Cox, B. & Forshaw, J. *The Quantum Universe* (2012)

Cox, B. & Cohen, A. *Wonders of Life* (2013)

Cox, B. *Forces of Nature* (2017)

Coyne, J.A. *Why Evolution is True* (2009)

Davis, P. *The Mind of God: Science and the Search for Ultimate Meaning* (1993)

Davis, P. *The Goldilocks Enigma: Why is the Universe Just Right for Life?* (2006)

Dawkins, R. *The Blind Watchmaker* (1986)

Dawson, A. *Extinction: A Radical History* (2016)

Diamond, J. 'How to Get Rich' *Edge Magazine* for June 6 (1999)pp. 1-24

Diamond, J. *Guns, Germs, and Steel: The Fates of Human Societies* (1997, 2017 ed.)

Edington, A. *The Internal Constitution of Stars* (1926)

Farrell, C. & Green, A. *This is Not a Drill* (2019)

Feldman, S. *Global Warming* (2009)

Flew, A. & Varghese, R.A. *There is a God: How the World's Most Notorious Atheist Changed His Mind* (2007)

Gould, S.J. *Wonderful Life* (2000)

Greene, B. *The Fabric of the Cosmos* (2004)

Greene, B. *The Hidden Reality* (2011)

Greene, B. *Until the End of Time* (2020)

Gribbin, J. & Rees, M. *Cosmic Coincidences* (1991)

Harari, Y. N. *Sapiens: A Brief History of Humankind* (2011)

Harari, Y.N. *Homo Deus: A Brief History of Tomorrow* (2015)

Hawking, S. *A Brief History of Time* (1988)

Hawking, S, *A Briefer History of Time* (2005)

Holt, J.C. 'Science Resurrects God' *The Wall Street Journal* (London edition, Dec. 24 1997)

Hoyle, F. 'The Universe: Past and Present Reflections' *Annual Review of Astronomy and Astrophysics* Vol. 20 No. 16 (1982) pp. 1-35

Hoyle, F. *The Intelligent Universe* (1983)

Juniper, A. *What's Really Happening to Our Planet?* (2016)

Krauss, L.M. *A Universe from Nothing* (2012)

Lane, N. *Life Ascending* (2010)

Lawson, N. *A Cool Look at Global Warming* (2008)
Linnaeus, C. *Systema Naturae* (1735)

Lovelock, J. *The Revenge of Gaia* (2006)

Marshall, M. *Human Origins* (2018)

McKie, R. *Ape Man: The Story of Human Evolution* (2000)

Michaels, P.J. *Shattered Consensus: The True State of Global Warming* (2005)

Malary, M. *Our Improbable Universe* (2004)

Needham, J. *Science and Civilization in China* (Vols. I-VII, 1954-2008)

Nurse, P, *What is Life?* (2021)

Penrose, R. *The Road to Reality: A Complete Guide to the Laws of the Universe* (2004)

Philip, B. 'Scrub Typhus in World War II' *The Journal of Parasitology* Vol. 34 No. 3 (June 1948) pp. 169-174

Panek, R. *The 4% Universe* (2011)

Reed, N. *The Naming of Parts* (1942)

Rees, M. 'Large Numbers and Ratios in Astrophysics and Cosmology' *Philosophical Transactions of the Royal Society* Vol. 310 Issue 1512 (Dec. 1983) pp. 311-322

Reilly, J. *The Ascent of Birds* (2018)

Rovelli, C. *Seven Brief Lessons on Physics* (2014)

Rovelli, C. *Reality is Not What it Seems: The Journey to Quantum Gravity* (2016)

Schrodinger, E. *What is Life?* (1944)

Shubin, N. *Your Inner Fish* (2007)

Soon, A. (ed.) *Global Warming: A Guide to the Science* (2002)

Stenger, V. *The Fallacy of Fine Tuning: Why the Universe is Not Designed for Us* (2011)

Stewart, I. *17 Equations That Changed the World* (2012)

Tamura, E.H. et al. *China: Understanding its Past* (1997)

Tegmark, M. *Our Mathematical Universe* (2014)

Tegmark, M. *Life 3.0: Being Human in the Age of Artificial Intelligence* (2017)

Wallace-Wells, D. *The Uninhabitable Earth* (2019)

Ward, P.D. & Brownlee, D. *Rare Earth: Why Complex Life is Uncommon in the Universe* (2004)

Woese, C.R. & Fox, G.E. 'Phylogenetic Structure of the Prokaryotic Domain: The Primary Kingdoms' *Proceedings of the National Academy of Sciences of the United States of America* Vol. 74 No. 11 (1977) pp. 5088-5090

Woese, C.R., Kandler, O. & Wheelis, M.L. 'Towards a Natural System of Organisms: Proposal for the Domains Archaea, Bacteria, and Eukarya' *Proceedings of the National Academy of Sciences of the United States of America* Vol. 87 No. 12 (1990) pp. 4576-4597

Ziurys, L. 'The Chemistry in Circumstellar Envelopes of Evolving Stars: Following the Origin of the Elements to the Origin of Life'*Proceedings of the National Academy of Sciences of the United States of America* Vol.103 No. 33 (Aug. 2006) pp. 12274-12279

On Politics

Acemoglu, D. & Robinson, J.A. *Why Nations Fail: the Origins of Power, Prosperity, and Poverty* (2012)

Adams, C.F. (ed.) *The Works of John Adams Esq., Second President of the United States* (1856)

Arout, F-M (Voltaire) *Micromégas* (1752)

Arout, F-M (Voltaire) *Candide* (1759)

Bentham, J. *A Fragment on Government* (1776)

Bentham, J. *An Introduction to the Principles of Morals and Legislation* (1789)

Bentham, J. *On the Liberty of the Press and Public Discussion* (1821)

Blackstone, W. *Commentaries upon the Laws of England* (1770)

Bodin, J. *Les Six Livres de la République* (1576)

Burke, E. *Thoughts on the Causes of the Present Discontents* (1770)

Bossuet, J-B. *Politics Drawn from the Very Words of Holy Scripture* (1709)

Bracton, H. *De Legibus et Consuetudinibus Angliae* (1268)

De Secondat, C-L. (Montesquieu) *Lettres Persanes* (1721))

De Secondat, C-L. (Montesquieu) *De l'Esprit des Lois* (1748)

De Secondat, C-L. (Montesquieu) *Considérations sur les Causes de la Grandeur des Romains et de leur Decadence* (1734)

Diamond, J. *Collapse: How Societies Choose to Fail or Succeed* (2005)

Diamond, J *Guns, Germs, and Steel: The Fates of Human Societies* (2017 ed.)

Dickens, A.G. *The English Reformation* (1978)

Diderot, D. & d'Alembert. J. (eds.) *Encyclopédie* (1751-72)

Epicurus of Samos *Principal Doctrines* (c. 300 BC) (2008 ed.)

Filmer, R. *The Necessity of the Absolute Power of all Kings* (1648)

Filmer, R. *Patriarcha* (1680)

Firth, C.H. *Oliver Cromwell* (1900)

Fortesque, J. *De Laudibus Legum Angliae* (1543)

Heine, H. *The History of Religion and Philosophy in Germany* (1834)

Hobbes, T. *Leviathan* (1651)

Hume, D. *An Enquiry Concerning the Principles of Morals* (1751)

Hutcheson, F. *An Inquiry into the Original of our Ideas of Beauty and Virtue* (1725)

Jesse, J.H. *Memoirs of the Court of England* (1840)

Juvenal, D.J. *Satires* (c. 100-128 AD)

Lapavitsas, C. *The Left Case Against the EU* (2019)

Lutz, D.S. 'The Relative Influence of European Writers on Late Eighteenth-Century American Political Thought' *The American Political Science Review* Vol. 78 No. 1 (March 1984) pp.189-197

Kelly, P.J. *Utilitarianism and Distributive Justice: Jeremy Bentham and the Civil Law* (1990)

Locke, J. *Two Treatises of Government* (1689)

Locke, J. *An Essay Concerning Human Understanding* (1690)

Locke, J. *Letters Concerning Toleration* (1689-1692)

Locke, J. *Some Thoughts Concerning Education* (1693)

Machiavelli, N. *The Prince* (1513)

Mackay, C. *Tubal Cain* (1851)

Masson, D. *The Life of Milton* (1880)

Mill, J.S. *Utilitarianism* (1863)

Paley, W. *The Principles of Moral and Political Philosophy* (1785)

Plato of Athens *The Republic* (c. 380 BC)

Ponet, J. *A Short Treatise of Politike Power* (1556)

Priestly, J. *An Essay on the First Principles of Government* (1768)

Prothero, G.W. *elect Statutes* (1906)

Proudhon, P-J. *An Inquiry into the Principle of Right and Government* (1840)

Rousseau, J-J. *Discours sur les Sciences et les Arts* (1750)

Rouseau, J-J. *Du Contrat Social: Principes du Droit Politique* (1762)

Rousseau, J-J. *Confessions* (1789)

Schmidt, K. 'Gobekli Tepe – the Stone Age Sanctuaries' *Documenta Prehistorica* Vol. XXXVI (2010) pp. 239-256

Shakespeare, W. *Richard II* (1595)

Sidney, A. *Court Maxims* (1666)

Sidney, A. *Discourses Concerning Government* (1698)

Stiglitz, J. *The Euro: How a Common Currency Threatens the Future of Europe* (2018 ed.)

Stuart, J. *The True Law of Free Monarchies* (1598)

Stuart, J. *Basilikon Doran* (1599)

Tyrrell, J. *Patriarcha non Monarcha* (1681)

Varoufakis, Y. *And the Weak Suffer What they Must* (2016)

Varoufakis, Y. *Adults in the room: My Battle with Europe's Deep Establishment* (2017)

Williams, B. & Smart, J.J. *Utilitarianism: For and Against* (1973)

Wilson, G. (ed.) *The Reports of Sir Edward Coke* (Report 12, 1777)

Winstanley, G. *A Declaration from the Poor Oppressed People of England* (1659)

On Economics

Brands, H.W. *Reagan: The Life* (2015)

Brooks, R. *The Great Tax Robbery: How Britain Became a Tax Haven for Fat Cats and Big Business* (2014)

Bregman, R. *Utopia for Realists and How We Can Get There* (2017)

Bullough, O. *Moneyland: Why Thieves and Crooks Now Rule the World, and How to Take It Back* (2019)

Cahill, K. *Who Owns Britain and Ireland?* (2002)

Campbell, J. *The Iron Lady: Margaret Thatcher: From Grocer's Daughter to Iron Lady* (2012 ed.)

Chang, H-J. *Bad Samaritans* (2008)

Chang, H-J. *23 Things They Don't Tell You About Capitalism* (2010)

Christophers, B. *The New Enclosure: The Appropriation of Public Land in Neoliberal Britain* (2018)

Crafts, N.F.R. *Economic Growth in Europe Since 1945* (1996)

Donnelly, J.S. *The Great Irish Potato Famine* (2005)

Du Pont, S. *Physiocratie, ou Constitution Naturelle du Government le Plus Advantageux au Genre Humain* (1768)

Fama, E. *The Theory of Finance* (1972)

Fama, E. *Foundations of Finance* (1976)

Friedman, M. *Essays in Positive Economics* (1953)

Friedman, M. *Capitalism and Freedom* (1962)

Friedman, M. *Inflation: Causes and Consequences* (1963)

Friedman, M. *The Counter-Revolution in Monetary Theory* (1970)

Friedman, M. *Free to Choose* (1980)

Friedman, M. *Two Lucky People* (1998)

Friedman, M. & Schwartz, A. *A Monetary History of the United States, 1867-1960* (1963)

Friedman, M. & Schwartz. A. *The Great Contraction* (1965)

Goodwin, M. et al. *National Populism: The Revolt Against Liberal Democracy* (2019)

Hampden-Turner C. & Trompenaars, F. *The Seven Cultures of Capitalism* (1994)

Harvey, D. *A Brief History of Neoliberalism* (2007)

Hayward, S.F. *The Age of Reagan: The Conservative Counterrevolution, 1980-1989* (2009)

Hayek, F.A. *Prices and Production* (1931)

Hayek, F.A. *The Pure Theory of Capital* (1941)

Hayek, F.A. *The Road to Serfdom* (1944)

Hayek, F.A. *Individualism and the Economic Order* (1948)

Hayek, F.A. *The Constitution of Liberty* (1960)

Hayek, F.A. *Law, Legislation, and Liberty* (1978)

Hayek, F.A. *The Fatal Conceit* (1988)

Jackson, T. *Prosperity Without Growth* (2017)

Jevons, W.S. *A General Mathematical Theory of Political Economy* (1862)

Jevons, W.S. *Theory of Political Economy* (1862)

Jones, B. & O'Donnell, M. (eds.) *Alternatives to Neoliberalism* (2018)

Joseph, K. *Why Britain Needs a Social Market Economy* (1975)

Kant,I. *Idea for a General History with a Cosmopolitan Purpose* (1784)

Kelton, S. *The Deficit Myth: Modern Monetary Theory and How to Build a Better Economy* (2020)

Keynes, J.M. 'Alfred Marshall, 1842-1924' *The Economic Journal* Vol. 34 Issue 135 (1924) pp. 311-372

Keynes, J.M. *A Treatise on Money* (1930)

Keynes, J.M. *The General Theory of Employment, Interest, and Money* (1936)

Kindleberger, C. *Manias, Panics, and Crashes: A History of Financial Crises* (1978)

Kishtainy, N. *A Little History of Economics* (2017)

Klein, N. *The Shock Doctrine: The Rise of Disaster Capitalism* (2008)

Lapavitsas, C. *The Left Case Against the EU* (2019)

Lengel, E.G. *The Irish Through British Eyes: Perceptions of Ireland in the Famine Era* (2002)

Le Pesant, P. *Le Détail de la France: La Cause de la Diminution de ses Biens et la Facilité du Remède* (1694)

Lippmann, W. *An Enquiry into the Principles of the Good Society* (1937)

Loveman, B. *Chile: The legacy of Hispanic Capitalism* (2001)

Lucas, R. *Studies in Business Cycle Theory* (1981)

Malthus, T.R. *An Essay on the Principle of Population* (1798)

Malthus, T.R. *Principles of Political Economy* (1820)

Marshall, A. *Principles of Economics* (1890)

Mason, P. *Postcapitalism: A Guide to Our Future* (2015)

Menger, C. *Principles of Economics* (1871)

Metcalf, S. 'Neoliberalism: The Idea that Swallowed the World' *The Guardian*, August 18, (2017)

Mill, J. *Elements of Political Economy* (1821)

Minsky, H. *Can 'It' Happen Again?* (1982)

Minsky, H. *Stabilising an Unstable Economy* (1986)

Monbiot, G. *Out of the Wreckage: A New Politics for an Age of Crisis* (2018)

Mosler, W. *Seven Deadly Innocent Frauds of Economic Policy* (2010)

Mosler, W. *Soft Currency* (2013)

Nelson, R. *Economics as Religion* (2001)

Obermaier, F. *The Panama Papers: How the World's Rich and Powerful Hide Their Money* (2016)

Piketty, T. *Capital in the 21st Century* (2013)

Piketty, T. Capital and Ideology (2020)

Quesnay, F. *Tableau économique* (1758)

Quesnay, F. *Le Despotisme de la Chine* (1767)

Ranelagh, J. *Thatcher's People* (1992)

Rapley, J. *Twilight of the Money Gods: Economics as a Religion and How it all Went Wrong* (2017)

Raworth, K. *Doughnut Economics: Seven Ways to Think Like a 21st Century Economist* (2018)

Rector, J.L. *The History of Chile* (2003)

Reinhart, C. & Rogoff, K. *This Time is Different: Eight Centuries of Financial Folly* (2009)

Ricardo, D. *Principles of Political Economy and Taxation* (1817)

Samuelson, P. *Economics: An Introductory Analysis* (1948)

Say. J.B. *Traité d'economie politique* (1803)

Sayer, A. *Why We Can't Afford the Rich* (2016)

Schultz, D. *Encyclopedia of Public Administration and Public Policy* (2004)

Senden, L. *Soft Law in European Law* (2004)

Shaxson, N. *Treasure Islands: Tax Havens and the Men Who Stole the World* (2010)

Shaxson, N. *The Finance Curse:How Global Finance is Making us All Poorer* (2018)

Shiller, R.J. *Irrational Exuberance* (2000)

Shiller, R.J. *The New Financial Order* (2003)

Shiller, R.J. & Akerlof, A. *Phishing for Phools: The Economics of Manipulation and Deception* (2015)

Skinner, B.F. *Schedules of Reinforcement* (1959)

Smith A. The Theory of Moral Sentiments (1759)

Smith, A. *The Wealth of Nations* (1776)

Standing, G. *Basic Income and How We Can Make it Happen* (2017)

Standing, G. *Plunder of the Commons: A Manifesto for Sharing Public Wealth* (2019)

Stiglitz, J. E. *Globalisation and Its Discontents* (2002)

Stiglitz, J. E. *The Price of Inequality* (2012)

Stiglitz, J. E. *The Great Divide* (2016)

Stiglitz, J. E. *Globalisation and Its Discontents Revisited* (2017)

Stiglitz, J. E. *The Euro and its Threat to the Future of Europe* (2018)

Stiglitz, J. E. *People, Power, and Profits: Progressive Capitalism for an Age of Discontent* (2020)

Tebbit, N. *Upwardly Mobile* (1991)

Tooze, A. *Crashed: How a Decade of Financial Crisis Changed the World* (2018)

Verkaik, R. *Why You Won't Get Rich: How Capitalism Broke Its Contract with Hard Work* (2021)

Wilkinson, R. & Pickett, K. *The Spirit Level: Why Equality is Better for Everyone* (2010)

Walras, L. *Elements of Pure Economics* (1877)

Woodham-Smith, C. *The Great Hunger: Ireland 1845-1849* (1991)

Zuboff, S. *The Age of Surveillance Capitalism* (2019)

Zucman, G. *The Hidden Wealth of Nations: The Scourge of Tax Havens* (2015)

Conclusion

Armstrong, S. *The New Poverty* (2017)

Blaug, M. 'The Poor Law Report Re-examined' *The Journal of Economic History* Vol. 24 No. 2(June 1964) pp. 229-245

Bond, B. & Exley, Z. *Rules for Revolutionaties: How Big Organising Can Change Everything* (2016)

Bregman, R. *Utopia for Realists and How We Can Get There* (2018)

Burgis, T. *Kleptopia: How Dirty Money is Conquering the World* (2020)

Cicero, M.T. *De Divinatione* (44 BC)

Collins, J.L. et al. (eds.) *New Landscapes of Inequality: Neoliberalism and the Erosion of Democracy in America* (2009)

De-la-Noy. M. *The Honours System* (1992)

Dorling, D. *Inequality and the 1%* (2019)

Eatwell, R. & Goodwin, M. *National Populism: The Revolt Against Liberal Democracy* (2019)

Geoghegan, P. *Democracy for Sale: Dark Money and Dirty Politics* (2020)

Gilbert, W.S. *Iolanthe* (1882)

Giroux, H.A. *Against the Terror of Neoliberalism: Politics Beyond the Age of Greed* (2008)

Goldsmith, O. *The Deserted Village* (1770)

Haig, M. *Notes on a Nervous Planet* (2019)

Hanlon, J. et al. *Just Give Money to the Poor: The Development Revolution from the Global South* (2010)

Harari, Y.N. *Sapiens: A Brief History of Humankind* (2014)

Hararie, Y.N. *Homo Deus: A Brief History of Tomorrow* (2016)

Henry, J. *The Blood Bankers: Tales from the Global Underground* (2005)

Jones, B. & O'Donnell, M. (eds.) *Alternatives to Neoliberalism: Towards Equality and Democracy* (2018)

Jones, O. *The Establishment and How They Get Away With It* (2014)

Milton, J. *Samson Agonistes* (1671)

Marx, K. *Theses on Feuerbach* (1888)

Maslow, A. 'A Theory of Human Motivation' *The Psychological Review* Vol. 50 No. 4 (1943) pp. 370-396

Monbiot, G. *Out of the Wreckage: A New Politics for an Age of Crisis* (2017)

Obermayer, B. *The Panama Papers: How the World's Rich and Powerful Hide Their Money* (2017)

Peston, R. *Who Runs Britain?* (2008)

Piketty, T. *Capital in the 21st Century* (2014)

Piketty, T. *Capital and Ideology* (2020)

Pinker, S. *The Better Angels of Our Nature* (2011)

Sayer, A. *Why We Can't Afford the Rich* (2016)

Shaxson, N. *Treasure Islands: Tax Havens and the Men Who Stole the World* (2012)

Shaxson, N. *The Finance Curse: How Global Finance is Making Us All Poorer* (2018)

Shrubsole, G. *Who Owns England?* (2020)

Smith, A. *The Theory of Moral Sentiments* (1759)

Standing, G. *Basic Income and How We Can Make it Happen* (2017)

Standing, G. *Battling Eight Giants* (2020)

Whyte, D. *How Corrupt is Britain?* (2015)